“INVESTIGATE EVERYTHING”

"INVESTIGATE EVERYTHING"

FEDERAL EFFORTS TO COMPEL BLACK LOYALTY DURING WORLD WAR I

INDIANA UNIVERSITY PRESS
BLOOMINGTON AND INDIANAPOLIS

Theodore Kornweibel, Jr.

This book is a publication of
Indiana University Press
601 North Morton Street
Bloomington, IN 47404-3797 USA

http://iupress.indiana.edu

Telephone orders 800-842-6796
Fax orders 812-855-7931
Orders by e-mail iuporder@indiana.edu

The paper used in this publication meets the minimum requirements of American National Standard for Information Sciences—Permanence of Paper for Printed Library Materials, ANSI Z39.48-1984.

Manufactured in the United States of America

Library of Congress Cataloging-in-Publication Data

Kornweibel, Theodore.
"Investigate everything" : federal efforts to compel Black loyalty during World War I / Theodore Kornweibel, Jr.
p. cm.
Includes bibliographical references (p.) and index.
ISBN 0-253-34009-8 (cloth : alk. paper)
1. World War, 1914–1918—African Americans. 2. World War, 1914–1918—United States. I. Title.
D639.N4 K67 2002
940.4'03—dc21 2001001891

1 2 3 4 5 07 06 05 04 03 02

For Daniel and James

CONTENTS

Acknowledgments • ix

Prologue. "Patriotism and Loyalty Presuppose Protection and Liberty" • 1

1. **"It became necessary to investigate everything":** The Birth of Modern Political Intelligence • 10
2. **"Very full of the anti-war spirit":** Fears of Enemy Subversion during World War I • 37
3. **"Slackers, Delinquents, and Deserters":** African Americans and Draft Enforcement during World War I • 76
4. **"The most dangerous of all Negro journals":** Federal Efforts to Silence the *Chicago Defender* • 118
5. **"Every word is loaded with sedition":** The *Crisis* and the NAACP under Suspicion • 132
6. **"I thank my God for the persecution":** The Church of God in Christ under Attack • 149
7. **"Rabid and inflammatory":** Further Attacks on the Pen and Pulpit • 164
8. **"Spreading enemy propaganda":** Alien Enemies, Spies, and Subversives • 188
9. **"Perhaps you will be shot":** Sex, Spies, Science, and the Moens Case • 199
10. **"Negro Subversion":** Army Intelligence Investigations during World War I • 226

Epilogue. "The Negro is 'seeing red'": From the World War into the Red Scare • 270

Notes • 277
Index • 317

Acknowledgments

This book is truly the result of collaboration between the author and numerous archivists, librarians, and colleagues, as well as the support and encouragement of friends and family members. Over the course of a decade of research I have amassed debts to many individuals and institutions. I first discovered this topic in the National Archives, and was greatly assisted by the staff of what are today called the Civil Reference and Military Reference Branches. The amount of records was staggering, but navigating them was made much easier with the assistance particularly of Susan Rosenfeld and Mike McReynolds. Ms. Rosenfeld continued to broaden my understanding of the federal intelligence bureaucracy after she became the FBI's official historian. While working in the National Archives, I hired several Howard University students to scan a hundred reels of microfilm containing hundreds of thousands of index cards for the purpose of identifying black suspects, who were designated with a "(c)" following their names. This tedious work was especially useful in compiling a list of draft suspects, and I want to acknowledge with thanks the students' labor. I also received assistance in locating documents from archivists at the following regional branches of the National Archives and Records Administration: Suitland, Maryland; Bayonne, New Jersey; Fort Worth, Texas; Atlanta, Georgia; and Laguna Niguel, California. The staff of the Library of Congress's Manuscript Division was similarly helpful. Although the FBI's Office of Public and Congressional Affairs processed several of my Freedom of Information Act requests, it unfortunately balked at releasing other files.

Librarians at a number of special collections likewise provided assistance as I probed their archival collections: State University of New York, Buffalo; the Hoover Institution; University of Texas; the Moorland-Spingarn Research Center at Howard University; Yale University; the New York Public Library; East Carolina University; and the A. M. Aiken Regional Archives of the Texas State Library. I also want to express my appreciation to the interlibrary loan staff at San Diego State University.

Each documentary search in the National Archives seemed to lead to new case files. Eventually I amassed approximately twenty-five thousand pages of federal documents. I benefited much from Randy Boehm's great familiarity with the National Archives, and it was he who shepherded the publication of most of those documents in a twenty-five-reel microfilm collection entitled *Federal Surveillance of Afro-Americans (1917–1925): The First World War, the Red Scare, and the Garvey Movement* (1986). Without the computer expertise of Gerald Sullivan, I could never have kept track of this mass of material. I also want to thank my research assistants for abstracting many of these documents: Sharon Odegaard, Margaret Grimshaw, Kathy Weakley, and T. J. Roman, and Michael Piasecki for designing the tables in Chapter 3. Financial support for these efforts, and for extensive travel to archives, was generously granted by the National Endowment for the Humanities, the American Philosophical Society, and San Diego State University.

No prudent scholar risks publication without first obtaining the criticisms and suggestions of colleagues. As I presented portions of my research at professional meetings, I benefited from the comments of a number of scholars: Ernest Allen Jr., Jay Beaman, Michael Casey, Murray W. Dempster, Vincent Fort, David J. Garrow, Charles H. Martin, Kenneth O'Reilly, Judith Stein, Roy Talbert Jr., Athan Theoharis, Emory Tolbert, and Patrick Washburn. Earlier versions of parts of Chapters 3, 4, and 6 appeared in the *South Atlantic Quarterly, American Journalism,* and *Southern Studies,* respectively, and I also wish to thank their editors and anonymous reviewers for helpful comments. However, my greatest debts in this regard are to three colleagues in the History Department at San Diego State University. Andrew Wiese gave the entire manuscript a thorough edit, and caught many gaffes. Francis Stites applied his knowledge of constitutional law to the whole book and greatly sharpened my understanding of how the First Amendment was understood during World War I. And the late Richard Steele wielded his pen—at times a scalpel—on every page, challenging my assumptions, playing devil's advocate, and teaching me much about the operation of the Justice Department. Despite their best efforts, this book undoubtedly still contains errors, for which I alone bear responsibility. Nevertheless, it is my hope that the analysis contained in this volume, when added to the discussion of the postwar period in *"Seeing Red": Federal Campaigns against Black Militancy, 1919–1925* (Indiana University Press, 1998), will provide a clearer understanding of American political intelligence activities and abuses as well as the role of the federal government in obstructing African Americans' aspirations for full citizenship in the twentieth century.

Without the encouragement of friends, this volume would not have been completed in a timely fashion. I want to thank all who have prayed for me and for this project, particularly my good friend and encourager Glen Scorgie. I would not have had the liberty to invest years of effort in this project without the patient understanding of family. My wife Catherine has been a saint, putting up with a husband's absences, making do with depleted finances, and enduring the clutter of documents, note cards, and manuscript pages throughout the home. There are not words sufficient to honor her support. I dedicate this work to my sons Daniel Aaron Kornweibel and James Andrew Kornweibel. They spent many weeks of their early childhood without a father, who was absent on yearly research trips. My greatest debt, however, is to God, for giving me the opportunity to pursue my scholarly passions and to bring this work to fruition.

“INVESTIGATE EVERYTHING”

Prologue. "Patriotism and Loyalty Presuppose Protection and Liberty"

We would rather see you shot by the highest tribunal of the United States Army because you dared protect a Negro woman from the insult of a southern brute in the form of a policeman, than to have you forced to go to Europe to fight for a liberty you cannot enjoy.

—Clara L. Threadgill-Dennis, writing in the *San Antonio Inquirer,* 24 November 1917

Southern Stunts Surpass Hun

—Headline of front-page article on lynching in the *Chicago Defender,* 8 June 1918

The Holy Ghost through me was teaching men to look to God, for he is their only help. I told them not to trust in the power of the United States, England, France or Germany, but trust in God. The enemy (the devil) tried to hinder me from preaching the unadulterated word of God. He plotted against me and had the white people to arrest me and put me in jail for several days. I thank my God for the persecution.

—Rev. Charles H. Mason[1]

I ain't got no business in Germany,
And I don't want to go to France.
Lawd, I want to go home, I want to go home.

—Sung by black draftees awaiting shipment overseas, 1918[2]

Mr. President, Why Not Make AMERICA Safe for Democracy?

—Signs carried by marchers, 28 July 1917, in a silent parade down New York's Fifth Avenue, protesting the East St. Louis race riot[3]

To Hell with President Wilson.

—Mattie Macon[4]

These voices reflect some of the profound changes that swept through Black America during the World War I era. What would later be called the "New Negro" or "New Crowd Negro" was being born out of the most dramatic domestic and international events to affect the race since Reconstruction. This New Negro had been conceived at the turn of the century, marked by the founding of Robert Abbott's *Chicago Defender* and W. E. B. DuBois's embryonic civil rights group, the Niagara Movement, in 1905. With the establishment of the National Association for the Advancement of Colored People (NAACP) in 1909, and the inauguration of its magazine, the *Crisis,* in 1910 under the editorship of DuBois, crusading journalism and attacks on the racial status quo took on broader dimensions. The militant black press expanded even more dramatically during the war with the addition of the socialist *Messenger,* the pan-Africanist *Negro World,* and the pro-communist *Crusader.* The NAACP and its monthly publication helped bring African-American issues back into national discourse, and even though few victories were won, their attacks on lynching, segregation, and disfranchisement lent encouragement to those unwilling to accept the racial status quo. The death of Booker T. Washington in 1915, ending the near-monopoly he had once exercised over setting national black agendas, opened further the door to new voices and strategies. But perhaps the greatest catalyst for the formation of the New Negro was the "Great Migration," which transported half a million southern blacks from sharecropper cabins and urban shanties "on the other side of the tracks" to the tenements and factory jobs of northern and midwestern cities between 1916 and 1919. Another million followed in the next decade. The act of migration was for many individuals a declaration of personal independence.

The foundation for this migration was World War I, which deprived northern industries of new immigrants from Europe and drained off millions of native and foreign-born whites, their customary laborers. But when conscription required black bodies as well, considerable numbers of African Americans responded to calls for patriotism and sacrifice with apathy or dissent. They frequently found themselves at odds with agencies and officials who did not hesitate to use the power of government—expanded exponentially by wartime legislation, executive orders, and court decisions—to compel black conformity to both racial subordination and national loyalty.

Among the most important effects of World War I was the enlargement of the federal government's police power. African Americans became one of its chief targets. Black militancy—often overtly political but also expressed more subtly through migration, religious conviction, draft dodging, and apathy—generated a strong response from the Justice and Post Office Departments and military intelligence. Armed with extraordinary coercive power granted by Congress and endorsed by the courts, the Wilson administration was determined to brook no dissent and to punish—if it could not coerce into submission—anyone who sought to use wartime exigencies to leverage racial change or who appeared to defy the demand for 110 percent patriotism. In this it had much popular support on its side.

Public opinion undergirded the heavy hand of government, approving nearly all suppression of wartime dissent, balking only when draft enforcement degenerated into egregious "slacker raids." Grand juries were quick to indict those suspected of disloyalty, which was very broadly defined. Supple trial juries, often acting on the flimsiest of evidence, voted to convict defendants accused of sedition. Individual citizens were eager to supply "tips" to agents of the Bureau of Investigation, as the FBI was then known. Most of these leads were groundless. In the case of black suspects, they arose from the widespread suspicion among whites that Germans or other enemy agents were actively subverting the loyalties of African Americans, who were believed to be uniquely susceptible to those who would manipulate them for sinister purposes.

By the end of the war, the twin fears of German subversion and black gullibility were being transformed into the conviction that conspiratorial Bolsheviks were plotting to exploit blacks' grievances and gain their allegiance. In the face of this perceived threat, war-swollen intelligence bureaucracies that were expected to shrink after the Armistice instead continued to expand. The result was the nation's worst "Red Scare." The federal government's efforts to suppress black aspirations during this paroxysm of fear is told in the author's sequel to this volume, *"Seeing Red": Federal Campaigns against Black Militancy, 1919–1925.* How the United States got to that point—how it developed mechanisms and methodologies of repression, how it transgressed civil liberties, how it demonized outspoken African-American leaders and publications—is traced in the chapters that follow. It is for the most part an unfamiliar story. This volume is the first work to probe deeply into the wartime intelligence bureaucracies' records and reveal the degree to which they brought African Americans under suspicion, surveillance, and siege.

Chapter 1 charts the evolution of America's modern political intelligence system, which was created during World War I. It reveals how the Secret Service, which historically had handled most domestic security investigations, was supplanted by a network of agencies that included the rapidly growing Bureau of Investigation, the army and navy intelligence branches, and the investigative arms of the Post Office and State Departments. In tracking down alleged German spies, draft dodgers, and other species of subversives, the Bureau and army intelligence were assisted by over two hundred thousand American Protective League "secret service" volunteers. Although these agencies deployed their operatives unevenly, they cast a broad net. Some of their actions, such as apprehending draft dodgers, were clearly mandated by law. But the business of catching spies, hunting subversives, and silencing dissenters rested on less certain foundations and was motivated not only by national security considerations but also by exaggerated fears of subversion and public demands for conformity to enthusiastic patriotism. Bureau agents and their civilian assistants were armed with draconian presidential executive orders and the Espionage, Sedition, and Trading-with-the-Enemy Acts. These acts' vagueness permitted federal prosecutors, who were often responding to political pressure to silence dissent, to define disloyalty and sedition very broadly and unevenly. The civil liberties of blacks and whites, non-citizens as well as citizens, took a beating—all with the approval of the federal courts. This was in good part because the extent to which the First Amendment actually protected speech and press freedoms had not yet been anchored in a substantial body of case law and legal doctrine. According to constitutional historian Paul L. Murphy, "the story of civil liberties during World War I is a dreary, disturbing, and in some respects, shocking chapter out of the nation's past. Americans . . . stood by on the domestic scene and saw liberty and justice prostituted in ways more extreme and extensive than at any other time in American history.[5]

World War I generated widespread fears, at times approaching the level of hysteria, that German agents were poised to sabotage the United States, either by their own acts or by sowing dissension among the population. There were enough isolated instances of actual destruction to give credence to the belief that enemy agents lurked everywhere. Many whites, particularly in the South, believed that such plotters were taking particular pains to propagandize African Americans. Blacks, it was imagined, were easy targets for manipulation, and their grievances readily exploited. Given such a climate of alarm in the South, any unfamiliar white person living, working, or trading among blacks; any reduction in blacks' accommodating behavior; or simply any nighttime gatherings were seen as evidence of enemy influence and disloyal intentions. Bureau agents investigated hundreds of such rumors. Chapter 2 details the prevalence of suspected but ultimately nonexistent German plots to arouse blacks to acts of treason, as well as the degree to which some blacks wished for German success as punishment for white Americans' record of racism. Some may actually have believed that a German victory would bring them economic and social equality. In the end, these phenomena produced new victims. Blacks suspected of harboring such sentiments were arrested, harshly interrogated, and jailed. In other cases, Bureau agents handed them over to local police for surveillance or punishment. Few whites, and certainly only a handful in federal or local law enforcement agencies, possessed the insight to understand that migration and war had raised blacks' aspirations and dissatisfaction with the racial status quo. It was simpler and more comforting to believe that a diabolical enemy was subverting an otherwise contented group of people.

Enforcement of the draft was one of the Bureau of Investigation's most extensive and time-consuming responsibilities during World War I, and it too had a disproportionate impact on blacks. Compared to whites, African Americans were nearly three times as likely to be charged with draft delinquency. White officials claimed that blacks' alleged ignorance, illiteracy, "natural inclination to roam," or "shiftlessness in ignoring civic obligations" explained the disparity.[6] Careful examination of the Bureau's draft case files reveals much more, however. Chapter 3 illustrates that while some blacks were indeed unaware of their responsibility to register, others had specific motives for failing to comply with the selective-service process. Thousands of migrating African-American men left not only the South, but also their draft responsibilities behind. Serving in the Jim Crow army did not fulfill their aspirations for a better life. Migrants often made no effort to inform their hometown draft boards of new northern addresses, and this inaction, for some, expressed how they felt about military service and the war in general. Indeed, many blacks—North and South, urban and rural—were apathetic about a war to preserve democracy for Europeans while that precious commodity was daily denied them at home. One of the signs carried by marchers protesting the East St. Louis riot in a silent protest parade down New York's Fifth Avenue read, "Mr. President, Why Not Make AMERICA Safe for Democracy?" Others expressed even more explicit dissent, articulating political grounds for opposing the war. Even after induction and the indoctrination inherent in military training, some black soldiers remained unconvinced of the reasons necessitating their service or the goals for which they might be fighting. Underlying black draft delinquency was the widespread sentiment that World War I was a "white man's war" and that blacks' main grievance was racist rule in the South, not German hegemony in Europe.

Not surprisingly, the Bureau's draft case files also show clear patterns of punitive enforcement against blacks. Southern agents, reflecting common patterns of racially tinged law enforcement in that region, routinely incarcerated black men who were unable to produce proof that they were not draft delinquents. Such agents sometimes persuaded local police and judges to jail blacks they believed should be serving in uniform, but whom medical examination boards had rejected. Some southern Bureau employees simply used incarceration to "set an example" for other blacks. Northern agents, on the other hand, while not immune to such abuses, were usually focused simply on enforcing selective-service regulations, not racial subordination. Viewing the cases as a whole, it is clear that blacks often suffered punitive treatment by draft boards and the whole apparatus of enforcement: the Bureau of Investigation, the American Protective League, and a host of local sheriffs, post office employees, and private citizens.

Chapters 4 and 5 reveal the array of government pressure brought to bear against the black press. Freedom of speech and the press was significantly tested during World War I. Periodicals that did not voice conventional patriotism became objects of suspicion and sometimes suppression. Socialists and members of the Industrial Workers of the World (IWW) were the prime targets of government hostility. Dissent was unpopular, and, given fears that African Americans were susceptible to manipulation by enemy agents, black protest was widely distrusted. Yet the equation is much more complicated than that. Just as the war provided a pretext for long-desired attacks on socialists, it also provided whites who opposed change in the racial status quo the opportunity to condemn the militant black press, which they already disliked, for allegedly harming the war effort and national unity. The periodicals that endured the most intense pressure to mute criticism of American society were Black America's most influential weekly newspaper, the *Chicago Defender,* and its most articulate voice of civil rights protest, the NAACP's monthly *Crisis.* During the war, agents of the Bureau of Investigation, the Post Office Department, and army intelligence waged a campaign to pressure these publications, providing an excuse to those who would silence their voices of rebuke and charging them with disloyalty for allegedly making blacks less patriotic. When the army's top black intelligence agent warned *Defender* editor Robert Abbott that every issue and word was being scrutinized, he recognized the need to tone down editorials, abjure criticism of the government, and give even more public professions of loyalty if he was to continue publishing. Abbott was a businessman, not a political activist, who could not follow the example of the socialist press by refusing to moderate his critiques of society. In order to avoid suppression, the *Defender* was forced to accept serious curtailment of its press freedom.

Government agents handled the *Crisis* somewhat differently because it had the backing of the NAACP, whose board included a number of influential whites. Military intelligence feared that the magazine was encouraging disaffection among black troops and sought, with mixed success, to exclude it from army posts. It also drew fire for another reason: the outspoken editorials of its editor, W. E. B. DuBois. Although he was not the only black journalist to bitterly assail discrimination by the army, he was one of the most articulate and his magazine was the most influential among educated blacks and liberal whites. Under pressure from the government and members of the NAACP's board, who wanted to avoid censorship of the magazine as well as government hostility toward the organization, DuBois reversed course and penned what quickly became an infamous editorial, "Close Ranks," in which he urged blacks to shelve, for the duration of the war, civil rights protest and join the rest of the nation in waging a single-minded fight against Germany. Historians are still debating the reasons behind DuBois's dramatic retreat, but one factor undoubtedly was a proposal to create a black morale branch within army intelligence, with DuBois playing a leading role. This idea was stillborn, and DuBois never donned a uniform; but he had already moderated the *Crisis,* probably realizing that the Justice Department was prosecuting other dissenters whose publications were no more outspoken than his own. Moreover, he surely knew that the Post Office Department had totally banned other periodicals from the mails on its authority alone, without the necessity of proving disloyalty in a court of law. As in the case of the *Defender,* a black editor was forced to censor himself if he was to continue publishing. While free speech was not fully muzzled, it was significantly eroded. Later, during the Red Scare, both the *Crisis* and the *Defender* would again become objects of investigation and pressure as their renewed civil rights advocacy was condemned, this time for allegedly dividing the nation and playing into the hands of Bolsheviks.

World War I also generated a major conflict between the federal government and the first black Pentecostal denomination. Chapter 6 reveals how the Church of God in Christ (COGIC), led by its founder, Bishop Charles H. Mason, first articulated and then stood fast upon a doctrine of pacifism. The government refused to acknowledge that its members were faith-based conscientious objectors like the Quakers and Mennonites, for two reasons: The church was a new denomination without a historic record of pacifism, and it had significant membership in areas where draft noncompliance among blacks was high. As a consequence, the Bureau launched numerous investigations of Mason and other leaders, including a white elder (the early COGIC was interracial), and twice tried to prosecute Mason. Unsophisticated in the ways of government and law, Mason and his elders held to their convictions, and a considerable percentage of the membership apparently followed suit. If persistence in claiming exemption from military service on the basis of conscience constitutes an act of resistance to governmental authority, and in a more general sense to white authority, then this was perhaps the most striking example of the new boldness being articulated by African Americans during World War I. It was also one instance in which blacks could claim at least partial victory in a direct confrontation with white power. White juries exonerated Mason and his fellow leaders of all major charges. In the process, they managed to rejoice in their suffering, attributing victory over persecution to their biblical faith. There was little knowledge of these events outside the church, however, so its impact on black militancy in general was negligible.

Chapter 7 describes additional attacks on blacks whose spiritual or political convictions impelled them to voice opposition to the war or conscription. None of the religious figures wielded influence over a numerous membership, as did Bishop Mason, but their relative insignificance was no shield against federal officials intent on suppressing all dissent. Surprisingly, the journalists and editorial contributors who found themselves federal targets were not, like Robert Abbott and W. E. B. DuBois, nationally known. A. Philip Randolph and Chandler Owen, editors of a new monthly magazine, the *Messenger,* were as yet largely unknown socialists and antiwar soapbox orators, but this did not diminish the zeal of federal prosecutors. Fortunately, racist judicial paternalism—a judge released the two "boys" because he believed they were incapable of authoring sophisticated antiwar polemics—saved them from punishment. Other journalists were not so lucky. The federal government's pursuit of G. W. Bouldin, editor of the *San Antonio Inquirer,* was nothing less than a vendetta. His alleged offense was to have allowed to be printed, without his knowledge, a stinging defense of the black soldiers who were on trial for their lives for participating in the 1917 Houston mutiny. His conviction on Espionage Act charges and federal prison sentence constituted one of the most egregious miscarriages of justice during World War I, comparable to that suffered by socialist leader Eugene V. Debs.

Fears that Germans were subverting the black population were vastly exaggerated during the war. No blacks were convicted of committing sabotage or espionage, either at an enemy's urging or on their own initiative. However, Chapter 8 reveals that the federal government prosecuted a handful of enemy aliens because they showed indiscreet loyalty for their central European homelands in the presence of blacks. These obscure individuals were zealots and sometimes fools, but if they harbored any genuinely subversive intentions, they were spectacular failures. One individual was different, however, and he became the center of a controversy that lasted for years after the war. Chapter 9 uncovers the trials and tribulations of Herman M. B. Moens, a Dutch amateur anthropologist intent on proving the equality of the races. Had America not been at war, had there been no fear that enemy aliens were undermining black loyalty, the Bureau of Investigation would have taken no interest in him. But anyone of Germanic background (he was thought to be an Austrian) who was seen consorting with blacks was automatically suspected of being a spy or a subverter. As in the case of the Bureau's pursuit of Marcus Garvey during the postwar Red Scare, any charges would do if they curbed someone who appeared to undermine the racial status quo. Army intelligence believed that Moens was "disseminating dangerous negro propaganda," but in fact there was no evidence of such actions. Instead, he was charged with possession and display of pornographic materials: His research methodology consisted of making ethnographic photographs of nude black females. Moens believed in the equality of the races and intended his research to help prove that point. Nonetheless, whatever contribution to science his work might have made was compromised by his immoral private conduct. Chapters 8 and 9 thus demonstrate that, if federal convictions are a measure, there was simply no systematic subversion of the black population by foreign enemies.

The final chapter focuses on one intelligence bureaucracy rather than on specific targets. While the Bureau of Investigation devoted considerable energy to tracking down suspected enemy subversives and pursuing outspoken journalists, religious objectors to war, and anyone else who was perceived to be pro-German or less than fully patriotic, its efforts were often enhanced by information gathered by military intelligence operatives. By mid-1917 the army was using its own agents and informants to pursue rumors of enemy activity on the home front. Its premier black investigator was Maj. Walter Loving, who also organized patriotic exercises to bolster black morale. On at least two occasions, Loving directly coerced individuals—Robert Abbott of the *Chicago Defender* and Howard University dean Kelly Miller—whose protests against lynching were regarded as undermining black loyalty. Military intelligence was in fact deeply involved in investigating alleged civilian disloyalty and subversion that had no direct link to military personnel or installations and which should have been handled solely by the Justice Department. In mid-1918, however, the focus of military intelligence shifted to monitoring the morale of black troops.

From the beginning of the war, black troops encountered discrimination at training camps all across the nation, and those who reached France continued to suffer indifferent or unjust treatment. These problems were so obvious that army intelligence's military morale section undertook a specific effort to investigate and, less often, ameliorate black soldiers' complaints. Loving and others inspected nearly every camp where black draftees trained, plus other stateside posts where black labor units performed the army's menial work. In a few instances the grievances proved inconsequential, but in the majority of cases the soldiers' complaints were real and the conditions egregious. Unfortunately, the army was more interested in quieting protests than ameliorating conditions, and in most cases military intelligence failed to protect or promote positive morale among black servicemen.

Readers will encounter much that is new in this volume, topics and themes only now revealed through a detailed examination of thousands of pages of wartime case files generated by four interlinked federal intelligence bureaucracies. The fear that enemy aliens were undermining black loyalty can now be seen as an important subtext of the greatly exaggerated fears of German subversion during (as distinct from prior to) World War I. No longer can historians assume that Black America was nearly unanimous in backing the war, or in faithfully cooperating with the draft. Bureau of Investigation, military intelligence, and Post Office Department files show the degree to which the two most influential black periodicals had to exercise self-censorship if they were to continue publication and enjoy the privilege of reduced mailing rates. The stubbornly conscientious stand of the

Church of God in Christ against military service is another chapter heretofore buried in court records and obscure Bureau files. Examination of the cases of other black religious figures and journalists who ran afoul of the vaguely defined and broadly interpreted Espionage and Sedition Acts now shows more clearly how legislation ostensibly designed for the protection of national security became an instrument to intimidate or silence those engaged in racial protest and dissent. Finally, the stories of military intelligence spying on civilians and how the army ignored the counsel of its most influential black officer by refusing to address blatant discrimination within its ranks are revealed in greater detail than before.

By November 1918, when the guns fell silent on the bloodied soil of France, the foundation had been laid at home for the tumultuous Red Scare and a permanent domestic intelligence apparatus. Repression of dissenters was perfected during the war, and in fact, the war provided the rationale for attempting to extinguish the most militant voices of the political Left. Given this opportunity, and capitalizing on the belief that blacks were particularly susceptible to subversion and manipulation by external enemies, federal intelligence agencies went after both black dissenters and those who spoke up in defense of their beleaguered race. In fact, black threats to national security or military effectiveness were vastly exaggerated, although New Crowd Negroes were indeed raising serious challenges to the racial status quo. By mid-1918 the focus on German subversion was rapidly replaced with the even greater fear of Bolshevism, which appeared to be marching westward across Europe and poised to invade American shores.

At the same time, the war and the Great Migration indelibly changed the mind and mood of Black America, inspiring more blacks than ever before to challenge the racial status quo with New Crowd Negro rhetoric and boldness. These voices demanded full civil rights—including freedom from racial violence—as a just reward for fighting to preserve freedom in Europe. But the African-American wartime generation was challenged by a racially and politically conservative intelligence establishment that de-legitimized its aspirations by convincing much of the nation that blacks were "seeing red," inflamed by Bolshevism to demand the unthinkable: true racial equality.

1

“It became necessary to investigate everything”: The Birth of Modern Political Intelligence

World War I brought far-reaching changes to the federal bureaucracy, vastly expanding the scope of governmental responsibilities. Nowhere was this more apparent than in attempts to ensure internal security. Indeed, such efforts are a legitimate and necessary role of government in wartime. Previously insignificant entities, like the intelligence services of the army, navy, and the Justice Department, mushroomed to investigate, spy upon, and suppress alleged enemies on the home front. At the same time, postal censors muzzled the dissenting press and the State Department instituted the modern passport system to hinder foreign travel by those thought to be disloyal. In addition to these, dozens of new agencies born of the wartime emergency also entered the field of domestic intelligence. This explosive growth not only required unprecedented numbers of new civilian employees, but also new levels of interagency cooperation as well. Conflicts over “turf” had to be reconciled and major allocations of responsibility hammered out in the cabinet and by Congress.

Out of these rapid changes emerged a modern political intelligence apparatus, with all the problems inherent in such systems. Distinctions between domestic and foreign intelligence blurred. Perceived dangers appeared on the domestic and international stages simultaneously, producing a widespread intolerance not only of Germans and other “enemy aliens,” but also of disgruntled or militant African Americans, pacifists, draft opponents, socialists, and labor radicals. As President Woodrow Wilson was reported to have said shortly before the war began, American involvement might unleash a “spirit of ruthless brutality” that would poison “the Congress, the courts, the policeman on the beat, the man in the street.” Yet he and his cabinet departments in fact fostered such passions. The president’s own rhetoric stigmatized many of the foreign born as domestic enemies. Once America entered the war, the Justice and Post Office Departments circumscribed freedoms of speech and press for both citizen and alien in the name of preserving the country from internal dangers. Peoples of all races and nationalities felt the oppressive weight of nationalist bigotry, which continued on into the postwar Red Scare. Over time, African Americans became particular targets because of purported efforts by “enemies” to buy their disloyalty with “German gold,” because of their unprecedented levels of outspokenness and heightened demands for racial improvement, and because many blacks insisted on linking their own struggles for political and social freedom to Wilsonian wartime rhetoric. The result was tragic. The period from 1917 to 1921, according to historian Harry N. Scheiber, was characterized by “an unprecedented sacrifice of civil liberty in the United States” due in good measure to the comprehensive new laws and executive orders which constituted the Wilson administration's "security program."[1]

As the several cabinet departments and the military services perceived worldwide threats to American security, they were ultimately obliged to cooperate with one another. But inter-agency competition came first, spurred by widespread fears, long before April 1917, of German and Austrian spies and their Irish, East Indian, Mexican, and Japanese surrogates. Although rumor far surpassed reality, there was sufficient plotting by the Central Powers and their sympathizers, including two spectacular examples of sabotage, to warrant some domestic surveillance. Great Britain was similarly eager to incite Poles, Czechs, and Slavs in the United States against German interests, and it was unabashed in its efforts to curry American support for the Allied cause. Americans recognized that their soil had become a playing field for the manipulations and subversions of friend and foe alike. Thus several bureaucracies began to conduct their own independent investigations and were soon competing jealously for dominance. The initial players were the State Department; the Justice Department's Bureau of Investigation (renamed the FBI in 1935); and the Treasury Department's Secret Service. After considerable jockeying for position and authority, the Secret Service was denied a significant role in wartime counterintelligence. At the same time, the Post Office Department and the army and navy intelligence services expanded their own surveillance activities. By the war's end, all of the agencies still involved in domestic spying were linked in cooperative relationships. This network, created without any statutory authorization or limitation, did not evaporate at the Armistice; the Red Scare left no opportunity to relax national vigilance. As America embarked on war in the spring of 1917, two goals for this intelligence apparatus quickly emerged: To curb alleged black disloyalty, and to halt the spread of a vibrant African American militancy, which threatened to upset the white-defined racial status quo.

By the time diplomats, spies, and agents of the warring European powers began to operate in the United States in the second half of 1914, four cabinet departments had investigative agencies. The State Department had a small number of intelligence operatives. Treasury agents (the Secret Service) and post office inspectors had long been responsible for catching smugglers, counterfeiters, and tax evaders, as well as protecting the mails. The initial responsibilities of the Justice Department's Bureau of Investigation, established in 1909, were few: peonage, antitrust, and bankruptcy cases; customs, internal revenue, and postal fraud; plus crimes committed on Indian reservations and government properties. The Bureau began to establish a national reputation for crime fighting after passage of the White Slave Traffic Act (Mann Act) in 1910 to combat organized prostitution. Even so, its "small and inept force of 219 agents" in 1915 was ill equipped to halt alleged German espionage and sabotage.[2]

Initially, Attorney General Thomas Watt Gregory believed that counterespionage had no sanction in existing federal laws and was thus beyond the jurisdiction of the Bureau of Investigation. In December 1915, he asked Congress for authority to monitor foreign agents, but legislators declined to act. When Secretary of State William Jennings Bryan sought surveillance of German embassy personnel, he turned to the Secret Service without seeking congressional approval. Treasury Secretary William Gibbs McAdoo, the president's politically ambitious son-in-law, recognized a high-profile issue in the investigation of suspected spies and was happy to pursue "German intrigues." Bryan's successor, Robert Lansing, approved continuation of the practice.[3]

Lansing's motives were mixed. On one hand, he was genuinely concerned about the activities of Germans operating in this country. Besides, he had no objection to whipping up national outrage against German spies so as to identify the United States more closely with Britain and France. Lansing thus continued to employ the Secret Service in widely publicized investigations and exposes. When agents got hold of a briefcase belonging to German commercial attaché Dr. Heinrich Albert, which he had left on his seat on a New York elevated train, its contents proved that he was a spy. This fortuitous event magnified the Secret Service's reputation for daring vigilance. At the same time, Attorney General Gregory and A. Bruce Bielaski, the head of the Bureau of Investigation, were humiliated by public criticism of their failure to catch German agents. Relations between Treasury and Justice became so strained that Wilson called a special cabinet session to address the competition between the two. A halfway solution to reduce discord and duplication was reached when the State Department appointed Counselor Frank Polk to decide when to request the services of the two competing investigative agencies.[4]

But conflict between the two agencies did not end there. The State Department continued to utilize the Secret Service to investigate matters that were not technically violations of federal law, while the Justice Department held with stubborn unhappiness to its belief that it had no jurisdiction. Finally, in mid-1916, Congress gave Justice broadened authority in matters that State wanted investigated. Invigorated with a new mission, the number of Bureau agents increased to three hundred by early 1917, with Gregory resolving to make the Justice Department dominant in counterespionage cases. Because the military branches were as yet without significant intelligence personnel and the post office was still focused solely on mail fraud, only the Secret Service blocked Justice from gaining supremacy in domestic surveillance. Yet the Treasury Department did not relinquish the field. The arrest of allegedly pro-German East Indians by Secret Service agents in March 1917 again brought protests from Justice, which saw its only defense against the usurpations of the Treasury Department in rapidly increasing its own personnel. Justifying such expansion proved no problem following exposure of the Zimmermann telegram, which proposed a German-Mexican alliance, on 1 March 1917. If not convinced before, the populace now believed that the country was "crawling with disloyal Germans," and when America entered the war a month later, public fears mushroomed still more.[5]

Investigative efficiency might have improved had President Wilson exerted leadership to ensure cooperation between the cabinet departments. But, as his close friend and adviser, Col. Edward M. House, confided in his diary, "the President does not know what is going on in any of the departments. He does not follow their work and has an idea that every department of the Government is running smoothly and well." Taking no pleasure in such criticism, House nonetheless concluded that Wilson "sadly lacks administrative ability." Treasury Secretary McAdoo shared that assessment, complaining that the president had no "business head" when it came to superintending his departments. What Wilson did know, however, was that his subordinates were not immune to the fears of German intrigues that engulfed the nation in the months immediately preceding war. Late in February 1917, members of the cabinet swapped rumors that German army reservists who had emigrated to the United States were poised for sabotage. Others repeated stories that the Japanese were secretly stockpiling munitions in anticipation of war. Still more rumors had Germans and Japanese conspiring in Mexico, awaiting the outbreak of hostilities. A month later the cabinet again discussed unconfirmed reports that German sailors on interned ships were planning to blow up American vessels. McAdoo believed this was a genuine threat, whereas Gregory thought the danger was much exaggerated. Just seven days before the United States declared war, the president himself told the cabinet some of the wild stories he had heard about alleged enemy threats. One tale concerned what Wilson termed an "inoffensive German" who tended the furnace in the White House basement. The president, who had a more level head than some of his cabinet secretaries, concluded, "I'd rather the blamed place should be blown up than to persecute inoffensive people."[6]

The declaration of war on Germany on 6 April 1917 did nothing to dampen interdepartmental rivalry. The president immediately imposed restrictions on enemy aliens. To strengthen his position, Attorney General Gregory had Wilson invest the Justice Department with sole responsibility for monitoring foreign nationals, but this did not deter Treasury Secretary McAdoo from continuing Secret Service investigations under the authority of the 1798 Alien Enemies Act, which the president had invoked. Seeking an even broader role, McAdoo proposed that Wilson issue an executive order creating a "Bureau of Intelligence" in the State Department to which all other agencies should report facts and information. Secretary of State Lansing initially embraced McAdoo's proposal since the State Department already employed agents in both foreign and domestic intelligence and had for several months acted as a "clearing house" for information gathered by the Justice and Post Office Departments and the Secret Service. Lansing stressed the necessity for coordination: "The various groups of secret agents should work in complete harmony otherwise there will be duplication of work and frequent 'crossing of wires.'"[7]

But when the ambitious McAdoo proposed centralizing intelligence activities (foreign as well as domestic) under Secret Service chief William J. Flynn, Lansing penned a "most confidential" letter urging the president to reject that plan. Flynn, he said, knew nothing of foreign affairs. Second, bitter relations between Treasury and Justice would preclude the cooperation of the latter. Lastly, Lansing argued, the State Department was best equipped to coordinate all intelligence work. Lansing for similar reasons rejected Bureau of Investigation head Bielaski for such a position. State already possessed competent, discreet, knowledgeable personnel. "The chief difficulty," concluded Lansing, "lies in harmonizing the domestic work. I do not think it can be done if either the chief of the Treasury [or] of the Department of Justice is given control. It will result in friction and jealousy. My suggestion is to select a man entirely outside the service and let all of the present secret service branches act under him through their respective chiefs. Moreover, he should be selected and employed by neither the Department of Justice nor the Treasury, for otherwise the same feeling of envy will exist." Attorney General Gregory, joined by the Post Office Department, protested this end run to preempt his authority. In any case, the president opposed a "unified counterespionage agency," whether proposed by McAdoo or Lansing.[8]

At the same time, various civilian departments were jockeying for position in matters of domestic security. The War Department, which was belatedly establishing a military intelligence capability of its own, saw the need for coordination of counterespionage if domestic security was to be protected. While not in favor of a unified agency, it advocated creation of a centralized registry of information gathered by all those involved in domestic as well as foreign investigations. Agents of the new Military Intelligence Section (MIS) were already collecting data on alleged enemy activities in Mexico and on German agents in the United States, some of it obtained from the Office of Naval Intelligence (ONI), the Bureau of Investigation, and the State Department. Enamored of the British and French models whereby the army General Staff controlled all of the nation's espionage and counterespionage activities, MIS suggested that it should house a centralized registry. Given the infancy of the army's intelligence system and its lack of trained officers, however, this proposal died aborning.[9]

Meanwhile, complaints and accusations flew back and forth between Treasury and Justice in mid-1917. William Flynn protested that "agents" of the American Protective League (APL) were passing themselves off as federal detectives. Practically anyone could join and, for a small sum, purchase a badge displaying the words "Secret Service Division." The APL was a private volunteer organization established in early 1917, whose letterhead declared: "Organized with the Approval, and Operating under the Direction of the United States Department of Justice, Bureau of Investigation." Its ostensible purpose was to "investigate and report disloyal acts and utterances." Attorney General Gregory encouraged citizens to convey their suspicions or tips to the Justice Department, so it is no surprise that the APL grew rapidly, numbering a quarter of a million members at its peak in 1918. As initially conceived, volunteers were supposed to furnish informal assistance to neutrality investigations. By the end of the war, however, the APL was officially investigating suspected draft dodgers, the loyalty of American Red Cross personnel seeking overseas duty, and applicants for commissions in the army reserve. Serious abuses occurred. As John Lord O'Brian later observed, "no other one cause contributed so much to the oppression of innocent men as the systematic and indiscriminate agitation against what was claimed to be an all-pervasive system of German espionage." The innocence and reputation of too many persons suffered from "the insistent desire of a very large number of highly intelligent men and women to become arms of the Secret Service [*sic*] and to devote their entire time to the patriotic purpose of pursuing spies."[10]

The Treasury Department's efforts to block the American Protective League proved futile. Treasury Secretary McAdoo warned the president that the APL would trample individual rights, stir up racial antagonisms, and foster a mood of suspicion with civilians spying on civilians. He again urged Wilson to authorize a central "Bureau of Intelligence" which, he claimed, would make the APL unnecessary.[11] Meanwhile, Attorney General Gregory reassured the president of the propriety of the APL while also justifying the need for an expanded paid investigative force. Despite the fact that a hundred new agents were added to the Bureau in the first two months of the war, its task was overwhelming: "There have been days when as many as one thousand letters came to my Department purporting to give more or less detailed information as to spies, disloyal citizens and plots to destroy ships, factories, railroad bridges, munitions plants, waterworks, arsenals, etc., etc., etc. In perhaps 90 percent of these cases the information furnished was of no value, but in a small number of them it proved to be very valuable indeed, and it thus became necessary to investigate everything called to our attention."[12]

Gregory's department was again embarrassed when Flynn's agents made headlines in pursuit of supposed German sympathizers employed by the State Department. Nor did McAdoo's suggestion that Secret Service personnel help the army and navy establish their own intelligence services reassure the Justice Department. In fact, many of the army's newly appointed and poorly trained intelligence officers were already seeking assistance from Secret Service men as they tried to get themselves organized. President Wilson, caught in the cross fire, suffered continued discord in his cabinet. Still unable to exert strong executive leadership, he wrote Gregory: "You may remember that the other day I spoke jestingly at the Cabinet about my perplexity concerning the varying counsels among the several departments having secret service with regard to a correlation of these services. Underneath the jest, of course, lay a very serious difficulty and I am writing now to ask if you would be generous enough to cooperate with the Secretary of the Treasury and Mr. Polk [of the State Department] in working out for me a plan for the cooperation of these services into which we can all enter with spirit and effect." The issue thus was not primarily cooperation, but rather one of turf.[13]

After several months of confusion, the interdepartmental battle was finally resolved in the summer of 1917 with a cooperative structure, which coincided with the establishment of investigative branches within the armed services. Although clear guidelines on the functions and jurisdiction of the new Military Intelligence Section, a part of the army's War College Division, had not yet been distributed to officers in the field, they were encouraged to cooperate with other federal agencies, local police, and volunteer groups like the American Protective League. But when many of these new intelligence officers "actively sought the assistance of the United States Secret Service to [help] organize their activities . . . the frequency of these inquiries tempted the vanity of the Secretary of the Treasury to renew his campaign on Woodrow Wilson for placing the control of these activities under his office." McAdoo again argued that he possessed the best-trained detective force in the country and urged that it be permitted to assist the army, navy, and State Department, as it had during the Spanish American War. Obliquely criticizing the War and State Departments for allegedly permitting German spies to run loose, he urged the president "to take action to make more effective the secret service agencies of the government." But Wilson was unwilling to deal decisively with the friction between his cabinet secretaries and, anyway, McAdoo's plea was too late. By the end of July, Justice, State, and the army and naval intelligence agencies agreed to share reports and meet weekly to coordinate investigations and strategy. These Wednesday conferences were held at the Department of Justice, underscoring its preeminence. The tens of thousands of APL volunteers afforded the Bureau of Investigation the manpower to dominate, although not monopolize, domestic intelligence operations. According to historian Joan Jensen, "by mid-July, [Bureau chief] Bielaski had convinced Gregory and Gregory had convinced Wilson that McAdoo's plan for abolition of the APL and substitution of Secret Service agents coordinated by a central intelligence agency was not necessary."[14] Thenceforth, the Secret Service would play a negligible role in domestic intelligence.

How well this relationship worked between the War, Navy, State, and Justice Departments depended upon one's point of view. In a pamphlet on "The Functions of the Military Intelligence Division" issued late in the war, the MID lauded the "enthusiastic cooperation" between the agencies. But beneath the surface lurked Justice Department fears, especially after passage of the Sedition Act in May 1918, that army intelligence was trying to supplant its own investigative prerogatives. These apprehensions stemmed particularly from overzealous army intelligence officers (IOs) in the Northwest, one of whom formed a civilian Volunteer Intelligence Corps. Others attempted to destroy the militant Industrial Workers of the World by arresting striking miners. Justice naturally was upset, whereas military officials believed that Gregory's department did not act decisively enough in halting alleged domestic subversion. Nevertheless, considerable cooperation existed among the organizations. Brigadier General Marlborough Churchill, who headed army intelligence in the latter months of the war, stressed on several occasions his willingness to go to any length to ensure cooperation with the Bureau of Investigation. For its part, the Justice Department's APL civilian volunteers were providing essential service to the army by forwarding information of military interest and investigating the ideological suitability of officers selected for sensitive duties.[15]

Predictably, with the Secret Service excluded from any significant role in political intelligence and domestic surveillance, relations between the Treasury and Justice Departments remained strained. Disharmony surfaced again in November 1917 when a Secret Service agent was charged with browbeating and trying to seduce a young stenographer while investigating her employer's loyalty. Gregory denounced the Treasury Department for acting "without authority of law" and "in defiance of the act of Congress limiting the activities" of the Secret Service. After the cabinet aired the issue, President Wilson admitted that he should have exerted decisive leadership months before, yet he did not know how to end the acrimony. McAdoo replied, "I am really deeply distressed about the attitude of the Attorney General concerning the Secret Service," and again offered "to try to devise some plan for getting a more effective cooperation between the two agencies." The result, however, was not greater teamwork but the departure of Secret Service director Flynn, who ostensibly resigned for health reasons. Later press reports emphasized Gregory's opposition to Secret Service pursuit of suspected German spies, so it is possible that the Attorney General was working behind the scenes to engineer Flynn's discipline or dismissal.[16]

McAdoo made one final attempt in early 1918 to establish a "coordinated intelligence system" that, he claimed, would make the American Protective League unnecessary. This proposal may well have been designed primarily to hit back at Gregory. In any event, McAdoo, clearly despairing of presidential decisiveness, suggested that Congress authorize a "government controlled and directed organization" that would protect the public from such abuses as those with which the APL was charged. Gregory's reply expressed regret that McAdoo still seemed hostile to the APL but offered no apologies for its volunteer sleuths.[17] The Justice Department had won this intramural battle. By the beginning of 1918, its relationships with the State Department, the armed services' intelligence branches, and the Post Office Department defined the structure of wartime political investigations and surveillance.

The Wilson administration's political intelligence program, which ultimately investigated hundreds of thousands of individuals and intimidated dissenters into silence or prudent conformity, drew its authority from legislation and presidential executive orders issued during the war. Three acts were preeminent. They became troublesome not because of what they authorized, but because of their vagueness and the absence of standards. The first was the Espionage Act, passed on 15 June 1917 after an exaggerated alarm sounded by the president: "From the very outset of the present war," Wilson wrote, Germany "has filled our unsuspecting communities and even our offices of government with spies and set criminal intrigues everywhere afoot." Continuing, he warned: "if there should be disloyalty, it will be dealt with with a firm hand of stern repression." Although Congress rejected Wilson's request for power to censor the press, the law authorized draconian punishments for anyone attempting to incite mutiny or disloyalty, obstruct enlistment or conscription, or make false or malicious statements intended to hinder the military effort. Under the Espionage Act, postal authorities could refuse second-class items "advocating or urging treason, insurrection, or forcible resistance to any [federal] law," and anyone trying to mail such material was liable to stiff penalties. These provisions gave the post office "vast powers for the suppression of critical opinion" and "virtually dictatorial control" over the foreign-language press and politically dissenting publications.[18]

Following the Espionage Act, the Trading-with-the-Enemy Act (6 October 1917) expanded press and mail censorship. Postmaster General Albert Sidney Burleson, already embarked on smashing anti-administration voices in the left wing and pacifist press, gained additional powers to cripple foreign-language newspapers. Although censoring mail had been an established practice since the 1770s, this law also authorized, for the first time in American history, censorship of cable, radio, and telegraph communications. President Wilson immediately created a Censorship Board dominated by Burleson, who used his new authority to pry into the private mail of even those whose only "crime" was having opposed intervention in the war.[19]

Completing the triad of oppressive laws were amendments to the Espionage Act known popularly as the Sedition Act, passed on 16 May 1918. In the words of a later attorney general, who did not hesitate to criticize his predecessors: "It provided drastic punishment for making false statements to interfere with military operations or obstruct the sale of United States bonds; inciting disloyalty or mutiny in military forces; obstructing enlistments; abusing the Constitution, the government, the flag, or the military establishment; provoking resistance to the United States; or in any way talking or writing in support of the cause of the enemy. Such a statute was a dangerous weapon in the hands of vindictive or fanatical prosecutors."[20]

These further restrictions on free speech stemmed in part from the president's belief that the enemy was using surrogates such as liberals and labor leaders who "have learned discretion" to undermine the American war effort. "They keep within the law. It is opinion they utter, now, not sedition." According to Attorney General Gregory, "some of the most dangerous types of propaganda were either made from good motives or else that the traitorous motive was not provable." Special Assistant to the Attorney General John Lord O'Brian later admitted that this act was so broad and vague that it covered "all degrees of conduct and speech, serious and trifling alike, and, in the popular mind, gave the dignity of treason to what were often neighborhood quarrels or barroom brawls." Indeed, as historian Richard W. Steele writes, the Sedition Act "provided for fines and imprisonment for anyone convicted of uttering *any* disloyal statement (true or not, regardless of intent)." In addition, Postmaster General Burleson was given new censorship power that allowed him to refuse to deliver mail to anyone who used the mails to violate the act. Gregory swallowed his misgivings about these postal provisions, but overall he approved the addition of new offenses, believing that "a reasonable amount of discretion and caution on the part of law officers" would prevent any abuse of power. This was not to be.[21]

Supplementing these three laws were additional legislation and presidential directives. On 6 April, the day that Congress declared war, President Wilson issued an executive order restricting the rights of enemy aliens and subjecting them to summary arrest and internment. The next day he issued a confidential executive order allowing the dismissal of Civil Service employees merely on the suspicion of disloyalty. The following week, Wilson created the Committee on Public Information (CPI) to induce "voluntary" self-censorship of the press. It organized a vast propaganda apparatus that "mobilized journalists, artists, writers, advertisers, and professors [especially historians] in a campaign that often seemed geared to persuade the American people that every German soldier was a violent beast; that spies and saboteurs lurked behind every bush . . . and that Russian Bolsheviks were merely German agents." O'Brian later blamed the CPI's "systematic and indiscriminate agitation against what was claimed to be an all-pervasive system of German espionage" for intimidating many innocent individuals.[22]

A second executive order, issued on 28 April 1917, empowered the navy to censor transoceanic cables and radio stations while giving similar power over telephone and land telegraph lines to the army. The Sabotage Act, passed 20 April 1918, "was designed to protect the country from an imagined network of saboteurs and spies." Finally, the Alien Act of 16 October 1918 hastened the government's evolution from suppressing German intrigue to combating Bolshevik subversion. This law allowed immigrants to be deported on the basis of proscribed (i.e., radical) political affiliations, thus legitimizing guilt by association in immigration and deportation proceedings and paving the way for the Red Scare. Historian Harry Scheiber calls the Alien Act "the capstone of a long succession of laws which removed those legal guarantees traditionally enjoyed by Americans against the arbitrary actions of hysterical or irresponsible government officials." Zechariah Chafee Jr., a constitutional scholar and outspoken contemporary critic of the Justice Department, saw it as "the greatest executive restriction of personal liberty in the history of this country."[23]

All these measures could be wielded punitively, given their vagueness and the absence of clear standards for their application, and disproportionate punishment was frequently a result. Despite congressional intentions that the Espionage and Sedition Acts would lapse at the end of armed hostilities, the United States remained in a technical state of war until mid-1921 since it did not sign the Paris peace agreement. The Justice Department thus continued to initiate prosecutions long after 11 November 1918, and the Post Office Department perpetuated censorship and intimidation of the press with a vengeance. Postmaster General Burleson is usually portrayed as the villain in using these statutes after the war, but President Wilson vetoed a bill in mid-1920 that would have repealed them. He thus must share the blame for the continuation of wartime excesses after the Armistice. The president's Progressive credentials notwithstanding, historian Roy Talbert Jr. agrees that Wilson was willing to accept erosion of civil liberties as the price for winning the war.[24]

None of the major domestic surveillance players during World War I began with either a strong organizational structure or clarified mission. Each one responded to the national emergency separately and only later became part of a network. By the end of the war, however, interdepartmental alliances constructed by the participants had been forged into America's first comprehensive political intelligence system.

Although the Bureau of Investigation hired new personnel in the early 1910s to crack down on Mann Act violations and other interstate crimes, it was dangerously shorthanded when the United States found itself on the brink of war. Only 219 agents conducted its investigations nationwide in 1915, although that number grew to about three hundred in early 1917. An additional hundred men were added by June, some transferred on a temporary basis from the Immigration Service, and others recruited from state and local agencies. After passage of national conscription in May 1917, the Bureau preferred lawyers between the ages of thirty-one and forty because they were exempt from the draft, although a few men of draft age were hired and thus gained exemptions. Even though the number of agents reached one thousand in mid-1918, at times even office clerks were pressed into investigative service, including at least two women who worked briefly on cases where a female could more likely establish rapport with witnesses. At its wartime peak in November 1918, the Bureau employed nearly fifteen hundred agents. The number of agents declined in early 1919, but again increased during the Red Scare. Although the Bureau had not previously employed black agents, the successful use of African American informants in the waning months of the conflict paved the way for hiring several black agents in the postwar years.[25]

Even with the dramatic increase in personnel, wartime responsibilities severely taxed the Bureau. According to the attorney general's annual report covering the period through June 1917, "hundreds of complaints were received daily of disloyalty, enemy activities, etc.," and thousands of enemy aliens were investigated and numerous Espionage Act cases opened. A year later he reported an even greater caseload: "Hundreds of investigations have been made under the provisions of the espionage act, as amended; thousands of delinquents under the selective-service act have been inducted into the military service, and hundreds of prosecutions instituted as the result of investigations. . . . The number of complaints daily examined by representatives of this bureau is extraordinarily large—sometimes numbering 3,000 per day and averaging well over 1,500 per day—it has been the uniform practice to examine and run down every complaint, however trivial on its face." This amount of work could not have been accomplished without the 250,000 volunteers of the American Protective League who conducted more than a million investigations for the Bureau, most of which concerned alleged "slackers" (draft evaders).[26]

A. Bruce Bielaski, who served as the agency's chief from 1912 into early 1919, led the Bureau of Investigation throughout World War I. His $3,500 salary in 1917, which his wife supplemented by teaching high school, was less than half that of an assistant attorney general, reflecting the relative insignificance of the Bureau at that time. Maryland-born, he earned a law degree from George Washington University a year before joining the Justice Department in 1905.[27] By the spring of 1917, Bielaski's three hundred agents were spread thinly across the country. Bureau field offices worked closely with the U.S. attorney and U.S. marshal assigned to each federal judicial district.

Although in theory Bielaski reported directly to the attorney general, soon after hostilities began a special War Emergency Division, headed by Progressive Republican John Lord O'Brian, was created to coordinate all the wartime activities of the Justice Department, including supervision of the Bureau's work. War, Navy, State, and Justice Departments' intelligence representatives met in O'Brian's office at least every Wednesday, and sometimes daily, to coordinate work on critical cases. Yet the Bureau exercised a considerable degree of independence (and had a great deal of influence because of its legion of APL volunteers) under the nominal authority of O'Brian while maintaining usually harmonious cooperation with the other intelligence services.[28]

Bielaski's agents were part of the machinery for administering wartime statutes and presidential proclamations. While Justice Department attorneys in Washington lobbied for and drafted numerous laws to govern the behavior of citizen and alien alike, the enforcement of these regulations depended upon the cooperative efforts of others. Bureau agents investigated alleged violations while U.S. marshals and their deputies arrested suspects, although Bureau agents likewise made arrests even though they had no statutory authority to do so. Meanwhile, U.S. attorneys and their assistants sought warrants, authorized arrests, prepared court cases, handled prosecutions, and interpreted statutes for agents and marshals.

The Justice Department promoted new legislation in the belief that existing treason and conspiracy statutes were totally insufficient for protecting the country against its enemies. Once enacted, the new wartime laws and executive orders were so thorough that even before American troops made the decisive difference on the battlefields of France, Attorney General Gregory pronounced the domestic war against subversion, disloyalty, and apathy won. Part of the credit, he believed, was due to the levelheaded, law-abiding character of the American people, who exercised "self-control and self-restraint" even during times of enemy-inspired "outrage and disorder." Moreover, "systematic disloyal propaganda became a failure during the first year of the war" because of the efforts of the Justice Department which, according to the attorney general, was "at all times mindful of the fact that this department is not only responsible for law enforcement, but, in a larger sense, is responsible for the protection of civil liberty. Its activities have been confined at all times strictly to the legal powers conferred upon it and no attempt has been made at any time to resort to extra legal process."[29]

It is true that Gregory resisted the urging of "extremists" outside the government as well as of Special Assistant Attorney General Charles Warren, who wanted to subject civilian dissenters to military trials. But Gregory was no civil libertarian. The Justice Department, including a large number of Bureau agents, took the lead in crushing dissent by radical labor unionists and socialists who condemned the "Wall Street war." Gregory agreed with the president that the IWW should be suppressed, and he approved use of the Espionage Act to convict one hundred "Wobblies" for alleged obstruction of the draft. After the war,

Gregory further embellished the myth that his department resisted assaults on civil liberties by "well-meaning but foolish people [who] were demanding that the Department should shoot spies and disloyal citizens." He approved vigorous prosecution of suspected seditionists and war opponents, claiming that those who deserted or tried to impede the military effort had "sinned against the sovereignty of America and I know of no crime so serious as this."[30] This illustrates the defects in the Espionage and Sedition acts, which did not elucidate clear enough standards for what constituted prosecutable offences. Gregory did not acknowledge the immoderation of those Bureau agents and U.S. attorneys who conducted dubious prosecutions of alleged enemies, draft evaders, and anyone else deemed insufficiently patriotic. The so-called slacker raids in the summer of 1918 particularly mocked the attorney general's claims to the probity of his department.

Beyond the actions of the Bureau of Investigation, protection of civil liberties was seriously weakened during World War I by the actions of U.S. attorneys. Wartime legislation was written broadly, and Gregory admitted that "great discrimination of judgment" was needed if "the rights of free speech and political agitation" were to be guaranteed. His annual report acknowledged responsibility for these rights. Wartime special assistants John Lord O'Brian and Alfred Bettman voiced commitment to these principles, but all shared responsibility for the excesses of prosecutors in the field. Federal attorneys were largely autonomous, given the decentralized structure of the Justice Department, and some pursued suspects with a vengeance "based on neither fair play nor common sense," often succumbing "to their own prejudices or to local pressure."[31] Thirteen of the eighty-seven federal districts accounted for nearly half of the total number of cases. O'Brian was quite afraid of vigilantism, and he feared that local prosecutors were responding to public opinion, but it was not until late in the war that the Department of Justice ordered that all prosecutions for sedition and related crimes be cleared in advance by O'Brian. Before that, U.S. attorneys had acted on their own. Gregory himself also enjoyed that same autonomy. President Wilson rarely interfered with his cabinet secretaries, trusting the attorney general when questions were raised about the department's actions, such as the wisdom of utilizing a quarter of a million amateur agents enrolled in the American Protective League.[32]

Of all the Justice Department's responsibilities, enforcement of the Selective Service Act was the most time consuming and demanded the greatest resources. It was this activity that was most likely to ensnare African Americans in the web of federal "justice." Gregory acknowledged that this statute was "the most important of the war laws" because it touched the lives of millions. It also required Herculean efforts by the Bureau's staff. In June 1918, Secretary of War Newton D. Baker informed Gregory that 308,489 presumably eligible men (the equivalent of twenty-five army divisions) had failed to register or fill out questionnaires, had made false claims for exemption, or had not reported for physical examinations or induction. Gregory forwarded Baker's letter to Bielaski for action. Having already proved the usefulness (if not the constitutionality) of slacker raids in Boston, Pittsburgh, and Chicago, the Bureau organized the most massive roundup yet, in New

York City. For three days a combined force of nearly four thousand Bureau agents, APL volunteers, soldiers, national guardsmen, sailors, and local policemen hauled some fifty thousand "suspects" into makeshift detention facilities. Fifteen thousand were alleged to be delinquent and referred to their local boards, but only 1,505 were immediately inducted. One Bureau agent inadvertently admitted to the press that ninety-nine out of a hundred men were mistakenly arrested. Following congressional and public outcries, Gregory insisted on continuing slacker raids while promising to avoid extralegal procedures.[33]

The Bureau had two additional responsibilities under the selective service law besides rounding up suspected draft dodgers. Some individuals encouraged others to resist the draft or to file fraudulent registration claims. Second, the Bureau exerted a great deal of effort in enforcing sections twelve and thirteen of the act, which banned prostitution and liquor from neighborhoods surrounding training and mobilization camps. Up to 1 July 1918, with many men still to be drafted, the Bureau and the APL had already investigated nearly a quarter of a million selective service cases and caused the induction of about twenty-five thousand men. No wonder, then, that even with the massive force of APL volunteers, Bureau agents worked at a feverish pace, preoccupied with violations of wartime statutes but responsible also for tens of thousands of run-of-the-mill civil and criminal investigations as well.[34]

Without the assistance of APL volunteers, neither the Bureau nor army intelligence could have accomplished more than a fraction of their wartime responsibilities. The creation of the nation's first modern political intelligence system was not possible without them. The consequent erosion of civil liberties was due in part to the unrestrained zeal of its amateur sleuths, some of whom also proved to be professional "patriots." Historian Roy Talbert Jr. has identified the source of the APL's motivations as well as its weaknesses: "Middle-class America poured its soul into the war effort on the home front. Flanders was far away, but spies, saboteurs, slackers, Socialists, pacifists, and neutrals [plus labor radicals] were right around the corner. Professional Americans vied with each other in signing members into their superpatriotic societies and vigilance committees" like the American Defense Society, National Civic Federation, National Security League, and state councils of defense. All these predated the APL, but it dominated the field of volunteer sleuthing by the summer of 1917. In addition to handling about a million draft cases for the Bureau and a much smaller number of investigations for the Office of Naval Intelligence, the APL claimed credit for handling over three million army cases. These statistics are explained in part by the fact that army intelligence did not leave the suppression of enemy agents, radicals, and subversives entirely to the Bureau of Investigation. For their part, many civilian volunteers had a "natural affinity for the military" and eventually parlayed their APL service into army commissions.

The American Protective League had been indispensable to both the Bureau of Investigation and to army intelligence during the war. But its participation in slacker raids and union busting had given the Justice Department too much unwanted notoriety, although military intelligence continued to strongly defend the

APL. Nonetheless, in late December, Gregory, O'Brian, and Bielaski agreed to officially disband the organization. The APL's national directors ordered its dissolution the following month, but many members voted to continue working as autonomous local units. Throughout the Red Scare and into the 1920s, former volunteers continued to feed information to and perform covert operations for individual intelligence officers. Most important, both the army and the Bureau "had created contacts with the ultraconservative community that would continue for two decades." The political intelligence network of World War I persisted long after the Red Scare ended because its members were ideologically obsessed with the Left. The American Protective League, during and after World War I, greatly encouraged this preoccupation.[35]

What is the significance of the wartime evolution of the Bureau of Investigation? Obscure and limited in jurisdiction before American entry into the war, it gained preeminence in domestic security and political intelligence in less than two years. Empowered by broad coercive legislation, it investigated the political beliefs and activities of socialists, anarchists, and other opponents of the war. The Bureau became the flagship among those agencies dedicated to preserving the nation from supposed threats, whether external or internal. Bureau agents and their APL volunteer assistants became guardians of a conservative status quo and an American way of life that sanctified free-market capitalism, decried socialism and communism, and narrowly proscribed the legitimacy of working class and racial minority aspirations. By the end of the war, as the Bolshevik revolution was spreading its influence over Europe and, to some, appeared poised to cross the Atlantic, fear that communism was infecting labor movements and ethnic minorities while further radicalizing established militant movements was widespread. The Bureau and its intelligence partners would skip nary a beat in making a transition from fears of German subversion to near panic over the march of Bolshevism.

The army entered World War I even less prepared than the Justice Department to respond to domestic security issues, yet, by the war's end, it too had developed an extensive intelligence capability. A distinct military intelligence division had been created in 1885, but by the early 1900s it had lapsed into invisibility. Not until 1915 did even small changes begin to take place, beginning when Maj. Ralph H. Van Deman, one of only a handful of trained intelligence officers, was assigned to the War College Division. He recognized the serious neglect of basic intelligence work and America's unpreparedness for war. Urging recreation of a separate intelligence agency, his views were supported by the head of the War College Division, Brig. Gen. H. H. Macomb, but the army chief of staff failed to move on the suggestion.

Despite this setback, the War College Division increased its collection and interpretation of information coming from war-torn Europe. In mid-1916, when the public became enraged by spectacular stories of German spies at work in America, the army took another step. Newly appointed Secretary of War Newton D. Baker, a progressive reformer who had pacifist leanings and no experience in military matters, ordered the establishment of a "Bureau of Information," headed by Maj. Douglas MacArthur, to control rumors and protect military secrets. Van Deman developed a system whereby each large army command was to have an intelligence officer, some of whom undertook occasional confidential missions to investigate enemy activities such as the rumor that Japanese soldiers were secretly training in Mexico. He also established liaison with the investigative branches of the Navy, Justice, and State Departments and the Secret Service. Thus the outlines of an organized military intelligence agency were being sketched in the two years before America's entry into World War I, but the army still had only two intelligence officers (including Van Deman), two clerks, and a few national guard officers receiving rudimentary intelligence training when hostilities commenced in April 1917.[36]

The development of a well-organized, efficient army intelligence agency took nearly the entire wartime period. This necessitated liberating intelligence from its burial within the General Staff organization. The few "dedicated military intelligence zealots" at the beginning of the war had to justify, build, and then expand their agency. Van Deman, the "father of military intelligence," spearheaded this effort. At first the chief of staff only gave permission to conduct "secret service work" as part of the War College's numerous other responsibilities. But Van Deman managed to get Secretary Baker's ear, and by early May 1917 a semi-independent Military Intelligence *Section,* headed by Van Deman, was established within the War College Division. When the General Staff was reorganized nine months later, the Military Intelligence *Branch* was put on an autonomous basis within a newly created Executive Division. Nonetheless, the secretary of war and the chief of staff had a "stubborn aversion" to true independence, which did not finally come until 26 August 1918. Five months previously, Maj. Gen. Peyton C. March had been recalled from France to become the new chief of staff. He was a forceful advocate of a Military Intelligence *Division* coequal with the other three General Staff divisions. Coincident with March's reforms came a change in leadership: Brig. Gen. Marlborough Churchill took command when Van Deman was detailed overseas.[37]

During the first few weeks of the war Maj. Van Deman (he was promoted to lieutenant colonel in May and colonel in August 1917) personally reviewed all major decisions and initiatives, but it soon became impossible for one person to accomplish this. Fortunately, the British military mission provided a model, which Van Deman adopted, dividing all responsibilities into espionage and counter-espionage. The terms positive and negative intelligence were used to distinguish these responsibilities. The Positive Branch focused on military, social, economic, and political situations abroad, whereas the Negative Branch was devoted to uncovering and suppressing enemy activity within the United States. Again following British practice, each branch had sections distinguished by function. The two directly concerned with domestic subversion, and which handled most investigations of black suspects or persons alleged to be sowing disloyalty among blacks, were

M.I.3, Counter Espionage in the Military Service, and M.I.4, Counter Espionage Among the Civilian Population. Both were housed in the Negative Branch, which also included M.I.10, Censorship.[38]

Secretary of War Baker, although more concerned for the protection of civil liberties than hardliners in the army and the Justice and Post Office Departments, nonetheless concurred in the army's "aggressive role in domestic security throughout the war." This necessitated much decentralization with branch offices established first in New York and later in several other cities. By the end of the war, MID also had intelligence units at ports of embarkation, plus "a multitude of field intelligence officers . . . operating at all major army posts, camps and stations, including airfields, hospitals, arsenals and war prison barracks." Other intelligence officers coordinated the protection of military plants from possible sabotage and helped censor postal, telephone, telegraph, and radio communications. Intelligence officers were instructed to collect information on suspected enemy sympathizers, whether civilians or military personnel, and cooperate with Bureau agents and local authorities. They were not, however, authorized to make arrests.[39]

An efficient command structure was not in place until relatively late in the war, in part because personnel increased so dramatically throughout the war. Although the number of General Staff (regular army) officers assigned to headquarters in Washington never exceeded ten, officers drawn from the several drafts and others recruited especially for intelligence duties numbered one hundred by the end of 1917 and 272 at the Armistice. In addition, more than a thousand civilians were employed by MID in Washington by that time. Its budget grew commensurately, and although officers like Van Deman and Churchill felt hampered by a shortage of trained personnel they never had to complain about a lack of funds.[40]

The rapid expansion of military intelligence operations necessitated a parallel growth in coordination with other governmental agencies. Prewar cooperation with the State and Navy Departments was handled informally or through a mutual exchange of liaison officers. High-level coordination was accomplished several months before America entered the war with the formation of the Council of National Defense, whose membership included the secretaries of war, navy, labor, commerce, agriculture, and the interior. A number of operating agencies derived from the Council, such as the War Trade Board and Censorship Bureau. They required military information and reciprocated by furnishing the army with the data they gathered. The closest links ultimately were established with those agencies directly engaged in counterintelligence: the Office of Naval Intelligence, the State Department, and especially the Bureau of Investigation. The army initially expected that treasury agents would share major responsibility for stopping spies and cutting the flow of goods and information to the enemy. But after July 1917, with the Secret Service essentially excluded, military intelligence assumed major responsibility for plant and waterfront security while the Bureau became preeminent in ferreting out suspected spies and enemy agents. In addition, the Navy, Justice, and Post Office Departments gave military intelligence all secret communications for decoding and deciphering.[41]

Censorship was another shared responsibility during the war. President Wilson's first executive order on this matter, issued a week after the war began, established the Committee on Public Information to implement a system of self-censorship by the nation's press. Two weeks later, another order gave the War Department censorship authority over telephone and telegraph lines leading out of the country, with the navy assigned similar responsibility for cables. The Post Office Department handled censorship of all mail to or from foreign countries where the Allies were not already maintaining such vigilance. All these duties multiplied chaotically in the first months of the war, eventually necessitating a third presidential executive order in October 1917 establishing the National Censorship Board composed of representatives from the two military services, the post office, the War Trade Board, and the CPI. The following year, the director of army intelligence officially became the chief military censor. By that time, newspapers, magazines, and books leaving or entering the country were being carefully examined. At the end of the war nearly three hundred military intelligence personnel, the majority of whom were civilians, worked on censorship.[42]

In like manner, control over foreign travel evolved into a shared responsibility during the war. Prior to 1918 American citizens traveling abroad were not required to have passports, and entry into the country was not strictly regulated. But the war emergency brought changes. The Passport Act of May 1918 assigned ultimate control over all travel to the State Department but gave six other agencies, including the War Department and the Bureau of Investigation, advisory roles. Since both maintained extensive lists of suspected enemy aliens, spies, and others deemed hostile to the war effort or the government, they were to comb their files for those who should not be permitted to leave the country. Military intelligence officers and State Department personnel examined outgoing and incoming travelers at strategic ports. Military attaches abroad helped screen visa requests. By the end of the war, no passports were issued without the applicants' names first being checked by MID. While the State Department had the final say over who would be granted visas and passports, the assistance of military and naval intelligence and the Bureau helped knit these four organizations together and enhanced their stature in security matters.[43]

One of the most serious obstacles faced by the Negative Branch was the shortage of trained officers. Not infrequently they were assigned this task because they had failed at other responsibilities. Many were uncertain whether they possessed arrest powers (they did not). Training gradually improved matters, but there was too much to learn in too short a time. Many of the most effective intelligence officers were ultimately recruited directly from civilian life, and several who held key positions were, like Van Deman and Churchill, Harvard graduates. Despite the Ivy League overlay, however, the deficiency of competent personnel was never completely resolved, forcing the army to rely heavily on amateur detectives.[44]

Although the Negative Branch was not formally created until relatively late in the war, its most important functions—the conduct of counterespionage within the military as well as the civilian population, and the management of censorship—

had been undertaken from the earliest weeks of the conflict. General Churchill later explained its justification for civilian counterintelligence:

> The investigative features of MID were a wartime necessity. Germany unquestionably expected to be able to thwart our military effort by causing sedition and disloyalty in our troops, by fostering the natural grievances of the enemy aliens included in the draft, and by sabotage and destruction in our munitions works, at our docks and on our transports. Neither the Department of Justice nor the Secret Service of the Treasury was adequate to do all the investigation required in the United States during the war. Moreover, although the idea of any investigation of individuals in the military service is repugnant to most military men, I am sure that they all agree that if a state of war makes such an investigation necessary, we want it done by agencies under our own control, and not by unsympathetic civilian bureaus.[45]

Colonel K. C. Masteller, who was succeeded by Col. Alexander B. Coxe, initially led the Negative Branch. Its most important components were M.I.3, responsible for investigations within the military service, and M.I.4, which conducted counterespionage operations in the civilian population. With millions of men conscripted into the army, fears abounded that persons of dubious loyalty, especially German nationals, were wearing the uniform and could harm mobilization. By the end of the war, M.I.3 also investigated the loyalties of civilian workers for the YMCA, Red Cross, and other organizations doing welfare work among army personnel. A subsection, M.I.3C, was formed to frustrate enemy infiltration in Washington, D.C. Under the leadership of Capt. Harry A. Taylor, it operated out of a "blind" office and investigated, among several targets, alleged subversion of blacks living or working in the district. This activity obviously blurred the distinction between M.I.3 and M.I.4. So, too, did M.I.3's role as official liaison with the American Protective League.[46]

The APL provided military intelligence with a "tremendous amount of invaluable assistance in the conduct of . . . many difficult investigative chores." Its headquarters were eventually moved from Chicago to Washington, and one of its national directors, Charles Daniel Frey, was commissioned as a captain so he could allocate military cases to volunteers. The number of cases became so large that a separate subsection of M.I.3 was created to maintain this liaison. American Protective League assistants were not confined to strictly military matters; in addition to performing "character and loyalty investigations" on officer candidates and overseas-bound civilian welfare workers, they assisted intelligence officers in various parts of the country by spying on labor radicals, participating in illegal raids on the IWW, and operating undercover against alleged enemy agents.[47]

Civilian intelligence was largely uncharted territory for M.I.4. Its largest and most important subsection was M.I.4B, which divided civilian counterespionage among the six geographical departments of the army. The Eastern and Northeastern Departments specialized in investigating alien enemies and foreign "racial" (i.e., European ethnic) groups. The Southeastern Department focused on "negro subversion and political demagoguery." The Central Department, headquartered in Chicago, devoted particular attention to Germans as well as "racial organizations." Investigation of "Mexican racial problems" along the border was the specialty of the Southern Department, whereas the Western Department focused on radical labor unionists in the IWW as well as Japanese and East Indian nationalists. Information came to M.I.4B from intelligence officers in the field, the Bureau of Investigation, postal censors, naval intelligence, the Secret Service, the APL, and the State Department.

The mission of M.I.4B was to counter specific threats to the nation's security, while a smaller subsection, M.I.4E, studied allegedly dangerous movements like the IWW, Russian Bolshevism, and the (Germanic) Lutheran Church. The chief of this subsection during mid-1918 was Maj. Joel E. Spingarn, chairman of the board of the NAACP and a prominent white liberal. His recommendation that military intelligence develop a nationwide "patriotic" counterpropaganda program, including an ambitious scheme to jack up sagging black morale, was not implemented. Meanwhile, the Negative Branch conducted widespread investigations of African Americans, focusing on the influence of militant newspapers and magazines and individuals suspected of encouraging noncompliance with the draft. Its most capable black officer, Maj. Walter H. Loving, also investigated many complaints lodged by soldiers and numerous reports of low morale.[48]

The concept of directly propagandizing soldiers, especially the foreign-born, was eventually embraced in mid-1918 with the establishment of a military morale section. When it became apparent that civilian enthusiasm had a direct impact on the patriotism of soldiers, a separate Military Morale Branch was created to coordinate both civilian and military efforts to stimulate positive views toward the war.[49]

By war's end the Negative Branch was the most significant stateside operation in the Military Intelligence Division, employing a headquarters staff of 202 officers, 65 volunteers awaiting commissions, 60 enlisted members of the Counter Intelligence Police, and 605 clerks. They in turn supervised "a veritable host of military and civilian personnel operating throughout the field." Strengthening these efforts was the work of many other government agencies. Army historian Bruce Bidwell has charted the spectrum of agencies with which military intelligence maintained liaison. Table 1 shows the resources available to the growing political intelligence system and the central role the Justice Department played in it.[50]

Van Deman and other military intelligence pioneers justified this network very early in the war. They saw subversion by German agents and sympathizers as the nation's chief domestic threat. Public opinion, if not hard evidence, held that blacks and other aggrieved minorities, as well as pacifists, isolationists, and German Americans, were particularly susceptible to enemy influence. There were enough tales of sabotage, including a few spectacular incidents, to convince many Americans that Germany was poised to wreak havoc in the United States. Anti-German sentiment was widespread. This dictated that the army take strong preven-

Table 1
Federal Agencies Engaged in Political Intelligence, 1917–18

1. Counterespionage in the United States (General)
- a. Bureau of Investigation (Justice Department)
- b. Office of Naval Intelligence
- c. American Protective League (Justice Department)
- d. Local chiefs of police and county sheriffs
- e. Credit associations
- f. Large American corporations

2. Counterespionage in the United States (Special)

ENEMY TRADE AND FINANCE
- a. War Trade Intelligence (War Trade Board)
- b. War Industries Board
- c. Alien Property Custodian (Justice Department)
- d. Internal Revenue Service (Treasury Department)
- e. Federal Reserve Board
- f. Federal Trade Commission

TRAVEL
- a. Bureau of Immigration (Labor Department)
- b. Customs Valuation Bureau (Treasury Department)
- c. Federal Railroad Administration (Railroad Police)
- d. The Pullman Company

COMMUNICATIONS
- a. Post Office Department
- b. Chief Cable Censor
- c. Committee on Public Information

LABOR PROBLEMS
- a. Secretary of War's Office
- b. American Federation of Labor

CITIZENSHIP AND RACIAL PROBLEMS
- a. Department of Justice
- b. Bureau of Naturalization (Labor Department)
- c. Department of State

PRODUCTION AND SUPPLIES
- a. United States Shipping Board
- b. Emergency Fleet Corporation
- c. U.S. Food Administration
- d. U.S. Fuel Administration
- e. Bureau of Aircraft Production
- f. War Industries Board

3. Counterespionage Outside the United States
- a. Foreign Service of the Department of State
- b. British Liaison Office
- c. French Liaison Office
- d. Italian Military Attaché
- e. Belgian High Commission

tive "negative" measures overshadowing the work of positive intelligence. But in the last half-year of the war the focus of military intelligence, like that of the Justice Department, shifted to fears of radical and racial movements. With the German threat extinguished on the home front, new obstacles to winning the war appeared to surface. Might not national morale, the draft, the safety of munitions factories, and success of war bond and Red Cross campaigns be undermined by the growth of leftist political movements? Sabotage, especially among discontented portions of the civilian population, seemed a concrete possibility by mid-1918. The heterogeneity of the population required army intelligence to probe deeply into social, economic, political, and religious trends among major racial and ethnic groups, particularly African Americans. Thus, the growing fear of Bolshevism by the war's end allowed no relaxation of military intelligence. Soon after the Armistice, linkages with the temporary wartime agencies evaporated as those entities were phased out, but bonds between the Military Intelligence Division and the Justice, State, and Post Office Departments remained intact.[51]

Postmaster General Burleson was proud of asserting that his was the only cabinet department "that had a nation-wide organization [so] thoroughly effective . . . that only in a few cases was it necessary to create separate organizations to meet the exigencies of war." In fact, every other part of the federal bureaucracy relied on the post office. Its new wartime duties included operating an international postal system for the armed forces; transporting millions of pieces of mail for new agencies (including 22 million draft questionnaires); administering parts of the Espionage and Trading-with-the-Enemy Acts; registering enemy aliens; using rural post offices as armed services recruiting stations and Department of Labor employment agencies; and promoting food and fuel conservation, Liberty and Victory Bonds, and war savings stamps. Finally, postal inspectors furnished valuable intelligence to the army and navy intelligence services, the State Department, and the Bureau of Investigation while safely handling "many thousands of communications of confidential character" to and from these agencies.[52]

The Justice and Post Office Departments share the distinction of most drastically inhibiting political expression during World War I. They were natural allies. When Treasury Secretary McAdoo proposed a unified "Bureau of Intelligence" in the spring of 1917, Burleson added his protest to that of Attorney General Gregory, urging President Wilson not to try to fix something that was not broken. No confusion or overlapping authority existed between the post office and other departments, he claimed. When postal inspectors discovered information of possible use in federal prosecutions they promptly sent it to the Department of Justice. No new intelligence bureau was formed, and the Secret Service was excluded from wartime investigations of subversives, dissenters, and enemy aliens while the post office joined the Bureau, State Department, and army and navy intelligence agencies in the network that allocated responsibilities and coordinated investigations and strategies.[53]

The Espionage and Sedition Acts, which denied use of the mails to printed matter alleged to incite treason or sedition, closely linked the Post Office and Justice Departments. (Sealed letters for domestic delivery were theoretically not to be opened.) Investigations of suspect publications were conducted not only by postal inspectors but also by military intelligence and Bureau agents, sometimes by all three. Justice, of course, was responsible for prosecution, but the post office wielded a powerful weapon in revoking second-class mailing permits (the second-class rate paid by periodicals covered only 15 percent of the actual costs to the post office, amounting to an 85 percent taxpayer subsidy).[54] Repeat violators could be banned from even first-class mailing. Burleson vowed to enforce the law in such a way that no loyal publication need fear, but he had a different view of the First Amendment than did the more outspoken journalists and publishers:

> Any newspaper of any political opinion or any shade of opinion can say what it chooses in legitimate criticism of the President, the Administration, the Army, the Navy, or the conduct of the war. Nothing will be excluded from the mails because of being politically or personally offensive to the Administration. Nothing will be considered except the welfare of the Nation, and only assaults upon this will bring about action.
>
> But there is a limit, and this limit is reached when a newspaper begins to say that this Government got into the war wrong, that it is there for a wrong purpose, or anything else that impugns the motives of the Government, thereby encouraging insubordination. Newspapers cannot say that this Government is the tool of Wall Street, or of munitions makers, or the tool of anybody. Nor can anything be published disigned [*sic*] and calculated to incite the people to violate this law. There can be no campaign against conscription and the draft law, nothing that will interfere with enlistments or the raising of an army, or the sale of authorized bonds, or the collection of authorized revenue. Nothing designed to hamper or obstruct in any way the prosecution of the war to a successful termination can be published and circulated. Nothing that is palpably intended to injure this Government and to aid the cause of the enemy can be so circulated.[55]

Complaints against these policies flooded into the White House and postal headquarters, prompting the president to warn Burleson that "we must act with the utmost caution and liberality in all our censorship." The postmaster general gave assurances that he would administer his responsibilities "with moderation and caution but with firmness and dispatch" and issued guidelines for the press, but he knew that Wilson's indecisive cabinet leadership would allow him to march to his own rather than the president's drumbeat. This in fact is what happened when Burleson announced the socialist *Milwaukee Leader* would not be delivered by the postal service. Wilson was not convinced such draconian measures were justified, but he did not attempt to rein in the postmaster general.[56]

Censorship of the press, ideally, was to be voluntarily implemented by editors and publishers. To a considerable degree this was the case, but self-censorship under the threat of punishment was in fact coercion. By late in the war, several periodicals had abdicated journalistic responsibility for "patriotic" compliance. The post office commended one New York newspaper that refused to quote the words of dissenters like Eugene V. Debs, Scott Nearing, and John Reed in order to avoid broadcasting allegedly seditious remarks. The paper only wrote that an individual disparaged the Allies or the war and that the offending words were known to the authorities. Burleson hoped this policy would be universally adopted by the press.[57]

The post office also joined representatives of the Navy and War Departments, War Trade Board, and the CPI on the Censorship Board. The chief postal censor chaired the board, so the post office largely dictated its policies. The board ostensibly was to review all incoming and outgoing international mail not already censored by England, France, or Italy. Yet despite assurances it would only interfere with domestic correspondence in cases of extreme necessity, the board in fact read mail to and from many opponents of the war. The postmaster general, who had been awarded "virtually dictatorial control" by the Espionage and Sedition Acts over the politically dissenting and foreign language press and given broad leeway to monitor the private correspondence of those deemed dangerous to the state, thus "proved to be neither a temperate nor a benevolent dictator." Perhaps anticipating the negative judgment of history, Burleson claimed that wartime censorship was the "most undesirable task ever imposed upon the Postal Establishment" but was nonetheless done "with moderation, justice, and fairness." Proof of this was the fact that the courts upheld the government in all litigated cases. After the war, Burleson's staff claimed that his censorship responsibilities were "quite irksome, as the Postmaster was by heredity and training a strong believer in absolute freedom of thought and speech, and especially did he believe in a free press." Evidence to the contrary, however, is more convincing.[58]

Strong wartime bonds were forged between the Post Office Department, army intelligence, and the Bureau of Investigation. A key player was postal solicitor William H. Lamar who sent lists of proscribed publications to the other two agencies. Once publications were barred from the mails Bureau chief Bielaski's office ensured that express companies would not deliver the offending pieces.[59] The post office established Bureau M-1, also known as the Translation Bureau, in New York. That city was seen as home to a large disloyal alien population and its nearly three hundred foreign-language newspapers, a veritable "hotbed of intrigue." Staffed by several "dollar-a-year" patriots, M-1 detected pro-German, anti-British, and anti-ally propaganda plus socialist attacks on capitalism and the government. More than four hundred college professors volunteered as translators to help monitor the foreign-language press. "Disloyal organizations" like the American Union Against Militarism (forerunner of the American Civil Liberties Union), the Women's Peace Party, and the IWW were also watched. Copies of black newspapers that criticized the government or treatment of African-American soldiers were also collected and, as was the case with suspect white publications, their offensive articles were blue-penciled and analyzed by Lamar for possible legal action. By 1918, pro-Bolshevik publications also came under heavy scrutiny.[60]

The State Department was the fourth major partner in the wartime political intelligence establishment, although it did not become significantly involved in attacks on black militancy until the Red Scare years. Before America's entry into the war, the State Department utilized the Secret Service to investigate German diplomats and spy suspects, but use of that agency largely ended with the formation of the interdepartmental political intelligence partnership in mid-1917. Even before this arrangement was formalized, the State Department was working in concert with the other agencies. An early example was the advocacy by Secretary of State Lansing, Secretary of War Baker, and Secretary of the Navy Josephus Daniels for an "authoritative agency to assure the publication of all the vital facts of national defense" so as to ensure the "confidence, enthusiasm and service" of all Americans in the war effort. They believed that both propaganda and censorship could be "joined in honestly and with profit" if administered wisely by a civilian who could "gain the understanding co-operation of the press," especially if they had a voice in such an effort. President Wilson quickly approved this Committee on Public Information, appointing George Creel as its head. Similar cooperation occurred in early 1918 when Justice, State, and the armed services' intelligence agencies jointly drafted a passport bill that included roles for all four intelligence services, with the State Department maintaining supremacy.[61]

Just as the Bureau of Investigation, military intelligence, and the Office of the Solicitor had responsibility for internal security matters within the Justice, War, and Post Office Departments, the Office of the Counselor (redefined as the Office of the Undersecretary in mid-1920) held similar importance in the State Department. The counselor was the secretary of state's chief of staff and principle adviser. His own staff monitored black militancy and the influence of revolutionary movements on race radicals in the postwar months as part of its larger focus on communists. Two assistants to the counselor, L. Lanier Winslow and William L. Hurley, became the resident experts on such matters and established liaison with their counterparts in army intelligence and the Bureau. In addition, the State Department's own Secret Service agents were directed by the counselor's office and would investigate black activism after the war.[62]

Cooperation between State and its political intelligence partners during World War I covered a wide range of activities. While Justice, MID, and the Office of Naval Intelligence searched their files for reasons why travelers should be denied passports, and attachés abroad helped screen visa applicants, the Division of Passport Control, with one of the largest staffs in the State Department, made the final decision. One result of this activity for African Americans was the effort to prevent black militants from traveling to France at the time of the Paris peace conference lest they raise embarrassing issues concerning the self-determination of Africans. Obstacles were also put in the way of a Pan-African congress running concurrently with the peace talks. The State Department later denied having barred black travelers as a matter of policy, but those who managed to reach France had to employ subterfuges and go without passports.[63]

One other intelligence partner was the Office of Naval Intelligence, led during the war by Rear Adm. Roger Welles and into the turbulent postwar months by Rear Adm. Albert P. Niblack. Although its interest in black militancy focused primarily on alleged Japanese influence over Marcus Garvey's black nationalist movement in the waning months of the Red Scare, ONI joined the other intelligence agencies in a wide range of investigations from 1917 onward. According to naval historian Jeffery Dorwart, the war "catapulted ONI into the complicated and murky work of secrecy, international espionage and counterespionage, code breaking, deception, surreptitious entry, eavesdropping, and domestic surveillance." Naval intelligence's capability and manpower at the beginning of the war were as meager as the army's, but by the end of 1918 its size rivaled that of the MID. As with the Post Office, War, State, and Justice Departments, "spying, surveillance, and secret operations" continued after the war as ONI made a quick transition to focus on Bolshevism, labor unrest (particularly the IWW), and black militancy.[64]

None of the political intelligence bureaucracies was equipped to understand and sympathize with the aspirations of African Americans in a period of both racial and national ferment. Few individuals held egalitarian views on matters of race. Major Spingarn was an obvious exception, but he had no long-term impact on governmental racial policies. Other white males who staffed the federal intelligence agencies in the 1910s, when they encountered racial issues, usually saw their role as preserving existing racial arrangements and proscriptions. Their personal interactions with blacks were usually limited to employer-servant relationships, which was the pattern in many white middle-class Washington households. Blacks who enjoyed federal employment worked typically as postal clerks (under segregated conditions) or as office "boys," janitors, and porters. Most of the State Department's black employees were messengers who escorted foreign dignitaries from reception rooms to offices, "humble but well-established functionaries who through long years of experience [had] themselves become schooled in the diplomatic tradition."[65]

One such man who witnessed the events of the world war was Edward Augustine Savoy, "the diminutive and, in the course of time, bent Negro" who served twenty-one secretaries of state from 1869 to 1933. As discreet a diplomat as any bred at Harvard, he was particularly artful between 1914 and 1917 in ensuring that envoys representing warring powers who chanced to enter the State Department at the same time would not suffer the embarrassment of meeting face to face. It was also Savoy's duty to present a diplomat who was being expelled from the country with his credentials.[66] But Savoy was, after all, only an attendant. Although his finesse in delicate situations might be appreciated on occasion, he and other black messengers—like their counterparts in other offices—were expected to be "invisible men."

Federal officials responded negatively to black aspirations during World War I because they so single-mindedly focused on preventing subversion and were so deeply influenced by fears and stereotypes. In a larger sense, though, they were also profoundly oblivious to African Americans' lives and issues. Woodrow Wilson's only consistent source of insight concerning how blacks felt was occasional correspondence from a few white liberals like George Foster Peabody, who urged the president to be more sensitive to racial issues, and from Booker T. Washington’s equally conservative successor at Tuskegee, Robert Russa Moton. Secretary of War Baker was perhaps the most enlightened member of the cabinet on matters of race. He received numerous communications from Peabody and benefited (indirectly, through the chain of command) from the wartime services of a black special assistant, the well-known racial moderate Emmett J. Scott. But letters from Moton and Peabody seemed not to have altered Wilson’s post-Reconstruction southern racial views, and Baker only rarely broached racial issues with the president. Two other cabinet heads whose departments reacted negatively to black aspirations, Attorney General Gregory and Postmaster General Burleson, were Texans (and fishing companions) who appear to have had no understanding of Black America and were, at best, racial paternalists. Burleson and Wilson on occasion told “darkey” stories and used offensive racial language.[67] Bureaucrats like army intelligence’s Van Deman and Churchill and postal solicitor Lamar might have understood racial issues more perceptively had they read their investigators’ reports through different lenses. But they, too, were captives of their own social and racial milieu. Moreover, they were fixated on threats, which they exaggerated, first from Germans and later from the Left.

Any chance that wartime labor requirements or the need to enlist the entire population in enthusiastic support for the conflict would result in concrete improvements in African Americans’ civil or social rights was scuttled by the Wilson administration’s deep suspicions of anybody or anything that challenged the status quo or participation in the war effort. The government’s expanding domestic intelligence network pursued its manifold suspicions with abandon, unhampered by strong internal restraints and advantaged by the fact that the first ten amendments to the Constitution were largely symbolic and theoretical, not yet concrete guarantees of civil liberties. Furthermore, the mood of the country sanctioned intolerance, including lynching and other mob action. Thus, although wartime repression of African Americans may appear to be merely illustrative of the paranoia of the times and the perceived necessity to crack down on all dissent, it was much more. National resolve required national unity. Unity required unquestioning adherence to the status quo, lest enemies gain opportunity to undermine either production or the country’s will. And maintaining the status quo meant fostering racism. Many blacks, however, were unwilling to offer enthusiastic support for the war without evidence that racism in civilian and military life was being genuinely addressed. However, the Wilson administration—including intelligence bureaucrats and military leadership—was uninterested in any meaningful racial reform. Intent on curbing any dissent that might undermine national unity, it was willing to use the war as a pretext for blunting African-American militancy and for reinforcing white supremacy.

2 "Very full of the anti-war spirit": Fears of Enemy Subversion during World War I

War with the Central Powers unleashed a flood of fears that internal enemies were preparing to sabotage America's war effort. This near panic stemmed from two sources. Support for war with Germany was far from unanimous. While most Americans saw war as inevitable in April 1917, and most leaders of public opinion favored it, the majority of those who would fight and sacrifice the most hoped armed conflict might be avoided. Congress received thousands of pieces of mail opposing American intervention and over a tenth of its members voted against the war declaration. In reaction to these widely held reservations, ardent supporters of the war fostered a superpatriotism that would eventually subvert the freedom to dissent. As one recent historian notes, "devotion to the flag became the symbol of a new harsh and unyielding patriotism. Patience and prudence were trampled underfoot during the months that followed as well-intentioned citizens rushed to 'stand by the President.'"[1]

Fear of subversion was also fed by rumors that Germans and German Americans were prepared to wage their own war on a vulnerable home front. Wild tales had German army reservists who had previously emigrated to the United States ready to form a guerrilla army. Evidence of sabotage seemed to appear everywhere. Alleged spies were said to be in government departments, shipyards, and munitions factories. When the cabinet discussed such issues shortly before America's entry into the war, Attorney General Thomas Gregory was convinced that the nation faced a real threat of internal subversion. This fear was not without some foundation. In July 1916, German saboteurs destroyed the Black Tom, New Jersey, railroad wharves where munitions were loaded onto vessels for shipment to the European Allies. Then, in January 1917, explosions set by German saboteurs who had sneaked into the country demolished a munitions factory in Kingsland, New Jersey, which produced artillery shells for Britain and Russia. Four days after Congress declared war, 112 workers at a large munitions plant in Eddystone, Pennsylvania, were killed in an explosion thought to have been engineered by German agents. Shortly thereafter, a German was caught before he was able to dynamite a dam on the Rio Grande. By that time, however, most would-be saboteurs had fled the country, and the number of suspected bombings decreased dramatically.[2]

Once America entered the war, the web of suspicion was spun much wider, including both the foreign born and natives. The Justice Department's vast civilian volunteer force, the American Protective League, magnified the climate of distrust and paranoid suspicion by hunting not only slackers (draft delinquents) and deserters, but also anyone suspected of disloyalty, sedition, or espionage. Although failing to apprehend even one actual enemy spy, the APL helped foster an intense anti-

Germanism that damned as subversive those with Teutonic surnames and led to the condemnation of all things associated with Germany, from sauerkraut and hamburger to Bach and Beethoven.

The result was an intense pressure for "100 percent Americanism." Intolerance became a virtue. Hatred and fear of Germany and things German coalesced. At the same time, the dictates of patriotism required obeisance to its national icons: pledging allegiance to the flag, singing patriotic anthems, publicly supporting the president, sacrificially contributing to Red Cross and Liberty Bond drives, and willingly fighting to crush the Kaiser. Uniformity of opinion was also required. One was either a patriot or a traitor, and any number of actions could earn the latter epithet.[3] This national mood held new perils for black Americans. Those who openly registered dissent received no more tolerance than whites. Others became suspect not because of any overt words or deeds on their part, but because of widespread white fears that America's subject race was a special target of German subversion and was, because of alleged racial characteristics, likely to be easily manipulated and deluded.

What is remarkable, given the pervasiveness of these white fears, is the degree of black dissent during World War I. It is proof of the fact that a generation of blacks, born neither in slavery nor the Reconstruction years but during the Jim Crow era, was able to confront the racial status quo in words and actions bolder than before. Such expression was clearly safer in the North, as many migrants found, but even some black southerners, in the first years after the death of Booker T. Washington, tested racial boundaries with new, albeit cautious, militancy. When such expression manifested itself as dissent or lack of interest in the war, however, whites often misinterpreted it as disloyalty plain and simple.

White southerners particularly feared German subversion of the black population. From shortly before the declaration of war in early April 1917 until well past the cessation of hostilities nineteen months later, white newspapers printed the wildest rumors as fact. Citizens wrote to the president, the secretary of war, the attorney general, the Secret Service, and their congressmen to voice almost unspeakable fears of plots and uprisings. As they had during the slave insurrection panic shortly before the Civil War, white southerners in 1917 and 1918 felt a particular vulnerability. Ancestral fears of outside agitators and black males' sexual desires and thirst for revenge again lay behind whites' apprehensions that neither blacks' loyalty nor passivity could any longer be depended upon. In such superheated times could local, state, and federal authorities sift truth from fiction and still maintain calm on the home front? If not, if public officials succumbed to the inflamed passions of the day and joined the chorus demanding suppression of disloyalty and dissent at any cost, then politically vulnerable minorities were certain to suffer. Such was the fate of black Americans in 1917 and 1918.

The federal government often lent support to the widening intolerance. Some Justice Department officials like Special Assistant to the Attorney General O'Brian and his assistant, Harvard law professor Alfred Bettman, attempted to curb the most egregious violations of civil liberties. But at the local level, where Bureau of

Investigation agents worked in conjunction with police and sheriffs to probe cases of suspected black disloyalty or German subversion of members of the race, the First, Fifth, Sixth, and Eighth Amendments to the Constitution were little regarded.

As the country prepared for hostilities in early 1917, some African Americans already sensed that war would spawn an intolerance not directed solely at enemy aliens. Blacks already experienced heightened hostility in the South as a result of their growing exodus to northern and midwestern cities in search of economic and social emancipation. Any hint of disloyalty to a nation embracing war might ignite new persecution. For some blacks, accommodationism appeared to be the safest stance. In March, for instance, residents of McDonough, Georgia, twenty-five miles southeast of Atlanta, found it prudent to reassure white neighbors of their acceptance of the status quo and loyalty to the government. A letter to the *Henry County Weekly* signed "Humbly yours, Colored Citizens," claimed McDonough the best place for blacks to live, given the kindness and goodness of the white populace, and promised to turn any "treacherous gossiper" over to the authorities, to discourage migration to the North, and to willingly shed one's last drop of blood for the country.[4] This obsequious posture illustrates the degree to which blacks sensed, even before the declaration of hostilities on 6 April, that nations at war do not tolerate internal dissent and that assertions of racial rights would only bring new dangers and persecutions. Nor, as would soon become apparent, would the United States tolerate any Germans who might seek to capitalize on black disaffection.

Signs of impending intolerance could be seen across the land in early 1917. White citizens communicated fears and demands for protective action to the nearest government officials. In March the Bureau of Investigation opened case file 3057 in what was later called the "Old German" series. This voluminous file on suspected German subversion of the black population would eventually include over a thousand pages reflecting three persistent anxieties expressed by whites nationwide, but especially by those in the South: alarms over disloyal speech, uneasiness that formerly subservient blacks were becoming "uppity," and, worst of all, fear of racial uprisings. The threat of German subversion of the African-American population seemed all too real to white southerners as the nation prepared for war.

Even before the country was officially at war, blacks' reluctance to support armed conflict seemed subversive to many white southerners. The *Wilmington (Delaware) Delmarva Star* printed an article written by John Richard Brown, a black chauffeur, which one Bureau agent described as "very full of the anti-war spirit," as were similar letters from two other blacks addressed to the *Wilmington Evening Journal.* Conferring with both papers' editors, the agent concluded that these letters were either not written by their signers or at least were inspired by someone else antagonistic to the country. While the federal officer made plans for further investigation, the editor of the *Evening Journal* promised to "print nothing in his paper in regard to the matter unless authorized to do so. He [also] suggested that at the proper time he might do some good by letting it be known to his paper that the government was carefully watching the activity of Germans in this respect."[5] If, in fact, such a warning ever was printed, individuals like John Richard Brown would have to weigh their actions more carefully. Entry into the war vastly increased their risks.

With the United States thrust into war, the national mood quickly turned hostile to anyone questioning the rightness of American involvement. Fears of black disloyalty mushroomed, particularly in the South, and especially in those areas with a high proportion of blacks in the population. Often it took no more than trivial or coincidental events to galvanize citizens or federal agents into action. Outside Hampton Roads, Virginia, for instance, a well-dressed white man was reported to be working on a farm near a black clubhouse. Informants could supply no name, but they assumed he was a German since he received no wages (he claimed to be studying farming) and mixed with local blacks. The real danger, according to the Bureau's special agent in charge (SAC) of the Norfolk office, Ralph H. Daughton, was the proximity of this activity to the fleet base at Hampton Roads. To modern eyes, this web of suspicion seems so loosely spun as to be ludicrous, but Daughton perceived sufficient danger to initiate immediate investigation.[6]

The outlines of a persistent southern fear that "outside interests" were inciting blacks to disloyalty are visible in this incident as well as others. Similar fears quickly surfaced in the North Carolina Piedmont, where a worried court official in Franklin County reported that blacks were reading and discussing disquieting ideas in their lodges. The offending material turned out to be a biting editorial from the *Topeka (Kansas) Plain Dealer,* a black paper whose editor, Nick Chiles, more than once earned the suspicions of the Bureau. Chiles's piece condemned blacks who eagerly volunteered to fight for a country that offered them no rights, even in the military. Locals once again linked unrelated events, for the North Carolina informant went on to describe two suspicious strangers in town, one speaking very broken English. The implication was that "outside interests" were subverting blacks, who composed 47 percent of the county's population and thus represented a significant danger if disloyal. Bureau chief Bielaski perceived enough danger in these unconnected threads to suggest an investigation, which a local agent vowed to undertake as soon as possible.[7]

Rumors such as those emanating from North Carolina shortly before the declaration of war and the deeply rooted dread of outside agitation spread fear of German subversion in other southern states. In South Carolina, for example, a *Florence Daily Times* headline warned that "Teutons Try Yankee Trick of Making the Negroes Rise in Rebellion Against Whites. Evidence of Plot in Various Places. It is also Charged that Hand of Germany is in Efforts to Crowd Negroes into Industrial Centers." Enemy agents, the paper elaborated, were using Elm Grove, a black settlement near Greensboro, to incite blacks and spread disloyalty into the tobacco and cotton belts of Georgia, Alabama, and Florida. These suspicions seemed to be confirmed by reputable sources: "The alleged work of Germans in the

South is believed by the [unidentified] federal agents to be closely allied to the recent exodus from the cotton belt to Northern industrial centers of large bodies of negro laborers." It was further rumored that the Ku Klux Klan was organizing to oppose a possible race uprising. The paper went on to quote federal officials who believed that German agents would seduce blacks into migrating to Mexico if war ensued so as to cripple southern agriculture.[8]

Such rumors did not always remain localized, but instead helped fuel the nationwide sense that blacks were susceptible to subversion. Metropolitan dailies far away picked up the Florence story, giving it their own slant. The *St. Louis Republic* revealed "Germans in Plot to Stir up Negroes. Work in South." Enemy agents were gathering support, on promises of social equality with whites, the paper reported. "German schools," many of which were run by the Lutheran Church, were said to be hotbeds of enemy activity. Other persons, representing themselves as doctors, were allegedly hiding out in Elm Grove urging blacks to rise up once whites became preoccupied with the war. Another paragraph, headed "Mammy Exposes Plot," told of "an 'old issue' household darky . . . inspired by the spirit of loyalty to 'her white folks' which marks out the negroes of the old regime, [who] went straight and reported the carryings on to Marse Pritchett." That gentleman confirmed that local blacks had contracted a dangerous virus, being "indifferent to discipline of late and . . . close-mouthed and mysterious. When a negro acts that way there is something in the wind. They don't need much encouragement, and once they get started they could do a lot of damage before we could stop them."[9] Indeed, many blacks were acting differently, and as they sought opportunities in northern war industries, whites (already worried by the Great Migration) blamed the accelerating exodus on the hidden hand of German intrigue. The loss of labor and the possibility of a racial uprising were thus closely linked.

With such fears given currency by the press, it is little wonder that rural whites in black-majority areas panicked on the eve of war. Such was the case in Cades, South Carolina, located in the cotton and tobacco coastal plains region where blacks composed sixty percent of the population, where an official of the Atlantic Coast Line Railroad reported that German agents were stirring blacks to revolt. The suspects were two insurance salesmen attempting to contact each black family in the district. Confiding his fears to his congressman, the railroad employee wrote: "we country people would be at the mercy of a mob of negroes headed by these Germans." Bureau chief Bielaski ordered an immediate investigation, but the subsequent inquiry unearthed nothing concrete.[10]

Farther South, the situation was no less worrisome to whites. In early April, a citizen of Athens, Georgia, where the two races were equal in population, expressed fears common among cotton-belt whites that blacks were morose and sullen, as if German agents had been inciting them to revolt. The situation was particularly grave because of the steep rise in prices. Admitting that blacks in particular suffered from the high cost of living, the citizen warned they were close to insurrection. If that came, a defenseless white populace would suffer rape, murder, and arson no less horrible than those occurring in Europe. Proof of such German subversion seemed all too clear in West Point, Georgia, along the Alabama border, where for a week before war began a man calling himself Dr. Pannkoke was said to have been meeting with blacks and "arousing them." Security demanded vigorous action once hostilities commenced, and local authorities jailed Pannkoke "for his own protection." Floridians experienced many of the same fears. In Tampa, when a grocer reported a black customer who vowed not to fight for the country, the Bureau agent's first instinct was to inquire whether there were suspicious whites in the community.[11] In short, both ordinary whites and federal agents were susceptible to forming panicky conclusions.

White Alabamians were equally stirred by rumors and fears of subversion of blacks as the nation embarked on war. United States Attorney A. D. Pitts notified Washington of "persistent" reports from Mobile and Selma of "a well-defined organization of various and sundry people of both Americans and alien enemies [who] are exciting the negroes throughout every county in this district." Supposedly they were undermining blacks' patriotism and encouraging them to emigrate to Mexico. "In one day I received messages from [the towns of] Lamison in Wilcox county, from Sprott in Perry County, from Demopolis in Marengo County and from Clarke and Choctaw Counties, all being of the same purport and tenor." Whites, he warned, were inclined to lynching. (Certainly they felt their control was threatened; blacks composed half the population in two of the counties and nearly three-fourths in the other three.) Pitts sought approval from the attorney general for averting mob action by prosecuting some individuals as an example to others. As the war progressed, the Justice Department became increasingly afraid of vigilantism, and in at least some cases prosecuted suspects without prima facie evidence so as to prevent a lynching.[12] Pitts's colleagues in the Birmingham area were not only equally alert to danger, but quick to act. Following the Senate's approval of the declaration of war, and not content to wait for the House to act, federal agents arrested two men, one black and one white, and accused them of plotting to incite blacks in Mississippi, Alabama, Louisiana, Georgia, and the Carolinas to sympathize with Germany. The conspirators were also said to be persuading them to flee to Mexico, promising special trains to carry them away on 15 April. Federal authorities announced that these plotters were spreading their evil while posing as Bible salesmen or ministers of the gospel. Two days later another pair of white men "believed to be Germans" were seized at a mining town north of Birmingham and likewise charged with inciting blacks against the government and encouraging their migration to Mexico. That same day, two blacks—Sheppard McKinney and William Ross—were arrested for treason in the southeast corner of Alabama for urging others to revolt and "stick with Germany."[13]

Nowhere during the first days of the war was there greater fear that enemy agents would turn blacks to violence than in Mississippi's northwest Delta region, where blacks represented 90 percent of the population. An alarmed postal official reported a meeting in Tunica County attended by five hundred enthusiastic blacks at which one of them supposedly urged the others to join Germany, Mexico, and Japan in attacking the United States. Coincidentally, "two foreigners of German appearance," ostensibly umbrella repairmen, had been spotted in the vicinity. The author of this report emphasized that the small white minority would be in grave jeopardy if trouble began. Even whites who seemed to be more level headed allowed their imaginations to run wild. The sheriff of Rolling Fork, between Greenville and Vicksburg, reported the recruitment of blacks for a German-Mexican army. Bureau agent Robert S. Phifer made an extensive investigation and concluded: "no nigger in the world is going to leave the Delta for an army in Mexico. But this kind of rumor is all over Mississippi." Most "German talk" among blacks, he believed, came from labor agents out of Chicago. But Phifer was nonetheless decidedly uneasy about possible subversion, adding: "if Germany succeeds in raising trouble among the negros [*sic*] in Mississippi, it is going to be a case of wholesale murder. In Sharkey County, for example, there are about 16 negros to one man. The negros are all armed. . . . The white people there are not going to take any chances if trouble starts; they are simply going to murder or massacre the negros until the trouble is quieted." Other reports echoed these fears, including one from two-thirds-black Panola County claiming that German and Irish agents were spreading "black republic" propaganda.[14] Such suspicious whites may have been traveling salesmen, peddlers, or other itinerants, but they were hardly guilty as charged. As Chapter Eight demonstrates, only a few individuals were found guilty of somehow meddling with the black population.

Even in parts of the South where proportionally far fewer blacks resided, white residents were not immune to exaggerated fears in April 1917. A citizen of Greenville, Tennessee, the hometown and burial place of Pres. Andrew Johnson, where only 5 percent of the population was black, wrote to the Department of Justice that gypsy fortune-tellers were sowing disloyalty among blacks, proof of which was the "truculent and impudent behavior of some of the race, on the streets" which was not manifested before the outsiders came to town. For this citizen, blacks' new boldness in refusing to yield the sidewalk to whites was a demonstration of "disloyalty" prompted by outside agitation.[15]

No greater exaggeration of danger during the first month of war occurred than in Chicot County, Arkansas, where four out of five residents were black. This region was directly across the river from Mississippi's Delta region. Events began with a letter from Lake Village deputy prosecuting attorney William Kirtin to the postmaster, reporting seditious speeches by blacks attending a lodge meeting, including remarks that Germany would win the war and blacks should avenge themselves on whites. Kirtin's information came from a prominent white planter who employed between three hundred and four hundred blacks on his acreage. Kirtin believed that a white man must have infected blacks with this propaganda. Adding that Germans were inciting the blacks, the postmaster forwarded Kirtin's letter to the district's congressman. He in turn sent both communications to the attorney general with the additional warning that whites were heavily outnumbered and apprehensive. Bureau chief Bielaski ordered a prompt inquiry by Agent C. M. Walser, who was posted in Little Rock.

By the time Walser arrived in Lake Village, passions had cooled somewhat. As news of the threatened uprising spread, whites had organized a "home guard" to forestall any sedition or other disloyalty. Apparently town officials had no objection to such vigilantism, for the sheriff, clerk of the circuit court, and marshal accepted the positions of captain, first lieutenant, and second lieutenant. This organization proved sufficient to terrify the local black population. The first targets were the principal of the local "negro school," William Mason, and one of his female teachers. They were charged with removing and desecrating the school's American flag, teaching the children that they lived in a country they could not call their own, and generally inciting prejudice against the white race. All this was on the testimony of one mischievous schoolboy, and hardly added up to a German-inspired uprising.

The school staff appealed to Kirtin for protection, fearing they would be lynched. Mason denied the student's allegation and described the boy's previous efforts to make trouble. Pleading for a hearing before the executive committee of the home guard, Mason managed to persuade them that the charges were unfounded. But to underscore its power and resolve, the white community organized a large patriotic gathering at the courthouse, which blacks found it prudent to attend and to pledge cooperation with local food conservation efforts. Kirtin appeared gratified with these demonstrations of black patriotism and compliance, but warned that "I do not doubt that seditious speeches were made" by blacks in the school, a lodge, or elsewhere. Moreover, he said, "our [white] citizens have very effectively by their prompt and vigorous manner brought the negroes to a full realization of the fact that at all times they will be kept under strict surveillance, and the first one that fails to obey the injunction of the President, 'Obey the law and keep his mouth shut' will be dealt with accordingly." Agent Walser concluded laconically that "this seems to dispose of the negroes causing any trouble in that locality."[16] Indeed, they must have been thoroughly terrified and thankful that the home guard had not enlisted "Judge Lynch." All this started with the vengeful story by a young schoolboy three days after America entered the war, and was then magnified into a German insurrection plot. Lake Village was not to be caught sleeping while the enemy worked its diabolical schemes.

Such events across the South in the spring of 1917 resembled ancient fears of Nat Turner and John Brown. Slavery had ended fifty years before, but many white southerners were still socialized into its twin mythologies of cheerfully subservient house servants faithfully enacting rituals of loyalty, and savage insurrectionists inflamed and manipulated by abolitionist conspirators. A white citizen of Atlanta, summarizing the intertwining of white nostalgia and fears, wrote to President Wilson's personal secretary, Joseph P. Tumulty, on 6 April that "the patriotism and loyalty of the Darkie of the Old School . . . is unquestioned, but the mental attitude of the modern Negro, induced by the tenets of an educational system the limitations of which he has not yet been able to comprehend, and swayed by a superstition and ignorance which renders him incapable of discerning the motives of his alien mentors, has created a situation of serious import." The result was plain: Germans were already at work to "attract and inflame the criminal and lawless element of the race" to acts of disorder and insurrection.[17]

This refrain would be repeated more and more often during the war and post-war years: The dependable antebellum "Darkie of the Old School" was being supplanted by the "modern Negro" (other southern whites used the term "new issue Negro") who failed to recognize the rightness of his "place" in the racial scheme of things. By the end of the war, whites throughout America would increasingly lament the emergence of this "new issue" and the waning of the accommodationist leadership of Booker T. Washington's generation. Even the once "safe" leaders associated with the Bookerite position were less dependably conservative. As whites saw it, there was reason to fear that their ordered and secure world, resting on racial privilege, was being threatened. Enemy agitators were conveniently blamed, but it was self-delusion for whites to believe they were the real source of danger. Rather, they were confronting a new black generation, insistent that the war against Germany was not its only fight. To many blacks, the "Huns of Georgia" were of more immediate concern than the Huns of Germany. As A. Philip Randolph's antiwar and pro-socialist *Messenger* said with sarcasm, "the Negro may be choosing between being burnt by Tennessee, Georgia or Texas mobs or being shot by Germans in Belgium. We don't know about this pro-Germanism among Negroes. It may be only their anti-Americanism—meaning anti-lynching."[18]

Although every southern state was rocked by reports that Germans or other foreign enemies were subverting local blacks, four areas experienced a much higher level of fear, even hysteria, than other regions. In most cases the principal context contributing to white apprehensions was not the identification of actual white suspects, but feelings of vulnerability, due at times to the ratio of nonwhites to whites, to the extent of black out-migration, and to traditional fears of black revenge.

Texas had the greatest number of investigations, many of which were fueled by fears of Mexican intrigue. Anglo Texans felt vulnerable with two subject groups in their midst, blacks and Hispanics, and feared particularly that Germany held influence over Mexico and was encouraging subversion from south of the Rio Grande. After all, had not the Zimmermann note proposed that Mexico declare war on the United States and then be compensated after a German victory by territory lost in the previous century? The German government had also proposed that Japan switch sides and join Mexico against the United States. Given these dreadful possibilities, it seemed logical to many Texans that blacks would be prime targets for German-Mexican-Japanese subversion, and that, given the supposedly childlike and easily manipulated nature of the race, blacks would be receptive to such overtures. The day after the United States declared war, the Bureau office in Dallas received a phone call from police reporting Mexican recruiting efforts. According to one black, the Mexicans had promised: "if you go to Mexico you can live in peace and luxury. The white people [in the United States] are the cause of the Negroes being held down." Two Mexican agents were said to have pledged that the Carranza government would welcome blacks, provide land, education for their children, and a new start in life. Agent F. M. Spencer searched futilely for the suspects, but only learned they had headed for Fort Worth. Authorities there were alerted and the entire police force sought the two men.[19]

Fears that blacks were being enticed to Mexico reached eastward into Mississippi and Alabama, a second region of particular white excitement about black loyalties. Two factors operated in parallel in these states. One was the fear that enemy agents were enticing away essential workers. In fact, a number of investigations found that such suspects were merely recruiters for northern industries. Since labor agents often had to operate secretly due to local hostility and personal danger, they often ignited magnified suspicions. A more important fear pervaded the heart of the Black Belt, however: In rural cotton counties blacks often outnumbered whites four to one, sometimes even more. The white minority had always ruled by force, threat, and lynching. Local white males had always been their first line of defense. Now, with many leaving for military service, those remaining behind felt doubly vulnerable. Particularly in the Mississippi Delta region, fears of disloyalty and rebellion ran unchecked.

Florida was a third region that experienced unusually high apprehensions of black unrest and enemy activity. Again the major background factor was the activity of labor recruiters. Thousands of migrants had already fled to the Northeast through Jacksonville, many on free railroad passes, and with the onset of war this movement took on ominous overtones. As in the Mississippi Valley, alarm over labor shortages coupled with suspicions that hostile forces had engineered the exodus at times led to panic.

Finally, Virginia whites felt a high level of anxiety throughout the war. The Bureau's Norfolk office conducted more investigations of black subversion than any other. Two factors explain this activity. There was legitimate concern for the safety of the huge naval installations, civilian shipyards, and coal piers at Hampton Roads, Portsmouth, Newport News, and Norfolk. The region was teeming with newcomers as civilian employment mushroomed, the naval presence increased, and hundreds of thousands of soldiers embarked for France. Enemy activity, if such actually existed, could indeed have had serious consequences there. But a second factor wildly exaggerated matters. Agents in the Norfolk office, led by Special Agent in Charge Daughton, seemed incapable of distinguishing fantasy from reality, flimsy rumor from likely occurrence. The volume of baseless rumors investigated in the tidewater region was greater than in any other part of the country, at least in part because of the credulity of investigators themselves. In the large majority of cases agents—as well as several black informants and even one of the office clerks, who doubled as an investigator—pursued hysterical reports of secret subversive meetings, which often turned out to be nothing more than church socials. The Bureau would have been remiss if it had not investigated the early rumors, but it continued to take them seriously even after it was clear that such stories were baseless.

The Bureau of Investigation conducted more than 450 separate investigations of alleged black disloyalty in the twenty-two months from March 1917 through December 1918, half of which were conducted between March and June 1917.[20] The earliest inquiries were included in its voluminous "Old German" case file 3057. By the fall of 1917, however, each separate investigation was assigned its own case file number. The total of these investigations thus includes several thousand pages of agents' reports; correspondence between the attorney general and his staff, Chief Bielaski, and U.S. attorneys; as well as numerous letters from private citizens warning of dangers or reporting suspicious activities of neighbors, chance acquaintances, and even relatives. Much of this latter correspondence, of course, was no more than rumor, some of it spiteful. During World War I, however, rumor was grist for the Bureau's mill, and many agents were inclined to regard even the flimsiest tale as likely true unless proved otherwise. A minority of agents correctly perceived that many Americans were prone to self-induced panic about German spies, saboteurs, and agents, as well as their Irish, East Indian, Mexican, and Japanese proxies. But many other agents failed to keep their own heads level, believing that the home front was in serious jeopardy and that they were the first line of defense. A good part of this anxiety was fueled by a parallel fear that more than a few blacks were disloyal or on the verge of revolt.

Two closely related types of Bureau investigations are prominent in its World War I case files: Rumored enemy attempts to provoke black disloyalty, and suspected seditious or otherwise unpatriotic actions by blacks themselves. The Bureau investigated more than 250 blacks in the latter category. This figure is in addition to the thousands of blacks investigated for failure to comply with selective service regulations or who evaded the draft. The largest numbers of black disloyalty investigations originated in Virginia and Texas, each with twice as many as any other state, South or North. It is impossible to tell from extant documentation whether there was actually more disaffection in these states in 1917 and 1918, or whether whites were simply more panicky. Northern and border localities, too, had their share of disloyalty suspects, particularly Chicago, Philadelphia, and Washington, D.C. Indeed, there was much disaffection with the war throughout Black America, from rural hamlets to big-city ghettoes. Bureau reports frequently noted individuals making a variety of allegedly seditious remarks, indicating that blacks who dissented from the nation's dominant patriotic mood often had numerous grievances against their country.

The most frequent accusation against blacks was the making of "disloyal" or "pro-German" statements or circulating pamphlets or newspapers reflecting such sentiments. What constituted disloyalty, of course, was by no means clear. Given the alarmed state of many whites, who feared that Germans were lurking in nearly every dark alley, many innocuous statements were labeled as subversive. But the volume of such allegations indicates how widespread were whites' fears that blacks were less than patriotic. Blacks were also charged with more specific sentiments regarding Germany. Several were reported, for instance, as stating that Germans were better people than American whites, or could be relied upon to treat blacks better. When whites argued that Germany had committed atrocities in Belgium, some blacks replied that lynching in America was equally bad. A few blacks, surveying the global issues, believed that Germany was right and the United States wrong in the present conflict. Others simply registered a blanket condemnation of the war. Even more dramatic were the statements of those who welcomed a German invasion or felt that blacks would be better off if Germany won the war. These individuals frequently asserted that a victorious Germany would grant blacks full rights, including social equality, and others believed that Germany would award them land. While only a few expressed a desire to emigrate to Germany, Bureau files reported that a dozen individuals had sought the opportunity to enlist in the German army to fight against the United States.

Some suspicions were the fabrication of hysterical minds, like the report of blacks displaying a German flag in a lodge hall. Others were based on the virulent anti-Germanism of the day, such as reports of a black man who had lived in Germany, spoke German, and had a German wife. When he offered his services to the government, the agent who interviewed him automatically assumed he was connected with the German government and was trying to spy. Another black man was suspected because he spoke German and had lots of money. Nearly identical was the lengthy investigation of a black couple that also possessed suspicious wealth and kept carrier pigeons. Much inquiry, however, failed to confirm suspicions that they were sending messages to the enemy by "air mail." In such tense times blacks' own wild fabrications were sometimes accepted as fact. The postmaster of Overton, in rural east Texas, reported to the Bureau with all seriousness the testimony of Jim Sanders, who told of two German airplanes landing near his residence at night. Sanders claimed to have actually seen and felt the airplanes and to have sold some chickens and cooking oil to the pilots, who possessed a four-foot-long automatic gun. Local whites who heard Sanders's story, including the postmaster, believed that German agents were indeed flying in at night from Mexico to spy, then returning to their sanctuary before daylight.[21]

In addition to stimulating some "disloyal" opinions about Germany among blacks, the wartime propaganda emphasis on ensuring freedom and self-determination abroad backfired by heightening blacks' grievances at home. Many Bureau reports indicate deep disaffection with the American government and the administration of justice. Some blacks stated outright that the United States could not hope to win. Others registered open hostility to the government or to President Wilson. A few said that they had no country and owed no allegiance to the United States. Nearly two dozen individuals were reported to have said they would refuse to fight until blacks were granted full rights. Others were accused of failing to support Red Cross drives or purchase Liberty Bonds. Over two dozen more were suspected of specific actions inhibiting enlistment or the operation of the draft.

Even more alarming to southern whites were suspicions that blacks were poised for revolt. The South's worst fears had always centered on slave insurrections and, assuaging their own sexual guilt, the belief that black men wanted to seize white women to satisfy both lust and the desire for vengeance. It had not mattered a hundred years before that slave rebels showed no such intentions; this belief was so deeply implanted in the white southern consciousness that evidence to the contrary would not uproot it. It is not surprising, then, that in 1917 and 1918 whites believed that, when sufficient white men were drafted and serving overseas, blacks would accomplish their long-sought revenge by attacking white women. These nightmares were fed by dozens of reports that blacks were plotting uprisings, race riots, or race war. White Texans in mid-1917, for example, feared that the black emancipation celebration, "Juneteenth," would be used as a cover for plotting insurrection. Such fears seemed to be validated by other reports throughout the South that the mood of Black America had turned surly, hostile, bitter, and antagonistic. Servants were allegedly more "uppity" and refused to work for poor whites under any circumstances. Blacks in Sanford, Florida, were said to be talking about no longer washing and ironing for whites, while east of San Antonio a black woman disdainfully told a white woman, "the white people better look out, the first thing they know they will be washing for the Negroes." Other blacks were less ready to yield the sidewalk to whites or observe other canons of racial etiquette. These actions were often attributed to German influence.[22]

Mexico was the source of many white fears in 1917 and 1918, particularly in Texas. Particularly ominous were frequent reports that German officers were organizing military units south of the Rio Grande, waiting to attack as soon as sufficient white American males had been sent overseas and the border area was defenseless. Such fears reached as far as Seattle, where the Bureau investigated a black confectionary chef who boasted that he was party to an agreement in which blacks would start a revolution, whereupon German army reservists in Mexico would invade the Southwest and turn captured territory over to blacks. Naturally these fears were based on suppositions that Mexico would seek revenge for past defeats and territorial losses. One of the most widespread rumors concerned an alleged "Plan of San Diego" to achieve an independent Texas republic. German and Japanese agents were said to be inciting Mexican and black plotters. Embittered Mexican Americans in Duval County were in fact sketching plans for reuniting with their fatherland. Needing allies, they included local blacks in their plot, without having recruited anyone. Authorities discovered the scheme before it could be hatched, and the conspirators fled. But nipping this incident in the bud did not quiet Anglo fears; it merely fed the raft of speculation that linked blacks with revolt.[23]

If blacks were growing more disloyal, as many whites believed, how did such sentiments spread among blacks, especially through the southern countryside? The Bureau received numerous reports of late-night secret meetings and the buying and stockpiling of firearms. This latter fear persisted into the postwar Red Scare months. Agents spent many fruitless hours tracing rumors of clandestine gatherings, either to find no evidence at all, or to discover that they were simply camp meetings, lodge assemblies, or church picnics. At times, whites' worst fears were their own self-fulfilling prophecies. That blacks claimed no knowledge of secret plots was sometimes taken as evidence that such plots were so successful they ensured blacks' silence.[24] Was there really, as whites alleged, an increase in black disloyalty? Blacks were, in fact, more restive. Their dissatisfaction was fueled by the war and migration possibilities. Some may have been attracted to settlement in Mexico. Others may have refused to buy war bonds. But if disloyalty is defined in conventional terms, blacks were not plotting anything approaching treason. Their major inclination was to absent themselves from voluntary participation in the war effort, not block such participation.

Finally, quite a number of blacks suspected of disloyalty, sedition, or pro-Germanism were simply voicing demands for justice and equality. One such group of men was only organizing a union to demand higher wages at a time when the cost of living was rising dramatically and wages elsewhere were on the increase. In another case, both Ferdinand Barnett and his wife, Ida B. Wells-Barnett, were suspected of enemy-inspired activities. He was a prominent Chicago attorney who, after the bloody East St. Louis riot in mid-1917, delivered a speech warning other blacks to arm so as to prevent another massacre. Bureau chief Bielaski ordered a thorough investigation after Chicago's division superintendent, Hinton G. Clabaugh, reported that Barnett was "rabidly pro-German" and spoke that language almost flawlessly. Clabaugh agonized over the fact that under weak Illinois laws, "a citizen may keep practically any amount of firearms and ammunition in his residence without violating any local law." Chicago's police chief believed that most blacks were armed, having bought surplus army rifles sold for two dollars or less in department stores. Thus, "men like Barnett . . . can very easily cause a good deal of trouble if they are not careful." The equation was simple: Barnett was pro-German; he advised arming for self-defense; many blacks had purchased arms; Barnett could cause much trouble. One plus one plus one equaled four, in the Bureau's worried calculus, particularly since its agents were unsuccessful in finding any witnesses to Barnett's speech.[25]

Later that same year, Ida Wells-Barnett, known nationally for her outspoken condemnations of lynching and promotion of black women's rights, came under Bureau pressure because of alleged disloyal activities. Her Negro Good Fellowship League sold buttons protesting the hanging of thirteen black soldiers convicted of mutiny and rioting in Houston. A Bureau agent, accompanied by a detective from the Chicago police force, demanded that she discontinue sale of the buttons. She maintained her right to protest and indicated a willingness to fight the issue in court. Agent Frank G. Clark sabotaged her effort, however, by warning the button manufacturer not to take any more orders or deliver any that had been made.[26]

Others charged with promoting Germany or being disloyal were southerners active in the NAACP. In the fall of 1918, blacks in Atlanta and Birmingham found themselves under suspicion when the American Protective League investigated the distribution of allegedly pro-German leaflets. An NAACP pamphlet entitled "Wake Up" declared: "you are dreaming if you think somebody else is going to give the Negro a square deal when the Negro does nothing to get it. You will get your rights when you go after them and not before." A second circular, "It's Up to You," questioned why blacks had fewer rights than resident aliens. At the same time, the APL, assuming links to "enemy propaganda," was investigating Dr. J. G. Robinson, an NAACP activist in Birmingham, for urging black enlistees to defeat Germany and then bring their rifles home to "blow hell out of prejudice in the south." According to the APL's Birmingham chief, this speech took place in a black church that "has been the scene of several other outbreaks of this kind, and

I feel that it is a very dangerous line for our enemies to be working." There was, in fact, no evidence of enemy involvement. That notwithstanding, the APL investigator closed by noting: "this negro Robinson is nearly white, and apparently pretty well educated, being for the reasons all the more dangerous." That Robinson's address was subsequently printed in leaflet form made matters appear even more serious to anxious white officials.

Local APL agents forwarded their suspicions to the headquarters of both the Bureau of Investigation and the Military Intelligence Division. Chief Bielaski ordered an agent in Montgomery to investigate further, amplifying the sense of danger by claiming that Robinson's remarks "have found a fruitful soil in this community and, as a result of similar views on the part of a lot of negroes here, . . . have found expression in a handbill which was strewn all over this city." That pamphlet did demand greater rights, but it also acknowledged the need for greater patriotism. Although efforts to identify the handbill's printer proved inconclusive, the head of the Atlanta APL concluded that the NAACP was the common thread linking the handbills and Robinson's speech and noted ominously that "such incendiary speeches and any such backing as this [agitation] is liable to lead to very serious consequences in the South as the troops return."

Bureau headquarters found itself in a quandary at this point, having agreed to halt investigation of the NAACP upon its promise to discontinue publication of any "objectionable" literature and confine its efforts to "legitimate work among the negroes." But the Atlanta leaflets and Robinson's speech/circular seemed a violation of the NAACP's pledge. Bielaski continued to believe there might be "enemy interests" behind Dr. Robinson. Not until January 1919, with the war at an end, was the matter put to rest when Special Assistant Attorney General Alfred Bettman instructed Bielaski: "there is nothing [in the leaflets] . . . which warrants any further action by this Department. The propaganda relates exclusively to domestic treatment of the negro and would seem to me to tend to encourage rather than discourage military service of negroes." Throughout all of this, no evidence of German or any other enemy influence was ever uncovered. However, as too often occurred in 1917 and 1918, the existence of black protest was prima facie evidence of subversive activity.[27]

Black challenges to the racial status quo were also often construed as disloyal or pro-German activities. On occasion, even simple aspirations for a better life brought such suspicions. For example, when the Charleston Navy Yard hired four hundred white women and girls to make uniforms in the spring of 1917, putting considerable expense and effort into recruiting and transporting them from the hinterlands, black women, not surprisingly, demanded a share of the jobs. They were rejected on the grounds that segregation required separate facilities and none had been constructed. Unwilling to passively accept this rebuff, the women initiated a well-publicized campaign organized by "some negro league," in the anxious view of Bureau agent Branch Bocock. He feared that "possibly German influence may be behind the trouble and inconvenience at the yard. The local facility is the only place supplying these needed uniforms, and any difficulty affecting the local facility can produce serious possibilities." Officials at the navy yard were perplexed over the insistence of the black women that they be granted employment opportunities. Bocock conferred with naval personnel and the assistant U.S. attorney and all agreed to search for signs of German influence.[28] Of course, they completely overlooked the obvious explanation: No German agent needed to persuade black women that government wages were preferable to what one earned from domestic service or sharecropping.

White northerners were also fearful, although to a lesser extent than southern whites, that blacks were being subverted or were planning violent action. Many of the same rumors present in southern localities also existed in northern cities, where the black population increased dramatically during the Great Migration. The exodus raised blacks' expectations. Many came north intending to better not only their economic position, but their political and social status as well. Race periodicals expressed a new racial militancy, and street-corner orators often spoke with even greater fervency. As long as the war lasted, employment for both races was plentiful. But whites, including many southern migrants on their own pilgrimages for greater opportunity, resented the encroachments of black newcomers. Competition for housing increased the level of racial friction beyond the tensions resulting from wartime anxieties. In short, many northern whites faced unaccustomed challenges to the racial status quo. Some people inevitably saw enemy influence in such changes. Nor surprisingly, northern agents of the Bureau of Investigation and their APL volunteers investigated numerous allegations that blacks were pro-German or disloyal. They suspected still others of impeding enlistment. In fact, some northern blacks echoed their southern kinsmen in arguing that it was a white man's war, or had positive things to say about Germany. But whites did not fear alleged German subversion of blacks in the North with the same gut level of panic that gripped southern localities simply because blacks did not outnumber whites in any northern locale or seem to have motives for revenge.

Even when obviously well-informed blacks spoke critically of the war, suspicious whites saw them as marionettes in the hands of enemy puppeteers. Such was the case of Eliza and Granville Martin. Eliza was reported to be spreading seditious rumors and hoping for the defeat of England and the United States. APL operative P. D. Gold was assigned to investigate the Martins, who had lived in New York for sixteen years since leaving the Carolinas. Granville was employed as a butler, while Eliza did day work. Gold flattered himself that his own southern background gave him particular insight into the Martins. He concluded that Eliza's offending statements could not have been her own. She clearly was of the "class of southern negro" that would easily be an "ignorant and innocent tool" of German propagandists. Certainly no black woman "of her type and training" would be so well versed in current history as to originate the critical remarks about England attributed to her. Gold was certain Eliza Martin was not the real culprit. "Knowing the negro race as I do," Gold suggested that someone representing authority should persuade the Martins of their mistakes and get them to reveal who was poisoning their minds. "I do not think there is a more fertile ground for German propaganda than playing upon the ignorance of the negro race and arousing them to enmity against our allies."

Later, when Gold interviewed the Martins together, he was faced with a troubling refutation of his stereotypes. Eliza Martin professed no sympathy for England, which had favored the South in the American Civil War, while her husband spoke knowledgeably about the CSS *Alabama* claims case and other Anglo-American issues. Mrs. Martin also discoursed on the Belgians' cruelties in Africa while her husband discussed King Leopold's policies at length, his views being mild compared to his wife's passionate condemnation of Britain and Belgium. She ended by saying that America must blot out lynching before going to the relief of foreigners, and proclaimed her refusal to buy Liberty Bonds to help the enemies of her race. Investigator Gold warned that her views might give aid and comfort to the enemy, or at least get her into trouble, yet she appeared unafraid of the consequences.

Having been the beneficiary of this course on recent history and international relations, Gold showed surprising ignorance in his summary of the case. While admitting that the Martins were well versed in current events and that other well-educated blacks might share their views, Gold could not rid himself of the belief that enemy subversion was the root cause. He suggested further investigation by a black operative to uncover the source of the Martins' opinions, suspecting that black churches might be teaching un-Americanism. Gold and other whites found it more comforting to believe that Germans were subverting blacks' loyalties than to acknowledge that blacks' disillusionment with the country's role in the war and the record of the Allied powers reflected deep-seated and logical grievances against white-dominated America.[29]

Northern whites' most common racial fear, however, was the possibility of rioting. Particularly after the East St. Louis riot in July 1917, whites worried most that blacks would respond to white aggression with equal militancy. Rumors of blacks arming themselves and stockpiling ammunition for future use were common in northern cities after mid-1917. Reports of secret meetings, which in the minds of many whites signified plotting against them, also exacerbated their fears. As in the South, such gatherings were probably lodge, church, or civic gatherings with no sinister intent. Nonetheless, many whites were unable to dispassionately sift truth from rumor, especially since they were convinced that more than a few of their own race were engaged in subverting blacks.

Over a third of the Bureau's black loyalty investigations focused on alleged German, Mexican, or American-born whites' conspiracies to subvert the black population. The majority of white suspects resided in southern localities, and Virginia and Texas again had the greatest number of cases. The Bureau investigated more than fifty non-German whites for making pro-German or disloyal statements to blacks, encouraging their resistance to military service, or telling blacks they had no stake in what was a white man's war. Some were clearly German sympathizers who had told their black listeners that Germany would treat them better or warned that black troops were used as cannon fodder on the battlefield so as to spare the lives of white soldiers. And the Bureau certainly had reason to investigate three other whites who were said to be encouraging riots or uprisings.

Given the heightened tensions in the South, a white man had to do no more than mingle with blacks or be an unfamiliar salesman to arouse suspicion. In fact, a number of cases suggest that native whites who, for whatever reasons, chose to associate with blacks were perceived as trying to "influence" them. Peddlers, evangelists, and insurance collectors were particularly likely to arouse such suspicions. However, the most hated white outsiders in 1917 were labor recruiters. It is likely that many charges of spreading German propaganda were simply justifications for expelling someone who was tampering with the local workforce. Some white recruiters were allegedly enticing blacks to Mexico, either to cripple the southern labor supply or to join a mythical German army ready to attack the lightly defended Rio Grande border. In cases where investigators knew nothing specific about whites operating in black neighborhoods or speaking in black churches or lodges, the suspect was usually accused of "inciting," "organizing," or "influencing" blacks or "stirring race trouble."

"Germans" accused of subverting African Americans were twice as numerous as American-born white suspects. Their "crimes," however, were nearly identical. Although over a hundred such individuals appear in Bureau case files, their precise identities are often unclear. In some cases a panicky citizen or Bureau agent assumed that any suspicious foreigner was German because of his activities or association with blacks. However, a German-sounding name was prima facie evidence of evil intentions. Germans also stood out by virtue of their numbers: The 1910 census counted 2.5 million German-born persons in the United States, plus nearly 6 million second-generation Germans. There were German settlements in many parts of the South, particularly Texas, Appalachia, and Virginia. A population mobilized for war against the hated "Hun" easily suspected those of similar nationality in America. To white southerners in particular, it was not inconceivable that the bestial German, the rapist of Belgium, would stoop equally low in attempts to destroy America, even going so far as to encourage blacks to rise up against the dominant race.

Encouraging disloyalty, impeding conscription, making pro-German statements, disparaging the American government, and spreading pro-German propaganda were the most common allegations against Germans suspected of subverting the black population. Others were simply accused of "influencing" blacks, and their specific statements were in character with their alleged disloyalties. Bureau reports quoted them as saying that the conflict was a white man's war and that blacks had no stake in the government and hence nothing for which to fight. Others proclaimed the German people's high regard for blacks, saying that they did not want to fight blacks, and promised full equality if Germany won. Most ominously, some told blacks that when millions of white males were fighting overseas, they should rise in revolt and claim what was rightfully theirs. A tenth of the German suspects were accused of having suggested such dastardly deeds. Still others were said to be organizing secret meetings for blacks or helping them stockpile firearms. Southern whites also perceived the influence of German enemies behind the allegedly more surly or intractable behavior of black servants since the onset of war. In short, Germans were a convenient scapegoat for changes in attitudes and behaviors that whites either found inexplicable or unacceptable.[30]

It was frequently alleged that churches with German-speaking congregations were also promoting subversion among blacks. The fear that Lutheran-run "German schools" were covertly undermining the loyalty of blacks surfaced early in the war and continued to be fueled by panicky whites. A white woman living near Waco, Texas, informed the Bureau of her suspicions about German agitators, especially one Pauline Leubner, whom she accused of encouraging blacks to revolt. The informant also reported that a fortune-teller was predicting that blacks would start an uprising. Despite the fact that the informant's allegations were almost incoherent, a Bureau agent proceeded to investigate. He found Pauline Leubner to be an older German woman sincerely engaged in "Negro uplift" through her local Lutheran church. Similarly far-fetched reports from North Carolina charged that Germans, operating through Catholic and Lutheran schools, were spreading the idea that once the German army occupied the South, blacks would be granted absolute equality, and that black children attending an allegedly integrated German Catholic school were treated with such impartiality. The postmaster of Buena Vista, Alabama, reported that German Lutherans there were spreading enemy propaganda.[31]

In addition to those charged with promoting the subversion of blacks, another tenth of the German suspects were accused either of recruiting blacks to fight for Germany or to join a pro-German army in Mexico. If there was any plausibility in either of these fears, it was only in the latter. Hysterical whites appear not to have thought through the difficulties involved in getting black recruits to Germany. Other Germans, presumably labor recruiters, reportedly were encouraging blacks to leave the South. Another recurrent rumor was that Germany offered financial rewards to seduce blacks into acts of disloyalty. For example, Bureau agents in Galveston investigated persistent tales that blacks were paid to sabotage ships bound for Europe by putting incendiary devices in their holds. Such concerns were justified, since anti-British Irish longshoremen recruited by German agents had performed such acts before the war.[32]

Finally, a few individuals from other ethnic groups faced the Bureau's scrutiny for alleged subversion of blacks. In three cases, gypsy fortune-tellers supposedly encouraged blacks to believe Germany would win the war and award them equal rights. Mexicans, not only in Texas but scattered in other locales, were believed to be in league with Germans and actively recruiting blacks for military service south of the border. Two Mexicans were also accused of fomenting race war within the United States, while another pair was supposedly discouraging compliance with the draft. Finally, one Mexican was believed to be promoting an alliance of all darker races to seek their collective liberation from the dominant white nations.

This same motive characterized the three Japanese and two "Hindus" (East Indians) suspected of promoting disloyalty and migration to Mexico. In sum, those individuals suspected of subverting the black population probably most often had their own axes to grind, and simply found encounters with blacks convenient opportunities to express their own grievances. If acts of outright disloyalty are a measure of their success, they failed miserably at sowing seeds of dissension that actually grew to acts of resistance. Moreover, by mid-1917 the federal government had equipped itself to deal severely with such enemies if actual subversion was detected.

The Justice Department sought to curb and punish subversive activity by and among blacks using three approaches during World War I: prosecution under federal statutes, cooperation with state and local authorities, and extralegal efforts to intimidate individuals into compliance. All three avenues were quickly utilized as the nation prepared to fight the Central Powers in Europe and suspected legions of enemy agents and subversives active on the home front. But until enactment of the Espionage Act in mid-June, prosecution of those believed to be disloyal was hampered by the absence of a clear legislative mandate for enforcing "loyalty."

The initial priority of the Bureau of Investigation was to gather evidence on suspected German agents. However, one difficulty the Justice Department faced in the first months of the war was the lack of specific federal statutes with which to effectively curb subversive activities by alleged domestic enemies. Early cases arising in Virginia, Alabama, and Tennessee forced Bielaski and the Justice Department to improvise. In one case, an American-born white man was jailed in Charlottesville, Virginia, and charged with publicly sympathizing with Germany and seeking to enlist blacks in a conspiracy against the government, promising them social equality if they should win. The day after war was declared, U.S. Attorney R. E. Byrd in Roanoke, recognizing the difficulties federal authorities faced in prosecuting such offenses, requested the commonwealth's attorney to indict the man under a provision of the old slave code, Section 3661 of the Code of Virginia, which provided a five-to-ten-year prison sentence should "any person conspire with another to incite the colored population of the state to acts of violence and war against the white population," even if no actual insurrection developed. Byrd doubted that prosecution could be sustained using that antebellum statute, but the federal criminal code was equally deficient. Only Section 5334 of the Revised Statutes, a Civil War statute that punished those guilty of inciting rebellion or insurrection with a jail term of ten years plus a $10,000 fine, was remotely applicable. Byrd sought the advice of the attorney general, who delegated the reply to Bielaski. The Bureau chief encouraged the state to prosecute. If that failed, he instructed Byrd to proceed with an indictment based on Section 5334. There is no record the case advanced to that point, perhaps because Byrd recognized the lack of clear evidence that a genuine rebellion was being incited.[33]

An almost identical situation arose on the same day in Tennessee when U.S. Attorney Lee Douglas reported numerous incidents of disloyal speech. A particularly flagrant miscreant was said to be a black preacher by the name of Gleaves. His influence in Davidson County, which included Nashville, could not be ignored, for over 45,000 blacks (more than thirty percent of the county's population) lived there. Gleaves was reported as saying that the president had wrongly led the country into war, that Germany was innocent of wrongdoing, and, because Germany was friendly to blacks, members of the race had no cause to fight them. Gleaves's talk generated considerable anger among whites. Even worse statements, Douglas wrote, were attributed to black teachers and preachers in Springfield, farther north, and Columbia and Shelbyville, south of Nashville. Local authorities pleaded for federal suppression of these voices. Recognizing the absence of applicable federal statutes, Douglas suggested that they employ Section 6663 of the Tennessee Statutes, the product of a slave insurrection scare shortly before the Civil War. It defined sedition in the broadest terms, punishing anyone guilty of "uttering seditious words or speeches, spreading abroad false news, writing or dispersing scurrilous libels against the state or general government, . . . instigating others to cabal and meet together, to contrive, invent, suggest, or incite rebellious conspiracies, riots, . . . thereby to stir people up maliciously to contrive the ruin and destruction of the peace, safety, and order of the government." Although this law might conceivably have been used, it lacked force since it only defined sedition as a misdemeanor. Douglas appealed to his superiors for counsel, knowing the public was looking to the national government for decisive measures and perhaps fearing vigilantism if he took no action. Surviving case files do not contain a reply, but Bielaski probably offered the same advice he had given U.S. Attorney Byrd in Roanoke.[34]

Other federal officials faced the same problem. When U.S. Attorney A. D. Pitts in Mobile reported persistent suspicions in four counties with black majorities of an organized plot to create disloyalty among blacks and transport them to Mexico, he recommended vigorous action as a deterrent but remained reluctant to act without the attorney general's approval. Again Bielaski urged that authorities handle the crisis using state laws. Should those not meet the emergency, however, he had a new suggestion: using the part of the federal criminal code that defined offenses against the *operations* of the government as distinct from the statutes against rebellion and insurrection, which outlined offenses against the *existence* of the government. Section 37 of the federal code punished conspiracies to commit any offense against the United States. Its penalties were less than the rebellion statute—two years' imprisonment and a $10,000 fine—but it would certainly be a potent deterrent if successful. Bielaski had his doubts, however. Application of Section 37 to the Alabama cases would stretch the statute "rather far." Nevertheless, until Congress might act, it was all the law books contained. Finally, assessing the cases realistically, Bielaski proposed the most expedient course: that "a grand jury investigation might have a deterrent effect on the instigators of this movement."[35]

Local whites often hoped that federal charges, or the threat of them, would inhibit the aspirations or militancy of blacks. A Georgia lumber mill official in league with a government timber inspector preferred charges against William Wright and Will Arbor for violation of the Espionage Act in July 1918. Wright and Arbor were employed loading lumber onto railroad cars at Jones, a flag stop on the Seaboard Air Line Railroad's main line in coastal McIntosh County, where blacks constituted more than 75 percent of the population. According to the white men, the two laborers' offense was saying "damn the government" and refusing to load government-contract timber. Bureau agent Goundry W. Bingham found matters somewhat more complex, however. Wright was spokesman for all the workers who were demanding to be paid forty cents an hour instead of the twenty-five cents they had been offered. When higher wages were refused, they stopped work. The employer threatened that they would get in big trouble if they did not load timber because it was "government work." In any case, he was unwilling to give in to their demands because it would set a precedent for future wages. Besides, he believed twenty-five cents was "plenty." Local whites clearly were trying to use the threat of federal charges to suppress wages and as a strikebreaking weapon. Bingham recorded statements from a number of blacks as well as whites, but, exercising official restraint, refused to take sides and filed no Espionage Act charges. Whether the black laborers won higher wages is not known.[36]

The search for a means to suppress dissent and unpopular actions continued throughout the war. Before the passage of the Espionage and Sedition Acts there were few avenues other than prosecuting violations of selective service regulations. In one case, the mayor of Okolona in the heart of northeast Mississippi's cotton belt charged that blacks were being enticed to Mexico. Senator John Sharp Williams, who was influential in Wilson administration circles, forwarded the letter to the Bureau. Chief Bielaski replied sensibly that recruitment for Mexico "in itself, does not constitute a violation of any Federal Law." Nevertheless, he urged Williams to ask the mayor for any other information that might form the basis for federal action.[37] In another case, a black man took the opportunity to voice long-suppressed sentiments about the defects of democracy in America, but he paid a price for his honesty when Bureau agents wielded informal coercion and threats. Seventy-year-old Jacob Sutton was described by a Bureau agent from Norfolk as an "old time negro," probably an ex-slave, who up to that point had a good reputation among Virginia Beach whites. Sutton had the misfortune to be overheard saying that since blacks were not regarded as citizens and had no rights they should not fight for the country, and that only a German triumph would improve matters. He also condemned the fact that white men could abuse black women with impunity, but if a black man so much as looked at a white woman he was likely to be lynched. Sutton allegedly added that, once whites went off to war, blacks would have a chance to redress the situation. The white residents of Princess Anne County, where the population was split evenly between the races, did not ignore these comments.

By the time Bureau agent Joseph M. Bauserman got to Sutton, local authorities had jailed him as talk of lynching rose in the community. Spirited away to Norfolk for safer incarceration and questioning, Sutton denied making any offending statements except saying that blacks need not fight in the war. Bureau personnel were not inclined to believe him, but they had no effective federal weapons to employ. So, after impressing Sutton with the seriousness of his "offense" and warning him against such conduct in the future, they let him return home and instructed him "to preach the doctrine of pure unadulterated Americanism." This assignment was clearly Bauserman's idea, not Sutton's. Nonetheless, it is likely he complied. The threat of lynching would be sufficient to force most blacks into complying with the growing demands for public patriotism.[38]

Even where agents found no violation of patriotic norms early in the war, they often began to enforce loyalty and support for the government on the black population. Another Norfolk-based agent was sent to an area so remote in North Carolina's Bertie County, near Albemarle Sound, that he had to travel by train, car, launch, and foot to reach his destination. No local whites could confirm the report that had sent him on this arduous journey: that German propaganda was circulating among blacks in nightly secret meetings. Interviews with fifteen blacks also failed to substantiate the suspicions, but the agent used the opportunity to inform them that "this was a time in which the white men and the colored men should stand together; that this was our common country, and that our rights and the rights of their families, were the same as ours; that we were all Americans, and that it was our duty to protect our country from enemies internal as well as foreign." After this pointed admonition the blacks naturally pledged to notify local whites if anyone came among them to stir up trouble. Certainly local whites did not want problems, as blacks outnumbered them three to two.[39]

In the absence of federal or state laws regulating expression, local and federal authorities often relied on intimidation to accomplish their goals. Bielaski did not disapprove of such efforts to ensure 100 percent Americanism, as is illustrated in a case brought by an assistant U.S. attorney in Bluefield, West Virginia, one of only four counties in the state with more than a 10 percent black population. He informed Bielaski of a local newspaper article, reprinted from the *New York Sun,* which appeared to be a subtle effort of "some alien enemy" to persuade blacks that they had no stake in the war. The article in fact stated that blacks' duty was to participate fully in the struggle, but questioned how willingly they would fight for a nation that segregated and lynched them. Clearly there was nothing illegal or unpatriotic in this piece, but Bielaski nonetheless ordered New York agents to investigate its author for having given encouragement to race prejudice.[40] Since there was no statute on which the writer of such sentiments could be prosecuted, it appears that Bielaski ordered an investigation in the hope that pressure would curb such viewpoints.

This practice of warning or intimidating "suspects" when they could not be prosecuted continued throughout the war and was often the only concrete action that Bureau agents and U.S. attorneys could take because violations of federal law had not occurred. In June 1917, for example, an elderly black named Henry Branch was accused of advising younger men to hide out so as to avoid draft registration. When the Bureau was unable to prove the allegations Bielaski nonetheless ordered an agent in North Carolina to warn Branch "of the consequences of such acts." In a similar case in Norfolk, a white man of German descent was suspected of encouraging blacks to form a dockworkers union. Obviously this was no transgression of law, but Special Agent in Charge Daughton and U.S. Attorney Mann subjected him to a threatening interrogation. He was eventually released "after being kept at the office for some time and cautioned." If the suspect failed to learn that federal and local officials believed that helping blacks organize for better working conditions was disloyal, then he was an obtuse man indeed.[41]

Such practices where federal charges could not be sustained were not confined to the South. In December 1917, for example, Chicago postal employee Mary Clark was "invited" to the Bureau office to account for allegedly seditious remarks. Despite denying such statements she was given a warning so strong that she vowed to be "totally loyal" in the future. In the same month and city, federal agents also pressured the militant anti-lynching crusader Ida B. Wells-Barnett to stop selling buttons protesting the hanging of black soldiers convicted in the Houston mutiny. Unlike Clark, however, she refused to repent of her activity.[42]

Similar tactics were applied elsewhere. Two generations of one black Kentucky family—Alfred W. Titus, an active churchman in Lexington, Kentucky, and his son John Kenneth Titus, a student at Iowa Wesleyan University—suffered comparable suspicions and pressures. They came to the attention of the Bureau after a local white judge delivered a patriotic address to Titus's congregation. In a discussion afterward, the elder Titus shared a letter from his son asking, "does the American flag really protect me?" The judge took this as evidence of growing pro-German sentiment among blacks and relayed his fears to Bureau agent L. O. Thompson, who drew the further conclusion that German propaganda was being taught at the university in Iowa. He saw a twin danger: Not only were students being propagandized, they were writing these same disloyal sentiments to family members who would believe them because they respected the wisdom of their college-educated children. Thompson urged an investigation of the university and an interview with young Titus to put him on notice that he was under surveillance. This would "have its effect on the negroes here [in Lexington]" as well. Five months later Titus's father was again overheard making this "suspicious" statement: "Germany now has more territory than she started out to get." When word of this reached the mayor of Lexington, Titus hurried to the Bureau office to proclaim his loyalty, saying that the offending statement had no disloyal intent. Just to be certain no unpatriotic propaganda was circulating, however, Thompson went to the post office and "intercepted," without a warrant, a letter from young Kenneth Titus in Iowa. That communication contained nothing disloyal, but by that time the intimidated father was promising to immediately inform the Bureau of any pro-German talk. He might have been even more frightened had he known the Bureau had sent copies of its reports on him to the Military Intelligence Division for its own possible surveillance.[43]

Whites were also subject to such intimidating treatment from Bureau personnel. In Norfolk a man said to be a German reportedly was telling blacks that Germany was their friend and that the war was a white man's war. When Agent

Ralph K. Dawson interviewed the suspect, he "of course, denied that he had any conversation with any negroes, but I took occasion to warn him that should such a report reach our ears again, he would be held to a strict accountability." Nonetheless, most of those subjected to such warnings were black. A theatrical troupe in Philadelphia included in its program a recitation that an agent felt was unpatriotic. Although he admitted the speech was not seditious, the agent told the actors to "voluntarily" delete it from their program rather than risk action by the U.S. attorney. When the actors refused to comply, the agent followed through and reported the matter to the federal prosecutor. Meanwhile, in Providence, an elderly black woman was overheard remarking that President Wilson was prejudiced against blacks. A federal agent warned her to keep such sentiments to herself and the intimidated woman promised to say nothing that was not patriotic.[44]

Federal agents forced some blacks to do more than keep their mouths shut. In rural Georgia, Bureau agent Charles E. Corgan opened a disloyalty investigation of Dan McCrady, "a wealthy darkey . . . [who] is influential among those of his race." His alleged crime was saying that he could not get his money returned after investing it in war savings stamps. McCrady claimed he needed the funds back, but Corgan preferred to believe that a white man had encouraged him to disparage the stamp program. Corgan conferred with the local head of the National War Savings Committee and the two agreed that it would have a "wholesome" effect on local blacks if McCrady publicly endorsed the benefits of investing. Succumbing to this pressure, McCrady took the platform, praised the stamp drive, and pledged to purchase $500 more. An additional reason for intimidating McCrady emerges from demographic factors. Burke County had been assigned a quota of $500,000 in the current stamp sales effort, and, since over 80 percent of the population was nonwhite, blacks held the key to meeting that quota. Someone as "influential" as McCrady had to be brought into conformity with patriotic norms lest local blacks march to a different drummer than their white overlords. At least McCrady did not suffer what Will Nance did in Dallas in mid-1918. Overheard saying, "to Hell with the war, it is not bothering me," he was arrested by local police. Called to the jail, Agent H. D. Bishop administered a "severe lecture," which he felt would prevent any further such remarks.[45]

The Bureau also employed informal but no less serious pressure on black newspapers and pamphleteers in its attempts to curb dissent and enforce conformity to the patriotic demands of the nation at war. In addition to systematic Bureau attempts to harass and intimidate black newspapers during the war, particularly the *Chicago Defender, Galveston New Idea,* and *San Antonio Informer,* agents openly attempted to manipulate the flow of news and opinion. In August 1918, for instance, agents approached news editors to dispel several rumors, namely that black soldiers were being annihilated on the battlefields of France, that the government was suppressing news that transports carrying black troops to Europe had been sunk with the loss of all aboard, and dozens of wounded black veterans lay in a secret ward in a New York hospital, their eyes gouged out and limbs hacked off by

German soldiers. Fred Roberts, editor of the *Los Angeles New Age,* was persuaded by an agent not only to print an article dispelling these rumors, but also to submit a draft of the article to the Bureau office for approval prior to being typeset.[46]

In another case in Washington, Bureau officers learned that several newsstands were selling the *New York Age,* which had printed an article critical of the army's segregation policies. Believing this was likely to cause disaffection, Agent F. C. Haggerly instructed two newsdealers to cease distribution until the Bureau could determine whether the *Age* was seditious. The offending article in the 17 August 1918 issue, "Color Line Tightly Drawn at Camp Dix," painted an accurate portrait of conditions at that New Jersey cantonment. Black troops were segregated in the baseball stadium; signs separated the races in the mess hall; and "nigger," "coon," and "darkey" were frequently used by whites despite their use being prohibited by War Department directives. In spite of the veracity of such charges (the traditional standard for libel), Haggerly concluded that such articles were "calculated" to lower morale among black troops, and were at least indirect criticisms of the War Department.[47]

Finally, New England's traditions of dissent meant nothing to a zealous agent in Boston who attempted to suppress a widely read pamphlet entitled *The Disgrace of Democracy.* Its author was one of the best-known African-American moderates, Kelly Miller, dean of federally funded Howard University in Washington. Agent Horace A. Lewis admitted that the content of the pamphlet was not in itself seditious—it condemned the East St. Louis riot and decried the lack of federal protection against racial violence—and he acknowledged it was lawful to bring the race's grievances to the attention of the government. He feared, however, that "our enemies" might use Miller's pamphlet as propaganda. And since it was distributed through the mails, it appeared to violate the Espionage Act. Lewis thus concluded that lawful speech that might be used by an enemy for propaganda was in fact unlawful, anticipating the "bad tendency" rulings of the Supreme Court in cases arising from the Espionage and Sedition Acts. Lewis aggressively pursued this issue with postal officials, but they were preoccupied with more radical publications. The post office solicitor ultimately declined to label the pamphlet as dangerous, and hence Lewis had to close his case in January 1919, nearly three months after the war ended, without the prosecution he sought.[48]

Although the federal government assembled a powerful arsenal with which to punish dissenters and alleged subversives during World War I, those suspected of disloyal activity sometimes faced a more grave danger: the threat of vigilantism. Opposition to the war or even halfhearted patriotism, whatever the motive—apathy, religious scruples, political opposition, personal reasons—was unpopular and often simply not tolerated. Both blacks and whites who expressed opposition to the war could expect no sympathy, but instead the fury of public opinion. Furthermore, the patriotic majority often had no way of filtering fact from rumor. Thus, not only were dissenters in jeopardy from the passions of a jingoistic populace, but those falsely accused or innocently linked to the supposed subversive activities of others could also be endangered.

Ironically, the presence of federal authorities was sometimes crucial to the protection of citizens' rights and the prevention of mob violence. Although blacks had little for which to thank the Bureau of Investigation during the war, it was true that whites felt less threatened if they were assured that the federal government had matters well in hand. A case from Okolona, Mississippi, illustrates this point. A few days after war began, the mayor reported a dangerous rise in local passions. The community had staged a mass demonstration of loyalty—actually two separate meetings, one for whites in the morning, another for blacks in the afternoon—but a few blacks had failed to demonstrate proper patriotism. When coupled with rumors that black agitators were conducting secret meetings to plan migration to Mexico for the duration of the war, after which they would return to seize control of the entire state, the mayor feared mob violence. He sought the calming effect of federal officers on the spot: "We feel that this is a matter that the National Government should handle, for you know what would be the result if the matter should be turned over to the general public in this section." Although Bureau chief Bielaski concluded that even if the rumors were true there was no violation of federal law, he nonetheless detailed an agent to see if other activities might provide the basis for federal intervention. Apparently this helped calm the local white panic.[49]

A few days later a similar scenario played out in Portland, fourteen miles away, where an alarmed resident telegraphed federal authorities in Little Rock to report a "treasonable demonstration" among blacks. The Bureau's Memphis SAC noted that "such a number of complaints have come in concerning the inciting of negroes and some few demonstrations of disloyalty that I am about convinced that such acts are not originating with the negroes," although he admitted he thus far had no proof of German subversion. The situation clearly warranted immediate Bureau action, and Agent E. J. Kerwin in Pine Bluff boarded a St. Louis, Iron Mountain, and Southern Railway train for Portland. When he arrived three hours later he learned the local postmaster had already spread the alarm, wiring the governor of "treasonable demonstrations here last night and speakers among negro teachers and pupils." After interviewing white residents and correlating their stories with the local newspaper's account, Kerwin isolated the essential details.

During closing exercises at the local black high school, two girls by coincidence gave identical recitations from an article in the *Arkansas Masonic Monitor* on "Negro Immigration and the Reason Why." Both fourteen-year-olds said they had chosen this article simply because it sounded good and appeared easy to memorize. Kerwin found no sinister motive in the girls' actions and nothing objectionable in their oratory. He next interviewed the school principal, who expressed surprise that anyone would take offense at the recitations. But all this was immaterial because terrified whites were hastily buying arms and ammunition. Agent Kerwin's role at this point was paradoxical. Either he hoped to head off mob violence by helping the community organize a defense, or he succumbed to panic himself. Whichever the explanation, while acknowledging that blacks were doing nothing suspicious, Kerwin instructed the "best citizens" of Portland on how to organize a home guard and urged them "to keep a lookout for all strangers that might come into their community or in the county and mingle with the negroes and report the same to me and it would be investigated." Mob violence by an alarmed and outraged white populace *had* been averted by Kerwin's presence, but blacks in Portland knew that henceforth the armed white minority would be especially alert to detect any deviation from the requirements for patriotism and submission.[50]

Although federal agents occasionally headed off impending violence, the war also led to the formation of white vigilance committees, which became widespread in the South by mid-1917. For example, when rumors of German subversion of blacks spread through the Lake Charles, Louisiana, area, New Orleans agent John B. Murphy raced westward on a Southern Pacific Railroad express to discover an armed committee of whites already organized with the blessing of the district court to deal with any black uprising, although that threat had diminished in Calcasieu Parish, where whites outnumbered blacks three to one. Murphy's presence was not needed to calm the situation, but local authorities elsewhere requested Bureau personnel as a signal to local whites that they need not organize vigilante action. All sorts of fearful rumors spread through Hampton County, South Carolina, in May. The local sheriff reported tales of a black uprising inspired by German agents and mysterious shipments of arms to local blacks. His fears may have been stimulated by the fact that whites constituted only 40 percent of the population. Agent Branch Bocock reached Hampton in the late afternoon on the once-a-day Charleston and Western Carolina Railway local. After reviewing the sketchy details and lack of concrete evidence, Bocock concluded that no federal violation had occurred. Nevertheless, the sheriff argued that a lynching was still possible unless he could convince the white populace that federal authorities had the matter well in hand.[51]

A similar situation developed in Cocoa, Florida, again in May. As was often the case, information reached the Bureau from a local postmaster who reported rumors that blacks were holding secret meetings and plotting the purchase of firearms. Upon being interviewed by Bureau agent Leverett W. Englesby, the postmaster repeated other tales: A black man was overheard saying blacks should not enlist as they had no country; another was grudgingly willing to serve if called but complained of how poorly blacks were treated; and an unknown white man was seen talking with blacks in "Nigger town." Even more suspicious was the visit of two black preachers who were picked up at the train station in an automobile. The Cocoa city attorney told Englesby about a black delivery boy who allegedly told a white lady that the black revolution in Cuba was tame compared to what might happen in Florida.

Englesby and local officials agreed that questioning local blacks was useless. They decided that a trustworthy black informant, perhaps a Mason or Odd Fellow, was needed. A quick check of a hardware store revealed that no guns had been sold lately but that blacks seemed to be purchasing pistol and Winchester cartridges in unusual quantities. Englesby concluded that this was a local matter but perceived that some "hot headed" whites were contemplating lynching a couple of blacks as an example to the rest, even though blacks numbered less than 30 percent of the county's population. He attempted to head this off by suggesting "it might be well to know first who the leaders were and that we should lay low till that was discovered." Gaining agreement to that plan, he was confident that "nothing will be done at present except as I advise." Although he averted the threat of an immediate lynching, Englesby seemed also to be giving implicit support for future mob action if matters worsened. On returning to his office in Jacksonville he wrote headquarters that the city attorney had agreed to try to handle matters locally in the future without bothering the Bureau for "useless assistance."[52]

At times, federal agents in the South appeared ambivalent regarding white racial violence and their role in suppressing it. Local whites clearly stepped up the employment of traditional threats of lynching and mob action to suppress black dissent during the war. At least one other Bureau employee approved of a lynching, after the fact. Birmingham agent Mark Hanna was detailed to investigate F. W. Matthews's "inflammatory statements" that when whites left for the army blacks would be able to have their own way and marry white women. Hanna learned that two other blacks had been lynched for publicly repeating his alleged boast. Their bodies were found buried side-by-side in a ditch, one with its head sticking out, the other with its feet exposed. Hanna's report concluded nonchalantly that the killings had put a "quietus" on local blacks, especially since Matthews had fled. The fact that two innocent men were lynched appeared not to concern him. This was common in Birmingham, whose fifty-two thousand black citizens (40 percent of the population) were accustomed if not reconciled to living in racial terror.[53]

On a number of occasions Bureau agents did intervene to protect blacks. Even Agent Hanna, who had been so callous in the Matthews case, recognized two weeks later the danger of wartime passions being exploited to settle old grudges. He was called to investigate charges that G. W. Scales was "stirring up" local blacks against the government. Traveling to rural Coatopa, in Black Belt Sumter County where blacks outnumbered whites four to one, Hanna interviewed an embarrassed white man, W. H. Coleman, who acknowledged he was the source of the complaint. Coleman admitted he had no foundation for his suspicion; he and other whites were simply whittling and gossiping at the post office when someone remarked that Scales needed watching. The agent deduced that Scales was disliked because he was well educated, influential in local black politics, and had recently been appointed county agricultural demonstrator. With nothing else to do and the Southern Railway's local to Birmingham not due for several hours, Hanna wiled away the time shooting at turtles in the creek.[54]

An herbal practitioner, "Doctor" Lonnie Jones, suffered similar community jealousies in the neighborhood of Lynchburg, Virginia. Hearsay had it that Jones was encouraging other blacks not to register for the draft. Although uneducated, Jones enjoyed a wide clientele among both "second class whites" and blacks. Bureau employee Charles E. Burks discovered that some blacks indeed had not registered, but only one of them had ever heard Jones speak. Burks concluded that whites were simply seeking a pretext for removing Jones from the county, which numbered 40 percent blacks. In any case, even if Jones had been encouraging noncompliance with the draft, he had failed. That ended the matter so far as Burks was concerned.[55]

Lynching and threats of mob action continued throughout the war. Exaggerated charges against Sam Doyle east of Waco, Texas, in September 1917, necessitated investigation by the Bureau. Whites mobilized on rumors that Doyle had organized other blacks to arm themselves and store up food to feed the Mexicans who would join their conspiracy once all the whites were drafted. Local whites, even though they constituted nearly 60 percent of the population, were soon "badly excited," fearing they all would be murdered. The county sheriff, who discounted the rumors, jailed Doyle, who denied knowledge of any plot. Because whites were determined that "a lot of niggers" would be killed if federal authorities did not intervene, the sheriff summoned Agent Charles B. Braun. He found the source of the rumors was another black man, Lige Price, who claimed he and several others had heard Doyle detail the plot. But every one of the witnesses denied hearing anything disloyal, and instead noted that Doyle and Price were enemies. After finally interviewing the suspect himself, Braun concluded that Doyle was "a pretty good sort of negro" in contrast to the "rather shifty and crafty" Price. The agent believed Doyle's story and closed his investigation. How long Doyle remained in jail is not known. However, if he stayed in the vicinity he undoubtedly remained under scrutiny by whites whose fears were abated but not totally eliminated by Braun's investigation.[56]

In Smyrna, Florida, local whites again prepared to use mob law to enforce wartime loyalty and the racial status quo, until their intended victim was saved from vigilantism by being jailed. Jesse Mosely had apparently boasted of what he was going to do when all the white men were sent off to France, and when questioned was found to be armed with a sawed-off shotgun and a pistol. Local whites, even though they outnumbered blacks three to two, were so incensed that Mosely had to be spirited off to Deland to avert a lynching. Agent Leverett Englesby conferred with the assistant U.S. attorney and the county sheriff, who by then had matters well under control, and decided to stay in the background unless the incident developed into more than simply a "sporadic case of a negro running amuck."[57]

The Bureau's general intolerance of black dissent, frequent disregard for the basic liberties of African Americans, and willingness to allow local mob rule to inflict informal local punishment is tragically illustrated in the case of Dr. J. H. Miller, a Vicksburg physician. When approached by whites to purchase war savings stamps, he agreed to buy only in proportion to the citizenship he was allowed to exercise, and bought merely half the amount the committee thought proper. Pressured to purchase more, he replied that he enjoyed only half the rights to which he was entitled because he was denied entrance to theaters and forced to sit behind screens on streetcars. The committee members would not brook Miller's temerity in demanding "social equality with whites" and tarred and feathered him, undoubtedly fearing Miller's influence in the city, where blacks made up nearly 60 percent of the residents. Miller exhibited defiance even after his punishment and the mayor, hinting at a formal lynching, advised him to flee. Agent L. P. Banville concluded that there was no federal offense in Miller's alleged disloyalty, but he was not concerned about the mob attack either. In fact, on learning that the physician had fled to Detroit, Banville warned the Bureau office in that city that Miller was "bitter toward whites" as a result of his punishment. The cruel ironies of this case are clear: Dr. Miller was the victim first of mob action, which understandably provoked anger on his part. This bitterness then became the basis for possible surveillance in the city to which he fled for refuge. Miller was now the suspect, his offense being resentment toward his white tormenters.[58] Even had Miller been spared mob violence, however, it is likely that, in the absence of federal action, he would have faced local charges initiated to punish a black man who had become far too "uppity."

Beyond the informal pressures of federal agents and the already familiar (in the South) threat of white vigilantism, local authorities used municipal law to punish disloyalty suspects and suppress dissent. Local officials probably handled more such cases than did the federal government. There are several reasons for the frequency of police action and prosecutions. In the first place, before the enactment of the Espionage Act in mid-1917, there was no unambiguous federal law on which to base indictments. Second, state and local prosecution was much easier and quicker in many instances; local juries, especially in the South, took little time deciding the guilt or innocence of blacks. In addition, Bureau agents and U.S. attorneys often eagerly shared evidence with local officials and urged them to prosecute when the likelihood of a federal conviction was slim. Finally, informal punitive "justice" was the most punishment that could be levied in many instances. A slacker might be jailed for days or even weeks prior to indictment or trial, only to have the charges dropped when the suspect was inducted into the service. Others might be charged with treason, incarcerated locally for a sufficiently punitive period, and then convicted of a misdemeanor. Occasionally local charges were unsustainable and suspects managed to get off relatively unscathed, but not before local officials had applied the powers of arrest, confinement, indictment, and intimidation. In short, there was a great deal of variance in the zeal with which local officials pursued cases of alleged subversion, and their willingness to proceed with only rumors as evidence.

Local officials often enjoyed the cooperation of the Bureau of Investigation. In fact, these cases are more numerous than instances where the Justice Department pursued a case all the way from investigation to federal conviction. In short, the federal government could take only partial credit for opposing antiwar dissent among blacks. Success in silencing or harassing opponents of the war relied more importantly on the zealous and often summary actions of state and local officials, APL civilian volunteers, and vigilante mobs.

Jailing for vagrancy or disorderly conduct was often the most expedient and effectual recourse, at least in the South. Such action proved to be politically useful: local sheriffs gained favor from being perceived by the electorate as vigilant in the face of danger. For instance, a week before the war began Bureau agents cooperated with Birmingham police in investigating two "Germans" who were circulating among blacks and supposedly discussing racist conditions in the South. From the perspective of local whites, the black population indeed seemed discontented, and many assumed that the suspicious pair must be responsible. Actual evidence of subversive activity was lacking, however, probably because the two were primarily concerned with earning their livelihood as automobile polish salesmen and only secondarily interested in engaging blacks in conversation. It later developed that one of them was interested not in promoting Germany, but socialism. The other man eventually recognized the danger of expressing unpopular beliefs and severed the partnership. While the Bureau's investigation progressed, Agent Mark Hanna conferred with the U.S. attorney and the two agreed that the only feasible legal action was to have local officials arrest the pair for violating an Alabama statute. The police readily obliged, agreeing with Hanna's desire to "break up the disturbing element amongst the Negroes."[59]

Many cases began with a local arrest for alleged disloyalty or some equally vague but unpopular charge, which then prompted police to request a federal investigation. Sometimes, however, Bureau agents determined that no charges, local or federal, were warranted or sustainable, as the following examples illustrate. A few days after the war began, police arrested a black woman in Pensacola for telling a white salesman that members of his race ought to do the dying in the war. A federal agent concluded that this was simply an argument between two individuals rather than a statement of opposition to the United States, thus ending the case. That same week, an argument over money prompted Henry Wilson of Norfolk to goad his white creditor by professing to be "a black pro-German enemy," adding that "I am not an American no how, and as soon as I do what I want too [*sic*] I am going to catch me a horse boat and go to Europe." Wilson was arrested by police and brought to the Bureau office, where he denied having made such statements and proclaimed his loyalty. This profession gained his release. The following month, W. W. Rourk was arrested by Birmingham police on charges of soliciting labor without a license, although it was rumored that he was recruiting blacks for military service in Mexico. Agent J. Reese Murray investigated and learned that Rourk was a "well-to-do" black West Virginia mine owner. There was no evidence of any Mexican plot. Rourk was released after promising to return home and tamper no more with the local workforce.[60] Others who were picked up by local sheriffs or police and who denied allegations of disloyalty did not fare as well. Two blacks were seized by Dallas police for allegedly recruiting men for a Mexican army to fight against the United States. When interviewed by Bureau officers, the suspects denied any such scheme. Agent F. M. Spencer decided that "in view of the fact that they were intoxicated and badly beaten up by a crowd of *American* citizens, and also evidence insufficient to warrant holding them on a *Federal* charge, they were confined to jail on charges of vagrancy." How long they enjoyed the city's hospitality is not known.[61]

In a number of cases local authorities filed charges against blacks so as to intimidate an entire community. This was little different, only less lethal, from the practice of lynching as an example to the black population at large. Whites in Kerens, Texas, for instance, accused Ollie Bryant in August 1917 of conspiring with other blacks to resist the draft, stockpile arms, and start an uprising once whites went off to war. He and two confederates were arrested by the sheriff, whereupon Bureau agent J. W. Harper, arriving after a six-hour train trip on the Southern Pacific and Cotton Belt routes, began an extensive investigation. The sheriff described Bryant as an "oracle" within the black community who "preyed upon their prejudices and weaknesses." However, Bryant's real offense seemed to be his philosophy that blacks need not depend on whites for anything and should "buy black." As the sheriff put it, "he was or is a forward nigger and calculated to do damage." Other white residents described Bryant as a notorious big talker. Several blacks—including his stepfather—also expressed dislike for him, but there was no evidence that he had obstructed the draft. Still suspicious that there might be a conspiracy, however, Agent Harper attended a meeting at the black Masonic Hall, but all he heard was "talk of heaven" and "long prayers." The agent masked his frustration with the comment that at least while thus occupied blacks were not conducting "raids on fowl roosts of their white neighbors." He next searched the houses of Bryant and his mother, without warrants, but found nothing. Harper finally acknowledged that Bryant had done nothing wrong. Instead, whites had orchestrated the complaint in order to prompt a federal investigation, believing the presence of an agent would scare blacks into behaving more compliantly. Harper nonetheless played his expected role, telling a "very wealthy" black to warn others that "no more complaints must come from the white people about them." Meanwhile, local whites insisted that Bryant and his alleged coconspirators remain in jail while they tried still harder to find better evidence against the trio. There is no record of how long the suspects languished there or what fate befell them.[62]

Bryant and friends were not the only ones to unjustly suffer incarceration for unproven wartime offenses. Local authorities routinely used the power of imprisonment as punishment for unproven crimes. Another case initiated by local authorities with later involvement by Bureau agents illustrates the abuses of power common during those intolerant times. In New Orleans, a Reverend Powell served at least twenty-nine days in the parish jail for alleged disloyal propaganda, although he was ultimately convicted only on local nuisance charges. While he was incarcerated the Bureau conducted a cursory inquiry into the matter and approved his punishment. Special Agent in Charge Forrest C. Pendleton noted smugly that "the action taken in this case has had a very good moral effect in that community and that no further complaints have been received regarding negro activities in that section of the town." Earlier in the war, authorities in Buckingham, Virginia, near Appomattox, were willing to keep an "enemy alien" in jail for twelve months by manipulating local charges so as to prevent him from "colluding" with the black half of the county's population. The Bureau agent cooperating on the case similarly raised no objection to this punitive treatment.[63]

The foregoing examples illustrate actions against alleged dissenters or subversives initiated by local authorities and then referred to the Bureau. In many other cases the process was reversed: Justice Department personnel made an initial response and then handed the case over to local officials. When agents found themselves too busy to further investigate a case, or could not free themselves to visit a remote rural area, or when it became clear that federal charges could not be sustained, they offered whatever evidence they had compiled to local prosecutors.

This occurred especially during the rush of events and flood of rumors in the first months after America entered the war. A week after hostilities began, for example, San Antonio's harried SAC wrote the postmaster of Marshall, Texas, asking to be notified immediately should rumors that Germans were recruiting blacks prove true. If there was substance to the rumors, however, agents instructed the postmaster to ask local police to apprehend the enemy agents.[64] That same month the assistant U.S. attorney in Clarksdale, in the Mississippi Delta, discovered the circulation of a flier addressed to young black men that asserted they had no reason to fight. Notified of this alleged danger, an overworked Memphis agent concluded that it would be a waste of time to undertake an investigation with no more evidence than the leaflet itself. Instead, he asked the city marshal to begin an inquiry. A similar case in the early days of the war concerned suspicions that Germans were trying to contact blacks in the predominately black cotton and tobacco district south of Florence, South Carolina, ostensibly to sell them insurance. The Bureau agent assigned to investigate, busy with many other matters, could do no more than telephone the informant on the spot and leave matters in the hands of the sheriff. Common to the Marshall, Clarksdale, and Florence incidents was the fact that Bureau agents in the spring of 1917 were so inundated with wartime responsibilities that they frequently delegated federal responsibilities to local authorities. In rural areas where local officials were willing to take action, agents gladly allowed them that privilege.[65]

A similar scenario occurred in early May when Bureau agent B. C. Baldwin conducted a futile inquiry in Hays County near Austin into reports of a well-dressed Mexican urging Hispanics and blacks to flee to Mexico to avoid fighting for the United States. When a rumored meeting did not materialize, Baldwin left matters in the hands of a sheriff who promised to search for the suspect. Local police were not the only ones federal agents enlisted to continue investigations. An agent named Stillson probed the case of a German who ran a saloon for blacks in Baton Rouge, allegedly discouraging patrons from registering for the draft. When Stillson learned nothing but hearsay he gladly accepted the mayor's offer to keep watch on the suspect.[66]

Bureau agents also found it convenient to leave matters in the hands of local authorities in times of exaggerated panic. Dunklin County, in Missouri's southeast boot heel, had a population of over thirty thousand whites and only about a hundred black residents, but the majority nonetheless became hysterical in August 1917 following the bloody East St. Louis riot in which over a hundred blacks—men, women, and children—were indiscriminately beaten, shot, stabbed, and hanged by rampaging whites resentful of black strikebreakers and the city's alleged "protection" of black criminals.[67] Fearing a black uprising, Dunklin County whites clamored for federal intervention. The city of St. Louis's overburdened SAC demurred, however, referring the matter to the local prosecuting attorney since there was no apparent federal violation and undoubtedly no real danger, at least to whites. That was not the case for blacks, who in this type of situation might easily become victims of an inflamed, panicky lynch mob. The following year, in San Diego, Agent W. A. Weymouth began to investigate a man identified by police as "nigger Blue." This individual seemingly did not care who heard him condemn the government for its mistreatment of black troops in Houston. He also spoke admiringly of Germany, claiming that blacks were treated well there and could marry whites. Weymouth suspected that these were not Blue's own ideas, but that he was being incited to disloyalty by German propaganda. When he could pin nothing down, however, the agent passed the case to a police investigator who handled "Negro" matters.[68]

Elsewhere, agents sometimes concluded matters even more informally. When George L. Darden investigated reports of blacks holding secret meetings, stockpiling arms and ammunition, and opposing the draft in Rapides Parish, Louisiana, he found no concrete evidence and left matters in the hands of "patriotic [white] citizens who are amply able to take care of any set of negroes who might 'start anything.'" (Whites made up slightly more than half the local population.) Some police departments had special units to which agents committed cases. Elsewhere, patriotic volunteers assisted local investigations to relieve the burden on busy agents. When vague rumors of German propaganda among blacks in Lexington, Kentucky, could not quickly be substantiated, a Bureau agent secured the cooperation of the local Council of Defense, the APL, and police in watching for suspicious activity or signs of black disaffection.[69]

Finally, Bureau agents sometimes referred matters to company police who were better situated to conduct inquiries than an outsider. When Agent Mark Hanna investigated an incident near Birmingham in which three black steelworkers came to blows with a white employee who urged them to fight only for Germany or Mexico, the company superintendent promised surveillance of the white instigator. The next month, Hanna and another agent probed reports that blacks employed at several graphite mines were sympathetic to Germany. The mine owners assured the agents that they would handle any situation that arose. A year later, when investigation of a black preacher accused of spreading pro-German sentiment in the western Kentucky coalfields proved fruitless, the Bureau turned the case over to company police who promised vigilance in discovering and reporting any subversive activity.[70] In short, Bureau agents often bestowed responsibility for ongoing investigations onto a variety of local authorities, and even company police, as a matter of simple expediency. Not only were federal agents faced with trying to investigate more cases than they could handle, but they found that the application of local punishment or intimidation was frequently more efficient, and certain, than initiating federal proceedings.

In the first month of war, an unsigned letter arrived at the Justice Department. Its white southern author, responding to newspaper pleas to report spies, poured forth a cornucopia of fears. Many blacks were being unwittingly influenced to favor Germany. Evidence of this was the black woman employed in the writer's home, who was fired after she expressed the wish that Germans would invade the United States and kill all whites. The anonymous correspondent refused to believe that the former servant had arrived at such views herself. He concluded that others must have influenced her. The letter went on to report another black woman who said: "this is the white folks' war. Let them fight it out. I ain't bothering myself one way or the other about it." These views correlated with a disturbing change in blacks' demeanor toward whites. Danger lay in the fact that practically every white family employed black servants, who possessed keys to the house. A "well executed uprising," therefore, would cripple the South. The writer's suspicions also focused on the "hundreds" of lodges and secret orders among blacks, again where they could easily be influenced. The letter ended with a plea for federal authorities to disguise white men as blacks so as to spy on the darker race. Every effort, the writer concluded, should be bent on promoting patriotism among blacks.[71]

Such suspicions, bordering on panic, were widespread during World War I. The Bureau of Investigation received and, insofar as possible, responded to hundreds of white citizens' reports that blacks were not only being subverted by enemy agents but were themselves inclined to disloyalty. How able was the Bureau to sift fact from fiction, reality from rumor? Complicating things further, Bureau agents themselves relayed hundreds of other suspicions up the chain of command. The sheer volume of such alarmist reports sent to the Bureau and numerous other branches of government, many sent directly to the president, created a powerful sense that the country was under siege and that enemy activity was ubiquitous in the land. The Bureau's inability to pin down concrete evidence or find actual culprits was not necessarily reassuring; conspiracies might be so effectively hidden as to defy easy discovery. Hence, the Bureau believed that it could not afford to ignore the legion of rumors that flooded its mail. Much detective work is by definition the pursuit of vague leads and second-hand information. But the war not only heightened irrational fears, it demanded an especially vigorous, systematic, and publicized Bureau response. In this politicized and highly public atmosphere, many citizens voiced their suspicions to elected representatives. It would have been politically disastrous for Chief Bielaski to ignore such communications when a congressman or senator forwarded them to him. In short, for both security and political reasons, the Bureau had to assume that any report, no matter how specious it might seem, required some investigation, some federal attention, so as to reassure an anxious public that subversion would be blocked and that everyone, black as well as white, demonstrated his or her patriotism.

The Bureau of Investigation was not oblivious to signs of patriotism among blacks. Old German case file 3057, on alleged enemy subversion of blacks, contains a few letters testifying to the loyalty of the race.[72] In addition, agents in the field, whose daily routine was often absorbed in tracing war-related rumors, occasionally commented on the loyalty of blacks and their imperviousness to German subversion. Only three weeks after the war began, for instance, Agent Edward S. Chastain reported from Jacksonville, one of the most excited areas of the country on account of the apparent success of labor agents in luring thousands of Deep South agricultural laborers to the North. Chastain was pleased to note that blacks had staged a patriotic mass meeting in the city park, with the mayor and other white dignitaries lending their presence. Beginning with a parade, the rally featured public-spirited speeches by prominent blacks and the passage of loyalty resolutions. Enemy attempts to encourage disloyalty were roundly condemned. Chastain concluded that, "judging from the patriotic attitude as evidenced by the parade and the declarations of the leaders among the negroes here, there does not appear to be the slightest foundation for the wholesale reports of possible disloyalty on the part of the negroes in this community." A similar patriotic exercise took place in Corpus Christi about the same time.[73]

Such reports notwithstanding, Bureau leadership strongly believed through 1917 that enemy influence on blacks presented a real and serious danger. In October, an internal memorandum entitled "Reports Covering Investigations of German Propaganda Among the Negroes" summarized the spectrum of suspected subversion, including attempts to recruit blacks for a Mexican army and the flow of German money to incite blacks against whites. Bielaski not only personally reviewed this memorandum, which covered reports from throughout the South as well as several northern locations, but sifted through all of the individual agents' reports.[74]

Chief Bielaski was a "hawk" within the Justice Department, a strong advocate of more severe laws with which to confront the enemy danger. Writing to the attorney general in early January 1918, he detailed the shortcomings of the Espionage Act:

> From reports of agents, conferences with various persons from different parts of the country, including quite a number of congressmen, I find that there is general complaint against the Department and its officers for failure to prosecute persons who are guilty of disloyal remarks. . . . There is, of course, no law under which action can be taken in such cases unless the persons involved are alien enemies, and it is my recollection that Congress left out of the Espionage Act a provision which might have made it possible to reach persons of this kind. The complaint is so general, the situation so misunderstood that it seems to me that the Department ought to take a rather aggressive attitude.

He concluded that if key congressional committees were made aware of the frequency of disloyal statements, enactment of more stringent provisions would be more likely. Bielaski was obviously operating on two levels here. First, he believed that disloyalty should be more vigorously punished. He also recognized the need to counter the public perception that the Bureau of Investigation was slow to root out disloyalty.[75]

Bielaski's analysis of African Americans' loyalty was, however, eventually reshaped by the accumulation of inconclusive reports and the paucity of prosecutable offenses. The greatest volume of rumors and demands for investigation came in the first three months of the war. Such reports never ended, but their frequency declined thereafter. Nevertheless, the Bureau generally acted on the belief, right up to the Armistice, that German attempts to subvert black loyalties remained a real danger to blacks and, by extension, to society in general. But Bielaski gradually understood blacks' priorities with clearer vision. In February 1918, U.S. Attorney J. O. Carr in Wilmington, North Carolina, brought to the Bureau's attention Kelly Miller's pamphlet *The Disgrace of Democracy* (which later excited Agent Lewis in Boston). Carr recognized there was nothing unlawful in the pamphlet itself, but he feared it might cause disaffection if circulated by pro-German interests. Bielaski replied: "the matter of negro propaganda has been under investigation by this office for some time past. This investigation, so far as it has been carried, would indicate that the negroes are not really endeavoring to disseminate any pro-German views, but are taking advantage of the present existing conditions to force federal legislation to prevent lynching, and also for the recognition of themselves upon the same plane as the whites."[76]

The chief's assessment demonstrates a level of insight that was not particularly common during the war, but also a conclusion that would lead the Bureau of Investigation into intense opposition to black aspirations in the postwar period. Many whites could not accept the proposition that both northern and southern blacks were, of their own initiative and without the prompting of outside agitators, mounting more militant challenges to the racial status quo. On one level, worried whites were more comforted with the fiction that German enemies were inciting an otherwise docile and happy black population. The exaggeration of enemy influence provided "evidence" to perpetuate the myth of black contentment. But Bielaski was being forced to recognize the new mood percolating through Black America. For the first time since Reconstruction, blacks perceived the possibility of significant changes in the status quo. Those who did no more than voice disaffection with the war were nonetheless articulating a new racial restiveness. As the next chapter will show, many expressed their grievances with their feet, joining in the Great Migration not only to free themselves from southern neo-servitude, but also to escape the draft. This generation of African Americans included some who were more politically motivated. These young blacks had freed themselves from Bookerite restraints and were determined to prevent the ascendancy of a new national accommodationist leader and to forthrightly criticize the remaining generation of conservative spokesmen. What the *Messenger* magazine would soon dub the

"New Crowd Negro" would demand much more meaningful alterations to the racial status quo than the incremental requests begged by the previous generation.[77]

The prospect of any racial change profoundly disturbed white Americans in all regions who had been raised in the post-Redemption racial order. Many whites could only deal with changes by assuming they were inspired not by blacks' own deep longings and disaffection but by enemy subversion. Some whites, like Bielaski, began to comprehend the changing currents somewhat more clearly. But a more accurate understanding of the new mood within America's subject race did not lead to approval of its agenda or timetable: White America would militantly reject alterations in the racial status quo in the months following the war.

3

"Slackers, Delinquents, and Deserters": African Americans and Draft Enforcement during World War I

The Bureau of Investigation was responsible for enforcement of conscription during World War I. Even though new agents were added throughout 1917 and 1918, they could not fully handle this and other new duties alone. Local police also apprehended alleged draft evaders or those who could not prove that they had complied with all requirements of the selective service system. With nearly half a million men identified as failing to report for induction, the Bureau was swamped with investigations. Most were handed over to APL civilian volunteers. Even with such assistance, the Bureau's agents spent countless hours investigating and apprehending slackers, delinquents, and deserters. Local boards used the term *slacker* to identify those who failed to register; more generally, slackers could be anyone failing to shoulder his fair share of the national defense. *Delinquents* were those who failed to fill out a classification questionnaire or who did not show up for a physical examination. Finally, anyone who failed to present himself for induction or transport to a training camp was classified as a *deserter*. Many men in this last category were sent induction notices after already being certified as delinquents. If they failed to appear at the specified date and time, they were considered inducted into the military and hence "passive" deserters, as distinguished from those who wore the uniform and absented themselves from duty. A $50 reward was payable to anyone other than a federal officer who caught a willful deserter (one who had been certified by his local board as physically qualified for service) and delivered him to military control.[1]

Nearly 24 million men registered for the draft during World War I. Of them, 2.75 million were actually inducted. Almost half a million were suspected of being deserters, although the number was reduced after the war to 337,649 when those who had enlisted but failed to inform their draft boards were subtracted from the total. Provost Marshal General Enoch Crowder praised the Bureau of Investigation's agents as "pioneers" in the apprehension of slackers, delinquents, and deserters. The Bureau handled over 220,000 cases from July 1917 to the end of 1919, a full year after the cessation of hostilities. Draft-age men were required to have in their possession at all times either a registration card or, after the classification system was instituted, a card identifying in which of five classes they had been placed. Class V included all who were completely exempt from military service, while those in classes II, III, and IV were deferred because of occupation or dependent wives, children, and/or parents. Men in Class I were qualified for military service, although not all served because their draft boards' quotas were filled by others.

Many men who were apprehended by local police and Bureau agents had lost registration cards, had never received classification cards because of changes in residence or failure to return questionnaires, or had simply left their cards at home. Such cases could take anywhere from a few hours to several weeks to resolve. Many thousands who were too young or too old for the draft were arrested by local authorities anyway or turned in by patriotic citizens who believed they were of age for military service. In numerous cases the informants' motives were influenced by the prospect of the $50 reward. Bureau personnel and APL volunteers tried to determine ages by examining school, life insurance, birth, marriage, immigration, and voting records. But agents did not depend solely on random tips and arrests. Large employers required job applicants to produce registration and classification cards, and they supplied the Bureau with the names of those who had none. Federal investigators also visited employment agencies and lodging houses in search of delinquents. Beginning in March 1918, large-scale "slacker raids" were conducted in numerous cities, culminating in the infamous four-day September raids in New York City, where fifty thousand men were snared so that their draft status could be examined.[2]

Statistics compiled at the end of the war by the provost marshal general's office claimed that the desertion rate for blacks was almost three times that of whites: 9.81 percent compared to 3.86 percent. Southern governors and draft officials offered two explanations that Crowder found convincing: Ignorance and illiteracy among rural blacks, exacerbated by "a certain shiftlessness in ignoring civic obligations." In fact, southern blacks ignored "civic obligations" because they were almost universally denied one such duty: the right to vote. Crowder also agreed with southern officials that blacks had a "natural inclination to roam from one employment to another," especially in response to new industrial job opportunities in the North and munitions plants like those in Muscle Shoals, Alabama. Southern whites were quick to add that willful neglect of duty was almost nonexistent, leading Crowder to assert after the war: "the colored men as a whole responded readily and gladly to their military obligations once their duties were understood." Moreover, he believed German propaganda attempts to persuade blacks to avoid military service were "a miserable failure."[3]

There is almost no evidence that Germans or other enemies attempted to subvert the loyalty of African Americans during World War I, and no evidence at all that any such attempts succeeded. But a deep current of apathy and disaffection ran throughout Black America. The views of Crowder, southern governors, and draft-board officials notwithstanding, the black desertion rate mirrored much more than ignorance and changes of residence. A much higher proportion of blacks than whites failed to report for induction in the South, where nearly 80 percent of draft-eligible black men resided (Table 2). Among the possible factors explaining this disparity is the likelihood that many black men were alienated from society and its rule of law.

Table 2
Desertions (failure to appear for induction or transport to a training camp) during World War I, by Race

	% of white desertions	*% of black desertions*
Alabama	2.96	13.22
Arkansas	2.11	9.32
Florida	3.28	21.32
Georgia	3.05	7.97
Kentucky	1.23	5.90
Louisiana	2.17	7.82
Maryland	3.48	9.12
Mississippi	2.25	9.95
Missouri	3.38	7.86
North Carolina	0.76	6.73
South Carolina	1.57	6.18
Tennessee	2.58	8.17
Texas	5.10	6.44
Virginia	2.18	7.67

Source: Second Report of the Provost Marshal General to the Secretary of War on the Operations of the Selective Service System to December 20, 1918 (Washington, 1919), p. 461.

On a more specific level, black men also must have sensed that the selective service system was giving them short shrift. Even given the likelihood that whites gained more deferments for holding essential jobs, draft boards granted fewer deferments to blacks who supported dependent families, and found blacks physically fit more frequently than whites.[4] Table 3 compares black and white induction rates in southern states, where discrimination was obvious.

Figures covering all but two of the wartime months indicate that 52 percent of all black registrants were placed in Class I, immediately eligible for military service, whereas only 32 percent of whites incurred such liabilities. Crowder explained this by saying, first, that the higher delinquency rate for blacks thus placed proportionally more men in Class I. Second, many southern whites enlisted in the military, thus reducing the number of whites in the Class I pool and exaggerating the proportion of blacks in that classification. Finally, many blacks were denied deferments even though they had dependent families because their sharecropper wages were so minimal that their kinfolk would live at least as well on a soldier's allotment.[5] Crowder saw no racism in either his statistics or his explanations, but clearly race played a role in the granting of exemptions and the classification of men as delinquent.

In 1919, as the draft machinery was being quickly dismantled, Crowder paternalistically applauded the cooperation of African Americans during the war:

Table 3
Induction Rates during World War I, by Race

	% of white inductions	*% of black inductions*
Alabama	27.27	31.57
Arkansas	27.13	34.28
Florida	21.62	33.08
Georgia	32.04	30.47
Kentucky	24.66	43.79
Louisiana	26.51	37.67
Maryland	22.40	34.85
Mississippi	25.40	29.51
Missouri	26.79	40.44
North Carolina	24.73	27.38
South Carolina	25.94	34.74
Tennessee	24.81	40.64
Texas	22.82	37.65
Virginia	24.55	36.57

Source: Second Report of the Provost Marshal General to the Secretary of War on the Operations of the Selective Service System to December 20, 1918 (Washington, 1919), p. 459.

> The part that has been played by the negro in the great world drama upon which the curtain is now about to fall is but another proof of the complete unity of the various elements that go to make up this great Nation . . . [S]ome doubt was felt and expressed, by the best friends of the negro, when the call came for a draft upon the manpower of the Nation, whether he would possess sufficient stamina to measure up to the full duty of citizenship, and would give to the Stars and Stripes, that had guaranteed for him the same liberty now sought for all nations and all races, the response that was its due. And, on the part of many of the leaders of the negro race, there was apprehension that the sense of fair play and fair dealing, which is so essentially an American characteristic, would not, nay could not, in a country of such diversified views, with sectional feeling still slumbering but not dead, be meted out to the members of the colored race.
>
> How groundless such fears, how ill considered such doubts, may be seen from the statistical record of the draft with relation to the negro. His race furnished its quota, and uncomplainingly, yes, cheerfully. History, indeed, will be unable to record the fullness of his spirit in the war, for the reason that opportunities for enlistment were not opened to him to the same extent as to the whites. But enough can be gathered from the records to show that he was filled with the same feeling of patriotism, the same martial spirit, that fired his white fellow citizen in the cause for world freedom.[6]

Granted that not all soldiers—black or white—fought for ideological reasons, it is clear that many blacks felt little personal stake in a war to preserve freedom for distant white people while they enjoyed so little of that precious commodity themselves. The treatment they often received from the draft system reinforced their skepticism and diluted their patriotism. Furthermore, once inducted into the army, blacks faced a host of new discriminations and indignities. News of this spread throughout the civilian population, further damaging morale.

Despite Crowder's glowing postwar assessment, prejudice toward African Americans infected the federal bureaucracy during the war. The higher black delinquency rate often led to punitive enforcement of the draft. Black disaffection—fueled in 1917 by the East St. Louis riot, the Houston mutiny, and a dramatic increase in lynching—was condemned by the public and government, not ameliorated. Overt opposition to the war by black religious sectarians and political dissidents was not tolerated, and by the end of the war, apprehensions that enemies were undermining black loyalties had evolved into the belief that anyone who dared challenge the racial status quo was subverting the foundations of American society.

African Americans' attitudes toward the war and the draft fell into four categories. Perhaps half the black population supported the nation's policies, either unequivocally or with reservations. But the other half encompassed large numbers who were clearly apathetic toward the war, those who engaged in overt antiwar actions, and many thousands who with some deliberation evaded the draft. In addition, others had no real sense of what the war was all about and hence could not even be said to be apathetic. Looking specifically at the southern black population, historian Mark Ellis concludes that opposition to military service ran the gamut "from vigorous abstention to aggression."[7]

Indifference is rarely newsworthy, so it is not surprising that historians have failed to perceive that World War I meant nothing to a portion of the black population. Nate Shaw, a poor Alabama farmer, recalled years later that even though he registered with the selective service, "I didn't definitely know who it was in war in them times. And it wasn't clear to me what that war was all about."[8] We have no way of quantifying how many other Nate Shaws there were, because the "inarticulate" rarely leave written records. But with the great majority of blacks still residing in the rural South, it must be deduced that others were similarly untouched by the issues and reality of the war. Bureau of Investigation case files reveal numerous individuals who appeared genuinely ignorant of the necessity to register for the draft. They can be said to be neither prowar, nor antiwar, nor apathetic: The war simply never became an issue for them.

There is much more substantial evidence of apathy. Lack of emotional commitment to or interest in the war ran deep among both rural and urban residents. Some felt Germany was no more oppressive than America. Black journalist George S. Schuyler had conversations with many persons who publicly mouthed patriotism but who privately would have shed no tears had German armies swooped down on the Black Belt. Germans could not be worse than white Americans, they felt, and what the country (i.e., whites) really needed was a good whipping.[9]

Others said they had no reason to hate or fight Germany. James Weldon Johnson reported that not a few Harlemites were unstirred by war rhetoric. "One coloured man came into a Harlem barber-shop where a spirited discussion of the war was going on. When asked if he wasn't going to join the Army and fight the Germans, he replied amidst roars of laughter: 'The Germans ain't done nothin' to me, and if they have, I forgive 'em.'" Meanwhile, unwilling black draftees, waiting in stateside camps for embarkation overseas, sang:

> I ain't got no business in Germany
> And I don't want to go to France
> Lawd, I want to go home, I want to go home.[10]

Some well-informed blacks, bitter over colonialism in Africa, felt no pity for the beleaguered Allies. J. C. St. Clair Drake told his friends he felt little sympathy for the suffering Belgians after what King Leopold's subjects had done to the Congolese. Washington, D.C.'s respected Rev. Francis J. Grimke, writing in his journal, rhetorically asked whether "atrocities committed against black people [were] less heinous than atrocities committed against white people." Although taking neither an antiwar nor an apathetic position, the *Crisis* exhibited the same bitterness: A biting cartoon depicted a mutilated Congolese telling the English king that "we could be of greater service to you now if your cousin [Leopold] had spared us our hands." These examples reveal a consciousness of the Black Diaspora, the recognition among African Americans that their lives were linked to those of black people scattered throughout the world. This outlook was particularly visible in Harlem, a mecca for radical ideas and news about the persecutions and progress of peoples of color around the world. It is not surprising, then, that throughout the war army recruiters were concerned over the lack of patriotic enthusiasm on the part of blacks in New York and elsewhere.[11]

Many blacks plainly were concerned more with events in the United States than abroad, in winning democracy in America before securing that right for Europeans. Newspaperman Roi Ottley concluded that apathy ran deep: "The truth is, Negroes exhibited little enthusiasm for the war—actually, their eyes were fixed on Washington, not London, Paris or Berlin." To black sociologist Ira De A. Reid, domestic issues stirred many blacks far more. Five thousand marched down New York's Fifth Avenue on 28 July 1917 in a silent parade protesting the bloody East St. Louis race riot. The banners participants carried show where many blacks' priorities lay. "Mr. President, Why Not Make AMERICA Safe for Democracy?" read one. "Patriotism and Loyalty Presuppose Protection and Liberty," read another. Yet another sign, this one censored by police, appealed to the president to "Bring Democracy to America Before You Carry It to Europe."[12]

Southern blacks also found little about which to be enthusiastic as the nation began to mobilize for war. A Mississippian identifying himself only as a "Negro Educator" distributed a flyer in April 1917 with the following exhortation: "Young negro men and boys what have we to fight for in this country? Nothing . . . If we fight in this war time we fight for nothing. Rather than fight I would rather commit self death . . . [W]e will only be a breastwork or a shield for the white race. After war we get nothing."[13]

A number of black newspapers in the early months of the war expressed skepticism that the conflict in Europe would bring benefit to blacks. The *Cleveland*

Gazette, reminding its readers that past black military contributions were often defamed, as in the currently popular film *Birth of a Nation,* proposed that blacks reconsider whether it was worthwhile to enlist in the current conflict. William Monroe Trotter's *Boston Guardian* took the position throughout the war that a German triumph posed a lesser threat to blacks' destiny than would an Allied victory. More than once the *Baltimore Afro-American* reported that blacks' attention was fixed more on domestic than foreign problems. Outrage over German U-boat attacks on American shipping seemed hypocritical when most whites were apathetic to the many more victims of lynching. The paper warned that black sacrifices on European battlefields would be pointless: "The solution of the problems that confront the colored people, especially those South of the Mason and Dixon's line would be postponed for the duration of the war, and . . . perhaps thrown back a decade." Although the *Gazette* and the *Afro-American* later supported the war, their early editorials mirror the widespread sentiment among blacks in the spring of 1917 that their more important fight remained the struggle against racism at home.[14]

Some blacks declared a simple racial reason for their apathy. Horace Cayton recollected: "I wasn't against the war, nor was I very bitter about the many injustices dealt out to Negro soldiers. It seems to me I felt much as all Negroes felt: this was their war, and since they weren't willing to accept us as civilians, then let them fight it. It was something that didn't concern Negroes. It was a white-folks' war." Other observers agree that this was the prevailing opinion in Harlem. On the West Coast, young William L. Patterson drew the same conclusion upon meeting Col. Charles Young, the highest-ranking black army officer in 1917 until he was medically discharged. There was no question Young was physically fit; the army simply was unwilling to accept a black general. According to Patterson, "the mistreatment my friend received strengthened my conviction that the war was a white man's war." Unfortunately, when Patterson proclaimed his views at an Elks picnic in Oakland, two black sailors reported him to the military police. He was arrested and held incommunicado for five days and only released after the intervention of friends and an NAACP attorney.[15]

If some concluded it was a white man's war, others added that it was a rich man's war. "Recrutin' Store" (also known as "Red Cross Store"), a blues song originating during the wartime period, reflects not only the "rich man's war" theme but also the belief among some rural blacks that Red Cross aid was used to trick them into the draft. Given the treatment of blacks by local police and Bureau of Investigation agents who enforced selective service requirements, apathy is understandable:

Chorus:
I told her no—o
Baby, you know I don't want to go.
Yes, an' I ain' goin'
Down to dat Red Cross Sto'.

She says, papa, I come here to let you know,
They want you down at that Red Cross Sto'.

She says, papa, I come here to set down on yo' knee,
Ain' you gonna fight for you and me?

She come here and she shook my han',
Ain' you goin' down and fight like a man?

She says, I come here 'cause they's feeding you mighty fine,
Mixing everything up with whiskey and wine.

She come back here an' says, they's feedin' offa ham,
Say, get away from here gal, I don't give a damn.

Listen, I'll tell you somep'n, somep'n mighty funny,
The rich mens they has got all the money.

She says, don't you know they need you to fight the war?
I says, listen baby, I got nothin' to fight for.

I ain' goin' down to no Red Cross Sto'.
I ain' playin in no rich man's show.*[16]

One of the most popular songs sung by black soldiers also expressed the frank observation that the war meant little or nothing to them even before they entered service:

Jined de army fur to git free clothes,
What we're fightin' 'bout, nobody knows.[17]

For other blacks, conscription—and the war itself—stimulated a fatalistic apathy, as expressed in Blind Lemon Jefferson's "Wartime Blues":

What you gonna do when they send your man to war?
Gonna drink muddy water and sleep in a holler log.[18]

The following two soldiers' songs reflect the resignation of men inducted for a purpose they could neither relate to nor understand:

I been diggin' in Mississippi, diggin' in Kentucky,
Diggin' in Georgia, diggin' all over God's heaven.
Lawd, lawd, guess I can dig in France.

Ruther be in corn-field workin' hard,
Than be buck private in national guard.
But I'm on my way, can't turn back.[19]

These complaints show clearly that many black servicemen had no positive motivations about the war that might have converted apathy into enthusiasm. As

*_Red Cross Sto'._ New words and music arranged by Huddie Ledbetter; edited with new additional material by John A. Lomax and Alan Lomax. TRO—© Copyright 1936 (Renewed) Folkways Music Publishers, Inc., New York, N.Y. Used by permission.

for the realities of training camp life, the black soldier sometimes responded: "Don't like it, don't know if I dislikes it, can't help it, nothin' to do about it." Even the act of enlistment was often motivated more by fatalism than patriotism. Years after the war, a Croix de Guerre–decorated veteran of the 369th "Hell Fighters from Harlem" Infantry Regiment frankly admitted that he joined only because he knew he would be drafted anyway and wanted to avoid onerous service in a labor unit.[20]

A number of African Americans took their opposition to a higher level, warning white southerners that at least some black soldiers did not intend to give up their weapons at the conclusion of the war. In a daring challenge, Pvt. Sidney Wilson, serving in the 368th Infantry, sent an unambiguous threat to his draft board, with a copy to a white newspaper in Memphis:

> It afoads to the soldier boys wich you have sint so far away from home a great deal of pledger to write you a few lines to let you know that you low-down Mother Fuckers can put a gun in our hands but who is able to take it out? We may go to France but I want to let you know that it will not be over with untill we straiten up this state. We feel we like we have nothing to do with this war, so if you all thinks it, just wait until Uncle Sam puts a gun in the niggers hands and you will be sorry of it, because we is show goin to come back and fight and whip out the United States, because we have colored luetinan [lieutenants] up here, and thay is planing against this country everday. So all we wants now is the amanation [ammunition], then you all can look out, for we is coming.

Wilson was subsequently court-martialed and sentenced to ten years at hard labor. A similar warning was contained in an anonymous letter to the federal government signed "the Black Nation": "You white folks are going to war to fight for your rights. You all seems to want us to go. If we was to fight for our rights, we would have a war among ourselves. The Germans has not done us any harm and they cannot treat us any meaner than you all has. Beware when you train 50,000 or 60,000 of the Negro race. When we get trained we are going to do the same [fight for our own rights]."[21]

Apathy and verbal protests against the war were widespread in Black America. Also noteworthy was overt opposition to conscription, Red Cross and Liberty Bond campaigns, and to the basic premise that the war against Germany was justified. Some black men who migrated North were both seeking economic betterment and fleeing their hometowns to avoid being drafted. Smaller numbers starved or mutilated themselves to become unfit for service. Newspaper editors and contributors condemned the conflict and black participation. Local leaders voiced similar views. Some blacks refused to perform military service, including whole church denominations, on the basis of conscience. The most ideological opponents of the war were socialists, particularly young A. Philip Randolph and his coeditor of the *Messenger,* Chandler Owen. The federal government took stern measures to intimidate, harass, threaten, and prosecute those who dared question the war's legitimacy or the necessity for blacks' loyal participation. As for conscription, federal authorities worried on two accounts: blacks failed to comply with selective service regulations more than twice as often as whites; and the influence and example of conscientious objectors and political opponents of the war might erode black participation even more seriously. The Bureau of Investigation could afford no complacency in tracking down black slackers, delinquents, and deserters.

Reconstructing the draft enforcement activities of the Bureau begins with the hundreds of thousands of pages of documents in its Old German case files, which focus on alleged spies and on individuals, organizations, and publications suspected of being less than totally supportive of the war effort. The Bureau investigated pacifists, anti-imperialists, socialists, anarchists, syndicalists, plus those expressing antiwar, pro-German, pro-Austrian, and anti-British views. Groups as diverse as the Industrial Workers of the World, the Nonpartisan League, the Jehovah's Witnesses, and the black Church of God in Christ were subject to hostile scrutiny.[22]

The Old German series also includes thousands of draft cases, including at least two thousand investigations of blacks who ran afoul of the selective service system.[23] These records unfortunately tell only a fraction of the story. Although some Bureau offices assigned agents to apprehend slackers, most cases were delegated to American Protective League volunteers. Nearly all of the APL's draft cases have been destroyed. Nonetheless, enough records survive to reveal enforcement patterns and attitudes in several large southern cities plus northern metropolises that received tens of thousands of wartime migrants (Table 4).

Blacks who failed, for whatever reason, to comply with selective service regulations frequently suffered unnecessary and sometimes lengthy jail terms. In other cases, agents used the threat of incarceration to "encourage" blacks to choose immediate induction into the army. Even those who presented strong evidence of having registered sometimes found themselves jailed while agents checked their stories. Some blacks appeared ignorant of the draft, requiring agents to judge whether failure to comply was willful or unintentional. If deemed willful, agents frequently coerced blacks into accepting immediate induction, brought complaints before U.S. commissioners so that prosecution could begin, or turned suspects over to local police for punishment (jailing) to be followed by induction. Whatever the case, blacks could hardly have confidence that the system worked with perfect fairness and justice.

Wartime passions brooked no hint of disloyalty or apathy and ran roughshod over due process and constitutional guarantees. Some agents saw themselves as judge and jury, meting out swift "justice." African Americans were not alone in suffering from this superpatriotic, intolerant public mood, but when suspected of being slackers or deserters they suffered more harshly than did whites. Not until the most egregious slacker raids, conducted during the summer of 1918, did significant numbers of whites criticize the methods of the Bureau of Investigation, U.S. attorneys, and local police, because few whites were victimized by them up to that time. Because blacks had no political voice and commanded no sympathetic interest in the white press, they suffered abuses that the white public would not

Table 4
Cities with the Highest Number of Black Draft Cases Opened by the Bureau of Investigation June 1917–November 1919
n = 2005

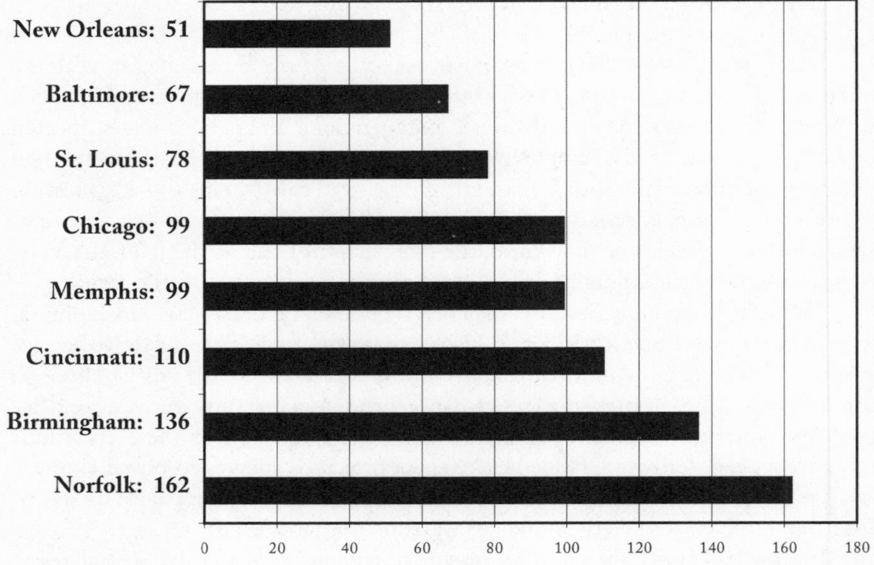

Source: Investigative Case Files of the Bureau of Investigation, 1908–1922, Record Group 65, National Archives and Records Administration.

have tolerated. White-staffed draft boards, white local police, and white Bureau agents were quick to arrest and sometimes callously abandon in jail poor and uneducated blacks whose only crime was being unable to prove on the spot that they were properly registered or classified. Despite official denials, the enforcement of the Selective Service Act was riddled with racial bias.

Three nationwide draft registration days, plus a supplemental registration, were held during World War I, the first occurring on 5 June 1917. The names of over 9.5 million men between the ages of twenty-one and thirty were recorded that day in a remarkably well-organized fashion considering that the administrative process had been established in only eighteen days. Because no one knew how many American soldiers would be required on French battlefields, and because there were not sufficient training camps ready to receive draftees, it was not until 1 September that the first 180,000 men were dispatched to cantonments. Since the army insisted on the segregation of troops but had not yet created separate training camps, no blacks were included in this first call.[24]

The initial pool of nearly 10 million men enrolled in mid-1917, even when drastically reduced by those granted deferments and found to be physically unfit, was sufficient until the early summer of 1918, when America's battlefield role increased dramatically in response to the massive German spring offensive. Over a million men were inducted during May, June, and July. A second registration was held on 5 June 1918, this time enrolling three-quarters of a million men who had turned 21 since the previous June. The rapid deployment of troops overseas necessitated a supplementary registration on 24 August of all men who attained the age of 21 after June 1918, resulting in 150,000 additional names being recorded. But the supply of men in Class I was exhausted in September, so the final (and officially the third) registration occurred on 12 September. With defense of the western front requiring more and more American soldiers, the nation faced two choices: Either induct family men and those in crucial occupations, or extend the draft age down to age 18 and upward to age 45. The latter option was chosen. More than 13 million new names were added to selective service lists on 12 September after using an unprecedented advertising campaign designed to make it "psychologically a certainty" that every eligible man would learn of the need for his services and "honestly and frankly come forward and register." Provost Marshal General Crowder congratulated himself and the nation for accomplishing "voluntarily in one day what the Prussian autocracy had been spending nearly 50 years to perfect." The results were gratifying: registrations were nearly 200,000 above estimates, and many men aged 17 and over 45 sought to volunteer by declaring themselves within the registration ages. The total of men enrolling in all registrations was over 24 million.[25]

Although Crowder claimed that the first registration, on 5 June 1917, succeeded in enrolling nearly every man between the ages of twenty-one and thirty, it failed to generate full compliance by African Americans. The vast majority of blacks resided in the South, and Table 5 shows that in several of those states less than half the potential registrants appeared as required. The first registration, which numbered 737,626 young black men, "missed" at least two hundred thousand more in the South alone.[26] The selective service system never acknowledged this disaster.

In the sample of more than two thousand Bureau of Investigation black draft cases, over 250 investigations took place in June, July, August, and September of 1917, before the first black draftees were called to camp on 22 September (Table 6). Agents in the South, from which 80 percent of the cases derived, believed that some blacks were not willfully disobedient because they honestly thought that they did not have to register since registering to vote was strictly a white man's prerogative. Moreover, some southern whites, desirous of keeping their farm laborers, instructed blacks not to register or withheld their mail. Other whites feared the consequences of blacks receiving military training and preferred that whites alone do the fighting.[27]

The Bureau's limited manpower, preoccupied with tracking down alleged

Table 5
Proportion of Black Registrants to Total Registrants, First Registration, 5 June 1917

	% of black registrants to total registrants	*% of blacks in 1910 census*	*% of blacks in 1920 census*
Alabama	20.40	42.50	38.40
Arkansas	4.79	28.10	27.00
Florida	33.28	41.00	34.00
Georgia	39.98	45.10	41.70
Kentucky	10.07	11.40	9.80
Louisiana	31.90	43.10	38.90
Maryland	15.97	17.90	16.90
Mississippi	23.85	56.20	52.20
North Carolina	9.88	31.60	29.80
South Carolina	46.18	55.20	51.40
Tennessee	18.03	21.70	19.30
Texas	17.14	17.70	15.90
Virginia	29.24	32.60	29.90

Sources: Report of the Provost Marshal General to the Secretary of War on the First Draft Under the Selective-Service Act, 1917 (Washington, 1918), p. 82; U. S. Department of Commerce, Bureau of the Census, *Negroes in the United States 1920–32* (Washington, 1935), p. 15.

enemy spies and saboteurs, could identify only a tiny fraction of suspected slackers in the summer of 1917. Many of its tips came from rural sheriffs and postmen who often knew which men were likely to be of military age. However, proving a suspect's age was made difficult by the paucity of birth records among blacks, nearly all of whom were born at home. Bureau agents frequently had to weigh the truthfulness of individuals' claims and their relatives' often conflicting statements. Birth dates entered in family Bibles were as definitive as records were likely to be, although some appeared to have been altered. Sometimes an agent had only his impressions of a young man's "youthful looks" on which to make a judgment.[28]

The greatest abuse of official power was the incarceration of black suspects while their claims—to being underage, overage, or having registered elsewhere—were being investigated. A pattern emerged in the early months of draft enforcement: Southern blacks were much more likely to be jailed than those apprehended in the North, some languishing there for weeks. The highest proportion of jailings occurred in Texas, raising suspicion that the Bureau's division superintendent in San Antonio encouraged punitive measures against black suspects. That young southern black men were often treated in such fashion should surprise no one familiar with the period 1890–1910, during which the white South employed lynching, convict leasing, and peonage along with disfranchisement and discrimination to deprive blacks of basic citizenship, economic independence, and personal security. Bureau personnel were usually native to the regions in which they served, and

Table 6
New Black Draft Cases Opened per Month by Bureau of Investigation Offices
n = 2005

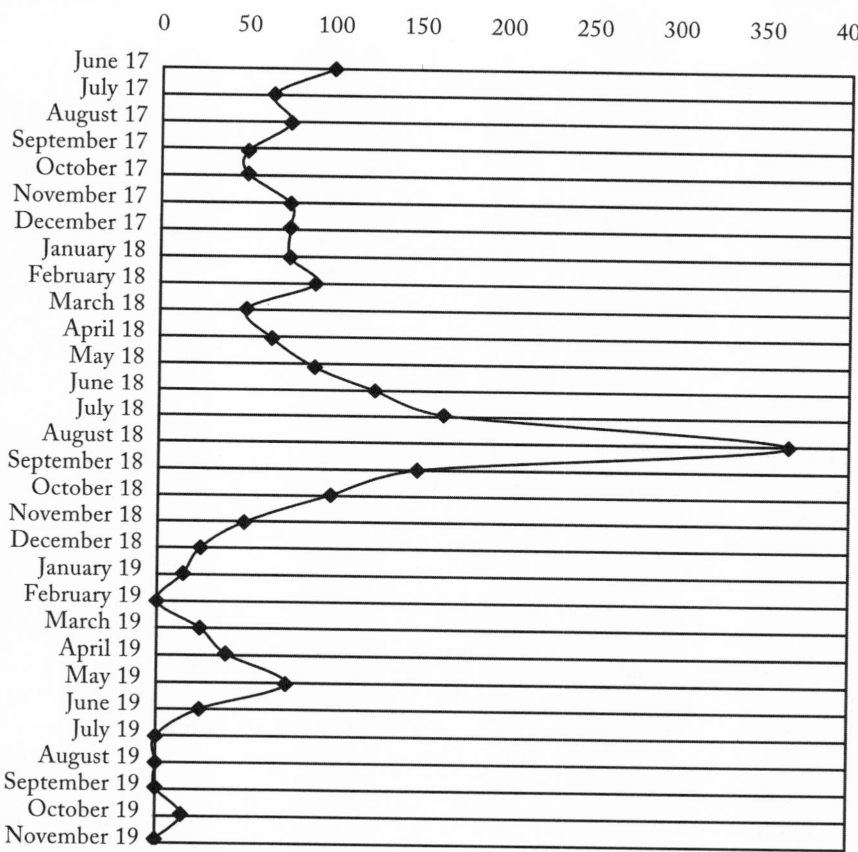

Source: Investigative Case Files of the Bureau of Investigation, 1908–1922, Record Group 65, National Archives and Records Administration.

it would be unrealistic to expect southern agents to have behaved much differently from others bred there.

Ollie Eaglin was jailed for failing to register in Beaumont, Texas, four days after the 5 June 1917 registration. He did not know his birth date, but guessed that he was perhaps twenty-one. Although Bureau agent Daniel Trazivuk telegraphed the U.S. attorney in Paris, Texas, of the arrest, and Eaglin secured a lawyer who found several witnesses to prove he was underage, the federal attorney did not instruct Trazivuk to investigate Eaglin's age until 27 June. Two days later he met with the suspect, who agreed to register, even though he still insisted he did not know his true age and had been ignorant of the requirements of the Selective

Service Act. Despite this willingness, Trazivuk kept him in jail until July, when Eaglin was finally released and drafted. A month in the county jail was clearly unwarranted.[29]

In early June Trazivuk also arrested twenty-six-year-old Perry Scott, who failed to register after some whites told him there was no need do so because he had lost his right arm. After several days he was released on his own recognizance by the U.S. attorney, who nonetheless prepared charges for presentation to the grand jury. Before it could deliberate, however, the one-armed man was drafted.[30]

Other federal officials in east Texas zealously pursued black suspects in mid-1917. Acting on a tip, Agent Charles E. Breniman jailed Dupree Newsome, who claimed he was only twenty. But witnesses testified he had willfully refused, saying that "they already had enough niggers." After spending five days in jail, Newsome was offered a deal: If he would raise $100 bond, admit to being twenty-one, and register, he would be spared prosecution. The extant case file does not reveal how Newsome responded. Elsewhere in Texas, blacks suffered similar fates. Jim Hardy admitted to being twenty-five and having arrived too late on 5 June to register. Seeking to make an example of him, a U.S. commissioner had him held on $200 bail and incarcerated for over a month until the federal grand jury convened to hear charges. Disposition of the case is unknown, but several weeks in Houston's Harris County jail was a severe punishment. In Waco, Frank James faced similar charges and an even higher bond. He, too, languished in jail until the next federal grand jury session.[31]

Persistence characterized other federal officers in pursuit of Bill Fulnettle, who had left Texas to work for the Santa Fe Railroad in Arizona. Agent Will C. Austin quizzed his sister, who had custody of the family Bible, only to find that the pages recording births had been destroyed. Before learning Austin's purpose, the sister said that her brother was twenty-three, but later claimed he was only nineteen. School records appeared to prove that Fulnettle was in fact twenty-two, and Austin concluded that he left the area to avoid conscription.

Fulnettle was arrested in Winslow, Arizona. Unable to make $1,000 bail, he spent the next two weeks in jail. Upon being returned to Texas, he secured affidavits from two women supporting his claim. One had a twenty-year-old son who she testified was born the same year as Fulnettle. The other was a former schoolteacher who possessed records attesting to the same age. Perhaps because of the conflicting evidence, Fulnettle was still in custody in early October, nearly two months after his arrest. Extant federal court archives contain no record of the case, which would indicate that the grand jury refused to indict him.[32]

The Bureau's Texas agents investigated more cases of alleged black slackers and deserters than their counterparts in any other state. They were at least partially responsible for the fact that, even though the first registration missed many blacks in the South, the proportion of Texas's black registrants nearly equaled the overall proportion of blacks in the state. Bureau personnel and U.S. attorneys in Texas appear to have been the most punitive federal officials in the nation when dealing with black draft suspects.

Other parts of the South also adopted a hard line when punishing black draft evaders early in the war. In Hopewell, Virginia, Elijah Scott admitted that he did not register, believing that farmers were not required to do so. Unable to raise $500 bail, he remained in jail for eighteen days until he was found guilty by a federal district judge, registered, and sentenced to an additional ten days.[33] Four weeks' incarceration was excessive, especially when men in other localities were allowed to register without penalty when presenting similar excuses. But federal agents and prosecutors were encouraged to take punitive action by Bureau chief Bielaski. The Norfolk office discovered several black sailors who were at sea on 5 June. Those who promptly registered upon their return were not prosecuted, but ones who procrastinated or quickly signed on for new voyages were shown no mercy. Bielaski instructed Norfolk SAC Ralph Daughton to personally ensure that such cases were "vigorously" pursued. No one knew, in the summer of 1917, how long the war might last, and federal officials, particularly in the South, were determined to set examples by severely punishing those blacks who failed to comply with selective service regulations.[34]

Federal employees were zealous in apprehending alleged non-registrants—already being called slackers by the general public—in the weeks immediately following the first registration. A marshal raided an Illinois Central train bound for Chicago shortly after it left New Orleans and arrested six blacks who were likely headed for industrial jobs and perhaps escape from the draft in the anonymity of a northern city.[35] Meanwhile, just days before the bloody race riot across the Mississippi River in Illinois, police in St. Louis were arresting any blacks on the streets who could not produce registration cards, with Bureau agents securing arrest warrants from cooperative U.S. attorneys.[36] In contrast, federal officers in Baltimore, another border-state city, saw their role as efficiently supplying men for the new national army, not acting as judge and jury in racially motivated actions. Agents there routinely took blacks found to be without registration cards before a federal judge who ordered them to serve one day in jail and then be registered.[37] Since there were no overall guidelines on how to deal with seemingly willful non-registrants, it was up to each Bureau office and U.S. attorney to decide on a course of action. Jailing hapless black laborers for more than a day or two when there was no evidence of political motives for avoiding the draft served no purpose other than to set a stern example or work out racial hostilities. If issuing a warning was the intent, the tactic failed.

The first black draft cases opened by the Bureau of Investigation in northern localities were typically handled differently from southern cases. By mid-1917, all urban centers were attracting black migrants from the South, with the earliest cases coming from smokestack cities like Chicago, Columbus, Cincinnati, Pittsburgh, Milwaukee, Philadelphia, and Detroit. Most suspects were recent arrivals who came to the Bureau's attention through tips from local police. Some were jailed for brief periods and released after registering.[38] Even though Charles Watkins was held under $1,000 bail in Chicago, it was canceled when he agreed to register. The case of Abraham Scott is perhaps more typical of the Bureau's Chicago office in the summer of 1917. Born in Louisiana, he migrated first to Toledo and then to Chicago where, two days later, Agent C. B. Ambrose questioned him. Scott claimed he had registered in Toledo on 5 June, giving a Louisiana address, but had never received a card. Ambrose wired the sheriff of New Iberia, who found no record of Scott's registration. Nonetheless, he concluded that since "there have been a great many mistakes made by registrars, and I was inclined to the opinion this man was telling the truth, he was given an opportunity to re-register."[39]

Examples from Pennsylvania also show the range of actions taken by Bureau personnel in the North after the first registration. Sheridan Johnson, jailed for having no card, claimed to be twenty years old and in prison in Kentucky on registration day. But Kentucky authorities reported that Johnson was released prior to 5 June and had claimed to be twenty-four years old. He remained in jail for the next several days while federal attorneys in Pittsburgh and Kentucky conferred, but before they reached a decision, Agent Edward M. Murphy visited Johnson in his cell, "carefully looked at the man and determined that he was not in conscription age" and ordered his release. Nine days of Johnson's life were wasted, but racial malice does not seem to have played a role.[40]

Philadelphia agents appear to have treated young black males with consideration in the summer of 1917. Local police brought several suspected slackers to the Bureau office, including brothers Dallas and Hollis Lewis. Hollis was obviously underage and was allowed to go home to get Dallas's registration card, whereupon both were released. Agent C. V. Mallet believed S. H. Ward's claim that he had registered in Toledo and released him with instructions to write for a new card and report back to the Bureau. Joseph Robert Walters claimed that his entire student military company at Delaware College had offered its services to the country and as a consequence been told not to register. Agent Webster Spates simply registered Walters and let him go. Nathaniel Mabb told Spates that he was not registered because he had been in town only two weeks and did not know of his obligation. Spates released him with instructions to proceed to city hall and register. Perhaps these agents were not punitive with black suspects because their boss, SAC Frank L. Garbarino, himself set a good example. He interviewed Foster Anderson, who said he could not read or write and had no knowledge of the registration requirement, whereupon Garbarino registered the man himself and released him. When Clarence Hairston came to the Bureau office to say that he had not registered because he thought he was only twenty but had since been informed by relatives that he was twenty-two, Garbarino registered him without penalty.[41]

Not every northern agent was free of racism or coercion at the beginning of the war. Bureau officials throughout the nation saw themselves as enforcing the national resolve as well as selective service regulations. But southern agents were more likely to employ racial "justice" in the form of lengthy incarceration, callous attitudes, and threats.

Pursuit of suspected black draft evaders by the Bureau continued after the summer of 1917 at about the same pace. Even though there would be no new registration until June 1918, there were still tens of thousands of men who had failed to register in mid-1917. Provost Marshal General Crowder recognized that the tiny force of Bureau agents could not possibly identify or apprehend most of them. Consequently, in November 1917 he issued orders to make every police officer in the nation "part of the army building machine" by giving them authority to arrest delinquents. Also recruited into the draft machinery were all postal employees, who were to give priority to delivering selective service notices and securing forwarding addresses for registrants who had moved.[42]

Crowder's orders did not preclude other means of catching alleged slackers. Late in November the New York state adjutant general published the names of 215 blacks said to have failed to comply with the draft and invited any federal, state, county, or city official to arrest them, even though he had no authority to confer arrest powers on anyone. It was believed that many men on the list had left for other parts, and their names were revealed in part so that friends and relations could urge them to comply with regulations.[43]

Patterns of enforcement established during the summer of 1917 persisted for the next nine months, with some Bureau offices operating more punitively than others. Within a given office, some agents adopted a hard line while others exercised grace and gave suspects the benefit of the doubt. Scattered across the South (and in two instances in the Far West) were a number of outrageous jailings far out of line with the gravity of the alleged offenses. The willingness of federal authorities to sanction such abuses illustrates the degree to which justice for blacks was of no importance to some of those who were sworn to uphold it.

A number of southern agents had arduous assignments, covering many rural counties and spending long hours traveling on slow branch-line trains in search of slackers. Perhaps because suspects and witnesses were so distant from federal attorneys and courtrooms, such agents frequently showed more leniency than those working on city cases. Agent George C. Calmes, who traversed portions of rural Georgia and South Carolina, was persuaded that the only reason twenty-six-year-old Marcus Nance had not registered was because his illiterate mother erroneously believed him to be six years older. When Nance agreed to comply, Calmes saw no need to punish him. Similarly, he believed that Fred Cofield was "ignorant," having no knowledge of his age, and accepted his willingness to register as proof of honorable intentions. Calmes had only a limited time to investigate individual cases and usually gave the benefit of the doubt to those he thought "ignorant" or who gave reasonable explanations for failing to execute some portion of the selective service requirements.[44]

Agent Harry D. Gulley covered practically every corner of rural Mississippi. Hiring cars, taking trains and buses, borrowing horses and buggies or automobiles from sheriffs and private citizens, he could not afford to spend days tracing the whereabouts or discovering the age of alleged black slackers. If suspects looked underage or overage, especially if they were illiterate, he released them without evidence. On other occasions he accepted reasonable excuses for not registering on time. Gulley was not averse to briefly jailing draft-age blacks who had not registered, were delinquent, or had failed to inform their local boards of changes of address, but he usually sought quick resolutions rather than allowing the men to languish behind bars. Getting eligible men into the service was his goal; executing racial authority over hapless individuals was not his method. Gully simply did his duty professionally, in many cases tempering justice with mercy.[45]

In the nine months after the summer of 1917, a significant number of blacks residing in southern cities could not prove they were properly registered and classified. Urban agents, in collaboration with draft boards, too often meted out gratuitous punishment. Mobile's Agent Calvin Outlaw believed that if a suspect "was delinquent in any manner" he should be immediately jailed. The number of days incarcerated varied from city to city, but it was common for men to spend weeks in jail while their status was being investigated or as punishment before sentencing. One of the worst cases concerned Frank Bailey, who was bedridden with a serious illness in Tampa on registration day. He admitted that he knew he should have registered after recovering but said he did not know how to do so at that late date. Federal officials believed Bailey to be educated enough to know his responsibilities and jailed him for ten weeks, at which time a federal grand jury accepted a family birth record showing that he had not been twenty-one years old on 5 June 1917. A miscarriage of justice had obviously occurred. One wonders if Bailey was given the opportunity to prove his true age while in the Tampa lock-up.[46]

Bureau agents in New Orleans collaborated with local police in unnecessarily lengthy jailings. Ed Grant was arrested for failure to have a classification card and waited eleven days before Agent J. F. Hote interviewed him. Admitting he had not registered, he remained in custody while charges were filed. How lengthy his stay in the parish prison was is unknown, but the wheels of justice were not rolling swiftly. Monroe Boyce was more fortunate: he had to wait only five days before Hote arrived to examine his registration card. However, since he had no classification card, he remained locked up while his local board was contacted. Hemp Young also became accustomed to jail, spending nine days there while Bureau agents and his draft board in Crystal Springs, Mississippi, took their time confirming his status. Peter Neal seems to have suffered the most heartless treatment at the hands of parish authorities. Arrested on 9 February 1918 for failure to have a classification card, he was placed in the local jail on orders from the Department of Justice. A wire was sent to his draft board in Marshall, Texas, requesting a questionnaire. Agent M. M. Schaumburger assisted Neal in filling out the document on 2 April, whereupon he was released. Did the Bureau need several weeks to send the telegram to Marshall? Did draft officials feel no urgency in responding?[47]

While some Texas agents accepted relatives' testimony concerning suspects' ages, others followed the pattern established in the summer of 1917 and continued to employ stern measures against alleged black slackers. On 20 April 1918, federal agents, military police, and local sheriffs and policemen raided all the pool halls in Houston. Among the many men netted was Charley Stewart, who had ignored an order to report for induction. Neither Bureau agents nor his local board in an adjacent county moved quickly and he remained in jail for fifteen days before being transported to Camp Logan. But this was a minor inconvenience compared to the suffering of James Griffin, whose only crime was that he had moved frequently and thus not received a classification card. Griffin was a gandy dancer for the Southern Pacific Railroad in June 1917, when, he claimed, his entire gang was brought to Houston to register. But when no record was found there, Griffin was jailed in Fort Worth. Two weeks later agents found that his registration had been transferred from Houston to Shreveport. Learning of his incarceration, the Shreveport board sent his papers to Fort Worth. Finally, seven weeks after he first landed in jail, Griffin was given a physical examination, found fit, and sent to a training camp. Bureaucratic ineptitude and a cavalier neglect on the part of federal officials had robbed him of nearly two months of freedom. Yet even that was not a Texas record. In Dallas, twenty-seven-year-old Archy Brown had been told by his mother that he did not need to register because the government would come and get him when he was needed. A Bureau agent concluded that his failure to register was "probably due to ignorance more than anything else." But for reasons not revealed in the case file, Brown remained locked up for the next ten weeks before an agent took him to be registered, whereupon he was released on account of physical unfitness. If his crime was in fact ignorance, his punishment was entirely undeserved.[48]

Norfolk agents investigated more suspected black slackers than any other Bureau office between the first and second registrations. That city, and neighboring Newport News and Portsmouth, housed many ship and navy yards as well as a major embarkation point for troops going overseas. The regional economy expanded rapidly in 1917 and 1918, bringing a flood of migrants from the Southeast. Many had registered with draft boards at home, while others registered for the first time in the Norfolk area. Some did not remain permanently in the lower James River cities but instead moved on to Baltimore, Philadelphia, and other points along the Atlantic seaboard, further complicating efforts to trace draft delinquents. Not surprisingly, agents were unable to locate many of them. So great was the press of business that at times Special Agent in Charge Daughton assigned cases to office clerk Joseph Polen. Investigations were time consuming when agents had to cross Hampton Roads on commercial ferries or the government steamer *Justice* to get to Newport News and Hampton. The Bureau was assisted by local police, who were particularly zealous in arresting suspected slackers, although half of those detained eventually proved to be properly registered and classified. Slacker raids also increased the number of those who had to be investigated.

Many suspects spent a day or two behind bars, but on average blacks in Norfolk were kept in jail for shorter periods than in other southern cities. They were also more likely to be released simply on an agent's belief that they looked too young or too old. In one case, the only evidence of age was the statement of a young man's father, but since the latter appeared to be a "respectable" individual, his word was accepted. Arrested by the police, Monroe Gainey told Agent Ralph K. Dawson he had been discharged from the army on account of physical disability. Since his "statements were straightforward" and it was obvious that he was physically unfit for military duty, Dawson ordered his release. Agent William L. Murphy not only released many men who appeared too young or too old, he also allowed those who were at sea on 5 June to register months later without penalty. Another agent allowed a suspect to go home after he promised to return the next day when a telegram from his out-of-state draft board was expected. And after Agents Dawson and J. R. Patterson questioned Tom Smith, "according to our discretion, we thought that his excuses should be accepted, and he was released."[49]

While not typical, federal officials in Norfolk occasionally jailed suspects for excessive lengths of time in the period between the first and second registrations. Isaac Cain, appearing to be twenty-one years old, spent nine days in jail during a fruitless effort to get a statement from his mother, residing in rural South Carolina. A U.S. commissioner eventually freed him, judging that on physical appearance he did not seem to be of draft age. James Arthur Carey suffered worse. Caught by police, he claimed to be eighteen, but several prominent whites said he was over twenty-one. After eleven days in jail, he was brought to trial, convicted, sentenced to an additional five days, and compelled to register.[50]

Two men in the Far West also suffered inexcusable treatment during this period, the first because of racism in the army. Rudolph Nathaniel Jacobs was jailed briefly in Spokane for allegedly failing to register, but was released on his father's statement that he was thirty-three years old. However, when the San Francisco office learned from Jacobs's mother that he was only twenty-nine, he was arrested again in Spokane. Admitting he had been mistaken about his age, he asked to be inducted. Unfortunately for Jacobs, his local board had orders not to allow voluntary enlistments by blacks unless an entire black unit was being formed, so Jacobs was sent to jail. A month later he was still incarcerated, with no prospect of induction. How much longer he remained behind bars is unknown, but clearly another miscarriage of justice had occurred.[51]

An inefficient draft board and a cavalier agent cost another black man weeks of liberty. In El Centro, California, William Conly Hayes, a laborer working on the new county jail, was placed in custody when he could not produce a registration card, having failed to notify his draft board in Duluth of his new address. Agent W. A. Weymouth sent a telegram to that board, which replied that it had no knowledge of Hayes. The prisoner stuck with his story, so Weymouth wired Duluth's police chief. On receipt of information identifying Hayes's draft board, El Centro's sheriff corresponded with its clerk, who ordered Hayes to fill out a questionnaire locally. Hayes was finally released after spending over three weeks in jail because federal and local officials took their time answering one another's queries. Clearly the confinement of an itinerant black laborer, who was daily literally within sight, seemed no matter of urgency.[52]

Bureau personnel in northern and border cities during late 1917 and the first five months of 1918 used incarceration sparingly. Chicago continued to be flooded with migrants, some of whom subsequently moved elsewhere. Telegrams to the Bureau office came from many other cities where blacks who claimed they had registered in Chicago had been picked up. If they were delinquent, Chicago agents simply ordered them to be inducted where they currently resided, not jailed. When the situation was reversed, Chicago agents customarily took men who had not registered elsewhere for physical examinations, sent the results to their boards, and allowed them to go free after they promised to keep in touch with those boards. Chicago's agents (and their APL assistants) were more concerned with making the selective service system work than with punishing delinquents.

Agents in Philadelphia likewise practiced leniency in allowing delinquents to register with minimal or no punishment. In nearby Baltimore several cases were concluded on the Philadelphia pattern: a night in jail, and then registration. Where men were registered but delinquent, immediate induction was the preferred course, not punitive incarceration. Cincinnati agents were also busy with draft cases involving migrant blacks and followed the pattern of Chicago and Philadelphia, accepting most unregistered men's statements of age if they were offered in a "straightforward" manner and their physical appearance corresponded with the claim to be under or over the draft age. Delinquents were usually inducted, not prosecuted. But tolerance was not unlimited, and it appears that Agent Albert D. Cash had sufficient reason for suspicion of Lee Martin. Martin first claimed to be only twenty years old, then said he had been working on the Pennsylvania Railroad on registration day. When he was found to have a registration card bearing another man's name, Martin explained that he had found it on the street. Cash decided to "allow him to stay in jail for a few days in order to make him tell the truth," meanwhile wiring his hometown in rural Alabama for information on his age. Eleven days later, having learned nothing from Alabama and with Martin sticking with his stories, Cash released the suspect.[53]

Draft enforcement accelerated drastically in mid-1918. The Bureau's roundup of non-registrants, delinquents, and deserters in the summer and early autumn greatly exceeded the rate of arrests and investigations during the previous twelve months (see Table 6). The second registration took place on 5 June. It, coupled with a supplemental enrollment on 24 August, yielded a total of nine hundred thousand men who had turned 21 since the first registration a year before. A third registration held on September 12 added over 13 million names of those aged 18 to 21 and between 32 and 45, but relatively few of these men were classified by the time hostilities ceased in November.

What explains the sharp increase in the number of investigations after the second registration, which increased the total number of registrants by less than 10 percent? What, particularly, accounts for the jump in black draft cases? Significant numbers of American troops were by then fighting in France. But many blacks had more immediate concerns which furnished ample reasons for apathy or cynicism toward the war and the draft: discriminatory draft boards; atrocious conditions at segregated training camps; insults to black officers; riots against black troops; reluctance of the army high command to trust black troops in combat; and a consequent concentration of black soldiers in stevedoring, supply, and other laboring details. Historians Arthur E. Barbeau and Florette Henri describe the scandalous training camp conditions which were becoming well known to black civilians by mid-1918:

> The men at Camp Humphreys still had no mess facilities by the middle of 1918; they ate in the open and were marched down to the Potomac River for their weekly bath. By far the worst of all was Camp Hill, where no provision had been made for the 6,000 black draftees who began arriving in October 1917. On arrival, the lucky ones had unfloored, unheated tents; others stood around fires all night or slept in the woods under trees. Very few had blankets. From October until January their only clothing was what they had worn when they came, and no bathing facilities were provided during that entire time. These men ate outside regardless of the weather; one group of 500 had only 150 mess kits among them. Their hospital was a floorless tent, and doctors ordered sick men to work without treatment. Eventually, some shelter was provided, with twenty to thirty men in each sixteen-foot-square tent. Every day was a workday, including Sundays and holidays.[54]

If anyone could be expected to be less than enthusiastic about military service, and less than conscientious about complying with selective service regulations, it was black men.

A second major explanation for the great increase in black draft cases in the summer of 1918 was the widespread use of "slacker raids." Led by Bureau agents and augmented by APL volunteers, local police, and military personnel, these dragnets occurred throughout the nation. In Chicago on 11 July, raiders targeted "cabarets, south side all night flops, dives, pool rooms, lodging houses, night movies, and other hangouts for young men." Commuter railroad terminals and elevated train stations were not neglected. Every man leaving the afternoon doubleheader at Cubs Park was stopped; dozens were detained, spoiling their pleasure at seeing "Shufflin' Phil" Douglas win both games for the home team. Thousands more were checked on the streets the following day, resulting in another one thousand overnight guests at various police stations. A month later the boardwalks, piers, and eateries of Atlantic City were raided. A similar dragnet was thrown over Tulsa. The most outrageous raids occurred in New York City, where a thousand soldiers, 750 sailors, and several hundred police and APL volunteers formed an anti-slacker strike force led by Bureau agents. One eyewitness was U.S. senator Joseph S. Frelinghuysen, who told his colleagues: "I stood on a street corner and saw soldiers armed with rifles, with bayonets fixed, hold up citizens, compel them to stand waiting while there were crowds around jeering at them, and when they failed to produce their registration cards [they] were put in motor trucks and driven through the streets amid the jeers and scoffs of the crowd; they were sent to the armories and there held for hours without food, practically without opportunity of communicating with their relatives and friends in order to procure the evidence demanded by the authorities."[55]

The number of men apprehended in the New York raids was estimated from 20,000 to 60,000. Nearly 12,000 were caught in Manhattan and the Bronx alone, although only 300 were found to be eligible for immediate induction. The Wilson administration was stung by widespread criticism. Attorney General Thomas Gregory accepted responsibility while claiming his orders forbidding use of soldiers and APL men in making arrests had been disregarded. Yet Gregory ultimately justified the process, saying, "some form of dragnet policy, within the law of course, was absolutely essential."[56] Gregory did not specify how a dragnet could be reconciled with the law. Most historians have concluded that the generally meager result of the raids hardly justified the draconian tactics used, even if constitutional scruples could somehow be satisfied.

Massive slacker raids were impractical outside the cities. Instead, a lone Bureau agent would spend several days in a rural region investigating men who had been reported delinquent by draft boards, county sheriffs, rural route mail carriers, and patriotic citizens. Blacks were common suspects in the southern countryside in the summer of 1918. The sheriff of Pike County, Georgia, drove Agent George C. Smith around to investigate eleven suspected violators. There was no time for in-depth sleuthing and justice was at times rudely administered, as in the case of four men who had no ideas of their correct age. Smith simply judged them to be of draft age and turned them over for summary induction. But he was not bent on inducting everyone. Investigating allegations that four other men had made false claims for exemption, Smith found all were supporting their families and indeed deserving of their classifications.[57]

Agent Fred Cotton of the Knoxville, Tennessee, office faced a monumental task in verifying the status of 260 blacks from Tapoco, North Carolina, in one day. Fortunately, only nineteen had failed to return their questionnaires, so he arranged to parole them to the local sheriff until such time as their draft board decided whether such failures had been willful.[58] As had been the case from the beginning of registration, determination of age was extremely difficult. Joe Chatman was questioned by Agent Charles E. Corgan in Saluda, South Carolina. Admitting he did not know his exact age, Chatman said his mother believed he was under twenty-one. Corgan was not convinced, and told him, "had he had a good look at himself . . . he would have known he was above registration age." Whether persuaded by logic or compulsion, Chatman agreed to register.[59]

Places of amusement were frequent targets of slacker dragnets, with one of the more unproductive ones involving black carnival workers in Raleigh, North Carolina. Agent Denver Graham organized two raids, first on the Brown and Dyer Carnival on 24 August. Twenty-one men—including seven whites, one of whom was described as a female impersonator and snake charmer—were determined to be delinquent and given physical examinations. Nine of them, including six blacks, passed and were given a choice: stand trial for draft evasion or accept immediate induction. Every one took the latter option. A larger raid was held on 5 September using APL volunteers, a provost marshal's contingent, a mechanics' training school cadet corps, and U.S. treasury agents and deputy marshals. Only federal agents had arrest powers, so each was given several assistants. Starting at 9:30 P.M., the raid on the Smith Greater Shows lasted scarcely forty-five minutes, after which three hundred men were interrogated throughout the night. Only nine men—all blacks—were found to be delinquent; seven were carnival employees. A doctor pronounced them to be "the best men physically he had examined since being on the board," after which Graham personally escorted them to Camp Jackson near Columbia, South Carolina, for induction. Riding one of the Seaboard Air Line Railway's dirty Jim Crow coaches for 202 miles must have been a novel experience for the white agent. Furthermore, the Raleigh draft board paid expenses only to Columbia, so Graham had to pay his own train fare home.[60]

Much of the daily work of federal agents was mundane. Men who had registered in another city but lost contact with their draft boards often voluntarily appeared at a Bureau office. In many cases, they had moved so many times that their questionnaires had been returned to local boards undelivered. Draft officials routinely classified such persons delinquent and advanced them on the list for physical examinations and possible induction. When they sought the Bureau's help in determining their draft status, agents telegraphed their local boards to ascertain their classification. More often than not the reply requested that the men be taken before the closest board, examined, and inducted.

By the summer of 1918 agents exercised wide latitude in deciding whether to simply induct or punish slackers. Southern agents commonly judged blacks to be innocent of willful evasion if they appeared to be ignorant or illiterate. If either was the case, such persons were simply escorted to an induction center.[61] This reflected southern racial paternalism in which even questionable ignorance could excuse behavior so long as acquiescence to white authority was observed. Where ignorance was not a mitigating factor, agents had to choose whether to quickly induct a delinquent or further burden federal attorneys and courts with relatively minor cases. In rural Oklahoma, Will Scott maintained he was exempt from the draft, but Agent Lewie H. Henry believed otherwise. However, the U.S. attorney decided that if Scott would abandon his claim and accept induction, prosecution would be dropped. It was an offer Scott could not refuse.[62]

While examples of fairness and even leniency can be found in the Bureau's draft case files for the summer and early autumn of 1918, punitive detention of blacks remained all too common. Agents referred cases for prosecution when they thought family members were lying about their sons' ages or their own dependency.[63] An extreme case was that of Thomas Green, who found no mercy from federal authorities in Galveston and Beaumont after his local board notified them of a probable false affidavit to gain a deferment. The investigating agent discovered that Green's first wife and two children received no support from him and that the date of his second marriage had been altered on the license. Unable to make bail in mid-August, Green languished in jail for months. When a November trial date finally approached, a Bureau agent persuaded him to plead guilty. Green was sentenced to an additional six months' term in January 1919, two months after the conclusion of the war and a halt in inductions. Another example of excessive detention comes from West Virginia, where federal agents believed that domestic servants were quitting work so that their husbands could claim them as dependents and thus gain deferments. George Wilson filed such a declaration but his wife was found to have had a "good-paying" job until she voluntarily reduced her hours. Wilson had indeed falsified his questionnaire, and he served ninety days in the county jail as a consequence.[64] However, his wife may have had a valid reason for quitting her job: What whites deemed "good pay" for a domestic's twelve-hour, six-and-a-half-day work week was often an exploitive pittance supplemented by cast-off clothing and kitchen leftovers.

Willie Green suffered similarly severe treatment in Louisiana when he was charged in August with failure to register. Even though Shreveport agent L. T. Stevens characterized him as "a negro of the ignorant class," he found it "unreasonable" to believe that Green did not know he had to register: "It appears that each and every one of the negroes, when caught up claim ignorance, but on the other hand, make absolutely no effort to find out whether or not they should register." An agreement was struck whereby Green consented to induction, but he was found to be physically unfit. The chagrined agent then got the U.S. attorney to reinstate the case for trial in the October term, with bail denied because of willful noncompliance. The Bureau's case file ends at this point, and the absence of notations in the federal criminal dockets and U.S. commissioner's record of proceedings suggest that Green was not brought to trial. In all likelihood, prosecutors or a grand jury concluded that the several weeks' time served were fit punishment. The severity of treatment seems grossly out of proportion to the offense, and appears to reflect racial bias in the administration of justice.[65]

In the summer of 1918, suspected black delinquents and deserters were routinely spending several days in southern jails while their draft status was investigated, enduring more judicial abuse than in the North, although ill treatment there was not unknown. Since individual apprehensions and slacker raiding frequently disregarded legal niceties anyway, it is not surprising that prolonged incarceration was common. To what degree blacks endured more lengthy detentions than whites cannot be determined with certainty, but southern officials often felt no urgency in expediting blacks' cases. Such was the fate of H. Harvey, jailed by the sheriff of rural Polk County, Texas, on 10 August 1918 for failing to register. Harvey admitted to being drunk on registration day. Three days later he pleaded guilty, told the court he wanted to enter the army immediately, passed his physical, and was approved for induction. Yet he remained in jail until 1 September, when he was at last transported to Camp Travis with other inductees from Houston.[66]

Innocent blacks also suffered lengthy incarceration. Willie Williams was jailed in Dallas as a suspected slacker. Even though his local board was in neighboring Fort Worth, he remained under lock and key for seven days until Bureau agents found him to be in a deferred classification. In Charleston, West Virginia, Edward Traylor was similarly jailed for failure to produce a registration card although he protested that he had in fact registered. He spent a week in the lockup before agents, conferring with local boards in that city and Atlanta, established the truthfulness of his claim.[67]

No state had more instances of abusive treatment of suspected black draft delinquents than Texas. From the beginning of the war white officials—federal, state, and local—cooperated in enforcing a pernicious brand of racial justice. The cases of Thomas Green, H. Harvey, and Willie Williams were not unusual. It was customary to keep delinquents in jail until they could be inducted. James Jackson luckily had to stay only five days in Dallas, but George Clay was jailed for sixteen days in Waco until being taken to a mobilization camp. This was inconsequential compared to the case of Andrew Felder, arrested in Brenham for draft evasion in September. He claimed to be thirty-six years old, and a statement by his mother, who was illiterate and had no family records, was inconclusive. After two months in jail, Felder was formally bound over for the federal grand jury, but when it failed to convene in January 1919, the U.S. attorney ordered him released because the four months he had been incarcerated was about equal to the sentence he would receive if convicted.[68]

Perhaps the worst spot in Texas for blacks accused of draft delinquency was the ill-named town of Liberty. Suspecting George Johnson of failing to register, its sheriff arrested him in June 1918, but did not notify federal authorities until August. Agent S. D. Bennett then picked up the prisoner and formally charged him after the illiterate man agreed that he "figured his age wrong." For reasons unknown, Bennett's office forgot about Johnson, who was confined in Beaumont's jail until 15 November, four days after the Armistice, when he told another federal agent that he wanted to plead guilty. He had to wait for trial another four weeks, however, and when his plea was finally heard he was sentenced to jail until 1 May 1919, bringing his total time behind bars to nearly eleven months. This was without doubt the greatest miscarriage of justice regarding a black slacker during World War I. There is no explanation for the draconian sentence, imposed at a time when the fighting was over and draft calls were suspended, other than simple racial punishment. By comparison Eugene Mack, another black from Liberty, was fortunate to serve only two months in jail. After being arrested by the sheriff, he was examined by a local board without a physician present and found to be deaf and thus disqualified for military service. Meanwhile, a Bureau agent found him to be delinquent and, believing Mack was exaggerating his deafness, insisted that he be examined again, this time by a proper medical board. Liberty's sheriff never received instructions to this effect and Mack remained in jail for six weeks. By the time Mack's draft board in San Antonio ruled that he was physically unfit he had lost nearly two months of personal liberty because of technical objections by a Bureau agent, official bumbling, and simple disregard for a black man's civil rights in Liberty, Texas.[69]

More suspected slackers came to the Bureau's attention because of arrests by local law enforcement officials than through the Bureau's own investigations. In southern localities, where blacks were frequently arrested for vagrancy or on "dangerous and suspicious" charges, police routinely detained anyone without a registration or classification card by the summer of 1918. The length of incarceration depended on how long it took for telegrams to be exchanged between Bureau offices and draft boards, whether or not the accused remembered accurately the precise draft board with which he was registered, the diligence of agents in concluding cases when men were already jailed, and bureaucratic ineptitude. This last circumstance resulted in several serious injustices, such as the case of Douglas Scott, who was arrested in rural Huntsville, Missouri, for failing to register. He claimed to have registered in Omaha, but no record of that act was found. After two months in the local lockup the Huntsville draft board declared him qualified for the army. But since federal charges had been filed, Scott was not inducted. The U.S. attorney recognized the injustice and sought induction papers from Omaha, but it took another month for them to reach Missouri. By that time the Armistice had been declared and draft calls suspended. In all probability Scott spent more than three months as a guest of the Huntsville jailer.[70]

Blacks who did not have classification cards could expect to be jailed in most southern cities in mid-1918, with induction into the military following some days later, whereas in northern localities they were more likely to be immediately inducted without suffering much jail time. Punitive attitudes characterized Bureau agents and U.S. attorneys in many cities other than those already mentioned. John Terry was apprehended in Chattanooga where a Bureau agent determined he was totally ignorant of his correct age and definitely not a willful draft evader. Nonetheless, after being registered and physically examined, he was remanded to the county jail until the next quota of draftees was scheduled to leave twelve days later. Similarly callous was the treatment of Carl Shafter Story in Roanoke who lost his registration card and had no knowledge of the requirement to file a questionnaire. He sat in jail for a number of days before Agent R. S. McKnight received authorization from his draft board in North Carolina to have him physically examined. But it took a Roanoke board another two weeks to do so, during which time Story continued to reside in jail. Ironically, he was found physically unfit and was released after enduring nearly three weeks' incarceration.[71]

Among punitive agents, none exceeded McKnight's vindictiveness in the case of Flin Washington. When arrested by police, he claimed to be registered in Richmond, but authorities there found no record of him. Upon being confronted by McKnight, Washington asked to be inducted so as to avoid prosecution. McKnight was agreeable and instructed Roanoke draft authorities to induct him. But the board "lost" Washington. When McKnight discovered him still in jail three weeks later, the angry prisoner stated that he was not of draft age and could not be forced to register. Now angry himself, McKnight wanted to initiate prosecution but a federal attorney advised that there was no way to prove Washington's age. But McKnight was not to be denied his pound of flesh: "In view, however, of the fact that he had wilfully made false representation regarding his Registration Status in the first place, and his defiant attitude regarding his age in the second place, which precluded the advisability of prosecution," McKnight determined "not to release Subject from custody without punishment of some kind" and persuaded local authorities to convict Washington of vagrancy and trespass. Thus, for being defiant to a white man with the power to make him pay, Washington spent the next sixty days on the chain gang.[72]

Although jail time without formal sentencing was generally shorter in Norfolk than in other southern cities, some men nonetheless suffered lengthy incarcerations while in the hands of the Bureau. James Knox was apprehended for failing to have a classification card. When agents quickly learned that his board had classified him as a deserter, they left him in the Newport News jail for eleven days before taking him before a local board for induction. Such a delay was clearly punitive. Ivanhoe Jones suffered nearly as long, although this may have been due to unintentional bureaucratic delays. It took nine days after receiving orders that he be inducted for the Bureau to take him for his physical, where he was rejected because he weighed only 109 pounds.[73] Unnecessarily long jailing of hapless black men was practiced by numerous southern Bureau agents. They may not have considered their actions malicious; such indifference was a common white response to the region's subordinate caste.

Southern racial folkways could also work in the other direction, as illustrated by the case of Guy Scott of Hampton, apprehended for failing to register. He was a personal servant to a Colonel Ellis, stationed at Camp Eustis, and explained that he had been traveling on registration day. In truth, he should have registered on 5 June 1917 and had also missed registering in June, August, and September 1918. Scott's excuse was clearly weak, but Agent Ralph Dawson released him after he finally complied.[74] The southern racial code dictated that a servant of an important person was not to be disciplined without that individual's permission. Scott benefited from his status and association, advantages not available to most black draft delinquents.

Although callous treatment of black suspects was more prevalent in the South, a few such instances occurred elsewhere during the frantic draft enforcement in the summer and fall of 1918. There is no rational explanation for the miscarriage of justice meted out to Herman Dickson in Erie, Pennsylvania. Arrested as a "possible draft evader" on 20 June, he informed agents that he was registered in Tennessee. Agents received a wire that same day informing them that Dickson was properly registered and subject to the next call, meaning he was not delinquent. Nevertheless, he remained in jail for more than a month, until 22 July, when the Erie board ordered him to entrain for Camp Lee, Virginia.[75]

George Taylor was a victim of bungling. He was picked up in Akron as a slacker, although he claimed to have registered in Louisville. When an agent wrote the Louisville office for verification, it "overlooked" the letter for twenty-one days until being reminded by a second message. Taylor was finally found to be delinquent and was inducted. His last three weeks before army duty were spent in jail because of poor management in both Bureau offices. Similar delays, resulting in a loss of freedom, occurred in other cities. In two Baltimore cases, men spent two weeks apiece in jail while investigations proceeded at a slow pace, although in a third instance an agent who was quick to jail alleged slackers nonetheless released a suspect after four days when his local board had not wired his status, requiring only that the man promise to contact the board personally.[76]

Two cases from the upper Midwest also show that other federal and local authorities could neglect black suspects as badly as in the South. Edward Ellis, caught as a slacker suspect in Bismarck, North Dakota, claimed to be registered in Philadelphia. An agent discovered that he had a cataract that rendered him nearly blind in one eye, but it took his Philadelphia board eight days to order a physical examination, during which time Ellis remained in jail. He stayed there another two weeks because the Bismark draft board failed to schedule an examination. Ellis was eventually registered after being incarcerated for three weeks.[77]

The most pathetic case in the Bureau's extant black draft cases chronicles the fate of William Penn Anderson. The Bureau's Milwaukee office received word from county authorities in Port Washington, twenty miles to the north, that Anderson had been in jail for several weeks for vagrancy and refusing to talk. Federal officials were notified because he appeared fit and of draft age. Agent Paul J. Kelly gradually pieced together Anderson's story. Born in Mississippi twenty-nine years before, he was sent to Seattle at the age of thirteen to live with relatives who subsequently died. About the age of twenty-two he was sent to a state institution for the insane, where he resided for six years. None of the inmates was registered on 5 June 1917. A year later a dozen of them were given new suits and five dollars apiece and put aboard a Chicago, Milwaukee, and St. Paul Railway coach in Seattle, accompanied by two guards. Several men were dropped off along the line. On reaching Milwaukee, Anderson detrained with one of the guards, who took him a short distance and then told him to keep walking. Agent Kelly concluded that Anderson seemed disturbed but was "very quiet and polite and causes no trouble to the authorities." Believing that the man was probably insane, Kelly's office washed its hands of the affair, instructing local officials to register and examine Anderson and then do with the helpless man as they saw fit. Whether Anderson was then released from jail, where he had spent the past three weeks, is not known. In any case, Anderson was a victim of federal, state, and local indifference toward a truly marginalized man.[78]

By the middle of 1918, Bureau offices were as well organized and staffed as they would get for investigating and apprehending suspected draft evaders. Some offices dedicated a few agents to conscription cases, whereas others assigned cases at random to any available agent. The number of cases handled varied greatly from city to city, due in part to the number of American Protective League volunteers, who assumed responsibility for many draft cases. Unfortunately, most records of APL draft investigations were discarded, so a city-by-city analysis of its actions is impossible to chart. Many more Bureau case files have survived. The busiest offices during the war are identified in Table 4. During the summer and early autumn of

1918, following the second and third registrations, three agencies managed a particularly heavy load of black draft cases: Birmingham (101 cases), Memphis (70 cases), and Cincinnati (69 cases).

Birmingham—the "Pittsburgh of the South"—housed the nation's seventh largest black urban population in 1920, with over seventy thousand residents plus another ten thousand in the industrial suburb of Bessemer. The region's economic mainstay was the iron and steel industry, which in turn depended on nearby coal mines. Blacks found plenty of wartime work, although skilled jobs remained the preserve of whites. Bureau agents not only spent much time on cases in Birmingham but also covered the nitrate plants at Florence and Muscle Shoals on the Tennessee River in the northwest corner of the state. In both Birmingham and Florence, the Bureau was assisted by company "secret service" agents who, along with APL volunteers, turned in suspected slackers. Despite the fact that nine hundred thousand blacks lived in Alabama during World War I, Bureau agents put relatively little energy into investigations in rural cotton belt counties where the black population was heavily concentrated.

Draft cases in Birmingham were a diverse lot. Not all suspects were legitimate military material: Some managed to prove they were below or above draft age, although most of them suffered jail time while their claims were being investigated. Others failed physical examinations, were mentally incompetent, or had legitimate deferments for supporting families. Much work involved wiring draft boards elsewhere for information on an individual's status, or sending telegrams to Bureau offices in other cities where suspects claimed to have registered. The Birmingham office was typical of all agencies in the summer and fall of 1918, resolving some cases, leaving others inconclusive, finding some suspects, and never locating others. The proportion of suspects who were jailed there was higher than in most other southern cities, though, and much greater than in the North.

Three agents handled the majority of black draft cases in Birmingham, and differences in their professionalism and personal attitudes indicate that special agents in charge of Bureau offices did not or could not always impose uniformity in the handling of cases. Agent Malcolm M. Stewart was a southern racial moderate and paternalist who often treated blacks with fairness so long as they appeared cooperative and honest. When company police at a nitrate plant in Florence apprehended Sam Harrison for not having a registration card, Stewart released him with instructions to return within the week to show his card, believing Harrison to be honest. Stewart likewise freed Odice Dixon from jail, believing he was legitimately deferred, having a dependent family in New Orleans, and confident that he intended to send them part of his earnings. While verifying Edgar Harrison's claim to being too young for the draft, Stewart released him with the understanding he would appear each day at the office until proof was received from his hometown. When Dudley Harris spent eight days in custody because his draft board failed to send information on his current status, Stewart took pity and paroled him. But Stewart was not unwilling to use jail to "persuade" an individual to cooperate. W. M. Jones was unregistered, claiming to be over age, although marriage records seem to indicate youthfulness. After being jailed Jones decided he was, in fact, within draft age, and the helpful agent made certain he was scheduled for induction.[79]

Unlike some agents elsewhere, none in Birmingham used racial epithets in their written reports. However, references to the ignorance of suspects betray a stereotypical view of blacks that is not surprising since most agents served in regions to which they were native. Walter Black and his common-law spouse, Mary Hammond, had been arrested, he for falsely claiming to be married and supporting a dependant spouse, she for signing the dependency claim. Black had previously been married and regarded that wife's move to another state as termination of the union. Stewart believed there was no willful intent to claim an undeserved exemption since both Black and Hammond were "very ignorant negroes, and this practice of marrying again among the negroes is so common and the state authorities do not take any steps to correct it." Exercising traditional southern paternalism, Stewart released them with instructions to go home and "gather their garden."[80]

Similar in attitude and action was Agent Mark Hanna. He discovered that Thomas Williams had never filed a questionnaire, an offense that many agents throughout the South felt warranted jail. But since Williams came to the Bureau willingly to ascertain his status, bringing along his white employer, Hanna had him fill out a questionnaire and released him without penalty. Like Stewart, Hanna generally conducted himself in a professional manner, seeming to take no pleasure in jailing or punishing suspects, usually giving them the benefit of the doubt, and exercising paternalism in exonerating those whose failure to comply with regulations was due to alleged ignorance.[81]

Agent C. L. Doggrell, who worked the Florence–Muscle Shoals beat, was markedly different from Stewart and Hanna, however. He was quick to assume the worst and throw suspects into jail on little pretext. When Joe McLendon "could not give a very good account of himself," Doggrell "was satisfied in my own mind that he had been called for service" and had him arrested. Similar treatment was given to Willie Suber, who never received his classification card. When he sought the Bureau's assistance, Agent T. F. McAdory slapped him in jail overnight while he contacted the man's local draft board.[82]

In fact, by the summer of 1918, Birmingham agents routinely incarcerated black draft suspects: The majority spent time behind bars, many for unjustifiably long periods. No Bureau office jailed a higher percentage of black suspects than Birmingham: thirty-five out of forty-five spent time behind bars, some for only one day, but at least a quarter for a week or more. Pete Walker believed registration was required only if one intended to vote, and he made plain to the white agents that he did not claim that right. Nonetheless, they kept him in jail for twenty days before arranging for his induction. After Doggrell arrested John D. Kelly as a possible deserter, he spent over three weeks in jail before it was learned he was deferred. Whether that was due to dilatory action on the part of Kelly's draft board or lassitude on the part of Bureau personnel cannot be determined.[83]

Birmingham agents succeeded in inducting over a third of the suspects they investigated. That proportion would have been higher had it not been for bureaucratic errors and the flu epidemic in the fall of 1918. In two cases delinquents were in jail for unrelated offenses, to be turned over to the Bureau at the completion of their sentences, but local jailers forgot this instruction and released them, to the chagrin of federal agents. In two other instances men were paroled from jail because of the epidemic; both escaped service entirely, for by the time the flu crisis subsided in November, local boards had no more calls for men. One of these individuals, however, did not get off scot-free: he served over two months in jail while agents investigated his claim to having registered and discovered it to be false.[84]

Bureau agents' morale was influenced by several factors. Some, like Doggrell, enjoyed catching delinquents in lies or inconsistencies and slapping suspects in jail. But reward-claiming "bloodsuckers" could rob one's satisfaction. When a private citizen or police officer apprehended a deserter expecting to claim the $50 reward, some agents felt little compulsion to assist them. A rural deputy sheriff seized Willie Brown for having failed to file his questionnaire. Once Agent Hanna determined the charge to be valid and understood that the sheriff intended to claim the reward, he left it up to him to take Brown for induction and escort him to camp. But other reward cases demanded intervention. Ellis Wimberly registered in the countryside but visited the Birmingham office to find out his status. Since he had not kept in contact with his board it had classified him as a deserter. Hanna took him to a medical advisory board, which pronounced him fit for service. Wimberly was inducted but remained free while others were gathered for transportation to Camp McClellan. Meanwhile, a bloodsucker seized him and had him jailed. It was only by accident that Hanna found Wimberly and freed him from the bounty hunter.[85]

The Birmingham office achieved a relatively high rate of inductions of black draft delinquents and employed incarceration to a needless degree. Agents in Memphis, by contrast, compiled a lower induction rate and used jail more sparingly and for shorter periods of time. Seventy extant black draft cases date from the summer and early autumn of 1918, at the height of the slacker drives and after the second and third registrations. Nine agents, with occasional assistance from postal authorities and APL volunteers, handled these cases. Many suspects had disappeared, most likely to northern cities. Although thousands of blacks found work in cotton and lumber mills and as stevedores on the Mississippi River docks, war production in midwestern industrial cities lured others into the Great Migration. Black men hoping to better their futures while simultaneously avoiding military service could act on both motives by leaving Memphis. The city was also a funnel for migrants from Mississippi, Alabama, Louisiana, and Georgia. Three large terminals sent passengers on five major railroads to stockyards in Chicago and St. Louis, steel mills in Gary and Pittsburgh, truck and tank factories in Detroit, and tire plants in Akron.

The Bureau office in Memphis also used incarceration to coerce suspects. Agents Young and Goggin, who along with SAC W. E. McElveen handled most of the city's black draft cases, cooperated on the case of Sam Thomas, picked up by the APL as a slacker. He twice claimed to have registered in nonexistent Iowa towns, his mother testified he was under age twenty-one although he looked much older, and his father named still another Iowa town where his son had supposedly registered. In frustration, Young wrote: "this negro and his whole tribe, seem to be lying about this thing, and it has been decided best to let this negro sweat for awhile until he makes up his mind to tell the truth." He sweated in jail for several days until agreeing to go into the army. However, when he was finally taken before the medical board he was found to be blind in one eye and "mentally defective, in addition to being very illiterate." Unqualified for even limited service, Thomas was released from custody. At least the urge to punish Thomas was satiated; no further prosecution resulted.[86]

Slacker raids in Memphis in the summer of 1918 led to the incarceration of blacks, some of whom were subsequently found to be in full compliance with draft requirements. The APL raided a circus in early September and apprehended George Lynn, who claimed to have been dishonorably discharged from the 25th Infantry four months previously. Despite having lost his papers he recited precise details concerning the date and place of discharge and the officer who signed the documents. After he had spent four days in jail, the Bureau decided to accept Lynn's story while compelling him to register with a draft board and report to it monthly. A victim of much greater callousness was Henry McKinney, who was arrested because he did not have a classification card. Young telegraphed his local board in Blytheville, Arkansas, to determine his status. That board never replied, and McKinney was held in jail for six weeks until Young released him on a promise to report to his local board two days later. Obviously sobered, McKinney obediently complied, was quickly examined, and immediately sent to a cantonment. Why the Memphis office did not send other telegrams to Blytheville, which was just fifty miles upriver, cannot be explained. Likely it would not have shown such disinterest in a white suspect languishing in jail. Charles Looney, by comparison, was lucky: Having failed to register, he was incarcerated for only fourteen days before being sent to camp.[87]

The Bureau frequently worked with local authorities on selective service cases. Warren Bonner was arrested on a larceny charge by Memphis police, who soon learned his draft board had declared him a deserter. So long as Bonner was indicted on the criminal count he could not be inducted, so Goggin persuaded a state assistant attorney general to withdraw the charge, whereupon Bonner was immediately inducted. Prosecution of slackers on nonfederal charges was also an option when agents concluded that blacks were not adequately shouldering their responsibilities. Aaron Wadley failed to return his questionnaire, so he was summoned for his physical. When the medical examiner found him unfit, Goggin arranged for his punishment: Wadley was fined $25 on an unspecified local nuisance charge—probably vagrancy—and, unable to pay, he was sent to the county workhouse to labor for his fine.[88] This case illustrates a common attitude in the South: If a black delinquent escaped the "sentence" of military service through some physical disability, then a criminal sentence would substitute nicely. Yet even Bureau officials who acted harshly in some instances were capable of compassion in others. John A. Moore failed to return his questionnaire, so Memphis agents escorted him through the induction process. Then, when word was received that Moore's mother was dying, Young arranged a four-day postponement in reporting to Camp McClellan so that the young man could fulfill his familial duties. Moore honored his part of the agreement.[89]

Blacks in Memphis also ran afoul of the nationwide "Work or Fight" order, a May 1918 amendment to selective service regulations. As explained by the provost marshal general, draftees marching through the streets on their way to entrainment often passed crowds of "sturdy idlers and loafers standing at street corners and contemplating placidly their own immunity. The spectacle was not a pleasing one to any right-minded citizen." Many of these men were in Class I but had high numbers and would not be called for months. The remedy was a requirement that such men go promptly to work or be subject to immediate induction. Other "fruitless immunes" were in classes II, III, and IV, exempt because they supported dependents, but were not employed in "productive industries." Deferring them did not promote the war effort. To retain that exemption they, too, were ordered to find useful work. Even men beyond draft age would, it was admitted, feel pressure to do strategic labor, and "wealth and social position were to afford no immunity."[90]

Memphis police seized a number of black men identified as "war loafers" in the fall of 1918. Arthur Myers gave his age as thirty-six and offered precise information on the date and place of his registration in Buffalo, New York, but Goggin nonetheless kept him in jail while his status was investigated. Six days later Myers's local board reported that he was not delinquent. Having punished him with nearly a week's loss of liberty, Goggin did not harass Myers on the work-or-fight issue. Local police picked up other war loafers as late as the day of the Armistice. The draft status of longtime Memphis residents was usually ascertained within a day so that such men did not have to stay overnight in jail.[91]

Bureau personnel in Memphis, Birmingham, and elsewhere in the South often found their jobs frustrating: Many black draft suspects had migrated and could not be found. Agents were also overworked, already inundated with investigations of enemy aliens and suspected spies and saboteurs. Not surprisingly, some conducted themselves with a professionalism colored by racial paternalism, others were callous regarding the liberties of black suspects, and not a few were abusive. Blacks in the South frequently suffered excessive treatment, and many must have concluded that evenhanded justice was designed only for white men.

Although nearly 90 percent of African Americans lived in the South in 1910, that proportion began to change dramatically between 1915 and 1930 as 1.5 million of them made their way to northern cities. Bureau of Investigation records reflect this population shift. Of the 2005 extant black draft investigations, nearly 30 percent took place in northern and border state cities that attracted large numbers of migrants. This proportion increased in the months of June–October 1918, when nearly 45 percent of the cases originated from such cities.

Surviving documents obviously do not include all investigations of suspected black draft evaders. No records from Cleveland, Akron, Newark, and Buffalo, for example, remain, even though these cities attracted many migrants. The largest number of extant cases comes from Cincinnati, followed by Chicago, St. Louis, and Baltimore. Only a few case files have been found for New York, where agents and APL volunteers had their hands full investigating suspected spies, saboteurs, anarchists, and enemy aliens. Some draft boards were forced to hire private investigators to track down delinquents. In other northern cities where few or no records have survived, APL men probably handled most or even all draft cases. Because they had the authority to take suspects directly to exemption boards, many men were ushered into the army without ever encountering any Bureau agents.[92]

Despite the gaps in the remaining record, a pattern emerges: Bureau agents in mid-1918 continued to treat suspected slackers with less racism in northern cities and Baltimore than in the South, including St. Louis. Typical of these was Agent William N. Doyas, who believed Jim Williams was telling the truth about notifying his board in North Carolina of his new residence in Baltimore, even though he had not received a classification card. Doyas generally treated black suspects evenhandedly and was more interested in making the draft system work efficiently than in using his authority to enforce racial domination. This pattern of evenhandedness had exceptions, however. Baltimore agent Billups Harris apparently learned little from Doyas's example, frequently jailing suspects for short periods of time while clarifying their draft status. In an especially egregious case, he let Roy Johnson remain in jail for fifteen days while awaiting instructions from a draft board in nearby Pennsylvania.[93]

Northern agents and federal attorneys late in the war were more likely than their southern counterparts to parole suspects rather than keep them in jail while their status was being investigated. In Chicago, Jesse Walker produced "proper correspondence" indicating he had "written his board anxiously on several occasions," even though he had no classification card. Agent J. P. Folsom released him in view of both the evidence and his "frankness." Folsom's colleague F. George Hadba was similarly fair with Ira Vincent McKissach, who was "very illiterate" and "did not intentionally mean to violate the draft law," having believed since childhood that he was actually a year older than he was.[94]

But Chicago agents, like those in Baltimore, differed in racial attitudes, resulting in a few cases of lengthy incarceration and unnecessarily high bail. Edgar Scott was arrested for failing to register. Having "no reasonable excuse," he was held in the county jail on $1,000 bond, a very large sum for that time and offense. After two months the district attorney decided to conclude the case by seeking Scott's induction. However, when it was discovered Scott had a cataract in one eye, federal officials sought to indict him for willful failure to register. The surviving record ends there, and it is unlikely that course was pursued. But this was already a flagrant abuse: Two months in county jail without being found guilty by a court was a more harsh punishment than was suffered by most men who neglected to register.[95]

High bail also characterized another Chicago case, that of Alonso Clinton

Smith, whose wife turned him in for not registering. When questioned, he said he had believed that only single men need register. When he subsequently found out differently, he was afraid of going to jail and thus never did comply. He offered to join the army forthwith, which was agreeable to the U.S. attorney handling his case. When a medical examiner found him unfit, however, the chagrined attorney had Smith arrested and held on $1,000 bond. He remained in custody for over a week until the grand jury convened. Unfortunately, there is no record of its decision. Exactly how long Smith languished in jail is unknown, but his plight was due not only to his failure to register, but to the desire of a federal officer to punish a man who could not be inducted.[96]

Of all the Bureau agencies in the North, the Cincinnati office stands out not only for the largest number of black draft cases in the extant files—110—but also for its fairness in dealing with black suspects. Agent Albert D. Cash handled exactly half of those cases, with ten others taking the remainder. Cash and his colleagues rarely incarcerated suspects and simply concentrated on ensuring that delinquents registered or filed their questionnaires. In the absence of conclusive evidence otherwise, Cash accepted the claims of those who said they were over or under draft age. Believing Ephiram Steed's excuse that he was out of the country on registration day and was unaware of his obligation, Cash allowed the man to register without penalty. His evenhanded professionalism stands out in contrast to the vindictiveness of many agents elsewhere. He recognized better than many others that his mandate was only to investigate and ensure compliance with selective service regulations, not to play judge and jury and issue his own summary punishments.[97]

The majority of northern black suspects in mid-1918 were not native to the cities in which they resided, but were born in the South. Many had already lived in another northern city, where they had registered. Their cases often were transferred to draft boards in their southern hometowns. When this happened, questionnaires or induction notices had to be mailed back to northern cities, where the addressees frequently moved from one boardinghouse to another or left the city in search of better employment elsewhere. Much of agents' time was spent trying to obtain current classification information or attempting to find men who were listed as delinquents by southern draft boards. Even though most communication was done via telegraph, the process could still be slow. Often a man would report that he had registered in a city with several different draft boards, but could not identify the precise one. Finally, not all men were truthful.

In another respect, however, there was little difference in northern and southern investigations: Few resulted in inductions. The longer the war lasted, the larger became the percentage of men in their twenties and thirties who were legitimately exempt from military service, most because they had dependent family members. Probably three-fourths of all persons rounded up in slacker raids were ineligible for the draft.[98] Of the black northerners investigated in the summer of 1918, only a small percentage was ultimately inducted. Most cases involved searches for men who were never found; inquiries resulting in proof that suspects were underage, overage, or mentally or physically unqualified; and cases where agents simply registered a subject or helped a migrant obtain his current classification.

Some men were suspected of being slackers because of conflicting statements or evidence of age. Rural southerners usually had only family Bibles or school documents to prove birth dates. Men who migrated to the North infrequently brought such records with them. Bureau agents experienced much frustration trying to verify ages. Two blacks in St. Louis compounded this problem by entering conflicting dates on other documents. John Webb said he did not register because he was born in 1870 and was thus overage. But on a 1917 voter application Webb had listed his age as forty-three. This was evidence enough for a federal attorney to issue an arrest warrant. However, officials soon concluded that Webb was indeed above draft age and had simply made a mistake when registering to vote. Jerry Webster's case was almost identical: He claimed to be forty-six but had listed his age as thirty-six on a recent voter application. On the strength of the latter evidence, he was bound over for grand jury action. The case dragged on until January 1919, two months after the war ended and conscription was halted. Only then did a grand jury find there was no valid case.[99]

There is no clear pattern as to why certain mid-1918 northern and border city cases were referred for prosecution, while Bureau agents working in concert with local authorities settled many others. Several factors influenced such matters. Draft prosecutions were popular, and someone seeking to advance his political career might be more likely to pursue such cases. Some U.S. attorneys were more caught up in the intolerance of the wartime months than others and sacrificed judiciousness to the popular mood. Finally, the merits of some cases undoubtedly required attempts at prosecution.

As in the South, agents in the North welcomed tips from private citizens. But the most common identification of suspected delinquents came from local police who had arrested individuals for sundry crimes and then became suspicious of their draft status. Another major source of suspects was APL raids. Draft boards also supplied the names of delinquents or those whose questionnaires were returned undelivered. In one case, the Bureau assisted British conscription efforts. When Agent J. W. Dolan apprehended alleged draft evader Henry Hall, he claimed British citizenship. A soldier being a soldier, no matter the cut of his uniform, Dolan sent Hall to the British recruiting mission in Philadelphia to be registered.[100]

In the end, northern and border state agents were no more successful in finding fugitives than their colleagues in the South. Massive migration out of the South and secondary migration from one northern city to another made the task especially difficult. Many cases ended in futility. Agents in Kansas City were asked by a draft board in Gonzales, Texas, to locate Isaac Green, who had fled to Missouri to avoid induction. After eight months, Green still could not be located.[101] Love Thompson migrated from West Virginia to New York to work in an aircraft plant. Advised that Thompson was delinquent, Agent Boyd faced a nearly impossible task of finding Thompson among the three hundred black men who lived in company bunkhouses in Albany. Boyd and local police raided the compound at 5 A.M. only to find that "somebody had no doubt tipped him off." All Boyd could do was ask the police to try to find him on payday. It seems doubtful that Thompson tried to claim his wages. Months later the police concluded that Thompson had fled the area.[102]

The cessation of hostilities did not end efforts to apprehend or punish suspected draft violators. All calls for the army were canceled on Armistice Day, 11 November 1918, and shortly thereafter draft boards were ordered to halt the classification of men who registered the previous September. Most draft records were sealed and taken from the jurisdiction of the provost marshal general, effectively ending the operation of the selective service system. But some files were not stored. According to Provost Marshal General Crowder, there was "a record of ignominy and unpunished delinquency that the Nation could not afford to leave undealt with." Even though thousands of men who were listed as delinquents had voluntarily enlisted in the armed services and simply neglected to inform their draft boards, all delinquency cases were sent to state headquarters where teams of inspectors, including Bureau agents and U.S. attorneys, would decide which ones were rightly accused. Their records were then shipped to the army, with the Bureau retaining copies so that it could attempt to find them. During the war most draft delinquents had been punished by immediate induction. Now, although the public was clamoring for a quick return to peacetime conditions, the prosecution of deserters was to be vigorously pursued. Attorney General Gregory vowed that every rich man's son who had fled the country would be brought to justice.[103] Poor blacks, too, would be shown no mercy.

The surviving black draft cases include over 250 postwar investigations of suspected delinquents and deserters. Only a small number of them were located, so for the most part the cases were never concluded. What is noteworthy, however, is the degree to which these postwar investigations remained a priority not only in the immediate weeks after the Armistice, but even into the fall of 1919.

The state of Georgia accounted for 55 percent of the extant cases and Texas another 20 percent, with the remainder spread over the rest of the country. In Georgia, Agent George Calmes labored to locate dozens of men who had worked briefly at rural cotton mills, registered in those locations, and then moved on, some undoubtedly to northern cities. Enlisting the aid of postmasters, rural-route carriers, sheriffs, chiefs of police, and other local whites, he managed to find several suspects but generally excused their failure to register or file questionnaires if they offered reasonable explanations or seemed to be "very ignorant." In other cases, allegations of delinquency were based on false reports. One investigation involved six men who asked a local black teacher to fill out their questionnaires. By that time the Armistice had been signed and the teacher did not send them in because he believed they were no longer required.[104]

Agents continued to receive tips on suspected draft dodgers in the postwar months. After Thomas McRae had an argument with his wife in April 1919, she notified authorities that her husband had failed to register the previous September. By the time Agent C. M. Muse got the case the pair was again on good terms and she claimed to have been mistaken. Muse concluded that McRae was probably beyond registration age, and recommended against prosecution. Lex Leo Lowe suffered a genuine miscarriage of justice long after the Armistice because a rural official tried to claim a $50 reward for turning in a deserter. Lowe was jailed until the Bureau concluded that, although his local board in Georgia had never received it, Lowe had probably sent in a completed questionnaire while residing in Milwaukee. But the loss of three weeks' liberty in September 1919 was entirely unjustified.[105]

Some agents still used suspected draft violations to impose racial punishment on hapless blacks, especially in areas where such abuses had been tolerated during the war. Such was the case of Frank T. Mason, who spent four months in the Illinois National Guard in 1916 until his unit was mustered out of service. A year later he registered in Shreveport, his hometown, while in the county jail. Nine months afterward he was again arrested, this time for claiming to be a current member of the Illinois National Guard and to have served in France, which, in fact, he had not done. When no record could be found of his registration he was given another jail sentence and subsequently reregistered. A few days before the Armistice, Mason left for Chicago, and police there picked him up in mid-December for being a slacker. In the meantime, his draft board in Shreveport declared him a delinquent and he was returned to Louisiana. Not until late February was Mason brought to trial, where he pleaded guilty and was sentenced to thirty days in the parish jail, with credit given for time already served. It appears that Mason was in jail in Chicago and Shreveport from at least mid-December to 21 February 1919. The war was over, and many men who had not filed questionnaires were being let off without prosecution. Why was Mason pursued? It appears that Agent J. B. Matthews was especially angered by the fact that Mason had boasted of having served in France and being properly discharged.[106]

Matthews and the U.S. attorney in Shreveport used their power to persecute another black man as the war was coming to an end. N. L. Thous was jailed in September for failing to file a questionnaire and spent eight days behind bars until he could raise bail, meanwhile being forced to work to pay the costs of his confinement. But federal officials were bent on more punishment. Because he had been delinquent for nearly five months, he was to be prosecuted as a willful deserter. According to Matthews, "his case is a fit one to make an example from." Trial was delayed until January, over two months after the war's end. Despite his not-guilty plea, Thous was convicted and sentenced to ten days in custody, with credit for eight days already served. It would have been far more efficient to simply induct Thous in September and give the army the benefit of his service. Society gained nothing from trying him after the war. His conviction would hardly serve to deter others since conscription had been halted. Vengeance seems to be the only motive.[107]

Although only a fraction of black draft cases have survived, the activities of the Bureau of Investigation can clearly be charted. The small number of federal agents would have been swamped by the responsibility for enforcing selective service regulations had it not been for the assistance of thousands of rural sheriffs and urban policemen, postal employees, and APL volunteers. Bureau offices had no motor pools, and were it not for automobiles provided by local APL groups or law officers, many investigations could not have proceeded. Cooperation with these agencies was a necessity if administration of the draft was to be effective. The task was overwhelming: ensuring that 24 million men complied with registration, questionnaire, examination, and induction procedures. But more than efficiency was at stake. Could federal agents and the U.S. attorneys with whom they worked conduct their responsibilities with reasonable fairness? Did the Bureau, the Justice Department's investigative arm, ensure that justice was upheld? Unfortunately, agents did not always divorce themselves from the patriotic passions of the day. Special Assistant to the Attorney General John Lord O'Brian, who oversaw prosecutions under various wartime statutes, worried considerably over the zealousness of federal attorneys (who were political appointees) and the activities of "slacker raiders." There was less concern, however, for those Bureau agents who were more eager to collar draft dodgers or coerce induction through jail threats than to ensure the rights of suspects. Other agents, to their credit, dealt with suspects more professionally, and exercised restraint at a time when summary judgment was popular.

Employees of the Bureau managed, for the most part, to distinguish between draft evasion and "pro-Germanism." Fears of German subversion were rife, particularly in the South in 1917. The press, politicians, patriots, and the public at large were much too quick to attribute black unrest or dissatisfaction—with the war, or with domestic political, social, and economic conditions—to enemy interference. Bureau agents often accepted rumors of enemy subversion as fact. Again to their credit, most agents shied away from spurious theories of German influence when investigating suspected black draft violators. Perhaps because of the sheer volume of cases, most conscription files are noteworthy for the absence of speculation about the motives of black suspects.[108]

Many black men who did not comply with the intricacies of the draft were simply taking advantage of the booming economy and pursuing their own self-interest. They failed to register, return questionnaires, or inform draft boards of new addresses when they found a better job or more desirable lodging in a crowded ghetto. Others reacted to the draft out of a fatalism born of generations of subjection. If one could maintain invisibility and stay clear of the white man—his police, his government, his demands—well and good. But if one was forced to satisfy his dictates, then acceptance rather than resistance was the prudent course. This explains the willingness of many accused delinquents to agree to induction without protest or appeal. To risk triggering the white system's wrath carried greater consequences than accepting its dictates. There was also the large number of blacks who were apathetic about the war, who had only negative incentives for complying with requirements. Others were simply untouched by the war until a postman delivered a government envelope.

But the country, and the Bureau of Investigation, ultimately cared little for blacks' feelings about the war. Compliant patriotism and loyalty were demanded, but not solicited through promises of inclusion in the body politic. The soldiers' blues, "Jined de army fur to git free clothes, / What we're fightin' 'bout, nobody knows," could have been echoed by countless civilians. Fatalism was a logical response to registration, classification, and induction into an army that was more likely to hand one a shovel than a gun. Under the circumstances, many placed no priority on obeying every requirement of the draft system. Some ran afoul of it. Whether one was summarily clapped into jail by Agent Doggrell in Muscle Shoals, or was treated with evenhandedness by Agent Cash in Cincinnati, was beyond a black man's control.

It was indeed a "white man's war," and it was certainly a white man's selective service system in which discriminatory local boards deferred proportionately fewer blacks than whites.[109] Furthermore, federal agents who by upbringing and habit were accustomed to treating blacks with condescension, racism, or even brutality were unlikely to change simply by pinning on the badge of the Bureau of Investigation. Those who were free of such social conditioning might treat black draft suspects civilly, but even those without an overtly racist upbringing could easily mistreat black slackers. To Americans whose passions were inflamed by the fears and emotions of war, draft dodgers of any race were traitors. Intolerance became one of the surest demonstrations of patriotism.

4

"The most dangerous of all Negro journals": Federal Efforts to Silence the *Chicago Defender*

If World War I had created a climate in which ordinary black individuals could be jailed for casual conversation, and in which even those who innocently neglected to comply with draft requirements suffered a similar loss of freedom, the black press was in real danger of censorship or outright suppression. The war created the opportunity for the federal government to crack down on all manner of despised publications, including those espousing socialism and pacifism, as well as a variety of foreign-language newspapers. Black publications challenging the racial status quo with a militancy that exceeded the bounds of white permissibility were also targeted.

Crusading black journalism had a venerable heritage from the abolitionist press to Ida B. Wells's crusade against lynching. Prior to the twentieth century, however, "race" newspapers and magazines rarely gained sufficient national circulation and influence to attract the attention of whites. Although the more outspoken journals at times condemned American society and the government along with the racism they fostered, such viewpoints were not threatening on a national scale. But the early 1900s witnessed an evolution in race journalism that laid the foundation not only for new roles and maturity for the press, but also for government surveillance and attempts at suppression.

First, the *Chicago Defender,* founded in 1905, inaugurated "yellow journalism" within the black newspaper fraternity and proved the success of that format. By 1915 Robert S. Abbott's weekly enjoyed a national circulation, with particular influence in the South, and the reputation not only for dramatic headlines but hard-hitting criticism of racial abuses. Second, the *Crisis,* the NAACP's official publication founded in 1910 by W. E. B. DuBois, quickly gained a circulation of ten thousand within its first year and an even greater authority among educated blacks and some white liberals. By 1917 it was the most influential voice of militant black opinion and protest in the country. These two publications laid a foundation for an even greater growth of black militancy in the second half of the decade. World War I and the Great Migration of hundreds of thousands of blacks out of the South into northern industrial cities (the migration heavily promoted by the *Defender*) spawned a dramatic ferment within the race. The New Crowd Negro, a term coined by the radical *Messenger* magazine, was no longer willing to be circumspect in discussing lynching and discrimination. Instead, it boldly demanded fundamental changes in America's racial patterns, including social equality for African Americans. This new militant spirit flowered and came to white attention at precisely the time when the nation felt itself at great peril. In 1917–18, America plunged not only into a worldwide war, but simultaneously into widespread fears that the enemy was diligently working to subvert and undermine domestic opinions and institutions, especially targeting blacks. In such passionate times a bold newspaper like the *Defender*, already known for vigorous denunciations of disfranchisement, segregation, and mob violence, and already hated by white southerners for urging blacks to desert their sharecropper cabins for the jobs and relative freedoms of the North, inevitably attracted the attention of the fledgling domestic intelligence network.[1]

The *Chicago Defender* first came to the attention of the Bureau of Investigation six months before America entered World War I, at a time when the collection of domestic intelligence was haphazard and without coordination between the various agencies engaged in it. Although not yet formally at war, Americans were poised to oppose Germany and had heard enough rumors to believe that its diplomats and agents were engaged in subversion. Believing that the country was already at peril from enemy aliens, many whites drew the conclusion that publications that challenged the racial status quo were either influenced by the enemy or unwittingly played into its hands by raising issues the preoccupied nation could ill afford to deal with at the time.

Surveillance of the *Defender* began in the fall of 1916 when a reporter for the *New Orleans Times-Picayune*, probing allegations that the Chicago weekly was inciting blacks against whites, passed his suspicions on to the Bureau of Investigation office in the Crescent City. Whether out of reportorial interest or to confirm his own racial fears, the white newsman took out a subscription and uncovered the names of the paper's local distributors. Bureau agent Clifford G. Beckham agreed that the *Defender*'s contents were offensive: The 25 September issue contained an attack on President Wilson's approval of segregation, and praise for Shreveport blacks who beat up an abusive white policeman. Grateful for the tip, Beckham promised the reporter a "scoop" should his own investigation prove fruitful.

New Orleans's SAC Forrest C. Pendleton concluded with Beckham that the *Defender* should be suppressed and sought the opinion of the U.S. attorney, who concluded that federal laws likely had been broken, especially since the newspaper used the mail to reach many of its subscribers. Pendleton wrote Bureau headquarters in Washington that the articles tended to "incite murder" and proposed a thorough investigation to determine what federal statutes were being violated. In the meantime, the newsman rifled the desk of one of the paper's local distributors, pilfering a list of subscribers and learning that he alone sold two thousand copies of the *Defender* each week. To assist the case, the reporter also supplied his own subscription copy and mailing wrapper as evidence that the newspaper circulated through the mails. Despite these leads, Bureau of Investigation chief A. Bruce Bielaski, preoccupied with the detection of alleged German spies, turned matters over to the post office inspector in New Orleans to determine if postal laws had been violated.[2]

Although nothing more came of this initial effort in the fall of 1916, the *Defender* immediately came under renewed scrutiny once the United States declared war on Germany on 6 April 1917. Within days worried southerners began to inform the Bureau of their fears about the paper. White civic leaders in New Orleans charged the *Defender* with inciting blacks against them and wired their senators to that effect. A similar report from Pensacola claimed the newspaper printed "a lot of stuff against the white people," a view confirmed by the local Bureau agent, who concluded: "this paper may prove to be the agency which is effective as a disturbing element among the negroes at this time." In Jacksonville another agent, reporting that two mass meetings to encourage northward migration had been prompted by the *Defender,* warned that some "pro-German" group might use it to create a home front distraction. And from Mississippi's Delta region came another agent's frank prediction that, if the *Defender* inspired blacks to "rise up and take by force the liberty which the white people of the south were withholding from them," local whites—outnumbered sixteen to one—would simply "murder or massacre the negros [*sic*] until the trouble is quieted."[3] In short, the war now seemed to provide the pretext to suppress a much-hated voice of black protest and racial advocacy.

While the *Defender* was hardly an advocate of revolt, Emmett J. Scott, the black special assistant to the secretary of war, recognized that it "voiced the unexpressed thoughts of many [southern blacks] and made accusations for which they themselves would have been severely handled." Two-thirds of its readership was outside Chicago, and its national edition was designed especially for southerners. Headlines in red ink routinely condemned the South: "100 NEGROES MURDERED WEEKLY IN UNITED STATES BY WHITE AMERICANS." One lynching story was illustrated with a picture of the victim's decapitated head and the caption: "NOT BELGIUM—AMERICA." Scott noted that the paper had a large circulation in Mississippi and usually sold out on the day it arrived. "Copies were passed around until worn out." A prominent Louisiana black claimed, "negroes grab the *Defender* like a hungry mule grabs fodder." If several individuals read every copy, then weekly readership probably exceeded half a million by the end of the war. No wonder, then, that local officials in several towns halted sales by confiscating copies from express or post offices; two southern "agent-correspondents" were murdered; and at least a dozen others were forced to flee for their lives.[4]

Bureau chief Bielaski was not about to ignore southern whites' alarmist reports about the *Defender,* particularly when a Mississippi senator endorsed allegations that the paper printed "seditious utterances." In the days immediately following America's plunge into war, fears of German subversion spread like wildfire, and white southerners saw nothing illogical in concluding that German enemies would try to influence the allegedly "ignorant" black population. Hence, only three days after America entered the war, Bielaski ordered his Chicago office to investigate the *Defender.* Agent J. E. Hawkins reported that publisher Robert S. Abbott was "a coal black negro" and "somewhat of an egotist" who built the paper's circulation on sensational stories that emphasized the oppression of blacks by whites. According to Hawkins, the paper was "not in good standing" with the city's "better sort" of blacks. More damning (and utterly erroneous), Hawkins alleged that the *Defender* was backed by the Hearst syndicate, which was then causing the government much heartburn by portraying the war as an economic conflict, criticizing President Wilson, championing the cause of Irish independence, and disparaging England.[5] Although the *Defender* shared Hearst's enthusiasm for "yellow journalism," it had no connection with William Randolph Hearst's press empire.

On 13 April, Hawkins summoned Abbott to the Bureau's Chicago office. Although probably aware that the government suspected his paper of encouraging disloyalty, he could not have known that his interrogation was linked to fanciful allegations that Mexican subversives in Chicago's Black Belt were attempting to weaken the war effort by fomenting racial antagonisms. Nor did he know that the Bureau was checking his credit rating. Under questioning, Abbott explained that he was the founder and sole owner of the *Defender*, which he began in 1905 at his kitchen table with twenty-five cents capital. Relating that he now sold sixty-seven thousand copies nationwide each week, he disavowed any connection with Hearst. He also refused to apologize for championing race causes, although he acknowledged that this was unsettling to some whites. Abbott stressed his patriotism, having given free advertising for recruitment appeals and editorial support for enlistment. If race advocacy was subversive, then Abbott readily owned up, but in the interview he saw no connection between patriotism and acceptance of the racial status quo. Summarizing the interview, another agent concluded only that Abbott "may have overstepped the bounds of propriety" in his zeal to improve the race's standing. Despite the fact that there were no substantive grounds on which to suppress the paper or prosecute Abbott, Bureau headquarters in Washington nonetheless reasoned that the *Defender* was an extremely radical publication, even though sedition had not been proven.[6] To Bureau observers, its outspokenness in defending the race and condemning racism was, in fact, the crime it was committing on a weekly basis.

Although the Bureau's first full investigation of the *Defender* led nowhere, the next time it came under scrutiny, the government had a new weapon to use against it. The Espionage Act, which became law in June 1917, directed the Post Office Department to bar from the mails "any matter advocating or urging treason, insurrection, or forcible resistance to any law of the United States." Even if only one issue was declared non-mailable, a periodical's second-class mailing permit could be revoked, which could easily prove economically fatal to a small publication. In addition, an offending editor or publisher, upon conviction by a trial jury, could be imprisoned for up to twenty years and fined $10,000 for any of the above transgressions. The next May, Congress passed the Sedition Act, an amendment to the Espionage Act, which made it a crime to say or publish anything "disloyal, profane, scurrilous, or abusive" about the armed forces, flag, or government, or bring "contempt, scorn, contumely, or disrepute" on them.[7] These two laws were far more threatening to the dissenting press than punishments authorized by postal regulations.

In spite of the Bureau's early failure to find any legal grounds on which to muzzle the *Defender,* complaints against the weekly continued to come from the South in the summer of 1917. For example, the Arkansas Council of Defense, a white citizens' organization, informed the government that blacks' "hitherto respectful demeanor" had changed. German influence, it alleged, was upsetting the racial status quo and enticing agricultural workers to leave for the North. It was no coincidence that in many homes, previously well-behaved servants were now reading the *Defender* and exhibiting less servile behavior. Arkansas officials pleaded with the Bureau for suppression: "Whether this is a part of the German propaganda or not, no more insidious and ingenious plan could be adopted for crippling the South and its resources, as well as necessitating very comprehensive steps to be taken for domestic defense." Chief Bielaski, aware of the need to avoid any impression that the Bureau was lax in protecting the nation from subversion, again referred these charges to his Chicago agents, but it was the 4 August *Defender* itself that led him to energize the investigation, particularly an article by Byron Gunner, president of the National Equal Rights League, urging blacks to defend themselves against attacks by whites. Bielaski believed this plea constituted "sentiments which are decidedly in opposition to the Government at this time."[8] That blacks asserted their right to self-defense in the summer of the East St. Louis riot is understandable. Less comprehensible is Bielaski's view that such action, especially given the absence of government protection against predatory white mobs and lynching, was somehow un-American.

The Justice Department was not alone in its fears concerning the *Defender*'s influence in the summer of 1917. The Mobile, Alabama, postmaster also alerted his superiors to Gunner's article and thought it was intended to incite riots or foment race hatred, either of which was "offensive to our government." Postal solicitor William H. Lamar, the department's chief legal officer, whose responsibilities eventually included all postal provisions of the Espionage and Trading-with-the-Enemy Acts, and who had authority to recommend that publications be banned from the mails, instructed Chicago's postmaster to forward copies of the *Defender* to Washington for scrutiny.[9] From that point on, the black newspaper was being monitored by two federal agencies; before long, a third intelligence agency would join this surveillance.

Meanwhile, Bureau personnel in Chicago and elsewhere continued to monitor the *Defender* through the fall of 1917. Predictably, southern agents kept up pressure to have the paper banned. San Antonio agents complained that it was fomenting race troubles in Texas. In Tucson, on learning that many local blacks were reading the 8 December issue, which graphically described a recent lynching, an unsophisticated agent wired the Chicago office that the *Defender*'s circulation was "apparently systematic" and the article in question "may be German propaganda." This prompted yet another investigation by Chicago agents, who concluded testily that the lynching story was identical to what had appeared in white dailies across the country. While noting that its circulation had grown to ninety-two thousand copies weekly, Agent B. D. Adsit pronounced the paper "loyal to the core. . . . There is nowhere connected with it the slightest evidence of German influence."[10]

Department of Justice headquarters apparently agreed in late 1917 that the *Defender*, compared with those publications that were actively opposing the war, was innocuous. Thus when complaints came from Columbus, New Mexico, that the *Defender*, as well as the *Crisis* and *Baltimore Afro-American*, were making black soldiers antagonistic toward whites, the Justice Department responded with less than full vigor, although a U.S. attorney threatened the editor of the Baltimore weekly with "consequences," which resulted in a quick agreement to keep the paper loyal and patriotic. The *Crisis*, as will be seen in the next chapter, had to be dealt with more gingerly because of the NAACP's influential white leadership. But federal agents were plainly tired of watching the *Defender*. The Columbus allegations resulted in no new investigation, although the Bureau was aware that members of the 24th Infantry, which was stationed there, were extremely bitter over the execution of thirteen of their comrades for participation in the Houston mutiny in August of that year. The Bureau also recognized that Columbus whites were fearful because black troops outnumbered white soldiers at the border garrison. Knowing that the black regulars received the three publications through the mail, the Justice Department responded correctly that barring them was a postal responsibility. The Bureau was willing to share information with postal and military authorities but was not going to become directly involved in their efforts to suppress the *Defender* at that time.[11]

During 1918 the Post Office Department and the army's Military Intelligence Branch maintained the heaviest pressure on the *Defender*. Postal officials, wielding authority under the dangerously broad Espionage, Sedition, and Trading-with-the-Enemy Acts, were particularly zealous in suppressing suspect periodicals. The latter two acts gave the Post Office Department radically expanded power with which to threaten unpopular publications. At the same time, the army rapidly expanded its "negative intelligence" capabilities to stifle alleged enemy influences within the United States. Millions of men were being prepared for combat in Europe, and federal officials wanted nothing to impede that effort. Disloyalty among civilians came under army purview because such actions were likely to adversely affect military personnel as well. These two agencies cooperated with the Justice Department in policing the nation's press, and by 1918 their relationships had been regularized. Citizens sent complaints about publications to their senators and representatives, the postmaster general, attorney general, or the president. By early 1918 most of these charges were routinely forwarded to postal authorities. But Solicitor Lamar was preoccupied with suppressing allegedly disloyal foreign-language publications and was not yet energized to pursue the *Defender*.[12]

Army intelligence was galvanized into action against the *Defender* in 1918, ironically, by a "Citizen's Committee of Patriotic Negro Citizens" that complained the newspaper's attacks on the government would erode the race's loyalty. This obsequious petition suggested that "a careful search into this paper and its methods might bring about a change and would no doubt benefit us colored folks as well as cease hurting the feelings of you who are white, and you to whom we owe our very existence." This appeal carried no date or indication of origin, although it appears to have come from a beleaguered southern black community where circulation of the newspaper had aroused the ire of local whites. How it reached the intelligence officer in the army's Central Department is also unknown, but he acted diligently upon its receipt, gathering information from cooperative Bureau of Investigation agents in Chicago for transmission to his own headquarters.[13]

Colonel Ralph Van Deman, head of the Military Intelligence Branch, lost no time in ordering an investigation of editor Robert Abbott. Accepting at face value allegations about the *Defender* in the Bureau's files, yet disregarding the fact that its agents had discounted any subversion on the newspaper's part, Van Deman predicted that the newspaper's alleged attacks on the government would lead to further erosion of patriotism among blacks, concluding that the *Defender* was "undoubtedly disloyal in most of its utterances."[14] The army clearly lacked statutory authority to suppress publications, but censorship, at least at army posts, might well be accomplished through coercion. This was Van Deman's intent, and the man he sent to twist Abbott's arm was Maj. Walter H. Loving, the distinguished founder and conductor of the Philippine Constabulary Band, which had performed at Pres. William Howard Taft's inauguration and at several world fairs. Loving was the army's most dependable black investigator during the war, and a conservative on racial matters. He was already at work trying to discover evidence of enemy subversion among blacks while also giving patriotic addresses to civilian audiences.[15] Like others of the black elite, Loving was disturbed by widespread evidence that the black masses were unenthusiastic about the war. Members of the "Talented Tenth" such as Loving hoped to convince the rest of the race that if they fought loyally, sacrificed willingly, and displayed public patriotism on the home front, America would reward them with long-overdue rights and privileges.

Loving determined to force Abbott to adopt a more satisfactory editorial stance. Visiting the office of "the most dangerous of all Negro journals" in May 1918, he concluded that threats would be more effective than appeals to Abbott's patriotism. In Loving's view, nothing must stand in the way of speedy, massive mobilization. Germany had embarked on its massive spring offensive in a desperate attempt to win the war before the arrival of large numbers of American troops would tip the balance. Delay at home could determine the outcome on the battlefields of France. So Loving issued an ultimatum: "Mr. Abbott has been told that he would be held strictly responsible and accountable for any article appearing in his paper in the future that would give rise to any apprehension on the part of the government. . . . I have . . . informed him officially that the eye of the government is centered upon his paper, and caution should be his guide."[16]

Although somewhat vaguely worded, Loving's threat worked its desired effect. Abbott's long written reply the following day reflected his realization that no black paper had sufficient public support or influential white friends with which to forestall governmental suppression. He also knew that local authorities were even less likely to respect First Amendment freedoms and that private citizens acting on their own initiative were already interrupting local distribution of his paper in the

South.[17] Abbott disclaimed all allegations of disloyalty, noting that the *Defender* had pledged $12,000 in the current Liberty Loan drive, money that had been set aside for a new press and building. In addition, he had presented a regimental flag to the 365th Infantry, joined the Committee on Public Information's speakers' bureau, and provided space generously to advertise war loan campaigns. In justifying the paper's editorial policies, Abbott admitted its outspoken criticism of lynching but denied attacking the government. He claimed that he had instructed his staff to avoid encouraging racial strife or disrespect for the laws, although Abbott believed the race's enemies were taking advantage of the times and position in which blacks found themselves. Still, Abbott recognized that the government, under pressure to catch spies and subversives, would tolerate no suspicions of disloyalty: "I realize the peculiar situation in which the administration is placed, and am also aware that the slightest form of criticism will move them to action." In closing, he thanked Loving "for the interest you have shown in my behalf." Mission accomplished, Loving forwarded Abbott's letter to MIB headquarters, noting: "the tone of this reply is all that we can expect, if the writer lives up to it, and I shall endeavor and try to see that he does."[18] Van Deman could ask for nothing better from his loyal racial investigator, although a month later, when he sought Loving's assistance in suppressing the *Crisis,* Loving found the idea repugnant and evaded Van Deman's order.[19]

The Military Intelligence Branch utilized both carrots and sticks to ensure the black press' patriotism during World War I. Threats were employed against the *Chicago Defender* and *Baltimore Afro-American.* But the MIB also hoped to persuade black editors to exercise voluntary restraint in discussing potentially inflammatory racial issues so as not to diminish black participation in the war effort. Persuasion reflected the joint efforts of Maj. Joel E. Spingarn and Emmett J. Scott, a special assistant to the secretary of war and the highest-placed black in the War Department. Scott's job included fielding complaints from black soldiers as well as working to ensure the better morale of blacks in and out of the service. Spingarn, the white chairman of the NAACP's Board of Directors, briefly worked for the MIB's "negro subversion" unit. Aware of "constant" complaints from military officers that the black press, including the *Defender,* was spreading "disaffection," and anxious to stimulate positive morale, Spingarn and Scott organized a conference, cosponsored by the Committee on Public Information, to let black editors and other public figures air their race's grievances and, more importantly, solicit their assistance in improving black morale.

Forty-one leaders and journalists attended this conference in Washington from 19 to 21 June, and Robert S. Abbott was among the thirty-one editors present. All agreed that unrest was widespread among blacks, with lynching the number one cause. Additional prevalent grievances included the Red Cross's refusal to enroll black nurses, federal unwillingness to hire black civil servants, and Jim Crow conditions on the government-controlled railroads. The assembly adopted resolutions written by the *Crisis's* editor, W. E. B. DuBois, demanding an immediate end to lynching but otherwise stressing the editors' loyalty and willingness to suspend much of the race's agenda while the war was being fought. Spingarn was pleased that nearly all the editors' grievances could be met "without any fundamental social readjustments."[20] The conference resolutions were nearly as abject a surrender of the black agenda as DuBois's "Close Ranks" editorial in the July 1918 *Crisis.*[21]

Abbott's participation in the editors' conference amounted to a public profession of loyalty, and for the remainder of the war the military had no complaint against the *Defender.* But success in tempering the newspaper's militancy was not due entirely to the army's efforts. Renewed pressure from the Bureau of Investigation and naked coercion from the Post Office Department in mid-1918 also helped convince Abbott to publish with much more circumspection. Local threats likewise influenced the beleaguered editor. After running an editorial cartoon depicting black troops being shot in the back by white American soldiers on the battlefield, local authorities threatened Abbott with jail, a fate he avoided by personally purchasing Liberty Bonds and promoting their sale in the *Defender.*[22]

Independent of army intelligence, Bureau headquarters in Washington continued to respond to complaints about the *Chicago Defender* from both private citizens (including patriotic volunteers enrolled in the American Protective League) and its own personnel in the field. In May 1918, Agent E. J. Kerwin in Pine Bluff, Arkansas, twice submitted copies of the newspaper and warned that its artfully worded contents only partly disguised attempts to "beget hatred and an inner feeling of getting even" on the part of blacks. Members of the race no longer seemed to be dutifully following whites' views of the war. Particularly dangerous in Kerwin's mind was the paper's effect on the more "ignorant" members of the race. By this he did not mean illiterates, but those, quoting Alexander Pope, for whom "'a little learning is a dangerous thing.'" In response, Chief Bielaski once again burdened the Chicago office with another investigation and once again agents found nothing startling to report except that circulation had climbed to 120,000.[23] Having insufficient evidence of criminal intent or punishable content, the Justice Department was unwilling to use the kind of coercion employed by army intelligence, and took no formal action against the *Defender.* Perhaps it was content to rely on Loving's "persuasion" and Abbott's promises, having learned of them at one of the weekly conferences in Washington where the various intelligence chiefs met with Bielaski. It is also quite possible that Justice Department attorneys read the *Defender*'s more cautious tone after May as sufficient evidence of change.

Even considering Major Loving's blunt warning to editor Abbott, it was postal officials who ultimately played the most decisive role in forcing the *Defender* to trim its editorial sails more to the government's liking. A sudden rush of post office pressure on Abbott in mid-1918 could neither be ignored nor misunderstood. Events began when the postmaster of Denison, Texas, sent the 8 June issue to Alabama-born postal solicitor William Lamar in Washington. What inspired his outrage was the front-page story, "Southern Stunts Surpass Hun," denouncing an inconceivably barbaric lynching in which a white mob tied its black victim to railroad tracks so that a speeding train decapitated him. Incredibly, the postmaster interpreted this article as "rank race hatred which shows the signs of German conspiracy. . . . It is precisely this form of public print that stirs in the negro's revolutionary mind not only the seditious thought but the seditious act," inflaming black against white when the two ought to be linked in mutual patriotic endeavor. Pending Lamar's decision, the local postmaster withheld all copies from delivery. One of the solicitor's attorneys, Charles E. Boles, drafted the memorandum that would guide policy toward the *Defender:*

> This issue is a fair sample of many issues of this publication and all other negro publications published in various parts of the country which have been brought to the attention of this office. Most of them play up in startling head lines all reports of violence against negroes at the hands of the Southerners and other whites. In the narratives the publications rarely, if ever, mention the provications [*sic*] furnished by the victims and if such provications are mentioned they are usually discredited. The victim is always characterized as an innocent victim of race prejudice or race hatred. Such articles can have but one effect on the negro and that is to cause him to hate the whites and the "white man's government." Any good that might be accomplished by matter of a loyal nature carried in these papers, is offset by this rotten race-hatred breeding stuff. The fomenting of race hatred among the negroes at this time is extremely unfortunate and flavors strongly of German propaganda.[24]

This quotation shows why the federal government and many white Americans had such difficulty understanding the origins of black discontent during World War I and the postwar Red Scare. What they viewed as promotion of race hatred black editors would have described as the righteous exposure of racial injustice. But to most whites, criticism of their behavior by the black press was no less than racial antipathy. In short, what blacks regarded as truth telling, whites considered likely to provoke disaffection, and the government clearly had legal authority to suppress disaffection. In addition, many whites, searching for comforting explanations for discomfiting events, fell back on the old "outside agitator" bogeyman, this time not blaming abolitionists or carpetbaggers for racial unrest, but "German propagandists."

To force the *Defender* into line, Boles drafted a letter for Solicitor Lamar to send to Abbott charging that the "Southern Stunts Surpass Hun" story incited race hatred and was a "possible" violation of the Espionage Act. While admitting that this one article alone was not sufficient to warrant exclusion of the 8 June issue from the mail (in fact, copies to destinations other than Denison had by that time already been delivered), Lamar warned Abbott to consider the "possible bad effect of this matter and . . . its possible interference with the Government's war program." Exaggerated attention to mob violence was preventing interracial goodwill, suggested Lamar: "Anything that tends to destroy this harmony and to cause friction between the two races, and that tends to create in the minds of members of your race the idea that they have no part in the struggle against the Imperial German Government and that they are being just as badly treated by the whites of America as they would be treated by the whites of Germany tends to interfere with the cause of the United States in the war against Germany and should have no place in a loyal newspaper." While concluding that he did not doubt Abbott's loyalty, Lamar pointedly stated his expectation that the black editor would perform his proper patriotic duty.[25] In fact, Abbott was fortunate to receive only a warning: The Post Office Department showed no such restraint in suppressing the Left-liberal *Masses* and the socialist *Milwaukee Leader.*

Other complaints against this and subsequent issues came to the Post Office Department, including a petition from residents of Madison County, Mississippi, with an endorsement by their influential senator, John Sharp Williams, charging the *Defender* with spreading lies and stirring up race trouble.[26] From July 1918 on, all complaints against the newspaper were routed to the Translation Bureau, a special section of the New York post office established to review foreign-language publications for mailability under provisions of the Trading-with-the-Enemy and Espionage Acts. This office eventually expanded its purview to English-language periodicals, including thirteen published by African Americans.[27] Its staff entertained some of the wildest racial fears and fantasies of any federal bureaucrats during the war. The Translation Bureau found an article in the 1 June *Defender* objectionable simply because it encouraged black emigration from the South where its labor was allegedly most needed. The 22 June issue seemed equally pernicious because race prejudice (meaning only black versus white, not the reverse) could be aroused by its contents. The censors urged that both issues be declared nonmailable. Fortunately, their recommendations were not implemented.[28]

For the remainder of the summer, the Translation Bureau closely scrutinized the *Defender.* The 20 July edition was noteworthy for attempts to "rub in the germs of dissatisfaction." Although Roger A. Bowen, who headed the office, found nothing illegal in the next week's issue, he discovered "plenty of evidence of an obstreperous negro spirit that is not the best way about for the negro to help to settle his 'problem.'" The editorial page contained "several of the usual incitements to race feeling." Bowen, apparently an Anglophile, complained that blacks were like the Irish, "always emphasizing their grievances and making grievances where they might evade them." Yet the Irish comparison was not to be taken too far, warned Bowen: "does it never occur to the negro . . . that there would be a source of independent strength to him if he were willing to be himself and not ape the white man?"[29]

The Translation Bureau found even worse in the 17 August issue:

> This violent negro paper not only put the attaining of their own objects, that is to say treatment which includes their being allowed to mix as freely as they choose among the white people, ahead of the winning of the war, but they apparently put this object ahead even of the safety of their own race. Surely they must realize that by the constant stirring up of the fires of race prejudice they are doing what is in their power to make lynching more, rather than less, frequent. Surely

> the frequency of lynching interferes with the war and thus, take it as you will, from whatever point of view, these papers are objectionists.

Postal censors likewise charged the following week's edition with fostering race hatred, while the last paper of the month featured editorials which, it was believed, would make blacks more sensitive to mistreatment and thus provoke even more bitter feeling between the two races. The Translation Bureau's logic was neatly circular and absolved whites of responsibility for racial violence, instead "blaming the victim" by putting responsibility on blacks for their own lynching.[30]

Following a long summer of pressure against the *Defender,* then, the Post Office Department, Military Intelligence Division, and Bureau of Investigation suspended close scrutiny of the newspaper in September 1918. The explanation seems simple: Numerous "visits" to the newspaper's office by Bureau agents, bald threats from the War Department, delay in mail deliveries, and threatening letters from postal censors had all made their point. Only doggedly persistent radical publications, which were not-for-profit ventures and were subsidized by political donations, were able to brave such pressures without altering editorial policy during the war. The *Defender* was Robert Abbott's livelihood. If for no other reason than financial survival, prudence required discretion. Cooperation was even better, as Abbott's increasing demonstrations of patriotism reveal, such as his decision in October to forward a black recruit's complaint of mistreatment to the army rather than publish it in the paper.[31] Other black editors were charting a similar course. While the *Defender* refused to abdicate its principles and continued to promote northward migration, criticize lynching and other injustices, and upbraid government officials who failed to deal fairly with the race, it now spoke in sufficiently temperate tones. The federal intelligence system had accomplished its goal, not to halt all criticism, but to ensure that criticism be sufficiently moderated so that it would not impede the prosecution of the war. By the time the war ended, however, the intelligence establishment had identified new threats to national security, bringing renewed pressure on Abbott and his paper.

In the half year after the Armistice, investigators in all three federal intelligence bureaucracies resumed critical scrutiny of the *Chicago Defender.*[32] Moreover, since World War I was not officially ended until a peace treaty was signed in 1921, wartime emergency legislation was still technically in force. Solicitor Lamar hoped to continue to use the Espionage Act against the radical press, and included the *Defender* in that category. The Bureau of Investigation made a quick transition from focusing on German subversion to combating alleged communist threats. Any militant black publication, even the *Defender,* was suspected of Bolshevik leanings or advocacy. Meanwhile, army intelligence, angered that Robert Abbott had reneged on his "promise" not to print anything "inflammatory," began to investigate his political associations and stole a copy of the subscription list.[33]

A wave of racial violence in the "Red Summer" of 1919 increased federal hostility to the *Chicago Defender.* Southern whites blamed it for inciting the riot in Longview, Texas, and while individual postmasters halted local mail delivery, Lamar's office came close to declaring the weekly unmailable. The most destructive riot occurred in Chicago, and when Bureau agents found no evidence of instigation by outside radical agitators they blamed local factors, including the *Defender*'s "decidedly rabid" articles. Finally, following the Phillips County, Arkansas, "riot," local whites laid part of the blame on Abbott's newspaper, resulting in further interdiction of mailed copies.[34] Prompted by these and other Red Scare events, the Bureau of Investigation created an antiradical section, called the General Intelligence Division (GID), to suppress or prosecute dangerous individuals, organizations, and publications. Headed by young J. Edgar Hoover, the GID collected voluminous data on black publications, including the *Defender,* but it failed to convince federal prosecutors that a case could be won against even the most militant of the lot, the socialist *Messenger.*[35]

The Military Intelligence Division lacked statutory authority to investigate civilian activities after the war. The Post Office Department's power still rested on the Espionage Act, but public opinion was leery of its having a formal postwar role in suppressing "radicalism." The Justice Department retained undisputed authority to deal with such threats, but when staff attorneys judged that successful prosecution could not be maintained against the *Messenger,* any hope of muzzling Robert Abbott's weekly disappeared. Nonetheless, the Bureau and army intelligence continued to monitor the newspaper into the early 1920s, regarding it as a threat to the white-dictated racial status quo.

The federal political intelligence system born during World War I reached maturity during the Red Scare. Among its initial premises was the fear that militant black journalism posed a threat to national security. During the war, the *Defender* evoked criticism and pressure because it dared to print the truth about racism at a time when government demanded of all Americans a united effort against both foreign and domestic enemies. In addition, many whites took advantage of wartime passions and prejudices to denounce blacks' protests against injustice as "anti-white," thus legitimizing opposition to any racial improvement. In other words, local and federal officials, urged on by white private citizens, used the war to attack their racial enemies, including the *Defender.* Beset on all sides, editor Robert S. Abbott had little choice but to modify his sharp rhetoric. Either he had to moderate its tone, or suffer repression through a mail ban, prosecution, or both. He need look no farther than post office attacks on the socialist and pacifist press to comprehend the consequences of defiance.[36] Abbott took the prudent course, and the *Defender* was safe, momentarily. But during the Red Scare, it was once again viewed by worried guardians of the racial status quo as a dangerously militant voice of a race in ferment, and again subjected to intimidation and attempts at suppression.[37]

The *Chicago Defender* was one of the most representative examples of black advocacy freed from the constrictions of late-nineteenth-century caution and accommodation. It was never a vehicle for pro-German subversion or Bolshevism, but its demands for racial justice posed greater challenges to the racial status quo than either of those much-exaggerated threats. Militant blacks confronted Caucasian hegemony in the pages of the *Defender.* To many whites, including those in the federal intelligence community, that confrontation was impermissible.

5

"Every word is loaded with sedition": The *Crisis* and the NAACP under Suspicion

As the United States entered World War I in early 1917, fears that some African Americans would not be fully loyal to the war effort quickly became widespread. In response, the Justice and Post Office Departments and army intelligence initiated broad investigations and sought to suppress a wide range of militant black activities. Although racial accommodationists were usually spared, others voicing even mild criticism of the war or the racial status quo were deemed disloyal and subjected to hostile scrutiny. The National Association for the Advancement of Colored People and its influential monthly magazine, the *Crisis,* edited by Dr. W. E. B. DuBois, came under aggressive investigation by three federal intelligence agencies. Moreover, this unwanted attention lasted beyond the Armistice as the Red Scare magnified the perception that black militancy posed a threat to the prevailing (white) American way of life.

The *Crisis,* in only seven years since its founding in 1910, had become Black America's leading journal of thought, just as the *Chicago Defender* had become its one national weekly newspaper. Representing most specifically the views and aspirations of the educated black elite—what DuBois called the "Talented Tenth"—the *Crisis* articulated the interracial NAACP's civil rights agenda in strongly worded editorials and in-depth reporting of examples of racial progress, as well as incidents of racial atrocity. DuBois, the best-educated and most insightful black intellectual of the day, was a sociologist and historian who, had he been white, would have risen to the academic peak in either discipline. But after a short career teaching at black Atlanta University, where his Harvard doctorate would have guaranteed him a voice of authority, he forsook academia for racial advocacy. In his editorial hands, the *Crisis* at times faithfully mirrored the NAACP's focus on achieving legal rights and battling discrimination, but at other times DuBois spoke in an independent Pan-African voice. To the NAACP's other officials, the *Crisis* was its house organ, but to DuBois it was often his own personal forum. What made the magazine distinctly valuable, to educated and politicized blacks, was DuBois's independent views. His editorial autonomy was at times a source of worry to the early NAACP's predominately white leaders, some of whom regarded him as unpredictable. As the war progressed and he spoke out on the treatment and employment of black troops, the federal intelligence establishment increasingly viewed him, and his publication, with disfavor.[1]

The *Crisis* managed to dodge a permanent postal ban or federal prosecution during the war, primarily because the Post Office and Justice Departments found bigger fish to fry. But in fact, the charge of disloyalty could just as easily have been pinned on the magazine as it was on the antiwar Left-liberal *Masses* and the socialist *Milwaukee Leader,* both of which were banned from the mails. The Espionage Act, according to constitutional historian Paul L. Murphy, empowered the postmaster general "to use his own judgment in determining whether mailing of certain kinds of matter constituted willful obstruction to the progress of the war. Material so designated could be excluded from the mails without a court order; the burden of proof in any resulting legal action would be on the person who mailed the allegedly subversive matter." Given such authority, the *Crisis* was fortunate that while individual issues were banned for no greater offenses than protests against lynching and letters to the editor criticizing the president or complaining of the mistreatment of black soldiers, it was not barred from the mails entirely. Moreover, DuBois could likely have been prosecuted under the Espionage Act for obstructing the war effort or recruiting and enlistment, simply by printing a play in which one of the characters argued that blacks had no cause for which to fight. Whom the government chose to prosecute often reflected public or political pressure on the government to silence particular dissent, rather than clear or consistent definitions of guilt or innocence or standards of disloyalty. In its vendetta against the Industrial Workers of the World, for example, government lawyers did not really have a case. However, determined to smash the organization, they made one and succeeded in crippling the radical labor union. In other words, disloyalty or sedition was ultimately defined by each judge's instructions to a jury, and each jury's verdict. The First Amendment existed largely in theory, but not yet in an extensive corpus of legal doctrine or case law, allowing the government during World War I to criminalize certain forms of association, expression, and belief.[2] The *Crisis* was fortunately less despised than the antiwar Left.

The Bureau of Investigation first investigated the NAACP and the *Crisis* in 1917 as the hidden hand of German subversion was thought to be present throughout the country, especially among blacks in the South. In fact, blacks *were* restive, but most whites could not distinguish between bitterness over lynching, discrimination, and economic exploitation, on the one hand, and rumors of enemy activity on the other. White southerners were so accustomed to believing African Americans were contented that black militancy could only be explained by resort to "outside agitator" theories. The federal government early on embraced such fears, first in late April 1917, when a prominent Memphis businessman notified the Justice Department that two "furiously pro-German" white women served on the *Crisis*'s staff. The Bureau's wartime investigation of the NAACP began when a New York agent interviewed the magazine's business manager, who gave assurance that no whites were even employed and invited perusal of recent issues to prove that nothing disloyal had been printed.[3]

Other scattered probes of the NAACP's activities continued throughout 1917 but the Bureau's interest was most quickened by fears that the *Crisis* was undermining morale among soldiers in the 24th Infantry.[4] Proud members of that unit, one of only four black regular army regiments, were posted to Houston in the summer of 1917, where they suffered racist treatment from police and local whites, who had long abused the city's black civilian population. Reaching the limit of endurance, about a hundred soldiers mutinied, seized arms, and marched through the city for several hours on the night of 23 August, leaving seventeen whites dead. Court-martial proceedings sentenced nineteen of them to hang while another sixty-three were given life sentences.[5]

Within days of the mutiny, the unit was removed to Camp Furlong at Columbus, New Mexico, site of Pancho Villa's 1916 raid. Disheartened that the War Department was unsympathetic to the degradation they had suffered in Houston, their reputation in ruins and now denied the opportunity to redeem it in combat, the troops' morale was unmistakably low. When the *Crisis* and other outspoken publications were found circulating in Columbus, the War, Justice, and Post Office Departments began efforts to ban the NAACP's magazine.

Suspicions first arose in November 1917, when Columbus postmaster L. L. Burkhead found an NAACP leaflet in the street. Littering was not his worry. He quickly forwarded it to Postmaster General Albert Sidney Burleson, a Texan who during his tenure had to dodge allegations that the plantations he owned exploited black convict labor. Burkhead, near panic, related that two additional battalions from the 24th were soon to depart Arizona to join their comrades in Columbus, where they would outnumber white soldiers five to one. With Villa's raid and the Houston mutiny fresh in everyone's memory, Burkhead reported that the possibility of "something worse" was making local whites decidedly nervous. He was not the only one giving credence to alarming rumors. Army officials in Deming, New Mexico, "learned" from a white visitor to Columbus that if members of the 24th Infantry were punished for the Houston tragedy soldiers in Columbus would tear up the town, seize machine guns, and cross the border to join Villa. These frightening reports reached the War Department, which sought confirmation from Colonel Wilson Chase, the regimental commander.

Coincidentally, the Post Office Department, which possessed significantly coercive power over the press, also began to investigate the *Crisis* at this same time. An issue of a magazine deemed detrimental to the war effort could be withheld from the mails on the authority of the postal solicitor alone, and all subsequent issues could likewise be banned regardless of content, all without action by the Department of Justice. Thus, responding to the exaggerated fears of a white woman in Twin Falls, Idaho, Solicitor William Lamar ordered the New York postmaster to forward copies of all future issues of the magazine for study by postal attorneys. Examination of the October, November, and December 1917 issues did not uncover anything egregious enough to justify a postal ban, much less a recommendation for prosecution, so Burleson forwarded Postmaster Burkhead's report of potential trouble in Columbus to the War Department.[6]

Meanwhile, Colonel Chase began his own investigation. He interviewed Burkhead, who admitted that black soldiers had been well behaved. That fact notwithstanding, Chase embellished his report with his own fears and exaggerations. Labeling the NAACP leaflet found in the street a seditious attempt to inflame blacks against whites, he urged that its publishers be prosecuted. But that was not his only worry: Troops were also reading the *Crisis,* the *Baltimore Afro-American,* and the *Chicago Defender.* Their editors, too, should be punished for sedition, Chase argued. In the meantime he sought authority to at least ban the offensive periodicals from Columbus so as to reduce pernicious influences on the soldiers.[7]

As Chase's report made its way up the chain of command, the head of the army's Southern Department, Maj. Gen. John Ruckman, added his recommendation that such "inflammatory literature" be suppressed because of its likelihood to encourage another mutiny. In early January 1918, Secretary of War Newton D. Baker sent all documentation to Attorney General Thomas W. Gregory, another Texan, noting that the publications in question tended to cause discord between the races. No proof was adduced for these charges, and Columbus, New Mexico, had not exploded in racial strife. The matter was handed to Gregory's wartime special assistant, John Lord O'Brian, who was in charge of Espionage Act prosecutions. A prominent Republican serving in the Democratic administration, he was a civil libertarian in the context of the times and by comparison to others in the Justice Department. O'Brian had already issued instructions that no prosecutions under the treason, espionage, or trading-with-the-enemy statutes be initiated by federal attorneys without prior approval from Washington, preferring instead the employment of informal coercion. Beginning with the *Afro-American,* he wrote to U.S. Attorney Samuel K. Dennis in Baltimore, relaying the War Department's concerns but noting that grounds for legal action did not yet exist. O'Brian suggested that its editor be warned of prosecution if he published anything impairing the morale or effectiveness of black troops. Dennis turned these instructions into a threat, telling editor John H. Murphy "what to expect" if he continued to publish such articles. Murphy expressed "great contrition" and promised to avoid printing anything that was offensive to the government. It is unlikely that O'Brian disapproved of this coercion, given his view that, at least during wartime, "liberty meant obedience to law, self-control, and self-restraint."[8]

O'Brian was undoubtedly well informed of the Columbus situation as well. "Intelligence conferences" took place weekly at the Justice Department headquarters in Washington, bringing together representatives of the Bureau of Investigation and military intelligence. One of the January meetings focused on Mexican border matters. O'Brian next instructed U.S. Attorney Summers Burkhart in Albuquerque to work with the Columbus postmaster and Colonel Chase to discover who was distributing the *Crisis, Defender,* and *Afro-American.* Not surprisingly, they learned that soldiers subscribed to them through the mail.[9] Because post office censors had found nothing egregious enough to warrant banning them from the mails, the Justice Department could do little more than pressure editors unless it was willing to risk unsuccessful prosecution. Murphy and Robert S. Abbott, editor of the *Defender,* received such coercion, but for the moment DuBois was spared, perhaps because one of the NAACP's board members was Oswald Garrison Villard, publisher of the *New York Evening Post,* who might push the organization to resist an attempt at censorship.

The postal solicitor's office, however, soon moved more decisively. Responding to complaints from Texas and Indiana, Lamar ruled in March that the January 1918 *Crisis* was non-mailable under provisions of the Espionage Act. This symbolic act did not affect circulation, of course, for copies had long since been delivered. But it put the magazine on a collision course with the Justice Department, which received a copy of Lamar's judgment. If subsequent issues also proved objectionable, in the subjective evaluation of postal censors, then grounds for a permanent ban and even prosecution would be established. In apprising the postmaster general of his action, Lamar's office labeled the NAACP's magazine "exceedingly dangerous," citing an editorial by a prominent white clergyman, John Haynes Holmes, who wrote that his race valued blacks' contributions to the labor force, Liberty Loan campaigns, and the army, but regarded them as dangerous when they demanded equal rights in return. How this statement could be possibly construed as seditious was not made clear by the solicitor's opinion. Also deemed offensive were letters to the editor, one from a black Canadian who expressed surprise that the *Crisis* could advocate loyalty at a time when blacks were slaughtered in the vicious East St. Louis riot. A second communication signed "A Voice From the Orient" condemned the war "to make the world safe for Anglo-Saxon supremacy" while excluding "the African and the Asiatic from the benefits of democracy." The writer similarly blasted the "great humanitarian who rules at the White House." The result of this after-the-fact ban was to show DuBois how vulnerable the *Crisis* was, and, although he was not willing to censor contributors to the magazine, DuBois promised to seek approval from postal authorities before quoting from articles in publications that had themselves been banned from the mail.[10]

DuBois was still far from insulating the *Crisis* from government pressure, however. In May 1918, Colonel Chase again complained about the "incendiary spirit" of the *Crisis,* which continued to circulate among his troops, adding the suggestion "that possibly enemy propaganda may be behind the publication." United States Attorney Burkhart alerted Bureau agent R. Gere, stationed in Deming, New Mexico, of the possibility of enemy subversion. Gere in turn sought instructions from Bureau of Investigation chief A. Bruce Bielaski, noting accurately that the *Crisis* featured protests against lynching and mistreatment of blacks but did not oppose the war. He obviously saw no grounds on which to halt its circulation. Bielaski's office sensibly concluded that prosecution was not warranted. Although the magazine contained strong attacks on discrimination in the army, it did not suggest withholding military service as a "hold-up weapon to force greater equality of treatment." Since the Bureau's New York office was sending each new issue to Washington, Bielaski promised that if any actual violations of the law were discovered, Agent Gere would be notified.[11] In the meantime, Columbus whites, including Colonel Chase and the postmaster, would have to live with their fears.

Bielaski was guided in this policy by another special assistant to the attorney general, Alfred Bettman, who was willing, along with his friend O'Brian, to protect freedom of speech under some circumstances. Bettman instructed Bielaski that the May *Crisis,* like previous issues, did not violate the Espionage Act, and that prosecution was unwarranted unless proof could be found outside the magazine's text of enemy origins, influence, financing, or purpose. One question merited investigation, however, Bettman claimed: the fact that many copies were distributed free at "colored YMCA huts" at army camps. Unfortunately, Bielaski let his imagination get the better of him and interpreted Bettman's suggestion to mean "German propagandists may be using this magazine in their work." He immediately ordered an investigation.[12]

The New York agent put on the case went directly to the source, interviewing Maj. Joel E. Spingarn, the white chairman of the board of the NAACP, who was assigned to the branch of the Military Intelligence Division responsible for "negro propaganda" and morale. Spingarn reassured him that the *Crisis* had no German connections and that DuBois was moderating its editorial content. But the New York office was apparently not convinced and had its civilian auxiliary, the American Protective League, probe deeper. W. T. Carothers, an APL volunteer, interviewed the *Crisis*'s business manager, Augustus Granville Dill, who again gave affirmations of loyalty. Ironically, Carothers also sought the opinions of A. Philip Randolph and Chandler Owen, iconoclastic soapbox orators and editors of the antiwar *Messenger* magazine, who were, unbeknownst to the APL operative, themselves currently under investigation by the Bureau. It must have given them unusual pleasure to be regarded as authorities on black militancy. Despite their view that DuBois was a timid and conservative race leader, they approved the NAACP's fight against lynching, segregation, and peonage. What appeared in the *Crisis,* according to Randolph and Owen, was largely truthful. Unable to resist a dig at their persecutors, the two young editors added: "May we not, in closing, congratulate this new method the Department of Justice has adopted in going directly to intelligent, honorable and capable colored and white people, to ascertain information. It is the only proper way, just as you did with us in the case of the *Messenger.* We trust your Department will continue this and dispense with ignorant white or colored detectives, sneaks, and scheming politicians as sources of information." Returning to the issue at hand, they emphasized that "there is no pro-German movement among Negroes—organized or unorganized," but rather deep discontentment over the very racism they and the NAACP were battling.[13]

The Bureau thus found itself stymied for the present in attempting to suppress the NAACP's monthly. Although the Justice Department won convictions on groundless prosecutions during the war, the *Crisis* had printed nothing so blatant or pernicious, using the Espionage Act as a measure, as to assure a guilty verdict. This did not mean, however, that the magazine was insulated from future legal attack. But for the moment the threat was remote: On 9 July 1918, Bettman instructed Bielaski to suspend investigation of the magazine, supplying the additional reason that the War Department planned to offer DuBois a captaincy and enlist him in efforts to promote black loyalty.[14] Although that plan was never implemented, the Bureau for a time would direct its investigations elsewhere. But this did not free the *Crisis* from hostile federal scrutiny. In fact, the Post Office Department was building a case for a postal ban.

By the spring of 1918, a new wartime unit, the Translation Bureau, housed in the New York Post Office, was conducting analysis of allegedly disloyal publications. Its alert readers perceived danger not only in the foreign-language press and the publications of the Industrial Workers of the World, but also in black periodicals. Postal solicitor Lamar was no less zealous in his own determination to ferret out subversive materials passing through the mails. The April, May, November, and December 1917 issues of the *Crisis* had been examined and found to be innocuous, as were the first three 1918 editions. But the Translation Bureau found the April issue far different. The leading character in a one-act play allegedly uttered "every reason that could be produced why the negroes should not go to war." An editorial criticized the Department of Labor for hampering the employment opportunities for blacks in northern industries. Several articles on lynching likewise drew condemnation as well as a photograph of a public park in Houston that displayed a sign reading "Negroes Keep Out." The magazine also questioned why America was fighting to restore Belgian liberty when that nation treated its African colonial subjects so despicably. Finally, a letter from a soldier overseas complained of white officers' attempts to poison relationships between black soldiers and the French populace. The Translation Bureau ended its brief with the conviction that "outwardly the tone of the magazine appears patriotic, . . . but it is full of suggestions, subtly expressed, as almost all of these disaffected [black] publications are, which in my mind would surely tend to make the negro discontented with the war, the Government and the draft." This conclusion, that bad tendencies were as pernicious as bad results, reflected long-established First Amendment doctrine and would be reaffirmed the next year in the Supreme Court's *Abrams* ruling, upholding the wartime Sedition Act. In fact, the Post Office Department did not even need to meet prosecution standards to impose a postal ban. So, on the basis of this Translation Bureau report, and disregarding the more moderate view of one of his own staff attorneys, Lamar ruled in mid-May that the April *Crisis* was nonmailable. As before, copies had already been delivered, so his action did not actually halt circulation.[15]

The May *Crisis* seemed even worse to postal censors in the Translation Bureau, who were by then reading the magazine through the lenses of their own racial anxieties: "This paper seems to exist principally for the purpose of exciting race prejudice." A lengthy description of a brutal lynching appeared to contain "an implication of hatred, if not contempt, of anybody so unfortunate not to be a Negro." The magazine's demand that the War Department restore Col. Charles Young to active duty was "not only excessively impertinent but clearly mutinous." (Young was the highest-ranking black officer at the beginning of the war, and in line for a general's star, but the army's white officer corps, deeply rooted in southern traditions, was not about to admit an African American to either a high command position or its own exalted company. Young was suddenly found to be medically unfit and was retired from active service. This was a slap felt all across Black America. No black officer attained general-officer rank until Benjamin O. Davis Sr. became a brigadier general on the eve of America's entry into World War II.)

The next month's *Crisis* had more of the same, charged the Translation Bureau, employing hints, suggestions, and innuendos to subtly condemn whites and the government. Postal censor L. How concluded: "continual dripping wears away a stone. I take it that the purpose of the editor of the *Crisis* is to do what he can to wear away the patience of the patriotism of our negro citizens." Despite this warning, Lamar did not interdict either the May or June editions of the magazine.[16]

Why Lamar did not impose bans, even ex post facto, on the May and June issues of the *Crisis* is not revealed in existing documentation. Perhaps he was discouraged by the fact that the Justice Department was not actively pursuing an Espionage Act case against the magazine. O'Brian may have advised against such a course, or the postal solicitor's legal staff may have been busy enough with other, seemingly more odious, cases. In any event, after-the-fact bans were Pyrrhic victories, although they were convenient ways to intimidate obstreperous editors. President Wilson did not encourage widespread restrictions on the press, although he failed to curb Postmaster General Burleson's excesses in that regard, contenting himself with pious remonstrances. But there clearly were far worse examples than the NAACP's monthly magazine.

Neither the Justice nor Post Office Departments was ready to move decisively against the *Crisis* in the spring of 1918, even though complaints against the magazine were increasing. Between December 1917 and August 1918, Bureau employees in Chicago, Washington, San Antonio, Waco, Norfolk, New York, New Orleans, Atlanta, and Palatka, Florida, charged that the magazine was disloyal or pro-German. Agent Albert Neunhoffer in Waco was typical, forwarding a copy of the *Crisis* to headquarters with the comment that "the contents of this magazine appear to be of a very agitating nature such as was manifested in the riot of colored troops at Houston, Texas."[17] Private citizens sent the Justice Department similar accusations. One complaint damning the April issue reveals the depth of whites' racial anxieties: "Every word . . . is loaded with sedition, treason, and dangerous unpatriotic meaning. It instills in the minds of its readers, prejudice, and hatred of our Government and the white race. . . . Please give this to the proper authorities and see that these devils are shot. You will find this bunch of vilany [*sic*] is financed by Germany." The offending pieces identified in this philippic were an editorial urging blacks to enlist in the field artillery and a short play by well-known poet Georgia Douglas Johnson in which the characters debate whether blacks ought to fight in the war, most agreeing that it was the race's patriotic duty to do so. Another white citizen, complaining about a different article in the same issue which claimed that Brazilian race relations were more enlightened than those in the United States, charged that the piece was "a direct effort to stir up sedition" among blacks.[18]

As early as April 1918, unaware that the Justice Department had determined prosecution to be unsustainable but undoubtedly aware that the Post Office Department could easily ban his publication from the mails on whatever "evidence" it found compelling, DuBois took steps to avoid suppression of the *Crisis*. Cognizant that federal authorities were looking over his shoulder, he informed the NAACP Board in May: "the Department of Justice has warned us against the tone of some of the articles in the *Crisis*. It will probably be necessary . . . to discuss the war hereafter very carefully."[19] First he sought a ruling from the Post Office Department prior to printing an excerpt from another magazine that had been banned from the mails. He also contacted Emmett J. Scott, the black special assistant to the secretary of war who had access to both Secretary Baker and army intelligence, to announce his itinerary for a lecture tour in the South, asking Scott to apprise the War Department, and any other concerned agency, of the patriotic purpose and content of his lectures on "The Negro in the War." DuBois planned to emphasize that the defeat of Germany was the highest priority and that blacks had already gained more from the war than any event since emancipation. "I am laying this matter before you because I am quite certain that unless I have my objects thoroughly understood, someone in North Carolina will discover that I am a German propagandist."[20]

But DuBois's precaution was for naught. Army intelligence had continued to conduct its own independent investigations in early 1918, assembling a file of magazines, many of which were submitted by worried intelligence officers at army camps. In fact, wherever black troops were stationed, white officers feared subversive outsiders were influencing them. Typical was the action of the intelligence officer at Camp Sherman in Chillicothe, Ohio, who submitted a marked copy of the January 1918 *Crisis* with the comment that it contained much "which would inflame and stimulate race feeling; it might even be considered to be a form of German propaganda." This kind of charge was common: Tolerance of wartime xenophobia led officials to misconstrue racial advocacy as resulting from enemy agitation.[21]

Reports of the *Crisis*'s alleged unwholesome influence at military camps precipitated renewed attempts at censorship by the army. This time the stimulus for such efforts came from the Young Men's Christian Association (YMCA), which recruited hundreds of men and women to staff "huts" for the recreation of soldiers as a wholesome alternative to off-base bars and brothels. The YMCA's facilities were segregated, of course, as was its staff. The association had its own intelligence department to investigate the loyalty of those who worked with the troops, headed by William G. Low Jr., who had become alarmed at the growth of black militancy. Writing in early May to Col. Ralph Van Deman, the head of military intelligence, he reported that large quantities of the *Crisis* were being distributed for free at Camp Lee, Virginia. Black YMCA secretaries had already "fallen for its insidious influence," which included alleged appeals to race prejudice. Accordingly, the magazine had been quietly removed from huts for black soldiers. Professing a neutral attitude toward racial progress, Low nonetheless questioned the advisability of such "agitation" during the war emergency and asked whether the *Crisis* should be removed from YMCA huts nationwide.[22]

This was the army's golden opportunity, and Van Deman took advantage of it in mid-May: "We strongly advise you to put this book [*sic*] on the list of those other books which it is deemed necessary and expedient to keep out of not only the YMCA huts, but all other places." Information received two days later only confirmed his resolve. The intelligence officer at Camp Gordon, Georgia, confiscated copies of the *Crisis* from the segregated YMCA hut, blaming it for inciting black troops to "guy" white soldiers and impugn their military abilities. Agent Howell E. Jackson, reporting that the magazine contained articles on lynching "which tend to excite the negro race in this section against the white people," ordered the black YMCA staff to cease distribution of the magazine. An identical order came from army intelligence.[23]

But Van Deman recognized the weakness of these actions: Neither the Justice nor Post Office Departments had ordered suppression of the magazine. Despite this shortcoming, Van Deman instructed Maj. Walter Loving, the army's most capable and dependably conservative black investigator, to press the attack. Just days before, Loving had conveyed the army's ultimatum to *Chicago Defender* editor Robert Abbott, insisting that he print only articles that supported the government and the war effort. Loving, however, reacted with shock when ordered to halt YMCA distribution of the *Crisis.* Addressing Van Deman, Loving noted that the censorship order was "so explicit and carries with it such drastic measures, that I thought it best to call your personal attention to it, before taking action to such an extent." Sidestepping suppression, Loving initiated his own investigation. A black YMCA official reassured him that his organization had no formal connection with the *Crisis;* rather, individual secretaries circulated it entirely on their own initiative at isolated camps where the magazine had no local distributor. Armed with this disclaimer, Loving played his hole card, writing to his superiors that "as Major J. E. Spingarn is Chairman of the Board of Directors of this Organization [the NAACP], and we know that he would not allow his name to be connected with any publication that the government would brand as being possibly pro-German, I respectfully request that a copy of this correspondence be forwarded to him before any further action is taken."[24]

Loving's artful strategy placed Spingarn in an awkward position. He continued to serve as board chairman while temporarily heading the army's effort to blunt German subversion and promote patriotism among black soldiers. He knew well that prosecution of the *Crisis* was a possibility. The preferable course was self-censorship rather than government suppression. The NAACP board had long regarded DuBois as a loose cannon, unpredictable in his volleys and targets, and would not oppose efforts to exercise more administrative control over his editorials. DuBois also recognized his vulnerability and had already acknowledged the need for editorial circumspection. Now the NAACP board appointed one of its members, white attorney Charles Studin, to render legal judgment on all articles before publication to ensure that if full support for the war could not be accorded, at least criticism would be constructive.[25]

Army pressure on the NAACP became absolutely transparent in a 3 June letter from the new head of military intelligence, Lt. Col. Marlborough Churchill, a letter actually written and cosigned by Spingarn. Addressed to Studin, it noted the "many" complaints about the *Crisis* and urged diligent efforts to remove any offensive material that would give cause for suppression:

> Congressional legislation authorizes the severe repression of seditious and disloyal utterances, and of all attempts to encourage discontent with American institutions during the progress of the war. The government is anxious that the legitimate grievances of loyal citizens shall have a fair hearing, and that all just causes of complaint be cured so far as the exigencies of the war permit; but it can not tolerate carping and bitter utterances likely to foment dissatisfaction and destroy the morale of our people for the winning of the war. This branch will be glad to cooperate with you in any constructive programme which you may suggest for the eradication of any just causes for complaint.[26]

In short, zero tolerance could be expected by anyone voicing discontent with American institutions. Such expression was no less than sedition. No matter how legitimate the grievance, wartime necessities must prevail. Even valid criticism was intolerable if it threatened to sap national morale.

To reinforce its threat, the army (under the same signatures) "requested" that the NAACP submit a list of all officers, including those serving in every one of its 117 local branches. Did military officials merely want the names so as to send them patriotic propaganda, or was there a more sinister motive? The threat of public exposure implied in this demand might well drive at least some southern black members out of the association. But the order was obeyed, and Studin promised Churchill that no pains would be spared to ensure that future issues of the *Crisis* would "comply with the wishes of the Government both in letter and spirit." He assured the army that the magazine's staff was completely loyal and would do whatever it could to back the war effort. Studin ended with gratitude for the army's offer to assist in any constructive program but failed to capitalize on the offer by insisting that the War Department investigate black soldiers' grievances. Given the thin ice on which the NAACP was skating—an outright ban of the *Crisis* and even federal prosecution were possible—abject acquiescence may have been the only realistic avenue.[27]

DuBois, recognizing the weight of such tactics, penned his famous "Close Ranks" editorial in the July 1918 issue at least partially in response to the events of the preceding weeks: "Let us, while this war lasts, forget our special grievances and close our ranks shoulder to shoulder with our own white fellow citizens and the allied nations that are fighting for democracy. We make no ordinary sacrifice, but we make it gladly and willingly with our eyes lifted to the hills." Few in the black Talented Tenth would disagree with DuBois's belief that winning the war was of supreme importance. Nonetheless, the language and imagery he employed—which even moderate critics considered rank betrayal—must be understood in terms of the pressure against him and his magazine. Spingarn attributed "Close Ranks" to the effectiveness of army policy, in a memorandum to Churchill, whose handwritten response was a succinct "Very Satisfactory."[28]

Soon after the publication of "Close Ranks," DuBois found himself the center of public controversy when it appeared he would be offered a captaincy to serve in the army's intelligence service. This was part of Major Spingarn's strategy to combat "Negro subversion" and promote positive morale. In June 1918, Spingarn proposed broad efforts to encourage black support for the war effort by conferring with black editors and leaders and recruiting a corps of black intelligence officers to be stationed throughout the country. Also necessary were specific measures to offset the chief sources of black disaffection, especially passage of anti-lynching legislation, a presidential statement condemning lynching, the recall of involuntarily retired Col. Charles Young to active duty (and a certain promotion to brigadier general), and curbs on anti-black vitriol in the white press.

To begin this ambitious program, Spingarn joined with George Creel's propagandistic Committee on Public Information in sponsoring a conference for black leaders and editors from 19–21 June in Washington. Attendees adopted a policy statement, written by DuBois, promising "active, enthusiastic and self-sacrificing participation in the war" by all blacks. While limiting grievances to lynching and discrimination, the statement was not as accommodating as the "Close Ranks" editorial. Spingarn made arrangements for morale-boosting press releases—boilerplate ready for printing—to be distributed to black newspapers. He also took credit for DuBois's agreement to submit the *Crisis* articles to Studin for clearance and his pledge to make the magazine, in Spingarn's words, "an organ of patriotic propaganda." To deal with lynching, Spingarn had Capt. George Sanford Hornblower, an attorney attached to army intelligence, draft a bill giving the federal government limited authority under its wartime powers to punish mob violence. Although Spingarn and Hornblower testified in support of the legislation before the House Judiciary Committee, the bill was never brought to a vote.[29]

The heart of Spingarn's plan to combat "Negro subversion" was his dream of a black "advisory committee to the Chief of Staff of the Army," a separate section of military intelligence to include "some of the ablest leaders of the colored people. . . . [W]hen this is organized a great deal of constructive work in countering unrest and disloyal propaganda among colored people will be possible." The *Crisis*'s editor would receive an army commission. Spingarn obviously hoped a Captain DuBois would be the central figure in such a force and gambled that his scholarly credentials would overshadow his reputation as a "race radical." Spingarn must have been aware that the nomination of DuBois would arouse opposition, but he knew that a committee stacked with timid accommodationists would be worse than nothing if black morale was to be bolstered. Several obstacles had to be overcome if DuBois was to receive a commission, however. He was initially disqualified because, as the result of an old surgery, he had only one kidney, but Spingarn apparently got that requirement waived. Another problem was the resistance of Special Assistant to the Secretary of War Emmett J. Scott, who had not always been kindly treated in the pages of the *Crisis*. But Spingarn reconciled differences to construct "an almost epoch-making alliance" between the two. Scott carried Spingarn's proposal to Secretary of War Baker, relating that "I saw the Secretary this morning: Showed him the Crisis editorial and told him of the spirit of our [leaders' and editors'] Conference last week, of Dr. DuBois' fine attitude."[30]

According to historian Mark Ellis, if Spingarn's plan to include DuBois in the army's counter-subversion effort was to succeed, he had to "deflect an intervention by the Justice Department." Bureau chief Bielaski had instructed New York agents to probe the *Crisis*'s finances, suspecting that "German propagandists might be securing copies for distribution." A copy of this order was passed to the army, probably at the weekly intelligence conference. Fortunately, Spingarn saw the document and went to the source of the rumor, Alfred Bettman, assuring him that the *Crisis* was uninfluenced by the enemy and that, with DuBois under close editorial supervision, it would henceforth be "an organ of patriotic propaganda." This averted danger to Spingarn's proposal from the Justice Department.[31]

Nonetheless, Spingarn's plans and maneuvers came to naught when army intelligence decided in late July to restrict its involvement in black matters exclusively to issues concerning troops. The separate section on civilian morale was never organized. The army was not indifferent to the deterioration of black morale. Indeed, the country's most prominent black accommodationist, Robert R. Moton, successor to Booker T. Washington as principal of Tuskegee Institute, wrote to both President Wilson and Secretary Baker that he had never seen more discontent among blacks, due primarily to the increase in lynching and mob violence. General Churchill took this so seriously that he drafted a letter for Baker to send to the president arguing that army efficiency required an end to lynching. Baker strongly endorsed Churchill's letter, urging Wilson to make a public statement against mob attacks. Military necessity, justice, and humanity all demanded a halt to the barbaric practice.[32]

Even so, army intelligence did not see fit to organize a black morale branch. DuBois was not offered a commission, if indeed he had ever seriously been considered for one. It seems likely that the Military Intelligence Division ultimately shrank from the controversy that was sure to ensue had one of the most prominent "race radicals" been given a commission. Moreover, Spingarn's plan would have expanded the army too far onto the Justice Department's turf. There was no clear warrant for MID attempts to influence civilian morale or to conduct surveillance outside of military jurisdictions, although it had undertaken just that sort of activity almost from the beginning of hostilities and continued to do so long after the Armistice. Another probable reason for scuttling Spingarn's proposal included the hostility of much of the regular army staff to black officers, whom they did not regard as social or even military peers. A separate, predominately black section within MID would have been an affront to racist officers who in consequence would likely have treated the blacks as pariahs. In addition, Spingarn was a Jew, and his sponsorship of the proposal might have fanned anti-Semitism, which was also widespread in the officer corps. Furthermore, many whites in MID undoubtedly remained unconvinced that the NAACP was a force for good, viewing it instead as promoting disaffection by raising embarrassing questions about discriminatory army policies. In the final analysis, the army was no more willing in World War I than it would be in World War II to engage in "social experimentation" or to alter entrenched racial patterns.[33]

What would have been the impact had DuBois been commissioned in the intelligence service? Spingarn must have known the risks involved, but Maj. Walter Loving analyzed them most candidly:

> A few days after the editor's conference, the Crisis carried a leading editorial under the caption "Close Ranks." . . . A storm of protest arose all over the country, for it was plain that the Crisis, which had pursued a radical policy for years had, after the conference of editors in Washington, abandoned its stand on the race question. And only a few days after this editorial appeared in the Crisis a further announcement was made that Dr. DuBois had been tendered a commission as captain in the National Army and would be assigned to the Intelligence Bureau under Major Spingarn. Following this announcement a mass meeting was held by the Washington Branch of the National Association for the Advancement of Colored People (July 10th) at which Dr. DuBois was bitterly assailed for the editorial appearing in the July Crisis. The same action has been taken by branches of this organization in other parts of the country, and while the changed attitude of the Crisis as expressed in the editorial of July issue may appear favorable to the government, it is in reality a boomerang, as the colored people throughout the country feel and frankly state that Dr. DuBois has abandoned the principles for which he stood so long and for which he was backed by the people, for an army commission. . . . A number of mass meetings have been held in New York during the past week in which Dr. DuBois has been bitterly assailed and called a traitor, while the Government has come in for its share of criticism for having brought about this condition by influencing Dr. DuBois to abandon his former principles. . . .
>
> It is my personal opinion that Dr. DuBois should not be commissioned in the army but that he should continue to edit the Crisis as heretofore, subject to the same laws that apply to all other publications. If he continues as editor of the Crisis I believe that the storm of popular resentment among the colored people will gradually die out, whereas his appointment to a commission in the army would give the radicals a continued theme for discussion and opportunity to implicate the government in this affair.[34]

Loving also had a personal reason for disfavoring a commission for DuBois: He opposed the stationing of any black officer at MID headquarters where such a person might read his own confidential reports or those submitted by other black operatives. But this aside, Loving's analysis had merit. Rightly or wrongly, African Americans suspected that DuBois had sold out to gain a commission. His placement in a strategic morale position could easily backfire and cause more problems than it solved. In the end, although he clearly desired the commission, DuBois insisted that the NAACP allow him to maintain control of the *Crisis* during his military service. When board support for that proposition proved lukewarm and the Washington branch of the NAACP registered its "passionate" objections, DuBois had the wisdom to withdraw himself from consideration.[35]

Historians have debated DuBois's motives in writing "Close Ranks" ever since. David L. Lewis believes he wrote the controversial editorial so as to gain the army commission. Mark Ellis substantially agrees, seeing DuBois in pursuit of a leading role in Spingarn's stillborn black intelligence corps. A different interpretation is presented by William Jordan, who sees DuBois's editorial not as a sellout, but as a pragmatic stance at a time where there was no absolutely clear strategy for racial progress. According to Jordan, "DuBois was not simply hopeful about what would happen if blacks supported the war unconditionally; he was also fearful of what would happen if they took any other course of action."[36]

By midsummer 1918, as a result of both federal pressure and DuBois's accommodationism, the *Crisis* was of little concern to federal authorities, and thereafter only the September issue aroused comment. Although the Post Office Department's Translation Bureau now deemed it "the most well-balanced and sane" of the current black periodicals, it disapproved of the magazine's graphic description of the lynching of Mary Turner. For protesting the injustice of her husband's murder at the hands of a white mob, the eight-months-pregnant woman was hung by her ankles from a tree, set afire, and eviscerated, her unborn child falling to the ground. When it emitted feeble cries, a member of the mob crushed its skull with his boot. Hundreds of bullets then ended the mother's torment. Although the *Crisis* used discretion in describing this unimaginably brutal act, the Translation Bureau questioned whether the obscenity statute had been violated, not because the lynching itself was obscene, but because its description seemed to be. Meanwhile, acting on his own, the postmaster in rural Dunnellon, Florida, withheld delivery of a bundle of copies of that issue. Postal solicitor Lamar's staff called the account of the lynching "both untimely and objectionable" but admitted that it did not violate the Espionage Act and thus must enjoy the privilege of mail delivery. There the matter might have ended had not postal censors in New Orleans intercepted a letter from a Jamaican resident of the Canal Zone to his sister in Roxbury, Massachusetts, citing the *Crisis* article. Some members of the censorship board refused to believe the truthfulness of the magazine's report and charged the letter writer with promoting race hatred and being pro-German. The MID representative on the board relayed the matter to General Churchill, who, in addition to being director of military intelligence, was the chief military censor. He urged the Post Office Department to take action against the *Crisis* but Lamar responded again that no federal statute had been violated. There the matter ended, although New Orleans censors remained of the opinion that such calumnies against the South should not be printed, law or no law.[37]

Despite the brief contretemps over the September issue, the crisis of the *Crisis* abated with the stillbirth of Spingarn's black counterintelligence proposal. It is unlikely DuBois learned of the indignation his description of the Turner lynchings provoked. He and his magazine had closed ranks with the war effort. But damage had been done: A legacy of prejudice against the magazine, its editor, and its parent association had been etched into the memory of the War and Justice Departments. In mid-July, while the army was still considering Spingarn's proposal, two MID officers composed memoranda that damned the NAACP, DuBois, and the *Crisis*. One came from Capt. Harry A. Taylor of the headquarters staff in Washington.

He labeled the periodical a "radical monthly magazine" and used twelve pages to quote extracts from articles "extremely radical and antagonistic in tone," concluding that "the magazine itself would seem to be responsible for a great deal of the present negro unrest and disaffection, and is apparently published for the sole purpose of creating antagonism and race prejudice with a view of exciting the colored races to acts of violence against the whites." Racial paranoia, the desire to sabotage the proposed black morale effort, and opposition to DuBois's commission may all have inspired Taylor's diatribe. He, like many other whites, confused protest against white racism with anti-white attitudes and actions. Whatever the case, Taylor's memorandum reached MID head Marlborough Churchill's desk.[38]

An even worse attack was a "Memorandum re Officers and Directors of the NAACP," written by Capt. James L. Bruff. Every individual official or board member save Spingarn, most of whom were white, was found deficient in patriotism or politics. Oswald Garrison Villard was labeled a pro-German pacifist and publisher of un-American propaganda. Reverend John Haynes Holmes was described as a "notorious pacifist" and supporter of the Civil Liberties Bureau. Although he allowed that Charles Edward Russell was patriotic, Bruff claimed that he was nonetheless an "extreme socialist" with strange ideas concerning racial equality. Bruff alleged that Florence Kelley's son was an IWW sympathizer, intimated that Jane Addams was notorious for her socialism, pacifism, and support for Henry Ford's peace expedition, and charged that Lillian Wald's pacifism extended only to America, not Germany. According to Bruff, William English Walling was an anarchist and a Wobbly while George W. Cook, who "seems to be a negro," was charged with obstructing the draft and being hostile to the Wilson administration. John E. Milholland was damned by Bruff as a "wealthy pacifist" and Archibald H. Grimke, also "believed to be a negro," was reportedly an agitator. Although Moorfield Storey was admittedly one of the country's leading lawyers, he possessed "exaggerated ideas" of the black race and was a pacifist. DuBois, according to Bruff, was brilliant but held extreme views such as belief in his race's equality with whites. The *Crisis* printed many "seditious articles," some of which had allegedly caused riots between white and black soldiers. Finally, Bruff noted that the NAACP shared the same street address with the National Civil Liberties Bureau and the antiwar People's Council.[39]

Whether paranoid, deliberately vicious, or simply ignorant, the two memoranda were obviously no help in the attempt to enlist DuBois in a constructive effort to bolster black morale. However, of even greater significance was their permanence in MID files and their influence on future policy. The return to "normalcy" in the 1920s found MID still damning the NAACP. One memo written sometime between 1921 and 1925 claimed that "the real object of the organization is to foment racial antagonism and demand social equality, and while the organization is not in itself radical, it lends itself to the exploitation of radicals and radical organizations." As evidence, the memorandum went on to repeat verbatim the canards against NAACP board members contained in Bruff's diatribe.[40] A similar repetition of outdated and inaccurate intelligence occurred in 1925 when white officers of the 25th Infantry Regiment, stationed at Nogales, Arizona, to guard the border, became worried that the NAACP was recruiting black soldiers into membership. As this fear spread up the chain of command, accusations of Bolshevik influence again surfaced. The MID headquarters staff in Washington had no difficulty pronouncing judgment: The NAACP and the *Crisis* were seditious, which was not surprising since their leaders—white as well as black—were radicals, pacifists, and advocates of social equality. No more evidence was needed than that contained in the documents written seven years previously by Taylor and Bruff. It seemed clear to MID that the NAACP's activities among black troops should be inhibited since "it is obvious that the aims and activities of this organization are not in harmony with the interests of the Army."[41]

Fears of subversion thus did not disappear with the end of World War I. Suspicions that the NAACP and the *Crisis* were endangering the racial status quo, temporarily allayed in the fall of 1918, revived soon after the Armistice. The federal intelligence network—whose central players remained the Bureau of Investigation, the Military Intelligence Division, and the Post Office and State Departments—monitored all phases of black militancy with renewed zeal as the Red Scare flowered. The magazine's stirring editorials and exposure of racism in the army and civilian life would again be deemed impermissible speech by those who saw the maintenance of traditional racial boundaries as their responsibility and prerogative. However, the *Crisis* would again manage to escape prosecution, but for different reasons than during World War I. In 1919, the Justice Department identified three other periodicals—the socialist *Messenger,* the pro-communist *Crusader,* and the black nationalist *Negro World*—as even worse examples of black militancy. Yet when federal prosecutors could not find sufficient grounds on which to mount a successful prosecution of the *Messenger*—deemed to be the most pernicious of the lot—they concluded that prosecution of the *Crisis* would be utterly futile. Postwar juries, reflecting a shift in public opinion, were unlikely to approve the use of the espionage and sedition laws to stifle verbal or written dissent.[42] Even so, the *Crisis* would feel the power of federal surveillance and hostility during the Red Scare. Perils to a free press did not cease with the end of World War I.

"I thank my God for the persecution": The Church of God in Christ under Attack

6

During World War I, alarms about enemy aliens, "Wobbly" anticapitalist labor agitators, and unpatriotic slackers gripped the emotions and prejudices of an anxious American public. With such fears rampant, the arrests of obscure black southern preachers on charges of obstructing the war effort elicited few national headlines. Although grand juries ultimately vindicated accused leaders of the Church of God in Christ (COGIC), the widespread efforts of government officers and vigilante mobs to compel patriotism and military service on the part of persons holding biblically based convictions against war reveal troubling pressures on wartime free speech and religious expression. The story of the federal campaign against the church also illustrates one of the infrequent instances where the wartime legal system resisted the inflamed passions of the day and ultimately protected, if not guaranteed, the free exercise of religion. In addition, this is one of the most striking examples of the more assertive mood growing within Black America: hundreds, and perhaps thousands, of African Americans, on the basis of their religious convictions, stood up to the federal government by refusing to perform military service, despite both broad public disapproval and the likelihood of prosecution.

By the onset of war, the Church of God in Christ was scarcely two decades old and had not yet established a tradition of pacifism. Its founder, Charles Harrison Mason, had been born in 1866, shortly after his parents exchanged slavery for wage labor on farms and plantations in Tennessee and Arkansas. As a child Mason attended school only to the fourth grade, yet he did not lack for scriptural training. His Missionary Baptist parents taught him, and even as a child he displayed unusual spiritual depth. In 1893, at age twenty-six, he assumed leadership of a revival in Preston, Arkansas, where many found repentance. Later that year, believing that formal education would make him a better preacher, he enrolled in Arkansas Baptist College, only to leave after three weeks: "The Lord showed me that there was no salvation in schools and colleges." Instead, salvation would come through the preaching of a twofold blessing: conversion—that is, a saving knowledge of Jesus Christ through a personal relationship with him—and sanctification—that is, the believer's purification from all sin. Meeting with like-minded preachers, Mason planted the seeds of a new Pentecostal church. They bore fruit in 1897 in an old gin house in Lexington, Mississippi, where Mason founded the first Church of God in Christ congregation.[1]

During the early years of the twentieth century, dormant spiritual embers burst into flame in widespread corners of the world, nowhere more dramatically than in the 1906 "Azusa Street revival" in Los Angeles led by black evangelist

William J. Seymour. He began "preaching the new doctrine of a third blessing—baptism by the Holy Ghost and fire—which empowered saints to cast out devils, heal the sick, and speak in other tongues." Soon hundreds of persons, white and black, made pilgrimages to Seymour's renovated livery stable seeking the anointing of the Spirit.[2] This "third blessing" provided Mason with the missing experiential and theological pieces of the holiness puzzle. Mason went to Los Angeles, received the gift of tongues, and returned to Memphis to spread the fire of revival. Five weeks of all-night meetings aroused dramatic interest in the new Pentecostal worship and belief.[3]

In 1907 Mason assembled fourteen congregations into a denomination, and the first General Assembly of the Church of God in Christ named Mason its chief apostle (bishop) that same year. Rapid growth took place among urban mill hands and rural sharecroppers, particularly in Tennessee, Mississippi, and Arkansas.[4] By the 1910s, as black Texans migrated to the West Coast, the church spread to southern California, where Elder E. R. Driver assumed leadership. Eastward, churches were planted in Norfolk, Pittsburgh, Philadelphia, Detroit, Harlem, and Brooklyn, while expansion up the Mississippi Valley led to outposts in St. Louis, Kansas City, and Chicago. By 1917 COGIC had congregations in the major urban centers to which blacks were streaming in the "Great Migration," although the majority of its members were still concentrated in Arkansas, Florida, Louisiana, Mississippi, Oklahoma, Tennessee, and Texas.[5] The church would have remained invisible to most whites, who little noticed the growth of urban storefront or rural southern sanctified congregations, had it not been for World War I. But the war brought unanticipated challenges and attention from public authorities and superpatriotic vigilantes. It was to be the church's time of persecution and testing.

In the supercharged wartime atmosphere, both public officials and superpatriotic organizations manipulated and exacerbated prejudices against conscientious objectors who were frequently accused of being enemy sympathizers. In that intolerant climate all but the most single-minded devotees of unpopular causes found it prudent to fall silent, comply, or both. Religious objectors to participation in war suffered considerable persecution, for neither the public nor the government was tolerant of those who believed that God forbade them to render military service unto Caesar. Nonreligious objectors, including some blacks, faced even greater hostility. One recent commentator concludes that "the treatment of the imprisoned World War I resisters was barbaric."[6]

Members and leaders of COGIC first drew the scrutiny of the federal government because their church forbade the shedding of blood, a belief that compelled their noncompliance with the draft. Enforcement of selective service regulations was the responsibility of the Department of Justice. United States attorneys prepared legal cases while the rapidly expanding Bureau of Investigation gathered evidence and apprehended non-registrants or refusers. The government's efforts often trampled constitutional liberties, the most spectacular example being the infamous 1918 slacker raids. Thus caught in a cross fire of public intolerance and zealous enforcement of conscription, COGIC members and other religious objectors refused to betray their understanding of Scripture by acquiescing to the draft.

Millions had already died on the battlefields of Europe when America entered the war in April 1917, and if the United States was to have a decisive combat role, it had to conscript soldiers quickly. In writing its draft law, Congress provided that exemptions be granted only to conscientious objectors who were members of religious bodies opposed to participation in war. Following this, President Wilson declared that members of "a well recognized religious sect or organization" that had a creed prohibiting war service were eligible, but they still had to perform noncombatant military service. (That is, the president made no provision for complete exemption or for alternative service under civilian direction.) To win such limited noncombatant status, applicants had to convince local draft boards of the sincerity of their beliefs. In practice the Quakers, Mennonites, Church of the Brethren, and a few smaller longtime pacifist groups such as the Brethren in Christ were the only denominations whose men had their pacifism recognized without undue difficulty. Moreover, the government demanded that even they don military uniforms and work under military command and discipline.[7] Many conscientious objectors refused to consent to noncombatant service, and hundreds of them were court-martialed and sentenced to long, abusive terms at maximum security prisons such as Alcatraz and Leavenworth. Seventeen received death sentences, although later, in saner times, the sentences were commuted; another seventeen died because of wretched prison conditions and, in some cases, outright torture. The officer in charge of Camp Funston, Kansas, where conscientious objectors were routinely mistreated, advocated harsh measures: "Not only are they refusing to play the part of loyal citizens, but they are also, by work and example, spreading discontent among other men. Their conduct is reprehensible in the highest degree, and if men of this character, in fact, enemies of the government, are not dealt with vigorously, their evil influence will be far reaching." Public opinion associated conscientious objection with pro-Germanism or Wobbly-style economic radicalism. An assistant secretary of war spoke of widespread "dislike and distrust of this small minority of Americans professing conscientious objections to warfare."[8]

The administration of the draft was also compromised by inconsistency and bias on the part of local draft boards. Staffed typically by middle- and upper-class white patriots, southern boards were ill-equipped to assess sympathetically the claims of members of the Church of God in Christ for exemption on the basis of conscience. Blacks in general were much more likely to be declared fit and available for induction than were whites, and they were less likely to receive deferments for hardship, family support, or agricultural necessity. Not surprisingly, the proportion of black to white draft "delinquents" was more than two to one.[9] Moreover, the general public often made no distinction between disloyalty and conscientious objection; for many, a refusal to bear arms was tantamount to treason. Given such policies and attitudes, Bishop Mason and the Church of God in Christ were guaranteed trouble in 1917 and 1918. Despite COGIC's assurances of patriotism and love for country, the public misunderstood the church's stand against participation in war. To many southern whites, conditioned by ancient fears of slave revolts, black unrest or dissent could be interpreted only as the product of outside agitation and the desire for vengeance.

Church of God in Christ doctrine, as defined during World War I, included an unambiguous prohibition against combatant military service. The virtue of brotherly love and the sinfulness of hating others were principles that Jesus Christ had stressed; therefore, so should all mankind. "We believe the shedding of human blood or taking of human life to be contrary to the teaching of our Lord and Saviour, and as a body, we are adverse to war in all its various forms." This view did not lead to sympathy for Germany, however. Addressing a large baptismal gathering at North Memphis on 23 June 1918, Bishop Mason preached a sermon entitled "The Kaiser in the Light of the Scriptures," referring to the German ruler as the "Beast" or Antichrist depicted in Revelation 13, a man of warfare, pillage, and suffering. Christ, by contrast, represented peace. Mason even found scriptural approval, in Matthew 5:42, for the purchase of Liberty Bonds, and eventually he claimed to have raised more than $3,000 for the government. His sermon ended in prayer not only that all peoples would beat swords into plowshares and study war no more in anticipation of the second coming of the Prince of Peace, but also that the "German hordes" would be driven back behind their borders.[10] Despite such patriotic and spiritual assurances, Mason encouraged male parishioners to seek conscientious objector status. In the eyes of many southern whites, that in itself was treasonable.

Bishop Mason first drew federal scrutiny in September 1917 when an alarmed chancery clerk at Lexington, Mississippi, warned authorities that he "openly advised against registration and made treasonable and seditious remarks against the United States government."[11] The church had many members around Lexington, situated in Holmes County in Mississippi's Delta region, where blacks constituted nearly 80 percent of the population and local whites worried about racial domination as well as meeting draft quotas.

Bureau agent M. M. Schaumburger, whose territory included rural Mississippi and Louisiana, tried to verify the allegations. Interviewing indignant whites who had attended Mason's assemblies, he learned that the "negro revivalist preacher" had conducted nightly meetings the first two weeks in August, always to overflow crowds of two or three thousand. A magnetic speaker, Mason was said to exert as much influence over his race as did Billy Sunday among whites—and to have amassed considerable personal wealth, including a $60,000 mansion in Memphis. Informants charged that he taught opposition to bloodshed and war and that he said his church's members need not register for the draft. Worse, Schaumburger was informed that Mason allegedly labeled the present conflict a rich man's war and a poor man's fight, a war in which blacks had no grudge against the Germans, a good people who treated blacks better than did other whites. At a baptism, Mason was said to have praised Germany so profusely that one of his fellow preachers threatened to quit the church. Schaumburger, accepting these allegations at face value, believed they were enough to convict Mason of treason, obstructing the draft, and giving aid and comfort to the enemy, especially since two church members had not reported for induction.[12]

Confident of indictment, Schaumburger took sworn statements from members of both races. Unfortunately for him, the affidavits of four members of the (black) Mississippi Cavalry who had attended Mason's meetings were couched in such racially guarded language that they proved to be useless. Schaumburger noted ruefully: "while all the men know by reputation that Mason is a menace to the country, they are unable to furnish direct testimony."[13] Hence, on its first attempt, the government, possessing only hearsay evidence, was unable to prosecute Mason. Of course this failure did nothing to allay the racial as well as patriotic anxieties of local whites and federal authorities.

The next person to come under government suspicion was Rev. E. R. Driver, overseer of COGIC churches in California and one of the denomination's founding elders. (Driver was later prominent in Marcus Garvey's Universal Negro Improvement Association.) Summoned to the Bureau office in Los Angeles in February 1918, he was accused of being "pro-German and bitter toward the Government." Although Driver insisted on his loyalty while defending the church's opposition to taking life, Agent George T. Holman remained skeptical of his patriotism. "This colored minister is supposed to have considerable influence among a number of people of his race and his attitude is very aggressive with reference to this country's entrance into the war," Holman declared, believing that "it would be possible for him to be of considerable menace to the country." The agent vowed to keep Driver under observation and curtail his activities should they become "pronounced."[14] Such a confrontation was typical. Bureau conscription files are replete with records of inquisitional interviews in which agents argued with suspects, assailed them with patriotic bombast, and threatened them to gain compliance with the draft.

But the most immediate danger to the church remained in the rural South, where many whites suspected that "German gold" was financing the subversion of blacks' loyalties. Such dastardly deeds seemed to be confirmed on 1 April 1918. A headline in the *Vicksburg Post* proclaimed, "Draft Evasion in Holmes County Due to Pro-German Teachings among Blacks." The state adjutant general's office, the paper reported, had found it "virtually impossible" to get blacks to comply in Lexington because of Mason's allegedly pro-German sermons and his advice to "resist" conscription. Investigators learned that three weeks earlier one Dimitrius Giannokulion had conducted a meeting at Mason's church, during which time he had also received a message in code. To worried whites there was no coincidence between this information and the allegation that Mason was "suddenly wealthy," enjoying a new brick-and-stone residence in Memphis. What made the situation seem all the more sinister was the fact that in the preceding two months only a small proportion of several hundred black registrants called up for service had reported for induction. In desperation, the state's adjutant general published the names of seventy alleged draft dodgers there, offering a $50 reward for each one delivered to the nearest military post. The story linking Mason, Giannokulion, and draft resistance was picked up by the national wire services, which spread the alarming tale of German intrigue across the country. Only the black *New York Age* debunked the idea of enemy subversion through Mason's church, calling instead for an investigation of southern draft boards, alleging that they inducted all black registrants regardless of fitness while exempting many eligible whites.[15]

The *Age* was correct; none of this "evidence" confirmed German complicity, much less "German gold." Nonetheless, these "revelations" prompted the Bureau to open a new case against Bishop Mason. At the same time, thanks to the patriotic zeal of a local representative of the U.S. Food Administration, the military intelligence section of the War Department was alerted to this perceived threat to preparedness. Henceforth the Bureau and army officers would share information on Mason and the Church of God in Christ.[16]

Bureau agent Harry D. Gulley found matters to be somewhat different from the description given by the excited press. Officials in Lexington told him that the number of black draft respondents was indeed alarmingly low but that part of the blame lay with the local board's inefficiency and poor record keeping. Nothing was learned about Giannokulion, although Gulley heard new rumors of five suspicious characters—three Germans, an Englishman, and a Frenchman—all of whom were believed to have some connection with Mason. Draft delinquents held in the local jail were interviewed, but only one had been to Mason's church, and he denied hearing any antidraft propaganda. Hearsay reports charging Mason with supporting Germany and holding secret antidraft meetings at 3 o'clock in the morning also surfaced. Gulley could substantiate nothing, however, and he concluded that most blacks "had evidently been admonished not to talk 'war talk.'"[17]

A church member who did agree to speak was James Lee, one of five ordained COGIC preachers in Holmes County, but Lee insisted that neither he nor Mason preached antidraft or antiwar messages. Gulley's only success was in obtaining several documents, including a doctrinal statement drawn up the previous August by Mason and Elders William B. Holt (white) and E. R. Driver. This piece affirmed loyalty to magistrates, civil laws, the Constitution, the president, and the flag, all as God-given institutions. Nonetheless, it also stated that shedding blood or taking life was contrary to the teachings of Jesus Christ, although it allowed church members to perform any other service that did not conflict with the no-bloodshed principle. Of subsequent great interest to the Bureau was a blank petition, signed by Mason and addressed to draft boards, to be used by registrants seeking exemption based on church doctrine. A final document was an earlier doctrinal statement, written by Holt several years previously, forbidding members to shed blood or bear arms.[18]

Despite finding no direct evidence of obstruction of conscription, Gulley was convinced that church leaders had caused blacks to disobey the draft law and that doctrinal statements against war were adopted merely to increase membership. Overcome by fears and disregarding Holt's 1895 statement, Gulley concluded that

COGIC's recent association with white churches in the West could well have resulted from German activities to hinder the draft. Nevertheless, he recognized the need for more concrete evidence, so he urged the U.S. attorney in Jackson and Bureau offices in Memphis and Los Angeles to further investigate Mason, Holt, and Driver.[19]

Ironically, Gulley's investigation gave Mason temporary protection from outraged white Lexingtonians by assuring the townsfolk that the "menace" was being taken seriously. Events elsewhere showed that when worried patriots felt that no governmental action was forthcoming, vigilante action was likely to occur. One victim of such action was Rev. Jesse Payne, a COGIC pastor in Blytheville, Arkansas, who was fortunate to escape with his life on 18 April 1918. Under the headline "Negro Preacher Tarred," the *Memphis Commercial Appeal* reported that this

> pastor of the colored holly [*sic*] roller church in the southeast suburbs of this city, was given a coat of tar and feathers last night as a result of alleged seditious remarks for some months concerning the president, the war, and a white man's war.
>
> Earlier in the evening the preacher is alleged to have said something about the kaiser being as good a man as the president, and that the kaiser did not require his people to buy bonds and some one landed a solar plexus on him sending him into the ditch, from which he got up running. . . . [After the tarring and feathering, Payne] repeated the soldier's oath, and promised to talk Liberty Bonds and Red Cross to the end of his life and the end of the war.
>
> It is said his flock has shown no interest in the war work, while the negroes of other churches have been most liberal, $2000 having been subscribed by the Methodist and Baptist churches Sunday night. This church is circulating literature which he says was sent to him by a brother preacher in Memphis, showing from Bible quotations that it is not right for Christians to fight. The literature is scattered broadcast over the country.

The newspaper ended its report by editorializing that the punishment inflicted "will result in great good to demonstrate to not only blacks but some whites that it is time to get into the war work and quit talking such rot as is attributed to Payne."[20]

Bureau investigations proceeded in the South and on the West Coast. Mason agreed to an interview with SAC W. E. McElveen in Memphis, in which he stressed that he had advised men of draft age who became church members after passage of the draft act to register but to claim conscientious objector exemptions, for he believed that church members should respect and obey current laws. Furthermore, Mason reported that he had sent a telegram to President Wilson after the draft act was passed, explaining the church's doctrines and offering to meet with him. Regulations concerning conscientious objection were sent to Mason, and he claimed to have followed them. In addition, Mason avowed his support for Liberty Bond, war stamp, and Red Cross drives. McElveen was particularly concerned about possible German influence in the church, but Mason denied both outside funding and pro-German preaching in COGIC pulpits. Finding little to confirm suspicions of subversion, McElveen concluded that the bishop was less extreme than other religious objectors such as the Seventh-Day Adventists.[21]

McElveen's lack of alarm notwithstanding, surveillance of Mason continued. When the preacher conducted a camp meeting in late May at E. R. Driver's Los Angeles church, the local American Protective League supplied the Bureau with an excited report of dramatic increases in COGIC membership due, it was charged, to members getting noncombatant status. The web of suspicion went farther, with the APL reporting that several Germans were members of Driver's church and that other wealthy Teutons gave generous donations. "Fine autos quite frequently stop at the above church and their occupants are of a strong German type." Neighbors did not appreciate the late-night revivals and reported angrily that their protests had brought threats in return.[22]

In the opinion of Bureau chief A. Bruce Bielaski, enough evidence from Mississippi, Tennessee, and California had been amassed by the late spring of 1918 to support prosecution of Mason. Believing that "there is some special basis for complaint of pro-German activities in these sections of the country," he directed that "a strong case should be prepared in order to make a striking example of some of the alleged agitators."[23]

At this point events overtook the Justice Department, forcing it to protect the life of the man it held under suspicion. Bishop Mason returned to Lexington in early June, perhaps not realizing the antipathy of local whites, who blamed him for the alarming decline in draft compliance. Many black registrants were unwilling to appear for induction. When apprehended, they exhibited COGIC petitions expressing religious objections to war. Moreover, white residents reported that Mason told would-be converts: "if you want to stay out of this war you must get right with God, and join my church. There is no occasion for the negroes to go to war; the Germans are the best friends the negroes have. Germany is going to whip the United States for the mistreatment accorded the negroes, if for no other reason. This is a rich man's war anyway." A lynching appeared likely, prompting the sheriff to quickly arrest Mason for obstructing the draft. This development, plus news of an imminent investigation by the Bureau, momentarily quieted the mob spirit. When Agent Eugene Palmer arrived in Lexington, however, he found local whites unpacified by the arrest. Fearing the worst, Palmer borrowed the sheriff's car, got Mason out of jail, and drove him to Durant, where he caught an Illinois Central train and took Mason to relative safety in Jackson. Arraigned on draft obstruction charges, Mason pleaded not guilty, waived a preliminary hearing, and posted a $2,000 bond guaranteeing his appearance in federal court in November. Meanwhile, back in Lexington, a "large number" of men said to have been influenced by Mason were summarily rounded up and sent to Camp Pike, Arkansas, for induction.[24]

In numerous cases during the war, alarmed southern whites found it difficult to believe that blacks could hold antiwar beliefs or be disenchanted with the war without such beliefs being the result of manipulation by enemy agents. On 19 June the *Jackson Daily News* hailed Mason's arrest as "an important step in countering German propaganda," saying that the preacher was responsible not only for the large group of Holmes County blacks who allegedly evaded the draft but also for "making false statements for the purpose of promoting the cause of Germany, and detrimental to the military welfare of the United States." When Agent Palmer examined Mason's suitcase for incriminating evidence, however, he found nothing to establish an enemy connection other than several pieces of "anointed cloth" and a bottle of German cologne with which to perform the consecration.[25]

Soon after Mason's arrest, military intelligence began mustering its own evidence against Mason. Any activity threatening to impair enlistments was of concern to its head, Col. Marlborough Churchill. He instructed intelligence officers in Los Angeles and St. Louis to investigate Elders E. R. Driver, W. B. Holt, and Randolph R. Booker to determine whether German influence was responsible for the church's nonparticipation policy. He addressed a similar letter to Bureau chief Bielaski recommending further investigation of COGIC propaganda and its leadership and urging that "the inquiry concerning William B. Holt should be especially rigid." Churchill explained that Holt "is a white man, very insulting and overbearing in manner, and [that he had] traveled all the way from Los Angles to Jackson to arrange bail for Mason, putting up $2000 in cash."[26]

In mid-July 1918, while army intelligence was advancing its investigation of COGIC leadership, the Bureau opened a case on Henry Kirvin, pastor of the Paris, Texas, COGIC congregation. Not only did the Bureau believe that his actions had undermined military preparedness; it also expected to implicate Bishop Mason. Agent DeWitt S. Winn, a former Burns detective, unearthed information that, if provable, would have damned the entire leadership. Kirvin was alleged to have referred to the Red Cross as the "blood of the Beast" described in the book of Revelation and to have warned his flock not to contribute to that charity or wear its button. More important, Kirvin's congregation had raised $125 so that he could accompany Mason to Washington to gain draft deferments from Woodrow Wilson. Not surprisingly, the two had not seen the president but had met with a draft official who supposedly arranged immunity from the draft and from Red Cross, Liberty Bond, and war thrift stamp contributions for every member. Henceforth each church member—adult and child—was assessed twenty-five cents monthly, allegedly on the authority of the president, to ensure their exemption. So ran the charges.[27]

Learning that Kirvin, Mason, and Holt were in Austin raising legal defense funds, Winn phoned Agent Claude McCaleb to urge investigation, although not a hasty arrest. McCaleb covered Mason's meeting but could report nothing incriminating.[28] Undeterred, Winn, McCaleb, and U.S. Attorney Clarence Merritt continued to prepare a case for prosecution. Records of the Paris church were examined. Holt, whom McCaleb believed to be a German, was already jailed in Paris on charges of possessing a gun, which suggests that state and federal authorities were cooperating on the case. But Mason and Kirvin were as yet uncharged. When grilled by McCaleb, Henry Kirvin detailed how on orders from Mason all members of the church had been registered the previous January and assessed twenty-five cents monthly for legal representation of men who might be drafted. He denied discouraging Red Cross participation and said, "I am now teaching that nations ought to chastise one another."[29]

Mason was again interrogated. He stated that although the part of the church creed detailing opposition to military service was first printed in 1917, after the draft law was passed, it had long been church doctrine; there simply had been no need to publish it earlier. As to unpatriotic motives, Mason claimed that he was "just trying to teach the scriptures." Answering questions about Holt, he declared that the white man had joined the church in May 1917 as its superintendent of Spanish missions. Concerning Holt's arrest for weapons possession, Mason explained that Holt carried a badge and gun as a deputy sheriff in California.[30]

Despite his explanations, Charles H. Mason was arrested on 16 July 1918, along with Henry Kirvin. They and William B. Holt were charged with pretending to be federal officers and conspiring to commit offenses against the government. The former infraction carried a maximum three-year sentence and $1,000 fine, and the latter permitted up to two years' incarceration and a $10,000 penalty. Mason was said to have told church members that he was an emissary of President Wilson with authority to collect the twenty-five cents monthly to ensure their exemption from military service. The *Paris Morning News* cynically simplified the issue, declaring that Mason was "charged with working holy roller negroes." Holt remained in jail in lieu of a $5,000 bond that he could not raise, and the others were released on their own recognizance. Given a climate in which suspicious white outsiders were assumed to be enemy agents, the white man was apparently deemed the more dangerous. A trial date was set for late October, which suited the federal prosecutors, who needed time to work up a credible conspiracy case.[31]

In Los Angeles, Bureau agent Killick gathered additional data on the three defendants by interviewing COGIC leader E. R. Driver—who, incidentally, denied he was a Negro, claiming his father was an East Indian who had married a black woman. Driver described Mason as being devoted heart and soul to his religious work but also as sometimes misunderstood because of his lack of education. He had never heard Mason criticize the government or encourage evasion of military duty. On the contrary, Mason had said that COGIC members who were drafted should seek positions "that did not necessitate their engaging in the actual taking of human life." Killick tried to trap Driver in a logical inconsistency by arguing that noncombatant soldiers were culpable, since they helped the combatants who did take life. Driver agreed, but he believed that noncombatants were absolved before God of any wrongdoing. Convinced of neither Driver's nor the church's sincerity, Killick concluded: "his attitude was very commanding and dictatorial, and his general personality very repugnant. I could easily imagine that this man, if crossed and aggravated, might become wildly fanatical on any issue which might confront him. In my opinion, I do not believe that the principle of opposition to warfare was ever established as a fundamental of this church prior to the entrance of the United States into the war. . . . I believe that the members of this church were anxiously desirous of evading military service in every respect."[32] But could such conspiratorial intent be proven in a court of law? The sum of the Bureau's evidence to this point was not likely to convince an impartial jury.

Meanwhile, the fear of German subversion still preoccupied army officials. In early August, the Bureau sent copies of Winn's reports to the MID, which in turn requested still more surveillance to determine whether enemy aliens were promoting obstruction of the draft laws. Military Intelligence Division operatives tapped Driver's telephone in a vain attempt to prove a German connection.[33] Colonel Churchill's office waited impatiently for the trial of Mason, Kirvin, and Holt, stressing to John Lord O'Brian, the special assistant to the attorney general overseeing Espionage Act cases, that prosecution was "fairly important for our counter-propaganda work, as there are outcroppings of this negro religious agitation in other parts of the country with which we have to deal." This was a reference to the Pentecostal Assemblies of the World, Churches of the Living God, Church of God and Saints in Christ, and black Church of Christ congregations, all of which similarly opposed bearing arms.[34]

If the Department of Justice was to succeed in prosecuting Mason and his associates, hearsay evidence would not be enough. Credible testimony by church members who were not themselves under indictment was essential. The most promising witness appeared to be Rev. W. C. Thompson, who had left the church in disagreement over the issue of military service. Interviewed by Bureau agents in Chicago, Thompson alleged that COGIC members were discouraged from buying Liberty Bonds because Mason wanted them to give money to him for his new house. He charged further that Henry Kirvin's antiwar stand was simply for personal gain. To the Bureau's chagrin, however, Thompson defended Mason and Kirvin as basically patriotic citizens, even if frauds. This was hardly the conclusive testimony that the Justice Department needed to convict the church leaders of conspiring against the government or posing as federal officials.[35]

The government suffered another setback when the sudden death of DeWitt Winn in the influenza epidemic left the Bureau without its most informed, diligent, and professional operative on the case.[36] His replacement, Agent Lewie H. Henry, continued with U.S. Attorney Merritt to prepare the case for presentation to the federal grand jury. Using the Paris church registry, Henry took detailed statements from thirteen members, including two lay preachers. They related how, after his trip to Washington to see the president, Pastor Kirvin instructed the congregation to pay twenty-five cents to register so that the president would know who were the saints of the church. All those paying and so registered would not have to go to war, but those who did not would be cut off from the church and afforded no protection from military service. Women were urged to register too, so as to avoid forced labor in Red Cross work. Members were also told to purchase, for fifteen cents, a document entitled "Doctrinal Statement and Rules for Government of the Church of God in Christ." This document stated that members believed "the shedding of human blood or the taking of human life to be contrary to the teachings of our Lord and Savior, and as a body we are adverse to war in all its various forms." If men were inducted, Kirvin was alleged to have said, they could use the pamphlet to plead for mercy and not be put in the frontline trenches. Members were admonished that in all circumstances they must "live the life" if they expected their church to stand behind them. The investigators also examined church finances, but nothing damaging came to light except the fact that Holt had failed to pay the printer for the doctrinal statements. None of this "evidence" was likely to guarantee a conviction. What most shocked Agent Henry was testimony that Holt had hugged and kissed Mason. Religiously ignorant, Henry interpreted this as a shocking display of interracial intimacy rather than what it was: the "holy kiss," a scriptural form of Christian greeting.[37]

On 29 October 1918, even as newspaper headlines were proclaiming the imminent collapse of Germany and its allies, a federal grand jury convened in Paris, Texas, to weigh the evidence against Mason, Holt, and Kirvin. A large number of church members attended the hearing, whose presiding judge, DuVal West of San Antonio, was no stranger to cases of alleged black disloyalty. Surprisingly, given local passions, the grand jury declined to indict on the charge of conspiring to hinder the draft, for it found that the three preachers' operations "were not conducted in a way that was covered by any federal statute." It found no more merit in allegations of impersonating government officials. Disappointed but not defeated, the assistant U.S. attorney prosecuting the case suggested that the three be charged in Lamar County Court for swindling in connection with the monthly assessments. Agent Henry persuaded county attorney Grady Sturgeon to prosecute, promising full access to evidence gathered by the Bureau, and on 1 November the defendants were back in custody.[38]

Local prosecution was potentially dangerous, for racial animosities might easily be manipulated. The press focused particularly on Holt because sworn affidavits reported him eating and lodging with blacks and hugging and kissing black fellow preachers. Kirvin and Mason made bond, but again Holt was not so fortunate. The *Paris Morning News,* in usage common to the southern white press, reported: "the white man who was arrested with the negro holy roller preachers on the charge of swindling is still in jail. None of the brethren have so far made bond for him, although the darkies have been released."[39]

The final attempt to prosecute the leaders of the Church of God in Christ must be pieced together from only a few extant clues. After 5 November the *Paris Morning News* did not mention the trio. The minutes indexes for both the county and district courts of Lamar County fail to note the disposition of the swindling case, and at that time the county grand jury did not keep minutes. It seems likely that its jurors declined to support the county attorney's attempt to prosecute using evidence supplied by the Bureau of Investigation. Only William B. Holt was convicted: On 6 December he pleaded guilty to vagrancy and was fined one dollar. That was the last recorded act of harassment against the white official of COGIC.[40]

* * *

Bishop Mason saw his legal travails in Mississippi and Texas as nothing less than persecution on the part of the federal government, and evidence supports his interpretation. In all likelihood the church's antiwar doctrines antedated the imposition of the draft in 1917. Clearly neither Mason nor other officials were pro-German. Mason's sermon "The Kaiser in the Light of the Scriptures" expressed a clear antipathy to German policy and a willingness to support Liberty Bond campaigns. Furthermore, there was simply no provable evidence of a conspiracy to obstruct either the draft or any other government operation. Nevertheless, public officials and ordinary citizens were not inclined to differentiate between religious objection to all wars and opposition to the immediate conflict. Part of the reason was that other blacks did express unmistakable political dissent. Socialists such as A. Philip Randolph and Chandler Owen, editors of the *Messenger,* viewed the war as the exploitive product of international capitalism. Some expatriate black southerners, trapped in northern urban ghettos where the Promised Land seemed as remote as ever, saw no reason to fight in the "white man's war."[41] By contrast, Church of God in Christ doctrine was apolitical.

Regarding the later charge that Mason impersonated a government official, the evidence is no stronger. The extant documents suggest that the twenty-five-cent assessments were to pay for the legal costs of Mason and other arrested leaders and of those seeking draft exemptions.[42] This was probably the easiest way to raise a defense fund, and the money collected seems to have gone for its intended purposes. The bishop may have naively assumed from his talks with draft officials in Washington that the government "recognized" his church's antiwar doctrines as sufficient to ensure exemption from conscription, at least for those men who were members before passage of the selective service law. Inexperienced in dealing with the wider world, Mason relied less on the nuances of law than on the strength of the sovereign God whom he knew far better.

But the mood of 1917 and 1918 was intolerant of any nonconformity. Even members of established peace churches such as the Mennonites and Quakers had difficulties. Despite scruples against participation in war, they were inducted into the army and forced to don a uniform, carry a rifle, and accept training. Those persisting in conscientious objection had only two options: request noncombatant assignments (still requiring one to wear a uniform) or resist (refuse to accept training) and be court-martialed.[43] Newer denominations without long-established traditions, or sects about which the government had no reliable information, were treated even less sympathetically. Given this climate, and the racially biased operation of many southern draft boards, it was almost inevitable that black religious objectors would be perceived as tools of the enemy and their leaders would be seen as traitors. In this respect, white southern responses to the Church of God in Christ simply echoed the vocal majority of the country, which had no patience for anyone, whether religious sectarian, political dissident, or slacker, who refused to demonstrate rabid patriotism. Wartime passions led to wartime excesses, and the Bureau of Investigation, whose agents were white, male, middle class, and patriotic, was not immune. Most agents worked in areas to which they were native, so those serving in the South were likely to hold traditional views on race relations and suspicions of black nonconformity. Considering the experiences of other groups and individuals who opposed the war on political or religious grounds, and a bigoted popular mood, the leadership of the Church of God in Christ was fortunate to escape conviction and draconian punishment after months of intense investigation.

Years later, Bishop Mason recalled his tribulations during World War I. His chronology was not exact, but his interpretation was clear:

> In 1918 I was called to appear before the judge of the Kangaroo Court in Paris, Tex. The presiding officers [*sic*] looked at me and laid down his books, and said, "You all may try him; I will not have anything to do with him."
>
> In 1918, at Lexington, Miss., I took a scriptural stand against the ungodly deeds of the various races, about how many souls were being hurled into eternity without chance of seeking God for their soul's salvation, knowing that without the hand of the Almighty there could be no remedy for the same.
>
> The Holy Ghost through me was teaching men to look to God, for he is their only help. I told them not to trust in the power of the United States, England, France or Germany, but trust in God. The enemy (the devil) tried to hinder me from preaching the unadulterated word of God. He plotted against me and had the white people to arrest me and put me in jail for several days. I thank my God for the persecution. "For all that live godly must suffer persecution." 2 Tim. 3:12.
>
> Later in the same year I was called to Jackson, Miss., to answer to the charge that the devil had made against me. The presiding officers talked with me, after which they told me that I was backed up by the Scripture, and would not be hurt by them. . . . If God be for you, who can be against you![44]

Reasons for the federal government's failure to prosecute Mason in Jackson must be inferred from sketchy evidence. It may be that proceedings were simply dropped after the Armistice on 11 November 1918. The Justice Department continued to pursue other wartime cases for many months after the end of hostilities, however, so it is more likely that a grand jury indeed indicted Mason (such bodies rarely failed to bring indictments in this period) and the prosecution dropped the case. Such actions were usually not recorded, and thus the absence of information in the minutes and dockets of the federal district court can be understood as mute evidence in support of that conclusion.[45] In any case, Mason, Kirvin, Driver, and Holt were indeed fortunate. Other religious leaders holding similar views were not so lucky. A pastor in another, much smaller, black denomination, Joshua Sykes of the Church of the Living God, served a three-year sentence at McNeil Island Federal Penitentiary for adhering to his church's proscription against standing for the national anthem or buying Liberty Bonds. Clarence Waldron, a white Pentecostal preacher from Vermont, was sentenced to fifteen years in prison for stating:

"a Christian ought not and should not fight." His sentence was commuted after one year.[46]

The Justice Department, charged with enforcement of selective service regulations, had a legitimate interest in the Church of God in Christ and its leadership. The tragedy in this case is not the fact of federal scrutiny but the degree to which an overenergized Bureau of Investigation, encouraged by military intelligence, succumbed to popular fears and prejudices that compromised its objectivity. Some agents, such as DeWitt Winn, conducted themselves professionally, but in this and other cases many of Winn's peers personified the anxieties and prejudices of the fearful white populace. The relentless pursuit of COGIC leaders and their arrests on farfetched conspiracy and impersonation charges lend credence to Bishop Mason's claim to persecution by federal authorities, his ultimate exoneration notwithstanding.[47]

But this story may be more than an example of persecution: There is likely a hidden story of resistance as well. No reliable membership figures for the COGIC during World War I seem to exist, but it is likely that several thousand members were drafted. An unknown number never showed up for induction; some may have hidden out, while others may have taken off for the anonymity of a northern city. Some undoubtedly submitted to induction, bearing copies of the church's doctrinal statement. Given the paucity of church members named in lists of those who became absolutist war resisters—those who refused to put on the uniform and who were court-martialed and imprisoned as a result—it must be assumed that COGIC objectors, once under the army's authority, were frightened or browbeaten into complying with military orders and shouldering a rifle. Unfortunately, extant records do not mention these individuals.

The Church of God in Christ's opposition to conscription was ultimately both religious and political. It began with the former. The church believed "the shedding of human blood or taking of human life to be contrary to the teaching of our Lord and Savior," who had stressed instead the substitution of brotherly love for the sin of hatred. However, on another level the COGIC stance was very political. The federal government never recognized the church in the sense of acknowledging the sincerity or legitimacy of its antiwar principles or conferring conscientious objector status on its members. Given that opposition, it is remarkable that black men, for the most part ill-educated sharecroppers and urban laborers who had not challenged government authority in such numbers and with such persistence since the Civil War and Reconstruction, continued to cling to their convictions. Although most of them likely had to submit to military discipline once they were inducted, their assertion of conscientious objection, which was in reality a challenge to white authority, was a very political declaration indeed—one that could not go unchallenged by those who had appointed themselves guarantors of white supremacy and black submission.

7

"Rabid and inflammatory": Further Attacks on the Pen and Pulpit

Freedom of speech often fell victim to the pursuit of suspected spies, traitors, and saboteurs during World War I. Legitimate concerns for national security evolved into suppression of harmless dissidents and hyperbolic bombasts. The Espionage and Sedition Acts gave license for broad restrictions on First Amendment freedoms during the war, and such abridgements were legitimized by the Supreme Court in 1919 in the *Schenck* and *Abrams* cases in which it ruled that curbs on free speech were justified in certain circumstances, that expression might be punished if a jury found it had even a remote tendency to cause disaffection. In short, speech that created a "clear and present danger," even if it was factually correct, was a violation of the law.

During 1917 and 1918 a chilling public intolerance made it unwise to question the war, the government, the draft, or patriotic exercises like Liberty Bond sales or Red Cross campaigns. One's motives—whether religious, political, or personal—were irrelevant. Although newspapers informed the public of a few spectacular cases like the trials of "Big Bill" Haywood and ninety-nine other members of the Industrial Workers of the World, much enforcement of the wartime statutes was little publicized. Many of its targets were simply victims of wartime paranoia or a superpatriotic frenzy who posed no danger to national security but whose bitter words, boastful dares, or biblical convictions offended the jingoistic expectations of others.

Charles H. Mason was not the only black preacher to endure persecution because of suspicions of harboring enemy sympathies. Other cases also reveal excessive zeal on the part of Justice Department agents who exceeded their investigative duties and acted as prosecutor, judge, and jury. Such was the fate of John W. Jackson, pastor of Roberts Chapel Methodist Episcopal Church in Alexandria, Virginia, across the Potomac from Washington, who first came under scrutiny after an altercation between white soldiers and members of that suburb's African-American community in August 1917. The finger of suspicion pointed to Jackson initially for no other reasons than the facts that he had studied in Germany some years earlier and was presently regarded by Alexandria's chief of police as a "smart negro." H. A. Barrett, an employee of the Government Printing Office and a member of Jackson's church who alleged that Jackson associated with few blacks and seemed to prefer the company of Germans, particularly fueled the Bureau's suspicions. Although part-time teaching at Howard University supplemented his $700 annual salary from the church, Barrett thought these sources of income insufficient to cover Jackson's free-spending habits and his purchase of a new Marion automobile. Barrett also reported that while Jackson did not openly advocate opposition to the United States, he nonetheless showed no public enthusiasm for the war and privately expressed sympathy and admiration for Germany. The informant promised to supply names of the preacher's German acquaintances.[1]

During the next few weeks the Bureau focused on gathering information at Howard. Since the school was federally funded, its administrators could be expected to cooperate. The treasurer promised a discreet investigation of Jackson's loyalty by having several "trusted" black faculty engage him in conversation regarding the war. But Jackson became wary and refused to express his opinion. A new lead developed in November, however, when the maid of a Justice Department employee reported that Jackson, whose church she attended, was "violently" anti-American and pro-German. Reverend and Mrs. Jackson, she claimed, spent much time at the Library of Congress reading German books. Based on this new allegation, Agent S. B. Pfeifer went undercover among Alexandria's black barbershops, posing as a New York reporter seeking information on local residents' attitudes toward the war. Several people acknowledged that "many" ministers were stirring up their congregations with militant sermons but none was willing to say Jackson was more rabid than others. Pfeifer then interviewed the editor of Alexandria's white daily newspaper, who expressed surprise at the allegations, believing Jackson to be a sycophant who was always seeking contributions from white businessmen. But on interviewing a black employee of the newspaper who was also a parishioner at Roberts Chapel, Pfeifer was told again of the preacher's pro-German sympathies. Still posing as a reporter, Pfeifer sought to "interview" Jackson but found only his wife at home in their sparsely furnished, humble cottage.[2] Apparently he made no further attempt to speak with the suspect, however, for the case went cold until February 1918.

Interest in Jackson was revived as the result of a trial in the Alexandria police court—unrelated to Jackson—during which a witness claimed the black preacher had delivered a strongly pro-German sermon months earlier, at the start of the war. On being interviewed, this witness's memory proved hazy, but he *was* certain that Jackson was a close friend to Kelly Miller, the outspoken dean of the College of Arts and Sciences at Howard and author of a scathing denunciation of recent race riots entitled *The Disgrace of Democracy: An Open Letter to President Woodrow Wilson*. Bureau agents and military intelligence officers were already trying to halt its circulation and intimidate Miller into silence or retraction, so Jackson's friendship with him rekindled suspicion of the Alexandria preacher.[3]

The black pastor undoubtedly held strong opinions about the war, saw no reason to hide his views, and, unluckily, was overheard by a progression of "patriots" who notified federal authorities. The next to do so was a friend of Bureau agent Warren W. Grimes, a white employee of the U.S. Geological Survey who commuted on the segregated electric streetcars of the Washington and Old Dominion Railway from her home in Alexandria to work in the nation's capital. In early March 1918, as she sat in the last row reserved for whites, she overheard two black preachers seated behind her. She identified one as Jackson and said he was comparing President Wilson unfavorably to the Kaiser, disparaging the purchase of Liberty Bonds, and claiming Germany was right and the United States wrong in the present conflict. On receiving this tip and reviewing the Bureau's files on Jackson, Agent Grimes recalled that he was an "intimate friend" of Kelly Miller and remembered having seen copies of *Disgrace of Democracy* on sale in Alexandria. On no other basis than this coincidence, Grimes concluded that Jackson was responsible for distributing the offensive pamphlet. He arranged for an informant to attend Jackson's services the following Sunday, and even though the minister said nothing "pro-German" Grimes ordered his "plant" to cover other church functions. In talking with parishioners the informant learned that much of Alexandria's black population was exercised over Jackson's views and doubted he would long remain at the church. Grimes determined either to punish Jackson or to engineer his removal.[4]

Reverend Jackson already ministered in precarious circumstances: The Methodist Episcopal Church was predominately white, and overwhelmingly so in its leadership. Black pastors were not the equals of their white counterparts. He could expect condescension at best and racism at worst from the hierarchy. Grimes capitalized upon this racial climate. Learning that Jackson was to attend a denominational conference, he contacted its bishop and learned that an investigation of the controversial preacher was already under way. Insinuating himself into the resultant inquisition, Grimes forced Jackson to admit he was responsible for the sale of Kelly Miller's pamphlet in Alexandria, although he denied any disloyal intent. In fact, there was nothing unpatriotic about Miller's protest, but it did criticize the government, which many persons viewed as a disloyal act during the war. Jackson acknowledged that he spoke German and had many white friends, and he admitted telling his church that Germany's legal system was superior to America's, but denied any "pro-German" intent. Regarding the streetcar conversation, Jackson claimed that he and his pastor friend frequently debated opposite sides of issues just for the sake of argument. But Jackson was not apologetic; in the presence of the bishop and others on the committee, he challenged Grimes to admit that African Americans lacked sympathy for the war and cited as authority Sen. Robert LaFollette. The upshot of this proceeding, however, was to Grimes's satisfaction. The bishop told him that Jackson was a "smart negro" who would be disciplined by being reassigned to a parish in another city. He promised to inform Grimes of that new location.[5]

Thus ended the Bureau's investigation of another black preacher. Reverend John W. Jackson was punished with the connivance of his denomination's white leadership, not for clerical misconduct or doctrinal heresy, but for being a "smart negro" who dared to question the wartime crusade against Germany. His penalty was not severe when compared to others who suffered incarceration. Nonetheless, the chilling weight of federal surveillance was plain, and he could not fail to understand that his words and actions at his new pastorate would be watched. The fact that his name does not again appear in Bureau reports, nor in a list of those prosecuted under the Espionage and Sedition Acts, is circumstantial evidence that Reverend Jackson kept his views to himself for the remainder of the war.

The farther removed from Justice Department headquarters in Washington, and the oversight of John Lord O'Brian, the more likely that U.S. attorneys and Bureau of Investigation agents might prosecute persons whose only crime was naivete or an individualistic religious faith. Harvey J. Anderson was such a victim of federal persecution. City police arrested him at Cincinnati's Sinton Park in August 1918 for allegedly making seditious remarks. A soapbox preacher, this was not Anderson's first attempt to share his prophecies with park visitors, and he willingly repeated them again for arresting officers and, later, Bureau agents. It was a shame, he said, that President Wilson had ordered troops to France, because the war was wrong and so were all those who took part in it. Anyone killed in battle would suffer eternal damnation in Hell as a murderer—as would the president, who Anderson said was equally guilty. Anderson believed himself called by God to deliver divine judgment to a wayward nation. Even if the president or the governor of Ohio personally directed him to register and go to war, he would refuse.

Bureau agent Claude P. Light interviewed Anderson at police headquarters and learned that the thirty-six-year-old suspect had been raised in rural Mississippi but had lived in Cincinnati since 1913, supporting himself intermittently as a barber, hod carrier, and common laborer. Sometimes he had to pawn clothes to survive. He became sanctified in 1915, receiving a call to preach, but only did so when the Spirit moved him. Anderson was arraigned two days after his arrest and admitted making seditious statements. Unable to post the $10,000 bond set by the judge, he remained in jail awaiting action by the federal grand jury, which was not scheduled to convene until October, two months later.[6]

Harvey Anderson languished in the Montgomery County lockup for nearly four months, without trial and without formal conviction. Did federal officials regard him as such a danger to the war effort that he needed to be incarcerated under such high bail? For someone who had to pawn his pants to get a meal, any bail was excessive. The Bureau thought no more about its jailed suspect until more than a month after his arraignment, when agents learned Anderson had written to his draft board proclaiming opposition to the war as a Christian and a "prophet" and indicated he was willing to die for his principles if need be. They concluded from this statement that Anderson was insane but did nothing to speed the helpless man's release.

The federal grand jury finally convened in October with a crowded calendar, so Anderson's low-priority case did not come up until 4 December 1918, sixteen weeks after his apprehension in Sinton Park. With the war now over, the attorney general issued orders that this type of case no longer be prosecuted. No evidence against Anderson was presented to the grand jury. The record is silent, but it is presumed he was soon set free. Indeed, prosecution was not "necessary." He had already been convicted and sentenced through excessive bail, legal disregard, and neglect. Harvey Anderson, preacher and prophet, was just another casualty of a system and public attitudes that so easily created victims.[7]

One of the most persecuted groups during World War I was the Jehovah's Witnesses, known then as the Russellites. Church founder Charles T. Russell died shortly before America's entry into the war, but his book, *The Finished Mystery,* decreed that war was un-Christian and must be opposed. Patriotism, he said, was a delusion of Satan and another form of murder. Russell's followers were often tenacious zealots. Bureau of Investigation raids on church offices, confiscation of *The Finished Mystery,* and arrests and trials were commonplace. Russell's successor and six other defendants were sentenced to twenty-year prison terms for allegedly obstructing enlistment and recruitment, although their convictions were reversed after the war. Individual members of the sect who were not leaders also felt the weight of government persecution. One such disciple was Dan McNairy of Marshall, Texas, described by Bureau agent DeWitt S. Winn as nearly white in complexion and possessing a good education. His crime, in Winn's words, was "of such a vile nature" and his advocacy so "bold" that he was jailed for six months.[8]

Just what had McNairy done? White and black informants alike agreed that he disparaged President Wilson, criticized the government's conduct of the war, and questioned the value of Liberty Bonds and war savings stamps. Beginning an investigation in early July 1918, Winn went undercover to talk with the suspect. McNairy did not hesitate to reveal his beliefs. Like other members of his sect he claimed to possess "secrets" that outsiders did not have. For example, he claimed that the Book of Revelation "proved" that Kaiser Wilhelm II was destined to rule the world. When Germany conquered America, blacks would be given rights that were presently denied them. Such events were imminent, McNairy claimed, for even then black troops in France were being taken prisoner in large numbers. Given such a future, investment in Liberty Bonds or war savings stamps was a waste of money; soon all American currency would be worthless. In expressing these views McNairy quoted liberally from *The Finished Mystery.* Further investigation brought allegations by local whites that McNairy exercised a dictatorial hand over a "very troublesome" group of blacks with whom he lived. These "reliable citizens" knew he managed to keep within the law but regarded him as dangerous. Winn feared that if McNairy's activities became more widely known a lynching might occur. Concluding that his suspect was "insane on the subject of the war" and particularly dangerous because he was well educated and had a white father—apparently believing that superior intelligence was the product of white parentage—Winn wanted to arrest McNairy immediately but could not do so because he was still working undercover.[9]

Dan McNairy remained free for another five weeks, during which time the government built its case. Arrested on 14 August 1918, McNairy was brought before U.S. Commissioner W. E. Singleton Jr., in Jefferson, Texas, and pleaded not guilty. Singleton quickly conducted a preliminary hearing to determine if sufficient evidence existed to proceed. Convinced by the testimony of two witnesses that

McNairy had violated the Sedition Act when he "unlawfully knowingly and wilfully . . . utter[ed] language tending to incite and encourage resistance to the United States in the war in which the United States is engaged against the imperial German Government," the commissioner ordered him held on $5,000 bail. His inability to raise that sum was to result in a prolonged residency in the Marion County jail.[10]

Not until nearly two months had elapsed did the grand jury hear charges against McNairy. Testifying for the government were Agent Winn, Deputy Sheriff S. B. Melton, and an African-American preacher, Rev. A. M. Moore. If what the sheriff alone reported was true, McNairy had expressed nearly the full panoply of dissenting attitudes held by African Americans across the country. Saying that he would prefer to do his fighting at home, where he would know what he was dying for, McNairy also claimed that black troops were glad to be shipped to France because, once armed, they were turning to fight for Germany. This explained why the government refused to arm them while in stateside training. President Wilson, he said, was a good man, but insofar as his chance of winning the war, he might as well be playing with his "peker." McNairy's opinion of Liberty Bonds and war savings stamps was even more obscene: They were so worthless he "would not wipe his ass on them." Melton testified that when he told the suspect that he had invested all his money in bonds, McNairy replied that it was already lost since the country had exhausted all its gold reserves and was only issuing greenbacks. But, he predicted, African Americans would be paid what the United States owed them for the past fifty years when Germany triumphed. Reverend Moore's testimony confirmed all that Melton said, adding only that he had warned McNairy about such "dangerous talk."[11]

The grand jury indicted McNairy on three counts on 8 October 1918. It is not certain that McNairy even had legal representation. That same day, U.S. Attorney Clarence Merritt, who led several other prosecutions of black dissenters during the war, rammed the case to trial. There was obviously no time for McNairy to prepare a decent defense. Four defense witnesses were hastily called but their testimony was not recorded. Federal district court judge Gordon Russell approved of the swift proceedings and brought the trial to a conclusion the following day, sentencing the defendant to four months in the Marion County jail, where he had been lodged since 14 August. His total incarceration would thus be nearly six months.[12]

McNairy's offense was the expression of apathy and dissent toward the conflict, views commonplace among African Americans who regarded it as a "white man's war" in which blacks had no grievance against Germany.[13] Most who held such views were never arrested or prosecuted simply because they confided their opinions only to friends and family or argued them with other patrons in barber shops and pool rooms. Dan McNairy was singled out because he was a known "Russellite"—hence already "guilty" of disloyalty—and because he was a vocal black opponent of the war. No testimony showed that his criticisms of the war or patriotic investments deterred others from buying Liberty Bonds or performing military service. But actual harm to the war effort did not have to be proved. Dan

McNairy, like Harvey Anderson, was clearly guilty—in the eyes of the courts as well as the general public—of the "bad tendency" of his speech. That was enough to convict yet another victim of the wartime demand for 110 percent patriotism. In fact, he was lucky not to have been convicted of Espionage or Sedition Act charges, which would have earned him a multiyear sentence to be served in a federal penitentiary, like the Russellite leadership. It was the decision of U.S. Attorney Merritt to conduct an immediate trial on lesser charges that saved him from more severe punishment.

The federal vendetta against Bishop Mason, the pressure applied to Reverend Jackson, the "lock-him-up-and-forget-about-him" treatment of Harvey J. Anderson, and the conviction and jailing of Dan McNairy were neither isolated incidents nor, indeed, confined to blacks. In addition to white Russellites, white members of the IWW were also vulnerable to such abuse. Blacks who were not inspired by religious convictions but who simply failed to respond with sufficient patriotism to the war also felt the weight of federal injustice. No victim suffered more than G. W. Bouldin, editor of the *San Antonio Inquirer,* a newspaper whose fifteen hundred weekly copies were "Devoted to the Up-building of the Negro Race." Black Texans were galvanized in the fall of 1917 with the trials of sixty-three black soldiers accused of participation in the Houston "riot" the previous August. That tragic event, which was more a mutiny than a riot, was carried out by members of a battalion of the segregated 24th Infantry Regiment, which broke into its arsenal, seized weapons, and marched on the city to avenge numerous acts of brutality against black residents of Houston and weeks of their own humiliation at the hands of local whites. Seventeen whites and two blacks died before the affair ended. The courts-martial were held in the post chapel at Fort Sam Houston in San Antonio, so naturally the *Inquirer* provided extensive coverage. The 24 November issue also included a signed article by a guest contributor entitled "Soldiers of the Twenty-Fourth," which expressed a militant defense of the black troopers. For the "crime" of printing—not writing—this essay, editor Bouldin faced a two-year ordeal of indictments, arrests, trials, and appeals, before finally being incarcerated in the federal penitentiary at Fort Leavenworth, Kansas.

What measure of dissent inspired such persistence on the part of federal agents and prosecutors? Clara L. Threadgill-Dennis, author of the guest article, was a former instructor at Tillotson College in Austin. She was saddened that the veteran soldiers were on trial for their lives for having avenged the honor of black women, who had been repeatedly degraded by Houston's white population, particularly its police force. Her bitter reflections gave birth to a stirring exhortation:

> Be brave, don't feel discouraged, rest assured that every woman in all this land of ours, who dares feel proud of the Negro blood that courses through her veins, reveres you, she honors you.
>
> We would rather see you shot by the highest tribunal of the United States Army because you dared protect a Negro woman from the insult of a southern

brute in the form of a policeman, than to have you forced to go to Europe to fight for a liberty you cannot enjoy.

Negro women regret that you mutinied, and we are sorry you spilt innocent blood, but we are not sorry that five southern policemen's bones now bleech [*sic*] in the graves of Houston, Texas.

It is far better that you be shot for having tried to protect a Negro woman, than to have you die a natural death in the trenches of Europe, fighting to make the world safe for a democracy that you can't enjoy. On your way to the Training Camps you are jim-crowed. Every insult that can be heaped upon you, you have to take, or be tried by court-martial if you resent it.

I needed you in Austin this week. If some of that sixty-three members of the immortal 24th, had been in Austin I would not have been insulted by a street car conductor when I asked for a transfer that was due me, my business manager of Scarborough's Store, my husband[,] would not have been insulted by a street car conductor, when he had paid his fare and had dared sit in a vacant seat in front of a white woman. The teachers of this city would not have been insulted in the Capitol of the Lone Star State when they were told by the Superintendent to go there to listen to the Governor of Texas tell them why they should take out liberty bonds.

Oh, no, colored soldiers, you will have died for what white men die every day, you will have died for the most sacred thing on the earth to any race, even the southern white man, his daughter's, his wife's, his mother's, his sister's, his neighbor's sister's protection from insult.

Be brave and face death fearlessly.[14]

The Bureau's special agent in charge of the San Antonio office took offense to the *Inquirer* article the day it was published and quickly secured a criminal complaint against Threadgill-Dennis, Bouldin, and contributing editor William L. Hegwood, all of whom were accused of violating the Espionage Act. Postal inspectors also noticed the article and secured authority to withhold the entire issue from the mails. The accused trio was arrested on 28 November and quickly made bail. Meanwhile, Bureau headquarters in Washington advised military intelligence of the case, the latter taking particular exception to Threadgill-Dennis's statement that blacks were better off dying for their race in America than preserving democracy for others in Europe.[15]

Exactly what transpired next is uncertain. A trial took place in December 1917, although who was charged with what offense cannot be established. The defendants were acquitted, but Bureau agents refused to abandon the case. They furnished their evidence to state authorities, who could use a new Texas disloyalty law "more drastic than the federal statute." Bouldin refused to be intimidated, and military intelligence agents continued to complain of the *Inquirer*'s militancy in demanding democracy for African Americans. Perhaps it was these new objections that reinvigorated the case, for in May 1918, six months after the offending article was printed, a federal grand jury issued a new indictment based on Section 3 of the Espionage Act, alleging that Bouldin "did unlawfully and wilfully attempt to cause insubordination, disloyalty, mutiny and refusal of duty in the military forces" by printing Threadgill-Dennis's article. The charge offered no proof other than the text of the article, and the only witness was Bureau agent Louis DeNette. Why Threadgill-Dennis was not also indicted is unexplained. Bouldin was immediately arrested and made $1000 bail. Although his attorneys sought to have the indictment quashed because there was no proof that anyone was influenced to commit mutiny or insubordination, that motion was quickly overruled, seemingly on the grounds of the article's presumptive "bad tendency."[16]

Editor Bouldin remained free on bond until his trial commenced on 13 January 1919, two months after the cessation of hostilities in Europe. Conscription had come to a halt and the huge American army was rapidly demobilizing, but federal attorneys were determined to prosecute those previously accused of disloyalty, subversion, or draft evasion. Even though one federal prosecution had failed, state charges had not proven successful, and nine months had elapsed since the most recent indictment, the U.S. attorney's office and agents of the Bureau of Investigation in San Antonio determined to pillory Bouldin.[17] He was the sole defendant.

The government called six witnesses against Bouldin, starting with contributing editor William Hegwood. A brick mason's helper for the Southern Pacific Railroad, he only worked in the *Inquirer* office three or four times a month and remembered little of the circumstances surrounding Threadgill-Dennis's article; he only confirmed that the paper circulated among blacks in San Antonio and Austin. Next, a postal clerk testified that the newspaper indeed circulated through the mails. The prosecution's key witness was Capt. R. K. Fisher, second in command of the company of white soldiers guarding the accused members of the 24th Infantry during their trial in San Antonio. Over the objections of the defense he testified that a copy of the 24 November *Inquirer* was sent to one of his prisoners (although it was confiscated before he could read it). The prosecution used this fact to "prove" that Bouldin intended to incite a new mutiny. Under cross-examination Fisher admitted he had no proof that the newspaper had actually been mailed to the prisoner. Two black barbers next testified that their shops subscribed to the *Inquirer,* which was available to patrons, including black soldiers. The final prosecution witness was a black elevator operator in the post office building who told of seeing Bouldin unload bundles of his newspaper there.

In addition to Bouldin himself, two witnesses were summoned by the defense. Irene Simmons, the newspaper's secretary, told of receiving the manuscript from Mrs. Threadgill-Dennis and sending it to the printer without Bouldin's knowledge; he only saw it after the issue was printed and being sold. Threadgill-Dennis had contributed previous articles, and it was not unusual for Miss Simmons to decide on her own to print unsolicited contributions. Bouldin only wrote editorials, spending most of his time on business matters and very little at all in the office. Under cross-examination Simmons denied knowledge of any subscribers on military posts and insisted that she alone was responsible for publication of the offensive piece. The second defense witness, the newspaper's printer, also confirmed that he got the article in question directly from Simmons, not Bouldin.

Before Bouldin testified, his attorney introduced evidence that Mrs. Threadgill-

Dennis was a "lunatic" and had been confined to an asylum a year before publication of her article. Then the defendant was called to the stand. He related a story familiar to black editors, of struggles to keep a newspaper alive by personally soliciting advertisements, collecting from subscribers, delivering bundles for shipment, and running numerous errands. With little time for writing or editing, those chores mostly fell to Miss Simmons. During cross-examination the prosecutor tried to establish that Bouldin must have known how articles on the Houston mutiny might adversely affect the morale of black troops stationed in San Antonio and the recruitment of others from that city. Failing to gain that admission, he asked Bouldin to agree that "every article you publish refer[s] to the activities of the negro people and the wrongs committed against them and the competency of the negro race." When the defense objected, the court ruled that the question should be withdrawn. But the prosecutor persisted, stating, "you threw your columns open to the ravings of maniacs." Bouldin denied knowledge of any such contributor, but by that point he was clearly intimidated and he proceeded to make damaging admissions. The prosecutor pressed his advantage, asserting that the editor had taken no steps to prevent publication of articles that might be "in conflict with the law." Bouldin acknowledged that, after finally reading Threadgill-Dennis's piece, he recognized it had better been left out because "I would not publish anything that might be contrary to the policy of the government."

Opening his defense, Bouldin's lawyer tried to establish his client's patriotism by asking him if the *Inquirer* promoted Red Cross work, but the judge halted this line of questioning as immaterial since Bouldin was not on trial for disloyalty. He did manage to introduce several patriotic articles printed in the newspaper, including one entitled "America Must Win the War." But on recross-examination the prosecutor, playing to the all-white jury and getting the last word, asserted that "you always published protests against any fancied or real wrongs against the colored race." Bouldin was too beaten to respond forcefully. Judge DuVal West, who also presided at Bishop Charles H. Mason's trial, rejected a defense request for a directed verdict of acquittal and the jury soon concluded the two-day trial by finding Bouldin guilty of violating the Espionage Act. Quickly jailed, he was sentenced on 16 January 1919 to two years in Leavenworth penitentiary, although he was then released on $2,500 bail pending appeal.[18]

No evidence had shown any harmful result from the publication of Mrs. Threadgill-Dennis's article. No testimony identified by name any civilian who read the article and was deterred from enlisting or complying with the draft. Nor was any soldier identified who had been encouraged to disobey orders and refuse to fight in France. What, then, explains the jury's hasty decision? Unfortunately, there is no surviving record of the judge's instructions on these points, but it is likely that he explained the current legal doctrine that the First Amendment did not protect speech or publication that might result in harmful effects. In addition to legal interpretations, the jury may also have been influenced by the racial nature of the case and the racial climate in Texas. The Houston mutiny was fresh in the minds of worried whites, a reminder that some blacks, at least, harbored the wish to avenge racial wrongs and that a few were willing to take up arms to accomplish that end. White Texans demanded stern justice for the mutineers, to ease their own apprehensions and to warn others that similar actions would be punished decisively. In the past, the heads of slave conspirators were impaled along the roadsides in warning to other would-be insurrectionists. The execution of mutineers would convey the same lesson. Bouldin must be punished, for all blacks must understand that self-defense or retaliation would be brutally punished. The prosecutor none-too-subtly played these tunes in persuading the all-white, all-male jury of Bouldin's alleged subversive intentions. Bouldin was convicted of circulating a provocative article at a time and place when African Americans were being disciplined for their militancy. Similarly, there was to be no justice for Bouldin in the white man's court.

Bouldin's attorneys moved for a new trial, and, when that was denied, mounted a second effort to quash the indictment. Judge West denied both motions. The circuit court of appeals, not scheduled to convene until November 1919, was asked to overturn the conviction on several grounds: That the offending article did not advise or recommend any disloyalty or mutiny or refusal of duty on the part of any servicemen, and was not even addressed to military personnel; that the original indictment failed to specify a violation of law or identify any specific military personnel whom the article attempted to influence; and that the article itself did not attempt to cause present or future mutiny or disloyalty, but merely commended the black soldiers' past acts. In short, the well-argued brief demonstrated that neither through motive nor direct or implied action, neither willfully nor inadvertently, had Bouldin incited any soldier to break any military regulations. But the federal circuit court was unpersuaded and upheld the verdict, without comment, on 11 December 1919, more than a year after the cessation of hostilities and, presumably, a cooling of wartime passions. Bouldin's attorneys filed a motion for a rehearing but it, too, was denied. Time was running out. Bouldin was placed in the Bexar County jail in March 1920. On 1 June the Supreme Court rejected his application for a writ of certiorari to stay the execution of his sentence. Bureaucratic details consumed another month and a half until 16 July 1920, when U.S. Marshal J. H. Rogers took Bouldin to the Missouri-Kansas-Texas Railroad depot where they boarded a train for Kansas City. From there a connection took them the final twenty-three miles to Leavenworth, where Bouldin was delivered to the warden on 18 July. His original two-year sentence was ultimately shortened, and he was paroled on 3 March 1921 after spending about a year in county and federal custody.[19]

Free at last. G. W. Bouldin's travail cost him hundreds of dollars in attorneys' fees and court costs, untold personal anguish, and a year of liberty. Was he unfairly convicted and sentenced? Between 1917 and 1921, 2,162 individuals were tried under the Espionage and Sedition Acts. Nearly half of them—1,055—were convicted. Only 181 were acquitted, while 655 prosecutions were discontinued and 135 quashed or dismissed.[20] Many of the people convicted were Wobblies, whose sole crime, in many instances, was simply membership in the despised IWW. Others were convicted for such offenses as publishing articles opposing the draft and

American intervention in the war; saying (not writing) that President Wilson was a "murderer" for sending American men to die in battle; circulating a speech by Sen. Tom Watson in which he criticized the selective service law; circulating the Jehovah's Witness publication, the *Watch Tower*, said to cause "disloyalty" or "insubordination" in the military; and, in the case of Socialist Party leader Eugene V. Debs, giving a speech lauding other socialists who had been convicted of antiwar activities. Debs served two years of his ten-year sentence, while many Wobblies served five or six years of their ten-year sentences.[21] In Bouldin's case, and many others like it, there was no evidence that the offensive words had actually hindered the military effort. But such proof was not necessary; only that such expression might hypothetically cause disloyalty. The courts had long held that one could be punished for the "bad tendency" of one's utterance, and the Supreme Court's 1919 *Abrams* decision merely reaffirmed that principle. It thus is not surprising that the circuit court did not reverse Bouldin's conviction. He *was* guilty, but at the same time he was a casualty of issues and legal doctrines much larger than the language of Clara Threadgill-Dennis's anguished appeal. Given widespread intolerance of dissent concerning the war, and the more specific intolerance of southern black protest against racial discrimination, it is perhaps remarkable that Bouldin got off so lightly.

Black editors in Texas walked a slippery tightrope during and immediately after World War I. The tribulations of the *San Antonio Inquirer*'s G. W. Bouldin must have been well known to other members of the African-American fourth estate. Yet they were not simply journalists: they were race spokesmen and advocates. Their capacity for silence was not limitless. Nor was the tolerance of agents of the Bureau of Investigation, who began to focus on the *Galveston New Idea* in late 1917. Edited by David T. Sheldon and S. H. Simpson, it was similar to other black papers, being issued every Saturday and containing pieces by local contributors. One such writer was Rev. Elijah C. Branch.

Galveston's federal investigators learned that an article in the 24 November issue entitled "Judge Lynch in Texas," written by Reverend Branch, was being posted in shop windows and sold as a broadside on the streets. While calling for national unity in the fight against Germany and highlighting blacks' patriotism, Branch underscored their oppression and compared lynching to Germany's most barbarous acts. Bureau personnel drew the wild conclusion that Germans were financing the paper to promote racial strife and radicalize the black population. Agent J. L. Webb urged its immediate suppression and Espionage Act prosecution of Branch, Sheldon, and Simpson.[22]

Having rushed to judgment, Webb had to find evidence. Other issues of the paper were perused. He found, among several egregious examples, an editorial saying that it was "Hell" to be black in Galveston. He was now even more certain that the paper was "so rabid and so inflammatory" that it was responsible for much "unrest among the colored people." Unrest hardly needed proving, in Webb's eyes, because at least seven upset whites had called the Bureau in recent days to complain about "insolent remarks" or other militant assertions on the part of blacks. One man even reported his own servant for having said that blacks soon would control the city and whites would do the cooking for them. Another individual overheard a black girl say she hoped white troops crossing the Atlantic would be drowned and predicted that whites would soon have their hands full coping with domestic racial unrest. Webb claimed that many similar instances could be told: "There is no doubt that these utterances are the result of the inflammatory articles being published in this negro sheet." Fearing that the newspaper was becoming even more "rabid," Webb wired his division superintendent in San Antonio, C. E. Breniman, who immediately sought permission to invoke the Espionage Act.[23]

This caused a dilemma for U.S. Attorney John E. Green. Breniman was impatient for action, but Green had no concrete evidence, only Webb's excited reports. Requesting advice from the attorney general, Green simultaneously asked Webb to forward copies of the *New Idea.* The agent secured issues from the previous three months and highlighted several articles. One encouraged migration to the North because of southern injustices like the recent death sentence imposed on a Galveston resident. Another piece denounced Houston's white power structure for failing to punish those who had provoked the mutiny of black soldiers. An article attacking Jim Crow laws was, to Webb's reading, bitter and "seditious." Concluding his analysis with a roundhouse punch, the agent charged the newspaper with being under German influence and intent on inciting civil war.[24]

Webb grew more alarmed on learning that Simpson, the paper's owner, was now employed by the *Houston Observer* "where no doubt he is writing rabid or [even] more rabid articles." This was, of course, pure speculation; Webb had no foundation for condemning Simpson's new endeavor, but this did not deter the agent's certainty. Others were not so sure, however. When Washington finally authorized prosecution, Webb asked U.S. Commissioner Jonathan C. Walker in Galveston to file a complaint. Although he admitted the *New Idea*'s language was "inflammatory," a prima facie violation of law did not seem to exist. Exasperated, Webb pointed out the relevant sections and titles of the Espionage Act but Walker still disagreed, saying that if Webb was insistent he should compose the complaint himself. To do so, Webb wrote Washington, was an act of futility given "the many humilitations [*sic*] Agents of the Department of Justice have been subjected to in the past before the Commissioner." Even if he agreed to a complaint, he would probably release the editors pending grand jury action, "which seems to be a hobby of the Commissioner." Giving up in Galveston, Webb persuaded the U.S. attorney in Corpus Christi to present charges to the grand jury there.[25]

In compiling additional proof for the grand jury Webb uncovered new evidence about Rev. Elijah C. Branch. A native of Huntsville, he had lived in Houston for twenty years, publishing in 1913 an outspoken pamphlet, "Judge Lynch's Court in America: The Number of Negro Convicts in Prison in America and other Injustice Done to the Negro in America." Embarking on ministerial studies that same year, he soon accepted a Missionary Baptist pastorate in Texas City and then moved to Galveston after the storm of 1915. He published several other attacks on conditions in the South, one of which was banned from the mail by the local postmaster. Webb was particularly interested in Branch's latest pamphlet, "An Appeal to Justice," which lamented the execution of thirteen soldiers but the punishment of no whites in the aftermath of the Houston mutiny. Learning that Bureau agents wanted to review his writings, Branch voluntarily brought copies to their office. When a federal grand jury convened in late January 1918, Webb presented Branch's pamphlets and copies of the *New Idea,* but jurors refused to indict Branch, Sheldon, or Simpson. Once again the Bureau and a U.S. attorney were stalemated.[26]

But state authorities had by this time marked Branch for prosecution. Among the most hated figures in the white South were labor agents promoting the Great Migration. Recruiters throughout the South enticed blacks northward with promises of good wages and, sometimes, free transportation. Powerful southern agricultural interests reacted with fury, unwilling to allow the depletion of their exploited labor supply and apprehensive that an exodus would drive up wages. Compliant state governments responded by passing laws to harass labor agents. In Texas, as elsewhere, they were required to purchase expensive licenses.

Neither the extent of Reverend Branch's recruitment activities nor the state's motive in singling him out can be determined from available evidence. It was not uncommon, however, for Bureau agents and U.S. attorneys to transfer their evidence to state or local authorities when they could not make federal charges stick. Thus it is likely that Webb encouraged Texas prosecutors to find some way to punish Branch. Whatever the scenario, he was hailed before the Galveston County court on 8 July 1918 for "engaging in the business of emigration agent without a license." No trial record survives, so it is impossible to tell the length or fairness of the proceedings. The jury found him guilty and he was fined $100 and sentenced to thirty days in the county jail. Remaining free on $500 bond, he petitioned for a new trial, which was denied, and he then took his case to the state court of criminal appeals. Six months later, on 22 January 1919, Judge Lattimore reversed Branch's conviction and dismissed all charges.[27] How great a toll this took on him is unknown, but the cost of legal representation must have strained his meager resources. More significantly, the threat of imprisonment, along with renewed federal investigations, must have been intimidating. A weaker individual would have decided that abject silence was more prudent.

Reverend E. C. Branch certainly did not need more difficulties after the summer of 1918, but the federal government, this time led by the Military Intelligence Division, renewed its pursuit of the outspoken preacher. United States postal censors, authorized to open mail from any overseas location where Allied governments did not censor outgoing mail, intercepted a letter to Branch from J. S. Moore in Bahia, Brazil. The writer, already on the postal censorship list, was unequivocal in his view of the current military conflict:

> The great war between the whites is the only salvation [for] the blacks and other mixed peoples. So, the white race is eating its own cooking; and God grant that it will lay heavy enough upon their stomachs to teach them the potancy [*sic*] of

> the devine [*sic*] laws. Stand up like men and declare against the wrong and offer no prayers to the devil. Do like the Mexicans or Germans. Stand up and fight the world with what you have without begging favors, when that you know that you are right. Why do you all forever talk of begging white people to contribute to the help of negroes, in seeking their revenge against white brutes?—They kill, ly [*sic*], steal or do any other kind of deviltry to carry out their plans. Nor will they give up their people to be punished by others afterwards.[28]

Moore, of course, was beyond the reach of punishment. But Branch, whose sin was receiving a letter, could at least be harassed.

A copy of the censorship report was forwarded to MID's intelligence officer in Galveston, Lt. G. R. Hoff, who compiled a detailed and damning report charging Branch with doing "everything in his power to incite prejudice and hatred against the whites" because of "alleged violence upon negroes." Hoff interviewed a black lawyer who denied that Branch had any German connections but admitted to his bitterness against the government. He also arranged for an undercover interview with Branch by a black city detective, although Branch must have known that person's identity. This did not deter him from bitterly assailing the government for censoring his mail. Both the detective and the lawyer agreed, however, that Branch had little influence among the local population.

Seeking more direct evidence, Hoff assigned one of his staff, a Sergeant Dillon, to another undercover "interview," but Branch would not talk until Dillon identified himself. The preacher then freely detailed his long-standing anger against the government stemming from 1915 when, following a storm in Texas City, Branch and other blacks were kept under army guard for five days, denied use of the mails, and compelled to clean up the town. Branch defiantly told Dillon that he was unafraid of the government, was as good as any white person, and would continue to urge his race to demand justice. (Dillon judged these remarks to be extremely "impudent.") Hoff proved as adept as Bureau agent Webb in drawing hysterical conclusions from shards of evidence and his own speculations. He concluded that Branch was "spreading dangerous propaganda," proof of which was reports from white employers and housewives that blacks had become "insolent and sullen and will not obey orders, and seem to be in a spirit of open rebillion [*sic*]. This would seem to indicate that some of subjects views have ladged [*sic*] in receptive minds." If in fact Branch had made laborers and maids more assertive—despite testimony that he wielded little local influence—was this a federal crime? Hoff thought so, and urged: "in view of the insolent attitude of this subject toward our Government, and his intolerable impudence while being interviewed, it is strongly advised that he be taken in charge."[29]

The MID's charges were referred to the U.S. attorney in Houston. Whatever he thought about Branch's alleged insolence, the attorney found insufficient evidence of any violation of law to warrant a prosecution. Unwilling to accept this decision, Hoff requested that the intelligence officer for the army's Southern Department, Maj. Robert L. Barnes, ask MID head Brig. Gen. Marlborough Churchill to use his personal influence with the Department of Justice to get a prosecution started. Here the linkage between MID and the Justice Department was especially close, for Barnes and his aide, 2nd Lt. Willard Utley, were a few months previously the special agent in charge and an agent, respectively, in the Bureau's San Antonio office. Churchill wisely decided not to push the case, although he sent the documentation to the secretary of war's black special assistant, Emmett J. Scott. But as Scott had no authority over alleged subversion or sedition, he took no action.[30]

Undaunted, Lieutenant Hoff, now cooperating with Agent Webb, continued to pursue his quarry even after the Armistice was signed. Webb confronted Branch concerning the letter from J. S. Moore in Brazil. At first denying any knowledge of it, Branch later admitted having received it but insisted that Moore was simply an advocate of emigration out of the United States while he, Branch, sought to encourage movement from the South to the northern states. While proclaiming his intention to continue writing against injustices, he unequivocally denied pro-German sympathies. Then Branch proposed a deal to the government: In return for it ceasing to open his mail, he promised to send all outgoing correspondence in unsealed envelopes. Meanwhile, another of Hoff's operatives, a Sergeant Goodman, secured the Galveston postmaster's agreement to help prove that Branch was in league with German agents. But when asked to allow all of Branch's mail to be opened and read, the postmaster retreated, saying that could only be done upon presentation of a proper warrant. He did, however, agree to keep a list of all correspondence addressed to Branch. Yet another MID agent, a Sergeant Abner, went undercover to try to trap Branch in conversation about political and labor issues. The preacher was understandably guarded and said nothing of an "incriminating nature." Hoff was not reassured, however, noting that "the agitative attitude assumed by Branch and the propaganda now being carried on by him among the members of his race, tends to antagonize and rouse a race hatred among the ignorant of his race" which, he was certain, was "directly harmful to the best interest of the country."[31]

Fortunately, all this was an exercise in futility. In late November 1918, the U.S. attorney resolutely refused to embark on what would have been a vindictive and frivolous prosecution. Branch's impassioned pamphlets condemning lynching and his mistreatment following the Texas City storm were hardly evidence of sedition. Nor were allegations of fostering impudence among domestic servants provable, much less a violation of federal statutes. But Lieutenant Hoff still did not see the light:

> In view of the many reports that have been made upon this subject growing out of numerous investigations concerning his loyalty, and in view of the fact that the United States District Attorney does not recognize the evidence compiled in each instance to be flagrant enough to warrant a breach of the Federal Law, it is thought useless to continue the investigation of this negro any further. His conduct upon the whole, is very reprehensible, and it is rather a disheartening undertaking for an investigator to call upon a negro, and hear himself and the white race in general insulted, and slurs cast at our form of Government. This is shown

> in the report of every investigation that has been had with subject. It is the opinion of this office that further investigation could not disclose a more unfavorable attitude toward our Government than has been depicted by subject from time to time.[32]

In the end, MID's dogged pursuit of Rev. E. C. Branch was based not on the wartime Espionage and Sedition Acts but on his transgression of a much more ancient code forbidding racial militancy and "insolence" toward whites. The case was summed up by MID's acting director at the end of November 1918. While acknowledging there was no evidence of pro-German activity, he emphasized that Branch's opinions were hostile to the government and the cause of "much injury" to "ignorant" blacks who were duped into hating whites.[33] Thus the federal government's persecution of the militant preacher-pamphleteer was really in the best interests of a race that could ill afford to endanger itself by harboring proscribed attitudes.

E. C. Branch and *Galveston New Idea* editors S. H. Simpson and David T. Sheldon were undeterred by their wartime tribulations and remained outspoken advocates for their race during the postwar Red Scare, as racial violence detonated across the nation. Even where outbreaks did not occur, the white populace feared the possibility of such explosions. When blacks and whites engaged in hand-to-hand combat in Chicago, rumors sped through Galveston that similar battles were about to occur there. Bureau agent J. L. Webb closely monitored the situation and once again alleged that Branch and Simpson were active agitators, even though both were absent from the city. Other agents as far afield as San Antonio and Fort Worth pinned the blame more directly on the 26 July 1919 issue of the *New Idea*. Denouncing a recent lynching by a "savage herd of white cannibals" that included the sheriff and deputies of Gilmer, Texas, Simpson demanded justice and protection for his race while advising blacks to trust God but keep their powder dry. Interpreting this as an invitation to stockpile ammunition and "incite trouble," San Antonio agent W. A. Wiseman urged prosecution of the paper's staff using the Espionage Act, which remained in force long after the war. But the likelihood of the attorney general approving new prosecutions was slim. Wiseman probably knew this, and certainly should have known that the Second Amendment to the federal Constitution protected one's right to own firearms. Prosecution was not initiated, but neither was any attempt to rein in overzealous agents eager to intimidate or trample on the citizenship rights of African Americans.[34]

Persistence in harassing Branch was more than an excess of zealotry on the part of Bureau and military intelligence agents. They reflected the widespread perception, especially in the South, that blacks were easily misled by those who would profess to be their friends or leaders, but who were in reality, wittingly or unwittingly, serving the interests of the German enemy. Webb, Hoff, and their colleagues were representative of whites who saw their roles in government as including the suppression of black militancy and dissent, both as a war measure and because the maintenance of white privilege was sacrosanct. Not only must the entire nation be of one mind in pursuing victory in Europe, but whites must also remain unquestionably committed to white supremacy, and blacks unquestionably acquiescent to their own inferior status.

Fears of black militancy did not die as the nation entered peacetime. Two years later, as the bloody 1921 Tulsa riot concluded the season of Red Scare racial violence, and as a resurgent Ku Klux Klan flexed its muscles nationwide, Bureau agents continued to fear the influence of outspoken black newspapers and their editors. By then S. H. Simpson had sold the *New Idea* but was publishing the *Galveston Colored American.* Once again agent Webb saw danger in its condemnation of America's "hellish, hunnish culture" and the "semi-civilized" South. His superintendent in San Antonio rejected labeling the newspaper "'ultra' radical" but nonetheless judged it guilty of printing articles "calculated to stir up race trouble."[35] This concluded the Bureau's final investigation of Galveston's militant black pamphleteer and journalists. No federal prosecution was formally undertaken against them, but they must have experienced considerable fear at that prospect. Reverend Branch's prosecution under state law was both worrisome and costly. Even though they were never arrested and tried, Simpson and Sheldon, along with Branch, were clearly victims of the federal crusade to suppress dissent—particularly African-American dissent—during and after World War I.

Dissenting black editorialists in the North were also vulnerable to federal persecution. Such was the case of the two most openly outspoken black critics of the war: young southern expatriates A. Philip Randolph and Chandler Owen. Both grew up experiencing the fullness of racism in the post-Reconstruction South: segregated schools, Jim Crow railroad coaches, disfranchisement, and lynching. Each independently concluded that he could not fulfill his dreams and ambitions by remaining under such circumstances. North Carolina–born Owen had studied one semester shy of a degree at Richmond's Virginia Union University, an institution that rejected Bookerite accommodation and dedicated itself to making Negroes men, not making men into Negroes. Breaking away from the South, Owen went to New York to study social work and later law at Columbia University. New York itself was an education for Owen, with libraries and schools and soapbox orators to challenge every orthodoxy. It was there that he met Randolph, the product of an educated but often poor Jacksonville, Florida, family. Frequenting its segregated public library, Randolph had read W. E. B. DuBois's *Souls of Black Folk* and was inspired to make himself an asset to his race. He attended high school at nearby Cookman Institute, which, like Virginia Union, refused to teach submission to black youth. But some of his greatest lessons were learned at home, from a father who exhorted him to fight for his rights and who set a concrete example by helping organize a group of armed blacks to prevent a local lynching.

Moving to New York shortly before the onset of the Great Migration, Randolph took evening classes at City College. When he met Chandler Owen, the two were intellectually prepared to test new ideas as they dug into sociology, politics, economics, and the theories of Karl Marx. While attending lectures at the

Rand School, a workers' institute, they met New York City's best-known socialist, Morris Hillquit, who recruited them into precinct work. Before long they were discussing history, economics, and sociology with Socialist Party leader Eugene Debs. By 1917 Randolph and his new wife, Lucille, ran for secretary of state and the state legislature, respectively, on the Socialist ticket. At the same time, he and Owen organized the Independent Political Council in Harlem in a disappointing effort to promote socialist discussion among blacks. But they quickly became preoccupied with editing a headwaiters' union journal, the *Hotel Messenger.* Soon disillusioned with that union, however, they transformed the periodical into the *Messenger* in November 1917, the inaugural issue of which, sold from Harlem street corners, condemned war profiteers, applauded antiwar groups, and promoted the Socialist Party. It is a mystery why the even more militant second issue, appearing in January 1918, escaped interdiction by Bureau of Investigation and Post Office Department censors: It demanded black representation in any postwar peace negotiations, acclaimed the spread of Bolshevism in Russia, and condemned southern "Prussianism" (lynching and mob violence) as worse than anything in Germany.[36]

Having already published *Terms of Peace and the Darker Races,* a tract expressing skepticism about the outcome of the war, Owen and Randolph were celebrities within the antiwar wing of the Socialist Party by the spring of 1918 when they embarked on what was intended to be a coast-to-coast antiwar lecture tour. Bundles of the magazine's third issue were freighted ahead to cities on their itinerary so that it could be peddled to audiences who gathered to hear the two young black socialists. It was in Cleveland that the Bureau finally took note of the *Messenger* and its editors. They arrived on 4 August and that evening addressed a large number gathered to hear them and white socialist speakers. Two federal agents mingled with the crowd, bought a copy of the *Messenger* for fifteen cents, and then arrested them while confiscating the remaining hundred copies. The agents' ire was aroused by two editorials that seemed to them to be clearly disloyal. One called for a confiscatory tax on all war profits so that there would be no economic incentive to go to war. The second editorial was destined to become the most quoted example of "Negro radicalism" during the Red Scare, which burst forth shortly after the Armistice. This piece, "Pro-Germanism among Negroes," discussed widespread fears among whites that enemy agents were subverting African Americans. Many blacks were undoubtedly disaffected, wrote Owen and Randolph, but on account of "peonage, disfranchisement, Jim-Crowism, segregation, rank civil discrimination, injustice of legislatures, courts and administrators." No wonder blacks were cynical about a "war to make the world safe for democracy" while they did not enjoy "economic, political, educational and civil democracy" at home. What was worse, the editors asked with sarcasm, "being burnt by Tennessee, Georgia or Texas mobs or being shot by Germans in Belgium. We don't know about this pro-Germanism among Negroes. It may be only their anti-Americanism—meaning anti-lynching." Were these words meant to be taken literally? Two years later, the editors told a white journalist, "with the characteristic stupidity of the Department of Justice, they did not understand that the article was satirical and sarcastic."[37]

Randolph, Owen, and two white socialists were arrested under Section 3, Title I, of the Espionage Act, which permitted a sentence of up to twenty years in prison for anyone convicted of inciting disloyalty, obstructing enlistment, or interfering with the efficiency of military forces. Neither of the young editors was able to raise the $1,000 bail set by the judge and they remained in custody until one of the Socialist Party's ace attorneys arrived from Chicago to represent them. Brought before a judge, they escaped trial through an ironic expression of racism. He refused to believe that the two twenty-nine-year-old "boys" were intelligent enough to have written such articulate, if inflammatory, editorials, and was convinced others must have used their names so as to conceal their own nefarious deeds. "Showing both judicial and racial paternalism, the judge dismissed the charges and, so he thought, sent the two home to their parents." Disregarding these instructions, the new celebrities in the antiwar movement caught a train for Chicago and their next speaking engagements. Large street meetings in other cities followed, with Bureau agents invariably watching them and recording their words. But with charges having been dropped in Cleveland, they could do little more than harass Randolph and Owen and warn them against criticizing the president and the war. Not intimidated, the pair proceeded to do precisely that, in Washington, D.C.[38]

What the Justice Department could not do, the Post Office Department was able to accomplish. Condemning "Pro-Germanism among Negroes," which appeared in the July 1918 issue, it revoked the magazine's second-class mailing permit, thus requiring it to pay much higher first-class rates. This punishment—a significant restriction on press freedom imposed without trial or jury that vastly increased the cost of publishing—would remain in force until 1921. Not surprisingly, the next issue of the *Messenger* did not appear until March 1919. In the meantime, Owen was drafted, and it is conceivable that his local board was "encouraged" by the Justice Department to induct him so as to silence his voice. But Randolph continued to speak out; he could not be muzzled like Owen because he was deferred on account of being married and supporting a wife. Bureau stenographers were commonplace at radical meetings, so Randolph's political activities remained under surveillance throughout the remainder of the war and, indeed, into the 1920s. On election eve in November 1918, shortly before the Armistice, New York socialists held simultaneous campaign rallies at four locations in the city, with fifteen speakers shuttled from one gathering to another. At one of the meetings in Brooklyn, a shorthand stenographer accompanied by city police recorded state assembly candidate Randolph's last-minute pitch for votes. The next day he polled 8 percent of the thirteen thousand ballots cast. Chandler Owen, unable to campaign because he was in the army, garnered only half as many votes in a neighboring district. But this poor showing was hardly comforting to the Bureau. Two days later, New York agent R. W. Finch predicted, "more agitation among the negroes by the Socialists may be looked for, as the Socialist Party considers this the psychological moment to strongly agitate among all classes." That was not all. Equally worrisome was a growing movement to secure black representation at the upcoming peace negotiations in Paris. A mass meeting in New York on 1 December selected Randolph, crusading journalist Ida B. Wells-Barnett, and a Haitian merchant and Pan-Africanist resident of New York, Elizer Cadet, to go to France to demand black participation in postwar settlements. None of the three actually embarked for Europe, but the Bureau nonetheless took this as a serious threat.[39]

Indeed, as Agent Finch had predicted, "more agitation" was forthcoming. The *Messenger* reappeared in March 1919 as bold and iconoclastic as ever and, in the view of the Military Intelligence Division, "frankly revolutionary." As the Red Scare unfolded in the following months, the magazine and its editors became the federal government's primary black target. The attorney general called A. Philip Randolph the "most dangerous negro in America," and labeled the *Messenger* "the most dangerous of all the negro publications." Strenuous efforts were made to suppress the magazine by prosecuting its editors, but even after Bureau agents conducted numerous investigations, federal attorneys could not find clear violations of the Sedition Act on which to build a successful case. Supple juries during the war would undoubtedly have found the magazine's editors guilty, but by 1919 public distaste for the excesses of wartime prosecution made it impossible, at least in New York, to convict editors on their flamboyant rhetoric alone, absent evidence beyond the printed page. This did not mean, however, that surveillance and harassment by the Bureau, MID, and the Post Office and State Departments would cease. As Randolph recalled many decades later, "I felt the force of the law and the force of public opinion . . . and I had no peace anywhere."[40] Chandler Owen dropped out of politics in the mid-1920s, but Randolph dedicated himself to labor and civil rights causes for the rest of his life. The Bureau, renamed the Federal Bureau of Investigation in 1935, kept a file on him for just as long.

One did not have to be in the public eye to run afoul of federal zealots who objected to expressions of black militancy coupled with dissent against the war. Preachers and publishers were likely to attract attention if they openly condemned the government or the racial status quo. But ordinary citizens could just as readily arouse suspicion and trigger federal investigations if a neighbor, employer, or coworker objected to one's views. Such was the fate of Mattie Macon, a chambermaid at the Hotel Morse in San Diego in mid-1918. Although she denied opposition to the war when summoned before a U.S. commissioner, a number of witnesses gave explicit testimony that she was indeed disillusioned by her nation's crusade abroad, now more than a year after America entered the war. If the recollections of coworkers and hotel residents were accurate, there is no doubt that Mattie Macon found the Wilson administration's defense of freedom and self-determination in Europe ironic if not cynical, given the denial of those rights to blacks in America. Although the fear of enemy subversion along the Mexican border had subsided since the early months of the war, the government was by then more fully prepared, with the passage of the Sedition Act in May 1918, to crack down on dissent.

Mattie Macon left no uncertainty about her personal identity and sense of history, expressing pride in the fact she was half Cherokee Indian and thus a more "full-blooded" American than most whites. She married Alec Macon, a Spanish-American War veteran, in 1906 and shared his anger over his alleged mistreatment by the army. The couple moved to San Diego in 1911 and by the time war came lived across the street from the police station. Her troubles began when a coworker took offense at her views and reported her to the police.[41]

In July 1918 the chief of police alerted the Bureau of Investigation that Macon was making "pro-German" remarks. San Diego's agents were extremely busy covering the entire Mexican border area as far east as Arizona, a region alive with rumors of enemy spies and agents, so it utilized its American Protective League civilian volunteers to conduct many initial investigations. Their reports usually did not identify them by name. "Operative 12" interviewed Edna Mills and Margaret Davis, the manager and housekeeper of the Hotel Morse, who had engaged in a heated discussion with Mattie Macon earlier in the month during which she allegedly criticized the government and said, "To Hell with President Wilson." She claimed he was an inept leader, but that hardly mattered as she did not care who won anyway. She also said blacks could not be treated any worse whether they were governed by white Americans or Germans. Perhaps to bait her listeners, she added that white American soldiers were "crazy" about marrying black women.[42]

This report convinced federal authorities that prosecution was warranted, and a more detailed investigation began. Davis and Mills repeated their statements while supplying a few new details, such as Macon's assertions that she wished she were a German and that the government was run on graft so that anyone with sufficient money could buy an army commission. Mills added that she finally fired Macon for so persistently favoring Germany and talking against the war. Davis regarded Macon as dangerous and expressed fear of her. The two women also supplied the names of others who could testify to similar unsettling conversations. With this evidence in hand, Agent W. H. Buck had no difficulty persuading U.S. Commissioner C. E. Burch to swear out a complaint against Macon for violation of Section 3 of the Espionage Act.[43]

A preliminary hearing was held on 3 September 1918. The government's witnesses testified first and then were cross-examined by Mattie Macon's attorney. Edna Mills repeated her accusations, remembering also that Macon had said on numerous occasions that American soldiers were bums and looked like slobs. Macon's attorney sought to impeach Mills by eliciting her admission that she did not fire the black chambermaid until after Macon reported Mills to military authorities for selling liquor to soldiers. Mills was followed on the stand by her grandmother, a resident of the Morse, who related how every morning, when Macon arrived for work, she would inquire about the progress of the war. If it seemed that Germany was faring badly, Macon would be unhappy for the rest of the day. Next to appear for the prosecution was a neighbor, Annie McLendon, who related a back-fence conversation in which Macon said she was glad her husband had not been drafted because he was so poorly treated by the army during the Spanish-American War. Macon's lawyer tried to impugn McLendon's motives by revealing that Macon had reported her to authorities for allegedly mistreating her son. Then

Margaret Davis reprised her earlier testimony but this time qualified her statements, saying she did not think Macon's views were likely to cause others to distrust the government.

Mattie Macon's witnesses painted a much different picture. Two neighbors, Oma Colley and a Mrs. Carlson, said they saw Macon nearly every day and had never heard her make any disloyal statements or criticize the president or government. Alec Macon said the same, adding that when he learned his wife was arrested for talking against the government he thought it was a joke. Mattie Macon was the last to testify, depicting herself as a loyal American, a purchaser of Liberty Bonds, who had spoken no unpatriotic words. Where did the truth lie? Only Macon herself contradicted the explicit, damning evidence of those at the Hotel Morse, but the testimony of neighbors raised the possibility of her innocence. Weighing the evidence, Commissioner Burch bound Macon over for the grand jury, setting bond at $500.[44]

At this point the paper trail vanishes. Newsmen covering the courthouse beat focused instead on a prominent banker accused of embezzlement, a man whose preliminary hearing occurred the same day as Macon's case was heard. San Diegans themselves were eager for news of the World Series and developments on the western front. Whatever transpired next is unknown, for grand jury and commissioner's records disappeared sometime in the next seven decades.[45] If Macon's case ever reached the grand jury, it probably refused to indict her, as there is no evidence at all of a trial. Mattie Macon, it seems, remained free, but she was undoubtedly chastened. Was she a victim of her own indiscretion? Perhaps. But she was also a casualty of the intemperance of the times. Were the charges levied by her employer, coworker, and neighbor simply spiteful fabrications, or did Macon actually disparage the president and government and perceive no personal stake in the war, as did many other African Americans? Anyone voicing dissent in the presence of others who felt more conventional patriotism was inviting at least a hostile response and the likely possibility of being reported, arrested, and prosecuted under the vague guidelines of the Espionage and Sedition Acts. Dissidents elsewhere were convicted and sentenced to prison terms for saying nothing more offensive than the statements attributed to Macon. She was one of the lucky ones, serving no jail time and paying only the cost of legal representation. Others were not so fortunate.

The wartime files of the Bureau of Investigation contain tens of thousands of cases of alleged disloyalty. Thousands of pages detail suspicions of unpatriotic activities or attitudes by blacks, and fears that Germans or their surrogates were sowing seeds of subversion among the race. Only a few of these inquiries unearthed evidence sufficient to warrant prosecution. Lacking statutory authority for summarily suppressing alleged enemies, Bureau agents, U.S. attorneys, and federal marshals frequently used the coercion of their badges, offices, and uniforms to intimidate or frighten suspects into silence or, even better, expressions of patriotism. They also frequently cooperated with state and local authorities who wielded antisedition and antianarchy laws plus nuisance legislation like vagrancy statutes or restrictions on labor agents. Particularly in the South, "racial justice" at the local level was a powerful weapon against any perception of black militancy, especially when armed with evidence and assistance from federal agents. But no one was policing the police.

It was because of insufficient safeguards against unrestrained executive power that the National Civil Liberties Bureau (later the American Civil Liberties Union) was born in June 1917.[46] The shortcomings of the Bureau of Investigation, many of whose personnel were incapable of impartially understanding the motives of a Bishop Mason or an editor like G. W. Bouldin, made such a watchdog necessary. Freedoms of speech, the press, and religious expression exist in delicate balance during times of national ferment, and for that reason a democracy must demand more scrupulous governmental protection of lawful expression by unpopular individuals and groups than existed during World War I.

8

"Spreading enemy propaganda": Alien Enemies, Spies, and Subversives

The patriotic passions of World War I created numerous victims. Some suffered for shorter periods, like those caught up in slacker dragnets. Religious sectarians experienced more prolonged persecutions. Anyone daring to voice disapproval of the government's policies or seeming to support the enemy risked prosecution. Some contributed to their plight by indiscretion while others endangered themselves because of the dictates of conscience. The temper of the courts and the times made few distinctions between intent and result. Local juries, months before the Supreme Court reaffirmed the doctrine in the *Abrams* case, followed judges' instructions and convicted suspects for the "bad tendency" alone of their speech, needing no proof that any harm had actually occurred. Among those who ran afoul of public opinion and the law were a number of whites charged with influencing African Americans to acts of disloyalty. Some were accused outright of being German agents or spies. Others simply voiced unpopular views under circumstances where, it was feared, blacks might be influenced by such words.

The fact that whites mingled with blacks and blacks with whites all across American society in the second decade of the twentieth century, and especially so in the South, may seem inexplicable in light of common assumptions about the nature of segregation. Even in deeply racist states like Mississippi, the color line was never so rigid as to prevent interracial contact. White males crossed sexual lines with impunity, and a small number of black males established intimate relationships with white women. But especially in daily life activities, the races were not and could not be separated. Both races came together in numerous places of business. White peddlers hardly shunned potential black customers. Employer-employee relationships were not infrequently personal as well as economic, in domestic service, agriculture, and other pursuits. Faith occasionally brought the races together, as in the early Church of God in Christ and the Jehovah's Witnesses. Many whites professed deep attachments to individual black families whose lives had been intertwined with theirs for generations. Some hunted and fished with longtime black companions. Segregation was intended to discipline both races, to remind them of their separate social categories and spheres, but it was never intended to isolate one race from another in all aspects of life. Such an endeavor would have been impossible to achieve. So while blacks experienced the indignities and degradations of segregation, their lives were also shaped by interracial contact.[1] The same was true for whites. However, when World War I generated new fears that unscrupulous whites might agitate the black population to acts of disloyalty, white-black contacts were viewed with unaccustomed alarm, in both the North and the South. Such was the case of a white man who called himself "Dr. Mea."

Federal authorities never learned Dr. Mea's Christian name, nor do court papers reveal his occupation. His alleged crime was disparaging the value of Liberty Bonds within earshot of a number of blacks lounging around a drug store in Marshall, in east Texas's Harrison County. African Americans made up nearly two-thirds of the population in that Black Belt county on the Louisiana border, and the possibility of their being infected by an unpatriotic virus was not ignored by anxious whites. Mea was engaged in conversation with another white patron, offering the opinion that the lack of rain and impending ruin of crops was understandable, since America could not expect the blessings of nature while it manufactured weapons of war used for the "wholesale butchery" of innocent women and children. He then remarked that the government would soon float another $3 billion issue of Liberty Bonds which "would not be worth twenty five cents on the hundred dollars" after the end of the war.

That conversation on 2 August 1918 began Dr. Mea's troubles. Word of the incident reached federal authorities, who arrested Mea seven days later for violating the Espionage and Sedition Acts, which made unlawful the willful and intentional obstruction of war bond sales. On Monday, 12 August, Mea was brought before U.S. Commissioner W. E. Singleton Jr. in nearby Jefferson, Texas. Singleton was simultaneously involved in the case against black Jehovah's Witness Dan McNairy. The commissioner held a "preliminary trial" during which two white witnesses repeated Mea's statement and verified that it was overheard by a group of blacks. Singleton bound Mea over for the next term of the district court, which was not to convene until October, and ordered $5,000 bail, which Mea was not able to raise, resulting in his being lodged in the Marion County jail.

Dr. Mea was eventually able to make bail but was again arrested on 8 October 1918 when a grand jury handed down indictments under the May 1918 Sedition Act charging him with obstructing the sale of government securities, favoring the cause of Germany, and opposing America's conduct of the war. All three charges were based simply on his statement that Liberty Bonds would be worthless once the war ended. The next day, U.S. Attorney Clarence Merrill, who had just won the conviction of Dan McNairy, prosecuted the case. The jury took little time in finding Mea guilty. Perhaps because he had already spent considerable time behind bars, Judge Gordon Russell sentenced him to thirty more days in the Marion County lockup, much less than the four months he gave McNairy. Racial bias may explain the difference since Bureau of Investigation agents damned McNairy as a dangerous influence among members of his race. In any case, Mea was fortunate to receive such a light sentence. Whites in east Texas remained apprehensive throughout the war that enemies were subverting the black population, evidence of which seemed to be the considerable number of black draft delinquents (including members of the Church of God in Christ) as well as the exodus of sharecroppers to the urban North. Mea could easily have gotten much rougher treatment.[2]

German citizens and subjects of the Austro-Hungarian Empire who resided in the United States were classified as "alien enemies" during World War I. Those from Bulgaria and Turkey were defined as "allied with the enemy" but were subject to the same suspicions and restrictions. Only a handful of resident aliens engaged in acts of subversion, but wartime hysteria made no distinction between overt hostile actions and the expression of views contrary to patriotic orthodoxy. Most of those who became targets of federal investigation and prosecution were guilty simply of expression deemed impermissible by the patriotic majority. Most dissident speech that was punished during World War I was so innocuous that it would have been unremarked during the Vietnam War. But the First Amendment was not the protector of political speech in 1918 that it was fifty years later. A case in point is that of an obscure Austrian-born insurance collector in New York City.

Max Freudenheim's real crime was nationalistic indiscretion. Affection for his homeland and dislike for American participation in the war found expression in conversations with urban blacks who bought small "industrial" insurance policies that provided minimal sickness and death benefits for as little as a nickel a week. The Secret Service was the first federal agency to learn of Freudenheim's views and knew that this was a matter for the Bureau of Investigation. Still smarting over exclusion from domestic counterintelligence, however, the Secret Service instead sent this information to the State Department, which earlier in the war had functioned as a clearinghouse for such cases. This petty snub only delayed action. Bureau agents in New York eventually received the report and arrested Freudenheim on 5 April 1918 for allegedly telling blacks they were fools to fight for a vain cause when the German people were better friends than white Americans. Agent D. Davidson, who spearheaded the case, found Freudenheim defiantly claiming that someone was trying to frame him, asking "what the word of a G--D--- nigger was good for along side of his." Davidson replied that "the Government would not tolerate any such remarks" and jailed Freudenheim overnight, telling him to think things over before the next interrogation. The only details he would reveal concerned his birth in Austria forty-three years earlier, arrival in New York in 1899, and the admission to having abandoned his wife and three children in 1915. Although he had resided in the United States for eighteen years, he had not applied for citizenship.[3]

New York agents proceeded to build their case the next day, while also apprising military intelligence of their investigation. Freudenheim's office at the Equitable Accident Company yielded the names of other policyholders to add to the list of witnesses. Further interrogation of the suspect was unfruitful and he remained in the Second Precinct jail for the weekend. Agents kindly gave him two dollars for meals. The next week, a parade of policyholders came to Bureau headquarters to give sworn statements that, by Monday afternoon, were sufficient to secure a presidential warrant for Freudenheim's arrest on charges of "spreading German propaganda." As a result he was transferred to the Essex County Prison across the Hudson River in Newark.

Meanwhile, Agent Davidson continued interviewing witnesses in Harlem. Forty-nine-year-old Isabella Holmes related how Freudenheim often discussed the war, confident that Germany would win but also warning that captured black soldiers would have their ears cut off and eyes gouged out, the same fate as the Congolese who suffered the displeasure of Belgium's King Leopold. Davidson also learned that Freudenheim had a habit of ridiculing black soldiers who were home on furlough and had barely avoided a beating for such effrontery. Freudenheim's wife confirmed that he had abandoned his family, leaving them destitute, and added that he had beaten her unmercifully. Davidson concluded that she was loyal and had no knowledge of her husband's alleged sedition. The suspect's mother similarly had no incriminating information. A search of his rooms—apparently without a warrant—proved uneventful, leading the Bureau to conclude that he was not spreading printed propaganda but only verbalizing his opposition.[4]

Bureau agents, like the public, were quick to believe in the existence of a German spy hierarchy in the United States that was allegedly directing individuals like Freudenheim in their disloyalty. In fact, a German spy and sabotage cell had operated before American entry into the war out of the rented brownstone of Frau Martha Held on West Fifteenth Street in New York, concentrating its efforts on halting the supply of weapons to the Allies. Its most spectacular success was the gigantic explosion in mid-1916 that destroyed the Black Tom railroad-marine terminal on the New Jersey side of the Hudson River, where ships destined for Europe were loaded with munitions. After the country entered the war, most members of this group fled to Mexico.[5]

Freudenheim almost certainly had no connection with this group. Not surprisingly, even after a week of interviews, interrogations, and searches, Agent Davidson concluded that Freudenheim was working alone, and thus simply urged his internment as a dangerous alien. But with persistent rumors of enemies sowing discontentment among African Americans and evidence that Freudenheim had spoken seditiously to at least fifteen persons, Davidson's colleagues deemed internment insufficient. An example needed to be set, and the New York office recommended prosecution for his "most contemptible kind of German propaganda." The government needed to act promptly, though, because some witnesses had already moved and could not be found.[6]

Nonetheless, the wheels of justice turned slowly after New York agents completed their investigation in mid-April. After languishing in jail for two months, Freudenheim petitioned the State Department to intervene on his behalf. Quoting from the attorney general's instructions on enforcement of the enemy alien statutes, he stressed the government's responsibility to avoid curbing legitimate criticism of the government or its policies. Claiming ill health and the ruin of his livelihood, Freudenheim alleged that his case was the product of "malicious personal elements of a private feud."[7] This plea did not, however, prevent a federal grand jury from indicting him on 28 June 1918 for "attempting to cause insubordination, disloyalty, mutiny and refusal of duty in the military forces," actions punishable under Section 3, Title I of the Espionage Act. A three-day trial conducted by Judge Learned Hand resulted in a guilty verdict on 24 July, even though most of the counts in the indictment were not proven to the jury's satisfaction.

Max Freudenheim was prosecuted by U.S. Attorney Francis G. Caffey, who after the war would be a voice of reason in the midst of a Justice Department campaign to suppress the *Messenger* and the *Crisis.*[8] One of his charges accused Freudenheim of uttering disloyal statements so as to discourage black men of military age from complying with the draft. Germany would win the war, he had told two black soldiers, and punish them by severing their limbs and ears and digging their eyes out. He allegedly added that if they would fight for Germany they would gain their rightful privileges. Freudenheim was found not guilty on this part of the indictment. Other counts charged him with telling black civilians that Germany would not sink troopships because it had contempt for the fighting mettle of American soldiers; that German submarines *would* attack all troop transports; that Germany possessed a gun so powerful that it could enter New York harbor and fire at the entire United States; that the Kaiser's army would smother American soldiers in the trenches of France like so many rats; that Germans liked the Negro race and would reward it with its own separate states or a kingdom after the war; and that blacks were fools to fight for "their" country. Freudenheim was similarly found not guilty on all these charges.

In the end, Freudenheim was convicted on only one count. The key prosecution witness was Ralph Calderon, who testified that the Austrian had told him that American troops were on a futile mission in France, with black soldiers having nothing for which to fight. The defendant was also reported as saying that Germany would allow troop transports safe passage to Europe but would then sink all provision ships so as to starve the Allied fighting machine. To make this incident punishable under the Espionage Act jurors had to believe that Freudenheim intended his statements to influence men liable for the draft. The case went to the jury on the third day of the trial. After only an hour and a half of deliberation, the panel told the judge that it was deadlocked with one holdout. Judge Hand, who during the war was one of the rare exceptions on the federal bench in believing that the protection of dissent served the social interest by preserving First Amendment rights, nonetheless ordered it to continue deliberations: "I should not think there would be any great difficulty in finding a verdict" unless it would "disregard the testimony of a number of people in the case, intelligently given." Despite the unsupported testimony of witness Calderon, Freudenheim was declared guilty on that single count and sentenced the next day to seven years in the penitentiary.[9]

Freudenheim's attorney filed a writ of error and succeeded in lowering his bail from $20,000 to $12,000, a sum still too large to permit him to post bond. Details in that writ support the conclusion that Freudenheim was convicted as a result of wartime passions. The sole charge that the jury found of merit was supported by the word of only one witness, although legally only one witness was necessary for conviction. In addition, argued Freudenheim's attorney, the government had not proved that his words were spoken "willingly, knowingly, and feloniously, for the purpose of and in an attempt to cause insubordination, disloyalty, mutiny and refusal of duty in the military forces." Furthermore, no testimony established that Freudenheim's words had actually impaired recruitment or enlistment. But Judge Hand, reflecting the existing understanding of the law, instructed the jury that if it believed Freudenheim had made the statements attributed to him it should find him guilty without probing whether there was disloyal purpose or intent. The circuit court of appeals affirmed his judgment.[10]

Max Freudenheim began serving his seven-year term at the Maryland State Penitentiary later in 1918. Existing sources do not reveal how long he remained incarcerated, perhaps for the entirety of the sentence. But it is also possible that, like other casualties of federal zealousness during the war, his sentence was shortened in the early 1920s. Others were similarly released early on the condition that they accept deportation. Long-term Sedition Act prisoners generally had to wait for presidential commutations.[11] Certainly the Austrian was guilty of indiscretion and a lack of appreciation for the country that had welcomed him and offered him a livelihood for nearly nineteen years. But his case reflects the operation of law, as it was then understood, not the First Amendment protections that later generations would enjoy. No evidence showed his words to have impaired the military effectiveness of the nation, but contemporary legal doctrine did not require such evidence. Max Freudenheim was in that sense the author of his own fate: His indiscreet conversations, expressing unpopular political views, were sufficient criteria for conviction and imprisonment. The fact that his intent appeared to be to undermine blacks' loyalty only guaranteed that he would pay the penalty.

Not all disloyalty suspects fared equally. Another enemy alien escaped prosecution although the offenses of which he was accused were more serious than those attributed to Freudenheim. The United States did not declare war on Bulgaria, but its citizens were considered enemy aliens because Bulgaria was allied with Germany and the Central Powers. How and why George Angeloff got to Natchitoches, Louisiana, is unknown, but he was in serious trouble there in the spring of 1918. Reports surfaced that he told a black farmer, Dave Hicks, that if he was drafted he would never return alive from Europe. In another conversation, this one with Pvt. Whit Patterson, home on leave from Camp Pike, Arkansas, Angeloff was said to have advised him how to reach the German lines and be taken prisoner rather than being shot. If true, both statements were violations of the Espionage Act, which prohibited interference with the draft or encouraging soldiers to mutiny or disloyalty. It was also rumored that Angeloff had a "following" among neighborhood blacks, which, if true, would make the white minority in the parish feel even more threatened.

The Natchitoches sheriff, fearing that local whites would form a lynch mob if these accusations became general knowledge, quickly arrested the suspect and notified the Bureau of Investigation. Angeloff just as quickly wrote to the Bulgarian legation in Washington for help, but the sheriff refused to mail the letter and instead gave it to Bureau agent J. B. Matthews. A volunteer post office linguist in Washington translated the letter, which proclaimed the accused's innocence: Angeloff professed not to know why he was arrested and asked the legation to secure bail so that he could get a quick trial and resume farming. Angeloff's plea eventually did reach his countrymen in Washington, who made a perfunctory inquiry to the Department of State. Informed by the Justice Department that it had a "strong case" against Angeloff, the State Department advised the Bulgarian legation of that "fact," leading it to wash its hands of the matter. What could it do, after all, for an obscure farmer living fifteen hundred miles away?[12]

By the time the translation was returned to Agent Matthews, Angeloff had been in jail for nearly two weeks, even though he had hired a lawyer. But Matthews and the U.S. attorney were a step ahead of him, having persuaded a U.S. commissioner to authorize a federal arrest warrant, preventing his release by a state circuit judge. If a conviction was to be gained, however, the testimony of Whit Patterson, now back at Camp Pike, was crucial. This brought army intelligence into the case, which agreed to let Bureau agent C. M. Walser, based in Little Rock, take a deposition from the soldier. Patterson was not the most forthcoming witness, but he eventually revealed that Angeloff had met with a number of blacks, asking them how whites treated them and telling them they could escape their draft liability. But that was not all. Patterson remembered Angeloff also encouraging him and other draftees to flee to Mexico, where they would then be taken to Germany to work. More incredibly, the Bulgarian was alleged to have said that blacks could kidnap white women, ravish them, and keep them as their wives. How much of this tale Patterson made up on the spot is unclear, but his signed statement reveals that Agent Walser asked many leading questions, giving the soldier ample opportunity to supply "correct" answers. Meanwhile, Matthews interviewed others in Natchitoches who knew the Bulgarian. Owen Bouie was himself in jail, which may have motivated him to accuse Angeloff of saying that blacks had no reason to fight. But Angeloff's cook and a neighbor, both black, claimed never to have heard him talk about the war. Although Matthews believed they were covering up for him, the neighbor turned over Angeloff's mail which, when translated, proved to be innocuous.[13]

Patterson's damning allegations pushed federal alarm buttons. The chief of military intelligence, Col. Marlborough Churchill, in a letter written by Maj. Joel Spingarn, head of the "negro subversion" unit, directed the intelligence staff of the army's Southeastern Department to investigate all reports of "disloyal propaganda" among blacks. Bureau agent Matthews and the federal attorney in Shreveport, convinced that Angeloff was virtually a spy whose white friends were either Bulgarians or Germans, pleaded for a special grand jury to expedite prosecution, especially since Angeloff had by then made bail.[14]

But the case almost immediately began to unravel. Matthews and the Natchitoches sheriff rounded up several new black witnesses. Five of them denied even talking with Angeloff. Another would only say that Whit Patterson had told him that Angeloff was a German spy. Two more could not be found. In the end, only a pair of witnesses would admit to having simply overheard a conversation about the war, and implicated Whit Patterson as much as Angeloff. Patterson was the key to prosecution, and military intelligence had taken steps, it thought, to keep him available for a trial. But on 10 July 1918 his unit, the 526th Engineers, set sail for France. Churchill assured Bureau chief A. Bruce Bielaski that the army was still interested in the case and wanted to cooperate. However, after examining copies of the Bureau's reports, military attorneys probably concluded the case was weak and hence not worth the trouble of bringing Patterson back. A search of the federal court dockets reveals no record of a trial and it is likely that Angeloff suffered no punishment other than spending nearly all of June in custody before making bail.[15]

Presuming that local authorities permitted a properly repentant Angeloff to return to his farm, he got off lightly. As questionable as was Whit Patterson's testimony, Angeloff could nonetheless have easily suffered the same fate as Max Freudenheim. The federal government prosecuted more than two thousand Espionage and Sedition Act cases during World War I, gaining numerous convictions from equally flimsy evidence. Whatever his purpose—and federal authorities never established a motive—George Angeloff paid cheaply for whatever indiscretions he actually committed. It is doubtful that he said all the things of which various individuals accused him, but he said enough to trigger a serious federal response. Given the xenophobic passions of the day, and the well-publicized internment of alleged German spies, Angeloff should have known enough to keep his mouth shut.

Native-born whites also were sometimes indiscreet in expressing opposition to the war. If they attempted to persuade African Americans of such views, they could expect no more tolerance from patriotic whites or law enforcement officials than could enemy aliens. Dr. Mea, whose nationality was unrecorded by the Bureau of Investigation, met such a fate. So, too, did Ernest B. Young. While his intent cannot fully be explained, his heedless imprudence is manifest.

As was often the case when the Bureau began investigating suspected subversion, the initial tip came from a civilian, in this case the manager of the Pacolet Mills in the hamlet by that name located twelve miles southeast of Spartanburg, South Carolina. Race relations were hardly placid in that region during the war. In the fall of 1917, when a regiment of black troops from New York was sent to Spartanburg's Camp Wadsworth for training, it had to be hastily removed twelve days later when the army feared another outbreak of violence like that which had occurred in Houston just a few months before. Local whites abused the doughboys, whom they regarded as "uppity" blacks from the North, and in fact the troops were in no mood to tolerate overt southern-style racism.[16] In the spring of 1918, the mill's manager, a Mr. Westmoreland, reported rumors that a German was spreading disloyalty with such effectiveness that a number of blacks believed that victorious Germans would grant them social equality, reduce high rents, and divide land equally between the races. Bureau agent Vincent W. Hughes was sent from Greenville to investigate.[17]

Initial inquiries did not exactly clarify matters. Hughes learned that two men were involved: a registered enemy alien named Charles H. Moore, and Young, a white sharecropper originally from New York. Hughes found most of the black witnesses cooperative. One of them alleged that Moore and Young possessed arms as well as papers relating to the war. But another black, a preacher named Mose

Johnson, denied knowing the suspects even though his employer accused him of holding secret "prayer meetings" inspired by German propaganda. After only one day's investigation Hughes believed he had sufficient evidence on which to obtain search and arrest warrants against the two suspects for violating the Espionage Act, even though there was no evidence of Young or Moore persuading anyone to resist conscription, commit disloyalty, or aid the enemy. But federal commissioners did not always require such evidence in issuing warrants and initiating judicial proceedings during the war. Testimony of allegedly subversive speech was usually sufficient. Consequently, Young was arrested and Moore detained, although Hughes was certain that only Young was actively involved in spreading "German propaganda."[18]

Agent Hughes was typical of many of his colleagues in recording in detail how he investigated cases and suspects. Leaving his office in Greenville, he took a Southern Railway express thirty-one miles up the main line to Spartanburg, then transferred to a train on the Charleston line that took him fourteen miles to Pacolet, where he met mill manager Westmoreland, who arranged for witnesses to be present at his office. How Hughes conducted himself with black informants can be inferred from the frequent use of the word "nigger" in his written reports and his admission that he interrogated one man, Jim Porter, for an hour until he changed his story and "admitted" to having spoken to a white man, although not Young or Moore. According to Porter, this man declared that blacks had no reason to fight because the Germans did not wish to kill them and in fact were sparing their lives in France. If blacks refused to join the army, Germany would win the war in Europe and then cross the Atlantic and defeat the United States. The victor would apportion land to everyone according to family size and require blacks to pay only one-tenth of their crops as rent instead of the customary third or half demanded of sharecroppers by crop lien holders. This unnamed white man was alleged to have called this "king rule." When asked how blacks could avoid a summons to military service, the man supposedly said that they should "all get together and just *refuse to go, and rebel.* They can't make you go." Porter finished by telling of hearing many blacks say they would prefer "king rule" to what now prevailed. Not surprisingly, Agent Hughes believed Porter was untruthful in denying that the white man was either Young or Moore.

Seeking more witnesses, Hughes hired a car and drove across open fields, finally walking a mile farther to locate Lester Wyatt. He and Young had conversed about sharecropping, both lamenting having to pay a third of their crops to landlords. So confident was Young of German victory, according to Wyatt, that he was certain he would only have to pay a tenth under "king rule" by harvest time. Since Wyatt was a compliant witness, Hughes took him back to Pacolet to await transportation to Spartanburg, where a preliminary hearing could take place. Two other witnesses were also assembled. Hughes then picked up Deputy U.S. Marshal Adams, who arrived on the afternoon train. His presence was necessary because Bureau agents did not possess formal arrest authority. Hughes and Adams found the two suspects at the cabin they shared. They arrested Young and insisted that

Moore accompany them because he was an enemy alien. Moore's wife chastised him for letting "that dirty white man . . . get them in trouble" and Moore himself echoed the criticism of Young. Moore also laughingly denied violating the Espionage Act or interfering with the draft. Searching the cabin, apparently without a warrant, Hughes found hundreds of undeveloped photographs and carelessly exposed them to the light, ruining any evidentiary value they might have. Young's suitcase was found to contain a number of photo postcards of Camp Wadsworth taken by a professional photographer, several pictures of a large military gun, and a bottle of developing fluid. But the only camera found was a small, broken No. 2 Brownie, hardly the equipment of a spy. Only one weapon was discovered, a .32-caliber revolver, which was left with Moore's wife.

Because the next train out of Pacolet did not leave until the dead of night, Hughes and Adams drove their prisoners directly to Spartanburg. Westmoreland, the helpful mill manger, had already delivered the three black witnesses to U.S. Commissioner Robert Gantt, who held a hearing that evening upon Young's arrival. After being identified by all three blacks, Young was bound over for federal court under $1,000 bond. Hughes immediately protested this figure, claiming Young had advised blacks to refuse military service and rebel, and Gantt obligingly raised it to $5,000. After depositing Young in the Spartanburg jail, Agent Hughes took Moore with him on the 8:30 P.M. train to Greenville, where he was incarcerated pending instructions from Bureau headquarters in Washington.[19]

Charles Moore was never prosecuted, but Ernest Young paid dearly for his beliefs and verbal indiscretions. Even the three black prosecution witnesses suffered the threat of federal punishment, each being forced to sign a recognizance in which they agreed that failure to testify would result in the attachment of $200 worth of their personal property—a sum that would have wiped out a sharecropper or mill worker. Why this was necessary is unclear, for they all seemed willing to appear in court. Ten days after his arrest Young was transferred to the county jail in Anderson, where the court of the Western District of South Carolina was in session. However, unlike defendants elsewhere, he did not languish long. A grand jury quickly indicted him for attempting to convince "negro citizens" that they had nothing to fight for and that a German victory would bring them land and social equality.[20]

Ernest Young's trial before Circuit Judge C. A. Woods lasted no longer than most other Espionage Act cases. He pleaded innocent on 3 June 1918, but by the end of the day he was found guilty and sentenced to serve a year and a day. On 5 June U.S. Marshal C. J. Lyons took his prisoner to the Charleston and Western Carolina Railroad depot in Anderson. They boarded a milk run for Calhoun Falls, thirty-four miles distant, where they caught a faster train on the Seaboard Air Line Railroad. Young was finally deposited in the federal penitentiary in Atlanta, a long way from his hometown of Fort Plain along the Erie Canal west of Albany, New York.[21]

Intriguing questions remain unanswered concerning the Young case. What impelled him to venture seven hundred miles to rural South Carolina, there to toil, as did numerous blacks and whites native to the region, as a sharecropper? What inspired his grievances against his country, or his preference for Germany? Why did he take such obvious risks in urging members of a race that was already under suspicion of disloyalty to resist conscription? Agent Hughes neither sought nor found evidence linking him to anyone who was actively pro-German. In fact, his only known "enemy alien" acquaintance, Charles Moore, turned against him and was ultimately exonerated by federal authorities. Perhaps Young was a farmer who left New York down on his luck, only to find another dead-end in South Carolina. If he was bitter over having to surrender a third of his crop to a landowner, he may have identified with similarly exploited blacks and urged their collective resistance when he found he could do little about his own circumstances. Possibly his New York roots allowed him to see through more understanding eyes those whom Hughes referred to as "niggers." In any case, Ernest Young was naive and indiscreet: as naive as others who mistook rural southern blacks' apathy to the war as a sign that they were ready for revolutionary action; and as indiscreet as those who took no heed in expressing their own antiwar sentiments. Whatever his motivations, whatever his sincerity, he was an easy target for federal authorities. Their investigation and his arrest and prosecution took no extraordinary effort. Given the superheated wartime passions and widespread fears in the South that enemy agents were subverting the black population, a guilty verdict was almost a foregone conclusion. Hard time in the pen was the price Young paid for his imprudence.

Civil liberties took a beating during World War I. Historian Paul L. Murphy writes that Americans, inspired to national sacrifice in the name of extending democracy throughout the world, "stood by on the domestic scene and saw liberty and justice prostituted in ways more extreme and extensive than at any other time in American history." Early-twentieth-century Progressivism empowered government with new authority for social control and the regulation of public policy. But now, "to assure patriotism and wartime victory, . . . a new policy of formal and prescriptive federal governmental action was adopted to repress individualism and diversity of opinion in order to secure the unwavering allegiance of immigrants, hyphenates, and a wide range of other Americans whose loyalty was in any way suspect." Some policies, like Americanism campaigns and Liberty Loan drives, stressed the positive. Others, like the Espionage and Sedition Acts, represented a federal assault on heterodoxy by criminalizing certain forms of belief, association, and expression. Victims of such repression were either unpopular or powerless, and sometimes both. They faced not only the expanded powers of government, but also an aroused public cheering on those who were blitzing slackers, tackling spies, and blocking saboteurs. Dissidents, whether native or foreign born, whether misguided or altruistic, found no tolerance for their views.[22] Most, including Dr. Mea, Max Freudenheim, George Angeloff, and Ernest Young, could have avoided trouble by keeping quiet or halting activities to which others took offense. In choosing not to do so, they ordained their fates.

9 "Perhaps you will be shot": Sex, Spies, Science, and the Moens Case

Cases against obscure "enemy aliens" like Max Freudenheim and George Angeloff drew no national headlines. But another individual who was suspected of subversive influence on the black population became the center of considerably greater controversy. No case was more spectacular, more convoluted, or more prolonged than that of Herman Marie Bernelot Moens.

When Moens arrived in the United States in 1914 bearing letters of introduction from the Netherlands minister of foreign affairs and the head of his country's legation in Washington, no one could have predicted the scandal that would embroil him with federal authorities for nearly a decade. These introductions described the forty-one-year-old bachelor as a distinguished professor of botany and zoology, although subsequent investigations proved he possessed no university degrees.[1] Prior to 1918 he supported himself as an "oil scout" for the Roxana Petroleum Company, a subsidiary of the Royal Dutch Shell corporation, gathering geologic information from government libraries and the U.S. Bureau of Mines. Yet his passion, both academically and lubriciously, was the study of race mixture through examination of the anatomies of young black women. His intent, he maintained, was to prove a single origin for all the races of mankind.

Moens's race equality theories and alleged scientific credentials opened doors into the world of the black elite. He first gained social acceptance in New York, where he met officers of the NAACP and the National Urban League. Dr. W. E. B. DuBois introduced him to Prof. Kelly Miller in Washington, where he was welcomed by black high society and was soon lecturing at churches and Howard University.[2] However, what first attracted the attention of the Bureau of Investigation and military intelligence were allegations that Moens was a German or Austrian spy. Eventually the State Department was drawn into the widening federal inquiry, by which time the interest of government agents was both professional and prurient. Science, sex, and alleged spying produced one of the most bizarre cases of wartime excess by the government, although Moens's own carnal behavior hardly makes him a martyr.

"Professor" Moens, as he was commonly known, claimed to have lucrative oil investments in Galicia but said that the war blocked access to this income. He therefore lived in Washington boardinghouses and apartments when not investigating potential oil sites in the western states. Given both the antialien sentiments of 1916 and the highly competitive nature of oil exploration and leases, Moens assured his employer, Roxana Petroleum, that "because of the confidential nature of my business and my being known in Washington, I shall live privately to avoid conjecture and questions of my acquaintances." He then added a statement that federal investigators would use to "prove" first that he was a spy and later that he was a pornographer and pervert: "For the same reason I shall remain interested in the race problems, especially 'the colored people' here. Prudence is necessary."[3]

By early 1917 the United States was poised for war, severing diplomatic relations with Germany in early February upon that nation's resumption of submarine warfare against unarmed merchant vessels. Exposure on March 1 of the Zimmermann note proposing an alliance between Germany and Mexico further unnerved a public that was already awash with fears of German spies operating everywhere. The nation's capital seemed a logical target for enemy intrigue. Anyone in Washington who "looked" German, spoke a Germanic language, or had such associations was likely to arouse the suspicions of "loyal" Americans.

Such a patriot was black attorney James Cobb, whose allegations stimulated the federal government's first probe of Moens. The record does not reveal whether Cobb had actually met Moens, or simply heard of him from other members of Washington's black elite, but in any case Cobb informed Bureau agent George W. Lillard that the "better class" of blacks was suspicious of Moens's comments on the indignities suffered by African Americans as well as his research, which included taking photographs of black schoolchildren and nude pictures of black women. (In fact, ethnographic photography, often nude, was a common methodology of physical anthropology in that era.) At Cobbs's suggestion, Lillard interviewed the principal and a teacher at Washington's Dunbar High School, one of the most prestigious black institutions in the country, but neither could name any students who had posed in the nude. Suspicions deepened, however, when Lillard discovered that Moens's landlady was a German and that the two often conversed in that language. All this seemed sufficiently dangerous to warrant assignment of a female informant to the case, a week before America entered the war.[4]

The precise identity of Miss M. Bagman and her motivations for undercover work remain a tantalizing mystery. When she went to Moens's boardinghouse to rent a room she saw him showing pictures of Indians to another woman. The landlady proved familiar with Moens's work, telling Bagman she could pay for part of her rent by posing for him since she appeared to have Indian ancestry. Bagman returned the next day and found him eager to describe his study of the different races in which he took X rays of certain subjects, photographed or made sketches of others, and used some as models for sculptures. Miss Bagman lived at the Massachusetts Avenue residence for the entire month of April, the Bureau paying all her expenses. While she found Moens unguarded in conversation about his scientific studies, the landlady, Mrs. Schwab, hovered over her male boarder and seemed intent on preventing Bagman from talking privately with him. Yet when the subject of German Americans' loyalties came up at breakfast, Moens reported hearing that they opposed their fatherland's militarism and were prepared to fight for the United States. Encouraged by her Bureau handlers to ingratiate herself with Moens, Bagman gained his promise to show her his photographs.[5]

Meanwhile, Bureau personnel in Washington probed more deeply into Moens's activities and sympathies, at a time when agents across the country were being deluged with citizens' suspicions of their neighbors, coworkers, or chance acquaintances. Such was the nature of the tips on Moens. The trail soon uncovered allegations that the professor was seen furtively studying maps with a woman thought to be bitterly anti-American. Another citizen complained that blacks visiting his rooms were being fed pro-German propaganda. Two federal employees who also boarded at Moens's address reported suspicions of both Mrs. Schwab and the professor, particularly his association with a scientific organization whose members all seemed to be Poles, Russians, and perhaps Germans. Moreover, when Moens placed an ad in the *Evening Star* seeking a young woman to assist in his study of the races, Schwab fielded the many callers. Agents also learned that when Moens attempted to affiliate with the Smithsonian Institution, officials there would not accept his unverified scientific credentials, although a staff photographer took many nude pictures for Moens's ethnographic studies. Finally, within the first month of war, the Bureau learned that black Washingtonians suspected Moens's research was a cover for spreading German propaganda, and that he was seen late at night entering the German embassy. Despite all these suspicions, however, no concrete evidence of spying or subversion was uncovered in the first weeks of investigation.[6]

Moens also had contacts with influential whites. One friend was Maj. Raymond W. Pullman, chief of the District of Columbia police force, who allowed Moens to accompany him into the "slums" and dance halls where blacks congregated so he could observe different "types" of blacks and persons of mixed racial background. The professor had also so impressed John Van Schaik, the president of Washington's Board of Education, that he allowed Moens to pursue his scientific studies in the District's black schools. Aware of rumors that Moens was a German spy, van Schaick wrote: "I personally know Mr. H. M. Bernelot Moens, that he is a Netherland [*sic*] citizen and deeply interested in scientific research, in particular in anthropology. I know of the accusation of him being a German spy only through Mr. Moen's [*sic*] own communication to that effect and have no reason whatsoever to believe that there is any foundation for this suspicion." The extent to which Moens abused this trust would only become apparent two years later.[7]

All that the Bureau knew in mid-1917 was summed up by wartime dollar-a-year agent H. Barrett Learned who was, coincidentally, a member of the District of Columbia school board. Putting the available pieces together, including information gained from Dutch diplomats who agreed to talk off the record so as to distance themselves should rumors of Moens's spying be proven, Learned concluded the following: Moens was an oil scout whose expenditures seemed to exceed his probable income from that source, the Netherlands legation knew him only slightly and indeed had its own suspicions, and evidence pointed to his being "pro-German." Learned was the first investigator to detail exactly why this foreign-born white man's activities within the black community were viewed with such concern: Moens "regards the negroes as an oppressed race—who should stand for their rights, such rights as are not acknowledged by the whites in the United States." This was the equation so often repeated during World War I: African-

American demands for racial equality were unacceptable even in peacetime and doubly illegitimate with the nation at peril. Promotion of such heresy by whites during wartime was an act of treason if done by natives, and subversion if the work of aliens. Advocacy of such misbegotten notions was ipso facto a "pro-German" act.[8]

By the middle of 1917, however, the Bureau's case against Moens flagged after it failed to uncover hard evidence of pro-Germanism. But at precisely that time the army's newly formed Military Intelligence Section (MIS) took interest in him and launched its own investigation. Having entered the war inexperienced in domestic counterespionage, army intelligence was forced to rely on at times unreliable civilian informants. Some of its initial data on Moens (and many allegations of disaffection among the African-American population) came from one of its most excited civilian sources, Hallie E. Queen, a black instructor at Howard University. She professed to have distrusted Moens from the beginning. Although she reported that he recruited young women to model for his sculptures, eventually resulting in an edict from the black high schools threatening dismissal of any students who went to his studio, military investigators seemed uninterested in this angle. More ominous was her statement that Moens claimed to know the ousted German envoy, Count von Bernstorff. (No verification for this charge was ever found by any of the intelligence agencies.) Moens apparently trusted Miss Queen and asked her to find subjects for his scientific study. By the end of 1917, however, army investigators had lost interest in her often exaggerated suspicions and were relying on the more levelheaded Maj. Walter H. Loving.[9]

Loving's first report, in late October 1917, revealed that Moens ingratiated himself into Black Washington's high society by capitalizing on his talent as "a pianist of considerable ability . . . [who] delights to entertain persons who appreciate his efforts." During November he tailed Moens and three times discovered him and a white woman, Mademoiselle Mattjour, entering a residence on Ninth Street. Loving initially suspected a sexual liaison but discarded that theory when he learned that the occupants of the house were a black woman and her daughter. When Moens helped get this daughter a job as a maid at the Russian embassy, MIS's interest quickened. It later learned that she posed nude for Moens's studies.[10]

Moens made no secret of his scientific interests and desire to mix socially with African Americans. Moreover, awareness that he was suspected of being a German spy did not deter him from asking the Dutch legation to write to the State Department, asking it to open doors for Moens at the Smithsonian Institution. In the summer of 1917 he also sought out Maj. Joel Spingarn, the white chairman of the board of the NAACP, and asked for the names of "radical negro leaders." Spingarn obliged, even though he had heard rumors that the Dutchman was inciting blacks "to stand up for their rights and make trouble." Meanwhile, both the MIS and the Bureau were seeking scientific assessment of Moens's professional qualifications. The results were mixed. One of the country's leading ethnologists, Dr. Ales

Hrdlicka of the Smithsonian Institution, told a military agent that Moens "is not Dutch and not a Scientist, as he claims. . . . Moens is an Austrian and needs watching." At least the MIS officer had the wit to observe that Hrdlicka was a Bohemian and rabidly anti-Austrian.[11]

The U.S. Geological Survey (USGS), where Moens was well known as a researcher on oil properties, conducted the most detailed probe of Moens's scientific credentials. One staff member insisted that Moens was not a trained ethnologist, geologist, or paleontologist but a science enthusiast doing "interesting and valuable" work on race mixture. This individual admitted being suspicious of foreigners but was convinced Moens was neither a spy nor a subverter of blacks' loyalties. A USGS geologist, George H. Girty, gave an even more positive assessment. He reported conversing with an officer on the surgeon general's staff who regarded Moens as "a man of high order of intelligence" with "no purpose or even wish to injure the nation from which he has received so much hospitality." Girty echoed the sentiment, calling Moens a "man of high social standing" whose studies of race mixture and serology were not only "perfectly harmless, but . . . tend[ing] to throw light on some of the most interesting and complex problems in biology." Politically, Girty was assured that Moens was "strongly opposed" to German militarism. On orders of the USGS director, its file on Moens was sent to the Bureau of Investigation, whose agents were concurrently monitoring his activities, interviewing neighbors and his new landlady, and identifying his visitors. Although there was indisputable evidence that numerous black women came to his rooms on a daily basis, nothing agents learned by the end of 1917 pointed conclusively to subversive activities, and the Bureau dropped its investigation. The MIS, however, soon received wild allegations that continued to fuel its own suspicions in the first half of 1918.[12]

One outlandish rumor accepted at face value by MIS operatives concerned Moens's association with a professor of theology at Howard University who was allegedly related to a member of the German General Staff. Other reports noted that Moens had traveled throughout the West and that he was "around the Mexican Border at the time of the trouble there." He always seemed to have plenty of money, but no apparent regular source of income. Among his acquaintances were a French "fancy woman" (Mademoiselle Mattjour) and a "line of 'clients'" who "appear to be German or of Teutonic appearance." An informant reported that Moens also had "a great many negro women calling to see him every day," sometimes as late as 11 P.M. When they were actually in his room he posted a sign reading "OUT" on the door. It was also discovered that one of his sculptures—a female nude—was exhibited in the National Museum.[13]

This assortment of suspicions seemed enough to justify a "black bag job" at Moens's lodging by military intelligence agents in March 1918, while he was away on an oil exploration trip to Texas. The burglars found "numerous visiting cards bearing the names of Japanese military officers and civilians, also a number of self-addressed envelopes to people in China." A second break-in five days later was less fruitful, discovering only that Moens burned all his mail. Upon his return,

Moens sought to hire two black women, one to handle office chores, the other to pose. Informant Hallie Queen again entered the picture, agreeing to recruit them. In May, on learning that a female employee of the Treasury Department had delivered a sealed envelope to Moens allegedly intended for the queen of Holland, MIS chief Lt. Col. Ralph H. Van Deman asked the Secret Service to investigate the woman. However, before Treasury agents could search their own files, an army officer did so in a fruitless effort to learn the identity of the mysterious courier.[14] Whether there was any truth to this "tip" is doubtful.

Much of the army's persistence in investigating Moens was due to Capt. P. F. Goodwin, the intelligence officer assigned to the General Engineer Depot in Washington. It is unclear how much authorization he sought or received, but Goodwin succeeded in intercepting Moens's mail, a telegram allegedly written in code, and a letter slipped under his door. Goodwin's operatives also recorded some of Moens's conversations. When it was discovered that he was acquainted with a Count Albert de Sarak who was passing himself off as an army surgeon, Goodwin wrote Van Deman that "this so-called Professor and Count must be up to something and I strongly recommend that one of our Heaviest Men be put on the case and follow it to the end." Soon thereafter the MIS began daily surveillance of Moens that lasted for three months, during which time mail coverage also continued.[15]

Little is known about the army's informant, E. Williams, who spied on Moens from late June through September 1918, or how he was recruited. He and his wife were either neighbors or resided in the same building where Moens took rooms. Williams was a physician or dentist; seemingly, his clientele was not large and he practiced out of his residence, for he had time to observe Moens on an hourly basis and sometimes accompanied him around the city. He also learned that Moens's circle of acquaintances included the Haitian minister, a secretary to the Honduras legation, the chancellor of the Chinese legation, and several scientists.

It was not long before Williams discovered that Moens's most valuable and loyal black friend was Charlotte E. Hunter, an unmarried, fiftyish teacher at Dunbar High School. She was utterly convinced that Moens was a legitimate scientist pursuing studies of great significance for her race. Trusting him completely, she helped secure "types" (often students from Dunbar) to be photographed or to pose for sculptures. Williams sometimes accompanied Moens to Miss Hunter's home and also witnessed her calling at his rooms with a prospective model. The informant also observed the traffic of young black women coming to Moens's rooms to pose, although he was never privy to such sessions. Moens did not suspect he was being spied upon. On one occasion, in a conversation with Mrs. Williams, he predicted race war in the United States within the next century even though, after the war, "the white race would see it was to their advantage to educate and uplift the colored people, that afterward it would be 'The Brotherhood of Man.'" Another time he proposed to Williams that the two share an office so that Moens could recruit "types" from his patients, and in return Moens would refer other "types" to Williams's practice.[16]

Williams submitted only one report after the end of September, for by then agents of the recently renamed Military Intelligence Division were trailing Moens daily. On one occasion they gained entry to a room adjoining Moens's apartment, but, lacking a sophisticated listening device, they were only able to record fragments of conversations. Despite this, they were certain that some of the unseen visitors were partially undressed. Military Intelligence Division operatives also interviewed Moens's acquaintances and kept logs on the dozens of persons with whom he met, including near daily contacts with Charlotte Hunter and repeated visits by other black women. Meanwhile, the post office began a thirty-day mail cover tracing all letters addressed to Moens. The MID also gained access to his bank records. Neither probe turned up any incriminating evidence.[17]

Until the end of August, the Bureau of Investigation remained aloof from the Moens case; since army intelligence maintained such tight surveillance there seemed no necessity for its involvement. However, a resurgence of black militancy in the second half of 1918 led it to reopen the case. Anticipating an end to the war, some blacks began to demand a voice in peace negotiations and the disposition of Germany's African colonies as just payment for their participation. Federal investigators totally misperceived the origins of this spirit and damned it as pro-German or in the interests of Germany. Of immediate concern was the Liberty Congress spearheaded by Hubert H. Harrison and members of William Monroe Trotter's National Equal Rights League. Moens had attended the Congress in June and was welcomed by Harrison. The Liberty Congress underscored the Bureau's weakness in depending on conspicuously white agents and hastily recruited and ill-supervised informants. Its logical and momentous next step was to hire its first "professional" black informant, Dr. Arthur Ulysses Craig, who was well educated, ideologically reliable, and willing to travel to whatever region needed attention. Craig's success in 1918 paved the way for the Bureau to hire its first black agent a year later.[18]

The Bureau's revived case against Herman M. B. Moens was initially based on allegations supplied by Craig, who had taught in Washington's black public schools for eighteen years and was currently a dollar-a-year man promoting conservation and patriotism for the U.S. Food Administration. Craig had known of Moens for some time, believed him to be a close associate of the "radical" Harrison, and was aware of his relationship with Charlotte Hunter. The record is not clear whether he ever met Moens, but Craig was strongly of the opinion that he was "a German agent and a master spy . . . for the colored race cause." Soon James Grover Cleveland Corcoran, the Bureau agent who "handled" Craig, was spearheading the pursuit of Moens. In a stroke of extraordinarily good fortune, Corcoran began to cultivate another of Moens's acquaintances, a young black woman named Helen Saunders. If she were offered a government job, would she cooperate with federal agents? Bureau chief A. Bruce Bielaski knew of no position available for her, but he did suggest that the Bureau offer money for her services.[19]

At first Miss Saunders was unwilling to tell Corcoran of her relationship with

Moens, but he was convinced the lure of a government job would allow agents to "keep our hands on her, and keep her in good Company, pending the investigation of Professor Moens." Yet even given wartime Washington's expanding federal bureaucracy, finding a decent job for a young black woman was not easy. Up to this point Corcoran suspected only that Moens's contact with militant blacks indicated some subversive purpose. But what he learned when Saunders agreed to talk forever changed the direction of the Bureau's case. This was the government's first big break.[20]

Helen Saunders proved to be a most uninhibited young woman whose candid admissions of a sexual relationship with Moens stirred Corcoran's prurient as well as professional interests. His secret dictaphone recorded her agreement to cooperate on the promise of money, a government job, and a lot of "trips." Abandoning all subtlety, Corcoran asked: "Can you go up there and screw him?" Expressing fear that her mother might find out, she hesitated, whereupon Corcoran promised protection if she proved trustworthy. She then agreed to "play square" so long as Corcoran did the same, announcing, "he [Moens] will go down in the bushes. I can do it with him anytime I want to." She had already had sex with him several times: "I just did it for the experience. You know I am this kind of a girl, I like to try new things, you know a new venture. . . . Anything that comes new to me in life its fun to see how it will turn out."

This was not prostitution, insisted Saunders; she had only accepted money for posing for nude photographs, not sex. Despite the fact his witness was a consenting participant and no federal crime was alleged to have been committed, Corcoran determined to have her arrange a tryst so he could witness "one of these performances between Professor Moens, and the co-informant." The agent at first wondered whether he could be hidden in her room. Next he proposed the ludicrous suggestion that she introduce him to Moens as one of her lovers. Finally, Corcoran pressed his subject, "How are you going to prove to me that you can fuck Moens? Can't you arrange to get me in?" Miss Saunders: "I will have to go to his house and look it over. Nobody can tell me how I work things." Corcoran admonished her not to tell anyone she was cooperating with the Bureau. "I don't know anything," she replied. "I am not working for the Government."[21]

Fornication was no federal crime. And in the South—Washington was a southern city—white men customarily went unpunished for even forcible sex with black women. Nonetheless, Corcoran was hot to trap Moens, casing his rooms in preparation for a surprise entry when the professor and Miss Saunders could be caught *in flagrante delicto.* Spy-catching and national security were no longer at issue; Corcoran was out to catch a dirty old man—but not until after first watching him and his lubricious paramour in action.

First, however, Corcoran had to coordinate matters with the MID, which did not want a premature arrest to jeopardize its own investigation of Moens and a young subordinate of Emmett J. Scott, the black special assistant to the secretary of war, who was believed to be responsible for mysterious calls to families of soldiers, informing them before official War Department announcements that their loved ones had been killed in France. The MID wanted to bug Moens's new rooms, which he now rented from the trusting Charlotte Hunter. Corcoran took MID's request to Chief Bielaski, who instructed his agent not to wait too long and miss the chance of convicting Moens. What federal violation Bielaski had in mind was not stated. He did, however, involve the State Department, asking it to investigate Moens's background and finances abroad. When no immediate answer was forthcoming, MID's new director, Brig. Gen. Marlborough Churchill, cabled the military attaché in The Hague for the same information. The MID still believed that Moens was "disseminating dangerous negro propaganda," but he caught the flu and remained at home for several days, preventing its operatives from wiring his room.[22]

The MID also hoped that Moens's mail might contain evidence that he was "fostering negro propaganda," but gaining access to it was not easy. Army agents particularly suspected a letter from Moens to W. A. J. M. van Waterschoot van der Gracht, Roxana Petroleum's representative in Tulsa, wildly imagining that Moens was "using secret means of communicating with the enemy" through "codes and invisible writing." Van der Gracht was alleged to be his contact with German agents. Postal officials held the unopened letter in Washington but would not permit it to be read, probably because they believed the government's case against Moens was flimsy. The MID thus asked the Bureau to devise a scheme for reading the letter. Chief Bielaski instructed the Tulsa office to learn when the letter was delivered and then interview van der Gracht on a pretext and secure the letter "without legal process." Agent John A. Whalen carried out these instructions perfectly, conning van der Gracht into "loaning" him the Moens letter. After all that effort, however, it proved of little consequence, as it was concerned only with oil explorations.[23]

Delays proved worrisome to Corcoran. When he could not locate Helen Saunders five days after his bargain with her, he feared "that Helen has been tampered with." Presumably seeking evidence and not simply feeding his carnal appetite, Corcoran went to the National Museum's photo lab and secured two dozen nude photographs of young black and mulatto women, including the daughter and sister of the Haitian minister. Not until the end of September did he succeed in again meeting Saunders, insisting that she maintain an intimate relationship with her Dutch friend so that Corcoran could photograph them having sex. He also conferred again with the MID, learning that it still had not bugged Moens's rooms, placed an informant in the house, or linked him to the suspicious phone calls. Discussions between Bielaski, the special agent in charge of the investigation in Washington, and their MID counterparts produced agreement to set a date for Moens's arrest. The State Department, however, felt no urgency, in the closing weeks of the war, in having its legation in The Hague investigate Moens's background.[24]

Agent Corcoran confronted the common problem of how to keep informants loyal, especially since the Bureau was hardly paying a munificent retainer. He proposed a specific evening for Miss Saunders to visit her paramour and again entered

Moens's rooms to inspect their layout and identify front and rear entrances. The MID had finally installed a two-week phone tap.[25] Events now moved swiftly. The MID kept Moens's residence under round-the-clock surveillance. Corcoran met daily with Saunders and laid plans for the anticipated photography, believing that a good picture would be worth a five-year sentence. Two agents, an American Protective League volunteer, and a photographer from the Department of the Interior practiced taking flash pictures. All participants in the raid were familiarized with the layout of Moens's residence. They counted on a young white woman who rented a room on the third floor allowing them to hide there until the proper time. One hitch developed: The U.S. attorney backtracked and refused to issue federal warrants for either Moens's arrest or a search of his accommodations, not that the absence of a search warrant had prevented Bureau and MID operatives from breaking in a number of times already. That official undoubtedly recognized that no federal case could be built simply on evidence of fornication.[26]

All was carefully plotted the evening of 19 October 1918. A District police detective named Kelly, who met agents Corcoran and Murphy at their office, carried a search warrant. Helen Saunders arrived later to receive last-minute instructions. Kelly and a fellow officer were to assist with photography and search the rooms. Corcoran recorded what transpired next:

> At 8 O'clock agent, accompanied Helen Saunders as far as Moens residence. She entered the house and then agent met special agent Murphy and went into the house next door, . . . through the yard and over the fence on to the back porch of subject's house, this porch is just off of his bed-room. Shortly after we were located, we heard subject and Helen talking in this room while we awaited the signal from Helen, that *both were in bed.* The[n] the girl opened the back door leading to the porch and left it unlocked, she looked out on the porch to see if I was there and then gave me the signal that everything was all right. We then stayed on the porch about half an hour and the light was put out in the bed room. Subject and girl were preparing to go to bed and at about 9.10 P.M. we heard subject say, "Oh, Helen, the door is open" which was the truth, due to the door only having a dead latch with no lock which Helen had unlocked. The wind evidently had blown this door open. After Moens discovered the door open, he is usually so careful about these things—he came to the porch and *discovered the agents* there. We saw our case had blown and *we ordered him to close that door,* under the subterfuge that we were using his porch to detect some radio outfit which was supposed to be operating across the street. Subject slammed door with an awful jam, ran back in his room and almost instantly returned to the porch with a *german gun and bayonet attached.* He was just about to use this bayonet on the agents when I drew my black jack on subject, the effects of which made him put his gun up and then I took it from him. In attempting to do so, Moens ran the bayonet in my arm.
>
> We then entered the room where subject had this girl who was partly undressed having her coat, ha[t] and over-skirt off and the light was out. Subject said he was a scientist studying colored mixtures. Agents told him he had spoiled

their plans detecting the radio outfit across the street. Subject took this for what it was worth and seemed satisfied that we really were watching the radio outfit.

Agent held a quick conference and decided it was not the proper time to execute the search warrant.

Later in the evening I met Helen Saunders and she advised me that subject believed our subterfuge and he thought everything was all right. The girl is willing to work further in the case and is now especially interested to get subject in an embarrassing position.

I might state, Prof. Moens never came closer in his life, being caught in the *perversion act* and having a flash-light taken of same, but due to the door being blown open and his discovering agents, that same was not taken.

To sum up the whole matter, there was not a mistake made by anyone but we had a bad break of luck.[27]

The Bureau's Keystone Kops caper scuttled all hopes of catching Moens in a compromising position, not that that alone would have ensured a federal conviction. What kind of a case could it now pursue? Although an informant in the Interior Department was tracing suspicions that Moens and his Roxana Petroleum associates were linked to German agents in Mexico, Corcoran had no real evidence on which to build a prosecution. He and the U.S. attorney had no recourse but to concoct charges based on the sexual aspects of the case, and Moens naively played into their hands. Learning that agents were looking for him and believing that alleged espionage was its only interest, he wrote to the Justice Department in hopes of staving off prosecution and preserving his income: "Though not convinced that my scientific work is of no value, I am willing to give it up and to avoid to go to colored people." He also offered copies of all correspondence with Roxana. But Moens's proposition was ignored. Instead, several agents went to his rooms on 23 October, where they interrogated him and seized his books, papers, and photographs. Moens later claimed this was done without a warrant.[28]

The next day, Moens was summoned to the Bureau office. No fewer than twelve agents grilled the "degenerate" about his "alleged propaganda activities and immoral relations with different colored types." It was undoubtedly the latter line of questioning that required the attendance of a dozen men. In fact, the former subject was hardly covered at all. Corcoran got Moens to contradict himself, first saying that his anthropological studies were limited to blacks but later admitting that a white woman had posed for him. Corcoran argued this was proof that Moens's studies were a "fake" and "nothing more than for the purpose of satisfying his degenerate passions." When asked whether he had sex with his subjects, Moens told Corcoran this "was not a gentleman's question." After persistent questioning, however, Moens admitted to being intimate with two women. When asked for names he at first refused, but when Helen Saunders was brought into the room he did not deny committing "an act of perversion." Corcoran recorded no details as to the particular "perversion," writing instead, "this report has to be condensed terribly, due to the very indecent language which would be necessary to explain from this point on. The line of questioning was so disgusting, it is useless to go further in this matter." There is no record, however, that any of the twelve agents found it so disgusting that they left the interrogation. In fact, one of them later admitted, "when Moens was dismissed from the room he went out hurriedly amidst a few jeers on the part of some of us." Corcoran's disgust was indicated in his own words to Moens: "You are going to spend ten years in the penitentiary, or perhaps you will be shot."[29]

Did the Justice Department have a plausible case? Corcoran believed so, noting that Moens advertised in the newspaper for models or assistants, and that he admitted to having sex with one of the women over a period of three years: "This shows conclusively he is not making scientific studies but is *trafficing* [*sic*] in *immoral activities.*" Although immorality was not a federal crime, the possession and display of pornographic materials was prohibited under Section 312 of the federal penal code. Conviction only required a witness to whom Moens had shown such items. Moens had never been reluctant to expound his theories to anyone willing to listen, so it was not difficult to find witnesses to whom he had shown nude photographs. Only one other matter needed attention: At the suggestion of the District police chief, Major Pullman, who now undoubtedly wished to distance himself from Moens, plans were made to keep the Netherlands legation out of the case. Indeed, Dutch diplomats offered to "expedite the return" of Moens to Holland if the United States so desired. A public trial would drag their own reputations through the muck since several had written letters of introduction or recommendation for Moens. But military and Justice Department officials did not intend to have their lengthy efforts wasted by an under-the-counter deal. They were out for blood.[30]

A search and apprehension warrant was secured and Moens was arrested while dining with Charlotte Hunter. Agents found his packed trunk along with train schedules for New York. More nude pictures were impounded. He remained in jail for six days until he could raise $5,000 bail. His mug shot depicted a stocky forty-three-year-old man with medium brown hair, full moustache, and Van Dyke beard. A grand jury viewed forty photographs, heard testimony from several witnesses including Helen Saunders and Agent Corcoran, and handed down felony indictments claiming Moens possessed and exhibited pictures of women "in obscene, impudent and indecent postures."[31] Moens pleaded for the opportunity to vindicate himself, writing in his somewhat fractured English to the Bureau soon after his release:

> I have confidence that you . . . will do me the justice to consider my scientific work and standing in the right way, that is purely scientific with the tendency to prove the descent of man and the development of the human races. The desire that by the knowledge a better understanding between the nations and races may come and so a real brotherhood of men is in several articles by me expressed.
>
> I hope that you will do me the justice to let me give you complete information about my work, based upon the facts in your possession, because the two

> afternoons that questions have been put to me in the idea that I was not right the impressions which you pronounced about me were wrong.[32]

One piece of possible evidence did not become available to federal investigators until after Moens's arrest: a letter of introduction for Moens written by J. Louden, the Dutch minister of foreign affairs. His brother, H. Louden, was a director of the giant Royal Dutch Shell Petroleum Company. Might Moens be an industrial spy?[33] His employer since mid-1916 was Roxana Petroleum, a subsidiary of Royal Dutch Shell. Bureau personnel gained access to Roxana's payroll records and Moens's bank account, while the MID also investigated his finances. Roxana's van der Gracht soon recognized the implications of this investigation and offered to meet personally with Chief Bielaski, informing the Bureau that all official connections with Moens were severed following his indictment. He was clearly attempting to steer clear of suspicions of disloyalty or industrial espionage, although he did, however, defend his countryman's character, stating that Moens did not favor Germany and that his study of "the negro and other alien races" was serious science.[34]

Bureau and MID investigators did not readily abandon the suspicion that Moens was linked to enemy-influenced industrial espionage. Bielaski took this so seriously that he instructed his New York office to have one of its "most diplomatic agents" investigate Royal Dutch Shell simply because it was a competitor to Standard Oil. Officials at Standard Oil's headquarters of course confirmed that Shell was a stiff competitor, but they knew little about Roxana Petroleum, van der Gracht, or Moens. In the meantime MID quizzed its attaché in the Netherlands concerning the Loudon brothers, learning only that they were "influential, wealthy, and respectable." This trivia was relayed to the attorney general, the U.S. attorney in Washington, the Alien Property Custodian, and the commissioner of Indian Affairs in hopes they might verify conspiratorial actions on the part of the oil companies or the two Dutchmen. But this proved to be a dead-end.[35]

Moens's livelihood was ruined by his indictment and the subsequent publicity when Roxana Petroleum stopped paying him at the end of October 1918. Moens foolishly believed that both would be spared further suspicion if there was no paper trail, and he consequently destroyed all correspondence between the two. But van der Gracht saw safety in cooperating with the government and furnished copies of all their communications to the Department of Justice. Naively hoping that van der Gracht was still his friend, Moens wrote him, "I am sitting with a colored lawyer, whom I now intend to replace by a white one since prejudice is stronger than justice." Yet he was confident of vindication: The "German spy idea is laughable" and the "power of the puritans" would be overcome although they had "almost put me out of business." If Moens thought this would bring sympathy or aid from his former employer, he was mistaken. Van der Gracht replied curtly that the notorious case had caused him "much annoyance." Writing to his own attorney, van der Gracht expressed hope that this "ridiculous upheaval" would not hurt Roxana. His only advice to Moens was to "come clean."[36]

In mid-December 1918 Moens once more addressed van der Gracht, this time claiming to have received an offer via the Netherlands legation allowing him to leave the country upon payment of $1,500. Moens was by then physically ill and burdened with a sizable legal bill. While asking van der Gracht for advice, he nonetheless seemed to have his mind made up, writing that new prints of the seized photographs had been made and endorsed by two members of Congress, the president of the Carnegie Institute, and other prominent persons who attested to their artistic and scientific value. Moens concluded by warning that if the case went to court there was no telling what embarrassing things might be revealed. Van der Gracht regarded this letter as "rather queer" and doubted that Dutch diplomats had arranged a bribe. Leaving all further communication with Moens to his lawyer, he professed to wanting justice for Moens but worried that "I don't want to expose myself to any entanglements in this matter and, least of all, to possible blackmail." Thus ended the relationship between the two Netherlanders.[37]

While there is no evidence of a bribe, Dutch diplomats clearly worried about embarrassing disclosures, having learned of the Justice Department's intention to try Moens and expose "acts of repulsive immorality." They had given Moens financial assistance and letters of introduction when he arrived in the United States in 1914. Besides that, they were also genuinely concerned that Moens was being unjustly treated and perhaps even framed by Bureau agents to divert attention away from the publicized immoral activities of some of their own peers. Hence they asked the State Department to find a way whereby a trial could be averted and Moens allowed to leave the country. The legation's secretary met with Justice Department officials, professing not to know of Moens's "unnatural practices with young negresses." Eager to squelch proceedings, the secretary proposed that Moens be expelled as a "social pest."[38]

The State Department recognized that a trial would be an embarrassment to the entire diplomatic corps in Washington, not just the Dutch. Third Assistant Secretary of State Breckinridge Long advised that the department be extremely firm in insisting that Justice drop the charges on condition that Moens be deported. The State Department's solicitor reluctantly supported this suggestion, but pleaded for compromise rather than issuing an ultimatum. The Justice Department was willing to reexamine the case to see "whether on the basis of evidence there is anything of serious interest to this Bureau [of Investigation], excepting this man's moral perversity." Unfortunately for diplomatic sensibilities, the attorney general's office decided that, in light of the "unusually unpleasant record," there was no justification for overruling the federal attorney prosecuting the case. The easiest way to avoid embarrassment, State was advised, was for Moens to plead guilty. This he was unwilling to do.[39]

The Justice Department was determined to convict Moens on pornography charges, and counted on the cooperation of the Military Intelligence Division. Up to the time of Moens's arrest, the MID's interest still centered on "the insidious form of propaganda being spread by Subject among his several negro acquaintances" but it had no hard evidence, even after maintaining a month-long mail trace. Its operatives admitted that a considerable number of his friends, both whites and "a very high grade of colored people," were strongly convinced that Moens was a serious scientist. Military investigators also interviewed several young women who had posed for Moens, but the issue of immoral behavior was beyond their official interest. Thus, although the MID gathered some useful data, it was not a major participant in subsequent proceedings.[40]

The Bureau of Investigation built most of its case in November 1918, soon after Moens's indictment, expecting a December trial. The war was coming to a close, with fewer selective service cases to be investigated, and the Washington office had nine agents with which to interview likely witnesses. In fact, Bureau personnel pursued the case with more zeal than an ordinary criminal case would warrant. Potential witnesses fell into two categories. Scientists connected with the Smithsonian Institution and the National Museum were prepared to testify that Moens was an "imposter" who possessed no scholarly credibility.[41] Black females proved more difficult to control. Several feared public exposure and only grudgingly talked with agents, who threatened to use "very stringent methods" if they did not cooperate.[42]

In the course of its investigations, the Bureau compiled a list of twenty-seven young women who were suspected of having posed for Moens. Some sat for photographs taken at the National Museum or Army Medical Museum, whereas others posed in his rooms while he sketched them or made sculptures. This list, including descriptions of Moens's relationships with them, was included in a ninety-six-page analysis compiled by Bureau agent (and Board of Education member) H. Barrett Learned in January 1919. Two older women were also included in the Bureau's investigation. Charlotte Hunter maintained her confidence in the scientific importance of Moens's work and, almost to the end, deluded herself concerning his sexual activities. The other woman was well-known poet Georgia Douglas Johnson, the wife of influential black Republican politician Henry Lincoln Johnson. Agents suspected that she and Moens had had an affair. Under questioning the embarrassed matron denied any improprieties or having recruited models, claiming to know Moens only superficially from attendance at lectures on anthropology. She did, however, admit to having introduced him to others who might be interested in his work.[43]

Of the more than two dozen younger women whom Moens considered as potential subjects, several were introduced to him by Miss Hunter, their former teacher at Dunbar High School. Others responded to newspaper advertisements, some of which were placed on his behalf by Hunter. Still more were recruited by women who had been selected to pose and even by those Moens had rejected. About half of them refused to pose nude, even after Moens showed them nude photographs of other young women whom they often recognized as their schoolmates. The poses were not sexually provocative, but merely ethnographic. Moens also showed them anthropology texts illustrated with pictures of deformed and disfigured Africans, telling them he wanted to publish a book with more flattering photographs so as to disprove racist theories. In all, ten young women posed unclothed. One other was Virginia Parsons, "a young white woman, of Indian strain, notably attractive," identified by Agent Learned only as Miss X. (Did racism explain Learned's decision to preserve the anonymity of the one white woman while recording the names of the ten nude black women?) However, what riveted the Bureau's attention most was Moens's relations with Helen Saunders, age twenty, and Rachel Custis, who was about twenty-one years old.[44]

The uninhibited Miss Saunders repeated, in a sworn statement given in late November, what she had earlier told Corcoran. By that time he had made good on his promise and secured a job for her in the Quartermaster Department's mail division. Again admitting to having sex with Moens soon after starting to pose for him for five dollars a week, she related how she eventually tired of his requests and pretended to have a venereal disease while taunting him sexually. Even though the crime for which he was indicted was possession and display of immoral pictures, Bureau agents were obsessed with proving that Moens was a dirty old man. When Saunders told them that Moens engaged in cunnilingus they labeled him a disgusting "degenerate" and "pervert." Assistant U.S. Attorney Arth, who would prosecute Moens, persuaded her to "admit" that she never intended to disrobe for Moens and was only persuaded when he showed her nude pictures of other girls. Testimony that Moens displayed "immoral" pictures to others was crucial, but her eagerness for new sexual experiences made her less than an ideal witness. Fearing that Moens might pay her to leave town, the Bureau assigned its black informant, Dr. Craig, whom she trusted, to keep Miss Saunders loyal to the prosecution.[45]

Rachel Custis came to the Bureau's attention when an anonymous letter accused Moens of being a sexual predator and suggested that agents contact her. The writer's information was correct. Miss Custis had been hired as a maid by Charlotte Hunter, who then suggested that Moens might find her a suitable model. On her first visit to his rooms she disrobed and he took measurements, but nothing else transpired. She returned a few days later and was again measured in the nude. Leaving the room, Moens returned naked, performed cunnilingus, and then attempted sexual intercourse, although she doubted he penetrated her. Attempting to excite Miss Custis, he showed her pictures he had taken of other young women. (This was the crucial evidence needed in court; testimony concerning his sexual performances could not prove Section 312 charges.) Moens then professed to be "desperately in love with her, and asked her if, in case he had to go away, she would go with him, and in case of death would they both die together." Miss Custis posed for Moens at other times but he did not again have sex with her. After revealing these details to Bureau agents she agreed to testify for the government.[46]

Prosecution witnesses were all lined up by early December, but the trial was postponed until the end of March 1919. Moens's attorney, Richard P. Evans, tried to quash the proceedings by alleging improprieties on the part of federal agents, writing Attorney General Thomas W. Gregory of "the unjustifiable misconduct of subordinates in your Department, in excess of their duty and authority, . . . of course, without your knowledge." Evans's charge was referred to Assistant Attorney General LaRue Brown, who was surprised to find the case still active. Two months previously, when the Netherlands legation attempted to have the matter settled quietly, he had concluded the case was both weak and insignificant, and now found no reason to alter that earlier judgment. There was no evidence of pro-German activity. Regarding the pictures, Brown was of the opinion that "their obscenity, if any, consists solely in the fact that they are photographs of naked women. The postures are, in the main, not objectionable." Brown found that the federal attorney's office had approached the case with unwarranted zeal, treating it as a felony whereas the District Code only classified it as a misdemeanor. Federal prosecutors seemed fixated on the issue of perversion, but evidence was weak, depending on "the unsupported testimony of a willing partner." Brown concluded that

> After hearing all of the facts [in December] I was of the opinion that it was desirable to get out of the case as easily as might be, and it is true . . . that an arrangement was attempted, with the assistance of the Dutch Legation, under which a plea of guilty was to be made, fine imposed and Moens was to be deported. I had supposed that this had been carried out, but it now appears that it has not . . .
>
> I did not and do not think it of very much importance. I have doubts of Moens' standing as a scientist and even graver doubts of his purity of his relations with the negro women of the town. I think he had better go back to Holland as soon as may be, but the case otherwise hardly seems to be one that warrants very urgent action by the prosecuting authorities.[47]

So what was to be done with Evans's charges and an admittedly insubstantial case? Acknowledging that the U.S. attorney and District of Columbia Supreme Court chief justice W. I. McCoy were eager to pillory Moens, Brown apparently bowed to their wishes and did not withdraw the case. The fact that McCoy, who would preside at the trial, was already emotionally involved in the case did not auger well for the defendant. McCoy denied Moens's petition to change his plea to *nolo contendere* if the charges were reduced to misdemeanors.[48]

Herman Marie Bernelot Moens's trial, which began on Monday, 25 March 1919, was a circus. The formal charge was possessing and exhibiting obscene materials, but the courtroom and corridors were packed with those more interested in the titillating details of the case. Marshals had difficulty maintaining order and hundreds were turned away, but those who gained admittance were not disappointed. Black editor Calvin Chase's *Washington Bee* made certain that no seats would remain empty, heading his lead story with a teaser: "Prominent Young Colored Women in Naked Poses and Unnatural Acts." Piously asserting that much testimony was "too revolting to publish," Chase nonetheless fed the public as much as he dared in covering "one of the most sensational cases that has ever been tried."

Agent Corcoran took the stand as the government opened its case. He described Moens's admission to having sex with Helen Saunders, showed the court two nude poses of the woman, and repeated details the *Bee* could not print. This testimony elicited such levity from spectators, including a large number of teachers, that Judge McCoy cleared the courtroom. Agent Learned, the next to testify, repeated Miss Saunders's unabashed admissions of trysts with Moens—testimony the black newspaper described only as "very revolting." Prosecutors then paraded a number of young women before the jury—but not Helen Saunders—who described Moens's persistence in requesting them to pose unclothed. One added that she accompanied Saunders to Moens's "studio," where the three danced in the nude. Several models also related how they were recruited by Charlotte Hunter. Also appearing for the prosecution was Dr. Ales Hrdlicka of the National Museum, who testified that Moens had neither the credentials nor knowledge of a genuine scientist. Examination of genitalia was unnecessary to determine racial differences, he said; rather, the head and gums allegedly revealed such factors.[49]

The case for the defense began with Moens himself defending the need for nude photographs in the study of ethnography. However, when his attorney attempted to explain Moens's scientific investigations Judge McCoy sustained the prosecution's objections and blocked that line of argument. Moens freely admitted to having sexual relationships with Helen Saunders and two other women but stoutly denied any improprieties with Charlotte Hunter.

Prosecutor Arth attacked Moens unmercifully. In a cross-examination that was irrelevant to the charge but calculated to prejudice the jury, he brought out that Moens possessed bank accounts in Belgium, Russia, and Germany totaling thousands of dollars. Secret letters the defendant had both sent and received were also introduced as evidence. Then Arth leveled his central charge. In the words of the *Washington Bee:*

> The prosecutor carried [Moens] through a rigid and scathing examination to test his knowledge of his profession. He failed to answer any question in the line of his profession, but he did say if he was given time to look up the questions he could answer them. This remark caused a smile to pass over the faces of the spectators. He was asked from what college or institution he graduated. He named an academy in Russia, something like our high school in this city. He was asked under whom he had studied as an ethnologist and what books he had read.
>
> The government prosecutor wanted to know whether any of those or his teachers state whether it was necessary to measure a female and do other acts. He could not name one. Neither could he state intelligently the teachings of the books to which he called the attention of the prosecutor. After his failure to answer any of the questions in science asked him, the prosecutor asked him to select his own questions in ethnology and give their meanings. The invitation was not accepted.

Moreover, when asked for records of his scientific examinations he replied that he kept no such data. Moens did, however, persist in defending his photographs as scientific and artistic and offered the endorsements of a number of well-known academics. (The judge was later quoted as saying that even if Pres. Woodrow Wilson had signed the pictures it would not have changed his view that they were obscene.)

Charlotte Hunter's appearance as a defense witness must have been a humiliating experience, because she still believed in the validity of Moens's scientific inquiries. The prosecutor implied that she, too, had an illicit relationship with him but she insisted that, although he rented rooms from her and she accompanied him to social gatherings, their relationship was simply that of friends. Her role in his work was to secure subjects and maintain records, but she admitted to having none of the latter.

The prosecutor's closing argument was described by the *Bee* as a "touching speech" that portrayed Moens as a "social pest." Why, if he was a genuine scientist, had he kept no records? And why was it necessary to show nude pictures of fourteen- and fifteen-year-old girls to anyone, for any purpose? Public purity had been violated. Moens's attorney made a spirited defense, but the jury quickly returned a guilty verdict on 1 April. Nine days later Justice McCoy imposed the maximum sentence of one year in jail and a fine of $500. Moens promptly appealed and was released on $3,000 bail.[50]

The proceedings also took their toll on the young female witnesses called by the prosecution. One such victim was Juanita Arthur, who was hired by Charlotte Hunter for secretarial duties and later worked as Moens's housekeeper. She eventually recruited several models and herself posed nude, eliciting "improper advances" on his part, which she repelled. She penned an anguished letter to prosecutor Arth regretting "that I ever consented to give the information I did concerning the Moens Case, for I have been brought to shame. Now I thought that I was acting as I should by telling the truth to you thinking you would protect me."[51] Hers was not the only ruined reputation in Black Washington; others were caught in the backwash of Moens's escapades.

Moens, convinced he was the victim of a frame-up, wrote once more to van der Gracht, saying that "I would rather they had persecuted [*sic*] me openly as a German spy, because it seemed that really that was the main purpose of their action against me." Everything had been distorted: "The entire case has been built up on crookedness, stupidity, and criminal activity in the brains of detectives, because the entire case against me has been formulated by the two detectives who have been sent to search my rooms." But the verdict was not unexpected: "You know out of what kind of elements a jury is composed in this country." Then followed a plea for financial assistance so that he could vindicate himself: "Where my connection with you and your company have caused me all this suffering, loss of money, and difficulties, I would naturally very much appreciate it if from this same side some help would be extended to me." Such help would promote justice and help salvage the reputation "of a Dutch scientist who is being judged so badly, merely on account of having done his duty. . . . If I can secure from you and your company the cooperation which I consider to have a right to expect, this will, at the same time, give me new courage." Van der Gracht regarded financial assistance as "silly" and "out of the question" and hoped that Moens could secure a suspended sentence and deportation.[52]

It was customary in cases where resident aliens were convicted of crimes for the Justice Department to notify the Bureau of Immigration so deportation might follow completion of a sentence. A summary of the case was prepared for this purpose, indicating "moral turpitude" as grounds for deportation, but this document was withheld pending consultation with the State Department, which was interested in preventing further embarrassment to the Netherlands legation. Indeed, State was caught in the middle. Dutch diplomats regarded Moens's treatment as unjust, and urged that no second trial take place and that Moens be allowed to return to Holland. They were particularly aggrieved with the Justice Department, having believed they had a promise that the government would not mention them in the trial; indeed, the embarrassed legation regarded itself as being prosecuted. When the State Department attempted to clarify the situation, the U.S. attorney's office replied that not only had no promises been made to the Dutch, but also that they owed an apology for foisting such a heinous criminal, armed with official letters of recommendation, on an unsuspecting America. There was no way the State Department could resolve this animosity between the Netherlands legation and the Justice Department: The latter was not about to drop charges.[53]

Moens took his conviction to the District of Columbia Court of Appeals, which reversed the judgment on the grounds that the original indictment did not state he had the photographs "knowingly" for obscene purposes. The government filed for a rehearing but the motion was denied and the original indictment quashed in early 1920. Still determined to pillory Moens, the Justice Department filed almost identical charges, persuading the grand jury to return a new indictment on 29 April 1920 based on the same violation (Section 312) and a new charge based on Section 872 of the District of Columbia code, which concerned the display of indecent publications. The former carried stiffer fines and prison sentences.[54] Moens's travail was not yet at an end.

Regarding his conviction as a rank injustice, Moens went on the offensive to marshal support for his case and reputation. He publicized the fact that reputable scientists endorsed his photographs as scientifically and artistically valuable and urged personal acquaintances to write the Justice Department asking why the case was being continued. His greatest supporter was a well-known physician, Dr. R. W. Shufeldt, who carried Moens's case to the scientific community through two angry articles in the widely read *Medical Review of Reviews.* Shufeldt was the author of *Studies of the Human Form* and had unabashed contempt for Anthony Comstock and anyone else using the power of government to punish those who violated their definitions of decency. A crusader against "Comstockery," Shufeldt published over thirty articles attacking such censorship. Comstock overreached himself in seeking Schufeldt's prosecution and a ban on his book, however, and the now-publicized volume was widely sold and added to law and medical libraries. Shufeldt also assisted in the publication of *Obscene Literature and Constitutional Law,* a volume intended to guide the courts away from unnecessary censorship.

Shufeldt considered Moens a distinguished and cultured scientist and saw nothing improper about his study of miscegenation despite believing, contrary to Moens, that race mixture in the United States was "terrible and most destructive." Shufeldt described Moens's "exceptionally fine anthropologic photographs" as "works of art, most tasteful and valuable." Shufeldt's first article in *Medical Review of Reviews* condemned the case as "a shameful and burning disgrace to the entire institution of scientific investigation." After the trial he again criticized the government's attempt to prove that a frontal nude photograph was "lewd." Neither art nor science could function without such illustrations. The prosecution's view that the mere possession of such photographs was criminal was "absurd." Schufeldt could not conceal his contempt for the courtroom proceedings nor, ironically, its black spectators:

> The 'court room' was filled with odoriferous negroes; it smelled of spittoons and cheap tobacco, and was as dismal in appearance as the Star Chamber of the days of the Inquisition. The jury, taken as a whole, appeared to be composed of honest, well-meaning, good, square American mechanics, with about as much knowledge of the requirements of art, medicine, and science for photographs of nude specimens of men and women, taken on anterior view, as a Government mule would have about singing *Annee Laurie*. . . . I naturally testified on the stand that the samples shown me were *not* lewd pictures—nor were they, except in the minds of those who habitually confuse the lewd, the nude, and the prude. . . . Neither judge nor jury appeared to be familiar with the art works in The Louvre.

Schufeldt concluded by accusing the government of "playing your game with fourteenth century cards . . . in the guillotine-cart at the rear end of the procession of advancing civilization."[55]

Prosecution witnesses had described Moens as a bogus scientist, so it was important to prove the contrary. The *Medical Review of Reviews* printed Moens's own article on "Intermixture of Races" in the fall of 1919, which was illustrated with some of the photographs he had been convicted of possessing and displaying. He began with the thesis that all present races were the product of both mixing and environmental influences, every human being descended from "protoman" who "stood between men and the anthropoid ape." Comparative anatomy, paleontology, embryology, and anthropology all substantiated that proposition. Moens was particularly interested in atavistic features—"the appearance in descendants of peculiarities which were possessed by their remote ancestors, but which in intervening generations have been suppressed or have become latent"—in persons of mixed race. He was convinced that American Indians were of Mongolian descent and that many Jews, as well as numerous other whites, possessed recognizable Negroid characteristics. Evidence of remote miscegenation could often only be detected in the lingering darker pigmentation of the external genitalia. Moens challenged nineteenth-century racist science by stressing that "history gives instances of human supremacy by people of all shades, hair forms, and varied craniological structures." His own studies, he predicted, would "afford impartial scientific conclusions and displace prejudice, hypocrisy and injustice. This will diminish the struggle between men who differ in race, nation, creed or cast [*sic*], and promote the universal brotherhood of humanity."[56]

Moens had his day in the court of science, but he could not clear his name before the bar of public opinion. Others were tarred with the same brush. Within days of his indictment in late 1918 black parents in Washington attacked the school system for allowing Moens access to their children. Naturally Charlotte E. Hunter, his loyal and naive assistant and a history teacher at Dunbar High School, received much public censure, but so, too, did the black assistant superintendent of schools, Roscoe Conkling Bruce. He in turn pinned the blame on the white president of the Board of Education, John Van Schaik, who authorized Moens to examine schoolchildren even after principals complained that nude photographs were being taken.[57] What stirred many Washington parents was their belief that Bruce practiced favoritism in the hiring and retention of black schoolteachers, and they seized on the tawdry Moens affair as a means to gain Bruce's ouster.

Seeking to navigate these treacherous waters, the white superintendent of schools asked the Bureau for information on Moens and Miss Hunter, receiving agent and Board of Education member Learned's ninety-six-page document identifying in embarrassing detail every young woman with whom Moens had contact as well as Hunter's role in facilitating their acquaintance. Learned recommended that she be allowed to retain her job if she had not known of Moens's actual activities, if her public influence was not destroyed by her "lamentable lack of judgment," and if she could "keep her poise after this experience." There was no conclusive evidence against her, and Moens had deceived others who were far more worldly wise: "What might seem incredible naivete to any shrewd man of the world might be fairly to be expected of a woman of innocent mind and fine aspirations for her race. . . . If her past record convinces you that her association with this man does not indicate her true character, it seems that she might well be let off with a probationary period of observation." On the other hand, if she was aware of what was going on, she was "obviously unfit to act as a teacher."[58]

Meanwhile, rumors swept through Black Washington. Stunned by the revelations at the trial, many now believed gossip that schoolteachers had posed in the nude. The Parents League, headed by prominent ministers and encouraged by the *Washington Bee,* began picketing Dunbar High School soon after the trial revealed Charlotte Hunter's relationship with Moens. Some whispered that she taught students to hate white people, spread German propaganda, and fostered disrespect for the American flag. The black community got its way: Miss Hunter resigned as a result of the protests. The Washington *Eagle* even refused to print a letter in her defense. But the Parents League was not satisfied. Assistant superintendent Bruce was charged with incompetence, questionable character, playing favorites, and helping suppress embarrassing nude photographs of those who were politically influential. Mass meetings in black churches demanded that the schools be "purified." A citywide boycott, if Bruce was not removed, was urged by the executive secretary of the Parents League, none other than the Bureau's former undercover informant, Dr. Arthur Ulysses Craig. Fifteen thousand signatures supported such action.[59]

The protest movement also criticized the Bureau because Agent Learned was a member of the Board of Education. Why had he not advised it of Miss Hunter's relationship with Moens so that she could be suspended? Such a revelation, of course, would have jeopardized the entire confidential investigation. But speakers at crowded Parents League meetings were in no mood to accept such reasons. Wild rumors charged that the Department of Justice had tailed Charlotte Hunter "from dive to dive" where she lured young women "for immoral purposes with 'Prof.' Moens," allegedly earning $10,000 for selling girls into prostitution through Moens. Others claimed that Washington NAACP officer Neval Thomas had been permitted to remove nude pictures of teachers from the Bureau's files. With an estimated thirty thousand persons attending mass meetings in April and May, the Parents League demanded a congressional investigation of the city school system and all government officials involved in the case. Friends of Bruce urged the Bureau to release information to prove his innocence.[60]

Finally, the *Washington Post* gained enough information from government sources to clarify the matter for the public. Only one teacher, Miss Hunter, was involved with Moens. The civic uproar finally died out in July 1919 when the Washington race riot monopolized the attention of all its residents. Public agitation was not revived even when a Senate committee investigated the public school system the following year. That panel found no evidence of participation by any other teachers in the Moens affair. Miss Hunter nervously testified, still insisting that she had no knowledge of Moens's sexual activities, never suspected any flaws in either his character or science, and saw no nude photographs until they were shown to her by Bureau agents.[61]

The Moens case disappeared from public view as the school controversy dissipated. Federal prosecutors obtained new indictments in April 1920, but exhibited no urgency in seeking a new court date. Keeping Moens under indictment and holding $2,000 bail money and all his papers, books, and photographs was certainly punishment, which seemed to be their intent. Undoubtedly sensing the animus of the Justice Department, Moens waited until the Harding administration took office to actively seek dismissal of the charges. But inquiries on his behalf in 1921 received the reply that "it is the intention of the United States Attorney to try these indictments when conditions permit" or "at the earliest practicable date." Still, nothing happened.[62]

The next year the weekly magazine *Issues of Today* sought to vindicate Moens, claiming that no second trial occurred because "the Wilson administration did not consider it opportune to bring a case to trial which was an outgrowth of the racial hatred fomented by Mr. Wilson's war propaganda" and that the Harding administration had no interest in the dirty affairs of its predecessors. The article concluded that "through the combined force of war hysteria, professional jealousy, and officious zeal of a bureaucracy anxious to establish a reason for its continued existence at the end of the war, a great injustice has been inflicted upon a scientist of an established international reputation." These factors did indeed figure in the persistence of the Justice Department. Meanwhile, Moens continued his work and in 1922 published *Towards Perfect Man*, which included a number of his nude photographs. He described himself in the book's advertisement as a "Naturalist and Philosopher" and its contents as a contribution to "Somatological and Philosophical Anthropology."[63]

In the spring of 1923 new inquiries prompted a Justice Department review of the case. Moens's supporters, including a defense committee of prominent figures in science and medicine that featured Franz Boas, hoped to persuade federal officials of three facts: that Moens's rooms were illegally searched in October 1918; that his photographs were anthropologic, not pornographic; and that Moens had suffered financially and emotionally from the lengthy proceedings. Their efforts bore fruit when the new U.S. attorney for the District of Columbia, Peyton Gordon, while agreeing with his Wilson administration predecessor that Moens was "a sexual pervert and degenerate" deserving of punishment, argued against a new prosecution:

> Apart from the great expense to the Government that would be involved in a re-trial of the case, a number of the important witnesses are far removed from this jurisdiction and the whereabouts of others would be difficult to ascertain. Again, a number of the colored girls who testified at the former trial are unquestionably in different situations than they were five or six years ago, perhaps having been married or engaged to be married since then, and I doubt if they, when called upon to testify, would make as full disclosures now as they did at the former trial. It is also important that we consider the undesirable effect that a reopening of this case—with all its attendant filthy detail—would have upon the colored people.

No public benefit would come in 1923 from reopening "this filthy, disgusting and revolting matter, especially so when it is questionable whether a conviction could be obtained." Gordon recommended that the cases be *nol-prossed*.[64]

Even though Attorney General Harry M. Daugherty, whose own dirty political linen would soon be aired, had no objection to this course of action, Assistant Attorney General John W. H. Crim, head of the Criminal Division, was still unconvinced and sought information from William T. Hornaday, director of the New York Zoological Park:

> Does this man know anything about the science he pretends to know? If he is a scientist, he is not guilty. If he is not a scientist, he is guilty. The fundamental claim of the prosecution was that he was entirely ignorant of the elementary principles and terminology of anthropology.
>
> If these pictures were the result of scientific effort, rather than salacious effort to exhibit them to the detriment of morals of others, then he is an innocent man, and deserves the sympathy of right thinking people.[65]

Hornaday gave a ringing endorsement, assuring Crim that Moens was "a real anthropologist, and a real man of science" who was discredited by others out of "scientific jealousy." Had his subject not been race mixture, he would never have gotten into trouble. Thus persuaded, Crim sent Hornaday's assessment to the U.S. attorney. Meanwhile, identical articles supporting Moens appeared in *Liberal* and *Culture Forum,* generating more letters to the Justice Department asking that

Moens be vindicated. Gordon entered a *nolle prosequi* on 19 November 1923. However, in one final act of vindictiveness, the Justice Department never bothered to inform Moens and it was not until the following May, and only after his own inquiry, that Moens learned he was no longer under indictment. Moreover, the department did not return his papers and photographs until February 1925.[66]

Not satisfied that the indictment was finally quashed, and seeking personal vindication, Moens wrote to Pres. Calvin Coolidge requesting redress, stating that his studies of race mixture were twisted into appearing as "a pretext to stir up the colored people to bring about a race war while the world war was fought." Still convinced that federal agents were determined to "get something" on him, no matter the injustice, he appealed for the same amends that the United States would demand of the Netherlands should one of its citizens suffer such ill-treatment. Moens received the curt reply that any complaint would have to pass through his legation in Washington. Knowing that Dutch officials would do nothing on his behalf, Moens waited for a year to ask the secretary of state to consider the case on its merits without involving diplomats from his country since they had suggested a "cowardly" plea of guilty when he was undergoing trial. But the State Department would not budge: Nothing would even be considered unless it came via the Netherlands legation.[67]

Moens's supporters renewed their efforts in 1926. While one tried unsuccessfully to get the chairman of the Senate Foreign Relations Committee to persuade the State Department to deal directly with Moens, others got Rep. Emmanuel Celler to introduce a bill that would award Moens $25,000 for "outrages committed upon his person, property, and professional reputation by agents of the Department of Justice in 1918." Whether the congressman believed this to be true or was simply obliging a constituent is unclear. At least one New York newspaper was unsympathetic, headlining its story: "U.S. May Pay 'War Spy' $25,000." The Bureau reviewed the cold case and, predictably, concluded that prosecution had been absolutely warranted, and that no official misconduct had taken place. The bill died in committee.[68]

By 1926 Moens had returned home and persuaded Dutch legislators to pressure the foreign minister to intervene with American authorities on his behalf. When the legation in Washington gingerly pressed the case, the Justice Department reminded it of the embarrassment the case had caused. The Dutch diplomats apparently had little genuine interest in pursuing Moens's claim and were content to have fulfilled their duty by meeting with State Department representatives. In fact, they gave assurance that their government would not press the United States to pass Celler's compensation bill. Thus ended the Dutch government's interest in its countryman.[69]

The final brief chapter in the Moens saga is quickly recounted. Supporters succeeded in getting Representative Celler to file his bill again in 1928. J. Edgar Hoover, who took over as head of the Bureau of Investigation in 1924, was asked to supply a digest of the case. The Bureau repeated its wartime rationalizations: the facts that Moens was an alien, resided in Washington, had contact with foreign governments, collected oil information for a Dutch firm, had suspicious sources of income, was not the scientist he claimed to be, and was active among blacks had justified the government's suspicions. Evidence that he was a sexual "degenerate" and "pervert" followed. Everything seized from Moens was taken under proper warrant. As to allegations that the government harmed his professional reputation: "Moens' reputation, either professional or personal, today is what he personally has made it, and if charity on the part of the prosecutors in failing to go the limit in prosecuting or removing from decent society a deceiver and hopeless moral degenerate, constitutes an outrage—then and only then can it be considered that the Department of Justice has committed an outrage." This memorandum convinced the Committee on Claims that it would be an embarrassment to favorably report the Celler bill, given the unsavory details of the matter. Herman Marie Bernelot Moens was for the last time denied official vindication.[70]

Was Moens a victim of wartime hysteria concerning enemy aliens, of paranoia that subversives were stirring the black population to disloyalty, of the science establishment's unwillingness to accept theories of racial development that did not posit white superiority, or of his own lust? Evidence supports all four conclusions. Nothing he did for Roxana Petroleum or its parent, Royal Dutch Shell, was remotely subversive, and was only disloyal if one defines working for a competitor of Standard Oil as disloyalty. Although uneasy whites often believed that any member of their own race who gave encouragement to the legitimate aspirations of African Americans was a subverter, Moens was guilty of nothing more than agreeing, as not a few foreigners did, that blacks suffered unjustly in the United States.

True enough, Moens was no university-trained scientist. But the fact that he gathered impressive support for the scientific and artistic value of his photographs and published some of them, along with his theories, in *Medical Review of Reviews*, shows that at least part of the scientific community regarded his ideas as worthy of consideration. That he failed to persuade others at a time when disciples of eugenics insisted on Caucasian superiority is not surprising. His ethnographic photographs were neither novel nor obscene in the eyes of members of that discipline. Even his scientific critics did not charge that his pictures were pornographic, only that he was a bogus scientist.

In the end, it was Moens's personal conduct that proved his downfall. His depravity, in the eyes of the Justice Department, was the reason for prosecuting him. But despite its major emphasis on Mann Act enforcement in the early 1910s, despite even the youthfulness of Moens's partners and models, the Bureau's main concern was not the virtue of black women. Rather, Moens's "Continental" sexual practices were simply disgusting. It was his "perversion," not his photographs, that was ultimately on trial. The evidence points to his having lured only one woman—Rachel Custis—into sexual relations on the pretext of science. Helen Saunders was clearly a willing partner. Furthermore, he was prosecuted for something else entirely: the possession and exhibition of allegedly obscene pictures. If the Justice Department had truly wanted to punish Moens as a "pervert," it would have encouraged local authorities to try him for sodomy or fornication. But it was bent more on persecution than prosecution. Moens's licentiousness provided the pretext. He was, in that respect, the author of his own troubles. Nonetheless, the doggedness of Justice Department employees also reveals their own prurient motivations. This *was* a case about sex. Agent Corcoran bluntly asked the uninhibited Helen Saunders if she could "go up there and screw him," and he wanted to *observe* them in the act. A dozen agents interrogated Moens after the abortive effort to photograph a tryst, forced him to describe his "perversions," and then taunted him as he left. Unable to admit their own sexual fascination with the lurid details of the case, Corcoran, other agents, and perhaps the federal prosecutor instead adopted a self-righteous stance of moral indignation.

Evenhanded justice did not prevail in the Moens case. He was a victim of the enemy alien–black subversion hysteria. Any white person who maintained relationships with blacks, especially one of purported Germanic background, was automatically suspect. But because evidence of subversion was so flimsy, prosecution, even using the broadly imprecise Espionage and Sedition Acts, was clearly foolish. So some other offense had to be found if the Justice Department was to "get" Moens. Yet even with all the ammunition supplied by Moens himself, obscenity charges were not provable. The most tragic victim, however, was Washington's black community, which regarded Dunbar High School and its faculty as exemplifying the intelligence, respectability, and progressiveness of the race. Indeed, Black Washington was home to substantial numbers of the Talented Tenth, whose responsibility and destiny were to lead and inspire those who were less educated and less fortunate. Instead they were drawn into an embarrassing scandal that undermined the respectability for which they had so mightily striven.

10

"Negro Subversion": Army Intelligence Investigations during World War I

World War I was already three months old when the army's fledgling Military Intelligence Section, headed by intelligence pioneer Lt. Col Ralph H. Van Deman, added to its burgeoning responsibilities the investigation of alleged enemy influences on the black population. The Justice Department's Bureau of Investigation had become convinced of such danger as soon as the United States declared war on Germany, and Van Deman was not far behind in fearing "Negro Unrest." As early as June, he became convinced of the existence of "an antigovernment attitude on the part of isolated groups among the negro population . . . which would tend to indicate German activity." Before long he was even more categorical, maintaining that "at the bottom of the negro unrest German influence is unquestionable." Moreover, Van Deman was gullible and frightened enough to give credence to rumors of Germans, masquerading as door-to-door sewing machine salesmen, who were said to be encouraging blacks to believe "that this country is not theirs and that they should not fight for it."[1]

By the summer of 1917 an intelligence partnership was being forged between the Bureau, army and navy intelligence, and the Post Office and State Departments, their representatives meeting weekly at the Justice Department to share information and determine responsibility for particular cases. The practice of supplying the other agencies with copies of one's own investigative reports was also begun. The MIS started a new case file on "Negro subversion" in July, and among its first items were copies of Bureau reports alleging German successes in encouraging disloyalty among blacks.[2] But the MIS had neither the manpower nor, more importantly, a clearly defined mission to investigate such suspicions. That mission soon evolved, however, spurred particularly by race riots in mid-1917.

The two white men who were most influential in constructing the army's "Negro subversion" mission held relatively enlightened racial views for that day. One was a newly commissioned major, Joel E. Spingarn, an educator and president of the board of trustees of the National Association for the Advancement of Colored People. His initial assignment was not, however, in intelligence, but with the infantry. The second newly minted officer, Maj. Herbert Parsons, was assigned immediately to intelligence. He was a former Republican congressman from New York who was active in a variety of urban social reform movements. While not previously involved in racial uplift efforts, he had a more sympathetic perspective on the less fortunate members of society than many other Ivy League–trained lawyers. Spingarn was eager to ensure black patriotism, believing it would be key to any future improvement in race relations. While desirous of uncovering any enemy attempts to subvert the loyalty of blacks, he was skeptical that such activities were actually taking place. His awareness that many blacks still embraced Bookerite conservatism and conventional patriotism helped him resist giving credence to panicky rumors that large numbers of blacks were pro-German or willing to cooperate with enemy agents. Neither man, however, would prevent army intelligence from identifying African-American militancy as a danger to national unity and purpose during the war. It would join the other federal intelligence bureaucracies in seeking to blunt the aspirations of the emerging young generation of New Crowd Negroes.

Military intelligence worried, of course, that enemy propaganda would interfere with the war effort, especially with conscription. Almost any tale, from whatever source, had to be investigated, and it was just such a rumor that prompted the MIS to probe black loyalty. The talebearer was Hallie E. Queen, a linguist and former Howard University student who had no formal connection with the MIS but would repeatedly warn it of fanciful enemy influences on the African-American population. Her first report, in August 1917, claimed that such subversion was going on in Washington itself. Major Parsons assigned Spingarn to make confidential inquiries as to the existence of enemy propaganda among blacks, warning him to conceal the fact that the government was concerned.[3] Spingarn had numerous contacts within the black Talented Tenth in New York, and within ten days had a memorandum written by "two of the ablest and most responsible colored men in the country," whom he unfortunately did not identify. The analysis was indeed sensible. While acknowledging press reports from all over the country of alleged enemy efforts to subvert blacks, and confirming that, nationwide, blacks were disheartened and dissatisfied, the authors pointed to domestic circumstances, not German subversion, as the explanation. African Americans clearly felt abused. They suffered discrimination in the draft, often viewing it as a method to enslave black labor. They were incensed that Col. Charles Young, the highest-ranking black officer and certain to become the first black general, was denied that opportunity when the army ordered his retirement on questionable medical grounds. Lynching and mob attacks continued unabated, the most bloody being the East St. Louis riot in mid-1917. Black troops suffered poor treatment from both the military and civilians at every southern cantonment, and some in Houston had even been driven to mutiny after being sorely abused by the local white population. But the memorandum ended with a powerful antidote: If the federal government took action to correct these injustices, if "the War Department will give early and definite assurance that Negro troops are to be used as soldiers in the same way as white men," and if President Wilson would publicly condemn mob violence, then "it is certain the country can count upon the loyalty of its colored citizens to the very end." Spingarn agreed that unrest due to pro-Germanism was probably rare and that blacks' despair, particularly fueled by the summer's riots, was caused by racism.[4]

The memorandum, with Spingarn's comments, went all the way up the chain of command to the chief of staff. Whether he read it or not is unknown. But army leadership, including those in its intelligence branch, had been clearly advised that positive black morale hinged on correcting domestic abuses, not on rooting out supposed enemy agents. This conclusion was confirmed a month later in another report on the "negro question," this one commissioned by MIS chief Van Deman himself. He ordered operatives in New York to identify the sources of current tensions there. One of them interviewed white police commanders in black neighborhoods who reported that there was no significant spirit of disloyalty within the city's rapidly growing African-American population.[5]

With dispassionate reports clearly pointing to discrimination and mob violence as the main causes of black disaffection, would the MIS (and its counterparts in the other intelligence agencies) acknowledge the impact of those issues and discount the existence of a German conspiracy to subvert black loyalties? Hardly. Their thinking was already steeped in conspiracy theories. Furthermore, most of their agents and operatives had a stake in preserving the racial status quo, which privileged whites over blacks. The Bureau of Investigation and the Post Office Department were the guiltiest of perceiving enemy influence in every expression of black grievance while refusing to credit racism as the central factor. Army intelligence did not as readily embrace this distortion, thanks to a handful of liberal whites and a talented black investigator, Maj. Walter H. Loving. But even they could not prevent it from marching down the same path trod by the other agencies in pursuit of alleged German agents and black subversives.

Identifying positive black morale as an important ingredient in achieving victory was a major breakthrough for military intelligence. Major Loving is identified with a second progressive step: the recruitment of black investigators to provide reliable information on racial conditions. This was a delicate task, because such men had to be conservative enough not to rankle the ultraconservative officer corps, which was disproportionately staffed with white southerners. Loving was an ideal choice, having already compiled a distinguished career as director of the 48th Infantry Regiment's band in the Philippines and later of the Philippine Constabulary Band, which he led until his retirement in 1916. In a farsighted move, Van Deman persuaded him to join army intelligence shortly before war commenced. To get him started, he arranged secret funding and secured a private office in Washington.[6] Loving's levelheadedness would become more and more valuable as the war progressed. The challenge to all intelligence operations was distinguishing rumor from truth. Tips and suspicions came from a variety of sources, but, as Spingarn warned, there were individuals like Hallie Queen who were prone to exaggerating danger. Indeed, sifting fact from fiction was not easy for anyone in the intelligence bureaucracies in 1917. Giving credence to unsubstantiated rumors created new victims, one of whom was Nannie Burroughs, a pioneer in education for black girls and founder of the National Training School for Women and Girls. This institution, located in Washington, emphasized industrial education, racial self-reliance, and the "3–B's"—Bible, bath, and broom—as keys to black progress. A deeply religious woman, she conducted well-attended early-morning prayer meetings. But alarmed whites, in the days following the East St. Louis riot in the summer of 1917, construed them as protest gatherings that might undermine the war effort. The specific charge against her was fostering "social prejudice." This was a twisted euphemism for hatred of whites. Miss Burroughs was, in fact, a patriot interested in promoting "positive propaganda" among the race. Nonetheless, the Bureau of Investigation and the MIS both launched investigations of her. Loving had little difficulty finding her to be loyal, but the Bureau took considerably longer to conclude that her opinions and actions were inoffensive.[7]

Loving was especially valuable to army intelligence in the early months of the war in sifting through the many rumors of enemy subversion and pro-German activity. Volunteer informants were frequently unreliable, and sometimes near hysteria. A. W. Williams, a citizen of Okmulgee, Oklahoma, advised the secretary of war, who passed his letter on to the MIS, not to train black soldiers because German spies who were inciting them to demand equal rights and intermarriage with whites had already poisoned the race. These enemy agents had also taught them that they should not fight the Germans, who were their friends, but should submit to military training, so as to be able to rebel. As Williams saw it, blacks had been so poisoned that it would be suicidal to arm them.[8]

Hallie Queen's several tips were likewise based on fear and imagination. In August and October 1917, she forwarded clippings from the black press to demonstrate that a spirit of unrest and "the seeds of revolt" were being planted within Black America. She also encouraged James Thomas, a former professor at Howard University, to convey his own excited suspicions to the MIS. Securing a meeting with Parsons, he alleged that several black leaders had been encouraged to create a "disturbance" against the government while the nation was preoccupied with war. When he interviewed two of those named by Thomas, Loving discovered that neither had been approached for any disloyal purpose and that Thomas was clearly an unreliable informant. While Loving was convinced that a "great amount of unrest among the colored population" existed, he was not willing to give credence to every alarm and stressed the need to question the veracity of volunteer informants if the MIS was not to be misled. Yet it was hard to ignore the rumors of even those who were demonstrably excitable. By the end of 1917, Parsons was receiving regular reports volunteered by Queen, none of which proved to contain anything of intelligence significance. These examples show that the MIS was no less able than the other intelligence agencies to distinguish alarmist reports and reporters from those offering genuinely credible information concerning black disaffection.[9]

Another early MIS informant was Robert Russa Moton, protégé of the late Booker T. Washington and his successor as principal of Tuskegee Institute. Like Washington, Moton was opposed to overt racial militancy and had a stake in preserving goodwill between the races. Moton's letters to the War Department and President Wilson were taken seriously. He believed it necessary to remain anonymous in delicate situations, stressing his expectation that the MIS would keep in confidence his report that a prominent black physician in Nashville, C. V. Roman, had been "approached" by a black "anarchist." Van Deman personally wrote to Roman, who was the editor of the *Journal of the National Medical Association,* the black counterpart to the whites-only American Medical Association, to say he was investigating all reports of "German propaganda." Roman would not name the individual in question but assured Van Deman that he was no anarchist, although he had suggested that retaliation might be the only solution for lynching and race riots. Roman claimed to have advised his acquaintance that violent methods would be suicidal. Van Deman was no more immune to exaggerated fears of racial unrest than many other white observers, however, and persisted in believing that Roman and his correspondent were willing to use force to accomplish their ends.[10]

While Major Parsons fielded Hallie Queen's alarmist reports, he also used a much more reliable source who was also a personal acquaintance: W. E. B. DuBois. Although DuBois's militant editorials in the *Crisis* excited Queen's fears and would later draw fire from the Bureau of Investigation, the Post Office Department, and army intelligence, in September 1917 Parsons solicited the editor's counsel regarding the morale of black soldiers. There is no record of DuBois's advice, but the fact that Parsons sought it demonstrates that he recognized the need for knowledgeable sources of information from within the black community.[11]

For the first six months of the war the Military Intelligence Section faced challenges simply in getting organized, having started almost from scratch in April. The majority of early "negro subversion" case files contained reports from Bureau agents, not MIS operatives. By October, however, each geographical department of the army had an intelligence officer (IO), and soon additional ones would be assigned to nearly every army facility in the nation. The division of responsibilities between the Bureau and the MIS was still indistinct, however. On 2 October, Van Deman ordered the Northeastern Department's IO to investigate William Monroe Trotter, editor of the outspoken *Boston Guardian.* Trotter was described as being "very radical in his views on the race question" and one who "might make some trouble." The same day, Van Deman instructed the IO for the Central Department to investigate "unrest" among blacks in Chicago. Why he wanted the MIS involved in these matters is unclear, for the Bureau had many more agents in both cities, and they were already monitoring black activism. On the other hand, the next day Van Deman asked the Bureau to investigate a black doctor alleged to be making "treasonable" speeches in Harlem. The MIS had a large contingent in New York, so it was not for lack of personnel that it passed the matter to the Bureau.[12] In fact, the relationship between the War and Justice Departments was still evolving during the second half of 1917.

In investigating black suspects or those thought to be subverting blacks' loyalties, the most important trend in 1917 was the growing reliance on Maj. Walter Loving to "keep his eye on negro agitation." As Van Deman later described the MIS's motivation,

> In the fall of 1917 it became evident that agents of the Central Powers were circulating among the Negro people of the United States. The method of agitation used was by word of mouth and it was evident that measures to counteract the

> influence of such propaganda must be taken if we were to avoid serious trouble with the Negro population. For this purpose two extremely capable and reliable Negro men were selected after most careful investigation. These men were instructed to circulate among the various communities where unrest was being reported among the Negro population. They were to remain long enough in each community to determine for themselves what the real trouble was and then by conversations and formal talks in Negro churches and other meeting places to persuade the Negroes in the community that the actions being suggested to them by persons who had previously circulated among them would lead to very serious consequences if not abandoned. In order to cover as large an area as possible these two men did not travel together but during the continuance of the war they covered practically the entire United States although their principal [*sic*] work lay among the Northern States. Neither of these men have ever had any public acknowledgment of the very fine constructive work which they accomplished.

The two men referred to were Loving and Charles Holston Williams, who was brought into the MIS in 1918. It is sad that Van Deman praised their accomplishments but did not see fit to include their names when he wrote this lengthy document, which named many white officers who made important contributions to military intelligence in World War I.[13]

Of the two responsibilities outlined by Van Deman—investigating suspicious events and individuals, and promoting loyalty and patriotism—Loving was used primarily for the first purpose in 1917. He was heartened by the appointment of Emmett J. Scott as special assistant to the secretary of war which, be believed, would generate widespread support for the government. Scott had for many years been Booker T. Washington's private secretary and for a time was touted as his successor. Loving probably exaggerated the degree to which Scott's appointment to an advisory position in the government shaped black perceptions on the war. The black middle class hailed every such designation as "recognition" of the race, but such jobs probably seemed irrelevant to most blacks, who never experienced the favor of government. Loving quite likely unintentionally misled his MIS superiors when he wrote that Scott's "judgment upon the vital points arising from time to time which will so nearly concern the race in general, may be accepted as the voice of the people which he represent [*sic*]."[14]

Loving's next assignment illustrates not only an expansion of his duties, but also the degree to which whites were willing to believe the wildest rumors concerning their black countrymen. Van Deman received information in mid-October, probably from a Bureau of Investigation report, that blacks in Glencoe, Illinois, were gathering arms and ammunition so as to prevent a repetition of the East St. Louis riot. Loving went to investigate, beginning a pattern of crisscrossing the country in response to rumors or incidents. What he found in that small community on the north side of Chicago was a classic instance of whites transferring their own guilty uneasiness over race relations into unwarranted suspicions that blacks were planning to attack them. A year before, authorization had been given to raise a black regiment, the Chicago Home Guards, with two companies to be recruited from Glencoe. The present rumors stemmed from the fact that the soldiers' wives had formed an auxiliary and given several public "entertainments" to raise money for their husbands' uniforms and equipment. What excited whites was a public letter from the ladies inviting participation—by whites as well as blacks—in activities supporting the companies, stating that the units stood for "patriotism, loyalty, and race pride." It was likely this latter phrase that unsupportive whites misconstrued into hostile racial motives. Fortunately, Glencoe remained quiet. Loving's task was easy to complete: He had only to ascertain the facts to quiet suspicions at MIS headquarters; there were no "fires" to put out in Glencoe. Not all of his subsequent missions would be accomplished that easily, however. White fears of black subversion or, worse, retaliation, were far too widespread.[15]

While in Chicago, Loving received orders from the Central Department commander to investigate labor troubles at the Inland Steel Works in Indiana Harbor. In actuality, he found himself an agent of an army general determined to keep black workers employed in a critical industry even though they feared friction with white workers and found available housing abominable. For its part, the company's only dissatisfaction was the fact that southern-born black workers tended to work a few weeks and then, flush with pay, leave for Chicago to "have a good time."

Major Loving met with a delegation of black employees and then investigated conditions in town. What lay behind the fears of black-white conflict was the existence of interracial prostitution at some of the more than two hundred saloons and dance halls surrounding the mill. Loving predicted that "this free intermingling of races . . . can but result in a serious race riot in the near future." The plant superintendent was less alarmed, however, having already formed and drilled a company of two hundred white workers that could quickly be mobilized to suppress any disturbance. Black workers understandably did not trust this force to protect them. Loving tried to reassure the black workers by forming a three-man committee which would have immediate access to the superintendent if they needed to report any trouble, whether in the mill or in town. What gave the workers more confidence, however, was a promise Loving secured from the Central Department that troops would be promptly dispatched from nearby Fort Sheridan should any dangerous situation arise. Loving's report to that officer reveals how much his intelligence assignment had been co-opted: "I carried to these [black] families and workmen the Commanding General's message, to stick to the work and ample protection would be given them. The families were unanimous in their expressions of gratitude to the Commanding General for offering them such consolation." They apparently were willing to endure crowded and filthy housing conditions, graphically described by Loving, as the price of having jobs and a promise that their personal security would be protected. Fearing violence stemming from interracial intimacies, Loving allowed himself to become the tool of management, local landlords, and the military production effort in failing to demand improvement in the quality of life for black employees.[16]

As 1917 came to a close, Walter Loving was given a new responsibility: investigating complaints of mistreatment of black troops as well as attempts to subvert their loyalty. Rumors of abuse, even if untrue, could seriously affect conscription, especially since blacks' compliance with the draft was considerably below that of whites. Loving himself initiated the first such inquiries in late October and early November, bringing to Van Deman's attention rumors he had heard in Chicago that only fifty doctors at the all-black officer training camp at Des Moines would be commissioned. Loving learned that the surgeon general had issued such an order but had stayed it after protests from the Colored Medical Society in Washington. This policy was a slap to the large number of physicians who sacrificed private practices and bought their own uniforms in order to serve their country and their race. The issue of commissioning black doctors persisted to the end of the war. For example, Dr. Robert B. Foster, of Athens, Georgia, was commissioned a first lieutenant in the Medical Reserve Corps (MRC) in April 1918 but was still wearing a private's uniform two weeks before the Armistice, even though there was a great need for qualified physicians for black troops. In another case, Dr. H. B. R. Orr, of Hillsboro, Texas, and Dr. James A. Franklin, of Evergreen, Alabama, held commissions in the MRC but, not having received orders to report to duty as officers, were drafted and sent to Camp Zachary Taylor as privates in the Hospital Corps.[17]

A second controversy was potentially even more damaging. Newspapers across the nation printed a report that black troops were to be rushed to France, not for combat, but to dig trenches. Loving learned that draftees at Camps Meade, Dix, and Upton were particularly discouraged by this report because they had only been issued fatigue, not combat uniforms, although he did not directly question the reported policy: "Whether or not it is the intention of the government to send these troops post haste to dig trenches, it is certainly unwise to release this information." Soon thereafter, Loving investigated "unrest" among black troops at Camp Lee, Virginia. Their complaint concerned the perception that they had no opportunity for promotion and were consigned to the ranks of trench diggers.[18]

At the same time, Loving also began to pay attention to the more militant voices in the black press, first taking alarm at an editorial printed in John Mitchell's *Richmond Planet* and reprinted in William Monroe Trotter's *Boston Guardian.* Mitchell would soon be warned by the Justice Department to moderate his rhetoric or suffer suppression. Trotter was a longtime opponent of the Bookerite school of racial accommodation and persona non grata with the Wilson administration, having argued with the president during a White House interview. Mitchell's editorial had an element of cynicism, but certainly not disloyalty:

> The longer the war and the bloodier, the better it will be for the Colored folks. When about a million white soldiers are fighting in France or somewhere else and the transports begin bringing the wounded to this country, then will the Colored folks come into their own. The white men at the top will not be able to distinguish a black soldier from a white one. All they will want will be help and the black trooper will give that help.
>
> When the war is over and the soldiers from the trenches and the plain march in review triumphantly before a grateful nation and a happy President of the

> United States, the long line of devoted black troopers will receive the encomiums of the nation and be welcomed to receive all of the rights and privileges of any other citizens. This can only come from a long and from a bloody war. From a short, quick war, Good Lord deliver us.

Loving cautioned Van Deman that the appearance of this editorial would have an immediate negative effect on black troop morale, as both papers had many subscribers in uniform, and he urged that Trotter and Mitchell be warned about such expressions. There is no record that the MIS took any action, but the Bureau of Investigation compiled an extensive case file on the issue. Loving was personally offended by the editorial: "I am most loyal to the race with which I am identified, but not to the extent that I would see the blood of thousands of American soldiers shed upon a foreign battlefield, before I would consent to lend my assistance." This is not exactly what Mitchell advocated, but Loving was clearly worried lest white America perceive any reservation on the part of blacks' patriotism.[19]

Loving's next major effort was to develop strategies for stimulating black morale. In November 1917 he arranged for Robert R. Church, a well-known black Republican and wealthy Memphis businessman, to introduce him to prominent, loyal, and well-to-do blacks in each large southern city who could serve as his informants on racial matters. This "information chain" would cost nothing and in fact save the expense of staffing each city with a black informant. Heartened by the eagerness of men to serve in this capacity, Loving predicted that his network would soon encompass the entire country. Van Deman gave his blessing to the scheme, not only because he trusted Loving but because Church was known to be reliably conservative. Although Loving's new contacts were not much used for the remainder of 1917, he would employ them the following year in staging a speaking tour to promote patriotism and quell unrest.[20]

By the end of the year, Loving was regularly receiving information from Bureau reports alleging pro-German attitudes among blacks as well as enemy subversion of the race. How much this convinced him that a dangerous situation had been reached is not known, but he showed judiciousness when he was sent in early December to Hampton, Virginia, to investigate charges that two whites alleged to be German sympathizers were propagandizing local blacks. This seemed especially serious because the Norfolk–Newport News area contained important shipyards and naval facilities and was an embarkation point for troops being sent to France. The intelligence officer stationed at Fort Monroe, who did not discount the possibility of subversion, had already made several inquiries. Loving first met with influential blacks, including the head of Hampton Institute, and then had informants keep a suspect and the alleged meeting point under surveillance for two days. The one individual who was said to be most propagandized proved to be an elderly, illiterate man who was so harmless that, in Loving's words, "if he were given the German Empire, he could not muster a corporal's guard among the negroes to help him protect it." Loving took only two days to puncture the case for subversion that white intelligence officers had been inflating for nearly a month.[21]

After finishing his business in Hampton, Loving entrained for Richmond, ostensibly to hear Roscoe Conkling Simmons, a well-known black orator, give a patriotic speech. Instead, Loving helped prevent a riot. African Americans all over the country were distraught on the night of 11 December, when evening newspapers brought word that thirteen black soldiers found guilty three days before of participating in the Houston mutiny had been hanged. The executions shocked many, especially since almost no time had been granted for appeals. Loving found a restive crowd of fifteen hundred interrupting Simmons with cries of "what about the hanging of the negro soldiers?" Simmons artfully abandoned his text and declaimed that "The American negro . . . knows but one government, speaks but one language, and claims but one flag—the flag that set him free . . . [T]he negro, with no voice in his government, has but one request. He asks for the gun of war, for the uniform of his country, and for the command from the officer who fears neither life nor death." As the audience wildly applauded, Loving had the orchestra strike up "The Star Spangled Banner," which brought the assemblage to its feet, singing the anthem. Concluding his report on this incident, Loving urged Van Deman to send Simmons all over the country to promote patriotism: "We need immediate action against German propaganda." This was indeed a strange conclusion, for Loving had just discounted German propaganda in Hampton, and he knew that the crowd in Richmond was stirred by the tragic executions of men who had been pushed to the limit by racist whites in Houston.[22]

The hangings sparked protests elsewhere. Hearing that indignation meetings would be held in Baltimore, Loving rushed there but found that the churches were taking the lead, setting a day of prayer for the executed soldiers. A week later he returned to Washington, where he lived when not out on investigations, and found that teachers at Dunbar High School, the pride of the local black community, were wearing mourning badges. He conferred with the principal and the black assistant superintendent of schools, Roscoe Conkling Bruce, stressing that teachers, parents, and children in other schools were likely to follow Dunbar's lead. "Then the situation would be serious." The two officials assured Loving that "immediate action would [be] taken."[23] This affair, and the event in Richmond, foreshadowed Loving's actions in 1918, when he would continue to investigate reports of suspected disloyalty, but also allow himself, in some circumstances, to dampen legitimate black dissent.

Army intelligence investigations of suspected disloyalty increased dramatically in 1918. The belief that disloyalty was widespread among African Americans increased even as the nation's defenses were strengthened. The "negro subversion" case file became even more a repository of unsubstantiated charges and impossible-to-prove rumors. Typical was the letter from a white resident of rural Georgia who reported hearsay that black soldiers felt no loyalty to the country because they had no voice in the government. Van Deman requested the names of those who had expressed such sentiments so that they could be investigated, but either the correspondent had no concrete information or was unwilling to get further involved. Another worthless tip, from the Office of Naval Intelligence, told of Gypsy fortune-tellers in the South who were said to be informing blacks that if Germany did not win the war, they would be re-enslaved. The State Department was also a source of similarly useless hearsay. One of its own intelligence agents related suspicions that Germans (fronted by Kuhn, Loeb, and Company) were buying up property and businesses in Harlem. In addition, a German was said to have told a black gathering that his countrymen would treat blacks kindly if they conquered the United States. It was also alleged that a Spanish family in Harlem was hatching a Mexican plot. Such tales, with informants supplying sketchy or fanciful suspicions, further strained an already overburdened army intelligence corps.[24]

The Military Intelligence Section (renamed the Military Intelligence Branch in February 1918, and finally the Military Intelligence Division in August) perfected the mechanisms for conducting domestic counterespionage as well as an abiding concern for "negro subversion" in 1918. Even though most suspect enemy aliens had been apprehended months earlier, the intelligence establishment acted for the duration of the war as if sabotage and subversion were realities. But almost no damage occurred to America's military and industrial capabilities after April 1917 that could not be explained by factors other than enemy activity. Moreover, hostile agents certainly enjoyed no great success in recruiting sympathizers from among even the most disaffected residents of the country. What happened instead was that intelligence agencies tended to explain opposition or apathy toward the war—by pacifists, radical labor unionists, religious sectarians, socialists, and a significant minority of blacks—as the result of enemy subversion, rather than the product of domestic political and religious issues. By fundamentally misunderstanding the nature of black apathy and dissent, all of the intelligence agencies created the myth that "negro subversion" was a real threat to the nation's ability to win the war, when in fact there was no concrete evidence that blacks' disaffection was translated into overt acts other than avoidance of the draft.

By early 1918 the army's domestic surveillance operations had become regularized. Intelligence officers were recruited, given minimal training, and assigned to every camp and post. They were supervised by departmental IOs attached to every geographical department within the continental United States. The departmental IOs in turn received instructions directly from the chief of military intelligence in Washington. When he received information concerning a suspect, the chain of command was activated, as in the case of Pat Murphy, who came to the MIS's attention via a report from the Bureau of Investigation. Murphy, a black man thought to have been born and raised in Germany, had worked for many years as a fireman on German ships. His alleged offense was photographing military buildings at Camp Travis and Fort Sam Houston, Texas. The IO at the latter facility interrogated him and learned instead that he was born in Fredericksburg, Texas, a town settled by Germans, which explained his ability to speak German. Murphy admitted he had lied on an employment application, listing his birthplace as Hamburg, Germany, because the employer believed American-born blacks were undependable. The IO also learned that Murphy had been to Camp Travis just once, to visit a soldier friend. Furthermore, he did not take any pictures because he did not own a "Kodak." Believing that Murphy was truthful, reassured by his promise to report any disloyal statements made by Germans, and satisfied that he was too old to be eligible for the draft, the IO recommended that the case be closed.[25]

Being an MID informant could turn unpleasant. Hallie Queen taught Spanish at Dunbar High School, and after Major Loving presented charges against another teacher in January 1918, she was identified in school gossip as a snitch. After she pleaded for vindication, Loving explained matters to her principal, which apparently defused the issue. Queen continued to submit unsolicited rumor-filled reports, apparently relishing her access to officialdom and the opportunity to demonstrate her own patriotism. By February she had extended her canvass as far as Harlem. She asserted that a number of Africans from German colonies—some probably seamen who had jumped ship—had taken up residence there, although local blacks appeared to be shunning them. Most butchers and druggists in the community, she claimed, were Germans, but there appeared to be no enemy propaganda in either Harlem or on the Lower West Side, which also contained a significant black population. All in all, she wrote, there was nothing worrisome in New York. She later returned to conditions in Washington, her hometown, calling attention to rumors that the government was withholding news that black regiments in France were being cut to pieces. A wounded black veteran recuperating at Walter Reed Army Hospital had supposedly exposed this cover-up. She later admitted that she had no definite source for the rumor, and an independent investigation reached the same conclusion.[26]

Investigations in the winter of 1918 covered a wide range of suspicions. An IO in St. Louis, hearing rumors of "propaganda" in the city, used black informants to canvass neighborhoods and fraternal organizations, only to find no evidence of organized sedition or even widespread disaffection. The propensity to exaggerate or misconstrue dissent was demonstrated in the response to an anonymous letter from a black soldier at Camp Meade, Maryland, who boasted that, now that they were armed, he and his comrades would do most of their fighting on the home front, not overseas, to avenge the wrongs done by whites. The MIB saw a wide range of possible motivations for the letter, imagining that it might have come from an enemy agent or someone else intent on blocking the use of armed black troops. "On the other hand, it is possible that it may represent a center of dissatisfaction and misunderstanding" regarding the camp hospital and the granting of leave. Van Deman ordered Loving to Camp Meade to uncover any actual grievance among the black troops and to attempt to correct any false impressions. Loving had recently completed a nationwide patriotic campaign aimed at black citizens and it was natural that Van Deman would hope that he could convince black troops of the need for uncomplaining patriotism and loyal self-sacrifice.[27]

Other anonymous "threats" were forwarded to military intelligence in the early months of 1918. A letter signed by "The spiritual Descendants of John Brown" warned that there would be far more sabotage if additional black soldiers were executed for participation in the Houston mutiny. Loving had no way of identifying its author. Another letter, this one from a soldier, declared that blacks felt no loyalty to a country that denied them political participation. The writer added that when they went into battle, German soldiers would not fire on them. A third unsigned letter, postmarked at Tylertown, Mississippi, and addressed to the secretary of war, boasted that blacks were praying for Germany to win the war out of hatred for whites who mistreated them, and claimed that God was equally tired of such mistreatment. Obviously there was nothing that military intelligence could do to track down the writers of such warnings. Reports from informants of unknown reliability were often equally difficult to verify, such as the accusation that two unidentified black ministers were preaching the benefits of peace and the horrors of war, or the story of an unnamed African American who urged others to protest the East St. Louis riots by refraining from enlistment.[28]

Major Walter Loving was the army's most reliable interpreter of black sensibilities. He shared in common with his white counterparts the fear that blacks might become seriously disillusioned with the war effort, but he knew that such views would likely be the product of American racism. Appalled at the escalation of racial violence during the war, he boldly addressed Van Deman in January 1918, describing the killing of Will Butler, who was stabbed to death with the complicity of white policemen by a mob determined to enforce segregation on a Memphis streetcar. Loving's conclusion was blunt: "It is this kind of justice which arouses the indignation of the colored people here, and it is lamentable that such JUSTICE is allowed to be meted out in any country which is inhabited by civilized people. No attempt has been made by the authorities here to even investigate the matter." Two months later, Loving was even more straightforward, writing Van Deman that "lynching is the world's greatest evil and the sooner it is on the wane, the sooner the unrest among negroes will disappear."[29]

In order to bolster black patriotism in such difficult times, Loving helped organize an ambitious cross-country speaking tour by two well-known black Republican orators: Memphis politician Robert R. Church and Booker T. Washington's nephew, Roscoe Conkling Simmons. Church had many political contacts and he planned the itinerary, booked many of the facilities, and gave a standard speech on "My Country and My Flag." Simmons was the more stellar orator, however, and he could also guarantee crowds on the basis of his association with the Tuskegee and Hampton Institutes. Although this patriotic road show targeted black audiences, prominent whites were platform guests and helped promote the notion of a biracial war effort. The tour began in the South, with stops in Marshall, Texas; Jackson, Mississippi; New Orleans; Tuskegee, Alabama; Atlanta; Nashville; and Memphis. Leaving Church behind, Loving and Simmons proceeded on to Little Rock, Oklahoma City, Los Angeles, Pasadena, San Francisco, Oakland, Colorado Springs, Denver, Kansas City, St. Louis, and ended in Columbus, Ohio. Loving's reports were ecstatic: Crowds of both races cheered the orators at every stop; hundreds of telegrams from other communities invited the speakers to stop there; and mayors, judges, and prominent white businessmen vied for the opportunity to be seen on the platform. Loving believed that an important additional benefit from the tour was an increase in interracial understanding brought about by the mutual patriotic fervor:

> No plan could have been organized to have brought the races closer together than the one formulated to instill patriotism and loyalty in the hearts of the colored people. I would that words would permit me to express here the sentiments of the colored people all over the United States. "Pressed to the wall to make room for strangers—mobbed, lynched, and burned to the stake—yet they are willing to cry out in the language of David, 'Tho you slay me, yet will I trust you.'" There can be no greater exemplification of patriotism and loyalty than is expressed in the above quotation. And as I sat beneath the trembling voice of the speaker and listened to the words of eloquence and pleading which fell from his lips, I saw prominent white men nod and bow their heads, and grey haired women weep.

Proof of the effectiveness of this patriotic orgy was the fact that, in the Midwest, Simmons received "many" anonymous letters, presumably from Germans, warning him to "stop trying to fool the people of his race to war against the German people for a nation that does not recognize them as citizens nor give them protection." Loving concluded that Simmons had succeeded beyond expectation in linking the races in "one common cause to make the world safe for Democracy." Moreover, the benefits would outlast the emotional moment: The solution to the "southern problem" was getting the races together to mutually attack lynching and guarantee police protection for blacks.[30]

While delighted by the apparent results of this patriotic tour, the Military Intelligence Branch remained convinced that there was still substantial danger from "negro subversion." This obsession is clearly revealed in the first of several investigations of Howard University dean Kelly Miller in February and March 1918. A mathematician and sociologist whose career at Howard lasted nearly half a century, Miller was also a nationally known lecturer and essayist who stood ideologically between Booker T. Washington and W. E. B. DuBois. It was his most widely read publication that spurred MIB's suspicion. *The Disgrace of Democracy: An Open Letter to President Woodrow Wilson,* which eventually sold 250,000 copies, was a protest against recent race riots, particularly the bloody affair in East St. Louis.[31] Van Deman wrote Loving a detailed memorandum, quoting several of Miller's militant statements: "The white people of this country are not good enough to govern the Negro. . . . Reproach is cast upon your contention for the democratization of the world in the face of its lamentable failure at home. . . . You have never done anything constructive for the Negro." To Van Deman, the greatest danger lay in the fact that Miller's voice was so well respected: "His intelligence and the authority with which he speaks can have but one effect, that of stimulating adverse propaganda among the negroes of this country." Racial militancy was dangerous, as Van Deman saw it, whatever the source or the grievance, and he ordered Loving to investigate Miller and his activities.

Loving did something entirely unorthodox for an intelligence officer: He showed Van Deman's letter to Miller, including its instruction that Loving investigate him. This is only understandable in light of the fact that Loving had already interviewed Miller the previous November, presumably to discuss the widely circulated pamphlet. Since that time Loving had reviewed all of Miller's newspaper columns prior to publication, so Miller was already feeling the weight of government pressure, if not outright censorship. Now, three months later, he was eager to assert his patriotism. *The Disgrace of Democracy,* he reported, had been entered into the *Congressional Record* by a senator who had characterized his analysis as temperate. According to Miller, it generated no criticism from any members of Congress. The purpose of the pamphlet was to urge the government to remedy injustices so that blacks' loyalty would be strengthened, not to "stimulate adverse propaganda." He then summarized his own patriotic credentials, which included numerous published statements, encouragement of Howard students to seek officer commissions, and support for Liberty Bond and Red Cross campaigns. Miller concluded his defense with understandable dismay: "In view of my utmost endeavor to serve the country at this critical hour, I confess that I am somewhat surprised and disappointed on finding myself under surveillance by the Intelligence Department of the government." Undoubtedly Miller had believed that by allowing Loving to preview his most recent publications, he would be spared the kind of pressure he was now experiencing.

Miller's response reached Van Deman, with Loving's assurance that he had gone over *The Disgrace of Democracy* paragraph by paragraph with Miller to point out phrases that might be "misleading" during the wartime emergency. Nothing written by Miller since November was objectionable. "I am confident that Mr. Miller has been made to see his mistakes and is now endeavoring to make amends for the same. However, I shall not turn my attention entirely from him, but will give him the benefit of the doubt until we should hear of some new activity on his part."[32] Loving must have been torn between his racial sympathies and his patriotism. As much as Miller, he deplored mob violence. But he also believed that the *agitation* of that issue was counterproductive during the war. Did Loving tell Miller that he would continue to be watched? While that is uncertain, it is clear that Miller had not insulated himself from criticism; he would again face hostile scrutiny in mid-1918.

As the investigation of Kelly Miller indicates, the detection and suppression of "adverse propaganda" had become a major priority for the Military Intelligence Branch by the spring of 1918. Walter Loving was often its point man. When he heard rumors that organizations might try to use the funeral of Cpl. Larmon Brown, one of the men executed for participation in the Houston mutiny, to spread "discontent" within Washington's black community, he persuaded the soldier's mother to allow no mention of the "unfortunate affair at Houston" at the funeral. To ensure that this was the case, Loving contacted the officiating minister and attended the funeral himself. Soon after that episode, he was sent to New York to investigate alleged connections between black and "Hindu" militancy, probably referring to efforts by the Indian nationalist movement to gain sympathizers among black Americans. Van Deman instructed the head of the MIB's New York office to "put every possible confidence in Loving and rely upon his work in every possible way." Apparently Loving initiated a counterpropaganda campaign, for when Van Deman alerted him to alleged "German propaganda" in Pensacola, he set up a similar program through black churches there. This scare was based on rumors circulating in Pensacola that the Germans would overrun the United States, "clean out the white people and put the negroes in their place." Panicky whites also believed that black food handlers were putting ground glass in their meals. While Loving was able to set up a preventive program in Pensacola without actually traveling there, he could do nothing to address problems at other distant locations. One case involved circulars found in San Antonio black neighborhoods stating that black soldiers were being sacrificed on the battlefields to spare the lives of whites. Another was the rumor of systematic enemy propaganda in South Carolina, Georgia, and Mississippi in which black domestics were supposedly told that as soon as Germany won, whites would become *their* servants. Van Deman also asked Loving to take whatever action he could to investigate two men, a Turk or Syrian and a German Jew, who were said to be spreading enemy propaganda in black lodges in Clio, South Carolina. It is likely that Loving checked the population of that tiny community and discounted the possibility of subversion there.[33]

Walter Loving could not be everywhere, so some matters were handled directly out of MIB headquarters. One was an effort to suppress an open letter against lynching that circulated through black communities across the nation. The names of a hundred black Atlantans were affixed to this protest, which was inspired by the murder of 222 blacks by white mobs in 1917. Such attacks, the document read, were "worse than Prussianism." Blacks were loyal and willing to sacrifice their blood on the battlefield, according to the petition, but they were not blind to the fact that white soldiers who killed innocent blacks in East St. Louis went unpunished while black soldiers found guilty in Houston were executed. The plea suggested that such realities would undoubtedly affect the morale of black soldiers in the trenches of France.

Van Deman perceived this protest as an attempt to "disorganize" the black population and sought to blunt its impact by intimidating its most prominent signatories. Letters to William F. Penn, M.D.; Dr. J. W. E. Bowen, president of Gammon Theological Seminary; *Atlanta Independent* editor Benjamin J. Davis; and two others asked if they had given consent to their names being used, whether the petition's sentiments reflected their own views, and what solutions they proposed for the problems identified in the petitions. Only two replies survive in the case file. Davis claimed to have neither seen nor signed the document, and added that he agreed with only portions of its contents. Whether this was true cannot be determined, but, as he depended upon the unhindered circulation of the newspaper for his livelihood, he undoubtedly knew that the Post Office Department had suppressed other publications that were construed to be "disloyal." Davis could not risk that fate. Dr. Penn, on the other hand, boldly acknowledged signing the petition, which he said represented his views entirely, even though he had a son serving under fire in France. As to the remedy for lynching and disfranchisement, he advised enforcement of the Fourteenth and Fifteenth Amendments and legislation making lynching a federal crime. Whether Van Deman was successful in halting circulation of the Atlanta petition is unknown, but his letter notifying its signatories that federal investigators were aware of their activity must have been chilling—at least to editor Davis.[34]

With Loving unable to handle all the investigations of suspected "Negro subversion," intelligence officers at army camps throughout the country also took up that issue. They, too, became busy in the spring of 1918. Perhaps in response to the Atlanta petition, the IO at Fort McPherson began to organize the "better class" and "leading" blacks, "telling them such things as we think they should know, and asking them to select for us negroes known to be entirely worthy to be used as [undercover] operatives." (As an equal opportunity employer, this IO was similarly recruiting white agents.) These efforts, prompted by fears that German propagandists were working among Atlanta's "ignorant" blacks, bore at least organizational fruit. Three of the most prominent members of the black elite—Benjamin Davis, Republican wheelhorse Henry Lincoln "Linc" Johnson, and businessman Harry Pace—agreed to constitute a committee to report any enemy attempts to subvert the black population. The IO stationed at St. Louis, meanwhile, spent considerable effort using black informants to learn about "secret meetings" organized by "Germans" to encourage blacks to gain their rights and organize unions. What actually occurred there is not revealed in the case file, but it was common for whites to damn any effort to pursue civil rights as inspired by the enemy.[35]

In reviewing the military intelligence "negro subversion" case files, it is difficult to determine the criteria used in deciding whether a particular suspect or incident would be investigated by an intelligence officer, or whether the matter would be turned over to the Bureau of Investigation. Decisions on the most significant cases were undoubtedly made at the weekly intelligence conferences held at the Justice Department. But for hundreds of other suspicions, the determination was probably made by Van Deman's office. In the spring of 1918 a number of cases were transferred to the Bureau, including those concerning Clem Kelly of Bond, Mississippi, whose alleged crime was saying that victorious Germans would decree equality between the races; William Kingsberry, of Alston, North Carolina, who told other blacks that Germany would win, making their war bonds worthless; George Brown, of John's Island, South Carolina, who allegedly boasted of how smart the Germans were and that their victory would benefit blacks; and a white man named McElrone who was said to be fomenting racial hatred in Philadelphia because he called himself a "negro liberator." Once a case was transferred to the Bureau, according to a policy announced by Van Deman, the MIB was not to interfere in it.[36]

The MIB kept other cases, however. The IO at Fort Sam Houston was instructed to apply pressure to the editor of *K. Lamity's Harpoon,* which objected to the arming of blacks, warning that he would not be permitted to obstruct conscription or foment racial friction. At Camp Meade, Maryland, the IO was alerted of a rumored agreement among local blacks not to fight against Germany. When five thousand black troops were slated to arrive at Camp Devens, near Boston, the IO there was told to immediately probe rumors that "equal rights agitators" (NAACP activists as well as William Monroe Trotter and members of his National Equal Rights League) would attempt to sow dissension among them. That officer enlisted the assistance of the YMCA, which reported that "agitators" had indeed visited the camp. The national head of that organization's intelligence department, William Gilman Low Jr., asked Van Deman to ban the *Crisis* from the camp's "Y hut" and require all black guests to be screened by the black YMCA secretary before being allowed to visit the troops. While Van Deman agreed to exclusion of the NAACP's journal, he sensibly rejected the second request: Such a policy could not be instituted if it were not applied to white visitors, too. An MIB operative probed this case of "Negro propaganda" further, however, and although he alleged that some visitors were promoting a disloyal agenda, he found that most dissatisfaction among the black troops was the result of Maj. Gen. Charles C. Ballou's infamous "Bulletin No. 35," which instructed black soldiers not to object to discrimination they encountered off base. Camp Devens issues died down in mid-May when most of the troops were transferred elsewhere, but later in the year the morale of new contingents would again concern army intelligence.[37]

Occasionally an investigation begun by the Bureau was subsequently turned over to army intelligence because it involved military matters. In June 1918, for example, the Bureau notified the MIB that black chauffeurs in Savannah were attending "German meetings" and no longer behaving with traditional obsequiousness. Why the Bureau decided not to keep this case is not revealed in extant documents. Van Deman's successor, Col. Marlborough Churchill, took this wild story completely seriously and ordered the IO at Fort Severin to investigate all instances of "enemy activity among negroes in that vicinity." Another case of the Bureau relinquishing responsibility to the MIB concerned a letter to a draft board in Binghampton, Tennessee, from Camp Meade, Maryland, signed by a "Capt. G. H. Hill." Employing "abusive" language, "Hill" claimed that blacks had no stake in the war and issued a warning: "Just wait until uncle Sam puts a gun in the niggers hands and you all will be worry for it." A records check found no Capt. G. H. Hill anywhere in the army, so Van Deman ordered Camp Meade's IO to investigate the handful of men who had been conscripted through the draft board in Binghampton. They were "assigned" to receive instruction in writing field messages. Text including words misspelled in "Capt. Hill's" letter was dictated to them, and Pvt. Sidney Wilson was easily identified as being the author. A handwriting expert corroborated the evidence, and Wilson was convicted by a court-martial board.[38]

How great was the threat of German subversion, or German encouragement of black disloyalty, in mid-1918? By then it had been a year since most suspect enemy aliens had been rounded up, and over a year since any major act of sabotage attributable to enemy hands. Black antiwar sentiment, as well as apathy toward the draft, was evident on the street corners of northern industrial cities, where soapbox orators like A. Philip Randolph and Chandler Owen frequently condemned the war. Furthermore, anyone serving on a draft board—as well as Bureau agents and their American Protective League volunteers—knew that proportionately more blacks than whites were failing to comply with conscription orders. But probably none of this was due to enemy machinations. Domestic issues were decisive for those African Americans who did not mount the patriotic bandwagon. But this reality was largely lost on the intelligence agencies. The hand of German enemies and their alleged Mexican allies was still suspected all over the country. In late spring, for example, when the acting IO at Camp Meade reported rumors of a black brotherhood dedicated to preventing blacks from fighting against Germany, Van Deman replied that headquarters had no evidence of such an organization, but he was certain that "there are yet very direct efforts being made in Texas and other Southern States by the Mexicans to induce the negroes to take up their residence in Mexico." Admitting that he had no real proof of the success of such efforts, Van Deman nonetheless vowed to take the necessary steps to neutralize this subversion.[39]

German conspiracies remained a convenient bogeyman throughout the war. The propensity to disregard racial and socio-economic factors and instead embrace conspiratorial notions persisted to the end. In October 1918, an undercover agent working for the MID's Military Morale Section speculated that a new riot could easily occur in East St. Louis. His report detailed an incident in which a hysterical white girl imagined that a black man looked at her in some inappropriate way. An "impetuous southern white youth, lawless in his thinking," came to her defense. Fortunately the confrontation was defused, but an explosive situation remained. Blacks, for their part, were on edge, with the 1917 riot fresh in their memory and feeling aggrieved about local injustices. That was a clear enough analysis, but the MID's agent could not shake the belief that an unseen enemy had set all this afoot, "for the stream of German money is said still to flow through in hidden courses."[40] Yet where was the corroborating evidence? Where were the enemy suspects? Military intelligence operatives intent on discovering those who were promoting disloyalty among blacks and uncovering the causes of low black morale had convinced themselves that the enemy was not only active, but at least partially successful in subverting the loyalties of black Americans. The truth, however, was otherwise.

What may have been the MIB's most thorough effort to counteract "adverse propaganda" occurred in Harlem in March 1918. "Tremendous rumors" were widespread: Blacks were only used as shock troops, their white officers abused them, Germans threatened to torture them if they were captured, and there was a military hospital in New York in which lay two hundred black soldiers who had been captured and sent back to Allied lines after having their eyes gouged out and arms cut off. While the MIB and Bureau agents tried to track down the source of the rumors, Walter Loving was instructed to "take whatever steps you think best to counteract this vicious propaganda." It was not long before at least one source of the tales was identified: a story in the *New York World*, supposedly based on interviews with six soldiers, that included details of torturing and maiming. When confronted, each soldier denied having told a reporter anything about alleged atrocities. Whether they testified truthfully did not ultimately matter, however; damage had been done. Loving took charge of the situation. First he took a reporter from each black newspaper, along with other "influential" blacks, to visit the hospital and see for themselves that there were no two hundred blinded amputees. The *New York Amsterdam News* subsequently printed a story with the headlines "Base Hospital Yarns Baseless. Investigation Reveals Utter Falsity of Rumors About Colored Soldiers." Loving then secured from the black ministerial association a pledge that every clergyman in New York and Brooklyn would use his pulpit to discredit the rumors. The ministers were also given a hundred copies of the *Amsterdam News* exposé for distribution to their congregations. Finally, he engaged two lecturers to speak against the rumors in every theater and club in Harlem. Apparently the harmful tales were squelched because Loving received the personal thanks of Col. Van Deman, and his report was read at an MIB staff conference, a genuine compliment indeed.[41]

Loving undoubtedly limited the damage to black morale from stories about enemy atrocities, but no one could guarantee that such tales were eradicated. Counterpropaganda could not completely eliminate beliefs that black troops were suffering abuse in the military or that the government was covering up news of inordinately large numbers of casualties, simply because African Americans knew from experience that life was filled with abuses. It is no wonder, then, that rumors of blacks being used as shock troops, and of their slaughter or maiming by the German army, cropped up elsewhere.[42] The MIB again had to try to extinguish such fictions in the summer of 1918. The idea for a new tactic actually came from a civilian, who suggested that wounded black soldiers who were furloughed home could stimulate morale by giving patriotic addresses that would dispel negative rumors. Major Joel Spingarn, who was in the midst of promoting a black morale effort, and MIB chief Churchill liked the idea and asked the port of embarkation at Hoboken, New Jersey, to supply the names of wounded or sick soldiers arriving on transports from Europe who seemed qualify to deliver "simple addresses." However, the plan was thwarted by the port's chief of staff, who had "the strongest kind of aversion against the use of returning soldiers along the lines suggested." The project apparently died without being implemented.[43]

The same rumors spread in the Savannah area in midsummer, prompting Georgia's adjutant general to warn that they could cause blacks to "rebel" against the draft. The War Department was by now doubtful that anything more could be done to halt such tales, which seemed to have taken on a life of their own despite the wide publicity in the black press and pulpit given to an official denial from Gen. John J. Pershing, the American commander in France. In Washington, stories emerged that the 1st Separate Battalion (colored) of the District of Columbia National Guard had been cut to pieces in France, with some of its wounded survivors secretly returned to stateside army hospitals. Many of these men, it was said, had been blinded, had lost limbs, and had their tongues cut out by the Germans. Teachers from Dunbar High School took it upon themselves to quell the rumor, while longtime informant Hallie Queen sought to track down its source. Whether she was successful is not revealed in surviving documents, but apparently the teachers were able to prevent the spread of the false story, at least for a while. In September one of the MID's part-time black informants, Quander E. Hall, reported a "whispering propaganda" in the nation's capital based on persistent rumors that families were receiving anonymous reports of their loved ones being maimed or killed in battle, always "accompanied by the statement that the casualties in Negro Regiments will not be included in the official lists." There is no record that Hall was able to identify the source of this rumor, much less halt it.[44]

For all the fears that enemies were manipulating and subverting the "ignorant" southern black population, army intelligence concluded in mid-1918 that as great a danger existed in its own backyard. A report pointed to a black preacher in a Washington suburb who, it was said, had spread the falsehood that wounded doughboys were ignored by white American medics but treated kindly on the battlefield by Germans. The preacher was also quoted as saying that when the Allies were defeated, blacks would be invited to Germany to receive full equality and the opportunity to marry white women. Churchill was convinced that "German propaganda among the negroes of Washington, D.C., and Prince George County, Md., is the most serious of any part of the country" and urged the propagandistic Committee on Public Information to find positive newspaper articles about black soldiers, have printing plates prepared, and get all the area's newspapers to publish them.[45] In fact, there was no hard evidence of German subversion in and around the nation's capital, and the city was not paralyzed by fears of sabotage or espionage. But concern among whites for maintaining the racial status quo was at a high level. Intelligence perception and policy were being highly colored by racial anxieties.

The gullibility of federal intelligence operatives during World War I is indeed noteworthy. In fairness, those involved in domestic espionage had to give at least cursory examination to hearsay and rumors. But many allegations that landed on the desks of investigators, particularly those in military intelligence, strained credibility; others were utterly trivial. Furthermore, when white agents' racial anxieties overlay their fears of conspiracies, their objectivity and sober judgment were often compromised. Washington MID agent K. A. Wagner serves as an example. Mere days before the Armistice, as an end to the war appeared in sight, he took seriously a report that a black laundress, who took in washing for the "better class" of whites, had suddenly become careless and begun charging higher prices. On being reprimanded by one of her customers, she replied that she could charge anything she wanted, and could take her time, because when Germany won the war, it would make blacks superior to whites. Another white informant told Wagner that German agents had gone so far in subverting blacks that they had shown them the exact houses in New York and Philadelphia that they could seize from whites after the expected German victory.[46] No wonder the MID's files were cluttered; no wonder the number of intelligence officers and investigators multiplied during the war.

Like the Bureau of Investigation, military officials were hard-pressed to distinguish fact from fiction and to keep themselves from acting on their own racial fantasies rather than on plausible evidence.

Army intelligence focused on "German propaganda" and unrest among blacks during its first year of wartime operations. But in the spring of 1918 a new problem came to the fore, one that would define its primary "black" mission for the remainder of the war: the morale of black soldiers. One of the characteristics of modern warfare is the recognition that military personnel do not automatically embrace their nation's war aims and unquestionably believe they are fighting for a worthy cause. Soldiers as well as civilians must be propagandized to ensure their full and enthusiastic support for war. This emerged as a critical issue in the wake of General Ballou's infamous "Bulletin No. 35."

Most black soldiers during World War I were denied a battlefield role; only two divisions saw combat. The 93rd Division was created out of three regiments of black national guardsmen, and a fourth regiment of draftees. The 92nd Division was filled entirely from the draft. Individual units of the 92nd trained at a number of northern cantonments and were not consolidated until they reached France. All of the field-grade officers were white. No blacks ranked higher than captain, and a third of the junior officers were white National Guardsmen who were assigned to the 92nd "not for their leadership qualities but because they were available and had 'some experience with colored men.'" In any particular unit, no black officer was to outrank one who was white. Commanding the division was General Ballou. According to W. E. B. DuBois, who collected numerous army documents for a never-published history of black participation in the war, Ballou operated from foundational racist assumptions: "Whenever any occasion arose where trouble had occurred between white and colored soldiers, the burden of proof always rested on the colored man. All discrimination was passed unnoticed and nothing was done to protect the men who were under his command." Furthermore, as DuBois saw it, Ballou undermined the dignity of black officers: "His action in censuring officers in the presence of enlisted men was an act that tended toward breaking down the confidence that the men had in their officers, and he pursued this method on innumerable occasions." Ballou claimed that he had the welfare of his troops at heart: "I worked through channels to secure from white officers and white soldiers tolerant treatment of the Negro, especially in the matter of refraining from the more offensive epithets." But he clearly saw his troops as Negro soldiers, not soldiers who simply happened to be black.[47]

Black military and civilian morale would never be the same after an incident in late March 1918, at Camp Funston, Kansas, where part of the 92nd Division was training. State law prohibited discrimination in public accommodations, but a black sergeant was nonetheless denied admission to a theater in nearby Manhattan. On learning of this incident, Ballou issued "Bulletin No. 35," in which he reminded his troops that they had been instructed not to go anywhere off base where they were not wanted. Even though the sergeant was "strictly within his legal rights in this matter, and the theater manager is legally wrong," the soldier was reprimanded for causing a disturbance: "No useful purpose is served by such acts as will cause the 'color question' to be raised." In Ballou's words, "the sergeant is guilty of the GREATER wrong in doing ANYTHING, NO MATTER HOW LEGALLY CORRECT, that will provoke racial animosity." Oblivious to the racist assumptions underlying his view, Ballou continued to alienate all blacks, whether in or out of uniform: "The Division Commander [Ballou] repeats that the success of the Division, with all that success implies, is dependent upon the good will of the public. That public is nine-tenths white. White men made the Division, and they can break it just as easily if it becomes a trouble maker." Ballou's bulletin created an "uproar of protest."[48] One of those thus outraged was Maj. Walter Loving.

It was not long before reverberations from "Bulletin No. 35" were felt elsewhere. At Camp Sherman, Ohio, where the 317th Engineers were in training, it caused considerable resentment, particularly the warning that whites could make or break the 92nd Division. But the white intelligence officer at the camp, while understanding that Ballou's order was creating the very sort of controversy it was intended to avoid, was as ignorant of its racism as the racism in his own perceptions: "We are cognizant of the extreme emotional temperament of the African and realize that his primitive nature is easily excited to passionate partisanship, rendering it extremely difficult to handle any question that may arise involving race issues."[49] There was nothing emotional or primitive, however, about the response of an anonymous "Negro Soldier" who wrote a letter to the editor of the 88th Division's newspaper asserting that blacks' chief motive in fighting to make the world safe for democracy was to make it a better place for themselves. But that better place hardly existed: "Free speech is forbidden," as blacks were commanded by white officers to be silent about lynching, segregation, disfranchisement, and the rape of their women. "God forbid that I would fight in defense of a government that doesn't protect me." This was no isolated protest. According to Loving, copies of Ballou's order were widely circulated among black troops, invariably causing much indignation. Black civilians were also outraged. Mass meetings were called to discuss it. In one theater, a Liberty Loan speaker departed from his patriotic text to denounce the general. Loving concluded that "Bulletin No. 35" was demoralizing soldier and civilian alike.[50]

Rumors alleging mistreatment of blacks were likely more easily believed following the controversy over Ballou's bulletin. If the army's policies were seen as racist in one situation, might others be similarly distrusted? At Camp Upton, New York, men of the 367th Infantry speculated that, once they reached France, allotments for their family members would stop. The 367th, known as the "Buffaloes," had a high esprit de corps and was commanded by a white officer who had confidence in its fighting mettle. But even these factors did not prevent the spread of rumors that questioned the army's fairness to black soldiers and their families, despite official denials to the contrary.[51]

"Bulletin No. 35" poisoned whatever trust blacks might have put in the military. Throughout the rest of the war, and into the postwar months, complaints would come from camp after army camp, more often regarding inferior conditions and assignment to noncombat roles than off-base problems. But Ballou's order made it much more likely that black troops would view their grievances—some of which were no different from whites' complaints—as racial affronts. By June 1918, reports of low morale were common. Some came from intelligence officers, others from the YMCA, as was the case at Camp Jackson, South Carolina. Black labor companies had to perform much Sunday labor, although some were given a choice of attending chapel or working. Some had not had holidays for a long time. Even though there were sufficient black noncommissioned officers, blacks were sent to work in squads and platoons commanded by white privates. When in town, white military policemen forced black soldiers to wait until all white soldiers had boarded streetcars. White civilians secured jobs in the black soldiers' canteen, denying jobs to black civilians. There also were no restrooms in camp for black women visitors. The YMCA report concluded that resentment ran deep. It can be presumed that this was an accurate description of camp conditions, as the report was forwarded to Van Deman without denial or reservation by the head of the YMCA's own intelligence department.[52]

The problems encountered by black troops at stateside army camps were so widespread that MIB leaders concluded more was needed than simply investigating abuses after they occurred. They ultimately authorized two extensive investigations in the last year of the war, out of which came a number of recommendations for improvement. Unfortunately, very few of the problems were seriously addressed, much less remedied. Charles H. Williams, the field secretary for the Federal Council of Churches' Committee on Welfare of Negro Soldiers, did the first thorough review of black soldiers' problems. Williams, a black minister, investigated twenty-five camps beginning in March 1918. A separate round of detailed inspections was made by Walter Loving, who wrote lengthy reports on his findings in the fall after visiting eleven army facilities. Camp life late in the war was much less chaotic than in the fall of 1917, when few preparations had been made for the flood of black draftees. Improvements had definitely occurred. Many more were needed, however, but they would not be accomplished by the time demobilization occurred in 1919.

Williams first visited thirteen camps between March and early August, spending from four days to two weeks at an installation, affording him opportunities to observe conditions in considerable detail. Overall he painted an optimistic picture. Initially, there was strong opposition at all southern and some western camps to training blacks as actual soldiers. But whites' fears of race conflict proved unwarranted, due primarily to the good conduct of the soldiers. Where trouble occurred, it was often due to camp commanders' unenlightened policies. Williams believed that blacks were generally treated well in terms of food, clothing, barracks, and equipment, although there were some notable exceptions. The greatest problem was the lack of a "proper atmosphere": "Its absence has not increased patriotism, but has tended to destroy that which already existed. It clouded the already doubting minds of many as to why they were in the war." Nonetheless, Williams believed that a "fine spirit of loyalty" had overtaken most skeptics. He was proud that camp life was transforming men in another way, but one which many whites would have viewed with concern, not approbation: "Many are being told for the first time that they are men and are required to do a man's work. For this the Negro manhood of the Country is stronger and better." Little could Williams know that, by the end of the war, "Negro manhood" would begin to mount strong challenges to the racial status quo.

A major source of racial friction observed by Williams stemmed from the fact that the majority of black troops, who served in noncombatant units, were under the command of whites. Commissioned officers often disliked their assignments and took little interest in the men under them. This apathy led to inferior medical care and a tolerance of mistreatment. Furthermore, "the greatest occasion for dissatisfaction in these units is found in the attitude of the white 'non-coms,' who, in many instances, were promoted to such positions because of previous knowledge of negroes, usually gotten on plantations, public works, turpentine farms and the like. The great trouble is that many times white officers, 'non-coms' and colored soldiers bring into the army civil life customs and attitudes." Unfortunately, military morale officers never forcefully pursued the problem of racist noncommissioned officers, and the problem remained for the duration of the war. Black officers were assigned almost exclusively to combat units. Perhaps because he, like other members of the upwardly mobile black Talented Tenth, so desperately wanted black officers to reflect positively on the race, Williams believed that "splendid relations" almost universally characterized their interactions with white soldiers and officers.

Williams's recommendations were hardly militant, but they got to the heart of black soldiers' experiences and implied a link between discrimination and low morale. White officers needed to take a more genuine interest in the welfare and good treatment of those under their command. The use of black sergeants, wherever possible, would significantly reduce dissatisfaction. Greater opportunity should be given for blacks to become commissioned officers. Finally, the social and religious needs of the soldiers required more sympathetic attention.[53]

Williams, and later Loving, also identified conflicts with white civilians as another impediment to high morale, and occasional remedial efforts were made. One was the response to a June 1918 incident in which employees of a depot lunch counter refused to serve food to uniformed officers and men whose Wabash Railroad train paused at Peru, Indiana. George W. Jackson, a local black citizen, reported the incident. The MIB took it seriously because a Military Morale Section had just been created to deal with precisely this sort of problem, and also because MIB chief Churchill demanded a genuine and timely inquiry: "As it is most desirable to conciliate our negro population at the present time it is desired that this matter be thoroughly investigated." If the facts proved to be true, he wanted Indiana authorities to prosecute the offenders. Army intelligence frequently used American Protective League men for investigations, and one of Peru's leading attorneys was such a volunteer. He found that the station restaurant, which was operated by an independent proprietor, had indeed refused service, but this was due to a "misunderstanding" on the part of employees. Although the misunderstanding was in all likelihood a deliberate act, the important result of the investigation was the message sent to local whites that there must be no more discrimination against blacks in uniform. The MIB felt this warning was sufficient, and that prosecution was not needed. To ensure there was no repetition, the head of the Military Morale Section wrote to George Jackson that "matters of this nature are of particular interest to this office. Such incidents do not contribute to a strong military morale and every one of them needs investigation, followed by such action as the circumstances warrant. It will be a favor to this office if you will keep us informed about any other incidents of this nature which may possibly come to your knowledge."[54] The MIB's motives in preventing further problems seem sincere, even if its interest was efficiency, not egalitarianism. The system worked pretty well in this instance.

The Peru case, unfortunately, was an uncommon example of strong efforts to prevent civilian discrimination against black troops. By 1 August 1918, the army had decided "to restrict military intelligence in the colored field entirely to colored troops," which narrowed its interest in incidents like that in Indiana. Historian Roy Talbert Jr. believes this may have been caused by Churchill's distrust of Maj. Joel Spingarn, the NAACP board president who dreamed of establishing within the MIB "a separate sub-section on negro subversion, which will be in charge of [i.e., led by] some of the ablest leaders of the colored people" which would focus on "countering unrest and disloyal propaganda." Spingarn intended for W. E. B. DuBois to be commissioned as a captain and assume a prominent leadership role in this new work. But in mid-July Spingarn was abruptly shipped overseas. His ouster from "negro subversion" work may also reflect suspicion on the part of Emmett J. Scott, the black special assistant to the secretary of war, who was more identified with the Bookerite than the DuBoisian position. Loving apparently did not trust Spingarn either, on account of his connection with the NAACP, which Loving at times seemed to regard as a dangerous organization. In any event, the renamed Military Intelligence Division did not entirely abandon all investigation of black civilian matters, despite its claim that all such cases were being referred to Scott. Loving continued his own domestic investigations for another year, even after the war ended.[55]

After Spingarn's departure, the task of addressing black soldiers' grievances devolved upon army intelligence's new Military Morale Section. And there was no lack of protests. From July through December 1918, complaints were reported from at least twenty army posts—most of the camps where large numbers of blacks were being trained—plus other installations where black labor units were detailed. At first intelligence officers at each installation were responsible for investigating grievances, but gradually that task was assumed by specifically designated "morale officers." Many complaints came directly from the soldiers themselves, sometimes in signed and sometimes in anonymous communications addressed to the secretary of war, Emmett Scott, or even the president.

The range of abuses was broad by mid-1918. Conditions at Camp Jackson, near Columbia, South Carolina, illustrate a number of all-too-common problems, many of which dated from the arrival of the first black draftees the previous autumn.[56] Men in a Sanitary Corps company, whose work was mostly digging ditches and clearing brush, protested that their white captain manifested a "spirit of hatred" toward them. Some soldiers also alleged they were forced to pay for passes to leave camp, while others charged that they could not get passes at all to see their families, who lived only a short distance away. Soon another letter from an engineer company detailed additional hardships. These soldiers were mostly high school and college graduates who deeply resented the absence of black non-commissioned officers. Instead, they were commanded by "slave drivers" and "Georgia crackers," sergeants whose only qualification was their purported skill in handling "niggers." Unfortunately, the Military Morale Section did not act on these complaints before the troops were ordered overseas. The head of that section lamely wrote to Emmett Scott that perhaps conditions would improve for them now that they had left Camp Jackson. One assumes, however, that the abusive white sergeants remained to afflict the next group of black draftees to arrive at the camp.

Since there was as yet no morale officer assigned to Camp Jackson, its intelligence officer investigated the complaints from the Sanitary Corps detachment. He admitted that a number of men in the unit were in such poor physical condition that they were not fit for the extremely hard labor to which they were put. Even the fit men needed to be rotated to less strenuous jobs. Penalties for infractions were too severe, and the soldiers' dependents had not received any allotments during the six months their men had been in the service. The camp IO concluded that morale was very low, but ignored his own findings and attributed that problem simply to the fact that they had been "poorly handled." Their captain's only fault was that, being of English nativity, he did not understand how to "handle negroes." Another white officer at the camp submitted even more nakedly racist recommendations. Black soldiers should only be commanded by southern men, as only they knew the different ways that blacks needed to be "handled." As for camp grievances, a board composed mostly of white southern officers should address those.

More anonymous letters arrived from Camp Jackson a month later. One complained that the battalion commander used a whip and stick to discipline the men. Another alleged that junior white officers carried whips on the drill field, treating the troops as if they were convicts. Sick men were forced to work, and some had died as a result. Officers frequently cursed the men, called them by comic names, or referred to them as "niggers." One officer was said to have promised a furlough to any white noncom who beat a black soldier. All of these letters passed through the hands of Emmett Scott, who finally gave vent to his feelings at the end of November, four months after abuses had first surfaced: "The complaints which continue to come out of Camp Jackson are all to the same effect and there must be something radically wrong with conditions at a camp where the men so uniformly complain of harsh and brutal treatment. Can anything be done to ameliorate these conditions?" A few of the complaints were based on misunderstandings. For example, some soldiers interpreted quarantining men with "bad diseases" as a discriminatory denial of furloughs. But the major issues seem never to have been truly addressed.

A board of inquiry was impaneled at Camp Jackson, but there is no indication that it ordered any substantive correctives. The Military Morale Section took its own feeble action, advising Scott that "every effort is being made from this end of the line . . . for an improvement of the conditions affecting the colored soldiers. Recently we have carried on what may perhaps be properly described as a bombardment by correspondence, of the military authorities at that camp. We hope that our efforts have brought some results." Still, no significant changes occurred. The same problems continued into 1919 and presumably did not end until the camp was shut down and the last black troops were mustered out of service. The Military Intelligence Division and its Morale Branch, commanded now by Capt. James E. Cutler, in civilian life an academic authority on lynching and a "liberal" on race questions, proved impotent to change matters or to protect the welfare of African-American soldiers at Camp Jackson.[57]

An attack on black soldiers at Camp Merritt, New Jersey, in August 1918 further illustrates the problems faced by black troops and the weakness of military intelligence in correcting abuses. The assault, leaving one dead and others wounded, precipitated a round of inquiries but no justice. The black troops were ultimately blamed because they did not behave properly when around southern white soldiers. The fullest description of the affair, which involved a regiment of white Mississippians and the black 15th New York Infantry, was provided by the camp's black YMCA secretary, William Lloyd Imes, who years later would become an important civil rights activist in New York. As there were no separate YMCA facilities, the one structure served men of both races. The Mississippians resented this and threatened to "clean out" the place. On a Saturday evening, twenty-five whites invaded the YMCA building and beat up five black soldiers. Trouble spread to the black barracks, where white guards lined up their occupants and opened fired on them with live ammunition. Somehow the black troops' officers prevented them from attacking these guards. Imes was naturally incensed, and resolved that the YMCA would not yield to prejudice and treat blacks differently from whites. Moreover, he recommended that the camp commander issue an "authoritative order" such as had been given by Brig. Gen. George Bell at Camp Upton following a racial clash. Bell had assembled all his officers, telling them that racial incidents would not be tolerated, and warning that any officer in charge of men involved in a racial incident would be held accountable. Each officer was also instructed to announce to all those under him that decisive actions would be taken against any participants in such disturbances. Ever since Bell's action, no racial troubles had occurred at Camp Upton. Furthermore, its YMCA remained desegregated and treated blacks and whites equally.

But white intelligence officers saw the Camp Merritt attacks, and the prevention of similar incidents, through their own racial lenses. Three boards of inquiry were impaneled, but no real amelioration or justice resulted. White officers agreed that General Bell's stern order had worked at Camp Upton, but only because both the white and black troops were from the North. At Camp Merritt and elsewhere, however, southern white and black soldiers shared the same facility. The problem, as whites saw it, was that the black troops did not know how to avoid giving offense to them. A case in point was the action of YMCA secretary Imes who proclaimed that his organization would not discriminate on the basis of race. According to Military Morale Section chief Capt. G. B. Perkins, Imes's statement "was not such, under the conditions described, as to contribute to a better mutual understanding and more harmonious relations." In other words, Imes was the source of the trouble; the onus was on blacks for maintenance of racial harmony by refraining from demanding equal or fair treatment. Military Morale went farther, however, instructing the YMCA to provide separate "huts" for the races. This order, written by Cutler, sidestepped overt racism by suggesting that signs not identify YMCA facilities by race, but instead designate each hut for use by specific units. In addition, Military Morale advised that at camps where both southern white and black troops trained, "some wise person, preferably colored, who understands relations between the races in the section of the country from which the troops were recruited, should talk to the [black] soldiers, advising them regarding their conduct and urging them to use every reasonable means to avoid disturbances."

There were additional victims in the Camp Merritt case as it wound down to its unjust conclusion. Four black officers were detained as witnesses to the riot, with the result that they were not allowed to accompany their troops when they went overseas, thus denying them any chance for eventual promotion. Trials finally took place in late November, after the Armistice. The white private in charge of the guards who did the shooting was acquitted. Only one of the black officers was called to testify, and he could not positively identify the private because he had not seen him since the incident more than two months before. A dozen other men were in the squad that fired the shots; they were charged with firing without orders and were put on trial to determine who fired the fatal shot. None of the four black officers testified at this trial. All the white soldiers were acquitted.

This case illustrates two common themes: Military justice was not assured for black troops during World War I, and army intelligence saw the maintenance of traditional racial roles and hierarchies as the best way to ensure an absence of racial friction. In one of the clearest cases of racism on the part of white troops, the Military Morale Branch "blamed the victim" and encouraged formal segregation where blacks and whites trained at the same facility. The MID's most "liberal" officer following the departure of Joel Spingarn, Captain Cutler, gave his approval to this approach. Major Walter Loving followed the Camp Merritt "riot," as the MID insisted on calling it, and concluded that "an unfortunate miscarriage of justice" occurred. He did not, however, raise his voice as he had in other instances. In short, the Military Morale Branch was more interested in maintaining racial calm than in advocating the rights of black soldiers, which would have been far more effective in generating positive morale among them.[58]

Strife continued to plague posts where black and white soldiers were billeted together. Simultaneous riots broke out in mid-August at Camps Sherman, Merritt, Meade, and Dix. These affrays were interpreted for the MID by one of its occasional black informants, Quander Hall. His conclusions, unfortunately, may have misled those who might otherwise have addressed the issues. Hall warned that unrest was due either to actual conditions at the camps or to a "propaganda system" intended to poison race relations. Having visited several of the facilities, he claimed that prior to the troubles good relations between the races had existed. Therefore, he concluded, there must be a plot to encourage black soldiers returning to camp after being out on passes to "resent the slightest thing." Previously "they would have understood and endured such matters." The culprits, according to Hall, were "Teutonic plotters."[59] Once again, if there was a chance for recognizing real racial problems and then taking steps to ameliorate them, it was lost in the confusion of paranoid thinking, this time promoted by a black informant.

In a minority of instances the mistreatment of black troops was acknowledged and steps were taken to correct the problems. The army's motive, however, was not necessarily to ensure that they received fair treatment. In addressing troubles at Camp Travis, Texas, a training facility for thousands of black draftees in the summer and fall of 1918, the MID's intent was to provide "less opportunity for German propaganda" to poison soldier morale. But if German propaganda was truly behind the disaffection of black soldiers, the army faced a massive task of purging its white leadership. According to the camp's black YMCA secretary, Tuskegee graduate Benjamin L. Joyce, blacks were routinely kicked and beaten by white officers and noncoms. This was not hearsay. Joyce wrote Emmett Scott that he had personally observed instances, including one on a troop train in which an officer kicked a man six times. In another case, white military policemen assaulted a group of blacks who fought back and forced the white guards to take refuge in the YMCA hut. The MID's response to this report was twofold: It instructed the Camp Travis intelligence officer to investigate Joyce's allegations, but it also ordered an investigation of Joyce and his influence on the black soldiers. Camp authorities moved on both fronts. At least some of the problems were addressed, for a month later Joyce informed Scott that conditions were much improved. But Joyce paid a personal price for being an advocate for black troops: Someone in the military hierarchy was encouraging the YMCA to fire him. Emmett Scott urged the MID to intervene: Joyce was a valuable YMCA secretary. "I very much hope we can be of some assistance to this man. Apparently he will be made to walk the plank for cooperating with us." Fortunately the interest of the Military Morale Branch in assuring at least due process for Joyce seems to have been sufficient warning to reconsider any punitive action, and Joyce apparently kept his job.[60] While the welfare of black troops was not the MID's primary motivation, its efforts to reduce the likelihood of "German propaganda" did redound to the soldiers' advantage in this instance.

Mistreatment seemed to be part of the diet of black troops in the summer and autumn of 1918, no matter where they were stationed. From Camp Wheeler, near

Macon, Georgia, an anonymous letter addressed to the president complained that, in addition to poor food and medical treatment, white sergeants hit black soldiers with clubs and docked their pay. The Military Morale Branch ordered the camp IO to investigate, but there is no record of his findings or any remedial action.[61] At Camp Pike, Arkansas, the black YMCA secretary informed the MID, a few days after Loving visited the post, of a white sergeant who had kicked two privates. The IO interviewed every sergeant, all of whom denied such actions. The Morale Branch decided that nothing could be gained from further investigation. The YMCA sent another report to Loving, notifying him that competent black corporals were not being promoted to sergeant. He declined to pursue the matter without the names of individuals who had been bypassed, and because promotion was an administrative action over which intelligence had no jurisdiction.[62]

What constituted mistreatment was sometimes in the eye of the beholder. Such was the case with a sanitary detachment at Camp Humphreys, Virginia, in August 1918. These men had been rejected for overseas duty and were supposed to be given only light work because of their disabilities. Nevertheless, they complained of laboring long hours, being abused by officers and noncoms, having no opportunity to become noncoms, being prohibited from receiving or sending mail, going without pay, and having to eat in the open and bathe in the Potomac. So disaffected were they that several had written to black newspapers to expose the poor conditions. Emmett Scott, who screened most black soldiers' complaints, urged the MID to investigate, but the Morale Branch saw matters through a different lens. Most of the men in the unit, it claimed, were of the "low type." Some had been tried for desertion, and part of their punishment was a denial of pay. Their white officers were not brutal, but simply running a "tight ship" and using extra work for discipline. Whether the punishments were justified cannot be determined from extant documents, but it is clear that camp conditions were atrocious. Permanent winter quarters with bathing facilities were soon to be built, to replace the miserably cold tents that earlier soldiers had endured the previous winter. Yet these improvements were still in the future. While the head of Military Morale acknowledged the need to keep watching the situation, he concluded that the complaints of ill-treatment were unjustified.[63] Would he have reached the same conclusion if the soldiers were white, or if he had been forced to bathe in a river?

Deplorable conditions existed at other camps in Virginia. Just days before the Armistice, the IO at the Newport News port of embarkation reported that black troops at nearby Langley Field were so discontented over poor sanitation, unhealthy conditions, and poor YMCA facilities that many of them had revolvers which, they claimed, were "for their own protection." Authorities at the base were debating whether to search every man for arms, but were undecided because 60 percent of the camp population was black.[64] A Camp Eustis soldier described extremely unhealthy conditions in a letter forwarded to Scott. The camp IO did not dispute that many men had sickened due to polluted water, no place to wash or bathe, and infestations of bedbugs. The MID admitted to Scott that the complaints were fully justified, but it was optimistic because new officers had been assigned and concrete improvements were being made.[65] In this case the army appeared eager to remedy appalling conditions, but why had it allowed them to get that bad in the first place? Prejudice must have been a major factor.

Southern camps had no monopoly on harsh treatment and poor facilities; black soldiers being trained in the North also suffered abuse and neglect. At Camp Sherman, near Chillicothe, Ohio, members of a reserve labor battalion—men rejected for overseas service—complained of being treated like convicts on a chain gang by being forced to labor on the public roads under the watch of white officers and noncoms. The camp intelligence officer, however, discounted their grievances.[66] Troops at Camp Grant, Illinois, complained of filth, not enough food, no bathing facilities, and abusive white officers. The IO there acknowledged that officers had cursed the men, but the camp commander had ordered this halted. Moreover, the unsatisfactory living conditions were being improved. New protests were received after a contingent of Tuskegee men arrived for training. Poor conditions were again found to exist, but the excuse was disorganization in the camp administration. The Morale Branch concluded, perhaps rightfully, that unfortunate conditions had existed, although not through racial malice, and had since been rectified.[67] The use of offensive language was apparently a common problem at northern camps as well as those in the South. When the MID learned of a white officer who spoke of commanding "niggers," General Churchill stressed that blacks would become prejudiced against their officers if they used such words. Apparently the camp commander agreed, for he issued general orders prohibiting the use of that offensive expression.[68] Of course, not all grievances were valid. Soldiers at Camp Dodge, Iowa, resented the denial of furloughs, which indeed had been canceled, but it was because the entire camp was quarantined for the Spanish flu.[69]

The validity of complaints could as readily be denied in the North as in the South, as is shown in the case of Camp Devens, Massachusetts, shortly before the end of the war. Unsatisfactory conditions first came to light when the NAACP informed Emmett Scott that soldiers were being verbally abused and physically assaulted by their young southern white officers. Some of the troops themselves reported that they were not receiving training, but instead were put to hard labor and treated like slaves. The Morale Branch ordered an investigation, but the camp IO denied that the men were really unhappy because, he claimed, they were better clothed and fed than in civilian life. Besides, blacks were naturally muscular, and best suited for unskilled labor. In fact, according to the IO, their officers treated them too easily, being under strict orders not to abuse them. The Morale Branch found these rebuttals to be valid and reported to Scott that some of the NAACP's information was erroneous. But the troops remained discontented for the remainder of the war and into the postwar demobilization period, believing they were unfairly denied discharges so that the army could keep them to perform labor that ought to be done by civilians.[70]

It must have been obvious to the Military Intelligence Division's morale staff that all was not well at training camps across the nation. The MID already had plenty of evidence of abuses and deterioration of black soldiers' esprit de corps. So what did it expect Walter Loving to accomplish as a result of his own personal inspection, in September and October 1918, of eleven camps? Problems were already well known at some of them. Was he ordered to put the best face possible on camp conditions? While that cannot be proven, he clearly accentuated the positive.[71]

Loving's itinerary took him on a zigzag course through the South, beginning with Camp Humphreys, Virginia, in the first part of September, where he found himself in the midst of the controversy over how poorly the 150-man sanitary detachment was being treated. Loving found "dissatisfaction" among the soldiers, who felt they had to keep their camp overly clean compared to a nearby camp that was not nearly as orderly. While the unit's white lieutenant believed that a third of the men were of the "lowest type," Loving found no evidence that he practiced or encouraged harsh treatment toward them. Loving concluded that in general the black soldiers' complaints were unjustified.[72] One is left to conclude that either the soldiers' manifold grievances were mostly fictitious, or that Loving participated in a bureaucratic whitewash.

The next stop on Loving's inspection was Camp Zachary Taylor, near Louisville. Morale of both black and white soldiers in mid-September appeared to be good, which Loving attributed to "conduct cards . . . issued to each soldier after he has passed a satisfactory examination in military courtesy. The soldier is then placed on his merits and is allowed to visit the city without a pass from retreat to call to quarters. Any commissioned officer may take up a card from a soldier for any breach of military courtesy. Every man tries hard to keep his card, for if it is taken up he must then be confined to the camp." This system seemed to Loving to prove his thesis that the attitude of a commanding officer set the racial tone for an entire camp. Three black units were stationed at Camp Zachary Taylor, all commanded by white sergeants and black corporals. Despite a few instances in which blacks were called "niggers," Loving did not observe "any harsh treatment meted out to the colored soldiers." Antagonism between soldiers and the military police was absent. Compared to other installations, this post was a model.[73]

Camp Pike, near Little Rock, also appeared to have good morale. Loving attributed this to the "untiring efforts of the YMCA agents to look out for the comforts of the men, assist them in their correspondence, give ear to their grievances, and console them in every way possible." In addition, the camp commander demanded that white officers and noncoms treat blacks well or suffer punishment. This order seemed to have had effect; Loving found "no sign of overbearance" on their part. Nor did white military police appear to be abusive.[74] A few days after his departure, however, Loving was informed that a white sergeant had kicked two privates. The allegation was neither proved nor disproved.

A seemingly enlightened officer commanded Camp Sheridan, near Montgomery, Alabama. Enlisted men with complaints could see him after retreat. Loving found that some of them did have legitimate grievances, but this was due to the fact that 95 percent of the eight hundred blacks suffered from venereal disease. Not surprisingly, they viewed their quarantining as race discrimination. He recommended the assignment of black morale officers so that soldiers could better understand why strict discipline was necessary. Such a step would have altered the complexion of leadership, as no black commissioned or noncommissioned officers served at the camp.[75]

Loving gauged the morale of soldiers at Camp Gordon, Georgia, to be "exceptionally good," which, if true, was remarkable given the evidence he found of justifiable grievances. No black officers served there, and five black sergeants, all college graduates, complained that they had no opportunity to enter officer training. Relations between the "Colored Combatant Unit" and its white officers were strained, although men in noncombat units felt they were treated well by whites. But the military police who patrolled nearby Atlanta often harassed black soldiers and their friends, requiring them to show passes for no good reason and subjecting them to racist language and other deliberate humiliations.[76]

In contrast, race relations appeared to be good at Camp Wheeler, near Macon, Georgia. Although there were no black officers and no noncoms above the rank of corporal, racial harmony seemed to prevail due, in Loving's view, to the fact that nearly all of the white noncommissioned officers came from the North. Military policemen in Macon did not interfere with blacks unless they became disorderly. Loving made no reference to the month-old charges of poor medical treatment and food and abusive white sergeants, which may have been swept under the rug in a cursory "investigation" by the camp intelligence officer.[77]

If morale at Camp Gordon was "exceptionally good," it was "excellent" at Camp Jackson, outside Columbia, South Carolina, in early October. Loving found practically no racial friction. A combat unit stationed there had white commissioned officers and black noncoms who seemed to enjoy good relations. A labor battalion was under the command of white sergeants and black corporals.[78] Loving's next stop was Camp Sevier, South Carolina, where he found a significant erosion in morale. No blacks exercised leadership above the rank of corporal in the 426th Labor Battalion, composed of fifteen hundred men from Baltimore and Washington. Its white noncommissioned officers were rejects from overseas service who were, in Loving's frank analysis, distinctly inferior to many blacks in the battalion who should have been considered for noncommissioned leadership positions. A quartermaster detachment was under the command of abusive white officers, while the military police, all of whom were white southerners, were at least as bad. Again Loving was blunt: "I can safely say that a colored soldier in this city [Greenville] has no more show, so far as safety or justice is concerned than a jack rabbit." Military police harassed black soldiers and their friends at will, cursed and beat them, demanded to see passes unnecessarily, and thrust revolvers into their faces without provocation. Unlucky was the black soldier assigned to Camp Sevier.[79]

By late October Loving was at Camp Greene near Charlotte, North Carolina, whose commander had decreed that black soldiers must be given fair treatment. Loving found little racial friction. Six black officers led a development battalion, and their relations with white officers in other commands were apparently cordial.

Complaints surfaced about rough treatment from white noncoms in several non-combat units, but Loving believed them to be exaggerated. The YMCA hut had a placard reading "No negro soldiers allowed by orders of the military authorities." If, in fact, the camp commander had given or allowed such an order, it stands in contrast with his announced policy of fair treatment.[80]

Loving inspected Camp Humphreys again in early November and discovered that "the morale of the colored soldiers is not particularly good." The problem was unrelated to the sanitary corps detachment that had been so demoralized there two months earlier. Rather, "this condition is due to assigning these Howard [University] graduates to these labor battalions, and failing to give them any recognition by appointing them non-commissioned officers." Loving was aghast at what he regarded as both racial and class discrimination: "I cannot believe that the War Department is aware of the fact that these university graduates are being made to dig ditches and perform other manual labor when their services are needed in combatant regiments as officers or non-commissioned officers." Company C of the 549th Labor Battalion had twenty Howard graduates, but not even one black corporal.[81]

Before completing his investigation of southern posts, Loving detoured to Camp Mills, near New York. There he found the best of race relations, not only between black and white soldiers, but also between black soldiers and neighboring civilians. Although there were no black commissioned officers, all of the noncoms in the labor battalions and depot brigades were black. Most of the white officers came from the North and Midwest. A southern white officer who was in the habit of calling soldiers "niggers" had been reprimanded. Loving gave no opinion on the camp commander's proposal to concentrate all black troops in one block and provide them with their own YMCA and "hostess house" for entertaining families and friends, so that they would not come into contact with southern white troops. That officer also promised Loving that he would review the demotion of a number of black sergeants and corporals and consider a protest against the consignment of educated blacks to labor battalions.[82]

Loving's last inspection returned him to Camp Lee, Virginia, in mid-November, where he had investigated "unrest" and low morale a year before. During this visit he found morale to be "good." Four black captains led a replacement battalion, and each of them had eleven white lieutenants in their command. But race relations were deplorable in the 407th Labor Battalion, whose many college graduates were commanded by "ignorant white non-commissioned officers." Fortunately, the military police did not practice harassment and abuse as in some other southern locations.[83]

Summarizing his investigations at eleven camps from September to November 1918, Loving concluded that, despite exceptions like Camp Pike, "very good" relations prevailed between black and white soldiers. Although black officers only served at Camps Taylor, Greene, and Lee, their associations with their men as well as with white officers were also positive. Loving was certainly overly optimistic, but this may have been a calculated strategy to build support for policy changes he would recommend later in his report. The performance of white noncommissioned officers in noncombat units, however, was unsatisfactory. Many were clearly inferior to the black high school and college graduates they led. Loving also criticized the fact that until the War Department issued orders in October requiring that noncombat units be given at least some instruction at arms, most blacks in such units received absolutely no military instruction. Even where blacks were taught close-order drill, the instruction was without weapons. At some locations noncombat units were worked so hard that there was literally no time for drill, or even, in some instances, time to wash their clothes.

The best white officers were those from the North or West, and Loving recommended that only such men be allowed to command blacks. Southern white officers should only lead white regiments. Black soldiers' medical care would improve, suggested Loving, if the army appointed black surgeons, especially since southern white doctors were not accustomed to treating blacks, especially those with venereal diseases. Loving also attacked the War Department policy of excluding blacks from commissions in noncombat units. Approximately seven hundred black officers graduated from the training camp at Des Moines early in the war and were assigned to combat regiments. But when labor battalions were organized, the War Department specified that their officers be white, even though there were at least thirty-three unassigned black officers at that time. Those thirty-three officers were still languishing at Camp Dix in November 1918, when they could have been leading the chronically officer-short labor battalions.

As Loving concluded his forthright analysis of the army's policies and their effect on morale, he highlighted a form of discrimination that had not existed before World War I, and which was racist in its assumptions and practice:

> Much of the unrest among colored troops at the various camps is due to the fact that white noncommissioned officers are assigned to colored units, viz: labor and service battalions. The assignment of white noncommissioned officers to colored units is a new departure in the history of the American army. Even in Civil War days colored units carried colored noncommissioned officers and the same practice has been followed in the regular army. . . . That most of these white noncommissioned officers view themselves in the light of the overseer of antebellum days is shown by their practice of carrying revolvers when they take details of men out to work. In all camps I found that there were colored men far better qualified to be noncommissioned officers than the white men under whom they were serving.
>
> There is general resentment in colored labor battalions because it seems that these organizations have been made the dumping ground for unfit white men who have been rejected for service in white units.[84]

But what would the War Department do with Loving's candid recommendations? The war was now over and demobilization would soon begin. Since that process took several months, the morale of black troops should have remained of concern to the MID. Although some of Loving's advice was embodied in proposed policies regarding the use of blacks in the postwar military, they were ultimately not implemented. The MID's willingness to allow a black officer to examine racial problems in the army and not discount his criticisms and recommendations because he was black was certainly a progressive step. But the army's failure to implement even moderate policy changes was in fact a ringing endorsement of its racist status quo.

Ill-treatment of black soldiers at stateside camps continued after the Armistice, requiring the MID to investigate, if not ameliorate, unsatisfactory situations. Exploitative conditions at Bush Terminal in Brooklyn came to light when the YMCA's own Intelligence Department learned that a labor battalion was being worked seven days a week, including nights. The commanding officer sought to paper over the men's unhappiness by asking the YMCA to raise morale, but its secretary was in sympathy with the soldiers, especially as they labored alongside civilians who were paid six to seven dollars daily for the same amount of work. Upon investigation, Walter Loving placed the blame on the terminal quartermaster, who had ordered the excessive work. The soldiers' immediate commanders wanted them to labor less and have more time for recreation, which Loving endorsed. The MID passed his recommendation on to the intelligence officer at the port of embarkation, asking for further investigation and recommendation. It may have passed the buck because it had no authority over the quartermaster. In any case, the port IO dismissed the issue as an attempt by white labor agitators to stop the employment of soldiers who were doing what they regarded as civilian work. Yet he and the quartermaster nonetheless recommended that henceforth only civilian labor be used. It appears that, when their abuses were discovered, the two absolved themselves of past wrongdoing by blaming white workers, and then cleared themselves in the present by recommending a benign policy.[85]

It was not uncommon when allegations of mistreatment surfaced in the early postwar months for camp or depot officers to admit that such conditions prevailed in the past, but to claim that they had since been rectified. It is impossible to tell from existing documents whether significant improvements in fact took place, or whether grievances generated only quick cosmetic changes. This is illustrated in the case of a black labor battalion at the Schenectady, New York, army depot. In December 1918, a black civilian complained of long hours of work and the lack of food, bathing facilities, and medical treatment. Emmett Scott requested an inquiry, which the MID placed in the lap of the depot quartermaster. Not surprisingly, he replied that the work was not onerous; food was sufficient, although it had been bad in the past, and for a time medical care was inadequate. Overall, he claimed, everyone at the depot had suffered in the past, but conditions had improved significantly. The MID took this at face value and dropped the matter. When and to what degree the black troops suffered harsh conditions, and whether this was greater compared to whites at the depot, cannot be proven with certitude, but while a black complaint was voiced, no similar white protest seems to exist.[86]

Another group of black soldiers who very likely labored under abusive conditions after the war was posted at Camp McArthur, near Waco, Texas. "Pvt. George Canada" wrote to the secretary of war that his unit was forced to work under the guns of local men who had been quickly made sergeants. In addition to suffering verbal abuse, they were also ill clothed and poorly fed. Scott asked the MID to investigate, although he cautioned that the "letter doubtless exaggerates some." There is no indication as to what gave Scott pause. How much his comment influenced the MID's approach to the issue cannot be determined, but its communication to the IO at Camp McArthur was an invitation to a not-guilty verdict: "It is probable that the charges made are scarcely worthy of investigation." Not surprisingly, the labor unit's white officer denied that any of the alleged conditions had occurred, claiming that the men were fed and clothed according to army regulations, and reporting that there was no "Pvt. Canada." In short, the charges need not be taken seriously. As with other inquiries of abusive conditions, the MID accepted these statements at face value and closed the case. It seems not to have occurred to anyone outside of Waco that the writer of the complaint had to use a false name to protect himself from reprisal, given the fact that he and others labored under hostile armed guards. Scott, at least, should have recognized this obvious point.[87]

As the war ended and millions of men were demobilized, army intelligence, mirroring the apprehensions of whites in society at large, worried that black troops were being stirred up by agitators and would return to civilian life emboldened in their demands for change. The MID particularly damned the *Crisis* in the immediate postwar months for allegedly radicalizing black troops. In fact, it was the war itself that heightened the racial consciousness of many African Americans, civilian and soldier alike. Those who served in the military believed they had earned the right to enjoy democracy at home for having fought to preserve it in Europe. And the Jim Crow army undoubtedly made many blacks, not only those in uniform, more impatient for racial change. Whites in the various intelligence bureaucracies had difficulty perceiving that the *Crisis* was more a reflection of the new black militancy than its source. DuBois's May 1919 editorial entitled "Returning Soldiers" articulated the new mood in three dramatic sentences: "*We return. We return from fighting. We return fighting.*"[88]

Five months before "Returning Soldiers," Camp Beauregard, Louisiana, went into a tailspin after a speech to the black troops by a white traveling YMCA speaker. Exactly what he said was never absolutely established. Some listeners, including some blacks, took him literally and believed he had said that blacks were as good as anyone, that all men were brothers, and that blacks should return to civilian life and be independent, their own bosses. Other blacks denied that this was his meaning. But according to some white officers, after this speech the black troops were less "obedient." How they expressed themselves is, unfortunately, not recorded. On reviewing reports from Camp Beauregard, the head of the MID urged YMCA headquarters to ban this man from ever again addressing black troops. The YMCA had already acted; the man was no longer speaking for the organization. One wishes for more details on the changing disposition of black troops as the war ended. Undoubtedly some were simply impatient to get out of uniform and back about their personal lives, but others had been transformed by exposure to the wider world and the wartime democratic rhetoric.[89]

This transformation was also expressed in black soldiers' growing unwillingness to passively accede to police brutality, mob violence, or nakedly enforced segregation. The peak of this unfolding spirit of resistance came in the summer of 1919 when blacks fought back against their attackers in several major urban riots, particularly in Chicago and Washington. But months before, as the war ended and demobilization began, this form of militant self-defense found expression in at least two now-forgotten "riots" in which soldiers battled police, other symbols of white authority, or local citizens. One such affray took place at Hampton, Virginia, in early December, when a "mob" of blacks, both civilians and soldiers, attacked a streetcar conductor. White military policemen were summoned to restore order, and on the surface racial tensions abated. But the city's white population remained uneasy despite the continued white military presence. The military police commander informed the MID that whites lived in constant fear of the blacks in their midst, whom they believed to be newly insolent, overbearing, and insulting. In fact, this was no exaggeration; blacks *were* manifesting such a spirit—civilians more than soldiers, although many civilians were discharged soldiers.[90] Southern whites especially found it difficult to understand the depth of black anger over segregation or manhandling by police, and found it easier to account for expressions of resistance as violations of the etiquette of race relations. Resort to explanations like "insolence" also allowed whites to delegitimize black aspirations and lay the blame for unrest, not on conditions perpetuated by whites, but on supposed character weaknesses inherent in the black race.

Another "riot" occurred on 8 December in Charleston, South Carolina, generating a thick MID case file. The chief perpetrators in two incidents were white. According to a white sailor who witnessed the first incident, a group of black soldiers was returning to camp, escorting one of their comrades who was drunk. A policeman "interfered" and tried to arrest him, but was opposed by the soldiers, who at the same time sent for a patrol. The policeman drew his pistol, hit one of the black soldiers, and threatened to shoot the others. At that point one of the black soldiers warned the policeman that he was not going to shoot any man in uniform, to which the policeman replied, "fuck the uniform and anybody that wore it." Fighting broke out when police reinforcements arrived. Several of the soldiers were arrested and taken to the police station, where a crowd of white and black soldiers and sailors soon gathered. It also appears that policemen, including their chief, beat some of the arrested soldiers after they were taken to the station. Meanwhile, the crowd outside remained orderly and, after being assured that the policeman who had insulted the uniform would be dealt with, dispersed peacefully and started back to camp. But as a group of black soldiers tried to board a streetcar, the motorman pushed them off and threatened to hit them with his air controller bar. One of the soldiers grasped the man's arm before he could hit anybody, whereupon the conductor drew a pistol, struggled with a soldier, and shot him. Other soldiers then disarmed the conductor.

The next day, three black soldiers, unable to pay fines, were sentenced to work thirty days on the municipal chain gang, a harsh punishment given the offenses. The military requested that the city charge various policemen and the streetcar conductor as well. Hearings took place, at which a number of policemen, including the chief, were called to testify, but no one was punished. The regional army commander, after reviewing a large file of affidavits, concluded, in a letter to the mayor, that soldiers, civilians, and the police were all to blame, and recommended that henceforth men in uniform who were charged with misdemeanors be turned over to the military police.[91] It does not appear that the soldiers' resistance to the policeman and the streetcar motorman and conductor was fueled by alcohol or the desire to start a fight. Rather, they were unwilling to bear insult to the uniform they were wearing, were not going to allow one of their comrades who was drunk but not belligerent be dragged off by the civilian police, and were not about to stand for being barred from a streetcar. It is also likely that the soldiers fought with police and responded forcefully to the streetcar crew because they symbolized white racial power. Those who were prepared to risk their lives defending their country had also prepared themselves to claim long-denied rights. Before the war, one could hardly imagine blacks fighting with white policemen over such an incident. But some black men had been transformed by the war, and southern whites did have something to fear. A new spirit of militancy—what the *Messenger* would soon call the "New Crowd Negro"—was emerging all across America. As the MID sensed with increasing apprehension in early 1919, many blacks were undergoing this metamorphosis.

With World War I ending, military intelligence faced serious racial issues, some of which it might address, others over which it had no control. Hundreds of thousands of black soldiers were preparing to reenter civilian life after enduring varying degrees of racial abuse while in the army. Members of labor units had at times been "worked like slaves," supervised by white noncommissioned officers who carried pistols, wielded whips, and kicked those who were not sufficiently compliant. Numerous black soldiers had endured appalling camp conditions—inadequate winter quarters, the absence of bathing facilities, lack of medical attention—although many of these circumstances were being remedied by the end of the war. Most of them served, at one time or another, under white officers who did not believe in their fighting abilities and thought them fit only for manual labor. Those who entered combat—and only a minority of black troops were allowed this role—found themselves being damned for allegedly failing to stand up under fire. Yet every man had undergone some degree of metamorphosis. Many encountered the wider world for the first time. Black southerners experienced regions where segregation was not rigidly enforced. Those who reached France met white people who did not view them as "niggers." Some of these men were becoming New Crowd Negroes as they experienced, while defending the flag and wearing their country's uniform, some of the most naked racism of that era, both in the military and in civilian life. One such recreated individual was Pvt. Charles Lewis, who was returning home on 16 December 1918 along with other black soldiers who had been honorably discharged the day before. When his train stopped at Hickman, Kentucky, a deputy sheriff entered their car and rudely began to search their luggage for whiskey. When Lewis objected to the officer's discourteous behavior, he was told: "shut up nigger, and open up your baggage." When he refused, Lewis was shot by the deputy, pulled from the car by a mob of whites which had already assembled at the station before the train arrived, taken to a nearby tree, and hanged.[92]

The growing tension between blacks' heightened aspirations and an uncompromising racial status quo was not lost on at least some military intelligence officers, especially those concerned with morale issues. But the army took no steps to protect men like Charles Lewis, who was not the only black soldier lynched while wearing his uniform, nor to press for punishment of such white murderers. Moreover, it took only feeble steps to deal with the "problem" of "colored troops." Not that it lacked concrete information and specific suggestion. Major Walter Loving, in a memorandum written in late December on the "Spirit of Unrest Among Negroes," was candid:

> 1. The fact cannot be denied that at this particular time there is a growing feeling of unrest among the negroes all over the United States. This condition seems to have arisen since the signing of the armistice. Negro journals all over the country are asking "What will be the negro's reward for helping to win the war for democracy?" No sooner had the President announced the names of the men who would compose the Peace Commission from the United States, colored societies and various organizations in the different large cities met and elected delegates who are to be sent to France and remain there during the Peace Conference. . . .
>
> 2. While the conventions were in session in the various cities and the people were filled with excitement . . . the startling news came to the attention of the convention holding session in Washington that a negro soldier had been lynched in Hickman, Kentucky, while dressed in the full regalia of a soldier in the United States Army . . . [B]efore the indignation which its members felt so keenly over the lynching of the negro soldier had subsided, another sad message bore intelligence of the lynching of four more negroes in Alabama, two brothers and two sisters.
>
> 3. Not since the East St. Louis riot have the colored people been so worked up as they are today. While their brave soldiers are absent on foreign soil answering the call of their country, their wives, brothers and sisters are being lynched and murdered in their own country while the government stands by and offers them no protection. View this matter as you may, and from any angle that you may, and you will see that something serious is going to happen unless the government takes some steps to protect the families of those negro soldiers who lost their lives while fighting on foreign soil for a democracy which offers their families no protection at home. The lynching of that soldier is entirely within the jurisdiction of the military authority, and the most rigid investigation should be

conducted so that the guilty, who are well known to the Kentucky officials, may be brought to justice and punished to the fullest extent of the law.

4. Indignation and mass meetings are being organized in many of the large cities and I am endeavoring to have operatives cover them all in order that any unwise movements on the part of the people may be promptly reported, and a repetition of the East St. Louis riot averted.

But the army was not about to assert jurisdiction over such atrocities and take an active role in protecting the lives of its discharged soldiers. The MID had once made an effort to combat lynching, in mid-1918, by sponsoring legislation to circumvent the prevailing legal opinion that mob violence was a state, not a federal matter. The MID's bill would have made it a federal offence to kill anyone in the military service, anyone subject to being drafted, or any close relative of such individuals. Despite being a well-crafted piece of legislation, and despite expert testimony by Major Spingarn, the bill died in committee.[93] In fact, it never had a chance. This was the MID's sole direct effort against mob violence, so it is not surprising that, six months later, its only response to the Lewis lynching was to advise the Department of Justice to "make a thorough investigation."[94]

Rather than learning positive lessons about blacks during World War I, the army instead reconfirmed its already deeply entrenched stereotypes and racial perceptions. Glimmers of insight were too often ignored. In June 1918, MIB chief Marlborough Churchill analyzed for the chief of staff the growing rejection of Bookerite conservatism and increasing support for the DuBoisian emphasis on civil rights. This more aggressive approach, Churchill argued, was not the result of German propaganda, but of blacks' growing racial consciousness, which made them more dissatisfied with white supremacy. But those higher up in the chain of command ignored his perceptive conclusion.[95]

Even problems right under the MID's nose could not honestly be addressed. Its headquarters was located in a six-story War Department office building in Washington. Among its many civilian employees were numerous black women, mostly messengers who worked on every floor, and a handful of typists who all worked on the sixth floor. A "Memorandum for Colored Women Employees" was issued in late October 1918 instructing them to use only a restroom on the first floor and banning them from all such facilities on the other floors. They, of course, regarded the order as insulting and discriminatory. Emmett Scott added his voice to their protest, quoting a recent War Department press release announcing that it would not tolerate discrimination on the part of draft boards. But the MID could not forthrightly face its own racism. Rather than simply decree that any women could use any restroom, Churchill agreed to "other arrangements" which apparently mollified the black women but continued to validate the objections of white women.[96] What had military intelligence learned in an intense eighteen months of war? In crucial respects its racial vision remained as obscured in late 1918 as it was when the war began in the spring of 1917. It might be argued that its function was solely to facilitate the war effort by minimizing disaffection, not to promote justice. But at least a few white MID officers must have been enlightened by Walter Loving, and come to realize that military efficiency would be promoted by positive black morale.

A "secret" bulletin on "The Negro Problem in the Army" written by Maj. James Cutler, one of MID's most "liberal" white officers, which was to be seen only by intelligence officers and the top command ranks, shows why the MID, in harmony with its intelligence partners in the Bureau of Investigation and the State and Post Office Departments, would continue to fear subversion of the black population and to oppose African-American militancy during the postwar Red Scare:

> The government is asking the entire colored population to take a full share in the war. Their men, their money, and their devotion are needed, to the greatest possible extent. As a result prominent negroes have raised, even more than in civil life, the question of the "equality" of the negro, and agitators have made what capital they could of the situation. "Why should we fight for America?" they ask. "What has she done for us? Are we still Jim Crow in the army?" So far there has fortunately been no difficulty of any disastrous kind, but there have been sufficient serious difficulties to make one grateful that more trouble has not resulted.
>
> There are certain evident facts about the drafted negro. . . . In the army he is more cut off from home associations than the white man, because the act of writing letters, if he can write at all, is a mental and physical strain. He does extraordinarily little reading of newspapers, but takes in his information through the ear. He is in every way more isolated than the white man, and, being isolated, is more gullible. The reason that enemy agents and agitators have had good success in proportion to the small effort among the negroes is found in this isolation and this gullibility.

Cutler went on to explain the psychology of the African-American soldier: "His habitual easy-going docility may prove either an asset or a liability according to how he is handled. Army life puts more snap and ginger into him than he ever dreamt of. By interfering with his easy-going habits these new qualities may lead to resentment of trivial things which otherwise he would hardly have noticed—or, if he is well fed and cared for, kept contented and free of race agitation." In other words, this "gullible" race was easily manipulated into believing that "trivial things"—i.e., racial slights and discriminations—justified agitation and resentment. Cutler was willing to admit that many issues might legitimately generate resentment: the difficulty in getting promoted, the army's preference for white noncommissioned officers, the concentration of the majority of black soldiers in noncombat units, differential treatment of black and white soldiers by both the military and nonmilitary agencies like the YMCA, inferior medical care, whites addressing blacks as "niggers" and using disciplinary measures not in conformance with army regulations, and the denial of military training to those in labor battalions. "Finally, there is the ever-present race question, . . . likely to be accentuated wherever large bodies of colored troops, concentrated and organized, are brought in close contact with equally well organized white troops."

Major Cutler admitted that "we cannot simply close our eyes and say that everything is going finely. There has always been in civilian life a contest over the 'dead line' drawn between whites and negroes, a contest as to the existence and extent of that line, and as to its necessity and advisability. We must equally recognize in the army that the same difficulty exists." In other words, the maintenance of white supremacy was a perennial issue in civilian society, and the army had to deal with that problem as well. But any real overhaul of race relations or etiquette was unthinkable: "It seems a sound point of view . . . that white troops and colored troops should be separated, but that colored troops should have every possible chance, within their domain, that white troops have in theirs. In a word, Separation *but* Equal Opportunity." Cutler apparently saw no contradiction between this extraordinary formula and a later statement that "all we are concerned with is the production of the highest possible efficiency and morale." In fact, he had just given evidence of unjust racial treatment causing an erosion of morale.[97]

From the beginning of the war, army intelligence placed a high priority on detecting subversion of the African-American population, particularly among those in uniform. By 1918 it was also seriously engaged in promoting positive morale among soldiers and civilians alike. This necessitated an examination of the experiences of black troops from their initial training to their shipment overseas and, for some, their entry into combat. Military intelligence unearthed no real evidence of enemy subversion targeted at blacks, but the absence of proof did not lead it to abandon the pursuit of imagined enemy agents. At the same time, those focusing on black morale—including officers like MID head Marlborough Churchill and Military Morale Section chief James Cutler—created their own dilemma: They recognized that blacks' support for the war was compromised by many discriminatory acts and policies imbedded in army culture. Yet they were so wedded to that culture that they could not contemplate initiating the changes that would have optimized morale. Instead, they had to accept the same tension that generations of slave owners and white supremacists were forced to live with: One cannot oppress a people without generating among them the aspiration to overcome that oppression.

Epilogue. "The Negro is 'seeing red'": From the World War into the Red Scare

The morale-building black editors' conference organized by Maj. Joel Spingarn, Emmett J. Scott, and the Committee on Public Information met in Washington from 19–21 June 1918 and was, by Spingarn's account, a rousing success. It succeeded in garnering more enthusiastic support for the war from the black press while giving black leaders the opportunity to voice their grievances over lynching, discrimination in federal hiring, the unwillingness of the Red Cross to employ black nurses, and the persistence of segregation on the government-controlled railroads. But there was a second motive: Military Intelligence Branch chief Col. Marlborough Churchill saw it as a checkmate to the long-planned Colored Liberty Congress organized by William Monroe Trotter, a well-known "race radical," editor of the *Boston Guardian,* and hostile critic of President Wilson and the editors' conference. The Liberty Congress was set for 25–29 June, also in Washington, and Churchill maneuvered to get it postponed or, better yet, canceled. He instructed the intelligence officer in Boston to warn Trotter that it was "highly undesirable before the policies to be adopted by this [editors'] conference are put in operation that any convention airing the grievances of the colored people should be held. . . . Mr. Trotter should be informed that in the opinion of the military authorities his convention or conference should be postponed for four or five months . . . [A]gitation likely to cause trouble at this time must be discouraged." The MID's most basic fear was that "Germans might take advantage of a movement of this kind."[1]

One hundred and fifteen delegates from thirty states attended the Colored Liberty Congress, drafting a petition to the House of Representatives "asking for the abolition of race discrimination and injustice to Colored Americans as a win-the-war measure." Hubert H. Harrison, whose new militant monthly, *Voice,* would soon be in print, chaired the meeting. It was a remarkable document, coming just three years following the death of the great conciliator, Booker T. Washington. Its content and rhetoric would not have been approved by the "Wizard of Tuskegee." The petition, in fact, is a dramatic example of the more militant approach to civil rights being forged by New Crowd Negroes like Harrison. Its first six points began with the phrase, "We are the victims." Victims of "civil proscription," barred from enjoying public accommodations in a majority of the states; victims of "class distinction," being segregated on railroads in a third of the states; victims of "caste and race prejudice" in the military and naval academies; victims of "proscriptive discrimination," barred from most federal civil service jobs and segregated when granted employment; victims of "political proscription" by being disfranchised in a third of the states; and victims in many states of "robbery, ravishing, mob violence, murder, and massacre." Then, citing the need to maintain high morale and national unity during the war, the delegates appealed to Congress for redress, undoubtedly recognizing that there was even less chance that presidential action would be forthcoming. They called for an end to segregation in federal buildings and discrimination in federal employment; an end to Jim Crow railroad practices; opening every branch of the military to blacks on an equitable basis; enforcement of the Thirteenth Amendment to end peonage, the Fourteenth to guarantee equal protection of the law, and the Fifteenth to assure the right to vote; and, finally, to make lynching a federal crime.[2]

Walter Loving attended the Colored Liberty Congress, along with army intelligence stenographers who transcribed what they regarded as particularly egregious rhetoric. From militant New Crowd Negro editor Hubert H. Harrison: "They take our brothers and lynch them and then expect us to go to war as loyal citizens." Mrs. M. Griffin: "Emmett Scott had a number of the colored editors to come to Washington to be wined and dined at the Government's expense for the sole purpose of muzzling them . . . [The] sole purpose in calling these editors to Washington was to thwart the plans of the Colored Liberty Congress." Trotter: "When I walk down Pennsylvania Avenue and see Old Glory flying over so many jim crow places, I hang my head in shame for disgrace." Trotter again: "Quite a number of people had tried to keep this congress from convening in Washington, but we could not be stopped by a Jew [Spingarn], nor a Jim Crow Negro [Scott]." Attorney Twining: "We are going to win this war, but when we win, I want the black fingers that are pulling the triggers to kill the Hun to be able to make a cross on the ballot in Oklahoma." J. W. Bell: "If I thought that God Almighty wanted the white men of this nation to have all the good things and the colored the bad, I would willingly return to him this Life as a precious gift." Mrs. Simpson: "We do not want a Jew to represent our race."[3]

The Bureau of Investigation also took interest in the Liberty Congress plus a follow-up meeting of Trotter's National Equal Rights League in September. Its agents were still fixated on German subversion, even at this late date in the war, and believed that Joseph Stewart, a black attorney residing in Washington who attended the Congress, was "a base for German propaganda among the negroes in this city." Their suspicion of German influence on the Congress stemmed in part from the fact that alleged German spy Herman M. B. Moens was one of the handful of whites to attend Trotter's June convocation.[4]

The attention of two major intelligence bureaucracies to the Liberty Congress illustrates an important transition taking place in the second half of 1918. The fear that "German agents" were seeking to subvert the African-American population was beginning to be replaced by what would become an even more widespread anxiety: that a growing black militancy was poised to challenge the racial status quo in more aggressive and unacceptable ways, and that behind such pressure lay a sinister enemy, Russian Bolshevism. By 1919, America's socialists and anarchists were debating whether to embrace Bolshevism, and even those who did not leave the Socialist Party and join one of the new American communist parties still found much to applaud in the overturn of czarism and in Russia's recreation as a proletarian society supposedly free of racism. Not surprisingly, then, as the Bolshevik Revolution overshadowed Europe and seemed poised to cross the Atlantic, many Americans feared that communism would further radicalize existing militant movements while also infecting aggrieved ethnic minorities and restive labor movements.

During the second half of 1918 the federal intelligence establishment underwent a major but remarkably easy evolution from the pursuit of one exaggerated threat to the creation of a horrific new bogeyman. The investigative agencies were by then well practiced in the techniques of domestic espionage. Even more significantly, they had convinced themselves and much of the public that they were the nation's first line of defense against internal threats. Agents in all the intelligence bureaucracies had taken on the mantle of guardians of an American way of life that narrowly proscribed the legitimacy of working class and racial-minority aspirations, sanctified capitalism, and damned communism and socialism. This represented more than the replacement of one scapegoat with another: An evil progression had taken place. Testifying before a Senate subcommittee investigating "Brewing and Liquor Interests and German and Bolshevist Propaganda," former MID and Bureau agent Archibald E. Stevenson made the connection explicit: "German socialism . . . is the father of the Bolsheviki movement in Russia."[5] Thus prompted, the senators voted to abandon their probe of distillers and instead investigate radical movements. The Red Scare, germinated in the fears of German subversion, was being born. Just as World War I–era intelligence agencies believed that African Americans were particularly susceptible to the lies and promises of Germans and other enemy aliens, blacks were again stereotyped as gullible and easily manipulated by those who would promise them the chimera of "social equality." According to the new attorney general, A. Mitchell Palmer, writing in 1919, "practically all of the radical organizations in the country have looked upon the Negroes as particularly fertile ground for the spreading of their doctrines. These radical organizations have endeavored to enlist Negroes on their side, and in many respects have been successful." No wonder, then, that "the Negro is 'seeing red.'"[6]

As the Red Scare unfolded in 1919, a number of individuals and movements that had become objects of suspicion and persecution during World War I found themselves continuing to be targets. The "Bolsheviki" brush was an indiscriminate weapon with which to tar anyone who challenged the status quo or advocated unpopular ideas. It was even applied to those who were, in fact, anti-Bolsheviks, like Pan-Africanist Marcus Garvey. But nuances and distinctions were often lost on the federal intelligence establishment. Palmer saw the world through apocalyptic lenses. Regarding the new crop of militant, iconoclastic black periodicals, he wrote, "defiance and insolently race-centered condemnation of the white race is to be met with in every issue of the more radical publications." Three of the most notorious examples were no strangers to the intelligence agencies; they had been the targets of intimidation and attempted suppression during the war. The tribulations of the *Chicago Defender, Crisis,* and *Messenger* did not cease with the disappearance of the German enemy; all three faced even stronger efforts to silence their militancy during the Red Scare. The *Defender*'s outspoken attacks on lynching and mob violence continued to outrage white southerners who pressed the Post Office Department to declare it unmailable. The *Crisis* was damned for several sins during the Red Scare. DuBois's bold criticism of the War Department's treatment of black soldiers during the war coupled with fear that his journal was radicalizing black troops kept the Military Intelligence Division focused on the magazine for several years after the Armistice. Its parent organization was also attacked for allegedly stockpiling arms and ammunition in anticipation of a black uprising.

But the most persistent and virulent attacks on a black publication during the Red Scare were reserved for the *Messenger* and its editors, A. Philip Randolph and Chandler Owen. Postal censors became apoplectic upon reading its flamboyant and often sarcastic editorials, which welcomed Bolshevism abroad, promoted the Industrial Workers of the World, advocated armed resistance to rioters and lynchers, and demanded full social equality between the races. The monthly took delight in tweaking the sensibilities of whites and conservatives with headlines like "Pro-Germanism among Negroes" and "The Hun in America." So hated was the journal that Randolph was branded "the most dangerous Negro in America," and the attorney general denounced the *Messenger* as "by all odds the most able and the most dangerous of all the negro publications."[7] Strenuous efforts were made to prosecute the two editors, and the magazine's second-class mailing permit was revoked for two years.

Yet another Red Scare target had already been relentlessly pursued during World War I: the Industrial Workers of the World. This radical syndicalist labor organization had long been hated by defenders of capitalism, and its opposition to the war provided a convenient excuse to seek its legal extermination. Two mass trials decimated its leadership in 1918, but the union survived, although significantly crippled, into the postwar years. The major black "Wobbly," Ben Fletcher, was in prison, but others, black and white, carried the banner and continued vainly to organize. In fact, however, the Justice Department blew the size and significance of the IWW out of all proportion during the Red Scare years.

The Justice Department was not inaccurate, however, in assessing the significance of another Red Scare target: Marcus Garvey, the charismatic Jamaican-born Pan-Africanist who established his headquarters in New York in mid-1917. His Universal Negro Improvement Association was the largest black mass movement up to that time, and its weekly newspaper, the *Negro World,* demanded justice for oppressed blacks all over the globe. Garvey would be accused of everything from being anti-white to pro-Bolshevik, although he was in fact neither. Because he was only first noticed by federal intelligence agencies in mid-1918, and not investigated seriously until the Armistice, the story of his early days has not been narrated here. Readers can follow the relentless efforts to prosecute him in this volume's sequel, *"Seeing Red."* That book also contains the story of another major black target of federal investigators, the communist African Blood Brotherhood and its militant magazine, *Crusader,* which had their origins in 1919.

The campaigns against black militancy during the Red Scare could not have been waged with such vigor, and at least partial success, had it not been for the organization and experience developed during World War I. Without the war and the security issues it raised—enemy aliens; spying, sabotage, and subversion; draft delinquency; allegedly disloyal publications and religious denominations; and antiwar activism—there would have been little justification for the meteoric growth of the Bureau of Investigation and army intelligence, plus new mandates for the Post Office and State Departments. In short, the war required each agency to hire and train new investigators, perfect their techniques, and define an intelligence mission.

As that mission evolved, it came to include suppression or muting of African-American dissent, enforcement of draft compliance on an often apathetic black male population, and harsh punishment of those, white as well as black, thought to be spies or subverters. Because First Amendment freedoms existed more as legal symbols then as concrete civil liberties guarantees, prosecution of anyone accused of "disloyalty" or "subversion" or "sedition" was possible under the broad and imprecisely defined Espionage and Sedition Acts, and given the susceptibility of U.S. attorneys to the pressure of inflamed public opinion. There was, in fact, no actual subversion of the black population by enemy agents, unless one defined a labor agent as an enemy. The "evidence" of subversion was almost always an instance of black discontent with racial subordination or the wish that Germany would administer a good licking to White America. There was, however, a significant absence of eagerness to serve in a segregated and hostile army, a mood that expressed itself in much higher rates of draft evasion among blacks than among whites. While only dimly recognizing the causes of black apathy and hostility to the draft, agents staffing southern offices of the Bureau of Investigation frequently acted as if they had a mandate to convict and punish "slackers" and even those who had been officially classified as ineligible for military service.

Anyone daring to print views critical of the country or the administration, or simply those deemed likely to hamper enlistments or impair soldiers' morale through something they wrote, risked at the least denial of second-class (reduced) postal rates, and at the worst, federal prosecution. Black editors or publishers, who had neither significant financial resources nor political clout, had little choice but to toe the line drawn by white officials. Even though army intelligence had no statutory authority to censor civilian publications, it added its own pressure to that of the Justice Department in the government's successful effort to compel the race's most influential periodicals—the *Chicago Defender* and *Crisis*—to more enthusiastically support the war and to mute if not bury criticism of it. But G. W. Bouldin, publisher of the *San Antonio Inquirer*, was not even afforded a chance to atone for the editorial sin of having permitted to be printed an angry protest against the government's treatment of the Houston mutineers. No other black journalist suffered as he did: an Espionage Act conviction and a year in a federal penitentiary. Young A. Philip Randolph and Chandler Owen, whose magazine and rhetoric were far more "seditious," in the contemporary understanding of that term, miraculously escaped with only a couple of days in jail. Prosecutors pursuing those who were in some way "disloyal" during World War I did not often take weak cases to trial, so it is surprising that Bishop C. H. Mason, founder of the pacifist Church of God in Christ, was not convicted of interfering with the draft, especially since his influence on the church's entire membership was much more direct than that wielded by any journalist. One did not have to be a religious leader, however, to experience federal prosecution. For Dan McNairy, simple adherence to the beliefs of the Jehovah's Witnesses was sufficient. McNairy was convicted under the Sedition Act, but in other cases, if such charges could not be made to stick, any others would conveniently do. So it was that accused enemy subverter Herman M. B. Moens was prosecuted for possession of obscene photographs.

The Bureau of Investigation used black informants on an ad hoc basis during World War I. Not until after the war did it regularize the employment of paid informants and then, based on their usefulness, hire its first black agents in the early 1920s.[8] Army intelligence, on the other hand, employed a very capable black officer during the war, Maj. Walter H. Loving, to track down rumors of subversion among blacks, both civilians and soldiers; organize patriotic rallies to counter black disaffection; and inspect army camps where black soldiers trained or served and from which complaints had been received. He was usually forthright in reporting flagrant examples of racial discrimination, while glossing over instances he deemed of less influence on troop morale. However, his most important recommendations, concerning the need for black leadership of black troops, putting an end to the practice of having southern white men lead (and discipline) black units, and guaranteeing black soldiers the same decency with which whites were customarily treated, were never seriously considered. As the army, along with the rest of white society, confronted increasing black militancy after the war, it had itself at least partially to blame: Many black men were radicalized by the experience of fighting in a Jim Crow army to preserve freedom for distant Europeans, while they enjoyed so little of that commodity at home.

The practice of political intelligence thus did not have to be invented during the Red Scare; it was already in place and functioning at a high level by mid-1918. The case can be made that the national hysteria of 1919–20 was only possible because the existence of extremely subversive domestic enemies had already become axiomatic as a result of the war. Previous wars ended with no demonic enemy remaining, but the magnification of suspected enemy plots during the war made it highly likely that paranoid thinking and the fear of conspiracies would continue to characterize political and social thought after 1918. In addition, informants and agents had to find a new mission or face unemployment if there seemed no purpose for their agencies' continued existence.

The postwar Red Scare campaign against African-American militancy seems inevitable, given the inescapable clash between a young generation newly emboldened by its experiences in World War I to challenge the racial status quo and powerful conservative interests determined to protect that status quo at all costs. Even before America's entry into the war, thousands of southern-born blacks were voting with their feet, declaring their independence by migrating to northern and midwestern cities in search of personal freedom and dignity as well as a paying job.

The postwar New Crowd Negro was conceived in the early years of the Great Migration, gestated during the turbulent wartime months, and was born into a postwar world filled with uncertainty. The migration, the new jobs, the war rhetoric, the soldiers' bitter experiences, the exposure to wider worlds, all generated a sense among more than a few blacks that America's racial patterns and balance of power might be altered. But the guardians of politics and the capitalist way of life saw nothing positive to be gained from racial change or reform. On the contrary, any alteration in traditional racial patterns would disrupt or threaten their privilege and well-being. New Crowd Negroes faced an adversary far better organized, more powerful, and more ruthless than they could ever be. The postwar months were the most militant era of African-American history until the modern civil rights period, but the political intelligence establishment born in World War I was able to block that militancy by making the maintenance of white supremacy part of the nation's security agenda, thus legitimizing the suppression of racial activism.

Notes

Prologue

The quotation in the title is from Roi Ottley and William J. Weatherby, eds., *The Negro in New York: An Informal Social History, 1629–1940* (New York, 1969), pp. 199–200.

1. Quoted in German R. Ross, *History and Formative Years of the Church of God in Christ* (Memphis, 1969), pp. 23–24.

2. Howard W. Odum, *Wings on My Feet: Black Ulysses at the Wars* (Indianapolis, 1929), pp. 155–56.

3. Ottley and Weatherby, eds., *Negro in New York,* pp. 199–200.

4. Agent W. A. Weymouth to Bureau, 27 July 1918, Old German case file (hereafter OG) 245212, Record Group (RG) 65, Investigation Case Files of the Bureau of Investigation, 1908–1922 (hereafter BI), National Archives and Records Administration, College Park, Md. (hereafter NARA).

5. Paul L. Murphy, *World War I and the Origin of Civil Liberties in the United States* (New York, 1979), p. 15.

6. *Second Report of the Provost Marshal General to the Secretary of War on the Operations of the Selective Service System to December 20, 1918* (Washington, D.C., 1919), pp. 199–200.

1. "It became necessary to investigate everything"

1. Harry N. Scheiber, *The Wilson Administration and Civil Liberties, 1917–1921* (Ithaca, N.Y., 1960), pp. 5–10, 59. Wilson is quoted on p. vii.

2. Sanford J. Ungar, *FBI* (Boston, 1975), p. 40; Max Lowenthal, *The Federal Bureau of Investigation* (New York, 1950), pp. 12–13; Don Whitehead, *The FBI Story: A Report to the People* (New York, 1956), pp. 23, 330 n7.

3. Joan M. Jensen, *The Price of Vigilance* (Chicago, 1968), pp. 10–13; Edward M. House diary, 3 Mar. 1917, in Arthur M. Link, ed., *The Papers of Woodrow Wilson,* vol. 41 (Princeton, 1983), p. 318.

4. Jensen, *Price of Vigilance,* pp. 13–15; Whitehead, *FBI Story,* pp. 27–31.

5. Jensen, *Price of Vigilance,* pp. 15–16, 21, 23, 29–30; Thomas Watt Gregory to William Gibbs McAdoo, 12 June 1917, in Arthur M. Link, ed., *The Papers of Woodrow Wilson,* vol. 42 (Princeton, 1983), pp. 510–511. At the beginning of World War I naval intelligence, like its army counterpart, was "a tiny, insignificant organization" (Jeffery M. Dorwart, *Conflict of Duty: The U.S. Navy's Intelligence Dilemma, 1919–1945* [Annapolis, Md., 1983], p. 7).

6. House diary, 14 Dec. 1916, in Arthur M. Link, *The Papers of Woodrow Wilson,* vol. 40 (Princeton, 1982), pp. 238–241; Josephus Daniels diary, 27 Feb., and 27 and 30 Mar. 1917, in Link, ed., *Papers of Woodrow Wilson,* vol. 41, pp. 298–99, 484, 506.

7. Robert Lansing to Woodrow Wilson, 8 Apr. 1917, in Link, ed., *Papers of Woodrow Wilson,* vol. 42, pp. 16–17; Jensen, *Price of Vigilance,* pp. 40–41; Col. Claud E. Stadtman and Capt. Carmelo J. Bernardo, *History of the War Department Military Intelligence Activities, 1885–1920* (Washington, D.C., n.d.), pp. 2–4.

8. Lansing to Wilson, 8 Apr. 1917, in Link, ed., *Papers of Woodrow Wilson,* vol. 42, pp. 16–17.

9. Stadtman and Bernardo, *History of the War Department,* chap. 6, p. 6.

10. Homer Cummings and Carl McFarland, *Federal Justice: Chapters in the History of Justice and the Federal Executive* (New York, 1937), pp. 420–21; Murphy, *World War I,* pp. 89–90.

11. McAdoo to Wilson, 15 May 1917, ser. 2, reel 89, Woodrow Wilson Papers, Manuscript Division, Library of Congress (hereafter Wilson Papers, LC).

12. Gregory to McAdoo, 12 June 1917, and Gregory to Wilson, 14 June 1917, in Link, ed., *Papers of Woodrow Wilson,* vol. 42, pp. 509–19.

13. McAdoo to Wilson, 2 June 1917, and Wilson to Gregory, 4 June 1917, in Link, ed., *Papers of Woodrow Wilson,* vol. 42, pp. 440–43, 446; Wilson to Gregory, 12 July 1917, in Arthur M. Link, ed., *The Papers of Woodrow Wilson,* vol. 43 (Princeton, 1983), pp. 154–55; Gregory to Wilson, 16 Apr. and 14 June 1917, Gregory to McAdoo, 17 Apr. 1917, Quartermaster General to Secretary of War, 28 June 1917, Secret Service operative Thomas J. Callaghan to Chief William J. Flynn, 29 June 1917, and McAdoo to Wilson, 5 July 1917, ser. 2, reel 89, Wilson Papers, LC.; Jensen, *Price of Vigilance,* pp. 43, 54–55; Stadtman and Bernardo, *History of the War Department,* chap. 6, pp. 16–17.

14. McAdoo to Baker, 9 July 1917, McAdoo to Wilson, 9 July 1917, and Thomas Callaghan to W. J. Flynn, 29 June 1917, ser. 2, reel 89, Wilson Papers, LC; Stadtman and Bernardo, *History of the War Department,* chap. 6, pp. 14–17. At the same time, the Post Office Department, in investigating alleged disloyalty of one of its employees, utilized Bureau of Investigation agents to assist its own inspectors. See Second Assistant Postmaster General Otto Praeger to Burleson, 16 and 17 July 1917, ser. 2, reel 89, Wilson Papers, LC; House diary, 7 Aug. 1917, in Link, ed., *Papers of Woodrow Wilson,* vol. 43, pp. 390–91; Daniels diary, 31 Aug. 1917, in Arthur M. Link, ed., *The Papers of Woodrow Wilson,* vol. 44 (Princeton, 1983), p. 107.

15. "The Functions of the Military Intelligence Division," War Department General Staff, 1 Oct. 1918, pp. 5, 30, in file 800.9-18, RG 59, Office of the Counselor, Central File, 1918–1927, Records of the Department of State (hereafter DS), NARA; Stadtman and Bernardo, *History of the War Department,* chap. 6, p. 23, chap. 7, pp. 8–10, 13, 18–20; Roy Talbert Jr., *Negative Intelligence: The Army and the American Left, 1917–1941* (Jackson, Miss., 1991), pp. 35, 45–54.

16. Memorandum, Rudolph Foster to Wilson 31 Oct. 1917, Wilson to Gregory, 1 Nov. 1917, and Gregory to Wilson, 5 and 12 Nov. 1917, ser. 2, reel 92, Wilson Papers, LC; Wilson to McAdoo, 19 and 22 Nov. 1917, and Daniels diary, 16 Nov. 1917, in Arthur M. Link, ed., *The Papers of Woodrow Wilson,* vol. 45 (Princeton, 1984), pp. 74, 75 n2, 101–102, 102 n1.

17. McAdoo to Gregory, 5 Jan. 1918, and Gregory to McAdoo, ? Feb. 1918, in *Wilson Papers,* vol. 42, pp. 518–19.

18. Scheiber, *Wilson Administration,* pp. 17–21.

19. Ibid., pp. 20–22.

20. Cummings and McFarland, *Federal Justice,* pp. 425–426. Cummings served as Franklin D. Roosevelt's attorney general from 1933–39.

21. Scheiber, *Wilson Administration,* pp. 22–26; Richard W. Steele, *Free Speech in the Good War* (New York, 1999), p. 4.

22. Scheiber, *Wilson Administration,* pp. 13–17.

23. Ibid., pp. 17, 22, 26–27; Zechariah Chafee Jr., *Free Speech in the United States* (Cambridge, Mass., 1941), p. 214.

24. Scheiber, *Wilson Administration,* pp. 27–28; Talbert, *Negative Intelligence,* p. 66.

25. Samuel J. Graham to Joseph P. Tumulty, 6 June 1917, case file 20, reel 173, Wilson Papers, LC; *Congressional Record,* 56th Cong., 2nd. sess., vol. 56, 22 June 1918, pp. 8138–39; Jensen, *Price of Vigilance,* p. 155; *Annual Report of the Attorney General of the United States for the Year 1918* (Washington, D.C., 1918), pp. 14, 16; *Annual Report of the Attorney General of the United States for the Year 1919* (Washington, D.C., 1919), p. 12; Theodore Kornweibel Jr., "Black on Black: The FBI's First Negro Informants and Agents and the Investigation of Black Radicalism during the Red Scare," *Criminal Justice History* 8 (1987): pp. 121–36.

26. Whitehead, *FBI Story,* pp. 14, 32, 34; *Annual Report of the Attorney General of the United States for the Year 1917* (Washington, D.C., 1917), pp. 82–84; *Attorney General Annual Report 1918,* pp. 104–105.

27. *Register of the Department of Justice and the Courts of the United States,* 24th ed. (Washington, D.C., 1917), p. 16; Obituary, A. Bruce Bielaski, *New York Times,* 20 Feb. 1964.

28. *Attorney General Annual Report 1918,* p. 14.

29. Ibid., pp. 14–22, 53–54.

30. Whitehead, *FBI Story,* pp. 3, 36–37; Lowenthal, *Federal Bureau of Investigation,* pp. 22–23; Thomas W. Gregory, "How the Rear of our Armies Was Guarded During the World War," address to the North Carolina Bar Association, 7 Aug. 1919, printed copy in John Lord O'Brian Papers, Hoover Institution, typescript copy in folder 18-2, John Lord O'Brian Papers, State University of New York–Buffalo.

31. Scheiber, *Wilson Administration,* p. 43.

32. *Attorney General Annual Report 1918,* p. 21; Scheiber, *Wilson Administration,* pp. 42–43, 46–51. I am indebted to my colleague, Richard Steele, who has examined the O'Brian papers in depth, for this analysis of his dilemmas in dealing with overzealous U.S. attorneys.

33. Whitehead, *FBI Story,* pp. 37–39; Lowenthal, *Federal Bureau of Investigation,* pp. 25–34.

34. *Attorney General Annual Report 1918,* pp. 24–25; Gregory, "How the Rear of Our Armies Was Guarded."

35. Jensen, *Price of Vigilance,* pp. 246–258; Talbert, *Negative Intelligence,* pp. 31–37.

36. Marc Powe, *The Emergence of the War Department Intelligence Agency: 1885–1918* (Manhattan, Kans., 1975), pp. 76–80; Bruce W. Bidwell, *History of the Military Intelligence Division, Department of the Army General Staff: 1775–1941* (Frederick, Md., 1986), pp. 95–99; Talbert, *Negative Intelligence,* pp. 6–7.

37. Powe, *Emergence of the War Department Intelligence Agency,* pp. 81–102; Bidwell, *History of the Military Intelligence Division,* pp. 105, 109–111, 113–15, 117–18; Stadtman and Bernardo, *History of the War Department,* chap. 14, pp. 1–2; Talbert, *Negative Intelligence,* pp. 8–9.

38. Bidwell, *History of the Military Intelligence Division,* pp. 122–25.

39. Ibid; Powe, *Emergence of the War Department Intelligence Agency,* pp. 94–95; Stadtman and Bernardo, *History of the War Department,* chap. 6, pp. 14–15.

40. Bidwell, *History of the Military Intelligence Division,* pp. 110–12; Talbert, *Negative Intelligence,* p. 9.

41. Lowenthal, *Federal Bureau of Investigation,* pp. 22–23, Bidwell, *History of the Military Intelligence Division,* pp. 132–34, 242; Stadtman and Bernardo, *History of the War Department,* chap. 7, p. 13, chap. 14, p. 21. The MID's phenomenal success in breaking codes is narrated by its chief cryptographer in Herbert O. Yardley, *The American Black Chamber* (Indianapolis, 1931).

42. Bidwell, *History of the Military Intelligence Division,* pp. 195–97; Stadtman and Bernardo, *History of the War Department,* chap. 9, pp. 25–26.

43. Bidwell, *History of the Military Intelligence Division,* p. 203; Stadtman and Bernardo, *History of the War Department,* chap. 14, pp. 38–39.

44. Stadtman and Bernardo, *History of the War Department,* chap. 6, pp. 25–26, 35–36. I am indebted to Talbert's book for illuminating the social class and educational background of the MID's leadership.

45. Marlborough Churchill, "The Military Intelligence Division, General Staff," *Journal of the United States Artillery* 3 (Apr. 1920): p. 294.

46. Bidwell, *History of the Military Intelligence Division,* pp. 179–80, 183, 186.

47. Ibid., p. 189; Jensen, *Price of Vigilance,* pp. 225–28; Stadtman and Bernardo, *History of the War Department,* chap. 7, pp. 1–6, 18; Talbert, *Negative Intelligence,* pp. 35–36.

48. Bidwell, *History of the Military Intelligence Division,* pp. 190–91.

49. Thomas M. Camfield, "'Will to Win'—The U.S. Army Troop Morale Program of World War I," *Military Affairs* 41 (Oct. 1977): pp. 125–28; Stadtman and Bernardo, *History of the War Department,* chap. 10, pp. 11–17.

50. Stadtman and Bernardo, *History of the War Department,* chap. 14, pp. 27, 39; Bidwell, *History of the Military Intelligence Division,* pp. 194–95.

51. Bidwell, *History of the Military Intelligence Division,* pp. 236–37; Stadtman and Bernardo, *History of the War Department,* chap. 10, pp. 1–2, chap. 14, p. 31. The MID also maintained links to the ONI in the postwar period but the latter limited its investigations quite narrowly, focusing mostly on Japanese activities.

52. "War Activities of the Post Office Department Under the Administration of Postmaster General Albert S. Burleson," typescript, (?) June 1919, Albert Sidney Burleson Papers, University of Texas, Austin (hereafter Burleson Papers, UT), also in Albert Sidney Burleson Papers, Library of Congress, Washington (hereafter Burleson Papers, LC); "Resume of War Activities," undated, Burleson Papers, UT; "Progress and Development of the Postal Service Under Postmaster General Burleson," typescript, no date (1919?), Burleson Papers, UT, also Burleson Papers, LC; *Annual Report of the Postmaster General for the Fiscal Year Ended June 30 1919* (Washington, D.C., 1919), pp. 7–8.

53. Burleson to Wilson, 17 Apr. 1917, and McAdoo to Wilson, 17 Apr. 1917, copies in Burleson Papers, UT, and Burleson Papers, LC.

54. "An Open Letter to Hon. Henry W. Taft from William H. Lamar, formerly Assistant Attorney General and Solicitor of the Post Office Department," 4 Nov. 1921, Burleson Papers, UT.

55. Burleson to Editor and Publisher, *New York World,* 3 Oct. 1917, Burleson Papers, UT, and Burleson Papers, LC.

56. G. S. MacFarland to Wilson, 12 Oct. 1917; Wilson to Burleson, 11, 13, 18, and 30 Oct. 1917; Burleson to Wilson, 16 Oct. 1917; and Burleson to Milton Brohner, 22 Oct. 1917, Burleson Papers, UT, and Burleson Papers, LC.

57. Postal Solicitor William H. Lamar, press statement, 18 Sept. 1918, Burleson Papers, UT, and Burleson Papers, LC.

58. Scheiber, *Wilson Administration,* pp. 19–21; Post Office Department order no. 2142, 18 Oct. 1918, Burleson Papers, UT; *Address of Hon. A. S. Burleson, Postmaster General, at a Conference of Representatives of Business Organizations and the Postal Service, at Washington, D.C., April 1, 1919* (Washington, D.C., 1919), p. 7, also quoted in Richard Winston Howard, "The Work of Albert Sidney Burleson as Postmaster General" (MA thesis, University of Texas, 1938), p. 82; "Burleson of Texas: The War Postmaster General," typescript, undated, Burleson Papers, UT.

59. Bielaski to all employees of Bureau of Investigation, 28 Jan. 1918, case file 49241; see also case file 50839, Records relating to the Espionage Act, World War I, 1917–21, RG 28, NARA.

60. Assistant Attorney J. B. S. to Postal Solicitor William H. Lamar, 2 Mar. 1918, unarranged file, Amendments to (Espionage and Trading with the Enemy) Acts, 1917–21; James A. Horton (?) to Lamar, 10 Feb. 1919, case file 51378A, "War Activities of Post Office Department, Office of Solicitor," RG 28, NARA; Lamar, "Open letter to Taft," Burleson Papers, UT.

61. Lansing, Baker, and Daniels to Wilson, 13 Apr. 1917, case file 3856, reel 355; Gregory to Wilson, 20 Feb. 1918, case file 20, reel 173; Lansing to Wilson, 20 Feb. and 25 July 1918, case file 40, reel 181; and John Lord O'Brian to Gregory, 18 Apr. 1918, ser. 3, reel 95, Wilson Papers, LC.

62. Bertram D. Hulen, *Inside the Department of State* (New York, 1939), pp. 59–63; *Register of the Department of State, 1918* (Washington, D.C., 1919); *Register of the Department of State, 1922* (Washington, D.C., 1922); Rachael West, *The Department of State on the Eve of the First World War* (Athens, Ga., 1978), pp. 56, 58.

63. J. M. Host to Joseph P. Tumulty, 14 Oct. 1920, and Sec. of State Bainbridge Colby to Tumulty, 26 Oct. 1920, ser. 4, case file 40, reel 182, Wilson Papers, LC; Charles Flint Kellogg, *NAACP: A History of the National Association for the Advancement of Colored People,* vol. 1, *1909–1920* (Baltimore, 1967), pp. 278–82; Stephen R. Fox, *The Guardian of Boston: William Monroe Trotter* (New York, 1970), pp. 223–25.

64. Dorwart, *Conflict of Duty,* pp. 5–13.

65. Hulen, *Inside the Department of State,* pp. 9–10.

66. Ibid.

67. See, for example, Wilson to Colby, 29 Sept. 1920, ser. 2, reel 108, Wilson Papers, LC; Joe P. Byrne to Burleson, 24 June 1919, Burleson Papers, UT; "Address of Hon. Thomas W. Gregory at the Meeting of the New York Southern Society, December 9th, 1914"; and "Reconstruction and the Ku Klux Klan," paper read before the Arkansas and Texas Bar Associates, 10 July 1906, Thomas W. Gregory Papers, UT; "Human Interest Stories About Albert S. Burleson," n.d., Burleson Papers, UT; Gregory, "How the Rear of Our Armies Was Guarded." Burleson, who was accused of using convict labor on his large Texas plantation, defended himself by saying that he had no control over the labor used thereon when the state government leased his land. Besides, he claimed the convicts were white. See Edward M. House to Burleson, 24 Apr. 1918, and press release from Burleson's office, 26 Apr. 1919, Burleson Papers, UT.

2. "Very full of the anti-war spirit"

1. Frederick C. Leubke, *Bonds of Loyalty: German Americans and World War I* (DeKalb, Ill., 1974), pp. 207–210.

2. Jules Witcover, *Sabotage at Black Tom: Imperial Germany's Secret War in America, 1914–1917* (Chapel Hill, 1989), pp. 152–170, 184–196, 231.

3. Leubke, *Bonds of Loyalty,* pp. 210–12, 218–20.

4. "A Tongue That Needed Taming," *Henry County Weekly,* 30 Mar. 1917, OG 3057, RG 65, BI, NARA.

5. Agent Todd Daniel to Bureau, 21 and 30 Mar. 1917, OG 3057, RG 65, BI, NARA.

6. SAC Ralph H. Daughton to Bureau, 2 May 1917, OG 3057, RG 65, BI, NARA.

7. J. J. Barrow to Chief, Secret Service, 7 Apr. 1917, OG 3057, RG 65, BI, NARA.

8. "Teutons Try Yankee Trick of Making the Negroes Rise in Rebellion Against Whites," *Florence Daily Times,* 5 Mar. 1917, in OG 3057, RG 65, BI, NARA.

9. "Germans in Plot to Stir Up Negroes," *St. Louis Republic,* 4 Apr. 1917, in Christopher F. Drews to Attorney General Thomas W. Gregory, 9 Apr. 1917, OG 3057, RG 65, BI, NARA.

10. D. J. Kirton to Hon. J. W. Ragsdale, 5 Apr. 1917, and Agent James B. Heyward to Bureau, 18 Apr. 1917, OG 3057, RG 65, BI, NARA.

11. Henry B. Mitchell to President Woodrow Wilson, 18 Apr. 1917, and Agent T. S. Marshall to Bureau, 7 Apr. 1917, OG 3057, RG 65, BI, NARA; *New York Times,* 8 Apr. 1917, sec. 1, p. 20, col. 5.

12. U.S. Attorney A.D. Pitts to Gregory, 13 Apr. 1917, OG 3057, RG 65, BI, NARA. I am indebted to my colleague Richard Steele for perspective on the Justice Department's fear of vigilantism.

13. "Detain Three in South as German Plotters," *New York Times,* 7 Apr. 1917; "Inciter of Negroes Held," *New York Times,* 9 Apr. 1917.

14. Post Office Inspector Arthur Smith to Inspector in Charge, Chattanooga, ? Apr. 1917; Sheriff George W. West to Hon. Jno. F. Cashion, 8 Apr. 1917; Agent Robert S. Phifer Jr. to Bureau, 30 Apr. 1917;and J. B. Markley to Chief A. Bruce Bielaski, 11 and 29 Apr. 1917, OG 3057, RG 65, BI, NARA. There were not sixteen blacks to every white in Sharkey County, but the 1910 census did report 89 percent of its total population was black, which made it one of the most densely black areas in the country.

15. John McFee to "Chief of Secret Service, Department of Justice," 25 Apr. 1917, OG 3057, RG 65, BI, NARA.

16. William Kirten to postmaster Hermon Carlton, 9 Apr. 1917, and Agent C. M. Walser to Bureau, 23 Apr. 1917, OG 3057, RG 65, BI, NARA.

17. Collier H. Minge to Joseph P. Tumulty, 6 Apr. 1917, OG 3057, RG 65, BI, NARA.

18. "Pro-Germanism among Negroes," *Messenger,* July 1918, p. 13.

19. Agent F. M. Spencer to Bureau, 9 Apr. 1917, OG 3057, RG 65, BI, NARA.

20. The actual number of investigations is undoubtedly higher. It was impossible to study all of the nearly four hundred thousand case files included in almost six hundred reels of Bureau of Investigation microfilm.

21. Agent R. L. Barnes to Bureau, 19 July 1917, OG 3057; Clerk J. Polen to Bureau, 12 Jan. 1918, OG 124054; Agent Billups Harris to Bureau, 1 June 1918; and Agent William M. Doyas to Bureau, 30 May, 1, 5, 15, and 24 June 1918, OG 209220, RG 65, BI, NARA.

22. Barnes to Bureau, 25 May 1917, OG 3057; and R. M. F. Berry to Gregory, 1 Feb. 1918, OG 22310, RG 65, BI, NARA.

23. Special Employee Beasley to Bureau, 13 Aug. 1917, case file 10218-4, RG 165, Records of the Military Intelligence Division (hereafter MID), NARA; Theodore Kornweibel Jr., *No Crystal Stair: Black Life and the Messenger, 1917–1928* (Westport, Conn., 1975), p. 5.

24. An example is a report from the postmaster of Overton, Texas, who believed it likely that blacks had clammed up because Germans and Mexicans had set them to plotting (Barnes to Bureau, 19 Sept. 1917, OG 3057, RG 65, BI, NARA).

25. Division Superintendent Hinton G. Clabaugh to Bielaski, 5 July 1917, and Agent J. C. Brantzburg to Bureau, 14 Sept. 1917, OG 37586, RG 65, BI, NARA.

26. Agent Frank G. Clark to Bureau, 2 Jan. 1918, and Clabaugh to Bielaski, 16 Jan. 1918, OG 123754, RG 65, BI, NARA.

27. American Protective League agent Copeland to APL, 30 Sept. 1918; Montgomery APL chief H. K. Milner to National Directors, APL, 14 Oct. 1918; John Lorenzen, APL National Directors, to Bielaski, 21 Oct. 1918; Bielaski to Brig. Gen. Marlborough Churchill, 22 Oct. 1918; Bielaski to Agent J. S. Edson, 22 Oct. 1918; Churchill to Bielaski, 30 Oct. 1918; Bielaski to Edson, 1 Nov. 1918; Edson to Bureau, 4 Nov. 1918; Edson to Bielaski, 4 Nov. 1918; Atlanta APL chief A. M. Schoen to National Directors, 4 Nov. 1918; A. M. Briggs, chairman, APL, to Bielaski, 21 Nov. 1918; Bielaski to Alfred Bettman, 22 Nov. 1918; Bielaski to Edson, 22 Nov. 1918; and Bettman to Bielaski, 9 Jan. 1919, OG 306451, RG 65, BI, NARA.

28. Agent Branch Bocock to Bureau, 10 and 11 May 1917, OG 3057, RG 65, BI, NARA.

29. APL agent P. D. Gold Jr. to APL, 21 Jan. 1918, OG 112508, RG 65, BI, NARA; Theodore Kornweibel Jr., "Apathy and Dissent: Black America's Negative Responses to World War I," *South Atlantic Quarterly* 80 (1981): pp. 324–25; idem, *No Crystal Stair,* p. 105.

30. Copies of many of the Bureau's reports found their way into the MID case files. See, for example, Agent L. O. Thompson to Bureau, 31 July 1917, 10218-2; and Agent Willard Utley to Bureau, 15 Aug. 1917, and Lt. Col R. H. Van Deman to Bielaski, 22 Sept 1919, 10218-6, RG 165, MID, NARA.

31. Agent Charles B. Braun to Bureau, 17 Aug. 1917, 10218-5; E. T. W. to ?, 19 Sept. 1917, 10218-16; and Post Office Inspector in Charge T. M. Diskin to SAC W. E. McElveen, 20 Apr. 1918, 10218-152-1, RG 165, MID, NARA.

32. Witcover, *Sabotage at Black Tom,* pp. 89–92.

33. U.S. Attorney R. E. Byrd to Gregory, 7 Apr. 1917, and Bielaski to Byrd, 13 Apr. 1917, OG 3057, RG 65, BI, NARA.

34. U.S. Attorney Lee Douglas to Attorney General, 7 Apr. 1917, OG 3057, RG 65, BI, NARA.

35. Pitts to Gregory, 13 Apr. 1917, and Bielaski to Pitts, 26 Apr. 1917, Mexican Files (hereafter MEX) 1538, RG 65, BI, NARA.

36. Agent Goundry W. Bingham to Bureau, 27 July 1918, OG 294585, RG 65, BI, NARA.

37. Bielaski to Sen. John Sharp Williams, 5 May 1917, and Bielaski to Agent W. E. McElveen, 5 May 1917, MEX 1538, RG 65, BI, NARA.

38. Agent Joseph M. Bauserman to Bureau, 10 Apr. 1917, OG 8714, RG 65, BI, NARA.

39. Agent William B. Matthews to Bureau, 23 Apr. 1917, OG 3057, RG 65, BI, NARA.

40. Assistant U.S. Attorney W. E. Ross to Bielaski, 25 Apr. 1917, OG 3057, RG 65, BI, NARA.

41. W. G. Kornegay to Secretary of the Navy Josephus Daniels, 22 May 1917; Bielaski to Agent Dorsey E. Phillips, 7 June and 3 July 1917, OG 20961; and Daughton to Bureau, 21 May 1917, OG 3057, RG 65, BI, NARA.

42. Agent B. Kahn to Bureau, 14 Dec. 1917, OG 106265, RG 65, BI, NARA.

43. Thompson to Bureau, 12 and 17 Dec. 1917, and 25 Apr. 1918; R. Harris to Capt. Harry A. Taylor, 2 June 1918; and Lt. Col. Marlborough Churchill to Bielaski, 6 June 1918, OG 106021, RG 65, BI, NARA; Thompson to Bureau, 4 Dec. 1917, 10218-61, RG 165, MID, NARA.

44. Agent R. K. Dawson to Bureau, 17 Jan. and 19 Feb. 1918, OG 159218; Agent C. V. Mallet to Bureau, 23 July 1918, OG 253404; and Agent T. Howick to Bureau, 25 June 1918, OG 237665, RG 65, BI, NARA.

45. Agent Charles E. Corgan to Bureau, 9 Aug. (four reports) and 3 Sept. 1918, OG 271659, RG 65, BI, NARA.

46. Agent V. W. Killick to Bureau, 21 Aug. 1918, OG 132476, RG 65, BI, NARA.

47. Agent F. C. Haggerly to Bureau, 19 Aug. (two reports) and 3 Sept. 1918, OG 271659, RG 65, BI, NARA.

48. Agent Horace A. Lewis, 19 Aug. (two reports), 20 Sept., 24 Oct., and 8 Nov. 1918, and 29 Jan. 1919, OG 329980, RG 65, BI, NARA.

49. Mayor W. J. West to Williams, 17 Apr. 1917, OG 3057; and Bielaski to Williams, 5 May 1917, and Bielaski to McElveen, 5 May 1917, MEX1538, RG 65, BI, NARA. Another reason for Bielaski's willingness to intervene was the widespread perception early in the war that the Bureau of Investigation was ill-equipped to deal with enemy subversion, and that the Secret Service was much better manned and capable for that task.

50. Agent E. J. Kerwin to Bureau, ? May 1917, OG 3057, RG 65, BI, NARA.

51. Agent John B. Murphy to Bureau, 16 May 1917, and Bocock to Bureau, 10 May 1917, OG 3057, RG 65, BI, NARA.

52. Agent Leverett W. Englesby to Bureau, 14 May 1917, OG 3057, RG 65, BI, NARA.

53. Hanna to Bureau, 21 June 1917, OG 34436, RG 65, BI, NARA.

54. Hanna to Bureau, 29 May 1917, OG 3057, RG 65, BI, NARA.

55. Agent Charles E. Burks to Bureau, 12 June 1917, OG 24181, RG 65, BI, NARA.

56. Agent B. C. Baldwin to Bureau, 13 Sept. 1917, and Braun to Bureau, 30 Sept. 1917, OG 3057, RG 65, BI, NARA.

57. Englesby to Bureau, 31 Mar. 1918, OG 166186, RG 65, BI, NARA.

58. Agent L. P. Banville to Bureau, 16 Sept. 1918, OG 294058, RG 65, BI, NARA. Vicksburg citizens had precedent for their lawlessness: In April their paper reported that a wealthy white Louisiana planter was tarred and feathered by his neighbors and driven from the state for alleged failure to buy Liberty Bonds. See James R. Mock, *Censorship 1917* (Princeton, N.J., 1941), pp. 33–34.

59. Hanna to Bureau, 31 Mar., 3 Apr., and 4 May 1917, OG 3057, RG 65, BI, NARA.

60. Agent A. W. Davis to Bureau, 18 Apr. 1917, and Agent J. Reese Murray to Bureau, 4 June 1917, OG 3057, RG 65, BI, NARA.

61. Agent F. M. Spencer to Bureau, 10 Apr. 1917, OG 3057, RG 65, BI, NARA.

62. Spencer to Bureau, 21 Aug. 1917; Agent J. H. Harper to Bureau, 26 Aug. and 17 Sept. 1917; and Acting SAC Utley to Harper, 22 Sept. 1917, OG 49980, RG 65, BI, NARA.

63. SAC Forrest C. Pendleton to Bielaski, 1 May 1917, and Prosecuting Attorney E. W. Hubbard to Byrd, 16 Apr. 1917, OG 3057, RG 65, BI, NARA.

64. SAC R. L. Barnes to Postmaster Marshall, 13 Apr. 1917, OG 3057, RG 65, BI, NARA.

65. McElveen to Bureau, 30 Apr. 1917; Kirton to Ragsdale, 5 Apr. 1917; and Heyward to Bureau, 18 Apr. 1917, OG 3057, RG 65, BI, NARA.

66. Baldwin to Bureau, 6 May 1917, OG 3057; and Pendleton to Bureau, 19 June 1917, and Agent Stillson to Bureau, 21 June 1917, OG 26527, RG 65, BI, NARA.

67. A good summary of the East St. Louis riot is in Arthur E. Barbeau and Florette Henri, *The Unknown Solders: Black American Troops in World War I* (Philadelphia, 1974), pp. 23–26. The most comprehensive treatment is Elliott Rudwick, *Race Riot in East St. Louis* (Cleveland, 1966).

68. SAC Edward J. Brennan to Prosecuting Attorney, Dunklin County, 6 Aug. 1917, OG 3057, and Agent W. A. Weymouth to Bureau, 2 Mar. 1918, OG 153778, RG 65, BI, NARA. Members of the black 24th Infantry endured outright persecution at the hands of Houston whites, especially the police, and finally mutinied, seizing arms and marching on the city, killing several whites before being captured or induced to lay down their weapons. Nineteen soldiers were eventually executed for this deed. See Robert V. Haynes, *A Night of Violence: The Houston Riot of 1917* (Baton Rouge, 1976).

69. Agent George L. Darden to Bureau, 1 Dec. 1917, OG 63793; and Thompson to Bureau, 25 Apr. 1918, OG 106021, RG 65, BI, NARA.

70. Hanna to Bureau, 10 May 1917, and Agent E. R. Beckwith to Bureau, 4 May 1917, OG 3057; and Agent L. H. Flinn to Bureau, 27 June 1918, OG 230336, RG 65, BI, NARA.

71. (Unsigned) to Department of Justice, ? Apr. 1917, OG 3057, RG 65, BI, NARA.

72. See, for example, J. Silas Harris to Wilson, 23 Apr. 1917; "Tongue That Needed Taming"; Bielaski to J. H. Ward, 24 Apr. 1917; and Herbert H. White to Bielaski, 18 Apr. 1917, OG 3057, RG 65, BI, NARA. Similar items are in the Wilson Papers, LC.

73. Agent Edward Chastain to Bureau, 9 May 1917, and Agent Manual Sorola to Bureau, 16 Apr. 1917, OG 3057, RG 65, BI, NARA.

74. "Reports Covering Investigations of German Propaganda Among the Negroes," 5 Oct. 1917, and RDR to Bielaski, 5 Oct. 1917, OG 3057, RG 65, BI, NARA.

75. Bielaski to Gregory, 10 Jan. 1918, 6 Mar. 1918, OG 83627, RG 65, BI, NARA.

76. U.S. Attorney J. O. Carr to Bielaski, 18 Feb. and 6 Mar. 1918, and Bielaski to Carr, 4 Mar. 1918, OG 151080, RG 65, BI, NARA.

77. Kornweibel, *No Crystal Stair,* pp. xi–xvi, chaps. 2, 7.

3. "Slackers, Delinquents, and Deserters"

1. *Final Report of the Provost Marshal General to the Secretary of War on the Operations of the Selective Service System to July 15, 1919* (Washington, D.C., 1920), p. 12*; Second Report of the Provost Marshal General,* pp. 199–200, 202–203. Local police were eligible for such rewards. Officers from a Brooklyn station house were $1,000 richer after apprehending twenty blacks who had failed to register in mid-1918 ("Score Caught in Myrtle Section as Draft Dodgers," *Chicago Defender,* 29 June 1918).

2. *Second Report of Provost Marshal General,* pp. 200–202.

3. Ibid., pp. 195–96, 205–206, 459, 461.

4. *Report of the Provost Marshal General to the Secretary of War on the First Draft under the Selective Service Act, 1917* (Washington, D.C., 1918), p. 46.

5. *Second Report of Provost Marshal General,* pp. 191–92, 194.

6. Ibid., pp. 193–94.

7. Mark Ellis, "W. E. B. DuBois and the Formation of Black Opinion in World War I: A Commentary on 'The Damnable Dilemma,'" *Journal of American History* 81 (Mar. 1995): p. 1584.

8. Theodore Rosengarten, *All God's Dangers: The Life of Nate Shaw* (New York, 1975), p. 169. "Nate Shaw" is the pseudonym for Ned Cobb.

9. George S. Schuyler, "Our White Folks," *American Mercury,* Dec. 1927, p. 386.

10. James Weldon Johnson, *Black Manhattan* (New York, 1968), pp. 232–33; Barbeau and Henri, *Unknown Soldiers,* p. 204; Ira De A. Reid, "A Critical Summary: The Negro on the Home Front in World Wars I and II," *Journal of Negro Education* 12 (1943): pp. 513–14; Ottley and Weatherby, eds., *Negro in New York,* p. 195; Odum, *Wings on My Feet,* pp. 155–56.

11. Theodore G. Vincent, *Black Power and the Garvey Movement* (Berkeley, Calif., n.d.), p. 34; Carter G. Woodson, ed., *The Works of Francis J. Grimke, III* (Washington, D.C., 1943), pp. 38–39; Ottley and Weatherby, eds., *Negro in New York,* pp. 195–96; *New York Herald,* 5 Apr. 1917, p. 1; Napoleon B. Marshall, *The Providential Armistice: A Volunteer's Story* (Washington, D.C., 1930), p. 12.

12. Roi Ottley, *The Lonely Warrior: The Life and Times of Robert S. Abbott* (Chicago, 1955), p. 154; Reid, "A Critical Summary," pp. 513–14; Ottley and Weatherby, eds., *Negro in New York,* pp. 199–200.

13. Agent W. E. McElveen to Bureau, 30 Apr. 1917, OG 3057, RG 65, BI, NARA.

14. "'Birth of a Nation' Won!" *Cleveland Gazette,* 14 Apr. 1917; *Baltimore Afro-American,* 10 Mar. 1917, p. 4, 7 Apr. 1917, p. 4, all quoted in William Jordan, "'The Damnable Dilemma': African-American Accommodation and Protest during World War I," *Journal of American History* 81 (Mar. 1995): pp. 1574–75.

15. Horace R. Cayton, *Long Old Road* (Seattle, 1964), p. 98; Ottley and Weatherby, eds., *Negro in New York,* p. 195; William L. Patterson, *The Man Who Cried Genocide: An Autobiography* (New York, 1971), pp. 33–35.

16. Alan Lomax, comp., *Hard Hitting Songs for Hard-Hit People* (New York, 1967), pp. 354–55.

17. John Jacob Niles, *Singing Soldiers* (New York, 1927), pp. 48–50.

18. Lomax, *Hard Hitting Songs,* p. 352.

19. Howard W. Odum, "Black Ulysses in Camp," *American Mercury,* Sept. 1929, p. 47; Odum, *Wings on My Feet,* pp. 99, 105.

20. Odum, *Wings on My Feet,* p. 49; interview with Isaac Freeman, Phillipsburg, N.J., 4 Apr. 1975.

21. Quoted in Ellis, "W. E. B. DuBois," p. 1585.

22. Good broad coverage of individuals and groups that were investigated and suffered various persecutions is in H. C. Peterson and Gilbert C. Fite, *Opponents of War, 1917–1918* (Madison, Wis., 1957); and Jensen, *Price of Vigilance.*

23. Each reel of Bureau of Investigation microfilm contains several thousand pages of documents. Short of viewing every document on each of the nearly six hundred reels, there is no foolproof method of locating every case file concerning black suspects. The best that

can be done is to comb the additional 111 microfilm index reels, each of which contains thousands of three-by-five note cards listing the names of individual suspects as well as organizations and publications. Black suspects were often, although not always, identified by the designation "(c)" following their names. I hired students from Howard University to scan these index reels to locate all black subjects. Their tedious labor produced the list of two thousand draft suspects on which this chapter is based.

24. *Report of Provost Marshal General on First Draft,* pp. 5–6, 26–27.

25. *Second Report of Provost Marshal General,* pp. 22–31.

26. *Report of Provost Marshal General on First Draft,* pp. 43–44.

27. *Second Report of Provost Marshal General,* p. 195.

28. These generalizations are based on all the June 1917 southern draft cases in the Old German case files, RG 65, BI, NARA. The following specific case files are pertinent: OG 3057, OG 20961, OG 21639, OG 21663, OG 21864, OG 22310, OG 22371, OG 22739, OG 22977, OG 23364, OG 23962, OG 23969, OG 24181, OG 24382, OG 24732, OG 26527, OG 26683, OG 26826, OG 27150, OG 28758, OG 29554, OG 29699, and OG 31865.

29. OG 23364, RG 65, BI, NARA.

30. Ibid.

31. OG 28758 (Newsome), OG 46494 (Hardy), OG 48439 (James), RG 65, BI, NARA.

32. OG 50094, RG 65, BI, NARA.

33. OG 56754, RG 65, BI, NARA.

34. OG 58898 (Hargrave), OG 57679 (Williams), OG 35162 (Dove), OG 35164 (Brown), Chief A. Bruce Bielaski to SAC Ralph H. Daughton, 31 July 1917, OG 35163 (Allen), OG 34916 (Earnest), RG 65, BI, NARA.

35. OG 41159, RG 65, BI, NARA.

36. OG 28790 (Winston), OG 28109 (Moore), OG 28789 (Witherspoon), OG 34017 (Clinton), OG 50636 (Alridge), OG 29064 (Wilson, Willis), OG 55730 (Duncan), RG 65, BI, NARA.

37. OG 32217 (Johnson), OG 33656 (Page), OG 33995 (Bailey), OG 34764 (Thomas), RG 65, BI, NARA.

38. Generalizations are based on all June 1917 northern draft cases in RG 65, BI, NARA: OG 3057, OG 20770, OG 21869, OG 22870, OG 23633, OG 25808, OG 26739, OG 27037, OG 27174, OG 27320, OG 27900, OG 28235, OG 28337, OG 28789, OG 28790, OG 28794, OG 28984, and OG 29434.

39. OG 28984 and Agent C. B. Ambrose to Bureau, 14 July 1917, OG 35769, RG 65, BI, NARA.

40. Agent Edward M. Murphy to Bureau, 12 Sept. 1917, plus other documents in OG 54551, RG 65, BI, NARA.

41. OG 28947 (Lewis and Lewis), OG 28994 (Ward), OG 52268 (Walters), OG 27915 (Mabb), OG 35503 (Anderson), and OG 47613 (Hairston), RG 65, BI, NARA.

42. "All Police to Help Round Up Draft Men," *New York Times,* 30 Nov. 1917, p. 8.

43. "List Draft Negroes Not Answering Call," *New York Times,* 30 Nov. 1917, p. 8.

44. OG 94162 (Nance), and OG 202362 (Cofield), RG 65, BI, NARA.

45. OG 80202, OG 102506, OG 61484, OG 122720, OG 172233, OG 178308, and OG 124845, RG 65, BI, NARA.

46. Agent Calvin Outlaw to Bureau, 2 May 1918, OG 189266; OG 98836 (Bailey), RG 65, BI, NARA.

47. OG 181527 (Grant), OG 183111 (Boyce), OG 158812 (Young), and OG 167127 (Neal), RG 65, BI, NARA.

48. OG 177647 (Stewart), OG 154001 (Griffin), and OG 110840 (Brown), RG 65, BI, NARA. Another case of bureaucratic ineptitude in Fort Worth involved Archie Williams, jailed for eleven days due to delays as paperwork coming from Oklahoma City was misdirected to Austin. He was eventually inducted. See OG 80883, RG 65, BI.

49. OG 169269, OG 125617, and OG 145201 (Agent Dawson); OG 104794, OG 117744, OG 118785, OG 132876, OG 118784, OG 118624, and OG 117311 (Agent Murphy); OG 130703, OG 147839, and OG 131269 (Agent Jenkins); and OG 118619 (Agent Patterson), RG 65, BI, NARA.

50. OG 112585 (Cain), and OG 146570 (Carey), RG 65, BI, NARA.

51. OG 157815, RG 65, BI, NARA.

52. OG 166584, RG 65, BI, NARA.

53. OG 163202, RG 65, BI, NARA.

54. Barbeau and Henri, *Unknown Soldiers,* pp. 51–52.

55. Peterson and Fite, *Opponents of War,* p. 231.

56. Peterson and Fite, *Opponents of War,* p. 234.

57. OG 277001, RG 65, BI, NARA.

58. OG 291974, RG 65, BI, NARA.

59. OG 273594, RG 65, BI, NARA.

60. OG 95344 and OG 290331, RG 65, BI, NARA.

61. OG 254565, OG 277005, OG 268957, and OG 289883, RG 65, BI, NARA.

62. OG 271797, RG 65, BI, NARA.

63. OG 294883, OG 257074, RG 65, BI, NARA.

64. OG 269734, OG 307785 (Wilson), RG 65, BI, NARA.

65. OG 269727, RG 65, BI, NARA; Barbara Rust, Federal Records Center, Fort Worth, Tex., telephone conversation with author, 18 July 1989.

66. OG 257831, RG 65, BI, NARA.

67. OG 273935 and OG 301373, RG 65, BI, NARA.

68. OG 162257 (Jackson), OG 262852 (Clay), and OG 314096 (Felder), RG 65, BI, NARA.

69. OG 258027 (Johnson) and OG 257279 (Mack), RG 65, BI, NARA.

70. OG 260951, RG 65, BI, NARA.

71. OG 239052 (Terry) and OG 316501 (Story), RG 65 BI, NARA.

72. OG 314051, RG 65, BI, NARA.

73. OG 276169 (Knox) and OG 285672 (Jones), RG 65, BI, NARA.

74. OG 279369, RG 65, BI, NARA.

75. OG 228730, RG 65, BI, NARA.

76. OG 229751 (Taylor), OG 260111, OG 309468, and OG 222165 (all Baltimore), RG 65, BI, NARA.

77. OG 258074, RG 65, BI, NARA.

78. OG 235787, RG 65, BI, NARA.

79. OG 249416 (Harrison), OG 262778 (Dixon), OG 267550 (Harrison), OG 280348 (Harris), and OG 285673 (Jones), RG 65, BI, NARA.

80. OG 300117, RG 65, BI, NARA.

81. OG 239005, RG 65, BI, NARA.

82. OG 284448 (McLendon) and OG 279055 (Suber), RG 65, BI, NARA.

83. OG 273690 (Walker) and OG 266905 (Kelly), RG 65, BI, NARA.

84. OG 254545, OG 253804, OG 270686, and OG 278163, RG 65, BI, NARA.

85. OG 271831 and OG 286687, RG 65, BI, NARA.

86. OG 269439, RG 65, BI, NARA.

87. OG 273301 (Lynn), OG 258363 (McKinney), and OG 268430 (Looney), RG 65, BI, NARA.

88. OG 288618 and OG 295487, RG 65, BI, NARA.

89. OG 300237, RG 65, BI, NARA.

90. *Second Report of Provost Marshal General,* pp. 75–76.

91. OG 306779 (Myers), OG 314095 (Wallace), and OG 322983 (King), RG 65, BI, NARA.

92. Jensen, *Price of Vigilance,* pp. 190, 198.

93. OG 273639 (Williams) and OG 260111 (Johnson), RG 65, BI, NARA.

94. OG 273639 (Williams), OG 260111 (Johnson), OG 273691 (Walker), and OG 244465 (McKissach), RG 65, BI, NARA.

95. OG 259724 and OG 259701, RG 65, BI, NARA.

96. OG 273818, RG 65, BI, NARA.

97. OG 250760, RG 65, BI, NARA.

98. Jensen, *Price of Vigilance,* pp. 192–93.

99. OG 294547 and OG 294543, RG 65, BI, NARA.

100. OG 294109, RG 65, BI, NARA.

101. OG 269746, RG 65, BI, NARA.

102. OG 269746, OG 301333, RG 65, BI, NARA.

103. *Final Report of Provost Marshal General,* pp. 7–11; Jensen, *Price of Vigilance,* p. 245.

104. OG 243484, OG 360008, OG 367821, OG 367822, OG 374801, OG 354053, OG 220491 (six men), and OG 296152 (Sales), RG 65, BI, NARA.

105. OG 354368 (McRae) and OG 260231 (Lowe), RG 65, BI, NARA.

106. OG 325512, RG 65, BI, NARA.

107. OG 281037, RG 65, BI, NARA.

108. Theodore Kornweibel Jr., "Apathy and Dissent," pp. 322–38.

109. Barbeau and Henri, *Unknown Soldiers,* pp. 33–35.

4. "The most dangerous of all Negro journals"

1. The birth of the *Defender* is charted in Ottley, *Lonely Warrior;* for *Crisis,* see Kellogg, *NAACP;* for the origins and growth of the "New Crowd Negro" spirit, see Kornweibel, *No Crystal Stair.*

2. Agent C. G. Beckham to Bureau, 26 and 28 Sept. 1916; SAC Forrest C. Pendleton to Bureau, 4, 5, and 7 Oct. 1916; Beckham to Bureau, 8 and 10 Oct. 1916; Pendleton to Bureau, 12 Oct. 1916; Beckham to Bureau, 14 Oct. 1916; and Chief A. Bruce Bielaski to Division Superintendent Hinton G. Clabaugh, 16 Oct. 1916, Miscellaneous Files 9969, RG 65, BI, NARA.

3. Pendleton to Bureau, 9 Apr. 1917, and Agent Edward S. Chastain to Bureau, 24 Apr. 1917, OG 5911; and Agent A. W. Davis to Bureau, 16 Apr. 1917, and Agent R. S. Phifer to Bureau, 30 Apr. 1917, OG 3057, RG 65, BI, NARA.

4. Emmett J. Scott, *Negro Migration during the War* (c. 1920; reprint, New York, 1969), pp. 29–33; Florette Henri, *Black Migration: Movement North 1900–1920* (Garden City, N.Y., 1976), pp. 62–65.

5. Bielaski to Clabaugh, 9 Apr. 1917, and Agent J. E. Hawkins to Bureau, 16 Apr. 1917, OG 5911, RG 65, BI, NARA; Peterson and Fite, *Opponents of War,* p. 94.

6. Clabaugh to Bielaski, 16 Apr. 1917, MEX 1651; Hawkins to Bureau, 16 Apr. 1917, and Agent P. E. Hilliard to Bureau, 17 Apr. 1917, OG 5911; and R. L. D. to Phifer, 8 May 1917, OG 3057, RG 65, BI, NARA.

7. Patrick S. Washburn, *A Question of Sedition: The Federal Government's Investigation of the Black Press during World War II* (New York: Oxford University Press, 1986), pp. 12–13; Scheiber, *Wilson Administration,* pp. 17–26.

8. D. Whipple to A. M. Briggs, 3 July 1917; Acting Div. Supt. Furbershaw to Bielaski, 10 July 1917; and Bielaski to Clabaugh, 17 Aug. 1917, OG 5911, RG 65, BI, NARA.

9. Postmaster J. Blocker Thornton to Postmaster General Albert Sidney Burleson, 28 Aug. 1917, and Postmaster, Chicago, to Solicitor William H. Lamar, 14 Sept. 1917, case file B-47522, Espionage Act cases, RG 28, Records of the Post Office Department (hereafter PO), NARA.

10. SAC Robert L. Barnes to Clabaugh, 19 Sept. 1917; Agent H. B. Mock to Bureau, 28 Dec. 1917; and Agent B. D. Adsit to Bureau, 22 Dec. 1917, OG 5911, RG 65, BI, NARA.

11. See case files 9-19-1713 and 189621, RG 60, Records of the Department of Justice (hereafter DJ), NARA.

12. See, for example, the complaint registered by Bolton Smith, a prominent Memphis businessman and New South exponent: Bolton Smith to U.S. Attorney W. D. Kyser, 14 Jan. 1918; Kyser to Postal Inspector in Charge T. M. Diskin, 23 Jan. 1918; Diskin to Chief Postal Inspector, 29 Jan. 1918; and Chief Postal Inspector to Lamar, 6 Feb. 1918, B-47522, RG 28, PO, NARA; Agent A. D. Dabney to Bureau, 19 Mar. 1918, OG 159218, RG 65, BI, NARA. Another citizen complaint is recorded in Lamar to Elizabeth T. Price, 5 Jan. 1918, B-47522, RG 28, PO, NARA.

13. Operative Leo Spitz to Col. Carl Reichmann, 25 Apr. 1918, 10218-133-1; and Reichmann to Col. Ralph Van Deman, Chief, Military Intelligence Branch, 29 Apr. 1918, 10218-133-3, RG 165, MID, NARA.

14. Van Deman to Maj. Walter H. Loving, 3 May 1918, 10218-133-4, RG 165, MID, NARA.

15. Research Guide, Walter Howard Loving Papers (hereafter Loving Papers), Moorland-Spingarn Research Center, Howard University, Washington, D.C. (hereafter M-SRC); Robert A. Hill, ed., *The Marcus Garvey and Universal Negro Improvement Association Papers,* vol. 1 (Berkeley, 1983), p. 327 n1.

16. Loving to Van Deman, 10 May 1918, 10218-133-5, RG 165, MID, NARA.

17. See, for example, the actions of whites in Griffin, Georgia, to suppress the *Defender,* recorded in case file 10218-160, RG 165, MID, NARA.

18. Robert S. Abbott to Loving, 11 May 1918, 10218-133-6; and Loving to Van Deman, 20 May 1918, 10218-133-7, RG 165, MID, NARA.

19. Loving to Capt. Henry Hunt, 23 May 1918, 10218-139-10; and Loving to Van Deman, 30 May 1918, 10218-139-14, RG 165, MID, NARA.

20. Col. Marlborough Churchill, Chief, MIB, to Maj. Joel E. Spingarn, 22 June 1918, 10218-154-14; and Churchill to Chief of Staff, 2 July 1918, 10218-154-15, RG 165, MID, NARA; "The Dawn of a New Era," *Indianapolis Freeman,* 20 July 1918.

21. See Mark Ellis, "'Closing Ranks' and 'Seeking Honors': W. E. B. DuBois in World War I," *Journal of American History* 79 (June 1992): pp. 96–124.

22. Lee Finkle, *Forum for Protest: The Black Press During World War II* (Rutherford, N.J., 1975), p. 46.

23. Agent E. J. Kerwin to Bielaski, 2 and 9 May 1918; Adsit to Bureau, 24 May 1918; Bielaski to R. E. Baily, 3 July 1918; American Protective League Operative 36 to Headquarters, 24 Sept. 1918; and APL National Director C. F. Lorenzen to Bielaski, 1 and 3 Oct. 1918, OG 5911, RG 65, BI, NARA.

24. Charles E. Boles to Lamar, 13 June 1918, B-47522, RG 28, PO, NARA.

25. Lamar to Abbott, 13 June 1918, B-47522, RG 28, PO, NARA.

26. Postmaster M. E. Nash to Lamar, 22 June 1918; Sen. John Sharp Williams to Burleson, 22 June 1918; and Burleson to Williams, 11 July 1918, B-47522, RG 28, PO, NARA.

27. Hill, ed., *Marcus Garvey Papers,* vol. 1, p. 453 n1, lists the thirteen suspect publications: the *Defender, Negro World, AME Zion Quarterly Review, Baltimore Afro-American, New York Amsterdam News, Boston Guardian, Challenge, Crisis, Messenger, New York Age, New York News, Pittsburgh Courier,* and *Veteran.*

28. Memorandum, Translation Bureau, 6 July 1918, B-47522, RG 28, PO, NARA.

29. L. How to U.S. Assistant District Attorney, 26 July 1918, and Robert A. Bowen to U.S. Assistant District Attorney, 26 July 1918, B-47522, RG 28, PO, NARA.

30. L. How to U.S. Assistant District Attorney, 16 and 26 Aug., and 2 Sept. 1918, B-47522, RG 28, PO, NARA.

31. For this cooperation see case file 10605, RG 165, MID, NARA.

32. The *Defender*'s postwar troubles with the Justice Department are narrated in detail in Theodore Kornweibel Jr., *"Seeing Red": Federal Campaigns against Black Militancy, 1919–1925* (Bloomington, Ind., 1998), chap. 3.

33. Burleson to Lamar, 25 June 1921, quoted in "Maryland War Service Record of William H. Lamar," RG 28, Office of the Solicitor, Official Records of William H. Lamar, NARA; Maj. Thomas B. Crockett to Churchill, 27 Mar. 1919, 10218-133-14, and 6 June 1919, 10218-133-20; Operative Charles Furthmann to Department Intelligence Office, 3 June 1919, 10218-133-19; and Crockett to Churchill, 11 Aug. 1919, 10218-133-16, RG 165, MID, NARA.

34. For reactions to the Longview riot, see Kellogg, *NAACP,* p. 236; Rep. William D. Upshaw to 1st Assistant Postmaster General J. C. Koons, 2 July 1919; Sheriff T. R. Hughes to Sen. Joseph E. Ransdell, 21 July and 16 Aug. 1919; Ransdell to Burleson, 21 Aug. 1919; and Postmaster H. C. Blalock to Acting 3rd Assistant Postmaster General H. J. Barron, 17 July 1919, B-349; and W. H. Rossman to Lamar, 28 June 1919; Lamar to Rossman, 8 July 1919; and Lamar to W. F. Keohan, 8 July 1919, B-47522, RG 28, PO, NARA. Analysis of the Chicago riot is in Agent M. Kitchen to Bureau, 2 Aug. 1919, and Agent A. H. Loula to Bureau, 2 Aug. 1919, OG 369914, RG 65, BI, NARA. The Phillips County affair is seen in Gov. Charles E. Brough to Burleson, 17 Oct. 1919; Brough to Acting Solicitor H. L. Donnelly, 4 Nov. 1919; "Committee in Charge of Race Relations" to Postmaster W. L. Jarman, 9 Oct. 1919; Jarman to Koons, 10 Oct. 1919; G. Wells to Hon. Joe T. Robinson, 7 Oct. 1919; Donnelly to Chief Postal Inspector, 10 Oct. 1919; Koons to James A. Horton, 10 Oct. 1919; Donnelly to Jarman, 18 Oct. 1919; Donnelly to Brough, 27 Oct. 1919; Lamar to Brough, 26 Nov. 1919, B-349; and Postmaster G. C. Thompson to Lamar, 21 Oct. 1919, B-47522, RG 28, PO, NARA. For background on the Phillips County riot, see Kellogg, *NAACP,* pp. 241–45.

35. For details on the General Intelligence Division, see Lowenthal, *Federal Bureau of Investigation,* and three recent biographies: Richard Gid Powers, *Secrecy and Power: The Life*

of J. Edgar Hoover (New York, 1987); Athan G. Theoharis and John Stuart Cox, *The Boss: J. Edgar Hoover and the Great American Inquisition* (Philadelphia, 1988); and Curt Gentry, *J. Edgar Hoover: The Man and the Secrets* (New York, 1991). Abortive efforts to silence the *Messenger* are detailed in Kornweibel, *"Seeing Red,"* chap. 5.

36. See Murphy, *World War I,* pp. 99–103.

37. See Kornweibel, *"Seeing Red,"* chap. 3.

5. "Every word is loaded with sedition"

1. The best biography of DuBois in these years is the magisterial work of David L. Lewis, *W. E. B. DuBois: Biography of a Race, 1868–1919* (New York, 1993).

2. Murphy, *World War I,* pp. 98–99 (quote), 192–93; William Preston Jr., *Aliens and Dissenters: Federal Suppression of Radicals, 1903–1933* (New York, 1966), chap. 5; Richard W. Steele, *Free Speech in the Good War* (New York, 1999), pp. 2–7. I am especially indebted to my colleague Richard Steele for sharpening my understanding of civil liberties during World War I.

3. Agent W. E. McElveen to Bureau, 30 Apr. 1917, and Agent Paul Hofherr to Bureau, 26 May 1917, OG 17011, RG 65, BI, NARA.

4. See, for example, case file OG 67118, RG 65, BI, NARA.

5. A comprehensive description and analysis of the Houston affair is in Haynes, *Night of Violence.*

6. Postmaster L. L. Burkhead to Postmaster General Albert S. Burleson, 26 Nov. 1917, 189621, RG 60, DJ, NARA; Etta Bullock White to Rep. Addison T. Smith, 8 Sept. 1917; Smith to Burleson, 13 Sept. 1917; Solicitor William H. Lamar to Postmaster T. G. Patten, 24 Sept. 1917; and Patten to Lamar, 1 Oct. 1917, 47732, RG 28, PO, NARA.

7. Col. Wilson Chase to Commanding General, El Paso District, 11 Dec. 1917, 189621, RG 60, DJ, NARA (this and other documents from case file 189621 are duplicated in case file 9-19-1713, RG 60, DJ, NA); Laffer to Chief, Intelligence Section, War College, 2 Dec. 1917; Chief of Staff, 34th Div., to Col. Ralph H. Van Deman, 3 Dec. 1917; and Van Deman to Chief of Staff, ? Dec. 1917, 10218-53, RG 165, MID, NARA.

8. Maj. Gen. John Ruckman to Adjutant General of the Army, 31 Dec. 1917, 189621; Secretary of War Newton D. Baker to Attorney General Thomas W. Gregory, 10 Jan. 1918; Special Assistant to the Attorney General John Lord O'Brian to Baker, 15 Jan. 1918; and O'Brian to U.S. Attorney Samuel K. Dennis, 14 Jan. 1918, 189621-1; and Dennis to Gregory, 21 Jan. 1918, 189621-3, RG 60, DJ, NARA. O'Brian is quoted in Murphy, *World War I,* p. 16.

9. O'Brian to U.S. Attorney Summers Burkhart, 15 Jan. 1918, 189621-1; and Burkhart to Gregory, 29 Jan. 1918, 189621, RG 60, DJ, NARA.

10. Postmaster William R. Sharpe to Chief Inspector, Post Office Department, 27 Dec. 1917; Post Office Inspector W. E. Greenaway to Inspector in Charge, 29 Jan. 1918; Chief Inspector to Lamar, 5 Jan. and 2 Feb. 1918; Lamar to Patten, 19 Mar. 1918; W. E. B. DuBois to Patten, 15 Apr. 1918; and Patten to Lamar, 18 Apr. 1918, 47732, RG 28, PO, NARA.

11. Chase to Burkhart, 22 May 1918, 189621; and Burkhart to Gregory, 24 May 1918, 189621-8, RG 60, DJ, NARA; Agent R. Gere to Chief A. Bruce Bielaski, 24 May 1918; Bielaski to SAC Charles DeWoody, 31 May 1918; and Bielaski to Gere, 31 May 1918, OG 17011, RG 65, BI, NARA.

12. Special Assistant to the Attorney General Alfred Bettman to Bielaski, 1 June 1918; Bielaski to SAC Ralph H. Daughton, 4 June 1918; and Bielaski to DeWoody, 4 June 1918, OG 17011, RG 65, BI, NARA.

13. Unidentified New York agent to Bielaski, 5 June 1918, and American Protective League operative W. T. Carothers to Bureau, 13 June and 24 July 1918, OG 17011, RG 65, BI, NARA.

14. Bettman to Bielaski, 9 July 1918, OG 17011, RG 65, BI, NARA.

15. L. How to Assistant District Attorney, 26 Mar. 1918; memorandum by James A. Horton, 3 May 1918; C. E. B. to Lamar, 17 May 1918; and Lamar to Patten, 17 May 1918, 47732, RG 28, PO, NARA.

16. L. How to U.S. District Attorney, 23 Apr. and 22 May 1918, 47732, RG 28, PO, NARA. For Young, see the entry in Rayford Logan and Michael Winston, eds., *Dictionary of American Negro Biography* (New York, 1982), pp. 677–79.

17. Agent Brautsburg to Bureau, ? Dec. 1917; Agent Manual Sorola to Bureau, 2 May 1918; Agent Leverett F. Englesby to Bureau, 5 May 1918; Bielaski to Daughton, 4 June 1918; Carothers to Bureau, 13 June 1918; unidentified APL operative, New Orleans, to Bureau, 8 July 1918; "special employee" Albert Neunhoffer to Bielaski, 10 May 1918, OG 17011; Agent F. R. Cotten to Bureau, 16 Jan. 1918, OG 369936; and Agent Charles P. Reynolds to Bureau, 2 Sept. 1918, OG 137812, RG 65, BI, NARA.

18. E. D. Holt to Sen. Ollie M. James, 21 Apr. 1918; James to Bielaski, 27 Apr. 1918; Bielaski to James, 10 May 1918; Clifford L. Butler to Bureau, 28 Apr. 1918; and Bielaski to Butler, 10 May 1918, OG 17011, RG 65, BI, NARA. Other communications from worried white citizens include John R. Tolar to "U.S. Department of Labor Employment," 14 Apr. 1918, and Bielaski to Tolar, 22 Apr. 1918, OG 17011, RG 65, BI, NARA; W. M. Searcy to Burleson, 18 Apr. 1918, 47732, RG 28, PO, NARA; *Crisis,* Apr. 1918, pp. 267–68, 271–75, 276–78.

19. Board of Directors minutes, 13 May 1918, *Papers of the NAACP* (Frederick, Md., University Publications of America), reel 1.

20. DuBois to Emmett J. Scott, 24 Apr. 1918, 10218-129-1, RG 165, MID, NARA.

21. Marked and unmarked copies of *Crisis* collected by army intelligence are found in case file 10218, RG 165, MID, NARA.

22. William G. Low Jr. to Van Deman, 2 May 1918, 10218-39-2, RG 165, MID, NARA.

23. Van Deman to Low, 6 May 1918, 10218-139-3; 2nd Lt. E. G. Moyer to Chief, MIB, 8 May 1918, 10218-139-6; and Capt. Malone to Capt. Henry Hunt, 25 May 1918, 10218-139-11, RG 165, MID, NARA; Agent Howell E. Jackson to Bureau, 18 May 1918, OG 17011, RG 65, BI, NARA.

24. Van Deman to Maj. Walter H. Loving, 16 May 1918, 10218-139-8; Loving to Hunt, 23 May 1918, 10218-139-10; Thomas E. Taylor to Loving, 29 May 1918, 10218-139-13; and Loving to Van Deman, 30 May 1918, 10218-139-14, RG 165, MID, NARA.

25. Board of Directors minutes, 13 May and 10 June 1918, *Papers of the NAACP,* reel 1; Kellogg, *NAACP,* pp. 271–72.

26. Lt. Col. Marlborough Churchill to Charles H. Studin, 3 June 1918, 10218-139-15, RG 165, MID, NARA. Churchill was promoted to colonel later in June and to brigadier general on 8 August 1918.

27. Mark Ellis believes Spingarn had more self-serving motives. Correctly observing that Spingarn knew there were anti-NAACP reports in army intelligence files, Ellis be-

lieves Spingarn drafted the communications from Churchill so as to protect his own position and reputation in the army: "Spingarn was using Studin to sanitize the NAACP" (Ellis, "'Closing Ranks' and 'Seeking Honors,'" pp. 105–106).

28. Studin to Spingarn, 12 June 1918, 10218-139-16; and Spingarn to Churchill, 6 July 1918, 10218-154, RG 165, MID, NARA; *Crisis,* July 1918, p. 111. Again, Mark Ellis sees things somewhat differently, believing that DuBois wrote "Close Ranks" primarily to gain favorable consideration for the army commission (Ellis, "'Closing Ranks' and 'Seeking Honors,'" p. 124).

29. Spingarn to Churchill, 10 June 1918, 10218-154-7, RG 165, MID, NARA; Elliott M. Rudwick, *W. E. B. DuBois: Propagandist of the Negro Protest* (New York, 1968), pp. 202–203; Robert L. Zangrando, *The NAACP Crusade against Lynching, 1909–1950* (Philadelphia, 1980), pp. 44–45; "To Protect Citizens against Lynching," hearings before the Committee on the Judiciary, House of Representatives, 65th Cong., 2nd sess., on H. R. 11279, pt. 1, 6 June 1918, pt. 2, 12 July 1918, serial 66 (Washington, D.C., 1918).

30. Spingarn to Churchill, 10 June 1918, 10218-154-7; and Spingarn to Scott, 1 Aug. 1918, 10218-154-38, RG 165, MID, NARA; Spingarn to Amy Spingarn, 18 and 26 June 1918, and Scott to Spingarn, 26 June 1918, Joel E. Spingarn Papers, M-SRC. Ellis believes Spingarn instructed DuBois to write "Close Ranks" so as to get the latter into the army (Ellis, "'Closing Ranks' and 'Seeking Honors,'" pp. 98, 124).

31. Ellis, "'Closing Ranks' and 'Seeking Honors,'" p. 107.

32. Robert R. Moton to President Woodrow Wilson, 25 June 1918, 10218-154-32; Churchill to Chief of Staff, ? July 1918, 10218-154-34; and Baker to Wilson, 19 July 1918, 10218-154-34, RG 165, MID, NARA; Baker to Wilson, 1 July 1918, reel 6, Newton D. Baker Papers, Library of Congress.

33. Baker to Wilson, 17 Aug. 1918, in Link, ed, *Papers of Woodrow Wilson,* vol. 43, pp. 506–507; Ellis, "'Closing Ranks' and 'Seeking Honors,'" pp. 113–14.

34. Loving to Maj. Nicholas Biddle, 22 July 1918, ser. D, folder 10, Loving Papers, M-SRC.

35. Ibid.; DuBois to Spingarn, 9 July 1919, Joel E. Spingarn Papers, Beinecke Rare Book and Manuscript Library, Yale University.

36. See Lewis, *W. E. B. DuBois,* p. 555; Ellis, "'Closing Ranks' and 'Seeking Honors,'" p. 124; idem, "W. E. B. DuBois," p. 1590; William Jordan, "'The Damnable Dilemma': African American Accommodation and Protest during World War I," *Journal of American History* 81 (Mar. 1995): pp. 1564–65, 1580–81.

37. How to U.S. Assistant District Attorney, 23 Aug. 1918; Postmaster W. H. Hoffman to Third Assistant Postmaster General, 6 Sept. 1918; Acting Third Assistant Postmaster General N.J. Barrows to Lamar, 17 Sept. 1918; memorandum, James A. Horton, 26 Sept. 1918; Lamar to Hoffman, 2 Oct. 1918; U.S. Postal Censorship report no. 22569, 19 Oct. 1918; Churchill to Lamar, 8 Nov. 1918; Lamar to Churchill, 16 Nov. 1918; Chief Mail Censor (Balboa Heights, C.Z.) C. H. Calhoun to Censorship Board Chairman R. L. Maddox, 19 Nov. 1918; and Executive Postal Censorship Committee (New Orleans) Chairman E. L. West to Maddox, 9 Dec. 1918, 47732, RG 28, PO, NARA.

38. Capt. Harry A. Taylor to Col. Alexander B. Coxe, 19 July 1918, 10218-139-45, RG 165, MID, NARA.

39. Memorandum, Capt. James L. Bruff, 13 July 1918, 10218-158-6, RG 165, MID, NARA.

40. A. C. Dunne to Capt. Kayser, undated (sometime between 1921 and 1925), 10218-158, RG 165, MID, NARA. Another example of this persistent negative attitude

toward the NAACP is in the notebook diary of Colonel Coxe, 12 Feb. 1920, 1919–1920 diary, Alexander Bacon Coxe Papers, East Carolina University, Greenville, N. C.

41. Lt. Col. W. T. Faulkner to Lt. Col. J. A. Moss, 27 Nov. 1925, 19218-158-29; Moss to Faulkner, 28 Dec. 1925, 10218-158-29; Moss to Acting Chief of Staff, G-2, War Department General Staff, 28 Dec. 1925, 10218-158-29; and Acting Chief of Staff, G-2, to Moss, 5 Jan. 1926, 10218-158-30, RG 165, MID, NARA.

42. Theodore Kornweibel Jr., *"Seeing Red": Federal Campaigns against Black Militancy, 1919–1925* (Bloomington, Ind., 1998), chaps. 5–7.

6. "I thank my God for the persecution"

1. German R. Ross, *History and Formative Years of the Church of God in Christ* (Memphis: Church of God in Christ, 1969), pp. 14–16; Lucille J. Cornelius, *The Pioneer: History of the Church of God in Christ* (n.p., 1975), pp. 9–12; I. C. Clemmons, "Mason, Charles Harrison," in *Dictionary of Pentecostal and Charismatic Movements,* ed. Stanley M. Burgess and Gary B. McGee (Grand Rapids, Mich., 1988), pp. 585–88.

2. Cornelius, *Pioneer,* pp. 3–5, 11–13; Ross, *History and Formative Years,* pp. 17–18; David M. Tucker, *Black Pastors and Leaders: Memphis,* 1819–1972 (Memphis, Tenn., 1975), pp. 88–90.

3. Tucker, *Black Pastors and Leaders,* p. 91. Not only was the church the first black Pentecostal denomination, but it also remains the largest. See Lawrence Neale Jones, "The Black Pentecostals," in *The Charismatic Movement,* ed. Michael P. Hamilton (Grand Rapids, Mich., 1975), p. 150.

4. Vinson Synan, *The Holiness-Pentecostal Movement in the United States* (Grand Rapids, Mich, 1971), p. 177; C. E. Jones, "Church of God in Christ," in Burgess and Moore, pp. 204–205.

5. Tucker, *Black Pastors and Leaders,* pp. 95–96. By 1926 there were seven hundred congregations and thirty thousand members, two-thirds residing in the South, with more congregations in urban areas than in country districts. See Charles E. Hall, *Negroes in the United States, 1920–1932* (Washington, D.C., 1935), pp. 532, 538–50.

6. Stephen M. Kohn, *Jailed for Peace: The History of American Draft Law Violators, 1658–1985* (Westport, Conn., 1986), p. 29 (quote). A good survey of this intolerance is Peterson and Fite, *Opponents of War.* Other useful sources are Chafee, *Free Speech in the United States;* Donald Johnson, *The Challenge to American Freedom: World War I and the Rise of the American Civil Liberties Union* (Lexington, Ky., 1963); Scheiber, *Wilson Administration;* William Preston, *Aliens and Dissenters: Federal Suppression of Radicals, 1903–1933* (Cambridge, Mass., 1963); Julian E. Jaffe, *Crusade against Radicalism: New York during the Red Scare, 1914–1924* (Port Washington, N.Y., 1972); Paul L. Murphy, *The Meaning of Freedom of Speech: First Amendment Freedoms from Wilson to FDR* (Westport, Conn., 1972); and idem, *World War I and the Origin of Civil Liberties in the United States* (New York, 1979). For details on treatment of black conscientious objectors, see Theodore Kornweibel Jr., "Apathy and Dissent," p. 331.

7. Peterson and Fite, *Opponents of War,* pp. 121–25.

8. U.S. War Department, *Statement Concerning the Treatment of Conscientious Objectors in the Army* (Washington, D.C., 1919), pp. 7–9, 14–19; Kohn, *Jailed for Peace,* p. 29.

9. Barbeau and Henri, *Unknown Soldiers,* pp. 35–37; *Second Report of Provost Marshal General,* pp. 459, 461.

10. Cornelius, *Pioneer,* p. 68; Ross, *History and Formative Years,* pp. 25–28.

11. Agent M. M. Schaumburger to Bureau of Investigation, 25 Sept. 1917, OG 144128, RG 65, BI, NARA.

12. Schaumburger to Bureau, 26 Sept. 1917, OG 64788, RG 65, BI, NARA.

13. Schaumburger to Bureau, 26 Sept. 1917, OG 172841; and 27 Sept. 1917, OG 64788, RG 65, BI, NARA.

14. Agent G. T. Holman to Bureau, 27 Feb. 1918, OG 64788, RG 65, BI, NARA. Driver's involvement in the UNIA is noted in Agent A. A. Hopkins to Bureau, 2 Apr. 1921, Bureau Section (hereafter BS) case file 198940-113, RG 65, BI, NARA; and in Emory J. Tolbert, *The UNIA and Black Los Angeles* (Los Angeles, 1980).

15. "Draft Evasion in Holmes County Due to Pro-German Teachings Among Blacks," *Vicksburg Post,* 1 Apr. 1918; "Negro Admits Preaching Objection to Draft," *New York Globe,* 2 Apr. 1918; "German Money Fights Draft," *New York Sun,* 2 Apr. 1918; "German Money," *New York Age,* 6 Apr. 1918.

16. H. Leider, field representative, U.S. Food Administration, to Col. Ralph H. Van Deman, 2 Apr. 1918, case file PF 1811-2; and Van Deman to Maj. Walter H. Loving, 12 Apr. 1918, PF 1811-3, RG 165, MID, NARA.

17. Agent Harry D. Gulley to Bureau, 2 Apr. 1918, OG 64788, RG 65, BI, NARA.

18. Ibid. The church's antiwar doctrine is printed in Cornelius, *Pioneer,* p. 68.

19. Gulley to Bureau, 2 Apr 1918, OG 64788, RG 65, BI, NARA.

20. "Negro Preacher Tarred," *Memphis Commercial Appeal,* 18 Apr. 1918, p. 11.

21. Agent W. E. McElveen to Bureau, 2 May 1918, OG 64788, RG 65, BI, NARA.

22. Agent V. W. Killick to Bureau, 3 and 17 June 1918, OG 64788, RG 65, BI, NARA. The presence of whites in the church was not unusual, for there were many mixed Pentecostal congregations in the early twentieth century, following the interracial Azusa Street revival (Jones, "The Black Pentecostals," p. 148).

23. Chief A. Bruce Bielaski to Agent J. P. Finlay, 17 May 1918, and Bielaski to Division Superintendent Forrest C. Pendleton, 17 May 1918, OG 644128, RG 65, BI, NARA.

24. Agent E. Palmer to Bureau, 20 June 1918, OG 227347, RG 65, BI, NARA (quotation); "Jail Pastor for Obstructing Draft," *Chicago Defender,* 29 June 1918. No record has been found to identify the men sent into the military or to determine whether they persisted in claiming to be conscientious objectors. Such summary "justice" obviously narrowed their options.

25. Palmer to Bureau, 20 June 1918, OG 227347, RG 65, BI, NARA; "Lexington Negro Pastor Held Under New U.S. Espionage Law," *Jackson Daily News,* 19 June 1918.

26. Col. Marlborough Churchill to F. Sullens, editor, *Jackson Daily News,* 25 June 1918; Sullens to Churchill, 29 June 1918; Churchill to Bielaski, 13 July 1918 (quotation); Churchill to Intelligence Officer, Los Angeles, 19 June 1918; and Churchill to IO, St. Louis, 13 July 1918, 99-7, RG 165, MID, NARA.

27. Agent DeWitt S. Winn to Bureau, 16 July 1918, OG 64788, RG 65, BI, NARA.

28. Agent Claude McCaleb to Bureau, 15 July 1918, OG 245662, RG 65, BI, NARA.

29. Winn to Bureau, 16, 18, and 19 July 1918, OG 64788; and McCaleb to Bureau, 15 July 1918, OG 245662, RG 65, BI, NARA (quotation).

30. McCaleb to Bureau, 15 and 16 July 1918, OG 245662, RG 65, BI, NARA.

31. "Charged With Working Holy Roller Negroes," *Paris Morning News,* 17 July 1918; Winn to Bureau, 19 and 20 July 1918, OG 64788; and McCaleb to Bureau, 16 and 18 July 1918, OG 245662, RG 65, BI, NARA. The trio was charged with violating Sections 32 and 37 of the U.S. Penal Code.

32. Killick to Bureau, 19, 23, and 25 July 1918, OG 64788, RG 65, BI, NARA.

33. Killick to Bureau, 6 Aug. 1918, OG 64788, RG 65, BI, NARA.

34. Alfred Bettman to Lt. Van Dusen, 8 Aug. 1918, OG 64788, RG 65, BI, NARA; Carlton J. H. Hayes to Special Assistant to the Attorney General John Lord O'Brian, 4 Sept. 1918 (quotation), and U.S. Attorney Clarence Merritt to Attorney General Thomas W. Gregory, 21 Sept. 1918, 195341, RG 60, DJ, NARA; Churchill to Bielaski, 26 July 1918, 99-7, RG 165, MID, NARA; Walter J. Hollenweger, "A Black Pentecostal Concept," *Concept* 30 (June 1970): pp. 61–63; Kornweibel, "Apathy and Dissent," pp. 330–31. Information on the other dissenting churches is in case files 99-7 and 99-68, RG 165, MID, NARA, and case file OG 27320, RG 65, BI, NARA.

35. Div. Supt. Charles E. Breniman to Div. Supt. Hinton G. Clabaugh, 31 Aug. 1918; Agent R G. Habda to Bureau, 10 Sept. 1918; Agent W. Neunhoffer to Winn, 16 Sept. 1918; and Neunhoffer to Merritt, 16 Sept. 1918, OG 64788, RG 65, BI, NARA.

36. Winn's death was mourned by his Bureau colleagues, who testified to his dedication and professionalism. Tragically, his daughter succumbed to influenza on the same day (personnel file of DeWitt S. Winn, obtained from the Federal Bureau of Investigation through the Freedom of Information Act).

37. Agent Lewie H. Henry to Bureau, 27 Oct. 1918, OG 64788, RG 65, BI, NARA; Capt. Moss, Los Angeles, to Department Intelligence Officer, San Francisco, 18 Oct. 1918, 99-7, RG 165, MID, NARA.

38. Henry to Bureau, 2 Nov. 1918, OG 64788, RG 65, BI, NARA; "Local News" columns, *Paris Morning News,* 30 Oct. and 2 Nov. (quotation) 1918.

39. "A Complaint Against Holy Roller Negroes," *Paris Morning News,* 2 Nov. 1918; "Local News," *Paris Morning News,* 3, and 5 (quotation) Nov. 1918.

40. Letter to author, 23 July 1982, A. M. Aiken Regional Archives, Texas State Library, Paris, Tex.; Criminal Minutes, Lamar County Court, book 12, Texas State Library, Paris, Tex., p. 290.

41. Kornweibel, *No Crystal Stair,* chap. 1; idem, "Apathy and Dissent."

42. Jones's and Cornelius's "authorized" histories of the denomination and Mason's own accounts do not provide any details on the assessment.

43. Kohn, *Jailed for Peace,* pp. 25–26.

44. Mason as quoted in Ross, *History and Formative Years,* pp. 23–24.

45. Letter to author, 3 Aug. 1982, National Archives and Records Administration, Southeast Region, Atlanta (hereafter NARA-A). I am indebted to my colleague Richard Steele for pointing out that federal grand juries rarely failed to indict, but that federal attorneys were more realistic in distinguishing winning from losing cases and dropping the latter before they came to trial.

46. Stephen M. Kohn, *American Political Prisoners: Prosecutions under the Espionage and Sedition Acts* (Westport, Conn., 1994), pp. 135, 137.

47. The Church of God in Christ's pacifist tradition faded after World War I. Anecdotal evidence suggests that during World War II the men whose membership antedated that conflict did not fight, but how many were successful in gaining recognition as conscientious objectors is unknown. Only twelve members worked in Civilian Public Service (CPS) camps, so very likely the total was small. The church's membership grew rapidly during the 1950s and 1960s, and its pacifist heritage faded from view. A new generation of members performed combat duty in Vietnam. Today, church doctrine still states that "the shedding of human blood or the taking of human life is contrary to the teachings of our Lord and Saviour, Jesus Christ, and as a body, we are adverse to war in all its forms." Should members be drafted, the official doctrine says they are to submit to induction as conscien-

tious objectors, undergo only basic training, and refuse any "advanced weapons training given to combatant soldiers," serving instead in noncombatant capacities. But few seem to know of, much less follow, that noncombatant doctrine.

The early restorationist Church of God in Christ nurtured pacifism. However, as happened in other sects that grew in membership and sought to enter the denominational mainstream, conscientious opposition to war became a forgotten tradition (David Daniels, McCormick Theological Seminary, Chicago, telephone conversation with author, 15 Oct. 1992; Bishop George D. McKinney, St. Stephens Church of God in Christ, San Diego, to author, 31 Aug. 1992). Regarding COGIC men in CPS camps, see Melvin Gingerich, *Service for Peace* (Akron, Pa.: Mennonite Central Committee, 1949).

7. "Rabid and inflammatory"

1. Agent R. A. Colorado to Bureau of Investigation, 15 Aug. 1917, and RSD to Agent G. W. Lillard, 10 Oct. 1917, OG 48323, RG 65, BI, NARA.

2. Agent S. B. Pfeifer to Bureau, 21 Nov. 1917, OG 48323, RG 65, BI, NARA.

3. Agent F. R. Cotten to Bureau, 5 Feb. 1918, OG 24323, RG 65, BI, NARA; "Kelly Miller," in *Dictionary of American Negro Biography,* ed. Logan and Winston, pp. 435–39.

4. Suzy M. Graves to Department of Justice, 6 Mar. 1918, and Agent Warren W. Grimes to Bureau, 11 and 19 Mar. 1918, OG 48323; and Grimes to Bureau, 11 Mar. 1918, OG 369936, RG 65, BI, NARA.

5. Grimes to Bureau, 20 Mar. 1918, OG 48323, RG 65, BI, NARA.

6. Agent Claude P. Light to Bureau, 17 and 23 Aug. 1918, and Agent Ora M. Slater to Bureau, 16 Aug. 1918, OG 270244, RG 65, BI, NARA.

7. Slater to Bureau, 30 Sept. 1918, and Light to Bureau, 10 Dec. 1918, OG 270244, RG 65, BI, NARA.

8. Peterson and Fite, *Opponents of War,* pp. 119–20; Agent DeWitt S. Winn to Bureau, 2 Aug. 1918, OG 258197, RG 65, BI, NARA.

9. Winn to Bureau, 2 and 4 Aug. 1918, OG 258197, RG 65, BI, NARA.

10. "Transcript of proceedings had before W. E. Singleton Jr., United States Commissioner, E[astern] D[istrict] Texas, at Jefferson, 31 Aug. 1918"; and "Commitment, U.S. vs. N. S. McNarry [*sic*]," 14 Aug. 1918, RG 21, U.S. District Courts, Eastern District of Texas, Jefferson Division, National Archives and Records Administration, Southwest Region, Fort Worth (hereafter Dist. Cts., NARA-FtW).

11. Indictment; testimony of S. B. Melton and A. M. Moore before U.S. Commissioner, 14 Aug. 1918, *U.S. v McNairy,* RG 21, Dist. Cts., NARA-FtW.

12. Subpoenas and record of verdict, *U.S. v McNairy,* RG 21, Dist. Cts., NARA-FtW.

13. See Kornweibel, "Apathy and Dissent," for additional details.

14. "Soldiers of the Twenty-Fourth," *San Antonio Inquirer,* 24 Nov. 1917.

15. SAC Charles E. Breniman to Agent B.C. Baldwin, 24 Nov. 1917; Baldwin to Bureau, 25 Nov. 1917; Agent Willard Utley to Bureau, 27 and 29 Nov. 1917; Breniman to Post Office Inspector in Charge C. B. Anderson, 28 Nov. 1917; and Agent Louis De Nette to Bureau, 20 Nov. 1917, OG 93286, RG 65, BI, NARA. Utley to Bureau, 27 Nov. 1917 is also in case file 10218-62, RG 165, MID, NARA.

16. Breniman to Chief A. Bruce Bielaski, 23 Apr. 1918; Agent R. C. Clayton to Bureau, 20 Apr. 1918; and Col. Ralph H. Van Deman, Chief, Military Intelligence Branch, to Bielaski, 3 May 1918, OG 93286, RG 65, BI, NARA; United States v. G. W. Bouldin,

indictment, presentment, and capias for Bouldin, 23 May 1918; defendant's motion to quash indictment, order overruling motion to quash indictment, 29 May 1918, United States District Court, Western District of Texas, San Antonio session, NARA-FtW).

17. Agent Fleet T. White to Bureau, 14 and 18 Jan. 1919, OG 341071, RG 65, BI, NARA.

18. Trial transcript, including exhibits; defendant's special charge, certified copy of judgment, sentence, and order, order admitting to bail pending writ of error, U.S. v. Bouldin, including exhibits, NARA-FtW.

19. DeNette to Bureau, 15 Dec. 1919, OG 341070, RG 65, BI, NARA; brief for plaintiff in error, motion for rehearing by plaintiff in error, motion to stay issuance of mandate, mandate of the U.S. Circuit Court of Appeals, order on petition for writ of certiorari, and clerk, Circuit Court of Appeals, to J. F. Hair, 11 Dec. 1919 and 19 Jan. 1920; E. D. Haltom to Circuit Court of Appeals, 22 and 23 Mar. 1920; Clerk Frank H. Mortimer to Haltom, 24 Mar. 1920; Mortimer to J. A. Grumbles, 6 Apr. 1920; Grumbles to Mortimer, 6 Apr. 1920; and marshal's return of certified copy of judgment, sentence and order, 29 Sept. 1920, U.S. v. Bouldin, NARA-FtW. Information on Bouldin's release from Leavenworth is in Cynthia G. Fox, National Archives, to author, 4 Dec. 1984.

20. Scheiber, *Wilson Administration,* pp. 48–49.

21. A list of those convicted under the Espionage and Sedition Acts, their offenses, sentences, and actual prison terms is in Kohn, *American Political Prisoners,* chap. 12.

22. Agent J. L. Webb to Bureau, 14 Dec. 1917, and Agent W. N. Zinn to Bureau, 14 Dec. 1917, OG 107212, RG 65, BI, NARA.

23. Webb to Bureau, 17 and 18 Dec. 1917, and Division Superintendent C. E. Breniman to U.S. Attorney John E. Green, 19 Dec. 1917, OG 107212, RG 65, BI, NARA.

24. Breniman to Green, 24 Dec. 1917, and Webb to Bureau, 29 Dec. 1917, OG 107212, RG 65, BI, NARA.

25. Webb to Bureau, 10, 14, and 18 Jan. 1918, OG 107212, RG 65, BI, NARA.

26. Webb to Bureau, 21 Jan. 1918, OG 107212, RG 65, BI, NARA; Webb to Bureau, 21 Jan. 1918, 10487-1027-1, and 23 Jan. 1918, 10487-1027-2; Zinn to Bureau, 23 Jan. 1918, 10487-1027-3; and Webb to Bureau, 15 Nov. 1918, 10487-1027-12, RG 165, MID, NARA; Haynes, *Night of Violence,* p. 85.

27. Court of Criminal Appeals Docket Book, docket no. 5253, University of Texas Law Library, Austin; Marilyn Robinson, reference librarian, telephone conversation with author, 16 Oct. 1991.

28. U.S. Postal Censorship Office, New York, 10 Sept. 1918, 10487-1027-4, RG 165, MID, NARA.

29. 1st Lt. G. R. Hoff to Col. Marlborough Churchill, Director, MID, 2 Oct. 1918, 10487-1027-4, RG 165, MID, NARA.

30. 2nd Lt. Winter R. King to Maj. R. L. Barnes, 10 Oct. 1918, 10487-1027-8; Barnes to Churchill, 10487-1027-9; Churchill to Special Assistant to the Secretary of War Emmett J. Scott, 16 Oct. 1918, 10487-1027-7; Churchill to Barnes, 22 Oct. 1918, 10487-1027-10; and Hoff to Barnes, 9 Nov. 1918, 10487-1027-11, RG 165, MID, NARA.

31. Webb to Bureau, 15 Nov. 1918, 10487-1027-12; and Hoff to Barnes, 20 Nov. 1918, 10487-1027-13, and 22 Nov. 1918, 10487-1027-14, RG 165, MID, NARA.

32. Hoff to Barnes, 20 Nov. 1918, 10487-1027-13, RG 165, MID, NARA.

33. Col. John M. Dunn, Acting Director, MID, to Scott, 30 Nov. 1918, 10487-1027-15, RG 165, MID, NARA.

34. Webb to Bureau, 28 July 1919, OG 369955; and Agent W. A. Wiseman to Bu-

reau, 20 July 1919, and Agent Will C. Austin to Bureau, 31 July 1919, OG 107212, RG 65, BI, NARA.

35. Webb to Bureau, 9 June 1921, BS 202600-667-52: Webb to Bureau, 18 July 1921, BS 202600-45-40; and Div. Supt. Gus T. Jones to Chief William J. Burns, 26 Aug. 1921, BS 202600-45-52, RG 65, BI, NARA.

36. A. Philip Randolph, interview with author, New York, 13 July 1972; Kornweibel, *No Crystal Stair,* pp. 24–32; idem, *"Seeing Red,"* pp. 76–77.

37. Agent J. F. Sawken to Bureau, 4 Aug. 1918, OG 234939, RG 65, BI, NARA; "Pro-Germanism among Negroes," *Messenger,* July 1928, p. 13; Frederick G. Detweiler, *The Negro Press in the United States* (Chicago, 1922), p. 171.

38. Sawken to Bureau, 10 Aug. 1918, OG 239339; and 10 Aug 1918, OG 265716, RG 65, BI, NARA; Kornweibel, *No Crystal Stair,* pp. 3–4 (quote), 33.

39. Agent R. W. Finch to Bureau, 9, 12, and 13 Nov. 1918, OG 208369; and Agent D. Davidson to Bureau, 6 Dec. 1918, BS 198940, RG 65, BI, NARA.

40. Kornweibel, *"Seeing Red,"* chap. 5; Randolph interview.

41. Agent W. H. Buck to Bureau, 5 Sept. 1918, OG 254212, RG 65, BI, NARA.

42. Agent W. A. Weymouth to Bureau, 27 July 1918, OG 254212, RG 65, BI, NARA.

43. Buck to Bureau, 26 Aug. 1918 (2 documents), OG 254212, RG 65, BI, NARA.

44. Buck to Bureau, 5 Sept. 1918, OG 254212, RG 65, BI, NARA.

45. Suzanne Dewberry, National Archives and Records Administration, Pacific Region, Laguna Niguel, Calif., telephone conversation with author, 10 Aug. 1989. I wish also to thank John Gilmore for checking the *San Diego Union*'s "morgue."

46. Murphy, *World War I,* pp. 154–56.

8. "Spreading enemy propaganda"

1. An excellent depiction of the shared world of whites and blacks is in Neil McMillan, *Dark Journey: Black Mississippians in the Age of Jim Crow* (Urbana, Ill., 1990).

2. Complaint, transcript of proceedings before United States Commissioner Singleton, testimony of T. L. Harold and Elmo Cook, indictment, and mittimus, United States vs Dr. Mea, U.S. District Court, Eastern District of Texas, Jefferson Division, RG 21, NARA-FtW.

3. Leland W. Harrison, State Department, to Chief A. Bruce Bielaski, 14 Mar. 1918; Bielaski to Division Superintendent Charles DeWoody, 25 Mar. 1918; Agent D. Davidson to Bureau, 15 Apr. 1918; Agent Fred H. Haggerson to Special Assistant to the Attorney General William Wallace Jr., 25 Apr. 1918, OG 173411, RG 65, BI, NARA; Agent A. B. Wallace to Haggerson, 9 Apr. 1918, PF 21645-1; and Davidson to Haggerson, 13 Apr. 1918, PF 21645-3, RG 165, MID, NARA.

4. Davidson to Bureau, 16 Apr. 1918 (four documents); A. B. Wallace to Bureau, 11 and 12 Apr. 1918; William Wallace to Attorney General Thomas W. Gregory, 8 Apr. 1918; and Gregory to William Wallace, 9 Apr. 1918, OG 173411, RG 65, BI, NARA. Copies of many of the Bureau's reports can also be found in case file PF 21645, RG 165, MID, NARA.

5. Witcover, *Sabotage at Black Tom,* pp. 3, 9, 15, 61, 151, 231, chap. 11.

6. Davidson to Bureau, 16 and 18 Apr. 1918; Haggerson to William Wallace, 25 Apr. 1918; and Agent Edward L. Newman to Bureau, 4 and 5 June 1918, OG 173411, RG 165, BI, NARA.

7. Max Freudenheim to Secretary of State Robert Lansing, 10 June 1918, OG 173411, RG 65, BI, NARA.

8. Kornweibel, *"Seeing Red,"* chaps. 4–5.

9. Indictment, *U.S. v Max Freudenheim,* U.S. District Court, Southern District of New York, 22 July 1918; and petition for appeal and assignments of error, *U.S. v Freudenheim,* 2 Aug. 1918, RG 21, National Archives and Records Administration, Northeast Region, New York (Hereafter NARA-NY). On Judge Hand, see Murphy, *World War I,* p. 210.

10. Petition for appeal and assignments of error, *U.S. v Freudenheim,* 2 Aug. 1918, RG 21, NARA-NY.

11. Kohn, *American Political Prisoners,* p. 75. Kohn's near-comprehensive list unfortunately lacks any information on Freudenheim.

12. Agent J. B. Matthews to Bureau, 8 May 1918; Div. Supt. Forrest C. Pendleton to Bielaski, 6 May 1918; Bielaski to Prof. Eugene Babbitt, Post Office Department, 13 May 1918; Babbitt to Bielaski, 14 May 1918; and Bielaski to Matthews, 15 May 1918, OG 188877, RG 65, BI, NARA; Special Assistant to the Attorney General John Lord O'Brian to Lansing, 12 June 1918; and State Department to Bulgarian Legation, 22 June 1918, Central Decimal File (hereafter CDF) 311.74/69, RG 59, DS, NARA.

13. Matthews to Bureau, 17 May 1918 (two documents); Bielaski to Babbitt, 24 May 1918; Agent C. M. Walser to Bureau, 28 May 1918; and Bielaski to Matthews, 31 May 1918, OG 188877, RG 65, BI, NARA; testimony of Pvt. Whit Patterson, 526th Engineers, 23 May 1918, 10218-159-3, RG 165, MID, NARA.

14. Lt. Col. Marlborough Churchill to Intelligence Officer (IO), Southeastern Department, 3 June 1918, 10218-159-2, RG 165, MID, NARA; Matthews to Bureau, 2 June 1918, OG 188877, RG 65, BI, NARA.

15. Matthews to Bureau, 5 June 1918; Churchill to Bielaski, 15 July 1918, 5 Aug. 1918; and Bielaski to Matthews, 18 July 1918, OG 188877, RG 65, BI, NARA; Churchill to Lt. Evans, 10 July 1918, 10218-159-5; Churchill to IO, Southeastern Dept., 15 July 1918, 10218-159-7; Churchill to IO, Port of Embarkation, Newport News, 15 July 1918, 10218-159-8; Churchill to IO, Camp Pike, 10218-159-9; and Capt. Henry G. Pratt to Churchill, 17 July 1918, 10218-159-10, RG 165, MID, NARA; Rust telephone conversation.

16. Barbeau and Henri, *Unknown Soldiers,* pp. 72–74.

17. Agent Vincent W. Hughes to Bureau, 21 May 1918, OG 171747, RG 65, BI, NARA.

18. Hughes to Bureau, 21 and 23 May 1918, and Hughes to Bielaski, 20 May 1918, OG 171747, RG 65, BI, NARA; affidavit for search warrant, search warrant, and charge, *U.S. v Ernest Young,* U.S. District Court, Western District of South Carolina, RG 21, U.S. District Court, NARA-A.

19. Hughes to Bureau, 23 May, 1918, OG 171747, RG 65, BI, NARA; depositions by Lester Wyatt, Arthur Stewart, and Herbert Morehead, 20 May 1918, *U.S. v Ernest Young,* RG 21, U.S. Dist. Ct., NARA-A. The Bureau of Investigation soon notified army intelligence and supplied it with a copy of Hughes's lengthy report cited above. See case file PF 12539, RG 165, MID, NARA.

20. Depositions, Wyatt, Stewart, Morehead; order to transport; recognizance; and true bill, *U.S. v Ernest Young,* RG 21, U.S. Dist. Ct., NARA-A.

21. Praecipe, indictment with plea and judgment, and commitment to undergo sentence, *U.S. v Ernest Young,* RG 21, U.S. Dist. Ct., NARA-A. A month later, Bureau chief Bielaski set in motion a routine investigation to determine if Young was an enemy alien. If

so, he was eligible for deportation upon expiration of his sentence (Bielaski to Agent Roland Ford, 3 July 1918, OG 171747, RG 65, BI, NARA).

22. Murphy, *World War I,* pp. 15, 25–29.

9. "Perhaps you will be shot"

1. Letter of recommendation from W. L. F. v. Rappard, Minister of the Netherlands to the United States, 27 Apr. 1914, in Bureau of Investigation case file 6002, obtained from the FBI through the Freedom of Information Act (hereafter FBI-FOIA).

2. Agent Jesse H. Wilson to Bureau, 9 Apr. 1917, 6002, FBI-FOIA; "The Alleged and the Real Moens' Case," *Messenger,* July 1919, p. 28.

3. Excerpts from Herman M. B. Moens's correspondence, 12 June 1916, and Paul Popenoe to Moens, 26 Feb. 1917, 6002, FBI-FOIA. Moens prepared an article for the *Journal of Heredity* at this time, arguing for the Mongolian ancestry of American blacks as traced through the interbreeding of American Indians and blacks. The journal rejected the manuscript and accompanying photographs as insufficiently proven.

4. Agent George W. Lillard to Bureau, 26 and 27 Mar. 1917, OG 3057, RG 65, BI, NARA.

5. M. Bagman to Lillard, 28 and 29 Mar., and 2, 6, 10, 11, (date obscured), and 28 Apr. 1917, 6002, FBI-FOIA.

6. Agent D. P. Ault to Chief A. Bruce Bielaski, 26 Mar. 1917; Leo E. Fox, Bureau of Naturalization, to ?, 4 Apr. 1917; Thomas P. Ivey to Bielaski, 5 Apr. 1917; J. K. Huddle, Department of State, to Bielaski, 7 Apr. 1917; Wilson to Bureau, 9 Apr. 1917; Bielaski to Lillard, 11 Apr. 1917; and Agent W. W. Grimes to Bureau, 13 Apr. 1917, 6002, FBI-FOIA.

7. Huddle to Bielaski, 7 Apr. 1917, and John van Schaick, "To Whom It May Concern," 24 May 1917, 6002, FBI-FOIA.

8. Agent H. Barrett Learned to Bureau, 19 June 1917, 6002, FBI-FOIA. An undated, unsigned memo from this period contained in the case file indicates that an official in the Netherlands legation was willing to talk about Moens so long as the conversation took place elsewhere.

9. J. W. Jenks to Maj. Herbert Parsons, 13 Aug. 1917, and Parsons, memorandum on interview with Hallie E. Queen, 23 Aug. 1917, 10218-1; Parsons, memorandum on interview with Queen, 29 Sept. 1917, 10218-24; Jenks to Parsons, 15 Nov. 1917, and Parsons to Jenks, 17 Nov. 1917, 10218-49; and Queen to Parsons, 9 Dec. 1917, 10218-56, RG 165, MID, NARA.

10. Maj. Walter H. Loving to Chief, Military Intelligence Section, 22 Oct. 1917, 9140-2222-6; and 30 Nov. 1917, 9140-2222-8, RG 165, MID, NARA.

11. Second Assistant Secretary of State Alvey A. Adee to Charles D. Walcott, Smithsonian Institution, 28 Jan. 1918, CDF 311.5621 Moens, RG 59, DS, NARA; memorandum, Parsons, 20 Aug. 1917, 10218-3; and Ahern to Office of Chief of Staff, War College Division, 31 Aug. 1917, 9140-2222-4, RG 165, MID, NARA.

12. George H. Girty to Dr. T. W. Vaughn, U.S. Geological Survey, 27 Oct. and 19 Nov. 1917; memorandum, David White, U.S. Geological Survey, 5 Nov. 1917; Vaughn to Dr. Philip S. Smith, acting director, U.S. Geological Survey, 30 Nov. 1917; and Smith to Bielaski, 3 Dec. 1917, 6002, FBI-FOIA; Agent Manuel de Aguero to Bureau, 20 and 21 Sept. 1917, 9140-2222-5; Lillard to Bureau, 31 Oct. 1917, 9140-2222-7; and Agent S. B. Pfeifer to Bureau, 21 Dec. 1917, 9140-2222-9, RG 165, MID, NARA. The Bureau's deci-

sion to abandon its investigation is discussed in Agent H. James to Capt. Harry A. Taylor, 15 Mar. 1918, 9140-2222-13, RG 165, MID, NARA.

13. Miles to Col. Ralph H. Van Deman, Chief, Military Intelligence Section, 29 Jan. 1918, 9140-2222-10; Edmund Leigh, Military Intelligence Plant Protection Service, to Van Deman, 7 Feb. 1918, 9140-2222-12; Capt. P. F. Goodwin to MIS, 11 Feb. 1918, 9140-2222-11; and James to Taylor, 15 Mar. 1918, 9140-2222-13, RG 165, MID, NARA.

14. Statement to Bureau, W. A. J. M. van Waterschoot van der Gracht, 5 Nov. 1918, 6002, FBI-FOIA; James to Taylor, 20 Mar. 1918, 9140-2222-14; Goodwin to Van Deman, 22 Mar. 1918, 9140-2222-16; Van Deman to Bielaski, 26 Mar. 1918, 9140-2222-17; Agent A. Roberts to Taylor, 26 Mar. 1918, 9140-2222-18; memorandum to Taylor, 1 Apr. 1918, 9140-2222-19; Goodwin to Van Deman, 21 Apr. 1918, 9140-2222-20; Van Deman to W. H. Moran, Chief, U.S. Secret Service, 8 May 1918, 9140-2222-23; Moran to Taylor, 17 May 1918, 9140-2222-24; and E. Williams to Taylor, 9 July 1918, 9140-2222-38, RG 165, MID, NARA.

15. Goodwin to Van Deman: 20 May 1918, 9140-2222-28, 21 May 1918, 9140-2222-26, 29 May 1918, 9140-2222-30, 29 May 1918, 9140-2222-31, 5 June 1918, 9140-2222-32, and 14 June 1918, 9140-2222-35; copies of intercepted mail include Girty to Moens, 19 May 1918, 9140-2222-27, and van der Gracht to Moens, 20 May 1918, 9140-2222-25, RG 165, MID, NARA.

16. Reports from Williams to Taylor, dated 6 July 1918 through 30 Sept. 1918, are in case file 9140-2222-36, -38, -39, 40, -42, -43, -44, -47, -50, -52, -57, -58, -59, -61, RG 165, MID, NARA.

17. Williams to Capt. Joseph A. Manning, 22 Oct. 1918, 9140-2222-72; and Agents Roberts and A. Harrison to Taylor, 1 Sept. 1918, 9140-2222-53, and 27 Sept. 1918, 9140-2222-60; C. Henry and A. Harrison to Manning, 21 Oct. 1918, 9140-2222-71; Taylor to Postal Inspector in Charge W. S. Bordum, 14 Sept. 1918, 9140-2222-58; and Capt. R. R. Bennett to Lt. Horten, 6 Sept. 1918, 9140-2222-54, RG 165, MID, NARA.

18. Agent George F. Ruch to Bureau, 9 Aug. 1918, 6002, FBI-FOIA; Theodore Kornweibel Jr., "Black on Black: The FBI's First Negro Informants and Agents and the Investigation of Black Radicalism during the Red Scare," *Criminal Justice History* 8 (1987): pp. 122–24.

19. Agent J. G. C. Corcoran to Bureau, 30 Aug. 1918, OG 369936, RG 65, BI, NARA.

20. Corcoran to Bureau, 31 Aug. and 4 Sept. 1918, OG 369936, RG 65, BI, NARA; Corcoran to Mr. Pike, 4 Sept. 1918, 6002, FBI-FOIA.

21. Corcoran to Bureau, 5 Sept. 1918, 6002, FBI-FOIA.

22. Corcoran to Bureau, 6 and 13 Sept. 1918, and Bielaski to Leland Harrison, Office of the Counselor, State Department, 9 Sept. 1919, 6002, FBI-FOIA; Brig. Gen. Marlborough Churchill to American Military Attaché, The Hague, 3 Oct. 1918, 9140-2222-62, RG 165, MID, NARA.

23. Agent W. L. Murphy to Bureau, 15 Oct. 1918, and Agent John A. Whalen to Bureau, 17 Oct. 1918, 6002, FBI-FOIA; Churchill to Bielaski, 10 Oct. 1918, 9140-2222-64; Henry and A. Harrison to Taylor, 15 Oct. 1918, 9140-2222-67; and Churchill to Bielaski, 16 Oct. 1918, 9140-2222-68, RG 165, MID, NARA. The MID also took note of the fact that van der Gracht's brother, Joseph Theodore van der Gracht, was issued a visa to travel to London to discuss oil deposits in Baja California. It advised the British military mission in Washington of this fact and that country's intelligence agency vowed to "keep an eye" on him when he landed on English soil (MID to Lt. Col. H. A. Packenham, 10 Oct.

1918, 9140-2222-63; and Packenham to MID, 18 Oct. 1918, 9140-2222-69, RG 165, MID, NARA).

24. Corcoran to Bureau, 19, 28, and 30 Sept. 1918, OG 369936, RG 65, BI, NARA; Secretary of State Robert Lansing to the American Legation, The Hague, 26 Sept. and 19 Nov. 1918, and Bliss, American Legation, The Hague, to Lansing, 20 Nov. 1918, CDF 311.5621 Moens, RG 59, DS, NARA.

25. Corcoran to Bureau, 1, 5, and 8 Oct. 1918; and Agent F. C. Haggarly to Bureau, 15 Oct. 1918, OG 369936, RG 65, BI, NARA; Taylor to Mr. McMahon, 11 Oct. 1918, 9140-2222-87; Churchill to Bielaski, 11 Oct. 1918, 9140-2222-65; and "Summary of Investigations to Date Case of Professor Bernelot Moens," 14 Oct. 1918, 9140-2222-66, RG 165, MID, NARA.

26. Corcoran to Bureau, 23 Oct. (two documents) and 26 Oct. 1918, OG 369936, RG 65, BI, NARA; Murphy to Bureau, 24 Oct. 1918, 6002, FBI-FOIA.

27. Corcoran to Bureau, 23 Oct. 1918, OG 369936, RG 65, BI, NARA.

28. Corcoran to Bureau, 22, 23, and 24 Oct. 1918; Agent Anatol L. Rodau to Bureau, 23 Oct. 1918; Agent Baggarly to Bureau, 24 Oct. 1918; and Moens to Department of Justice, 23 Oct. 1918, 6002, FBI-FOIA; notarized statement, Moens, 19 June 1920, 197783, RG 60, DJ, NARA.

29. Corcoran to Bureau, 25 Oct. 1918, and Learned to Acting Chief W. E. Allen, 19 Feb. 1919, 6002, FBI-FOIA; notarized statement, Moens, 19 June 1920, 197783, RG 60, DJ, NARA.

30. Corcoran to Bureau, 25 Oct. 1918, and Learned to Allen, 19 Feb. 1919, 6002, FBI-FOIA; Capt. G. C. Van Dusen to Capt. Grosvenor, 5 Nov. 1918, 9140-2222-90, RG 165, MID, NARA; notarized statement, Moens, 19 June 1920, 197783, RG 60, DJ, NARA; Netherlands Legation to Department of State, 20 Nov. 1918, CDF 311.5621 Moens, RG 59, DS, NARA.

31. Corcoran to Bureau, 29 Oct. 1918 (3 documents), and Murphy to Bureau, 2 and 4 Nov. 1918, 6002, FBI-FOIA; Moens's police booking card, 25 Oct. 1918, 9140-2222, RG 165, MID, NARA; presentments and true bills, *U.S. v Herman M. Bernelot Moens,* criminal case file 34490, Supreme Court of the District of Columbia, RG 21, NARA; "Indicted as Possessor of Improper Pictures," *Washington Star,* 31 Oct. 1918; "Hollander Is Indicted Also on Immoral Picture Charge," *Washington Post,* 1 Nov. 1918.

32. Moens "To the head of room 711" (Bureau of Investigation), 9 Nov. 1918, 6002, FBI-FOIA.

33. Col. Edward Davis, The Hague, to MILSTAFF: 28 Oct. 1918, 9140-2222-76; 7 Nov. 1918, 9140-2222-91; 15 Nov. 1918, 9140-2222-94; 16 Nov. 1918, 9140-2222-95; and 17 Dec. 1918, 9140-2222; Churchill to Bielaski, 13 Nov. 1918, 9140-2222-93; and 18 Nov. 1918, 9140-2222-96; Bielaski to Churchill, 26 Nov. 1918, 9140-2222-98; Acting Director John M. Dunn, MID, to Davis, 11 Dec. 1918, and Dunn to Bielaski, 17 Dec. 1918, 9140-2222, RG 165, MID, NARA; L. Harrison to Bielaski, 22 Nov. 1918, and J. E. Haynes, Alien Property Custodian Office, to Allen, 31 Jan. 1919, 6002, FBI-FOIA; Bliss, The Hague, to Lansing, 20 Nov. 1918; Ambassador, The Hague, to Lansing, 2 Dec. 1918; and Garrett, The Hague, to Lansing, 11 Jan. 1919, CDF 311.5621 Moens, RG 59, DS, NARA.

34. Van Dusen to Grosvenor, 5 Nov. 1918, 6002, FBI-FOIA; interview, van der Gracht, 5 Nov. 1918; van der Gracht to T. F. Lydon, 6 Nov. 1918; Whalen to Bureau, 29 Oct., and 2, 9, 29, and 30 Nov. 1918; accountant R. M. Huston to Bureau, 29 Nov. 1918; APL agent H. G. Bell to Bureau, 30 Nov. 1918; Bielaski to Whalen, 2 and 26 Nov. and 3 Dec. 1918; James M. Sheridan to A. W. I. Tjarda van Starkenberg-Staehouwer, Netherlands

Legation, 7 and 14 Feb. 1919; and van Starkenberg-Staehouwer to Sheridan, 8 Feb. 1919, 6002, FBI-FOIA.

35. Agents K. A. Wagner, A. Harrison, and Henry to Capt. Henry G. Pratt, 20 Oct. 1918, 9140-2222-78; Bielaski to Dunn, 2 Dec. 1918, and Davis to Capt. Johnson, MIL-STAFF, 14 Dec. 1918, 9140-2222; Bielaski to Div. Supt. Charles DeWoody, 7 Nov. 1918; Agent W. B. Matthews to Bureau, 14 Nov. 1918; Corcoran to Bureau, 30 Nov. 1918; Bielaski to Alien Property Custodian A. Mitchell Palmer, 20 Dec. 1918; Bielaski to U.S. District Attorney John E. Laskey, 20 Dec. 1918; Learned to Assistant Attorney General H. LaRue Brown, 20 Dec. 1918; Bielaski to Commissioner of Indian Affairs Cato Sells, 20 Dec. 1918; and Allen to Palmer, 22 Jan. 1919, 6002, FBI-FOIA.

36. Moens to van der Gracht, 30 Oct. and 11 Nov. 1918; van der Gracht to Moens, 8 and 21 Nov. 1918; van der Gracht to Sheridan, 8 and 21 Nov. and 2 Dec. 1918; and Laskey to Bielaski, 4 Jan. 1919, 6002, FBI-FOIA. As was customary, the Bureau used a civilian volunteer, Prof. E. H. Babbitt, to translate much of this correspondence.

37. Van der Gracht to Sheridan, 23 Dec. 1918, 6002, FBI-FOIA.

38. Netherlands Legation to Department of State, 20 Nov. 1918; Secretary, Netherlands Legation, to Breckinridge Long, 30 Nov. 1918; and memorandum, C. B. H, Division of Western European Affairs, 15 Jan. 1919, CDF 311.5621 Moens, RG 59, DS, NARA; Learned to ?, 27 Nov. 1918, 6002, FBI-FOIA.

39. Long to Mr. Ruddock, State Department, 30 Nov. 1918; L. H. W., Office of the Solicitor, to Adee, ? Dec. 1918; Long to Diplomatic Branch, 10 Dec. 1918; Long to Minister, Netherlands Legation, 11 Dec. 1918; Long to Attorney General Thomas W. Gregory, 11 Dec. 1918; and Brown to Lansing, 13 and 16 Dec. 1918, CDF 311.5621 Moens, RG 59, DS, NARA; memorandum, Learned, 27 Nov. 1918, and Learned to Mr. Offley, 10 Dec. 1918, 6002, FBI-FOIA; Brown to Laskey, 16 Dec. 1918, 197783-3, RG 60, DJ, NARA.

40. Churchill to Bielaski, 2 Nov. 1918, 9140-2222-85, and 30 Nov. 1918, 9140-2222-100; A. Harrison to Pratt, 8 Nov. 1918, 9140-2222-92; and Agents A. Harrison, Wagner, Henry to Manning, 26 Oct. 1918, 9140-2222-77, RG 165, MID, NARA.

41. Bielaski to acting Special Agent in Charge C. H. Oldfield, 1 Nov. 1918; Oldfield to Bielaski, 2 Nov. 1918; Oldfield to Bureau, 9 Nov. 1918; Corcoran to Bureau, 5 and 22 Nov. 1918; and U.S. Attorney to Chief, Bureau of American Ethnology, Smithsonian Institution, 17 Mar. 1919, 6002, FBI-FOIA.

42. Corcoran to Bureau, 30 Nov. 1918, and Agent W. N. Dannenburg to Bureau, 2 Dec. 1918, 6002, FBI-FOIA.

43. Regarding Hunter: Corcoran to Bureau, 20 Nov. 1918, and Agent W. F. Prescott to Bureau, 4 Dec. 1918, 6002, FBI-FOIA. Regarding Johnson: Corcoran to Bureau, 20 Nov. 1918, and sworn statement of Mrs. Johnson to Assistant District Attorney Arth, c. 20 Nov. 1918, 6002, FIB-FOIA; Learned, "Memorandum in re Herman Marie Bernelot Moens, Suspect," ? Jan. 1918, 9140-2222, RG 165, MID, NARA.

44. Learned, "Memorandum re Moens," ? Jan. 1918, 9140-2222, RG 165, MID, NARA. Interviews with black women are described in Agent H. P. Alden to Bureau, 6 Nov. 1918; Baggarly to Bureau, 6 Nov. 1918; Corcoran to Bureau, 5 Nov. 1918; Dannenburg to Bureau, 6 and 9 Nov. 1918; Prescott to Bureau, 7, 12 (2 documents), and 29 Nov. 1918; Ruch to Bureau, 9 Nov. 1918 (2 documents); Agent E. J. Wells Jr. to Bureau, 6 and 12 Nov. 1918; and sworn statement of Juanita Arthur to Arth, c. 20 Nov. 1918, 6002, FBI-FOIA. Interviews with Virginia Parsons are in Baggarly to Bureau, 29 Oct. 1918, and Corcoran to Bureau, 5 (2 documents) and 30 Nov. and 2 Dec. (2 documents) 1918, 6002, FBI-FOIA.

45. Sworn statement of Helen Saunders to Arth, 23 Nov. 1918, and Corcoran to Bu-

reau, 10 Nov. 1918, 6002, FBI-FOIA; Learned, "Memorandum re Moens," ? Jan. 1919, 9140-2222, RG 165, MID, NARA.

46. "A friend of Justice to the Official in Charge," 30 Oct. 1918; Corcoran to Bureau, 5 and 10 Nov. 1918; Corcoran to Learned, 12 Nov. 1918; and sworn statement of Rachel Custis to Arth, c. 20 Nov. 1918, 6002, FBI-FOIA.

47. Richard P. Evans to Gregory, 15 Feb. 1919; Gregory to Brown, 18 Feb. 1919; and Brown to Gregory, 18 Feb. 1919, 6002, FBI-FOIA.

48. Brown to Gregory, 18 Feb. 1919, 6002, FBI-FOIA; motion for leave to substitute plea of *nolo contendere,* and order denying leave to change plea, *U.S. v Moens,* criminal case files, RG 21, NARA.

49. "Moens Case—Sensation," *Washington Bee,* 29 Mar. 1919; "Moens is Found Guilty," *Washington Bee,* 5 Apr. 1919.

50. Details of the trial have been pieced together from the following sources: U.S. Attorney Peyton Gordon to Attorney General Harry M. Daugherty, 22 Sept. 1923, 197783-19, RG 60, DJ, NARA; Rodau to Bureau, 3 Apr. 1919, 6002, FBI-FOIA; Maj. H. B. Arnold to Pratt, 21 June 1919, 9140–2222, RG 165, MID, NARA; "Had Objectionable Pictures," *Washington Evening Star,* 2 Apr. 1919; "Art Study Gets Moens in Prison," *Washington Post,* 18 Apr. 1919; "Moens is Found Guilty."

51. Juanita Arthur to Arth, 30 Mar. 1919, 6002, FBI-FOIA.

52. Moens's letter is quoted in van der Gracht to Sheridan, 8 Apr. 1919, 9140-2222, RG 165, MID, NARA.

53. Abstract of Moens case prepared by Justice Department for the Immigration Bureau, ? Apr. 1919, OG 369936, RG 65, BI, NARA; Allen to L. Lanier Winslow, Office of Counselor, 14 Apr. and 5 May 1919, 6002, FBI-FOIA; C. B. H., Division of Western European Affairs, to ?, 19 May 1919, and Winslow to Ruddock, 21 May 1919, CDF 311.5621 Moens, RG 59, DS, NARA.

54. Moens, notarized statement, 19 June 1920, and Special Assistant to the Attorney General John Lord O'Brian to Edward H. Bierstadt, American Red Cross, 24 July 1920, 197783; and Laskey to Daugherty, 7 May 1921, 197783-11, RG 60, DJ, NARA; motion for new trial, motion for arrest of judgment, motion to extend time for submitting bill of exceptions, order extending time to submit bill of exceptions, prayers on behalf of defendant, motion for bill of particulars, bill of exceptions, assignment of errors, motion for order upon mandate (criminal no. 34395), motion to quash indictment (criminal no. 34490), true bill of indictment, motion for bill of particulars (criminal no. 36507), true bill of indictment (criminal no. 36508), *U.S. v Moens,* criminal case files, RG 21, NARA.

55. R. W. Schufeldt, M.D., "On the Exhibition of the Organs of Sex in Medical Museums Open to the Public," *Medical Review of Reviews* 25 (Apr. 1919): p. 212; idem, "Enemies of Art, Sculpture and Anatomy in the Law Courts of Washington, D.C.," *Medical Review of Reviews* 25 (Oct. 1919): pp. 599–604.

56. Herman M. Bernelot Moens, "Intermixture of Races," *Medical Review of Reviews* 25 (Sept. 1919): pp. 531–43.

57. Assistant Superintendent Roscoe Conkling Bruce to Superintendent Ernest L. Thurston, 7 Nov. 1918, 6002, FBI-FOIA.

58. Thurston to Learned, 7 Nov. 1918; Learned to Thurston, 3 and 6 Dec. 1918; and Agent John Hanna to Thurston, 6 Dec. 1918, 6002, FBI-FOIA; memorandum for files, Capt. J. E. Cutler, 26 May 1919, 9140-2222, RG 165, MID, NARA.

59. S. M. Kendrick, District of Columbia NAACP, to Learned, 16 Apr. 1919, and Assistant Attorney General Samuel J. Graham to Kendrick, 21 Apr. 1919, 197783-4,

RG 60, DJ, NARA; handbill, "Moen's [*sic*] Affair Mass Meeting," 22 Apr. 1919, and George E. Hamilton, president, Board of Education, to Mrs. C. M. Tanner, president, Parents League, 25 Apr. 1919, 6002, FBI-FOIA; "The Alleged and the Real Moens' Case," *Messenger,* July 1919, p. 28; "May Withdraw Pupils to Emphasize Protest," *Washington Star,* 16 May 1919; Josephine Redfield Hallinan, "Hunter Case a Lynching in Washington," *Richmond Planet,* 24 May 1919; articles in the *Washington Bee,* 12, 19, and 26 Apr.; 3, 10, 17, 24, and 31; 7, 14, 21, and 28 June; and 5 and 12 July 1919; memorandum for files, Cutler, 26 May 1919, 9140-2222, RG 165, MID, NARA.

60. William H. Wilson, M.D., to Learned, 18 May 1919, 6002, FBI-FOIA; memorandum for files, Cutler, 26 May 1919, 9140-222, RG 165, MID, NARA; "Public-School System of the District of Columbia," Hearings before the Select Committee of the United States Senate, 66th Cong, 2nd sess., pursuant to Senate Resolution 310 (Washington, D.C., 1920), pp. 1276–85.

61. "Moens Mystery Man," *Washington Post,* 30 May 1919.

62. B. H. Clark to Daugherty, 27 Apr. 1921, 197783-9; Daugherty to Clark, 10 May 1921, 197783-11; Sen. Hiram W. Johnson to Daugherty, 11 July 1921, 197783-13, and 2 Sept. 1921, 197783-14; and Daugherty to Johnson, 14 July 1921, 197783-13, 7 Sept. 1921, 197783-14, and 13 Sept. 1921, 197783-15, RG 60, DJ, NARA.

63. "The Case of Herman M. Bernelot Moens," *Issues of Today,* 11 Feb. 1922, pp. 417–18; advertisement in *Culture Forum,* June 1923.

64. "A Miscarriage of Justice or Injustice? Which?" *Culture Forum,* June 1923; Daugherty to Gordon, 26 Apr. 1923, 197783-16, and 29 Aug. 1923, 197783-17; and Gordon to Daugherty, 22 Sept. 1923, 197783-19, RG 60, DJ, NARA.

65. Daugherty to Gordon, 1 Oct. 1923, 197783-19; and William T. Hornaday to Chief Clerk Sims Ely, 13 Oct. 1923, and Assistant Attorney General John W. H. Crim to Hornaday, 24 Oct. 1923, 197783-20, RG 60, DJ, NARA.

66. Hornaday to Crim, 26 Oct. 1923, and Crim to Gordon, 29 Oct. 1923, 197783-21; J. A. H. Hopkins, National Bureau of Information and Education, to Dept. of Justice, 1 Nov. 1923, and Daugherty to Hopkins, 6 Nov. 1923, 197783-22; Hopkins to Crim, 9 Nov. 1923, Daugherty to Gordon, 14 Nov. 1923, and Crim to Hopkins, 14 Nov. 1923, 197783-23; Gordon to Daugherty, 19 Nov. 1923, 197783-24; Moens to Daugherty, 22 Apr. 1924, and Attorney General Harlan Fiske Stone to Moens, 7 May 1924, 197783-25; Attorney John H. Mariano to Department of Justice, 16 Aug. 1924, Assistant Attorney General William J. Donovan to Gordon, 28 Aug. 1924, and Donovan to Mariano, 28 Aug. 1924, 197783-26; Gordon to Stone, 21 Oct. 1924, and Donovan to Mariano, 23 Oct. 1924, 197783-27; Mariano to Donovan, 31 Oct. 1924, 197783-29; Gordon to Stone, 9 Dec. 1924, 197783-30; and Stone to Mariano, 19 Feb. 1925, 197783-31, RG 60, DJ, NARA; "A Miscarriage of Justice or Injustice? Which?" *Culture Forum,* June 1923; "One of Those 'Spy' Cases," *Liberal,* Nov. 1923.

67. Moens to President Calvin Coolidge, 23 Sept. 1924; Moens to Secretary of State Charles Evans Hughes, 5 Nov. 1924; Moens to Secretary of State Frank B. Kellogg, 29 July 1925; and Assistant Secretary of State J. Butler Wright to Moens, 10 Aug. 1925, CDF 311.5621 Moens, RG 59, DS, NARA.

68. *Culture Forum,* 24 Feb. 1926; "U.S. May Pay 'War Spy' $25,000," *New York Evening Journal,* 30 Apr. 1926; Director J. Edgar Hoover to Mr. Dodge, 4 May 1926, and memorandum, Bureau, 4 May 1926, 6002, FBI-FOIA. Correspondence regarding bypassing the State Department is in CDF 311.5621 Moens, RG 59, DS, NARA.

69. H. van Asch van Wyck, Charge d'Affaires, to Kellogg, 4 Nov. 1926, 15 Dec. 1926;

Kellogg to Attorney General John G. Sargent, 19 Nov. and 22 Dec. 1926, and 21 Jan. 1927; and Sargent to Kellogg, 24 Nov. 1926, and 5 and 25 Jan. 1927, CDF 311.5621 Moens, RG 59, DS, NARA. These letters are also in 197783, RG 60, DJ, NARA.

70. Assistant Attorney General O. R. Luhring to Bureau of Investigation, 18 Jan. 1928, and Hoover to Luhring, with memorandum, 20 Jan. 1928, 6002, FBI-FOIA; Rep. Charles L. Underhill to Sargent, 6 Jan. 1928, and Luhring to Assistant Attorney General Marshall, 26 Jan. 1928, 197783-36; and Underhill to Sargent, 1 Dec. 1928, 197783-39, RG 60, DJ, NARA.

10. "Negro Subversion"

1. Quoted in Talbert, *Negative Intelligence,* pp. 113–14. This book is an essential source for understanding the history and scope of military intelligence in this period.

2. Agent L. O. Thompson to Bureau of Investigation 31 July 1917, 10218-2; Agent Beasley to Bureau, 13 Aug. 1917, 10218-4; Agent Charles B. Braun to Bureau, 17 Aug. 1917, 10218-5; and Agent Willard Utley to Bureau, 15 Aug. 1917, and Lt. Col. Ralph H. Van Deman, Chief, Military Intelligence Section, to A. Bruce Bielaski, Chief, Bureau of Investigation, 22 Sept. 1917, 10218-6, RG 165, MID, NARA.

3. Maj. Joel E. Spingarn to Maj. Herbert Parsons, 12 Aug. 1917, and Parsons to Spingarn, 15 Aug. 1917, 10218, RG 165, MID, NARA.

4. "Memorandum on the Loyalty of the American Negro in the Present War," n.d., Spingarn to Parsons, 25 Aug. 1917, and Parsons to Spingarn, 27 Aug. 1917, 10218-7, RG 165, MID, NARA.

5. Acting Chief of War College Division to Chief of Staff, 1 Sept. 1917, 10218-7; and Nicholas Biddle to Van Deman, 25 Sept. 1917, 10218-10, RG 165, MID, NARA.

6. Talbert, *Negative Intelligence,* p. 117.

7. Maj. Walter H. Loving to Van Deman, 11 July 1917; F. W. Scheick to Capt. Harry A. Taylor, 4 Oct. 1917; and Taylor to Parsons, 17 Dec. 1917, 10218-11, RG 165, MID, NARA. The MID's file on Nannie Burroughs also included sixteen pages of the Bureau's more extensive probe. Today those documents can be found in OG 51311, RG 65, BI, NARA. A good sketch of her life is in Logan and Winston, eds., *Dictionary of American Negro Biography,* pp. 81–82.

8. Van Deman to A. W. Williams, 30 Oct. 1917, 10218-42, RG 165, MID, NARA.

9. Hallie Elvira Queen to Military Intelligence Section, ? Aug. 1917, 10218-10; Queen to Dr. J. W. Jenks, ? Oct. 1917; Loving to Van Deman, 16 Oct. 1917; and memorandum, Parsons, 5 Oct. 1917, 10218-33; Queen to Jenks: undated, 10218-56-1; undated, 10218-56-2; 20 Nov. 1917, 10218-56-3; and 21 Nov. 1917, 10218-56-4; Jenks to Parsons, 22 Nov. 1917, 10218-56-5; Queen to Taylor, undated, 10218-56-6; and Parsons to Queen, 11 Dec. 1917, 10218-56, RG 165, MID, NARA.

10. Robert Russa Moton to Van Deman, 12 Sept. 1917; Van Deman to C. V. Roman, 18 Sept. 1917; Van Deman to Moton, 18 Sept. 1917; Roman to Van Deman, 21 Sept. 1917; and Van Deman to Felix Frankfurter, 26 Sept. 1917, 10218-15, RG 165, MID, NARA.

11. Parsons to W. E. B. DuBois, 20 Sept. 1917, 10218-22-3; and DuBois to Parsons, 25 Sept. 1917, 10218-22-4; and 29 Sept. 1917, 10218-22-5, RG 165, MID, NARA.

12. Van Deman to Intelligence Officer, Northeastern Department, 2 Oct. 1917, 10218-26; Van Deman to Intelligence Officer, Central Department, 2 Oct. 1917, 10218-24; and Van Deman to Bielaski, 3 Oct. 1917, 10218-25, RG 165, MID, NARA.

13. Van Deman to Third Assistant Secretary of War Frederick P. Keppel, 14 Dec.

1917, 10218-61-2; Ralph H. Weber, ed., *The Final Memoranda: Major General Ralph H. Van Deman, USA Ret., 1865–1952, Father of U.S. Military Intelligence* (Wilmington, Del., 1988), pp. 33–34.

14. Loving to Van Deman, 11 July 1917, and Taylor to Parsons, 17 Dec. 1917, 10218-11; and Parsons, memorandum, 5 Oct. 1917, and Loving to Van Deman, 16 Oct. 1917, 10218-33, RG 165, MID, NARA; George William Cook to Loving, 15 Oct. 1917, and Loving to Van Deman, 18 Oct. 1917, box 113-1, folder 9, Loving Papers, M-SRC.

15. Van Deman to Loving, 20 Oct. 1917; Loving to Van Deman, 26 Oct. 1917; Illinois Adjutant General H. P. McCain to Col. Frank Stewart, 6 Dec. 1916 and 6 Jan. 1917; Adjutant General's Special Orders No. 16, 23 Jan. 1917; and public letter from Glencoe Dept. of the Ladies Auxiliary, ? Oct. 1917, 10218-37, RG 165, MID, NARA. This case file originally included a Bureau of Investigation report, but it was removed prior to the file being made available to researchers.

Whites' racial fears sometimes reached truly fanciful proportions during the war. A woman resident of Cleveland sent the secretary of war a publisher's announcement of a scholarly book entitled *The Slaveholding Indians, as Secessionists, Participants in the Civil War, and Under Reconstruction,* by Yale-educated Annie Heloise Abel. The alarmed correspondent labeled the volume "seditious" and added, "at *this* time *no* one should try to agitate the Negro Problem. (Dr. Abel *may* be a 'pro-German.')" (Adelaide W. Bridgman to Secretary of War Newton D. Baker, 22 Oct. 1917, 10218-40, RG 165, MID, NARA).

16. Loving to Commanding General Carter, Central Department, 29 Oct. 1917, box 113-1, folder 9, Loving Papers, M-SRC; Loving to Van Deman, 26 Oct. 1917, 10218-43, RG 165, MID, NARA. Loving's report to General Carter provides a detailed description of the type of slum conditions which black urban workers were forced to endure during the wartime "Great Migration."

17. Loving to Van Deman, 31 Oct. 1917, 10218-44; Capt. G. B. Perkins, Chief, Military Morale Section, to Commanding Officer, Camp Zachary Taylor, 30 Sept. 1918, 10218-295-1; and Perkins to Provost Marshal General's Office, undated (late 1918?), 10218-295-2, RG 165, MID, NARA.

18. Loving to Van Deman, 9 Nov. 1917, 10218-47-2, and 12 Dec. 1917, 10218-61-1, RG 165, MID, NARA.

19. Loving to Van Deman, 9 Nov. 1917, 10218-47-2; and "Long War Race's Hope," *Boston Guardian,* 3 Nov. 1917, 10218-47, RG 165, MID, NARA. Thirty pages of Bureau of Investigation documents were originally part of this case file but were removed prior to making it available to the public.

20. Loving to Van Deman, 23 Nov. 1917, and Van Deman to Loving, 28 Nov. 1917, 10218-50, RG 165, MID, NARA.

21. Capt. A. Morton to Department Intelligence Officer, 14 Nov. 1917, 10218-51-1; Intelligence Officer, Fortress Monroe, to Morton, 16 Nov. 1917, 10218-51; testimony of John Strong, 17 Nov. 1917, 10218-51-4; Department Intelligence Officer to Morton, 17 Nov. 1917, 10218-51-5; Van Deman to Loving, 1 Dec. 1917, 10218-51-3, and 5 Dec. 1917, 10218-51-6; and Loving to Van Deman, 12 Dec. 1917, 10218-61-1, RG 165, MID, NARA.

22. Loving to Van Deman, 12 Dec. 1918, 10218-61-1; Van Deman to Keppel, 14 Dec. 1917, 10218-61-2; and Keppel to Van Deman, 17 Dec. 1917, 10218-61-3, RG 165, MID, NARA.

23. Loving to Van Deman, 14 Dec. 1917, 10218-64, and 21 Dec. 1917, 10218-70-1, RG 165, MID, NARA.

24. Van Deman to Loving, 28 Dec 1917, 10218-74-2; Fred A. Sale to Baker, 9 Jan. 1918, 10218-80-1; Van Deman to Sale, 23 Jan. 1918, 10218-80-2; Office of Naval Intelligence Section A-2 to Military Intelligence Section, Justice Department, and State Department, 11 Mar. 1918, 10218-112-1; and Leland Harrison, Office of the Counselor, State Department, to Van Deman, 2 Aug. 1917, 10218-113-2, RG 165, MID, NARA.

25. Van Deman to Intelligence Officer, Southern Department, 24 Jan. 1918, 10218-84-2; and Lt. E. V. Spence, Ft. Sam Houston, to Intelligence Officer, Southern Department, 22 Feb. 1918, 10218-84-3, RG 165, MID, NARA.

26. Taylor to Loving, 27 Feb. 1918, 10218-100-3; Queen to Taylor, 23 May 1918; 1st Lt. Thomas M. Gregory to Spingarn, 10 July 1918; and H. C. Stratton to Spingarn, 19 July 1918, 10218-56; Queen to Chief of Staff, War College, 13 February 1918, 10218-93-1; and Van Deman to Queen, 26 Feb. 1918, 10218-93-2, RG 165, MID, NARA.

27. Stratton to Parsons, 22 Jan. 1918, 10218-87-1; anonymous to R. M. Gates, n.d. (Feb. 1918), 10218-94-1; Van Deman to IO, Camp Meade, 26 Feb. 1918, 10218-94-2; and Van Deman to Loving, 26 Feb. 1918, 10218-94-3, RG 165, MID, NARA.

28. "The spiritual Descendants of John Brown" to Sir, n.d. [Jan. 1918], 10218-75 10218-1; Fred A. Sale to Baker, 9 Jan. 1918, 10218-80-1; Van Deman to Sale, 23 Jan. 1918, and Emmett J. Scott to Van Deman, 25 Feb. 1918, 10218-96-2; H. D. Williams to Taylor, 23 Feb. 1918, 10218-99-1; Office of Naval Intelligence to Military Intelligence Service, 11 Mar. 1918, 10218-112-1; and Van Deman to Loving, 14 Mar. 1918, 10218-112-2, RG 165, MID, NARA.

29. Loving to Van Deman, n.d. (Jan. 1918), 10218-78-3, RG 165, MID, NARA; Loving to Van Deman, 10 Mar. 1918, box 113-1, folder 10, Loving Papers, M-SRC.

30. Loving to Van Deman: 10 Jan. 1918, 10218-78-4; 15 Jan. 1918, 10218-83-1; 19 Jan. 1918, 10218-83-3; 1 Feb. 1918, 10218-83-4; 3 Feb. 1918, 10218-83-5; 20 Feb. 1918, 10218-83-7; 21 Feb. 1918, 10218-95-1; and 10 Mar. 1918, 10218-111-2, RG 165, MID, NARA.

31. "Kelly Miller," in *Dictionary of American Negro Biography,* ed. Logan and Winston, pp. 435–39.

32. Van Deman to Loving, 28 Feb. 1918, 10218-91-6; Kelly Miller to Loving, 8 Mar. 1918, 10218-91-7; and Loving to Van Deman, 14 Mar. 1918, 10218-91-8, RG 165, MID, NARA.

33. Loving to Van Deman, 5 Mar. 1918, box 113-1, folder 10, Loving Papers, M-SRC; Van Deman to Biddle, 18 Mar. 1918, 10218-114-1; Van Deman to Loving, 17 Apr. 1918, 10218-122-2, and 17 Apr. 1918, 10218-123-2; Loving to Van Deman, 26 Apr. 1918, 10218-123-3; and Van Deman to Loving, 3 May 1918, 10218-124-3, and 26 Apr. 1918, 10218-126-2, RG 165, MID, NARA.

34. Petition to Secretary of Agriculture David F. Houston, 5 Mar. 1918, 10218-117-1; George Creel to Van Deman, 27 Mar. 1918, 10218-117-2; Van Deman to Creel, 7 May 1918, 10218-117-3; Van Deman to William Driscoll, William F. Penn, Dr. J. W. E. Bowen, Benjamin J. Davis, H. R. Rucker, 7 May 1918, 10218-117-4 through -8; Davis to Van Deman, 22 May 1918, 10218-117-9; and Penn to Capt. Henry T. Hunt, 26 June 1918, 10218-117-10, RG 165, MID, NARA.

35. Lt. Col. C. G. Lawrence to IO, Southeast Department, 10 Apr. 1918, 10218-121-1, and 17 May 1918, 10218-149-1; and Capt. Roy Britton to Van Deman, 27 Apr. 1918, 10218-128-1, RG 165, MID, NARA.

36. Maj. M. D. Wheeler to Bureau of Investigation agent Branch Bocock, 8 May

1918, 10218-143-1; Van Deman to Bielaski, 10 May 1918, 10218-143-1; Wheeler to Bocock, 8 May 1918, 10218-146-1; Van Deman to Bielaski, 14 May 1918, 10218-146-2; Wheeler (?) to ?, 14 May 1918, 10218-148-1; Capt. Spencer Roberts to Van Deman, 22 May 1918, 10218-147-3; Van Deman to Bielaski, 25 May 1918, 10218-147-4; and Van Deman to Loving, 28 Feb. 1918, 10218-74-2, RG 165, MID, NARA. This pattern of referring domestic issues to the Bureau of Investigation continued throughout the remainder of the war. See, for instance, Brig. Gen. Marlborough Churchill, Director, Military Intelligence Division, to Bielaski, 22 Oct. 1918, 10218-240, RG 165, MID, NARA.

37. Lt. Col. Marlborough Churchill, Chief, MIB, to IO, Fort Sam Houston, 8 June 1918, 10218-164-1; William Gilman Low, chief, Intelligence Department, YMCA, to Van Deman, 22 Apr. 1918, 10218-130-1, and 27 Apr. 1918, 10218-138-1; Van Deman to IO, Northeastern Department, 4 May 1918, 10218-130-2; Van Deman to Low, 11 May 1918, 10218-138-2, and 31 May 1918, 10218-138-4; MIB operative E. R. Barnard to IO, Northeastern Dept., 14 May 1918, 10218-130-3, and 31 May 1918, 10218-130-6; IO, Northeastern Dept., to Van Deman, 16 May 1918, 10218-130-5, and 31 May 1918, 10218-130-7; and Low to Lt. Col. K. C. Masteller, 17 May 1918, 10218-138-3, RG 165, MID, NARA; Talbert, *Negative Intelligence,* pp. 115–116.

38. Col. Marlborough Churchill, Chief, MID, to IO, Ft. Severin, Ga., 17 June 1918, 10218-308-2; "Capt. G. H. Hill" to Dr. H. B. Everett, 27 Apr. 1918, 10218-145-1; Bielaski to Van Deman, 8 May 1918, 10218-145-2; Van Deman to Capt. Harold F. Butler, 23 May 1918, 10218-145-3; Churchill to Butler, 22 June 1918, 10218-145-4, and 5 Aug. 1918, 10218-145-7; and Butler to Churchill, 27 July 1918, 10218-145-6, and 7 Aug. 1918, 10218-145-8, RG 165, MID, NARA.

39. Roberts to Van Deman, 10 May 1918, 10218-147-1; and Van Deman to Roberts, 17 May 1918, 10218-147-2, RG 165, MID, NARA.

40. Undated undercover report, Military Morale Section, 10218-237-1; and Maj. Roy Britton to Capt. T. K. Schmuck, 3 Oct. 1918, 10218-237-2, RG 165, MID, NARA.

41. Raymond B. Fosdick, Chairman, Commission on Training Camp Activities, War Department, to Dr. F. P. Keppel, MIB, 23 Mar. 1918, 10218-116-1; Van Deman to Bielaski, 4 Apr. 1918, 10218-116-3; Van Deman to Loving, 9 Apr 1918, 10218-116-5; Capt. Robert M. Ewing to Commanding Officer, U.S. Army General Hospital No. 1, 14 Mar. 1918, 10218-116-11; Loving to Van Deman, 16 Apr 1918, 10218-116-22; and Van Deman to Loving, 22 Apr. 1918, 10218-116-27, RG 165, MID, NARA; "Our Soldiers' Eyes Gouged Out by Germans," *New York World,* 8 Mar. 1918; "Base Hospital Yarns Baseless," *New York Amsterdam News,* 17 Apr. 1918.

42. Agent/informant Quander E. Hall to Taylor, 22 Aug. 1918, 10218-215-1, and 23 Aug. 1918, 10218-215-2, RG 165, MID, NARA. The Bureau of Investigation handled a similar incident that occurred in March, although the MIB was apprised of the issue. A flyer was reported to be circulating in black neighborhoods in San Antonio, saying that it was War Department policy to place blacks in the front lines so as to save white soldiers. It was claimed that this circular—which was characterized as "German propaganda"—had caused many blacks who had been drafted to flee the city. Bureau agents, however, were unable to secure a copy or find the source of the rumors (Agent Louis DeNette to Bureau, 29 Mar. 1918, 10218-122-1; Agent R. E. Corder to Bureau, 16 Apr. 1918, 10218-122-3; and Van Deman to Loving, 17 Apr. 1918, 10218-122-2, RG 165, MID, NARA).

43. E. P. Bellows (citizen) to Secretary of War, 8 June 1918, 10218-169-1; Spingarn to Churchill, 15 June 1918, 10218-169-6; Churchill to IO, Port of Embarkation, Hoboken,

22 June 1918, 10218-169-2; Maj. L. B. Dunham, IO, Port of Embarkation, Hoboken, to Churchill, 16 July 1918, 10218-169-3; Maj. Henry T. Hunt to Col. Masteller, 24 July 1918, 10218-169-7; Masteller (?) to Hunt, 24 July 1918, 10218-169-8; Churchill to Surgeon General of the Army, 25 July 1918, 10218-169-9; and Col. Winford H. Smith, for the Surgeon General, to Chief, MIB, 30 July 1918, 10218-169-13, RG 165, MID, NARA.

44. For the Savannah rumors: F. T. Saussy to Adjutant General, 3 Aug. 1918, 10218-214-7/W; Maj. Gen. Frank McIntyre to Adjutant General, 18 Sept. 1918, 10218-214-7; and Churchill to Chief of Staff, 12 Sept. 1918, 10218-214-6, RG 165, MID, NARA. For the Washington rumors: Agent C. Henry to Capt. Harry A. Taylor, 22 June 1918, 10218-291-1; Taylor to Queen, 16 July 1918, 10218-291-2; Henry to Capt. Henry G. Pratt, 5 Nov. 1918, 10218-291-3; Quander E. Hall to Taylor, 28 Sept. 1918, 10218-286-1, RG 165, MID, NARA.

45. Capt. A. P. Wagner to M. I. 4, 30 Aug. 1918, 10218-259-1; Churchill to Emmett J. Scott, 3 Sept. 1918, 10218-259-2; and Churchill to George Creel, Committee on Public Information, 17 Sept. 1918, 10218-259-3, RG 165, MID, NARA.

46. K. A. Wagner, M. I. 3-C, to Pratt, MID, 4 Nov. 1918, 10218-254-2, RG 165, MID, NARA.

47. This background on the 92nd and 93rd Divisions, and the quotations from DuBois and Ballou, come from the best published history of black participation in the war: Barbeau and Henri, *Unknown Soldiers,* chap. 5, esp. pp. 82–83.

48. A copy of "Bulletin No. 35" is in 10218-120-3, RG 165, MID, NARA. See also Barbeau and Henri, *Unknown Soldiers,* pp. 86–88.

49. Capt. Howard F. K. Cahill, Acting Div. IO, 93rd Div., Camp Sherman, to Chief, MIB, 11 Apr. 1918, 10218-120-5, RG 165, MID, NARA.

50. Capt. George N. Northrop, Asst. IO, Camp Dodge, to Chief, MIB, 11 May 1918, 10218-120-20; Van Deman to Chief of Staff, 22 Apr. 1918, 10218-120-15; and Loving to Chief, MIB, 16 and 18 Apr. 1918, 10218-120-14, and 25 Apr. 1918, 10218-120-17, RG 165, MID, NARA.

51. 1st Lt. Emery L. Bryan, IO, Camp Upton, to Chief, MIB, 3 June 1918, 10218-168-1; Churchill to Bryan, 22 June 1918, 10218-168-2; and Capt. Emery L. Bryan to Chief, MIB, 23 June 1918, 10218-168-3, RG 165, MID, NARA.

52. Low to Van Deman, 5 June 1918, 10218-165-2, RG 165, MID, NARA.

53. Charles H. Williams, "Resume of Conditions Surrounding Negro Troops," 5 Aug. 1918, 10218-279-1, RG 165, MID, NARA.

54. George W. Jackson to Baker, 11 June 1918, 10218-184-1; Churchill to W. P. Harod, 16 July 1918, 10218-184-3; Herod to Chief, MIB, 2 Aug. 1918, 10218-184-7; and Perkins to Jackson, 12 Aug. 1918, 10218-184-10, RG 165, MID, NARA.

55. Talbert, *Negative Intelligence,* pp. 125–27; Churchill to Scott, 2 Aug. 1918, 10218-193-1, RG 165, MID, NARA.

56. Barbeau and Henri, *Unknown Soldiers,* pp. 79–80.

57. Camp Jackson soldiers' complaints: Anonymous men of Sanitary Corps P.2 Company, to Secretary of War, 30 July 1918, 10218-201-1; anonymous, 16 July 1918, 10218-201-7; E. W. Scott to Emmett J. Scott, 4 Aug. 1918, 10218-201-6; anonymous to Emmett J. Scott, 8 Aug. 1918, 10218-201-9; anonymous to Emmett J. Scott, 19 Oct. 1918, 10218-201-22; anonymous to Emmett J. Scott, 20 Oct. 1918, 10218-201-23; anonymous to I. F. Simmons, Secretary, Army YMCA, Hampton Institute, 5 Nov. 1918, 10218-201-25; and (eight soldiers) to Simmons, ? Nov. 1918, 10218-201-29, RG 165, MID, NARA. Official responses are: Emmett J. Scott to Capt. J. E. Cutler, Military Morale Section, 8 Aug. 1918,

10218-201-2; Perkins to Capt. C. W. B. Long, IO, Camp Jackson, 10 Aug. 1918, 10218-201-4; 3 Sept. 1918, 10218-201-8; Perkins to Emmett J. Scott, 3 Sept. 1918, 10218-201-11; Capt. Ralston Fleming, Acting IO, Camp Jackson, to Perkins, 1 Sept. 1918, 10218-201-18; Perkins to Fleming, 13 Sept. 1918, 10218-201-21; Churchill to Fleming, 22 Nov. 1918, 10218-201-24; Simmons to Emmett J. Scott, 10 Nov. 1918, 10218-201-26, and 17 Nov. 1918, 10218-201-30; Emmett J. Scott to Gen. E. L. Munson, Chief, Morale Branch, 23 Nov. 1918, 10218-201-31; and Masteller (by Cutler) to Emmett J. Scott, 26 Nov. 1918, 10218-215, RG 165, MID, NARA. For details on Cutler, see Kornweibel, *"Seeing Red,"* p. 56.

58. William Lloyd Imes, YMCA Secretary, Camp Upton, to Emmett J. Scott, 18 Aug. 1918, 10218-209-15; Maj. L. B. Dunham, IO, Port of Embarkation, Hoboken, to Chief, MIB, 21 Aug. 1918. 10218-209-2; Capt. G. B. Perkins, Chief, Military Morale Section, to Dunham, 28 Aug. 1918, 10218-209-3; Dunham to Perkins, 30 Aug. 1918, 10218-209-4; Capt. Emery L. Bryan, IO, Camp Upton, to Dunham, 11 Sept. 1918, 10218-209-19; Perkins to Dunham, 25 Sept. 1918, 10218-209-21; Perkins to Scott, 27 Sept. 1918, 10219-209-23; Scott to Churchill, 23 Nov. 1918, 10218-209-8; Cutler to Low, 26 Nov. 1918, 10218-209-22; Loving to Perkins, 29 Nov. 1918, 10218-209-26; and Dunham to Acting Director Military Intelligence, 15 Jan. 1919, 10218-209-28, RG 165, MID, NARA.

59. Churchill to Emmett J. Scott, enclosing handwritten memos from Quander Hall, 31 Aug. 1918, 10218-215-3, RG 165, MID, NARA.

60. Benjamin L. Joyce, YMCA Secretary, Camp Travis, to Emmett J. Scott, 4 Sept. 1918, 10218-216-4, and 18 Oct. 1918, 10218-216-9; Perkins to Capt. G. D. March, IO, Auxiliary Units, Camp Travis, 5 Sept. 1918, 10218-216-3; Scott to Perkins, 11 Sept. 1918, 10218-216-5; Perkins to IO, Camp Travis, 19 Sept. 1918, 10218-216-6; Capt. Samuel L. Gill, IO, Camp Travis, to Director, Military Intelligence, 14 Oct. 1918, 10218-216-7; Scott to Cutler, 25 Oct. 1918, 10218-216-10; Brig. Gen. E. L. Munson, Chief, Military Morale Branch, to IO, Camp Travis, 31 Oct. 1918, 10218-216-12; Masteller (by Cutler) to Scott, 22 Nov. 1918, 10218-216-15; and Cutler to Low, 31 Nov. 1918, 10218-216-11, RG 165, MID, NARA.

61. Emmett J. Scott to Perkins, 31 Aug. 1918, 10218-220-2; and Perkins to IO, Camp Wheeler, 5 Sept. 1918, 10218-220-3, RG 165, MID, NARA.

62. Luther F. Simpkins to Emmett J. Scott, 3 Oct. 1918, 10218-243-1, and 18 Oct. 1918, 10218-243-6; Cpls. Elijah Freeman and Fred W. Cary to Scott, 17 Oct. 1918, 10218-243-5; Brig. Gen. E. L. Munson to IO, Camp Pike, 24 Oct. 1918, 10218-243-3; Loving to Cutler, 8 Nov. 1918, 10218-243-8; Maj. Eugene E. Barton, IO to Munson, 15 Nov. 1918, 10218-243-3; and Masteller to Scott, 21 Nov. 1918, 10218-243-4, and 23 Nov. 1918, 10218-243-9, RG 165, MID, NARA.

63. Anonymous to Maj. J. E. Spingarn, 29 Aug 1918, 10218-221-1; W. P. Kemp, editor, *Detroit Leader,* to Scott, 30 Aug. 1918, 10218-221-8; Peter J. Smith to Scott, 3 Sept. 1918, 10218-221-5; anonymous to "My Dear Sir," 3 Sept. 1918, 10218-221-6; Perkins to IO, Camp Humphreys, 11 Sept. 1918, 10218-221-4; Scott to Cutler, 14 Sept. 1918, 10218-221-9; "One of Them" to Scott, 16 Sept. 1918, 10218-221-16; Perkins to Scott, 17 Sept. 1918, 10218-221-10; Perkins to IO, Camp Humphreys, 2 Oct. 1918, 10218-221-11; Perkins to Smith, 3 Oct. 1918, 10218-221-12; and Col E. L. Munson, Chief, Morale Section, to Kemp, 11 Oct. 1918, 10218-221-14, RG 165, MID, NARA; Barbeau and Henri, *Unknown Soldiers,* p. 51.

64. Capt. Harry A. Taylor, IO, Port of Embarkation, Newport News, to Director, Military Intelligence, 5 Nov. 1918, 10218-258-1, RG 165, MID, NARA.

65. "Friends of the Camp" to Emmett J. Scott, 27 Sept. 1918, 10218-238-8; Corp. Robert Edward Williams to "Dear Pastor," 1 Oct. 1918,10218-238-1; Brig. Gen. E. L. Munson to IO, Camp Abraham Eustis, 16 Oct. 1918, 10218-238-2; Capt. G. U. Gates, IO, Camp Eustis, to Chief, Morale Branch, 19 Oct. 1918, 10218-238-3; Munson to Scott, 25 Oct. 1918, 10218-238-11; Churchill to Gates, 5 Nov. 1918, 10218-238-5; and Masteller to Scott, 14 Nov. 1918, 10218-238-7, and 21 Nov. 1918, 10218-238-10, RG 165, MID, NARA.

66. Anonymous to "Dear Sir," 31 Aug. 1918, 10218-226; "A Friend to the boys" to Emmett J. Scott, 1 Sept. 1918, 10218-226-1; "The Colored boys of the 418th Reserve Labor Battalion" to Scott, 12 Sept. 1918, 10218-226-7/W; W. L. Anderson to Scott, 13 Sept. 1918, 10218-226-4; Brig. Gen. E. L. Munson to IO, Camp Sherman, 19 Oct. 1918, 10218-226-6; Capt. Robert M. Sohngen, IO, Camp Sherman, to Munson, 24 Oct. 1918, 10218-226-8; and Munson to Scott, 29 Oct. 1918, 10218-226-9, and 23 Nov. 1918, 10218-226-13, RG 165, MID, NARA.

67. "A Soldier for the Country" to Madam, 28 Aug. 1918, 10218-227-1; Mary F. Waring to Emmett J. Scott, 3 Sept. 1918, 10218-227-2; eight privates, Camp Grant, to J. D. Stevenson, 10218-227-8; Perkins to IO, Camp Grant, 25 Sept. 1918, 10218-227-4; 1st Lt. P. J. Krausnick, IO, Camp Grant, to Chief, Military Morale Section, 2 Oct. 1918, 10218-227-5; Munson to Waring, 7 Oct. 1918, 10218-227-6; Munson to Scott, 7 Oct. 1918, 10218-227-7; Munson to IO, Camp Grant, 26 Oct. 1918, 10218-227-11; 2nd Lt. J. Murray Mitchell, IO, Camp Grant, to Munson, 31 Oct. 1918, 10218-227-12; and Masteller to Scott, 26 Nov. 1918, 10218-227-13, RG 165, MID, NARA.

68. Anonymous to "Miss Maddox," 12 Sept. 1918, 10218-260-1; anonymous to Emmett J. Scott, 18 Oct. 1918, 10218-260-2; Churchill to IO, Camp Greene, 22 Nov. 1918, 10218-260-5; and 1st Lt. R. J. McCandlish, IO, to Churchill, 25 Nov. 1918, 10218-260-6, RG 165, MID, NARA.

69. "Colored Servicemen of Camp Dodge" to Emmett J. Scott, 9 Sept. 1918, 10218-233-1; and Maj. Jackson R. Day, Asst. IO, Camp Dodge, to Military Morale Section, 9 Oct. 1918, 10218-233-4, RG 165, MID, NARA.

70. Anonymous to Emmett J. Scott, 28 Sept. 1918, 10218-239-3; Archibald Grimke to Emmett J. Scott, 12 Oct. 1918, 10218-239-1; Brig. Gen. E. L. Munson to IO, 12th Div., Camp Devens, 15 Oct. 1918, 10218-239-2; Scott to Cutler, Oct. 16, 1918, 10218-239-10; Capt. Ernest J. Hall, Asst. Div. IO, to Munson, 18 Oct. 1918, 10218-239-6; Munson to Hall, 23 Oct. 1918, 10218-239-7; Munson to Scott, 23 Oct. 1918, 10218-239-8; Hall to Churchill, 21 Oct. 1918, 10218-239-15; Churchill to Hall, 29 Oct. 1918, 10218-239-16; Hall to Munson, 3 Nov. 1918, 10218-239-24; Masteller to Scott, 25 Nov. 1918, 10218-239-26; "Negroes Charge 'Slavery' at Devens," letter to the editor from "Soldiers 800 Strong," *Boston American,* 25 Feb. 1919, 10218-239-30; 1st Lt. Royal H. Place, IO to Acting Director Military Intelligence, 26 Feb. 1919, 10218-239-32; and Maj. Gen. H. P. McCain to Acting Director Military Intelligence, 26 Feb. 1919, 10218-239-33, RG 165, MID, NARA.

71. Loving to Chief, Military Morale Section, 24 Nov. 1918, 10218-279-8, RG 165, MID, NARA.

72. Loving to Cutler, Chief, Military Morale Section, 14 Sept. 1918, 10218-280-1, RG 165, MID, NARA.

73. Loving to Cutler, 23 Sept. 1918, 10218-280-11, RG 165, MID, NARA; Barbeau and Henri, *Unknown Soldiers,* pp. 62–63.

74. Loving to Cutler, 27 Sept. 1918, 10218-280-10, RG 165, MID, NARA.

75. Loving to Cutler, 2 Oct. 1918, 10218-280-9, RG 165, MID, NARA.
76. Loving to Cutler, 4 Oct. 1918, 10218-280-8, RG 165, MID, NARA.
77. Loving to Cutler, 9 Oct. 1918, 10218-280-7, RG 165, MID, NARA.
78. Loving to Cutler, 10 Oct. 1918, 10218-280-6, RG 165, MID, NARA.
79. Loving to Cutler, 13 Oct. 1918, 10218-280-5, RG 165, MID, NARA.
80. Loving to Cutler, 28 Oct. 1918, 10218-280-4, RG 165, MID, NARA.
81. Loving to Cutler, 2 Nov. 1918, 10218-280-2, RG 165, MID, NARA.
82. Loving to Cutler, 8 Nov. 1918, 10218-280-3, RG 165, MID, NARA.
83. Loving to Cutler, 16 Nov. 1918, 10218-280-1, RG 165, MID, NARA.
84. Loving to Cutler, 24 Nov. 1918, 10218-280-12. The same document is in 10218-279-8, RG 165, MID, NARA.
85. Low to Col. John M. Dunn, Acting Director, MID, 29 Nov. 1918, 10218-265-1; Dunn to Loving, 3 Dec. 1918, 10218-265-2; Loving to Director, Military Intelligence, 6 Dec. 1918, 10218-265-3; Dunn to Maj. L. B. Dunham, IO, Port of Embarkation, 19 Dec. 1918, 10218-265-4; and Dunham to Dunn, 28 Dec. 1918, 10218-265-5, RG 165, MID, NARA.
86. Mrs. E. H. Jefferson to Emmett J. Scott, 19 Dec. 1918, 10218-270-1; Dunn to Capt. Geo. J. Lyon, 20 Dec. 1918, 10218-270-3; Capt. A. H. Toole to Maj. R. C. Smith, 2 Jan 1919, 10218-270-4; and Lt. Col. D. G. C. Garrison to Scott, 7 Jan 1919, 10218-270-6, RG 165, MID, NARA.
87. Pvt. George Canada to Baker, 25 Nov. 1918, 10218-267-1; Emmett J. Scott to Cutler, 2 Dec. 1918, 10218-267-2; Dunn to IO, Camp McArthur, 10 Dec. 1918, 10218-267-3; 2nd Lt. Warner Keyser to IO, Camp McArthur, 28 Dec. 1918, 10218-267-4; and Masteller to Scott, 4 Jan. 1919, 10218-267-6, RG 165, MID, NARA.
88. Kornweibel, *"Seeing Red,"* pp. 55–57.
89. S. F. Shattuck, General Secretary, YMCA to Capt. R. G. Heard, Asst. IO, 17 Dec. 1918, 10218-273-2; 1st Lt. John C. Grout to Commanding Officer, 419th Reserve Labor Battalion, 16 Dec., 1918, 10218-273-3; 1st Lt. Terry H. Kaner to Commanding Officer, 419th Reserve Labor Battalion, 17 Dec. 1918, 10218-273-5; 1st Lt. N. R. Harned to Commanding Officer, 419th Reserve Labor Battalion, 17 Dec. 1918, 10218-273-6; Heard to Director, MID, 17 Dec. 1918, 10218-273-7; Dunn to Wilman E. Adams, YMCA Headquarters, 2 Jan. 1919, 10218-273-8; and Adams to Dunn, 7 Jan. 1919, 10218-273-9, RG 165, MID, NARA.
90. 1st Lt. Gordon F. Stephens to ?, 20 Dec. 1918, 10218-276, RG 165, MID, NARA.
91. Statements of Sgt. Cyrus W. Perry, Pvt. Fletcher Brewer, and Seaman William B. Dulshire, 11 Dec. 1918; memorandum, 1st Lt. James C. Scarff, 10 Dec. 1918; and memorandum of conference, 14 Dec. 1918, 10218-272-3; Maj. Thomas W. Davis, Judge Advocate, to Commanding General, Southeastern Department, 19 Dec. 1918, 10218-272-5; and Maj. Gen. Henry G. Sharpe, Commanding, Southeastern Department, to Charleston Mayor Tristam T. Hyde, 20 Dec. 1918, 10218-272-6, RG 165, MID, NARA.
92. "Kentucky Mob Hangs Hero of Democracy," clipping, unidentified black newspaper, ? Dec. 1918, 10218-274-1, RG 165, MID, NARA.
93. Barbeau and Henri, *Unknown Soldiers,* pp. 22–23; Talbert, *Negative Intelligence,* pp. 124–25.
94. Loving to Director, Military Intelligence, 23 Dec. 1918, 10218-274-2; and Dunn to Bielaski, 30 Dec. 1918, 10218-274-3, RG 165, MID, NARA.
95. Talbert, *Negative Intelligence,* p. 124.

96. Capt. J. C. Auchincloss, "Memorandum for Colored Women Employees," 24 Oct. 1918, and Miss Juanita M. Curtis et al. to Emmett J. Scott, 26 Oct. 1918, 10218-252; Scott to Churchill, 7 Nov. 1918, 10218-252-1; Auchincloss to Churchill, 13 Nov. 1918, 10218-252-2; and Churchill to Scott, 13 Nov. 1918, 10218-252-3, RG 165, MID, NARA.

97. "M. I. 3 Bulletin for Intelligence Officers. No. 31," 21 Oct. 1918, 10218-279-7, RG 165, MID, NARA.

Epilogue

1. Capt. Fred W. Moore, IO, Northeastern Dept., to Col. Marlborough Churchill, Chief, Military Intelligence Branch, 5 June 1918, 10218-153-5, and 19 June 1918, 10218-153-7; and Churchill to Moore, 13 June 1918, 10218-153-6, RG 165, MID, NARA.

2. The petition is printed in Trotter's *Guardian,* 6 July 1918, copy in 10218-153, RG 165, MID, NARA.

3. Excerpts from Addresses at Colored Liberty Congress, n.d., 10218-153-8, RG 165, MID, NARA.

4. Agent J. G. C. Corcoran to Bureau, 11, 20, and 28 Sept. 1918, OG 369936, RG 65, BI, NARA.

5. Lowenthal, *Federal Bureau of Investigation,* pp. 48–50.

6. U.S. Senate, *Investigation Activities of the Department of Justice.* 66th Cong., 1st sess., Sen. Doc. 153 (Washington, D.C., 1919), p. 13.

7. Ibid., pp. 172–73, 179, 181–82, 184; Kornweibel, *No Crystal Stair,* chap. 3.

8. Kornweibel, "'Black on Black,'" pp. 121–36.

Index

Abbott, Robert, 1–2, 5, 7, 8, 118, 120, 121, 124–130, 141

Abrams case, 138, 164, 175, 188

Adsit, B. D. (Bureau Agent), 122

African Blood Brotherhood, 273

Agents, Bureau of Investigation: Adsit, B. D., 122; Ambrose, C. B., 92; Austin, Will C., 90; Baldwin, B. C., 70; Banville, L. P., 67; Bauserman, Joseph M., 58–59; Beckham, Clifford G., 119; Bennett, S. D., 102; Bingham, Goundry W., 58; Bishop, H. D., 61; Bocock, Branch, 51–52, 64; Boyd, N., 113–144; Braun, Charles B., 66; Breniman, Charles E., 90, 176; Buck, W. H., 185; Burks, Charles E., 66; Calmes, George C., 93, 114; Cash, Albert D., 97, 112, 117; Chastain, Edward S., 73; Clabaugh, Hinton G., 50; Clark, Frank G., 50; Corcoran, James Grover Cleveland, 205–210, 214, 215–216, 225; Corgan, Charles E., 61, 99; Cotton, Fred, 99; Craig, Arthur Ulysses (informant), 205, 214, 220–221; Darden, George L., 71; Daughton, Ralph H., 40, 46, 60, 91, 95; Davidson, D., 190–191; Dawson, Ralph K., 61, 95–96, 104; DeNette, Louis, 172; Doggrell, C. L., 107, 108, 117; Dolan, J. W., 113; Doyas, William N., 110; Englesby, Leverett, 64–65, 66; Finch, R. W., 183, 184; Folsom, J. P., 111; Garbarino, Frank L., 92; Gere, R., 136; Goggin, 108–110; Graham, Denver, 99–100; Grimes, Warren W., 165–166; Gulley, Harry D., 93–94, 154–155; Hadba, F. George, 111; Haggerly, F. C., 62; Hanna, Mark, 65, 68, 71, 107, 108; Harper, J. W., 69; Harris, Billups, 111; Hawkins, J. E., 120–121; Henry, Lewie H., 100, 159–160; Holman, George T., 153; Hote, J. F., 94; Hughes, Vincent W., 195–198; Jackson, Howell E., 141; Kelly, Paul J., 105; Kerwin, E. J., 63–64, 126; Killick, V. W., 158; Learned, H. Barrett (dollar-a-year agent), 201, 213, 216, 220; Lewis, Horace A., 62; Light, Claude P., 167; Lillard, George W., 200; Mallet, C. V., 92; Matthews, J. B., 115–116, 193–194; McAdory, T. F., 107; McCaleb, Claude, 157–158; McElveen, W. E., 108, 155–156; McKnight, R. S., 103–104; Murphy, Edward M., 92; Murphy, John B., 64; Murphy, William L., 96, 208; Murray, J. Reese, 68; Muse, C. M., 115; Neunhoffer, Albert, 139; Outlaw, Calvin, 94; Palmer, Eugene, 156–157; Patterson, J. R., 96; Pendleton, Forrest C., 69–70, 119; Pfeifer, S. B., 165; Phifer, Robert S., 43; Schaumburger, M. M., 94, 152–153; Smith, George C., 99; Spates, Webster, 92; Spencer, F. M., 45, 69; Stevens, L. T., 101; Stevenson, Archibald E., 272; Stewart, Malcolm M., 106–107; Stillson, 70; Thompson, L. O., 60; Trazivuk, Daniel, 89–90; Walser, C. M., 43–44, 194; Webb, J. L., 175–180; Weymouth, W. A., 71, 96; Whalen, John A., 207; Winn, DeWitt S., 157–158, 159, 163, 168, 169; Wiseman, W. A., 180; Young, 108–110

Alien Act, 19

Ambrose, C. B. (Bureau Agent), 92

American Protective League: and draft enforcement, 76; and Moens case, 208; and NAACP, 50; mentioned, 3, 14–15, 16, 17, 20, 21, 22, 23–24, 28, 29, 37–38, 50–51, 52, 68, 71, 76, 77, 85, 97, 98, 99, 105, 106, 108–109, 111, 113, 116, 126, 137, 185, 244, 250–251

American Union Against Militarism, 33
Anderson, Harvey J., 167
Angeloff, George, 193–195, 199
Apathy, of blacks toward draft, 2, 4, 80–83, 84, 85, 97, 117, 243, 274
Army intelligence, in WWI: and *Chicago Defender,* 123–124, 129, 130; and *Crisis,* 6, 140; Military Morale Section, 250–257, 269; and Moens case, 202–205; mentioned, 3, 8, 9, 10, 11, 12, 14, 16, 17, 21, 23, 24–32, 33, 34, 130, 132, 144, 199–226 passim, 235–238, 247–250, 275. *See also* Military Intelligence Branch; Military Intelligence Division; Military Intelligence Section
Atlanta Independent, 241–242
Austin, Will C. (Bureau Agent), 90
Austro-Hungarians, in U.S.: Freudenheim, 190–193; mentioned, 189–193

Bagman, M., 200
Baker, Newton D., 22, 24–25, 26, 34, 36, 135, 140, 143, 144
Baldwin, B. C. (Bureau Agent), 70
Ballou, Charles C., 243, 247–249
Baltimore Afro-American, 82, 123, 125, 135
Banville, L. P. (Bureau Agent), 67
Bauserman, Joseph M. (Bureau Agent), 58–59
Beckham, Clifford G. (Bureau Agent), 119
Bennett, S. D. (Bureau Agent), 102
Bettman, Alfred, 22, 38, 51, 136–137
Bielaski, A. Bruce: and *Chicago Defender,* 119, 120, 122, 126; and COGIC, 156, 157; and *Crisis,* 106, 136–137, 144; and Moens case, 205, 207, 211; mentioned, 12, 14, 16, 20–21, 22, 24, 40, 41, 43, 47, 50, 51, 56, 57, 58, 59, 63, 72, 73–74, 75, 91, 194–195
Bingham, Goundry W. (Bureau Agent), 58
Bishop, H. D. (Bureau Agent), 61
Bocock, Branch (Bureau Agent), 51–52
Bolshevism: in *Messenger,* 182; in publications, 33; mentioned, 3, 9, 19, 24, 29, 31, 35, 129, 271–272, 273
Boston Guardian, 82, 230, 233, 270
Bouldin, G. W., 7, 170–175, 274
Bowen, J. W. E., 241
Bowen, Roger, 128
Boyd, N. (Bureau Agent), 113–114
Branch, Elijah C., 175–180, 181
Braun, Charles B. (Bureau Agent), 66
Breniman, C. E. (Bureau Agent), 176
Bruce, Roscoe Conkling, 220, 221, 235
Bryan, William Jennings, 12
Buck, W. H. (Bureau Agent), 185
Bulgarians, in U.S., 193–195
Bulletin No. 35, 243, 247–249, 312n48
Bureau of Investigation: and *Chicago Defender,* 119–123, 126, 129; and COGIC, 150, 152, 157, 159; and *Crisis,* 132, 133–134, 136, 137; and *Messenger,* 137, 184; and Moens case, 200–202, 205–225 passim; mentioned, 2–3, 4, 5, 8, 9, 11, 12, 13, 14, 15, 20–21, 22–23, 24, 26, 31, 32, 34, 38–39, 46, 47, 48, 49, 51, 55, 56, 60, 61, 63, 64, 65, 66, 67, 68, 69, 71, 72, 73, 76, 80, 85, 87, 91, 92, 94, 95, 97, 102, 103, 110, 115, 116, 117, 130, 135, 167, 168, 171, 177, 186–187, 190, 195, 226, 228, 229, 230, 243, 247, 271, 272, 274, 275. *See also* Agents, Bureau of Investigation; Justice Department
Bureau M-1. *See* Translation Bureau
Burks, Charles E. (Bureau Agent), 66
Burleson, Albert Sidney, 18, 19, 31, 32, 33, 36, 134, 139

Caffey, Francis G., 191–192
Calmes, George C. (Bureau Agent), 93, 114
Camp Merritt case, 253–254
Cash, Albert D. (Bureau Agent), 112
Chastain, Edward S. (Bureau Agent), 73
Chicago Defender, 1–2, 5, 8, 61, 118–131 passim, 132, 135, 141, 272–273, 274
Chicago Home Guards, 232
Church, Robert R., 234, 238–239
Church of God in Christ (COGIC): and conscientious objectors, 151–152, 297–298n47; and racial mingling, 188; mentioned, 6, 8–9, 85, 149–163 passim, 274–275
Churchill, Marlborough: and COGIC, 159; and Moens case, 207; mentioned, 16, 25, 26, 27, 28, 36, 141–142, 146, 178, 194–195, 243, 245, 246, 250, 251, 257, 267, 269, 270
Clabaugh, Hinton G. (Bureau Agent), 50
Clark, Frank G. (Bureau Agent), 50
Cleveland Gazette, 81–82
Cobb, James, 200
Colored Liberty Congress, 270–272
Committee on Public Information (CPI) 19, 27, 33, 34, 125, 143, 246, 270
Conscientious objectors: and COGIC, 8–9, 149–163; mentioned, 7, 84, 85, 151–152
Conscription, enforcement of: in Alabama, 106–108; in California, 96; in Georgia, 114; in Illinois, 111–112; in Louisiana, 93, 101,

115–116; in Mississippi, 93; in Missouri, 103; in New York, 98–99; in the North, 91–93, 96–97; in North Dakota, 105; in Ohio, 112; in the South, 93–96; in Tennessee, 103, 109–110; in Texas, 89–90, 93, 100, 101, 102, 114; in Virginia, 91, 95–96, 103–104; in Washington, 96; in West Virginia, 100–101; in Wisconsin, 105; mentioned, 76–117 passim. *See also* Draft evasion, accused of
Coolidge, Calvin, 223
Corcoran, James Grover Cleveland (Bureau Agent), 205–210, 214, 215–216, 225
Corgan, Charles E. (Bureau Agent), 61, 99
Cotton, Fred (Bureau Agent), 99
Council of National Defense, 26
Craig, Arthur Ulysses (Bureau Informant), 205, 214, 220–221
Crisis, 2, 5, 6, 81, 118, 123, 125, 126, 132–148 passim, 192, 230, 243, 263, 272–273, 274. *See also* DuBois, W. E. B.; National Association for the Advancement of Colored People; Spingarn, Joel E.
Crowder, Enoch, 76, 77, 78–79, 80, 87, 93, 114
Crusader, 2, 148, 273
Culture Forum, 222
Cutler, James E., 253, 254, 268–269

Daniels, Josephus, 34
Darden, George L. (Bureau Agent), 71
Daughton, Ralph H. (Bureau Agent), 40, 46, 60
Davidson, D. (Bureau Agent), 190–191
Davis, Benjamin J., 241–242
Dawson, Ralph K. (Bureau Agent), 60–61
Defender. See Chicago Defender
DeNette, Louis (Bureau Agent), 172
The Disgrace of Democracy, 62, 74, 165–166, 239–240
Disloyalty, accused of: Anderson, Harvey J., 167–168; Angeloff, George, 193–195, 199; Arbor, Will, 57–58; Arthur, Juanita, 217; Bouldin, G. W., 7, 170–175, 274; Branch, Elijah C., 175–180, 181; Branch, Henry, 59–60; Brown, George, 242; Brown, John Richard, 39–40; Bryant, Ollie, 69; Burnett, Ferdinand, 50; Burroughs, Nannie, 228–229; Chiles, Nick, 40; Clark, Mary, 60; Doyle, Sam, 66; Freudenheim, Max, 190–193, 199; Hammond, Mary, 107; Hegwood, William L., 171, 172; Hunter, Charlotte E., 204, 205, 213, 216–217, 220–221; Jackson, John W., 164–167, 170; Jones, Lonnie, 65–66; Kelly, Clem, 242; Kingsberry, William, 242; Lewis, Charles, 266; Martin, Eliza, 52–53; Martin, Granville, 52–53; Mason, Charles H., 1, 6–7, 149–163, 164, 170, 274–275; Mason, William, 44; Matthews, F. W., 65; McCrady, Dan, 61; McKinney, Sheppard, 42; Miller, J. H., 66–67; Moens, Herman Marie Bernelot, 7–8, 199–225 passim, 271, 275; Moore, Charles, 195–196; Mosely, Jesse, 66; Murphy, Pat, 236–237; Nance, Will, 61; Patterson, William L., 82; Powell, Reverend, 69–70; Robinson, J. G., 50–51; Roman, C. V., 229–230; Ross, William, 42; Rourk, W. W., 68; Saunders, Helen, 205–210, 214, 215, 216, 224, 225; Sutton, Jacob, 58–59; Threadgill-Dennis, Clara L., 1, 171–175; Titus, Alfred W., 60; Titus, John Kenneth, 60; Wilson, Henry, 68; Wilson, Sidney, 84; Wright, William, 57–58; Young, Ernest B., 195–198, 301–302n21
Doggrell, C. L. (Bureau Agent), 107, 108
Dolan, J. W. (Bureau Agent), 113
Doyas, William N. (Bureau Agent), 111
Draft evasion, accused of: Anderson, Foster, 92; Anderson, William Penn, 105; Bailey, Frank, 94; Black, Walter, 107; Bonner, Warren, 109; Boyce, Monroe, 94; Brown, Archy, 95; Brown, Willie, 108; Cain, Isaac, 96; Carey, James Arthur, 96; Chatman, Joe, 99; Clay, James, 102; Dickson, Herman, 104; Dixon, Odice, 106; Eaglin, Ollie, 89–90; Ellis, Edward, 105; Felder, Andrew, 102; Fulnettle, Bill, 90; Gainey, Monroe, 95–96; Grant, Ed, 94; Green, Isaac, 113; Green, Thomas, 100–101, 102; Green, Willie, 101; Griffin, James, 95; Hairston, Clarence, 92; Hall, Henry, 113; Hardy, Jim, 90; Harris, Dudley, 106; Harrison, Edgar, 106; Harrison, Sam, 106; Harvey, H., 101, 102; Hayes, William Conly, 96; Jackson, James, 102; Jacobs, Rudolph Nathaniel, 96; James, Frank, 90; Johnson, George, 102; Johnson, Roy, 111; Johnson, Sheridan, 92; Jones, Ivanhoe, 104; Jones, W. M., 106–107; Kelly, John D., 107; Knox, James, 104; Lewis, Dallas, 92; Lewis, Hollis, 92; Looney, Charles, 109; Lowe, Lex Leo, 115; Lynn, George, 109; McKinney, Henry, 109; McKissach, Ira Vincent, 111; McLendon, Joe, 107; McRae, Thomas, 115; Mabb, Nathaniel, 92; Mack, Eugene, 102; Martin, Lee, 97;

Mason, Frank T., 115; Moore, John A., 110; Myers, Arthur, 110; Nance, Marcus, 93; Neal, Peter, 94; Newsome, Dupree, 90; Scott, Abraham, 92; Scott, Douglas, 103; Scott, Edgar, 111; Scott, Elijah, 91; Scott, Guy, 104; Scott, Perry, 90; Scott, Will, 100; Smith, Alonso Clinton, 111–112; Steed, Ephiram, 112; Stewart, Charley, 94–95; Story, Carl Shafter, 103; Suber, Willie, 107; Taylor, George, 104; Terry, John, 103; Thomas, Sam, 108–109; Thompson, Love, 113–114; Thous, N. L., 115–116; Traylor, Edward, 101; Wadley, Aaron, 109; Walker, Jesse, 111; Walker, Pete, 107; Walters, Joseph Robert, 92; Ward, S. H., 92; Washington, Flin, 103, 104; Watkins, Charles, 91–92; Webb, John, 113; Webster, Jerry, 113; Williams, Jim, 111; Williams, Thomas, 107; Williams, Willie, 101, 102; Wilson, George, 101; Wimberly, Ellis, 108; Young, Hemp, 94
Driver, E. R., 153, 154, 157, 158
DuBois, W. E. B.: and "Close Ranks" editorial, 142, 145–146; mentioned, 2, 6, 118, 125–126, 132–148 passim, 181, 199, 230, 239, 247, 251, 263, 273

East St. Louis riot, 1, 4, 50, 53, 62, 71, 80, 81, 122, 136, 227, 228–229, 231, 238, 239, 241, 244, 266, 285n67
Englesby, Leverett (Bureau Agent), 64–65, 66
Espionage Act: and *Chicago Defender,* 121, 122, 123, 129, 130; and First Amendment, 164; and Freudenheim case, 191, 192; and Moens case, 225; passage of, 17–18, 19; and radical press, 133, 136, 137, 146; mentioned, 3, 7, 9, 20, 21, 22, 31–32, 33, 56, 57–58, 62, 73, 121, 135, 139, 166–167, 170, 171, 174, 175, 176, 180, 183, 185, 186, 191, 192, 196, 197, 198, 274

Finch, R. W. (Bureau Agent), 183, 184
First Amendment: and *Abrams* case, 164; and *Schenck* case, 164; mentioned, 3, 32, 39, 133, 138, 190, 192, 193, 274
Florence Daily Times, 40
Flynn, William J., 13, 14, 15, 17
Folsom, J. P. (Bureau Agent), 111
Freudenheim, Max, 190–193, 199

Galveston Colored American, 181
Galveston New Idea, 61–62, 175–177, 180, 181
Garbarino, Frank L. (Bureau Agent), 92
Garvey, Marcus, 153, 272, 273
General Intelligence Division (GID), 130, 291–292n35
Gere, R. (Bureau Agent), 136
Germans, in U.S.: suspected, 54–55; mentioned, 10, 11, 12, 24, 25, 29, 37, 189–190
Giannokulion, Dimitrius, 153–154
Goggin (Bureau Agent), 108–110
Graham, Denver (Bureau Agent), 99–100
Great Migration: and churches, 150; mentioned, 2, 4, 9, 41, 52, 74, 84, 108, 110, 118, 177, 181, 276
Gregory, Thomas Watt: and Moens case, 214; mentioned, 11–12, 13, 14, 15, 16, 17, 18, 21–22, 24, 31, 36, 37, 99, 114, 125, 135
Grimes, Warren W. (Bureau Agent), 165–166
Grimke, Francis J., 81
Gulley, Harry D. (Bureau Agent), 154–155

Hadba, F. George (Bureau Agent), 111
Haggerly, F. C. (Bureau Agent), 62
Hall, Quander E., 246, 255
Hanna, Mark (Bureau Agent), 65, 68, 71, 107, 108
Harper, J. W. (Bureau Agent), 69
Harris, Billups, (Bureau Agent), 111
Harrison, Hubert H., 270–271
Hawkins, J. E. (Bureau Agent), 120–121
Henry, Lewie H. (Bureau Agent), 159–160
Hoff, G. R., 178–180
Holman, George T. (Bureau Agent), 153
Holt, W. B., 154, 155, 157, 158, 159, 160, 162
Hoover, J. Edgar: and General Intelligence Division, 130; and Moens case, 223
Hote, J. F. (Bureau Agent), 94
Houston mutiny, 7, 50, 80, 123, 133–134, 235, 238, 240, 241, 274, 285n68
Houston Observer, 176
Hughes, Vincent W. (Bureau Agent), 195–198
Hunter, Charlotte E., 204, 205, 213, 216–217, 220–221
Hurley, William L., 34

Imes, William Lloyd, 253, 254
Industrial Workers of the World: attempts to suppress, 5, 16, 21, 133, 273; and Haywood trial, 164; mentioned, 28, 29, 33, 35, 85, 138, 149, 170, 174
Issues of Today, 221

Jackson, Howell E. (Bureau Agent), 141
Jackson, John W., 164–167, 170
Jehovah's Witnesses: and Bouldin trial, 170–175;

and McNairy case, 168–170, 275; and racial mingling, 188; mentioned, 85
Johnson, Georgia Douglas, 213
Johnson, Henry Lincoln, 213, 242
Johnson, James Weldon, 80–81
Journal of the National Medical Association, 30
Justice Department: and *Chicago Defender,* 122; and COGIC, 150, 156, 159, 163; and *Crisis,* 6, 134, 139–140, 144; and *Messenger,* 182, 183; and Moens case, 205–225 passim; mentioned, 2, 10, 12, 13, 14, 15, 16, 17, 19, 21, 22, 25, 26, 28, 31, 35, 37, 43, 56, 67, 70, 72, 73, 94, 116, 130, 135, 137, 164, 167, 176, 178–179, 192, 226, 273. *See also* Agents, Bureau of Investigation; Bureau of Investigation

K. Lamity's Harpoon, 242–243
Kelly, Paul J. (Bureau Agent), 105
Kerwin, E. J. (Bureau Agent), 63–64, 126
Kirtin, William, 43–44
Kirvin, Henry, 157–158, 159, 160, 162
Ku Klux Klan, 41, 181

Lamar, William H.: and *Chicago Defender,* 122, 126–128, 129; and *Crisis,* 134, 135–136, 138, 139, 146; mentioned, 33, 36
Lansing, Robert, 12, 13–14, 34
Learned, H. Barrett (dollar-a-year-agent), 201, 213, 216, 220
Lee, Douglas, 56–57
Lewis, Horace A. (Bureau Agent), 62
Liberal, 222
Light, Claude P. (Bureau Agent), 167
Lillard, George W. (Bureau Agent), 200
Longview riot, 129–130, 291n34
Los Angeles New Age, 62
Loving, Walter: and Moens case, 202; mentioned, 8, 29, 124–125, 126, 141, 145, 228, 230, 231–242, 244, 245, 248, 249, 250, 251, 254, 256, 258–261, 262, 266–268, 271, 275
Lynching: and *Chicago Defender,* 1, 8, 122, 125–127, 128–129, 273; and *Crisis,* 133, 125, 138, 141; of Charles Lewis, 266; and *Messenger,* 45, 192, 273; of Mary Turner, 146; and Ida Wells-Barnett, 50, 60; mentioned, 2, 42, 43, 47, 53, 58, 65–66, 67, 74, 80, 82, 88, 118, 137, 143, 144, 175, 179, 180, 227, 238, 239, 241–242, 266–267, 270

M.I.3, 26, 28
M.I.4, 26, 28–29

MacArthur, Douglas, 25
Macon, Mattie, 1, 184–186, 275
Mallet, C. V. (Bureau Agent), 92
Mason, Charles H., 1, 6–7, 149–163, 164, 170, 274–275
Masses, 128, 132
Matthews, J. B. (Bureau Agent), 115, 116, 193–194
McAdoo, William Gibbs, 12, 13, 14, 15, 16, 17, 31
McAdory, T. F. (Bureau Agent), 107
McCaleb, Claude (Bureau Agent), 157–158
McElveen, W. E. (Bureau Agent), 155–156
McKnight, R. S. (Bureau Agent), 103–104
McNairy, Dan, 168–170, 189, 275
Mea, Dr., 188–189
Messenger, 2, 7, 45, 74–75, 84, 118, 130, 137, 148, 161, 182–184, 192, 265, 272–273
Military, black soldiers in: and morale, 29, 144, 227–228, 232–234, 247; postwar, 262–267, 275–276; mentioned 5, 8, 78–80, 83, 84, 97, 98–99, 117, 238, 241–245, 266. *See also* Conscription, enforcement of; Draft evasion, accused of; Houston mutiny
Military Intelligence Branch, 25, 123, 124, 125, 240–245, 249, 250–251, 267, 270. *See also* Military Intelligence Division, Military Intelligence Service
Military Intelligence Division (MID): and black informant Quander E. Hall, 246, 255; and *Chicago Defender,* 129; and COGIC, 159; and Moens case, 205, 206–207, 211, 212–213; and NAACP, 50–51, 144, 146, 147–148; mentioned, 16, 25, 26–28, 29, 31, 34, 35, 60, 129, 137, 177–180, 184, 244, 246, 261–265, 267–268, 269, 270, 273. *See also* Military Intelligence Branch; Military Intelligence Service
Military Intelligence Section (MIS), 14, 202–203, 204, 226–230. *See also* Military Intelligence Branch; Military Intelligence Division
Miller, Kelly, 8, 62, 74, 165–166, 199, 239–240
Milwaukee Leader, 32, 128, 133
Mitchell, John, 233–234
Moens, Herman Marie Bernelot: trial of, 215–220; mentioned, 7–8, 199–225 passim, 271, 275
Moton, Robert Russa, 144, 229–230
Murphy, Edward M. (Bureau Agent), 92
Murphy, John B. (Bureau Agent), 64
Murphy, William L. (Bureau Agent), 96

Murray, J. Reese (Bureau Agent), 68
Muse, C. M. (Bureau Agent), 115

National Association for the Advancement of Colored People (NAACP), 2, 6, 29, 50–51, 118, 123, 125, 132–148 passim, 199, 243, 251, 257. See also *Crisis;* DuBois, W. E. B.; Spingarn, Joel E.
National Civil Liberties Bureau, 147, 187
National Equal Rights League, 122, 205, 243, 271
Navy intelligence, 10, 11, 12, 16, 17, 21, 23, 26, 29, 31, 34–35
Negative Branch, 25–26, 27–28, 29
Negro World, 2, 148, 273
Neunhoffer, Albert (Bureau Agent), 139
New Crowd Negro, 1–2, 9, 74–75, 118, 227, 265–266, 270, 276
New York Age, 62, 154
New York Amsterdam News, 245
New York Sun, 57
New York World, 244–245
Niagara Movement, 2

O'Brian, John Lord, 14, 18, 21, 22, 24, 38, 116, 135, 136, 139, 159, 167
Office of Naval Intelligence (ONI), 23, 26, 34–35, 236
Old German case file 3057, 39, 46, 85
Outlaw, Calvin (Bureau Agent), 94
Owen, Chandler, 7, 84, 137, 161, 181–184, 244, 273, 274. *See also Messenger*

Pace, Harry, 242
Pacifism, 6–7; in publications, 118. *See also* Conscientious objectors
Palmer, A. Mitchell, 272
Palmer, Eugene (Bureau Agent), 156–157
Parsons, Herbert, 226, 227, 230
Passports, control of, 27, 34
Patterson, J. R. (Bureau Agent), 96
Payne, Jesse, 155
Peabody, George Foster, 35–36
Pendleton, Forrest C. (Bureau Agent), 69–70, 119
Penn, William F., 241
People's Council, 197
Pfeifer, S. B. (Bureau Agent), 165
Phifer, Robert S. (Bureau Agent), 43
Phillips County riot, 129–130, 291n34
Pitts, A. D., 42, 57
Positive Branch, 25
Post Office Department: and *Chicago Defender,* 121, 123, 126, 129, 130; and *Crisis,* 132, 138, 139, 146; and *Messenger,* 183, 184; mentioned, 2, 3, 5, 8, 10, 11, 13, 14, 17, 19, 26, 31–32, 33, 35, 132, 137, 148, 226, 228, 230, 241, 269, 274
Publications: *Atlanta Independent,* 241–242; *Baltimore Afro-American,* 82, 123, 125, 135; *Boston Guardian,* 82, 230, 233, 270; *Chicago Defender,* 1–2, 5, 8, 61, 118–131 passim, 132, 135, 141, 272–273, 274; *Cleveland Gazette,* 81–82; *Crisis,* 2, 5, 6, 81, 118, 123, 126, 132–148 passim, 192, 230, 243, 263, 272–273, 274; *Crusader,* 2, 148, 273; *Culture Forum,* 222; *The Disgrace of Democracy,* 62, 74, 165–166, 239–240; *Florence Daily Times,* 40; *Galveston Colored American,* 181; *Galveston New Idea,* 61–62, 175–177, 180, 181; *Houston Observer,* 176; *Issues of Today,* 221; *Journal of the National Medical Association,* 30; *K. Lamity's Harpoon,* 242–243; *Liberal,* 222; *Los Angeles New Age,* 62; *Masses,* 128, 132; *Messenger,* 2, 7, 45, 74–75, 84, 118, 130, 137, 148, 161, 182–184, 192, 265, 272–273; *Milwaukee Leader,* 32, 128, 133; *Negro World,* 2, 148, 273; *New York Age,* 62, 154; *New York Amsterdam News,* 245; *New York Sun,* 57; *New York World,* 244–245; *Richmond Planet,* 233; *San Antonio Informer,* 61–62; *San Antonio Inquirer,* 170–174, 175, 274; *St. Louis Republic,* 41; *Voice,* 270; *Washington Bee,* 215–217, 220

Queen, Hallie E., 202, 204, 227, 228, 229, 230, 236, 246

Randolph, A. Philip, 7, 45, 84, 137, 161, 181–184, 244, 273, 274. *See also Messenger*
Red Scare: and the press, 129–130, 148; mentioned, 3, 6, 7, 9, 11, 20, 24, 33–34, 49, 127, 130, 132, 148, 180, 181, 268, 272–276
Richmond Planet, 233
Russellites. *See* Jehovah's Witnesses

Sabotage Act, 19
San Antonio Informer, 61–62
San Antonio Inquirer, 170–174, 175, 274
Saunders, Helen, 205–210, 214, 215, 216, 224, 225
Savoy, Edward Augustine, 35
Schaumburger, M. M. (Bureau Agent), 94, 152–153
Schenck case, 164
Schuyler, George S., 80

Scott, Emmett J., 36, 120, 125, 140, 143, 179, 206–207, 231, 251, 252–253, 254, 255, 256–257, 262, 263, 267, 270, 271
Secret Service, 3, 11, 12, 13, 14, 15, 16–17, 25, 26, 28, 29, 34, 190, 204
Sedition Act: and First Amendment, 164; and *Messenger,* 184; and Moens case, 225; mentioned, 3, 9, 16, 18, 19, 22, 31–32, 33, 58, 112, 121, 123, 138, 166–167, 169, 170, 174, 180, 184, 186, 193, 198, 274, 275
Selective Service Act, enforcement of, 22, 23, 89. *See also* Conscription, enforcement of; Draft evasion, accused of
Sheldon, David T., 175–177, 180
Simmons, Roscoe Conkling, 235, 238–239
Simpson, S. H., 175–177, 180, 181
Slacker raids: in Memphis, 109; mentioned, 2, 22–23, 77, 85, 98–99, 116, 150
Smith, George C. (Bureau Agent), 99
Socialism: and *Messenger,* 89, 183; and *Milwaukee Leader,* 32; mentioned, 5, 10, 21, 24, 183, 271–272. *See also* Bolshevism
Spates, Webster (Bureau Agent), 92
Spencer, F. M. (Bureau Agent), 45, 69
Spingarn, Joel E.: and Moens case, 202; mentioned, 125–126, 137, 141, 142, 143, 144, 194, 226–228, 245, 251, 267, 270, 271
St. Louis Republic, 41
State Department: and Moens case, 212, 218, 223; mentioned, 3, 10, 11, 12, 15, 16, 17, 21, 25, 26, 27, 29, 31, 33–34, 35, 148, 190, 191, 194, 226, 236, 274
Stevens, L. T. (Bureau Agent), 101
Stevenson, Archibald E. (Bureau Agent), 272
Stewart, Malcolm M. (Bureau Agent), 106–107
Stillson (Bureau Agent), 70
Sykes, Joshua, 162

Thompson, L. O. (Bureau Agent), 60
Thompson, W. C., 159
Threadgill-Dennis, Clara L., 1, 170–175
Topeka (Kansas) Plain Dealer, 40
Trading-with-the-Enemy Act, 3, 18, 31, 122, 123
Translation Bureau, 33, 128–129, 138–139, 146
Trazivuk, Daniel (Bureau Agent), 89–90
Treasury Department, 11, 12, 13–14, 15, 16–17
Trotter, William Monroe, 82, 205, 230, 233, 243, 270, 271

Universal Negro Improvement Association, 153, 273

Van Deman, Ralph H., 24, 25, 26, 27, 29, 36, 124–125, 140–141, 226, 228, 229–245 passim, 249
Van der Gracht, W. A. J. M. van Waterschoot, 207, 303–304n23
Vigilantism during WWI, 22, 62–67; and church leaders, 149
Voice, 270

Waldron, Clarence, 162–163
Walser, C. M. (Bureau Agent), 43–44, 194
War Department, 14, 16, 21, 26, 33, 35, 62, 129, 134, 135, 137, 138, 206–207, 227, 229, 245, 261, 267, 273. *See also* Military Intelligence Branch; Military Intelligence Division; Military Intelligence Service
Washington, Booker T., 36, 38, 45, 144, 229, 231, 238, 239, 270
Washington Bee, 215–217, 220
Webb, J. L. (Bureau Agent), 175–180
Wells-Barnett, Ida, 50, 60, 118, 184
Weymouth, W. A. (Bureau Agent), 71, 96
Whalen, John A. (Bureau Agent), 207
Williams, Charles H., 231, 249–251
Wilson, Woodrow: and conscientious objectors, 150; and racial views, 35–36; mentioned, 10, 12–13, 15, 16, 17, 18–19, 22, 31, 32, 34, 35, 61, 119, 139, 144, 151, 155, 167, 168, 175, 227, 229, 270
Winn, DeWitt S. (Bureau Agent), 157–158, 159, 163, 168, 169, 297n36
Winslow, L. Lanier, 34
Wiseman, W. A. (Bureau Agent), 180
Wobblies. *See* Industrial Workers of the World
Women's Peace Party, 33

Young (Bureau Agent), 108–110
Young, Charles, 82, 138, 143, 227

Zimmerman telegram, 12, 45

Theodore Kornweibel, Jr., professor of African-American history in the Africana Studies Department at San Diego State University, is the author of *No Crystal Stair: Black Life and the Messenger, 1917–1928; In Search of the Promised Land;* and *"Seeing Red": Federal Campaigns against Black Militancy, 1919–1925* (Indiana University Press, 1998).